State of the Art MARKETING RESEARCH

A. B. Blankenship
George Edward Breen

 American Marketing Association
Chicago, Illinois

 NTC Business Books, a division of
NTC Publishing Group, Lincolnwood, Illinois, U.S.A.

Library of Congress Cataloging-in-Publication Data

Blankenship, Albert Breneman.
    State-of-the-art marketing research / A.B. Blankenship, George
Edward Breen.
        p.   cm.
    Includes bibliographical references and index.
    ISBN 0-8442-3457-5 (NTC Business Books)
    1. Marketing research.   I. Breen, George Edward.
HF5415.2.B555   1992
658.8′3—dc20   91-3834
                                                                  CIP

Published in conjunction with the American Marketing Association, 250 South Wacker
Drive, Chicago, Illinois, 60606.

Published by NTC Business Books, a division of NTC Publishing Group
4255 West Touhy Avenue
Lincolnwood (Chicago), Illinois 60646-1975, U.S.A.
2 3 4 5 6 7 8 9 RP 9 8 7 6 5 4 3 2 1

CONTENTS

PREFACE

This book is about state-of-the-art marketing research. Despite the enormous impact the information/computer age has had on the practice of marketing research, no book has yet recognized just how pervasive that influence has been on research theory and application.

As with any discipline, the fact that "state-of-the-art" methods are new and modern does not necessarily mean that they are infallible or even that they are superior to more traditional research methods. In writing this book, we followed the advice of a Spanish Jesuit priest-philosopher: "Do not always be carried away by the latest." We have tried to provide the best of both worlds and have stated the shortcomings of state-of-the-art methods where we have found them.

This book is aimed primarily at the two partners in any research project: the marketing firm and the marketing researcher. While it is the researcher who needs to know how to conduct marketing research that provides the right kind of information, the marketing firm also must understand the entire research process so that it can decide exactly what type of information is needed to solve specific marketing problems. Using a minimum of technical language or jargon, the book is written for both as they work side by side as members of the marketing team.

Top management can also profit from reading this book. It will show what kind of information marketing research can provide, how such information is obtained, and how it should—and should not—be used. With a firm grasp of the basic concepts of marketing research, top management can communicate effectively with research staff to produce information that will influence executive-level decision making.

Throughout the book, our emphasis is on the practical. We recreate as closely as possible real-life research situations. We take the student step by step through the key research concepts, but we omit much of the theoretical background. Our discussion of statistics, for example, is limited to how the results are used; we do not show how they are derived or calculated. We stress applications and talk about specific sources of services, facilities, and specialized programs that can help researchers in on-the-job situations. Throughout, we are writing for the doers—those faced with marketing decisions.

For this reason, the book is not encyclopedic. We do not attempt to present every detail of the development and conduct of marketing research. Rather, we provide an overview of the subject, emphasizing the knowledge and skills needed to plan and implement effective marketing research. For in-depth coverage, we provide a bibliography at the end of each chapter and, when relevant, sources for additional reference.

The book is organized into three distinct sections. Part One introduces the key concepts and methods of traditional and technology-driven research. Part Two leads step by step through the entire process of planning and building a research study. Part Three tells how marketing research can be used in solving the specific problems of makers and distributers of products, service providers, retailers, and advertising agencies. It also describes methods of monitoring the market and forecasting. Finally, Part Three addresses the needs of marketers of business and industrial goods and services.

Marketing research is in a state of turmoil in the 1990s. New techniques are constantly being introduced, most of them related to technology. Mergers and acquisitions occur almost monthly. State-of-the-art marketing research has meant the development of a broad range of computerized technologies and services. Some are accessible and affordable for organizations of all sizes. Others, such as the major national syndicated services or specialized research services, are necessarily costly and are used on a regular basis only by the largest marketers. However, we have included these as we want to cover the entire range of technologies and services available and to explain the applications of each. This is important because even the smallest organizations involved in research regularly use and apply the results of larger research studies. To use them meaningfully, they need to understand exactly how such results were obtained. Also, as we show, some of the technology is available on a less costly basis. Moreover, these smaller organizations need to prepare for the happy tomorrow when they grow to become market leaders.

To ensure that this book is as current as possible, we enlisted the help of many specialists in the field. To all the research scholars and professionals—many of whom are listed in the chapter endnotes—who have contributed to the field of marketing research, we owe a general acknowledgment.

We also have many specific acknowledgments. Critical reviews of specific chapters were provided by William S. Rubens (retired vice president of research, NBC), Dr. Raymond F. Barker (professor emeritus of marketing, Bowling Green State University), and Laurence N. Gold (founder and principal of the Center for Business Decisions).

At the American Marketing Association, three names deserve special mention. Francesca Van Gorp worked with us far more caringly and thoroughly than any other editor we have dealt with. Lorraine Caliendo, director of the Information Center and warm friend and information source for many years, provided essential information. Carla Windhorst, executive director, Academy for Health Sciences, was most generous in providing research material in the field of health care.

We also express our gratitude to three people at the Advertising Research Foundation. Michael J. Naples, president, opened the door to its Information Center, and Roslyn Arnstein, director of information, went through the library shelves to provide information. Dr. Allan D. Ballanger, senior vice president and director of research, also contributed significantly.

Jack Honomichl, of the Marketing Aid Center, provided much information through his newsletter, *Inside Research.*

At NTC Publishing Group, Anne Knudsen, editor, and Karen Shaw, associate editor of business books, did a brilliant job of editing the manuscript. Our thanks also to Gregg Cebrzynski and Mary Englehart for their very thorough copyediting.

There is no way to acknowledge in this preface all of the research sources utilized. Without their assistance, this book would have not been possible. They are recognized in the References at the end of each appropriate chapter.

A. B. Blankenship
George Edward Breen

PART ONE

INTRODUCTION

1

WHAT IS STATE-OF-THE-ART MARKETING RESEARCH?

What's in This Chapter

In Chapter 1 we begin by explaining the role of research in today's organizations and show why it is key to every marketing—and top management—decision that is made. We describe the extensive changes in marketing and marketing research that have taken place during the late 1980s as a result of the application of powerful new technologies. These changes will continue through the 1990s at an even faster pace. We explain why it is critical for marketing researchers—and for top executives and marketers—to understand the new conditions that technological advances have created in the marketplace.

The purpose of a business is to create and keep a customer. There can be no corporate strategy that is not in some fundamental fashion a marketing strategy, no purpose that does not respond somehow to what people are willing to buy for a price. *Theodore Levitt*[1]

The purpose of this book is to bring the reader up to speed with technologies that have revolutionized the entire discipline and the day-to-day practice of marketing research. We will show how such technologies can be used to produce and manage market information that is vital to more profitable marketing activity. This will lead to a realization that marketing and marketing research, working together, can greatly augment the economic strength of business.

In today's fast-paced business environment, market information is an increasingly valuable asset. Today's companies are introducing more new products and services than ever before, there are more frequent changes in ownership and more mergers, and companies are switching from field to field and expanding into international markets, while fighting to maintain strong market positions at home. All this means that to keep moving ahead, companies need wiser research, planning, and decision making than in the past.

This book treats research as an integral marketing strategy, a function that—as Dr. Levitt[1] says—cannot be separated from the planning strategies of the entire organization.

J. Walter Smith, senior vice president of Yankelovitch Clancy Shulman, was among the first to recognize that marketing research is undergoing a technological revolution. While the 1970s and 1980s saw advances and improvements in research methods, the phenomenal growth of electronic technologies in the late 1980s and early 1990s can do more than just change methods; these technologies can revolutionize the whole field of marketing.

New methods allow us not only to find out more about consumer attitudes, behaviors, and desires today, but to predict who tomorrow's consumers will be, what products and services they will want, and how they will want to buy them. A recent study by Whirlpool Corp. is an excellent illustration of this point. It shows how today's top corporations are combining traditional research methods and consumer information with new technologies and thinking.

Most of our market research for new product, service and feature development is done with focus groups [see Chapter 10] comprised of consumers who represent our target market. With a mature market, such as dryers, this market is the replacement purchaser—primarily the female head of household in the 35 to 54 age group.

We asked focus groups in our target market to respond to a new dryer design and features. One of these designs included a dryer with a voice-activated control and synthetic speech response. Our purpose was to measure consumer reaction to the new technology which is readily available for appliance use and is currently being used on other consumer products. As we look at the demographics in the population now and around the year 2000, it seemed logical to begin assessing consumer reaction to a technology that will be useful in such new housing concepts as the Smart House, and to meet the needs of the elderly, disabled, and visually impaired consumer. We also noted that youngsters' response to computers, synthetic toys, and high-tech products in general indicates a need for more, automated, technologically advanced products for their future homes.

What we found was that our target market consumers aren't ready for talking appliances. They do not see the need for them and anticipate no advantage to having this technology. We are a market-driven company. We consumer-test new concepts and delay introduction of products and services that offer no perceived consumer benefit.

This does not mean that we abandon the product idea. For the reasons mentioned above, we see talking/hearing appliances as viable products within the next 10 to 15 years. We will continue to develop such products in order to be ready when there is a market demand.[2]

Whirlpool Corp. is examining the past, measuring the present, and planning for the future. This is the job of marketing and marketing research as a part of the larger role of deciding the future directions of the corporation.

THE NEED FOR RESEARCH AS A MARKETING STRATEGY

In the past, marketing research has been viewed by many companies as an activity somewhat removed from the "action" of sales and marketing. Marketing research measured the potential of proposed new products (often after the design had been completed and prototypes produced), measured results, solved "problems" of marketing, sometimes helped in planning, and occasionally pointed an unwelcome finger at those who had created "mistakes" that drained profits or created losses. The point is, marketing research spent most of its time looking backward or at the present. Seldom was it asked to look into the future and work as a team with others to plan for more profitable years ahead.

This book assumes a larger, more strategic role for marketing research in the future. It should be a working part of the marketing function, contributing its knowledge and skill to every phase of marketing. George Santayana once said that "Those who cannot remember the past are condemned to repeat it."[3] This is often repeated and just as often ignored by those who do not use the full strength of marketing research.

American Demographics, in a feature article written by the editorial staff, makes the same point:

There is more than one way to miss a market. That's what many businesses discovered in the 1980s. During a decade when knowing the customer became increasingly important, many companies—and even whole industries—failed to understand their markets. Some companies ignored core customers in favor of the fringe; others ignored important market shifts. Many failed to recognize when a market had peaked; some launched products with no target in sight. Others knew their market but failed to reach it.[4]

Take a look at just six of what *American Demographics* calls "Ten Blunders of the 1980s":

1. Coke "ignored the baby boom." The formula was changed to attract teenagers who like a sweeter taste. What was ignored was the strength of the 21 to 29-year-olds. They grew up with old Coke, were deeply attached to it, and rebelled when it was taken away.

2. "Women grew up but the fashion industry did not notice." There had been a short-skirt push in 1987 which failed. Almost three-quarters of the baby-boom women were working outside the home. They could not and would not wear these skirts. The result was a dreadful time for the fashion industry. At the time of this writing, the fashion industry is attempting to bring back the short skirt. Will it be more successful this time? Is the industry, unable to remember the past, repeating itself?

3. When the middle class melted away, Sears began to lose many of its customers. While such chains as K mart and Wal-Mart were flourishing, Sears appeared to ignore its changing customers. Now, many middle-income consumers, looking for affordable prices in an inflationary period, have moved to K mart and other chains. Wal-Mart has grown tremendously in this period as well.

4. "World Fairs were most important in the days of mass markets, media innocence, and slow travel. . . . Now with so many of us becoming world travelers and television watchers, we do not feel the need to go to a fair for education or even enjoyment." Seventeen percent of all Americans have seen a foreign country. And most of us have visited at least 20 states.

   Was there a need for another World Fair? Apparently not. Knoxville only drew about half the crowd that went to the Chicago Fair in 1893. Better research, planning, and forecasting might have prevented this disaster.

5. Because of the instant popularity and subsequent rapid decline of Cabbage Patch Kids, Coleco's sales blossomed and then dropped precipitously. Large losses were incurred. The company has been sold.

Could better research and planning have prevented this disaster? Of course. Intelligent people planned this product. Too much faith was placed in a single product planned for an ever-changing children's market. Better research and certainly better planning was needed.

6. Burger King still is seeking a new image. Advertising and promotion of recent years has made burger-buyers think of Burger King only as Number 2, always behind McDonald's. What can be done? Herb the Nerd in television spots did not help to create a more favorable image.

What next for Burger King? Well, better research, better planning, and new advertising messages must do the job.

These and many other stories continuously show the need for better, wider, and more thorough research. They also highlight the need for marketing research to be more aware of and thoughtful about the implications of social and demographic changes.

Now let us consider what good marketing planning—the means of avoiding disasters like the ones above—entails. Here is a simplified list:

1. Determine the basic goals of the company. Where have we departed from these goals in the past?

2. Decide which products or services best lead to these goals.

3. Decide the minimum market share we need in these products or services to produce a satisfactory profit and return on investment.

4. Determine a pricing strategy that would best lead to this profit and return on investment.

5. Forecast probable demand for several years in advance.

6. Decide on the best distribution channels to produce continuous satisfactory sales and profits.

7. Decide on the best promotional strategy to produce these sales and profits.

8. Anticipate problems that may arise as these decisions are implemented.

Clearly, this oversimplifies the tasks facing companies in the 1990s. The list simply illustrates a point: A wise firm can use marketing research in all these activities. Certainly, research staff should be consulted in determining the basic goals for the firm, and in selecting products or services to best lead to these goals. Market share has always been a concern of marketing research, as is pricing strategy. Forecasting probable market demand for the firm's products always has been a marketing research function. Hardly anything done by a company in its marketing efforts would not benefit from intelligent and thoughtful research.

The point is, marketing research has a role in all of the key decisions that affect the direction any organization takes. Without good, timely, and relevant research, companies are hindered from moving ahead.

WHAT IS MARKETING RESEARCH?

Philip Kotler has defined marketing research as "the systematic design, collection, analysis, and reporting of data and findings relevant to a specific situation facing the company."[5] The American Marketing Association (AMA) offers a much broader and more comprehensive definition, one that indicates the changing role of research in modern marketing:

> [Marketing research] links the consumer, customer, and public to the marketer through information—information used to identify and define marketing opportunities and problems; generate, refine, and evaluate marketing actions; monitor marketing performance; and improve understanding of marketing as a process. Marketing research specifies the information required to address these issues; designs the method for collecting information; manages and implements the data collection process; analyzes the results; and communicates the findings and their implications.[6]

Another way of defining marketing research might be to state that it is a continuing participant in all areas of marketing, providing timely and accurate information about specific and general marketing problems, viewing past experience, the present situation, and the probable future so that marketing managers can make sound decisions.

Each of these definitions shows the increasing role of research in all phases of marketing. Research becomes a part of a team that guides the marketing efforts of the organization.

Kotler was quoted as saying that marketing research should work on specific marketing situations facing a company. Of course, this is true in part. But marketing research in the broader role that we foresee will study more than specific problems or specific situations. If it is viewed as a means of *avoiding* problems, its broader role in the corporation, as defined above, becomes clear. It is a research, fact-finding, forecasting function that will be used by all phases of marketing and other functions as required for greater sales and profits.

Other departments and functions that can and should use marketing research include product development, engineering, traffic, among others. Even top management will require accurate information about markets and products and competitive activity.

The recent changes in marketing at the Campbell Soup Co. represent the type of new thinking that is affecting the role of research. Campbell once represented mass marketing in its true sense: products were the same for every region and sales methods were the same. Now Campbell is beginning to use different products, advertising, promotion, and sales methods for different regions of the country. At least it is experimenting cautiously with such differences.

Because of new information about specific markets that is being made available through advanced research methods, it is possible to begin changing from mass marketing, which depended on national advertising and identical products for all regions and customers. The new market and media research technologies are helping companies to come to grips with local variations in competition, distribution, and consumer attitudes.

THE ROLE OF COMPUTERS IN MARKETING RESEARCH

Before we look at the role of computers, it's important to realize that traditional research methods can never be fully replaced by technology. In addition to collecting objective information about customers and markets, research requires marketers to find out *why* customers do what they do. Research must collect highly subjective information. It looks forward and measures changing tastes and changing ways of life, and it tries to determine how a manufacturer or distributor can understand and take advantage of these changes. Here, traditional marketing research methods still dominate. Tools such as questionnaires, focus groups, telephone interviews, mall intercepts, and store observations are still the way to go. While computers can aid in recording, categorizing, and presenting the results, they offer little help in evaluating personal opinions and beliefs that influence consumer behavior.

Peter Drucker, a leading management thinker, touches upon the applications—and limitations—of technology in research. He says that business information ". . . has progressed beyond the data stage. Data were what early marketing consumer technologies delivered in the 1960s and 1970s." Now, he continues, research-based data and information in the 1990s will seek to answer "why" questions. Though computers can help, certainly, it is dangerous to become so entranced with technology that desires, wishes, dreams, objections, misconceptions, and changing buying habits of consumers are lost in a sea of numbers and charts.

Despite this reservation, computers have become essential for the research studies and analyses that are conducted in today's business firms.

THE GROWTH OF COMPUTER TECHNOLOGY

Let us look, for a moment at the history of computers, as reviewed by R. F. Barker.[7] We take the liberty of condensing his writings for the purposes of this chapter.

The First Generation: Mid 1940s to Mid 1950s

- MARK 1, Harvard, was the first high-speed calculating machine with a stored program.

- ENIAC (Electronic Numeral Integrator and Computer) was used by the University of Pennsylvania to calculate trajectories of artillery shells.

- 1953 marked the first business application of electronic computers with the delivery of the first Remington Rand UNIVAC to the Bureau of the Census. A year later General Electric was the first commercial firm to get a UNIVAC.

- Early—mainframe—computers were nonelectronic; they used vacuum tubes in the central processing unit, hence were huge. Primary storage was on magnetic drums, with magnetic tapes providing secondary storage. Input was on punched cards, output on printers and cards.

The Second Generation: Mid 1950s to Mid 1960s

- The development of transistors (replacing the vacuum tubes) provided electronic computers and initiated the process of reducing the size of computers.

- Second-generation computers were smaller, required less power, gave off less heat, were far more reliable, and allowed up to eight times as much storage as first-generation mainframes.

- Second-generation computers allowed input and output onto both punched cards and magnetic tape.

- Improved software was developed for second-generation computers.

The Third Generation: Early 1960s to Mid 1970s

- The minicomputer was introduced, with integrated circuits on tiny silicon chips (single chips held both central processing and memory units).

- Minicomputer technology offered a wide variety of input/output equipment (cards, tapes, disks, keyboards, cathode-ray monitors, etc.). Other advantages were reduced size, increased speed, greater storage capacity (up to eight times as much as second-generation computers), and faster access times.

- The early desktop computers offered easier languages and software that allowed users to "talk to" the machine. Users no longer needed to deal with technicians but could work directly with the computer.

- Reservations systems for airlines and rental cars first appeared.

- By 1965 executives in one department store chain were getting daily reports on the previous day's nine-store dollar sales by store and department, instead of the previous year-to-date sales reports.

The Fourth Generation: Mid 1970s to Present

- The microcomputer, still smaller than the minicomputer, appeared. Whole sections of a computer were built into single chip.

- Computer networks, through which users in different locations can communicate both with a mainframe and with each other, were developed.

- During 1977 computer terminals started to replace cash registers in stores.

- Management information systems, connecting microcomputers to a central mainframe, were developed. These systems offered "a set of procedures for the regular planned collection, analysis, and presentation of information for use in making marketing decisions."[8]

The Fifth Generation

- Significant refinements and developments in the minicomputer, such as hand-held terminals with two-way communication between minicomputers, laptop computers, and a proliferation of user-friendly applications programs for almost any business function.

APPLICATIONS OF COMPUTER TECHNOLOGY

The computer now permeates the entire process of data collection. Here are some marketing research applications for which technology has quickly become indispensable.

Demographic Data Application

Working with demographic bases, the user of a desktop system can:

1. Identify the growing metropolitan areas where marketing efforts can yield the best sales and profits.

2. Match these areas with the company's records to see whether profitable areas are being missed.

3. Inform marketing executives where increased sales effort will yield increased profits.

Scanners

Scanners are becoming almost universal, mostly in large supermarkets. Scanning gives the store and its central office an immediate record of sales by product and dollar volume. But there has been progress beyond this. Procter & Gamble is linking its computer system to the systems of some of its customers, thereby simplifying the entire ordering, shipping, and billing process. A 1989 annual report states that "the use of state-of-the-art computer software has helped build business volume for both P&G and its customers, while improving service." To illustrate, P&G used computer-generated data to discover that vacuum-packed coffee was popular in the south. P&G repackaged its Folger's brand for this market and achieved a very satisfactory increase in sales.

The avalanche of data stemming from scanners at checkout counters can be used to get a better feel for exactly what a price cut, coupon blitz, or store display actually does for sales and profits.

Marketers now can get weekly information about every item and package size. Scanner data are available from research companies such as Control Data, SAMI, Dun & Bradstreet, A. C. Nielsen, and Information Resources Inc. The data collected come from more than one chain or location; they are available by region, state, and locality. Along with product sales, these national firms track displays and much other point-of-sale advertising information. Nielsen buys sales data from 3,000 stores across the country. A scanner analysis system, according to Nielsen, allows managers to determine almost instantly how well a promotion is working and what effect price changes, amount of inventory, and arrangement on shelves will have on sales.

Scanner data can be linked with demographics of areas to guide consumers on what to buy. Foods on supermarket shelves can be tied more closely to the demographics of the particular area. Thus inventory can be matched to local needs, and turnover rate can be increased.

Single-Source Research

Scanner information can be used to develop a single-source technology. Ukrops, in its 20-store supermarket chain, uses a "valued customer" card system provided by Citicorp to develop a consumer database. Each customer card has a bar code that is read by the checkout scanner. Scanner data then gives Ukrops up-to-the-minute information on what its customers are buying, how much they are buying, and how often they buy. The effects of store displays, the impact of its monthly newsletter, and advertising can all be measured. It is thus possible to follow the buying habits of individual customers and get in touch with those who appear to be wandering to competitors.

Information Resources Inc. (IRI) pioneered single-source research in 1979. Now it has over 70,000 panel households in 27 markets. An identification card similar to Ukrops' is issued to all customers on the panel. When these identification cards are read by the scanner, information becomes instantly available to the store and very quickly available to IRI. Of the 70,000 panel households, 10,000 (as of 1989) also are equipped with television meters. IRI also keeps track of panelists' print subscriptions.

The obvious weakness of such tracking systems, of course, is that there is no means as yet to determine the effect of print advertising, billboards, and the like. And there is no means as yet to determine what types of stores sales originate from.

Simplified Glossary of Computer Terms

Database   The information stored in a computer. *Database* is used in this book to mean an extremely large amount of systematized data organized for a specified purpose. It might, for example, be a list of customers and their characteristics or it might be a national or regional report of the nature of consumer buying or television viewing.

Desktop computer   A small computer, literally of desktop size, for use in business.

Disk or diskette   Since the material in RAM (random access memory) is lost when the power is turned off, the disk or diskette is used to store material for future use.

Disk drive(s)   The location within the desktop computer for the disk(s).

Downloading   the transfer of data from an outside database into the user's system.

Floppy disk   A removable, flexible disk that provides separate but changeable RAM (random access memory).

GIGO (garbage in/garbage out)   The use of poor input data, leading inevitably to the production of poor output data.

Hard disk   A permanently sealed storage medium within a desktop computer. Allows access faster than working on floppy disks.

Hardware   The "fixed" elements of a computer system, typically including the computer, disk drive(s), keyboard, monitor, and printer.

Magnetic tape   Reels used for data storage. Magnetic tape allows more storage capacity than disks and is generally used to provide database material from an outside supplier to the mainframe of a user.

Mainframe   A large, centralized computer system, usually connecting desktop workstations throughout an organization.

Point-of-Sale Computers

The Limited, the very successful women's apparel chain with over 1,000 stores, tracks consumer preferences through point-of-sale computers. Illustrations of popular styles and designs go via satellite around the United States and to suppliers in the Far East. Within days, stock of the required clothing collects in Hong Kong. Four times a week chartered airplanes bring the merchandise from Hong Kong, and 48 hours later the clothing is in the stores in the United States.[9]

Menu   A list of elements of a program offering the user a choice of options that instruct the computer.

Modem   A connection between computers or terminals making it possible to send or receive data over a distance, usually by telephone line but sometimes within an internal system.

Monitor   The display screen that accompanies a computer. Depending on the phase of the operation, this displays the requests being made of the computer (generally in the form of a menu) or the status of the tasks being performed.

On-line   One computer system being connected to another, generally through a modem, for access to that system's database or a part of it.

PC (personal computer)   An IBM trade name, now generally used to indicate a desktop computer.

Program (or software)   A prepared system of instructions for end users designed to make the computer perform special applications or tasks.

RAM (random access memory)   The temporary, working memory of the computer, which the machine can locate and utilize at very rapid rates. Data accessed through RAM is "lost" when the power is turned off, and so must be stored on disks if needed for future use.

ROM (read only memory)   A memory permanently stored within the computer system instructing it to get ready for use when the start switch is turned on.

Software   See *Program.*

Terminal   The keyboard and monitor elements of the hardware.

User-friendly   Designed for ease of use.

Workstation   Any physical location in which a multiuser system can be accessed.

Database Marketing

A bank of information about individual customers is prepared and put into the computer. Information is obtained from orders, inquiries, distributors, and so on. The databank can be supplemented by information from outside sources. Large companies such as AT&T and IBM are investing heavily to build these databases.

Database marketing is an effort to learn as much as possible about the ultimate purchasers of a firm's products. Corporations commonly gather their lists of potential customers from credit card companies, from change-of-address forms sent to the Postal Service, from lists of catalog subscribers, and from other such sources. For more specialized products, organizations pull consumer information from targeted databanks. For example, computers can name persons with small children or can select people within a particular profession or with a particular hobby or interest.

The ability to direct sales messages only to the most probable prospects can save advertising and promotion money that, as marketers are all too aware, is otherwise wasted on people who do not buy. Through effective database marketing, customers receive only those catalogs or are exposed only to those ads that are directed to their own needs and interests.

These are just some of the marketing applications for which technology-driven research is indispensable as a time- and money-saving tool.

THE CHANGING ROLE OF RESEARCH IN THE 1990s

Marketing research in the 1990s will be greatly affected by the following factors:

- Markets will mature, with little real growth. There will be a continuing struggle in many industries and for many product lines for a bigger slice of the same pie. To an extent, this will change the type of research conducted and the goals of research studies.

- The number of new-product introductions will increase, as will the number of new products that fail in their first three years, before profits are realized. Organizations will demand better, deeper, more comprehensive research to survive, especially in maturing markets.

- The cost of new-product failures will be higher. Managements will look to research to help reduce the escalating costs of advertising in a crowded marketplace, the costs of getting the product on store shelves, development costs, overhead costs, and the like.

- Organizations will demand faster research to respond to market trends. Marketing research must plan its studies to be done more quickly. Modification in the structure of the research may be required, stressing more dependency on internal sources such as databases. There must be much more careful planning to achieve valid information—for example, from smaller samples or by new, faster techniques of contacting the users and buyers of products or services.

- There will be significant changes in the characteristics of consumer markets. The story of the Campbell Soup Co. illustrates this well. As we saw, Campbell is learning how to market in an increasingly fragmented marketplace by segmenting consumers by regional differences, ethnic areas, metropolitan areas, and similar characteristics.

In the chapters that follow we will show how marketing research can be used to solve a variety of problems, from selecting new products and measuring the success of existing ones to setting up effective distribution methods and building customer loyalty. We will explain how the research function can be effectively managed as a marketing activity, and how the research team can work together with top management, marketing personnel, and suppliers to keep the organization moving ahead.

ENDNOTES   1 Theodore Levitt. *The Marketing Imagination.* New York: Free Press, 1983.

2 Letter from Joy A. Schrage, Manager, Appliance Information Service, Whirlpool Corporation, 1989.

3 George Santayana. *Reason in Society,* The Life of Reason Series, Vol. 2. Peter Smith, 1905.

4 Reprinted with permission from *American Demographics,* December 1989, Ithaca, N.Y.

5 Philip Kotler. *Principles of Marketing.* Englewood Cliffs, N.J.: Prentice-Hall, 1983.

6 Peter D. Bennett, *Dictionary of Marketing Terms.* Chicago, Ill.: American Marketing Association, 1988, 114.

7 R. F. Barker. *Marketing Research.* Reston, Va.: Reston Publishing, 1983, 344–350.

8 G. A. Churchill. *Basic Marketing Research.* Hinsdale, Ill.: Dryden Press, 1988, 724.

9 "The Winning Organization." *Fortune,* Sept. 26, 1988, 50.

2

BASIC METHODS OF GATHERING INFORMATION

What's in This Chapter

In this chapter we discuss the major methods of collecting the information that enables the organization to solve its marketing problems. We examine the sources of secondary data, chief among them the U.S. census. We outline the steps to be followed in doing exploratory research, and we describe the major news sources and specialized secondary sources for information. We conclude with a discussion of the use of surveys in the collection of primary data.

What makes an automobile run? It is easy to say that it is the fuel. But without a driver who has some idea of where he or she wants to go and the way to get there, there is simply no need or purpose in moving that car.

So it is with the marketing effort. The fuel that drives it is sales. But without some guidance provided for the marketing manager running the effort, the fuel may give out before there is any cash to replenish the supply.

Information helps the organization solve its marketing problems, to make marketing decisions. But there is a sharp distinction between information and data. Data are news, facts, and figures about any kind of topic you care to define. They are unorganized. They are the sorts of things you discuss with your friends when you are simply chatting.

Information is quite different from facts. It is a body of facts organized around some specific topic or subject. It is what the military might term "intelligence," not merely a recitation of facts, but facts organized and presented to help solve a problem or develop a plan or program. It is the sort of factual accumulation you would put together if you were trying to solve budget problems: limited income vs. necessary and other expenses. In the case of this chapter, it is factual accumulation and organization to help solve a marketing problem.

SOME BASIC CONCEPTS

SECONDARY VS. PRIMARY DATA

When you *read* about auto theft, that is secondary data. When you *experience auto theft yourself,* you have collected primary data. Unlike collecting material about auto theft, however, collecting information for marketing purposes has a basic rule: Never collect your own information (this is called primary research) if the material has already been collected by someone else. (If it is already available, it is secondary data.) Doing your own thing in marketing research if you don't have to is not only like reinventing the wheel, but also expensive and time-consuming. So you always start by examining the secondary sources.

THE WAYS IN WHICH SECONDARY INFORMATION CAN BE USED

Secondary data can be useful in one or more of three ways in marketing research: in exploratory work, as a news source, or in marketing decisions.

The use of secondary data as part of an exploratory study often is tied in with a long-range consideration by a firm—such as whether to think seriously about taking on a completely new product or service area. The manufacturer of cosmetics and toiletries, for example, might want to consider the feasibility of establishing a chain of beauty salons. The first step obviously involves a great deal of secondary research.

Secondary information as a news source helps tell the marketer or researcher what is going on in the world, both in terms of the economy and the particular industry.

And some secondary information, as we will show, contributes directly to making a marketing decision. Here is an example. A grocery retailer consulted census material to check income, housing values, and ethnicity for its trading area. The data made it possible for the store to expand its delicatessen and add specialty items.

But one secondary source—the census—is both so extensive and intensive that it cuts across these three categories. There are also some other general information sources that may apply to one or more of the three. That is why this first portion of the chapter is divided into five major areas of discussion: the census, other general sources, secondary information as an exploratory step, secondary information as a news source, and secondary information as direct input into marketing and research decisions.

THE CENSUS

The Bureau of the Census is the largest single source of secondary data in this country. The range and amount of information available from the Bureau of the Census is too great to describe in depth as a part of a chapter in a marketing research book. The material covers both population and business. All interviews done by the bureau, points out Dr. Barbara Everitt Bryant, director,[1] falls under Title 13, United States Code. This means confidentiality, including address as well as name, since sometimes address alone reveals identity.

We start by providing a few examples of how the census data may help, and then list the major types of information available—usually without charge—from the bureau.

- An older couple visited a regional office of the bureau. They wanted to find out about the population of seniors and its distribution. By use of census data they were able to identify metropolitan areas having sufficient population numbers to warrant their service: a trade show promoting new and unusual travel and vacation opportunities for seniors.
- By studying the growth trends of production data over a period of years, a furniture manufacturer felt justified in offering a line of metal office furniture.
- Census data may help in determining business location. A Chicago businessman evaluated marital status and age distribution before deciding to open a singles bar in a particular neighborhood. A lawn mower manufacturer set up sales territories for its salesmen on the basis of census data showing single detached dwelling units.

These examples provide only a general idea of the broad range of census material available and the ways in which the information can be used. Presented below is a summary of the sources and types of census material.

CENSUS OF POPULATION

Conducted every ten years, the Census of Population provides details on the nature of the population of the United States. It covers demographics such as sex, age, ethnicity, family size, marital status, occupation, income, and education.

The major innovation for marketers and marketing researchers that has resulted from the 1990 census is TIGER (Topographically Integrated Encoding and Referencing), a cross-referencing of basic demographics with computerized maps of every city block across the country. Since we see TIGER primarily as helping to solve ongoing marketing problems rather than as an exploratory research tool, we mention it here only in passing; details are presented later in the chapter.

CENSUS OF HOUSING

The Census of Housing provides information on number of rooms, whether the premises are owned or rented, value of home or rent paid, plumbing, air-conditioning, and number of cars owned. Such information is particularly useful for firms considering the market for household items such as furniture, rugs, and major household appliances.

ECONOMIC CENSUSES

Economic censuses include the Census of Manufactures, the Census of Retail Sales, the Census of Wholesale Sales, and the Census of Service Industries.

The Census of Manufactures provides data on shipments (in both units and dollars) of thousands of products manufactured in the United States. Shown by SIC numbers and descriptions, these data can pinpoint exactly where particular items are produced.

The three other censuses (retail sales, wholesale sales, service industries) provide sales and number of establishments by product line, states, and counties, and by SMSAs.

The total detail of census data is overwhelming. The information specialist in the library often knows enough about the census to be a guide, particularly if the library (usually an academic library) is a depository for these materials.

COUNTY BUSINESS PATTERNS

In a series of separate reports for each state, the Bureau of the Census provides information on employment and size of firm reporting, including payrolls. The reports can be particularly useful in measuring market potential, establishing sales territories and quotas, and suggesting the location of business establishments.

THE CENSUS AS A MARKETER

Fortunately for marketers and marketing researchers, the Bureau of the Census is now itself a marketer—of its own information. The bureau publishes a general catalog, *Statistical Abstracts,* and other items.[2]

OTHER GENERAL SOURCES

Other general sources include local government sources (state, county, municipal) and chambers of commerce. For business and professional markets, trade, business, or professional associations are another possibility.

State sources are usually not very helpful. Their greatest competency is in providing information about specific laws and regulations. The department of commerce or the department of development, if either exists in a state, might provide useful information or background. But in such departments the availability of statistics is secondary to the tasks of attracting new business to the state and maintaining the health of businesses already in the state.

Local governments (county, city, village) are another source of information. While they should not be overlooked, they tend to be an even poorer source than the state government. These must be checked out, but their data are generally limited, often not current or accurate. The agencies to be checked are the economic development commission, redevelopment commission, industrial development board, or downtown planning committee. It is likely that they will be able to provide helpful insight rather than sound statistics.

BUSINESS AND PROFESSIONAL GROUPS

The business or professional association is often a good source of business and other statistics. Every type of organization—industry, profession, or service group—seems to have one or more associations. For some product lines there are associations that both compete and overlap.

If a particular organization is not a member of such a group, the association can be identified by checking the *Encyclopedia of Associations,* published by Gale and almost sure to be in the local library. But the quality of the material varies by association. Some are purely public relations firms, aimed at influencing the public and/or legislative bodies. Others do collect and disseminate sound data that might aid in the search for market information, although a membership fee may be required to obtain the information.

Local chambers of commerce are likely to offer more enthusiasm than hard facts. Still, they are a good source in understanding the psychology of the community: its thinking about expansion and growth, community planning and development, transportation facility plans, and taxes.

SECONDARY INFORMATION AS AN EXPLORATORY STEP

Exploratory research, you will recall, is generally a study that provides a broad understanding of an industry, a service, or an area in which a firm has limited knowledge. There are three steps: defining the information needs, searching to locate promising leads by title or apparent content, and chasing down promising published material. The concepts of the last two steps are similar when a researcher is working either with hard data (print data) or with computerized material (database sources), but the specifics differ significantly.

Since the terms are used repeatedly throughout this chapter, it is necessary to distinguish between *print format* and *computer format*. Print format includes not only material that is in print form (books, periodicals, and other print forms), but also microfilm, microfiche, and slides. Computer format refers to material transmitted from a computer, either onto a screen or in the form of hard copy (a printout).

It may be difficult for the marketer or researcher to decide between print format and computer format. The computer novice may find it easier to depend on print sources, feeling at home with these. Although readily available print sources rarely cost anything, checking out print sources, as the college student well knows, takes considerable time. Use of on-line sources is far less time-consuming and can provide much more pertinent information. But its use costs money, and the novice or even the person with computer experience is likely to need some expert assistance.

But there is a real caveat. When dealing with printed material, there is no great cost—other than time—if you make a few mistakes here and there in the search and come up with some poor leads. However, if the decision is to go the computer search route, the investigator—with help, to be sure—has to know what he or she is looking for and how to find it. Otherwise, it can cost a lot of money. The computer is a tremendously efficient search machine. But because its hourly costs are high, additional setups and runs become costly.

STEP 1: DEFINING THE INFORMATION NEEDS

Chapter 1 outlined the importance of starting any marketing research with a statement of the problem. This is crucial, not only in the search for secondary data, but in *any* kind of marketing research investigation.

A statement of the marketing problem will outline the particular marketing decision(s) to be made. In turn, this leads to a statement of the kinds of information required to come to that decision. The nature of the information should always be spelled out, never left open-ended. Otherwise, the search for secondary information will be unfocused and unending.

STEP 2: THE BASIC SEARCH

With Traditional Hard Data

Generally libraries are the most promising source for print material. Libraries as a group include the community or public library (city, county, or state), the college or university library, and the special library.

The nearby *public library* is often the best starting point. Even in a small community, the public library may be hooked up to a computer system, which can be of considerable help through access to databanks. Even better is the *college or university library,* if there is one readily available. If the state capital is nearby, chances are that there is an excellent *state library.* The state library typically has not only state materials, but good general facilities as well.

The investigator also will want to check whether there is a special library in the community. Typically found in metropolitan areas, these usually are privately maintained (by a business or an association) and carry considerable depth of material within some specialized topic, such as advertising, direct-mail selling, and the like. Gale Research Company publishes a list of the thousands of these special libraries, including their specialties and addresses. A good public library may have this list available, though it may be necessary to talk to the head librarian to obtain it, since often it is not readily available to the public. In some larger metropolitan areas, there is a specially prepared list of such local libraries, although, again, a chat with the head librarian may be the only way to gain access to this. It is also possible that a local library is a member of the Special Libraries Association. Based in New York, this is a group of members (usually business firms) who maintain specialist libraries in their field of interest, whether it be advertising, chemistry, or whatever. Usually, if the researcher is in a noncompetitive situation, these libraries will be happy to cooperate, and often have materials that other libraries do not.

The reference specialist in a library is known as the reference librarian. But not all persons who sit at the reference desk are equally qualified. Some are part-timers, and, in an academic library, some may be students who don't know much more about the job than you do. So the first point is to be sure that the person at the reference desk is capable of helping you. If the investigator starts by knowing his or her own business, this is easy to check.

You should arrive armed with a complete knowledge of the business problem (see Chapter 1). As the investigator talks with the person at the reference desk about the problem, it soon becomes clear whether that person knows how to help. If the person at the desk cannot help, he or she will generally refer you to someone else. Also, inquiry may indicate that there are specialists in other library systems who can be of help.

But let us say you are mainly on your own. Then the starting point is a "guide." A guide, in the sense used here, is a directory of specific sources of information that may be relevant to the search for secondary information. The first step is a broad sweep of possibilities to uncover promising specific leads.

The *Reader's Guide to Periodical Literature* provides (annually and periodically) a listing of articles in some 200 major periodicals (magazines and journals) classified by topic. Because of the choice of periodicals reviewed, it tends to provide general rather than specific information.

The *Business Periodicals Index* covers some 400 business periodicals. The *New York Times Index,* published annually, provides abstracts of news items listed chronologically by subject. The *Wall Street Journal Index* lists business and financial stories published in that publication. One section of the index lists items by subject other than by companies.

The *Statistical Abstract of the United States* is another good starting point. Published annually by the Department of Commerce, it provides over 1,000 pages of tables and data about many different aspects of the United States. It offers a broad overview of the kinds of data available and their sources.

With Database Material

With database material the concept of the basic search is similar to that described for print material. But the actual procedure is rather different.

To start with, the specialist in the field is now a database information specialist. In some cases this may be the reference librarian, but that depends largely on whether the particular library has on-line facilities to be in touch with databank sources. Further, the database specialist may actually be a broker in a firm that specializes in making data searches.

While the concept of the search using database material, as we have said, parallels that for print, skill is required in communicating with the information specialist firm or with the library person in pursuing information from databanks. If the researcher does not clearly understand the marketing problem, it will be impossible—even for a knowledgeable information specialist—to help the searcher come up with "key words," which is the way a databank has to be searched. Mistakes can be costly and can lead to acquiring useless information.

There are over 5,000 databanks, covering topics ranging alphabetically from aborigines to zymogenesis; discipline-wise from anatomy to zoology; marketing-wise from advertising to wholesaling. Unless the computer operator is a specialist in dealing with these databanks, it's a confusing world.

The data within a particular databank may be bibliographical, a list (directory or dictionary), news, or statistics. A particular databank may cover items for a period of ten years or for only the most recent six months.

There are directories of on-line sources. An informed reference librarian can assist in spotting these. To provide an idea, here are three of them.

The *Directory of On-Line Information Resources* is published annually by CSG Press (Rockville, Md.). The indexing by topic is broad but it is specific under each heading. There is a statement about the years of coverage for each category, and each sublisting includes specific contents and the organization offering access to the database.

The *Database Catalog*, published by Dialog (Palo Alto, Calif.), an information retrieval service, lists database sources by marketing topics (found in their general listings under many different headings) from advertising to trade opportunities. In each case the specific listing provides the organization source, dates of coverage, types of information available, and costs.

At one time used primarily by librarians and home consumer buffs and only occasionally by marketing researchers, *Dialog Information Services* is now increasingly being used by both marketing researchers and brand and product managers who have their own PCs. Miller[3] reports that Dialog has some 350 databases, about a third of which are on business subjects. The topical headings include directory entries, journal articles, conference papers, patents, books, trademarks, and statistics. The Dialog Business Connection Service has six application areas, of which three are the most directly related to marketing: corporate intelligence (information on companies' locations, financial position, officers, directors, and products), products and markets (market share data, product development, and manufacturers' trade names), and sales prospecting (company listings listed by location, industry type, and size.)

The possible uses in marketing and marketing research are so broad that we mention only four. One is in the exploratory phase of research (Chapter 4), where the particular firm has had little experience in the particular product or service field and needs information to help provide background material. Another is in working through some of the stages of new-product development. A third use is in the tracking of competitive efforts and results. Yet another is in developing a list of companies to be surveyed for a particular purpose.

The system has extensive possibilities for marketing, including statistics (demographic, economic, and financial), market potential, and identification and tracking of competitive products and services.

STEP 3: CHASING DOWN THE SOURCES

The basic search has come up with published titles and a list of sources, which in themselves give some idea of their promise in this exploratory phase. It is time for weeding out and for settling down to pursuing and perusing only those titles and sources that are promising.

Somewhat similar to the database sources are some sources reporting the availability of specific published material. One of these, *Off-the-Shelf* (Off-the-Shelf Publications, Northport, N.Y.), offers a free bimonthly catalog. This provides brief descriptions and prices for specific business reports, listed by foods and beverages, specialty chemicals, electrical and electronic equipment, home and office furnishings, machinery, industrial equipment and supplies, consumer products, leisure products, and the service sector. Reports are reproduced by computer printout and sent to the buyer.

The Cambridge Information Group (Bethesda, Md.) annually publishes *FINDEX, The Directory of Market Research, Reports, Studies and*

Surveys. This publisher says that its annual volume covers over 11,000 research reports on some 90 industries. A telephone service provides updating in the field of interest to particular subscribers.

The *Marketsearch International Directory of Published Market Research* lists research reports for both industrial and consumer goods. Approximately half of these concern studies of the U.S. market. On this basis there are some 9,000 relevant entries. There is both a product index and an SIC index.

Another promising source of leads is the *Directory of Industry Data Sources*, published by Ballinger (Cambridge, Mass.). This provides sources primarily by industry. It also has a section listing data publishers and producers, by various industry topics. Each listing gives the name of the publisher, the specific title, a brief abstract of the contents, and price.

Over 7,000 directories in more than 300 major categories of business, industries, and the professions are listed in *The Guide to American Directories* (Klein Publications, Coral Gables, Fla.). Publisher names, frequency of publication, cost, and a brief description of the directory's contents are included.

Some suppliers will take on the assignment of making a custom search for the investigator. M/A/R/C is an example.[4] This large Dallas-based marketing research firm undertakes searches of secondary sources (such as statistics, reported trends, economic factors, and industry news and views) for any marketing topic or industry. It offers the marketer the advantage of dealing with an agent well-versed in marketing, thereby making the dialogue a lot easier.

SECONDARY INFORMATION AS A NEWS SOURCE

We have seen that continuing information can provide understanding of the dynamic economic (financial) environment. It also helps to explain the environment of the general industry or business of the marketer or marketing researcher.

THE MAJOR NEWS SOURCES

About the Economy

To have an understanding of the economic climate, since all marketing effort operates within this framework, the marketer or marketing researcher must have a continuing and current understanding of the state of the economy. Daily reading of *The Wall Street Journal* or of the financial section of the *New York Times* is essential.

The *Federal Reserve Bulletin*, published by the Federal Reserve System, is a monthly publication that emphasizes financial information.

The *Survey of Current Business*, published by the Department of Commerce, provides information such as gross national product, national income, and international balance of payments. It covers data on personal income, employment, and prices and has a special section on current business statistics.

Trade Papers

The marketer or marketing researcher who wants to work in an environment of knowledge about his or her field of business makes it almost a ritual to read trade papers covering the field. These also can be helpful in getting a general feel of a particular business or industry field that the firm is considering entering. We mention only two publications in marketing that help the marketer gather general information about what is going on. One is *Advertising Age*, a weekly publication providing news about advertisers, agencies, media, and people in the field. The other is *Marketing News*, published biweekly by the American Marketing Association, which provides news about marketing generally and has issues covering topics such as marketing research and media.

A good source to locate trade papers in specific fields is provided by the *Standard Rate & Data Service*, usually available in any good library.

Newsletters

There are a number of newsletters relating to marketing research. Some are aimed at top management, some at marketing management, some at the researcher. Some hit more than one of these segments.

Published twice monthly, *Research Alert* (Alert Publishing Company, Long Island City, N.Y.) summarizes Bureau of the Census trend data, public and proprietary studies by nationally recognized marketing research firms, media research findings, and more. Some issues cover topics as varied as health care marketing, who shops at supermarkets, coupon users, the female Hispanic executive, health foods, and convenience foods. Typically running about eight pages, it is tersely and interestingly written, clearly aimed at the busy marketing research executive who lacks the time to dig through all the sources needed to keep up with consumer market information and trends. It is sold on an annual subscription basis. At an additional cost, the subscriber can receive newsletters reporting on key consumer market segments, such as the affluent, the youth market, and minority markets.

The *American Marketplace* is a privately published, biweekly newsletter that reports trends. It may feature dining trends, airport shops, buying of books, or whatever its editors decide are important current marketing topics.

Published for marketing executives, *The Consumer Research Center* (The Conference Board, New York) quarterly informs its subscribers about demographic changes in the marketplace, based on ongoing material produced by the Bureau of the Census.

The American Marketplace (Business Publishers, Silver Spring, Md.) is a biweekly publication that tracks census and consumer trends and reports these in terms of their marketing implications for varying industries.

Another subscription publication is the *Directory of Market Research Reports, Studies and Surveys,* which provides annual information on some 10,000 research reports covering about 90 industries.

American Demographics (published monthly by Dun & Bradstreet, Ithaca, N.Y.) is a tersely written, glossy-paper publication reviewing some of the specific changing markets and marketing methods in the Untied States. Aimed mainly at marketers and marketing researchers, it contains many advertisements for research services and firms.

The *Yankelovich MONITOR,* published since 1970, regularly reports consumer social values, attitudes, life-styles, and demographics. The Roper Organization (New York) publishes *The Public Pulse,* a monthly newsletter reporting what Americans are thinking, doing, and buying.

There is also a monthly newsletter aimed at keeping the marketing researcher up to date on what is happening to research firms, facilities, and personnel. Jack Honomichl's *Inside Research* is just that: a current newsletter on what is going on in research, usually beating the trade media on research activity.

We report only a single research newsletter published by a research firm, simply because it happens to be the only one we know of that seems to be concerned more with the basic issues of research methodology than with out-and-out promotion of the firm. This is *Datapoints,* a "periodic" newsletter published by Survey Solutions and sent without charge to some 1,500 marketing research professionals (along with a handful of marketing service people) in various types of corporations and in advertising agencies. Individual issues cover topics such as benefit impact analysis, brand personality, positioning studies, and concept research. A case history is typically included.

SECONDARY INFORMATION AS DIRECT INPUT INTO MARKETING AND RESEARCH DECISIONS

Secondary information sometimes can provide direct input in helping to arrive at marketing decisions. We have already mentioned the case of the couple who used census data to help them select a metropolitan area with enough senior citizens to support a business aimed at the elderly. This is a good example of the first way in which secondary information can often help provide direct input: by providing market statistics. In other cases secondary sources may provide specific lists of potential customers.

These two kinds of secondary data are available for the consumer market and for the business or industrial market. But except for the use of geographic categories, where listings tend to be parallel, the specifics of statistics and of lists vary between the two types of market. We therefore discuss first the geographics (applying to both), then consumer secondary information, and finally industry secondary information as direct input.

THE GEOGRAPHICS

The geographics apply to both the consumer and the industrial or business market. These are convenient and accepted geographic definitions used by marketers, whatever the particular area of marketing or marketing research.

When statistics are used for marketing, they are most often considered in geographic terms. The geographic breakouts most often used are given in Exhibit 2.1, starting with the largest divisions typically used in marketing research and working down to the smallest. These terms are frequently used throughout the text, sometimes as initials only.

Definitions are fine, but let us see why these geographic descriptions are of crucial importance to marketing.

In marketing research there are two ways in which an understanding of these terms is critical. One has to do with defining the geography

---

Exhibit 2.1 GEOGRAPHIC TERMS (SOURCES AND DEFINITIONS) FREQUENTLY USED IN MARKETING RESEARCH[5] (ARRANGED IN ORDER OF SIZE OF UNIT)

Total United States (political): All 50 states plus the District of Columbia.
Continental United States: All states within the North American continent (the contiguous states plus Alaska).
State (political): A territorial unit of government. Average population is 4,571,000, but with ranges of from some 24 million (California) down to some 402 thousand (Alaska).
Region (census): The Northeast, South, Midwest, and West.
Division (census): The four regions are split into nine divisions, with individual states combining to form divisions.
Telephone Exchange (AT&T): There are currently 34,443 of these, with an average of 2,479 telephone households per exchange (statistics courtesy of Survey Sampling).
Area of Dominant Influence, ADI (media research): A county where the dominant share of TV viewing hours is spent with "home" stations. Originally used by a TV audience service, it is now a common geographic designation about statistics.
Total Survey Area, TSA (media research): A broadcast media term, a county where the net weekly circulation of "home market" stations occurs. Now broadly used in describing an area for any sort of marketing research data.
Metropolitan Statistical Area, MSA (census): An area composed of one or more counties including a large population nucleus and nearby communities having a high degree of interaction. Formerly known as Standard Metropolitan Statistical Area (SMSA). Primary Metropolitan Statistical Areas (PMSAs) are SMAs that make up Consolidated Metropolitan Statistical Areas (CMSAs).
County (political): A subdivision of a state whose boundaries are politically defined. The United States contains 3,141 counties, with the average county in the United States having a population of some 73,000.
County Size: Defined by A. C. Nielsen Co., county size is now commonly used throughout media research particularly but all marketing re-

---

within which a sample is drawn. As will be shown, little marketing research is done on a census-type basis, where every unit is enumerated. That would be too demanding in terms of time and cost, and often it would produce no more dependable results than using a well-defined sampling plan.

The other way has to do with analysis of the data by market or submarket. Because more often than not results are shown by geography, you have to know these terms to understand the results.

search generally:

A: All counties in the 25 largest metropolitan areas.

B: Counties having over 150,000 population excluding those in A, and counties that are part of the metropolitan area in such B counties.

C: Counties having over 35,000 population, excluding those already in A or B, and counties that are a part of the metropolitan area in C counties.

D: All remaining counties.

City (political): An incorporated municipality whose boundaries are defined by the state in which it is located. Currently the 100 cities of heaviest population range from over 7 million to some 162,000. So it is impossible to place the city accurately in a hierarchy of geographic categories by size, though it is typically smaller in population than the county.

Census Tract (census): County subunit, defined by local committees following guidelines of the Bureau of the Census, typically having some 4,000 population of roughly comparable socioeconomics.

Block Numbering Area (census): Similar to a census tract, a term used by the Bureau of the Census for areas lacking census tracts.

Block Group (census): A subunit of a census tract or block numbering area, typically having 1,000 residents.

ZIP Code (Postal Service): Each of the ZIP codes covers an average of some 4,000 families. The country is divided into 10 major regional segments (the first digits in the number), and into sectional or, in the case of major metropolitan cities such as New York, Chicago, and San Francisco, neighborhood locations (the next two digits) that are centers for the sorting of mail, and neighborhoods (the last digit). There are about 43,000 ZIP codes.

ZIP + 4: For residential listings this might mean the side of a block or a group of apartments. While it is difficult to state a number of dwelling units in a +4 segment, it is estimated as something less than a dozen.

Postal Delivery Routes: The path followed by specific letter carriers. Applies to both urban and rural routes.

Block (census): These are the smallest of the census geographic designations. They are roughly equivalent to a city block and provided for areas lacking census tracts. Blocks in rural areas are generally larger in area than those in more densely settled areas. In the 1990 census, for the first time the entire country was divided into blocks.

INFORMATION ABOUT CONSUMERS

Consumer Geographics, Demographics, and Psychographics

The term *geographics* has already been discussed, along with its applications. In terms of consumers, it means where people live. The word *demographics* is just about as easy to understand. It concerns the statistics of an area's population, such as number of households and their composition, income, sex, age, education, and occupation.

Combining geographics and demographics has coined the word *geodemographics,* which is simply a demographic description of those within specific geographic areas. The data sometimes are presented as descriptions of localities; in other cases the marketer predefines the characteristics of what are considered his best customers or prospects, and gets a list of where such people live.

The term *psychographics* has long been used by psychologists to mean the personality characteristics of an individual. Now that its usage has been adapted to marketing research, its meaning has been expanded. It is used to describe people not only in terms of their personality characteristics, but also in terms of their interests and life-styles as a reflection of these characteristics. Chapter 15 covers this topic in more detail.

Information Sources for Statistics

Both the census and private sources provide statistics about consumers.

The census has the most prolific and the most profitable of all existing data for the marketer in the immediate solution of problems. We will give a few examples.

Since the census provides details about where and who consumers are (specific geography by characteristics such as age, sex, ethnicity, size and nature of the living unit, type of dwelling, and rental or value of dwelling unit), it has many immediate marketing applications. A national retailer such as K mart can use local data to tailor neighborhood promotions. McDonald's can use local data to evaluate possible locations for new franchise sites. A chain bank can make use of local data to paint a demographic picture of the neighborhoods surrounding its locations. By singling out neighborhoods most closely matching its profiles of typical purchasers of personal loans, mutual funds, CDs, and other banking services, it can effectively target its advertising and direct-mail efforts.

Campbell Soup Co. regularly uses census data to guide it in developing new products or changing the market of an existing one.[6] For example, marketers in the company noticed that household size was declining and two-income families were rising. It was safe to assume that there were no longer group breakfasts, and since the woman in the family most likely worked, there was less time to prepare breakfast. Following further exploratory research that confirmed these assumptions, a broadly expanded line of single-serving frozen breakfasts was introduced. At last reports Great Starts owned 17 percent of this expanding market. As another example, aging of the population, indicated by census data, and evidence that older people are increasingly health-conscious led Campbell to market its Special Request line of reduced-salt soups.

Here is another example, provided by the census itself.[7] A grocery chain wanted to open a supermarket in one of three counties in a metropolitan area. The company was particularly interested in economic and population growth. Census data provided change measurements over time in population, income, household composition, housing value, car ownership, and grocery store sales. The retailing firm thus had solid data on which to make the county choice, and it planned to use census tract and ZIP code data to help it make the best location choice within the selected county.

Also, one California retailer found, to its surprise, that Hispanics were the largest group of purchasers of bottled water,[8] perhaps because they were used to the poor quality of tap water in Mexico. This retailer used market data much better than the manager of the New York World's Fair Spanish Pavilion, one of the better restaurants there. Being Spanish himself, he stocked up with thousands of bottles of water, knowing from his experience that Americans almost always ordered bottled water with their meals. The difficulty was that he didn't know why!

TIGER[9,10,11]

TIGER, the detailed mapping provided by the 1990 census, will lead to many different kinds of direct marketing applications. An anagram for Topographically Integrated Encoding and Referencing, it can be termed a "smart map"—it can be asked questions about a specifically defined area (the asker's choice) and will deliver. It will be able to pinpoint small clusters of prospects for a particular kind of business. The business will start with a demographic definition of the kinds of people it is looking for and then can spot the best locations for retail and consumer service establishments. Wholesaling and distribution points also can be established on the same sort of data considerations.

The maps provide incredible detail, showing not only every street and road, but also even bridges and tunnels. The detailed computer information, even to street and number of each residence within the unit, will have been checked out by the most rigorous methods. (Of course, no information is available on individual households, but only on clusters.) This will make it possible for marketers to be more precise than ever before, since each unit may contain as few as 100 people.

The information is available for every city, town, and village in the country. It is even possible to get—at cost—data for specific ZIP codes, neighborhoods, or blocks, information often crucial to a small enterprise.

The individual company wanting to use the data will need either a mainframe or PC plus appropriate software (from the private sector). There are many private suppliers of information that are or will be offering TIGER data to meet the specific needs of marketers.

There are several other good sets of statistical data about geographic areas available from private sources. The *Sales and Marketing Management Annual Survey of Buying Power* is a source that should be in the local library. For metropolitan areas it provides data on population, number of households, effective buying income, a buying power index, and total retail sales, broken out by household for various types of retailer.

The *Editor & Publisher Market Guide* also is generally available in a good library. For metropolitan statistical areas it provides information about population, household income, and retail sales by category. For counties and cities it goes beyond this, including disposable income and income per household.

Other available data may be geographically broader or narrower than this. Some are available regionally, by state, by metropolitan area, by county, by census tract, by ZIP code, or even by mail carrier route.

But this chapter is discussing only the *basics* in the information search. The highly detailed possibilities of geographic market description are better left for Chapter 15.

Information Sources for Specific Consumer Customer Possibilities

The two types of information sources for possible customers are a straight list and a database list, and we make a real distinction between the two. The straight list provides a minimum amount of information about the possible customer. It may be as little as the individual's name and address, such as found in a directory, or a mailing list available from a mailing list firm or broker, perhaps listing by name and address persons who have a particular hobby or who have children in their teens living at home. But little else is known about them. In the case of the database list, a considerable amount of information may be available about each person on the list, perhaps including household income, education of the household head, ownership of a car, and numerous other demographics, psychographics, and buying habits. Chapter 15 is completely devoted to this sort of database marketing.

One possible source of customer lists are the alphabetical listings in telephone books. There are limitations to these, however: They are out of date on the day of publication; they exclude those with unlisted telephone numbers; and it is not always possible to tell which listings are men and which are women.

City directories, published by R. L. Polk & Co., are a source for business names in various cities and are also valuable in providing lists of residents. For every person over 18, these lists include name, address, telephone number, whether residence is owned or rented, and nature and place of employment.

INFORMATION ABOUT BUSINESS AND INDUSTRY

General Categorization of Business and Industry

Business and industry, like consumers, is generally sorted out, in marketing, by one or more of the geographic classifications. But grouping by kind of business is just as important for business and industry as demographics is for consumers.

One of the most significant and commonly used methods of classifying business and industry by type is the *SIC (Standard Industrial Classification) Manual,* published by the Department of Commerce, which lists all types of business and assigns classification numbers to each. Exhibit 2.2 shows two pages from the *SIC Manual*—as good a method as any for showing what we are talking about. Major Group 27 is Printing, Publishing, and Allied Industries. The first broad category below that is 271, referring to Newspapers: Publishing, or Publishing and Printing. The digits 2711 represent the next subdivision; in this case they cover the same category. But if you look at the second page, you will see Books as 273, followed by 2731, meaning Books: Publishing, or Publishing and Printing; and then 2732, covering book printing. The broad category of 27 runs the gamut down to 279, Service Industries for the Printing Trade. The categorization of the SIC is formulated so that no industry is missed. Only with knowledge of the SIC number is it possible to search most sources for material relevant to the particular marketing problem.

Information Sources for Specific Business and Industrial Customer Possibilities

A directory, in the sense used here, is a listing. Many directories are available in the library without charge, whereas others must be purchased. Some are almost impossible to obtain.

Here are some of the more valuable print directories for business and industrial firms usually available in libraries.

The *Dun & Bradstreet Million Dollar Directory,* generally available in a good library, is one of the first sources to be consulted to learn about companies in a particular industry or business. The first volume covers firms with a net worth of $1 million of more. The second includes those valued from $500,000 to under $1 million. Each listing gives the firm name, trade name, state where the firm is incorporated, parent company (if any), headquarters address, division names and functions, annual sales, SIC codes, and names and titles of executives.

One of the most important directories is the *Thomas Register of American Manufacturers.* This 17-volume list of some 123,000 manufacturers, classified by products and by city within state, provides information on total assets, trademarks, and subsidiaries.

The *state industrial directory* typically includes listings for all or most industrial firms, by cities, towns, and villages in the state, and by product. These directories vary in size and quality. If the local library does not have a directory for a particular state, contact the State Industrial Directories Corporation (New York, N.Y.), where it is available for a fee.

Another important directory source is *Moody's Manuals.* These cover industries, public utilities, and transportation. Information is updated biweekly. These manuals provide a "feel" of an industry being studied, though they cover only the largest corporations and so are not a source for small, privately held firms. Published by Moody's Investment Services, these manuals are available in most banks and investment firms.

High on the list of sources of information about specific companies is *The Corporate Directory* (Cambridge Information Group, Bethesda, Md.). Published annually, this volume lists some 10,000 firms in the United States, providing information not readily available in any other single source: names of officers and directors, SIC code, subsidiary firms, and more.

There are the *yellow pages* of the telephone directory, a good source of company names by type of business. Frequently the library has yellow pages for other communities as well. If not, these are generally available at the telephone company. There is one limitation, however: There is no quality control of the companies listed; a listed firm might be a one-man operation handled on a part-time basis.

There are a few specialized kinds of telephone listings. One is the *crisscross directory,* which is a listing of residences and business by block numbers along streets. These are published by some 12 different firms, members of the International Association of Cross-Reference Directories, and they publish 375 such directories throughout the country. There are also special summaries from the yellow pages. One of these, for instance, is published by the Yellow Page Research Group, and is titled *Statistical Reports.* By county, it is possible to get a listing by business type or a count by SIC code.

There are also *city directories,* which provide both business and residential listings. They usually include the crisscross type of listing. Each firm is categorized by type, and names of owners, partners, and corporate officers are provided. R. L. Polk & Co. publishes these for over 1,400 cities. The information is generally based on personal interviews made on the premises.

There are several specialized lists. R. R. Donnelley offers current detailed information on over 24,000 *shopping centers* nationwide. It also provides databases for the health care industry, including information about *physicians* and *hospitals.*

There is also a specialized list relating to state governments: *The National Directory of State Agencies.* For each state, this shows state agencies by function, and state-elected officials. It provides an alphabetical telephone listing for over 23,000 state representatives, state officials, and staff members.

Although *mailing lists* are not examined at this point (they are discussed in Chapter 8), these are available from list firms. Specific names of companies can be provided for particular categories or for particular types of individuals: antique auto owners, wealthy women, and photography hobbyists. The *Standard Rate & Data Service,* usually available in a library, provides sources for various kinds of such lists. A multivolume set of annual issues includes one for mailing list sources (at a price, of course). The firm that wants to reach aircraft owners, for example, can get a list of all individual and corporate aircraft owners currently registered in the United States.

Other important sources of specialized names are *trade and professional associations.* Some associations hold their lists of names in private, not permitting their use by anyone other than an association member, and perhaps even then restricting the types of use. Other associations will provide the list for a fee. The researcher interested in

Exhibit 2.2   TWO PAGES FROM THE SIC MANUAL

126

Major Group 27.—PRINTING, PUBLISHING, AND ALLIED INDUSTRIES

The Major Group as a Whole

This major group includes establishments engaged in printing by one or more common processes, such as letterpress; lithography (including offset), gravure, or screen; and those establishments which perform services for the printing trade, such as bookbinding and plate-making. This major group also includes establishments engaged in publishing newspapers, books, and periodicals, regardless of whether or not they do their own printing. News syndicates are classified in Services, Industry 7388. Establishments primarily engaged in textile printing and finishing fabrics are classified in Major Group 22, and those engaged in printing and stamping on fabric articles are classified in Industry 2396. Establishments manufacturing products that contain incidental printing, such as advertising or instructions, are classified according to the nature of the products—for example, as cartons, bags, plastics film, or paper.

Industry Group No.	Industry No.	
271		NEWSPAPERS: PUBLISHING, OR PUBLISHING AND PRINTING
	2711	Newspapers: Publishing, or Publishing and Printing

Establishments primarily engaged in publishing newspapers, or in publishing and printing newspapers. These establishments carry on the various operations necessary for issuing newspapers, including the gathering of news and the preparation of editorials and advertisements, but may or may not perform their own printing. Commercial printing is frequently carried on by establishments engaged in publishing and printing newspapers, but, even though the commercial printing may be of major importance, such establishments are included in this industry. Establishments not engaged in publishing newspapers, but which print newspapers for publishers, are classified in Industry Group 275. News syndicates are classified in Services, Industry 7383.

Commercial printing and newspaper publishing combined
Job printing and newspaper publishing combined

Newspaper branch offices, editorial and advertising
Newspapers: publishing and printing, or publishing only

272		PERIODICALS: PUBLISHING, OR PUBLISHING AND PRINTING
	2721	Periodicals: Publishing, or Publishing and Printing

Establishments primarily engaged in publishing periodicals, or in publishing and printing periodicals. These establishments carry on the various operations necessary for issuing periodicals, but may or may not perform their own printing. Establishments not engaged in publishing periodicals, but which print periodicals for publishers, are classified in Industry Group 275.

Comic books: publishing and printing or publishing only
Magazines: publishing and printing, or publishing only
Periodicals: publishing and printing, or publishing only

Statistical reports (periodicals): publishing and printing, or publishing only
Television schedules: publishing and printing, or publishing only
Trade journals, publishing and printing, or publishing only

Industry Group No.	Industry No.	

273   BOOKS

2731   Books: Publishing, or Publishing and Printing

Establishments primarily engaged in publishing, or in publishing and printing, books and pamphlets. Establishments primarily engaged in printing or in printing and binding (but not publishing) books and pamphlets are classified in Industry 2782.

Book club publishing and printing, or publishing only
Books: publishing and printing, or publishing only
Music books: publishing and printing, or publishing only

Pamphlets: publishing and printing, or publishing only
Textbooks: publishing and printing, or publishing only

2732   Book Printing

Establishments primarily engaged in printing, or in printing and binding, books and pamphlets, but not engaged in publishing. Establishments primarily engaged in publishing, or in publishing and printing, books and pamphlets are classified in Industry 2731. Establishments engaged in both printing and binding books, but primarily binding books printed elsewhere, are classified in Industry 2789.

Books: printing or printing and binding, not publishing
Music books: printing or printing and binding, not publishing

Pamphlets: printing or printing and binding, not publishing
Textbooks: printing or printing and binding, not publishing

274   MISCELLANEOUS PUBLISHING

2741   Miscellaneous Publishing

Establishments primarily engaged in miscellaneous publishing activities, not elsewhere classified, whether or not engaged in printing. Establishments primarily engaged in offering financial, credit, or other business services, and which may publish directories as part of this service, are classified in Division I, Services.

Atlases: publishing and printing, or publishing only
Business service newsletters: publishing and printing, or publishing only
Calendars: publishing and printing, or publishing only
Catalogs: publishing and printing, or publishing only
Directories: publishing and printing, or publishing only
Globe covers (maps): publishing and printing, or publishing only
Guides: publishing and printing, or publishing only
Maps: publishing and printing, or publishing only
Micropublishing
Multimedia educational kits: publishing and printing, or publishing only

Music, sheet: publishing and printing, or publishing only
Patterns, paper, including clothing patterns: publishing and printing, or publishing only
Race track programs: publishing and printing, or publishing only
Racing forms: publishing and printing, or publishing only
Shopping news: publishing and printing, or publishing only
Technical manuals and papers: publishing and printing, or publishing only
Telephone directories: publishing and printing, or publishing only
Yearbooks: publishing and printing, or publishing only

275   COMMERCIAL PRINTING

2752   Commercial Printing, Lithographic

Establishments primarily engaged in printing by the lithographic process. The greater part of the work in this industry is performed on a job or custom basis; but in some cases lithographed calendars, maps, posters, decalcomanias, such a list will have to check with the appropriate association. Earlier in this chapter it was suggested that the *Encyclopedia of Associations* (usually available in a library) is the way to locate associations in different fields and to learn about the interests, nature, and size of their membership.

SPECIALIZED SECONDARY SOURCES FOR THE MARKETING RESEARCHER

In this section we list several specialized secondary sources—excluding books—that may help the marketing researcher to perform more effectively.

DIRECTORIES OF RESEARCH SOURCES

There are a fair number of these. However, since Chapter 6 covers the whole area of using outside assistance, we will discuss these directories there.

RESEARCH JOURNALS AND MAGAZINES

This review excludes any journal that covers primarily academic research, because this book is concerned with applied marketing research rather than with theory and academic approaches to marketing.

Marketing Research is a journal published monthly by the American Marketing Association (Chicago). It is aimed at the manager and the practitioner of marketing research. Mainly through articles and regular departments, it presents a range of current applications of marketing research and management of the research function. Its topics include emerging technology and computer applications, integrating the research function, legal issues facing the research professional, new techniques in comparative research, and qualitative research as part of the research mix. It is sold on a subscription basis.

The Advertising Research Foundation publishes the *Journal of Advertising Research* six times a year. A subscription publication, it has a circulation of some 5,500. It too is aimed at covering applied research, mainly, but not completely, advertising research. Many of its articles are on other applied marketing topics as diverse as target marketing, qualitative marketing research, and research quality.

One monthly magazine is aimed at buyers of marketing research. With a controlled circulation of 13,000, *Quirk's Marketing Research Re-*

view stresses the applications of marketing research procedures. Case histories and discussions of techniques are provided, along with new product/service announcements and personnel news. Quirk also publishes several directories of research sources annually.

COLLECTING PRIMARY DATA IN MARKETING RESEARCH

INTRODUCTION

We are first going to waffle a bit on our definition of primary research in our discussion of marketing research. For now, we are going to include all forms of current collection of data, whether this is done by the user or by an outside source. So a particular firm—Procter & Gamble, for instance—doesn't run its own continuing studies to measure how much of one of its brands it is selling at retail for each period of the year. It more likely is depending on an ongoing service such as Nielsen for such information. The Nielsen Scantrack service, discussed in Chapter 13, provides such measurements from summarizing retail store scanner material on a nationwide basis.

We have to make it clear early on that, in our view, almost all primary studies in marketing research fall under the broad heading of surveys. So we must define surveys.

A *survey,* in the sense in which we use the term, is the use of some sort of sample—a piece used to represent the whole group. Most researchers—and marketers too—think of surveys as being limited to studies that ask questions. We use the term more broadly, since virtually all primary marketing studies use sampling as their basic tool.

In addition to the usual *questionnaire* survey, there are electronic devices and single-source research.

Electronic Devices

Again, we do not regard the use of electronic devices in data collection as a basic method. Nevertheless, these devices have permeated almost every aspect of data collection in marketing research. We can separate them into two broad groups: monitoring devices (for observation) and interaction devices (for questioning). Some of the monitoring devices we have already discussed briefly.

Interactive devices require the participating consumer to respond by means of an electronic device when he or she is asked a question or otherwise prompted, usually by the same electronic device. A brief example: One method of checking a household's purchase of products marked with a Universal Product Code (UPC) is to have the family draw a hand-held wand, used at home, over each product purchased. (This information is electronically recorded and stored in a compact home computer provided by the research firm.)

Another example of an interactive device is the electronic people meter—about which more later—attached to a television set that flashes a reminder light when the set is turned on, reminding the household member who is tuning to indicate by pushing a button which particular member he or she is (so that tuning can be isolated by identity of the family member).

There are many more examples, mainly devices used in connection with direct questioning or response studies. Virtually all of these are described in later chapters.

Single-Source Research

Single-source methods, one of the "in" procedures in today's marketing research, are methods that use various kinds of information—buying behavior, media behavior, and the like—obtained from the same set of specific consumers. The argument is that using measurements from the same group of respondents solves the problem of relating cause and effect. Admittedly, it was often impossible, for instance, to make sure whether repeated viewing of a commercial—measured in one or a series of separate studies—had anything to do with brand buying, perhaps measured quite separately through store auditing methods. The correlation of repeated commercial viewing and higher sales was no proof that viewing caused purchasing.

Since single-source studies depend on questionnaire surveys and/or monitoring, we do not consider them a basic method. Rather, we regard the term *survey* as the umbrella term.

SOME WAYS OF CLASSIFYING SURVEYS

We have already looked at one method of classification: questioning surveys versus electronic measurements. We now examine other methods.

Syndicated Ongoing Surveys versus Customized Studies

Some surveys are conducted on an almost continuous basis (with perhaps periodic scheduled omissions, ranging from a few weeks to a month). Using one or another means of collecting data (such as by tele-phone, consumer reaction via a machine—usually electronic—by mail, or a combination of these), the research firm supplies information to its clients. The syndicated survey tends to have basically frozen proce-dures, modified only as improvements in technique or needs for new types of information arise. Syndicated surveys are studied in later chap-ters.

A custom-tailored survey is undertaken to help answer a particular marketing problem faced by a specific firm. It may use *any* of the basic survey data-collection methods to be outlined, and it will typically run the gamut of all stages of the survey.

The Common Elements of Questioning Surveys and Electronic Monitoring

Without going into specifics at this point, we will merely highlight the identical or near-identical elements and concepts common to both ques-tioning and observation.

Consider *problem definition.* In all surveys the marketing problem must be stated before the particular data available from an external source or an internal study are pertinent.

The *nature of the sample*—people, stores, or some other type of total—must be agreed upon. The *method of data collection* must be given seri-ous consideration to ensure that it is the best method of providing the information aimed at the problem solution. And the methods of *summa-rizing results* and *presenting results,* while perhaps taking somewhat different forms in the two cases, definitely require the same basic con-siderations.

SOME BASIC POINTS

Aspects of Reaction Measured

Three aspects of human reaction can be measured in surveys: the per-son's knowledge, attitudes, and behavior.

Measurement of *knowledge* is often crucial to the study. A survey of advertising effectiveness may have to determine what proportion of the target audience (those at whom the advertising is aimed) recalls the ad-vertising message or slogan. Moreover, many studies call for classifying or qualifying questions, where only those with some understanding of the issue are asked for specific responses. It makes little sense to ask about advertising recall of a brand the particular respondent is not aware of. Obviously, the measurement of knowledge calls for some form of questioning survey.

Measurement of *attitude* is common. Attitude, psychologists tell us, means readiness to act. Here the term is used in a broader sense, to mean a person's feelings about a topic or a thing (such as a product, a brand, or a company). Measurement of attitudes is not a simple process, as will be shown in Chapter 13. It takes considerable skill, and at best it may not be very accurate. People may not be fully aware of their attitudes, let alone know how to express them. This kind of study also generally requires a questionnaire study.

Measurement of *behavior* may be the most crucial kind of measurement in marketing research. It has rightly been said that the consumer's most accurate expression of attitude toward producers is their buying behavior in the marketplace—that every time a purchase is made, it is a vote favoring the brand. While this discounts the role of such factors as promotion, price, and the salesperson, it probably is not too far off the mark.

Measuring behavior has not been easy for marketing research. In questioning procedures, behavior has sometimes been spelled out in terms of recall, as in asking what products and brands were purchased (along with quantities), or what television shows were watched and who in the family watched them. More recently, electronic monitoring devices have been introduced. Thus the measurement of behavior may use either a questionnaire survey or an electronic monitoring system.

Today, as we shall see throughout this book, electronic recording of behavior has progressed far beyond the elementary stage. At least one device does not even require the person whose behavior is being measured to take steps to see that his or her actions are being recorded—it is all automatic. The scanner, used at the retail checkout counter to provide information about product movement by reading information on the UPC (Universal Product Code), is now common on many consumer products. The system is used extensively by grocery outlets and increasingly by drugstores and discount stores. It is spreading to many other type of retail outlets as well.

Although the system was designed for other reasons, scanning is in the process of revolutionizing much of marketing research. Scanners now provide virtually instantaneous measurements of customer behavior. Combined with other measurements, they can give a good idea of the effectiveness of a given promotion (such as a price offer or a particular advertising campaign). It has even been said that the scanner will revolutionize marketing research for the next ten years. The collection of data through scanners is discussed throughout much of this book, particularly in Chapter 13.

Another behavior-monitoring tool is a device attached to a television set that begins recording the moment the set is turned on, and therefore measures tuning.

It is estimated that about half the primary information in marketing research comes from monitoring studies and half from questionnaire surveys.[12]

BASIC METHODS OF SURVEY DESIGN

The term *design* refers to the pattern of the survey. There are several basic designs in marketing research.

The One-Time Study

The one-time study is the most common form of survey. It is a still photograph of what is happening. Respondents are questioned or observed at a single point in time. With a well-done study, results reflect reaction at that single point.

For example, assume a company has developed a new product and wants to know how its particular public reacts to that product. It has a sample of consumers try its new product and gets their reactions as a guide as to whether it should be marketed. There is no need to do more than a single study of that particular product. (Of course, reactions of the people studied may lead to product modification, in which case a new one-time study might be indicated.)

The Longitudinal (Panel) Study

The longitudinal study is simply a fancy name for a continuing study of specific consumers who are questioned or observed over a period of time. In contrast to the one-time study, it is a videotape, not a still photograph.

In one case, a cereal manufacturer with a new product wanted to know the staying power of the proposed offering. Cold cereals, each typically with a small market share, must have loyal buyers to survive. The study gave each family that tried and liked the product an opportunity to continue getting no-charge samples over a period of weeks. It was found that the new product had no staying power, and as a result it was dropped.

Experimental Design

In using an experimental design, the researcher sets up conditions in which one group of respondents is exposed to a particular stimulus (such as advertising) and another group is exposed to a different stimulus. There may be additional groups responding to still other promotional efforts, and perhaps a control group for which there is no promotional effort at all. The differences in sales, in awareness of the campaign, or in whatever measurements are used then indicate the impact of each stimulus.

Basic Questioning Survey Methods

In questioning surveys, people who are intended to represent those in whom the sponsor is mainly interested are asked to respond to a set of generalized or specific questions. A questionnaire is usually the instrument.

With the *mail questionnaire,* the researcher begins with a list of those whose responses it is important to measure. A questionnaire is sent to these people, perhaps with some incentive to reply. The recipient fills in the replies and mails back the questionnaire. The responses are used to estimate total reaction.

The mail survey is a self-administered study in the sense that the respondent fills in the form without any outside assistance other than that offered in the covering mail materials. There are other forms of self-administered questionnaires, the major one being the form used by many service firms, such as hotels, motels, and restaurants. Typically left at a desk or table for the customer to fill in, the form asks for reactions to the service received.

Frequently the purchaser of a durable product (toaster, washing machine, television set) is asked to complete and mail an enclosed questionnaire covering circumstances of purchase and purchaser demographics. (Often such responses are used to sell names of people with particular characteristics and purchasing behavior to other firms for use in their direct mail efforts.)

Another form of questioning survey is the *personal interview,* a face-to-face meeting between questioner and respondent. Today such interviewing most typically takes place in shopping malls. A few years ago the most common location was in the home, but today's security consciousness has made home interviews an outmoded practice. However, the mall interview may, as a follow-up on the person's reactions to a product, result in an in-home interview or, more likely, a telephone interview.

Sometimes personal interviewing is conducted in a store. More rarely it is done on the street, but on-the-street questioning cannot produce a reliable cross section.

Interviewing by telephone is perhaps the most common method of obtaining survey information today. It is relatively inexpensive, can be done regionally or nationally with little effort, and is fast. Also, the interviewing can be supervised, which is difficult or impossible with mall or in-home studies.

Chapter 7 examines these methods in detail.

Group interviewing is such a highly specialized tool that we put it in a class by itself. It might be included as a type of questioning study, though it is far more than that. In the group interview (often called a *focus group*), a small group of people, generally no more than 12, is assembled for a discussion of a particular product, commercial, or company, and is led by a trained moderator. The group's reactions and interactions are measured. The technique offers many advantages but it also has disadvantages, as outlined in Chapter 10.

SOME TECHNICAL ASPECTS OF CONDUCTING A SURVEY

Conducting a survey that will give dependable results requires considerable knowledge, skill, and judgment. An overview of the major aspects is provided here, but the fine points will be discussed in later chapters.

Problem Definition

To make sure that the appropriate study is bought or conducted for the firm, the basic starting point is definition of the problem. This means a statement of the marketing problem or problems that the study is supposed to help solve.

The Sample

The sample is a cross section of the particular group of people or companies that the study is intended to represent. The process of selecting and getting information from the sample is a complicated process, as is the decision about the number to be included in the sample.

In the early days of marketing research, determining the sample was not considered a problem. A leading news magazine of 1936 (the *Lit-*

erary Digest) predicted that President Franklin Roosevelt would be defeated by the Republican candidate, Alfred Landon. The magazine depended on mail returns—in the millions—to ballots circulated to people with telephones and owning automobiles. At that time—still the Great Depression—such people were in the affluent class. George Gallup was only then starting his polls. Through personal, in-home interviews, he predicted not only that the magazine would be wrong, but by dividing his respondents into those who did and did not own telephones and automobiles, he was able to predict what the magazine results would show. The *Literary Digest* folded a year later.

Chapter 8 considers and evaluates all of the major sampling methods.

Choosing the Method of Collecting Data

Each of the methods of data collection briefly described earlier in this book is better adapted than others for particular kinds of problems and topics. The data collection method chosen considers all of these elements in relation to the nature and requirements of the particular problem.

The Questionnaire

If the study calls for a questionnaire, then this too is an important technical point. Bruce Barton, founder of a major advertising agency, said many years ago that "most people will frankly admit that they can't direct a dance orchestra—that they wouldn't know how to operate for appendicitis—but almost everyone seems to feel that he (or she) can work up an effective questionnaire." It is not that easy.

Although putting together a good questionnaire is an art, not a science, questionnaire testing in advance of final use is crucial. If results are to be valid, the questionnaire must be understood and responded to in the way in which it is intended. Chapter 9 discusses the problems and techniques of questionnaire preparation.

Summarizing Results

The process of summarizing survey results has been considerably eased by computers (and computer programs), but the method cannot be automatic for the user. The astute researcher must not only know the form required for the basic data, but must also be aware of the possibilities of specialized and sophisticated data analyses described in Chapter 11.

Presenting Research Results

If there is, indeed, a need for a report in these days of the marketing information system, it must be a dynamic, action-getting report to management. It may be an oral report with visual and sound presentations, or it may be simply a written document. Chapter 12 discusses this topic.

ENDNOTES

[1] B. E. Bryant. *Research Differences: Taking the 1990 Census Versus Market Research Surveys.* Address to the Market Research Council, Feb. 22, 1991.

[2] *The Search Begins Here.* Washington, D.C.: Bureau of the Census, 1989.

[3] Cyndee Miller. "Dialog Moves Out of the Libraries." *Marketing News,* July 9, 1990, 21ff.

[4] *M/A/R/C Information Services.* Dallas: M/A/R/C, undated.

[5] *Census '90 Basics.* Washington, D.C.: Bureau of the Census, 1990.

[6] V. P. Goel and M. L. Carnevale. "Devouring the Data." *The Wall Street Journal,* Mar. 9, 1990, R30.

[7] *Census ABC's: Applications in Business and Community.* Washington, D.C.: Bureau of the Census, 1989.

[8] *1990 Census: Today's Technology for Tomorrow's Business.* Fairfax, Va: CACI Marketing Systems, 1990.

[9] R. W. Marx. "The TIGER System: Automating the Geographic Structure of the United States Census." *Government Publications Review* 13 (1986): 181–201.

[10] R. W. Marx. *GIS, TIGER, and Other Useful Acronyms.* Washington, D.C.: Bureau of the Census, 1989.

[11] *TIGER Questions and Answers.* Washington, D.C.: Bureau of the Census, 1989.

[12] Jim Spaeth and Mike Hess. *Single Source Data . . . The Missing Pieces.* Single Source Data Workshop, Advertising Research Foundation, 1989.

3

TWO BASIC RESEARCH SYSTEMS

What's in This Chapter

In this chapter we discuss two of the most important marketing research systems: competitive marketing intelligence and the marketing information system. We indicate how each of these systems is aimed specifically at making the marketing operation more effective. We show how a marketing research data system is an integration of broadly based information (information collected by many methods and generally from numerous sources maintained on an ongoing basis). We describe the marketing information system, which integrates vast amounts of computerized information into forms useful in the solution of marketing problems and in the monitoring of marketing activities.

COMPETITIVE MARKETING INTELLIGENCE

On a pleasant June evening, many automobile company executives were at a large cocktail party in Detroit. A Chrysler executive overheard a comment that Ford's top advertising photographer was in Paris. Since June is the month when automobile company photographers are typically hard at work to help put the fall campaign together, this seemed odd. The Chrysler representative in Paris was alerted and found that new Fords were being photographed with the Eiffel Tower as background and that Hong Kong was the next step.

Chrysler "scooped" the Ford campaign with one that highlighted its cars at U.S. landmarks, figuring that the American public could identify more easily with these than with landmarks abroad.

But competitive marketing intelligence is rarely of the cloak-and-dagger variety. " . . . We don't peek through keyholes or lift curtains to do our job," says James E. Touhy, former manager of marketing intelligence for A. C. Nielsen Marketing Research. "People think we have to steal information to make ourselves useful, but all the information we need is available from public sources."[1]

Says Bob Margulies, manager of competitive assessment for McDonnell Douglas Corp.: "Ninety-five percent of the information anyone needs is available through computers and on-line databases."[1]

Two weeks after the opening of a new Bergdorf Goodman men's store in Manhattan, the chairman of Bergdorf Goodman discovered the president of Brooks Brothers checking out the store. The visitor was late; executives of several other competitors had been spotted earlier, busy making notes.[2]

INTRODUCTION

Competitive intelligence, a broader term than *competitive marketing intelligence*, is the collection, evaluation, synthesis, and interpretation of information about a specific competitor that is useful for a company's planning and operation. Note the emphasis on a single competitor, though a particular firm may choose to focus on more than one.

There is a considerable amount of information about competitors that is readily available, through brochures, articles, speeches, and networking at marketing and industry conferences. But there is no substitute for an organized information search, one that includes both existing (secondary) information and primary data, as in the Chrysler example above. Whatever the method of getting the information, it is legitimate. There is little need for the cloak-and-dagger approach.

The Japanese seem to have this down to a science. They reputedly use business and trade newspapers, personal contracts, trade books, and company reports to keep up. Firms hold weekly meetings where competitors' strengths and weaknesses are evaluated against the firm's.

Competitive marketing intelligence is competitive intelligence of a marketing nature. This includes information that may help a firm in its marketing efforts against a competitor. It may provide an early warning of some specific customer move.

Importance and Common Use of Marketing Intelligence

Marketing intelligence is widely collected and used. As a shopper, you may have noticed a person in a grocery store with a hand-held computer walking down the aisle. It has been estimated that as many as one-quarter of these are employees of competing retailers. Others are members of firms that sell information about brand share and movement to grocery producers and chains.

Some firms make it a point to check on the competition's every move, if they can do it. The manufacturer of a shaving lather had its research lab working hard on a hot lather product. The company placed a number of samples of the product's first run in homes where the shaver tried it and gave his reaction. Each sample was picked up after the trial to prevent any possible pickup by competing manufacturers. After four such tests, the "bugs" seemed to have been ironed out, for the testers gave glowing reports. A fifth test was run as a final check. This time, since the product was ready for marketing, no product pickups were made. Within 24 hours the company president had a telephone call from the president of his major competitor congratulating him on the fine product, a sample of which was on the competitor's desk.

When a product is being test-marketed—especially in a controlled test market situation in which the research firm acts as distributor (discussed in Chapter 13)—the marketer may make the product directly available to the competition to avoid shelf-depletion by nonconsumers.

Why should a firm monitor competition? For one thing, surprises can be avoided. There is early awareness of threats and opportunities. The company can react more quickly to competitive action. Decision making will be improved, and overall marketing planning will be improved.

Key Areas of Competitive Marketing Intelligence

Competitive marketing intelligence provides *information about the competitor's product commitment*. The firm needs such information to plan and carry out its own marketing. Is the competitor really aggressively pushing the product, or just allowing it to sit quietly in the marketplace? If the latter, the firm may see an opportunity to move in and capture a significant share of the market.

Competitive marketing intelligence also provides *information about the competitor's product quality*. In one case a food manufacturer found that market share of one product—its instant pudding line—was being captured significantly by a particular competitor. There was nothing different from before in terms of the nature of the marketing by either firm. A quick kitchen test of the competitive product line was made, and it was then obvious that the competitor had made significant product improvements, obviously noted by consumers. The company got busy and improved its own product. Although it finally was able to recapture most of the lost market share, it got that important bit of product information far too late.

Competitive marketing intelligence also produces *information about the competitor's attitude toward new products*. Some competitors are, by intent, followers, rarely spending the money to develop new products, and content to follow the lead of others. Others may spend considerable money on product development and may be among the leaders in new-product introduction. If it is to compete successfully, the firm has to know into which category each of the major competitors falls.

A good competitive marketing intelligence system also determines the *competitive attitude toward the bottom line*. The question here is whether each competitor being watched is interested primarily in immediate profits or takes a long-range view without insisting on continuing short-term gain.

Only if a firm knows this can it market effectively in the competitive environment. A firm competing against Procter & Gamble, for instance, knows that P&G is willing to back its judgment about a new product with millions of dollars of marketing money, sometimes over several years, with no insistence on immediate return. Only a well-capitalized, successful firm can take such a stance. The smaller competitor may find it necessary to take a short-term view.

The marketing intelligence program also provides *information about the specific nature of the competitor's market*. Whether the firm is in the business market or the consumer market, it is important to know the nature of the specific market for the competitor. A fast-food restaurant should realize, for instance, that McDonald's originally was typically after the business of families with younger children and of teenagers. But now, with further growth locked in by its obtaining such large shares of these target markets, McDonald's is experimenting. It has opened family-style restaurants in small towns. It is trying fixed breakfast meals in many restaurants. In one small community—Edgewater, Fla.—it is now trying out buffet breakfasts on Friday, Saturday and Sunday. It has several full-service restaurants in larger cities.

A firm offering office supplies should know how its major competitors are concentrating their marketing by nature of major business categories, such as professional offices (physicians, lawyers), small versus larger business offices, and the like. It is not too difficult for a firm to get the names of the major accounts of its competitors.

Then there is *information about market share and trend*. The firm should have a pretty clear idea of the market share of each major competitor. A brewer, for example, has to be able to have running reports of the market shares of its major competitors. In this extremely competitive market, one national brewer keeps tabs on share of four major domestic brands and three import brands. A half-point share gain nationally by a competitor may mean millions of dollars of loss for the brewer, so it is crucial for the firm to spot changes early and to be aware of the geographic areas, and even cities, where such changes are concentrated. Being able to localize such changes enables the brewer to find what differences in marketing are being introduced and to take marketing action accordingly.

Another area is *information about competitive distribution channels*. It is important to know whether the major competition is using distribution channels similar to those used by the firm, or whether these are different. The success of the competition—and therefore of the firm—may depend on such knowledge and awareness of any competitive changes in distribution channels. For example, one major national brewing firm recently introduced a snack line. It began by introducing the line into bars, a logical enough step since this utilized its current distribution channels. A major snack company was not disturbed, since it marketed primarily to grocery stores. But it didn't take the brewer long to expand efforts to include such diverse outlets as airlines and groceries, already two of its important outlets for its beer. The established snack firm was hurt badly by the inroads of the beer firm into the grocery field and has never fully recovered. An early warning system would have alerted it and given it a chance to fight back early.

Finally, the competitive marketing intelligence system measures *competitive flexibility in marketing strategy*. Is the competitor a wheeler-dealer, responding quickly, decisively, and aggressively to marketplace pressures? Is the competitor likely to use such tactics as price-cutting and advertising to respond quickly? Does the firm have funds and the willingness to use them as long as it believes the end justifies the means? The firm keeping tabs on its competition needs to know this, because such knowledge helps it make its own marketing decision.

TWO BASIC SOURCES OF COMPETITIVE MARKETING INTELLIGENCE

As with all research methods, there are secondary data and primary data.

Secondary Data

Many of the kinds of secondary data used in competitive marketing intelligence are not easy to come by; they are often unobtrusive published material, not easily located by the company. It may be crucial to go to an outside supplier of such information to get all that is required. Whether or not they are simple to locate, many of them cost money to obtain.

Two important starting points are *The Wall Street Journal Index* and the *New York Times Index*. One portion of the *Journal* index provides a list of news items classed by company name, so it is a source of competitive news. The *Times* is commonly regarded as the best newspaper in the United States. Its index offers abstracts of news items listed chronologically under subject headings, so it too is a rich source of information about major competition.

There is *federal government information* available. But the firm has to know what it is and how to get it. One such source is congressional hearings on various topics that may reveal competitive information. Often the office of a congressman or senator is delighted to check out this source for a firm located in the voting district. The Environmental Protection Agency makes studies of firms that might pollute. The Consumer Product Safety Commission may have competitive information from its investigations of products considered potentially hazardous. Studies by the National Institute of Occupational Safety and Health may reveal interesting intelligence about specific firms.

If the competitor is large enough to be traded on a stock exchange, the Securities and Exchange Commission is a fertile source. Firms must reveal many of the facts they would prefer their competition not to have—not only specific financial information, but many operational facts as well.

If information about a small firm is needed, it may be available from the Small Business Administration, which keeps files on small companies working through it in seeking primary or subcontracting work from the federal government. These firms must provide information such as type of business, number of employees, products and services produced, year established, current year's sales, and type of ownership. All this is included in its Procurement Automated Source System (PASS). In addition, the Department of Commerce maintains files on some 27,000 minority businesses.

State governments sometimes are good sources of secondary information about competition. One possibility is court records. If the competition has been involved in any litigation, it is almost certain to have revealed information about itself that is nowhere else available. An attorney is a help in determining how to locate such material.

A second possibility is at an entirely different level. The geographic distribution of a competitor's customers can often be obtained through a check of the license numbers of vehicles in a parking lot. While most states will not provide such geographic checks directly, in most cases they can be provided by R. L. Polk & Co., a commercial source in Detroit.

Another source of competitive marketing intelligence is *the competitor*. The annual report of the competitor is not likely to provide any trade secrets, but chances are that it will stress the strong points and minimize or omit the weak aspects. It still may provide marketing information of which the checking firm was not yet aware.

Press reports about the competitor are another way in which a firm can keep the tabs on the competition. Two possibilities (*The Wall Street Journal* and the *New York Times*) have already been mentioned. However, with few exceptions, the mentions in these two sources will be of larger firms. The company interested in smaller or localized competitors cannot count on such sources. The local library typically contains back issues of local newspapers, but this requires digging out the material. A good press-clipping service can generally be located for about a $30 basic monthly charge plus 70 cents per clip.

Then there is competitive advertising. Three types of advertising may provide key leads about the competition's marketing-related plans. By keeping a running record of the general nature and frequency of competitive advertising, it is possible to get a focused idea of what rival firms are trying to do in their marketing efforts. Any sudden changes will also be apparent.

Leading National Advertisers (LNA) provides clippings of newspaper ads and of magazine ads, with tapes available for television and radio commercials.

The yellow pages are another useful competitive advertising source. If a firm wants a good idea of the marketing area of a competitor, all it needs to do is check the telephone books in which that competitor is listed in the yellow pages. When the competitor markets in so many areas that it is difficult to locate all the appropriate books, there is the possibility of using the Electronic Yellow Pages, a service available through Dialog.

Local want ads may be valuable. Through these it is possible to spot when a competitor is hiring and the kinds of employees being sought. Such competitive information may reveal when a competitor is planning a new product or production expansion for an existing product.

Another good secondary source is *specialized published material*. One such source is Poor's Register of Corporations, Directors and Executives. Published by Standard & Poor's, this provides in-depth information on publicity and privately held firms. There is an SIC index to direct the user to companies in selected product and service fields. The corporate listings then typically provide company sales and number of employees.

FINDEX (Bethesda, Md.) provides a publication including a 750-

page directory that helps the subscriber locate appropriate firms, as well as reports on 2,000 of these prepared by top Wall Street analysts. The Corporate Directory (from Cambridge Information Group in Bethesda) covers some 9,500 firms and their subsidiaries, with SIC numbers, numbers of employees, sales history, and the basics of ownership.

Trinet (Parsippany, N.J.) provides marketing, sales, and financial data for U.S. firms with 20 or more employees.

Finally, there are *miscellaneous secondary sources*, such as media reports, credit reports, and even litigation. Studies covering the major competitors may have been conducted by an advertising medium. In a local area such a study may have been done by a newspaper, television station, or radio station. On a national basis, a major medium may have done a larger but parallel study on national and regional competitors. Such studies may be market or consumer studies showing the ranking of major competitors in the market, or studies that are "desk" research, examining the firms within the market and describing them and their operations based on available data.

Credit reports may be available from Dun & Bradstreet or from a local credit bureau. The main value in such reports is the credit history and creditworthiness. Occasionally they provide competitive information not available elsewhere. Dun & Bradstreet, when updating a report, sometimes provides material from an interview with one or more company executives. The input is limited and is often biased to present the firm's best case, but occasionally new plans are revealed.

Coors, for example, was aware that one of its competitors was being sued. Through a careful study of many pieces of isolated testimony in the case, Coors was able to make an accurate calculation of the amount of beer produced and shipped by the competitor each quarter.[3]

Primary Data

Sometimes the available (secondary) data do not provide all of the desired competitive information. It may be necessary for the firm to collect some of its own data.

Primary competitive marketing intelligence information is collected primarily through observation and surveillance. There are three basic methods: formal surveillance, informal observation, and informal questioning.

A structured approach of what is going on at a competitor's location is *formal surveillance*. It is used sparingly because it is generally expensive and not really necessary very often.

A Canadian gasoline company, for example, conducted a massive controlled observation study of four service-station restaurants along a major Ontario highway over a two-week period. Each place of business was observed during all business hours, which was often around the clock. This was done from a post across the highway. There was no attempt to secure cooperation from the service stations. One parent firm sent out observers to observe the observers!

Specific information was obtained on each service station and its restaurant. Station data included vehicle counts (at islands, bays, parking lots), recording of license numbers, gasoline gallons pumped, and gallons received. Restaurant data included vehicle counts in parking lots, numbers of people entering the restaurant, and dollar amounts of purchases (from cash register observation).

Few formal surveillance studies are on such a grand scale. It is possible to observe traffic flow, as mentioned earlier, through use of license numbers to get customer locations. If an estimate of the number of employees is needed, the employee parking lot can be checked by shift and number of people in each car. The estimate of total employees won't be too far off.

If the firm's business is retailing or consumer service (restaurant, hotel, motel), there are additional options. The competitor's premise may be visited (comparison shopping) to learn what the offerings are—their services, their pricing, and so on. A professional service can be employed to handle this if there is a good reason to spend the money.

A second and less formal type of study is *informal observation*. Company people keep their eyes and ears open to pick up clues about what the competition may be doing in a marketing way. The Chrysler example at the beginning of this chapter is an example. Usually the input of the sales force is crucial; these people can be the eyes and ears of the organization, picking up competitive marketing clues.

A Corning buyer visiting a supplier noticed crates of a glass-making material on a shipping dock addressed to the new factory of a competitor. His trip report, filed by computer to the home office, included that information, which was soon in the hands of an engineer. It took little time to figure what kind of glass the competitor was planning to make, and that information became part of Corning's background for marketing strategy.

Bacardi representatives visit trendy bars and listen to customer orders, bartenders, and wait staff. Their reports provide a possible guide to what is happening to drinking patterns and to competitive trends. New executive trainees for Seagrams, for example, visit bars and learn to keep their ears open, reporting back key observations.

By listening in, a company employee may get wind of significant competitive events or possibilities. A single report may not prove anything, but it may provide a clue that can be checked out. The waitress in a coffee shop may mention a layoff at a nearby plant and comment that it is too bad there is no promise of when the "poor fellows" may be called back. A regular there may say it's due to poor sales of a particular product.

The practice of listening can and should be well planned. Business places that cater to employees and families of a competitor can be spotted rather easily, usually being close to the competitor's place of business. Types of business where people linger and chat, such as restaurants and bars, should be chosen. The crisscross telephone directories discussed in Chapter 2 can be used to spot such establishments. Then the observers can arrange to be there during periods when the competitor's employees or families are most likely to frequent those locations.

The third basic method of obtaining marketing intelligence information is through *informal questioning*. This is not the survey questioning approach discussed in Chapter 2; it is far less structured. There is no specifically designed sample of people to be questioned, and there is no specific questionnaire.

One form of informal questioning is networking. The company employee primarily responsible for competitive marketing intelligence builds a list of every informed person he or she can think of who might be able to provide unpublished information about the competition. This list might include peers in other business firms. Such people, in addition to suggesting other sources, often are able to provide information about what the competitor is doing. If the competitive marketing intelligence person within the firm is able to build peer contacts in other geographic areas, the search might be even easier. The peer in a distant firm may be able to obtain information about a local competitor that is not otherwise available. Naturally, from time to time, reciprocity will be requested and expected.

One researcher in a manufacturing firm developed such a responsive group of peers in similar firms that it was relatively easy to determine market shares and to spot when a firm was developing a new or improved product.

The media sales representative from a magazine, newspaper, television, or radio station can be another fertile source of competitive information. One of the most obvious areas concerns advertising plans and details about the nature of campaign claims, coverage, and amount. The astute media rep goes far beyond this.

The real estate agent may know about a competitor's expansion plans. Particularly in a small community, the agent is often the first to know not only about the kind of real estate being sought (location and size), but also about the firm's plans that lead to such needs.

The shopping center manager is another good source, assuming that the competitor is either a current or an incoming tenant. The manager may know the general plans for the firm but will definitely know square footage, cost per square foot, and lease arrangements.

Associations should not be overlooked. The association executive is likely to know specific plans about a competitor and may be willing to discuss them, assuming that he or she has not been told them in confidence. But the firm that really wants to pick up competitive information should be an active member of the association and attend its meetings. The in-the-hall discussions almost invariably bring out competitive information that otherwise could not be learned. Sometimes, too, the publications of the association provide competitive marketing information.

Customers are another viable source of competitive marketing information. These might be the firm's own customers (many of whom also use competitive products or services) or customers of the competitor. But the organization has to be careful in reactions obtained from its own customers about competitors. Many or most are likely to be loyal, preferring not to come up with comments they feel are disloyal. The same sort of problem may be faced in reverse if the firm wants reactions from customers of a competitor. There is a solution: An outside research service can be used to handle the informal questioning. There is more about how to select such a firm in the last part of this section of the chapter.

Company suppliers are another important source. Most of them also serve one or more of the firm's major competitors, and these people often have news and information about what the competitor is doing or considering in the way of marketing.

THE ORGANIZATION OF COMPETITIVE MARKETING INTELLIGENCE WITHIN A FIRM

While this discussion emphasizes competitive *marketing* intelligence, probably most companies with a competitive intelligence function run it on an overall business basis for the firm, and do not concentrate on marketing intelligence alone. However, even where this is true, the competitive marketing intelligence function is likely to be under the management of someone within the marketing operation.

Some firms—the smaller ones have little choice—handle competitive marketing intelligence on a small-scale, casual basis, using a do-it-only-as-absolutely-required schedule. Larger firms that have gone into competitive marketing intelligence typically have done so on a large-scale, well-organized, continuing basis. When Motorola began its intelligence operation, for example, it hired a former CIA agent as its full-time person to head the function. Coors has a competitive intelligence manager. AT&T has a competitive information and analysis manager. But most firms with a competitive intelligence system fall between these two extremes, having a loosely organized function. To speed up its intelligence system, one firm even set up a hot line to speed communications from its sales force.

OUTSIDE ASSISTANCE IN COLLECTING COMPETITIVE MARKETING INTELLIGENCE

Frequently a company decides that it has neither the time nor the manpower to set up its own competitive marketing intelligence operation. Even if it does, there are likely to be numerous kinds of information it must get from external rather than internal sources.

The Specialist Information Broker

This is the specialist, described in Chapter 1, that usually deals primarily in information banks. Such firms do not typically stress marketing information, but they can be used to obtain competitive marketing intelligence if they have the necessary resources.

Three firms that serve as information brokers are the Competitor Intelligence Group (Chicago, Ill.), FIND/SVP, Predicasts (Cleveland, Ohio), and Washington Researchers (Washington, D.C.).

The Specialist in Primary Information

Two names come up most often in discussions of primary information specialists. One is Information Data Search (Cambridge, Mass.); the other is Combs Moorehead Associates (Chicago).

The user firm may make its own search for a competitive intelligence research house, although this may not be an easy task. It is too soon in the history of this sort of research to find appropriate listings in the yellow pages. Still, the firm does have some options.

If the firm deals with an advertising agency, a management consultant firm, or a marketing research firm, one or more of these could be the starting point in the quest. If the firm lacks such contacts, it can get them from the yellow pages. The names of the more prominent firms will be recognized. They should be able to handle a search for the firm, or even to suggest immediate possibilities.

The networking contacts previously discussed are another possibility. One or more persons should have had some contact with such firms.

There is no reason why the right person in the firm should hesitate approaching knowledgeable people in some of the larger of the Fortune 500 companies. A few firms with established intelligence functions have been mentioned in this section of the chapter. In any case, the contact should begin by getting the name of the marketing research director, the marketing planning director, or, if there is one, the competitive intelligence director. That person should be approached by telephone, not by letter; response to the latter is often indefinite.

THE MARKETING INFORMATION SYSTEM

SOME BACKGROUND

The Concept and Its Meteoric Rise

The marketing information system is a broader concept than the competitive marketing intelligence system. The marketing information system assembles all pertinent marketing data about a product line (or a single product)—both from external and internal sources—and assembles these so that they can be integrated into any combination to help solve a problem or to monitor ongoing marketing activities.

The concept is really not quite new. The basic elements were developed in the early 1970s. But it was not until the early 1980s, along with the development of the desktop computer, that the marketing information system really began to take hold. The UPC (Universal Product Code) was one major factor. Use of the UPC at the checkout counters in food stores rapidly led to the development of scanner services to measure the movement of merchandise, as explained in Chapter 2. This in turn led to a geometric increase in the generation of data. It has also been estimated that in 1990 the marketing data per brand rose to 150 times that in 1970.

It has also been estimated that the information produced in just one year is today equal to the total amount of world information in existence at the start of World War I. This increase was at least partially due to the computer and is its greatest contribution in the marketing intelligence system: the assimilation and analysis of data.

But the basic marketing needs were there too. Product life cycles were declining. There was a continuing drive toward greater productivity. There were pressures for improved product quality and lower prices. In short, competition was getting tougher.

Companies most often achieve competitive advantage through front-end marketing systems and databases. Today's firm has to be fast, nimble, and able to strike first. No company can compete effectively today without electronic order processing.

DEFINE THE MARKETING INFORMATION SYSTEM

Before beginning this discussion, we need to define three background terms.

Data file: This is a specific data set that is ready for reporting or that can be easily processed. Typically the data are aggregated in some form. For example, case shipments of a brand for three years in twenty markets is a data file.

Database: This is a collection of disaggregated data identified by attributes and characteristics. Generally there are several related databases, each with its own common or related attributes/characteristics. These are separated for each subsequent processing. For example, scanner sales and prices (UPC/STORE/WEEK) are separate from causal factors, (i.e., display, feature ads, special pricing) but these may be combined into processing for reports.

Databank: This is a loose term that generally refers to a repository of data.

We start with the term *management information system*. This term refers to a program for a company databank containing all possible useful information that a company management might want—everything from financial information to production, research and development, and marketing data. The *marketing* information system is most often a segment of this broad-scale databank—material that is important to the marketing end of the business.

The emphasis in this book, because of its marketing slant, is on the marketing information system. Its definition must be considered at further length.

The marketing information system includes all of the kinds of data discussed earlier in this chapter. It includes secondary and primary data for the firm. It includes specific kinds of survey data collected by and for the organization. Competitive marketing intelligence material of all types relevant for the particular organization also is incorporated.

The definition may be further expanded to include the purpose of the databank accumulation. A limited definition holds that the marketing information system is *a computerized accumulation that provides information*. It is the accumulation and dissemination of marketing information of various types—an integrated database for marketing. It can be updated at any time with new information, by disk or by on-line sources.

A more sophisticated definition is that the marketing information system is *a database tool to help in marketing decision making*. The product manager has the responsibility for deciding on marketing objectives and strategies and tactics for a single product or line of products for the firm. Programming is so constructed that the material is electronically abstracted and summarized to assist the product manager. The system provides a basis for simulation. Marketing programs can be tried out with the computer rather than through test marketing. The machine can be asked "What if?" for any number of conditions.

NATURE OF USERS

Until recently, the marketing information system has been largely limited to use by large manufacturers and retailers of consumer goods, most likely because of the huge volume of information generated by and for such firms, and the highly competitive environment in which they work. Among the firms that have such systems—many of them as a part of a general management information system—are AT&T, Campbell Soup, Carnation, Colgate-Palmolive, Frito-Lay, General Mills, General Motors, Johnson & Johnson, Kraft-General Foods, Lever Bros., J. C. Penney, Pepsico, Philip Morris, and Procter & Gamble.

SOME THINGS A MARKETING INFORMATION SYSTEM CAN DO

Ideally the marketing information system assists in *marketing planning* and in *producing solutions to marketing problems*. It achieves the former through monitoring its own and competitive marketing activities and by collecting and analyzing data constantly, before there are problems, to make marketing plans. It helps produce solutions through the identification of problems and, perhaps, within the limits of the material in the system, providing a solution. On the other hand, it indicates the lack of information needed to assist in problem solution and thus helps the researcher or product management executive to determine what additional information is needed to solve the problem. A good marketing information system will provide the basis for decisions, and not merely play back masses of data.

These syntheses of information should be by product. There are a number of specific types of information that the system should produce. One is *sales analysis*, a breakout of sales by regions, by customer types, by major customers, or other groupings.

The system should also provide *spotting of sales changes* on a daily basis, so that unusual rises or drops in sales can be seen by geography, by price, by variety, or by size of the product. Such data give an early alert about changes in spending patterns. One national retail chain uses terminals at all of its customer checkout points, and detailed records of each sale are automatically and immediately entered into a central computer, covering item number, brand, size, and price. A major toiletries firm can provide its managers with daily reports about the sales of its brands by geographic district.

Another important output of the system is *customer information*. Customers can be profiled in changing patterns by their demographics and psychographics. Their buying behavior and any changes in it can be spelled out, as can their reactions to new products.

Then there is *market information*. Sales potential and sales predictions can be indicated by geographic area, and so can market change. The system can generate information that will determine the size and location of the best markets for a new product.

An important output is *promotion effects*. Promotion refers to all the marketing functions of informing, persuading, and especially influencing the buyer's purchase decision. It covers personal selling, advertising, sales promotion, and public relations. The relationship of specific promotional efforts to sales is an output of the modern marketing information system.

Yet another possible output is *site selection*. As we will show a little later, it is now possible to use sophisticated analyses to select business sites, and the relevant raw data can be entered into the system to provide these analyses.

POSSIBLE TYPES OF INPUT FOR THE MARKETING INFORMATION SYSTEM

The following partial review of the types of data that might be entered into the marketing information system covers both internal and external data.

Internal Data about Customers

This could include, depending on company needs, ongoing reports from company material on sales, customer characteristics, target market data, and primary research studies done by the company.

Internal Data about Sales to Various Kinds of Middlemen

This might include the sales volume, perhaps on a monthly basis, to middlemen, entered by type, such as brokers and wholesalers. It might indicate buying frequency and number of items bought on particular orders.

Company-Secured Competitive Information

This might include ongoing reports from company employees (most often the sales force) about the major competitors: when and where new products were introduced, the sales effort put behind these, the degree of success. It would also include company-secured data such as the marketing efforts of the competition (as outlined in the first section of this chapter). Material from competitive brochures and price lists belong here, as do material from competitive corporate literature and reports and any other relevant bits of company-secured competitive marketing intelligence.

External News Material

VU/TEXT[4] is Knight-Ridder Newspapers' entry to the electronic access of the full text of newspaper materials from many publications in the United States, including the *Washington Post*, the *Boston Globe*, the *Philadelphia Inquirier*, and the *Chicago Tribune*, as well as business information from 2,000 worldwide journals. It is possible to dig into regional newspapers for local marketing information. What is selling in a specific market? What are various firms doing in a marketing way? What is the competition there? Financial, price and volume data, and SEC filings are available for thousands of companies. All this is on-line.

The *New York Times* offers a similar service, covering abstracts from the *Times* as well as from many other newspapers and some magazines. The Dow Jones News/Retrieval Service provides complete and abridged articles from *The Wall Street Journal* and *Barron's*. First Release Service provides access to other databases such as Reuters, Knight-Ridder Financial News, McGraw-Hill News, PR Newswire, and Businesswire; it is updated throughout the day.

There are three broad-based vendors that may have databases useful to particular marketers: The Source, CompuServe, and Dialog. The kinds of information they carry are broad and varied. Dialog offers abstracts of articles in the *Harvard Business Review*, for example. Dialog Alert sends a subscriber the latest information when something happens to a firm or market segment in the user's field of interest.

What we have presented above are examples of outside databases on a broad scale—news items and feature articles—that may be relevant for a firm's use in its marketing intelligence system. On a more narrow and targeted basis, there are external data collected as secondary data and those collected as primary data.

External Data Collected as Secondary Data

Many external sources provide already existing information as data-bank material. In addition to many other kinds of secondary data, external sources can provide census data, such as descriptions of the population in many or most of the ways described in Chapter 2. Census data on businesses may well be part of the offering.

External Data Collected as Primary Data

While all external data going into the system is by definition secondary, some of this information was collected by the particular source as primary data, and is thus distinguished from straight primary data. These data are collected largely from surveys. Information such as market share (both for the company itself and for its competition) is collected at the retail level, with prices, nature, and size of shelf displays collected and reported by the A. C. Nielsen Co. Similar types of information are reported through scanner data by Information Resources Inc. (IRI).

Then there are consumer data. Longitudinal studies provide continuing input for each consumer detail of the purchase, such as frequency, amount, and brand. All this can be entered by the nature of each customer (demographics and perhaps psychographics).

Research Information: The AT&T System[5]

Because too often the researcher is eager to start a new study or a new management team wants to show how good it is, there may be neither awareness nor interest in earlier, possibly pertinent research. In the AT&T system the researcher tells the information manager his best guess on what the key words are. The information manager is then able to check not only the company's own past studies, but also other public databases.

FACILITIES NEEDED FOR A MARKETING INFORMATION SYSTEM

If the firm has its own internal files within the marketing information system, it is almost certain that a mainframe will be required, because these files tend to be massive and to continue to build. Of course, if there are no internal files, it is questionable whether the system is truly a marketing information system, for any system that depends only on external sources is merely a system that accesses existing external databanks.

For the system to be effective, it should have workstations for the major users. These most often take the form of PCs with display units and keyboards. Sometimes the external source—particularly if it is a marketing research firm providing syndicated data—will provide its data in the form of magnetic tape to be put into the mainframe. Where this is the case, the individual user has no access to certain outside data, such as news sources.

More often the ideal setup of facilities seems to be a PC with a modem so that the user can get whatever external data are useful on an on-line basis, directly from the vendor. Nielson and IRI have on-line reporting systems that use the supplier's mainframe for processing. Or the vendor may supply the material on disk to be used with the PC.

SOME PRACTICAL PROBLEMS OF A MARKETING INFORMATION SYSTEM

Most existing marketing information systems have inherent problems, some of which we will now examine.

A Mass of Undigested Data

More data are going into these systems than can serve anyone's needs. For example, there are some 200,000 scanner reports from 16,000 supermarkets going into research systems daily. It is little wonder that so many of these facts remain unexplained.

The hope is that, with time, an increasing number of marketing information systems will mean that the computer assimilates the billions of figures and comes up with the desired executive summaries that can lead to marketing decisions.

Too Little Interpretation of Unusual Events

Rapid and unexplained changes in sales may occur in a specific city or even in a specific neighborhood. There should be a way to anticipate many of these so that they are understood when they do occur.

Too Many Data within the System Are Not Dependable

People meters are the current major method for measuring the size of television audiences. (A discussion of people meters is not really relevant until Chapter 18.) However, people meters require active participation of the viewer if they are to provide reliable data, and there is certainly a big question as to how much participation is secured.

Especially with survey data, as we will show in Chapter 7, there are many sources of error. Some panel studies ask people to record their television viewing, radio listening, or purchasing. But people often forget to record their behavior. Such shortcomings are seldom seriously considered in the search for masses of data at low prices rather than reliable data at more costly prices.

SETTING UP A MARKETING INFORMATION SYSTEM

When the management and marketing functions of a firm have agreed that the firm should have a marketing information system, what is the way to go about setting it up? It is generally agreed that there are four issues to be considered: information needs, organization, degree of sophistication, and development strategy.[6]

Whatever form of information system is established, perhaps the key element is the needs of the users. The system must consider user needs in determining the information to be entered into the system. Potential users should be questioned to learn their information requirements. The long-range plan for system development must be based on such requirements.

The organization must include a number of both marketing and nonmarketing functions, such as sales, marketing, marketing research, computer operations, and finance and accounting. The approach must have the acceptance of all. One approach proposes use of a special task force committee representing all areas using or supplying information and headed by the top marketing executive.[6] Another approach suggests appointment of an information coordinator who reviews and coordinates the contributions of all those participating in the system and who represents the needs of the marketing users of the system.[6]

It is also argued that a balance between the sophistication of the user and that of the system is crucial, in that the users will reject the system if the sophistication of the system is above their own. Psychologically, this recommendation makes good sense.

The firm moving into a marketing information system typically upgrades the methods it is using rather than starting from scratch. In line with this, Kotler proposes that existing flows of information should be traced so that their timeliness and degree of completeness may be improved. Close to this is the idea that each subsystem should be separately constructed from the existing system.[7] Other writers suggest using the existing system as a base on which to build improvements.[8,9]

THE PHYSICAL ASPECTS OF MARKETING INFORMATION SYSTEMS

The physical aspects of any marketing information system vary with the needs of the firm. These needs include *the capacity required to handle the amount and nature of information that the organization demands*. As a simple example, the firm that is going in for a management-wide information system will need considerably more capacity in its hardware and software than will a small firm wanting to handle only marketing information needs.

There is also the question of the need for external data. While most firms will want to have external data incorporated into the system, the few generally smaller organizations not demanding such data can have a less involved system, with simpler hardware and software.

Some Hardware Considerations

There are few strictly marketing information systems that need the hardware of a mainframe. At most, even an involved marketing information system does not need capacity over what a microcomputer can provide. A strictly in-house system can generally get by with a microcomputer.

The marketing information system designed to provide information to more than a single user, such as to multiple product managers, needs to have a workstation for each user.

The Basic Types of Marketing Information Systems

There are two basic types of marketing information systems: the custom-designed system and the off-the-shelf system.

The *custom-designed system* is built to meet the exact needs of a specific firm. Although it can be argued that it better meets company requirements, it is expensive to develop and takes a long time to implement.

The *off-the-shelf* or *package system* is much better adapted to the needs of an organization wanting primarily a marketing information system, as opposed to a management information system. However, some of the package systems do offer the broader application.

The firm that opts for an off-the-shelf system typically starts with the package system and chooses from among standard options for the system. But special needs and internal company input can also be handled.

Most package systems have taken years to develop and have been user-tested all along the way. There is no need for the designers to start from scratch and reinvent the wheel. These package systems, therefore, tend to be practical, usable systems. They seem to meet most companies' needs.

EXAMPLES OF PACKAGE SYSTEMS

A Broad-Based Management Information System: METAPHOR[10,11]

This system provides desktop availability to each user in the organization. But to get its foot in the door, the METAPHOR firm uses an approach to the marketing people in the user organization and, after the first hurdle is passed, then goes to the management information people to talk about the broader applications and to complete the sale.

The system requires a mainframe and microprocessors and provides from 15 to 20 workstations, with every 2 workstations sharing a laser printer. The basic system was designed to synthesize a packaged-goods company's internal data with external data from firms such as A. C. Nielsen and IRI.

The METAPHOR company gives a brief case example. The client was a brand (marketing) group of a diversified packaged-goods manufacturer. The brand group wanted to be able to allocate advertising budgets to take advantage of regional sales opportunities. It wanted to be able to select areas for a new-product launch and create programs to minimize share loss of established brands. It wished to be able to respond quickly to competitive needs.

The manufacturer already had a mainframe system. Factory shipments were in the mainframe. Nielsen audit data were available on a time-share service basis. Other information was available in print form. The systems were not integrated, were not connected, and used different commands. Reporting categories were predefined and often inappropriate for the particular analysis required. The systems were overloaded.

The solution was to put all data into a common METAPHOR database. This gave the brand group the opportunity to create its own analyses as required. The network structure and workstations eliminated bottlenecks, permitting rapid access.

As another example, Frito-Lay, with 32 divisional sales managers, has an ongoing sales information system that is aiding its marketing effort.[12] For each snack line, it reports weekly the sales in every type of store. Reports go to everyone from sales representatives to the chief executive. The system quickly showed the company that it could move from a national sales strategy to a local sales strategy.

A divisional sales manager can spot which sales reps in a territory are really performing, and what marketing moves, such as pricing, are being introduced by the competition. Divisional sales manager Mary Ellen Johnson quickly spotted stores in her division not yet stocking Jumping Jack Doritos, a new product being introduced in Michigan.

Frito-Lay is so delighted with the system that expansion is under way. Soon will be added a feature to enable an executive to add questions or comments to a report before it goes to subordinates or superiors. Data about sales and advertising support are soon to go into the system. It also will spot stores that can increase profits by displaying more Frito-Lay products.

All this is made possible by the firm's providing each of its 10,000 sales reps with a brick-sized, hand-held computer to track inventories and enter orders for every store. The devices are designed to tell the sales rep what items should be restocked on the next visit to each retailer, and to send all weekly information to headquarters.

This is an example of micromarketing, a relatively new idea in marketing made possible by the computer. The 1990s marketer knows that trade deals must be tailored to individual accounts and that the sales force might even be given discretionary funds for local promotions. Micromarketing goes far beyond this, as we will show in later chapters.

DOES THE USER OF RESEARCH INFORMATION NEED A DESKTOP COMPUTER?

The answer to this question depends on two factors, the second a reflection of the first: the types and quantities of information used and the size of the organization.

Types and Quantities of Information Used

Certainly, where the individual is either in the marketing research end of the firm or a product manager, if the firm has a marketing information system, a desktop computer is a must.

As the types and quantities of information drop off from the maximum level, the individual may or may not require a desktop computer.

If the firm, at a minimum, does its own primary research (surveys), the marketing researcher and perhaps even the product manager should still have a desktop computer, because of all of the assistance this can provide for processing survey and other primary research data. Some of these tools are discussed more specifically in Chapters 8 through 12. At this point only a brief summary is needed of the types of program available for the desktop researcher whose company does some or all of its own research, or even those that buy custom-tailored studies from outside sources:

1. Sampling (design, selection, administration)

2. Questionnaires (design, administration)

3. Interviewing (mainly telephone interviewing)

4. Data processing (producing summary tables)

5. Statistical treatment (special analyses, discussed in Chapter 15)

6. Reports and graphics from surveys

There are also software programs to assist in group interviewing. Group interviewing and the software tools to help handle it are discussed in Chapter 10.

Size of the Organization

The large organization performs more information functions than the small group. In the large firm, desktop computers almost surely are desirable.

In the smaller organization the need for a desktop computer for the person responsible for research depends on whether there are other uses for it. Since the person responsible for marketing research in a small group will have additional areas of responsibility, as explained in Chapter 1, it becomes a question of whether these total responsibilities warrant that person's having a desktop computer.

A side note: There are few organizations with ten or more employees that cannot profitably make use of a computer. But that is not the issue being considered here.

ENDNOTES [1]Bruce Buursma. "Spy Image Comes in from Cold." *Chicago Tribune*, Nov. 5, 1990, sec. 4, p.1.

[2]Deidrem Fanning. "Only the Best for the Bergdorf Man?" *New York Times*, Sept. 16, 1990, F23.

[3]C. H. Deutsch. "007 It's Not. But Intelligence Is In." *New York Times*, Dec. 23, 1990, Sec. 3, p.24.

[4]*VU/TEXT*. Philadelphia: VU/TEXT Information Services, undated.

[5]J. D. Raphael and Richard Kitaeff. "The Research Information Center." *Marketing Research*, June 1990, 50–52.

[6]D. W. Nylen. *Marketing Decision-Making Handbook*. Englewood Cliffs, N.J.: Prentice-Hall, 1990, pp.G-342–G-343.

[7]Philip Kotler. "A Design for the Firm's Marketing Nerve Center." *Business Horizons*, Fall 1966, 63–74.

[8]C. E. Cox and R. E. Good. "How to Build a Marketing Information System." *Harvard Business Review*, May-June 1967, 145–154.

[9]Jane Hulbert, J. E. Farley, and J. A. Howard. "Information Processing and Decision Making in Marketing Organizations." *Journal of Marketing Research* 9 (Feb. 1972):75–77.

[10]"Desktop Metaphor Gives MIS a Weapon." *Information Week*, Mar. 16, 1987.

[11]*Metaphor Computer Systems*. Mountain View, Calif.: Metaphor Computer Systems, undated.

[12]B. J. Feder. "Frito-Lay's Speedy Data Network." *New York Times*, Nov. 8, 1990, C1 ff.

REFERENCE McConagle, J. J., and C. M. Vella. *Outsmarting the Competition*, Naperville, Ill.: Sourcebooks, 1990.

PART TWO

BUILDING THE RESEARCH STUDY

4

DEFINING THE MARKETING PROBLEM

What's in This Chapter

In this chapter we discuss the importance of defining completely and precisely the nature of the marketing problem facing the organization. We examine the importance of enrolling all of the affected personnel in defining the marketing problem. We explain why it is important to make sure that the proposed definition is agreed to before proceeding to prepare the research plan and proposal, and we show why it is important to state the problem in writing.

MARKETING PROBLEMS ARE ALWAYS WITH US

There never is an end to marketing problems in any business or organization. Some are important enough to threaten sales, profits, and the general welfare of the organization. Others are less drastic and often can be solved through the good judgment of the managers and executives of the firm.

The Avon Products Co., for example, recently used marketing research to help solve a major company problem. According to the *New York Times*,[1] Avon always has done business by using "Avon ladies" to sell its largely cosmetic products to their neighbors, friends, and lately even co-workers in offices and factories.

Avon sales and profits have been rising satisfactorily. Recent purchases of nonrelated companies (such as Tiffany and Co., the luxury jewelry store based in New York) have in turn been sold. Avon continues to rely on its "ladies," although now they are better trained and better supervised.

With the movement of women into the work force, particularly women who would be the best customers for Avon, customers increasingly are not at home during the day. Many buy their cosmetics from convenient retail stores near their workplaces.

Market research showed that 14 percent of Avon's customers accounted for 56 percent of its sales. These women were primarily over 50 and most did not have a college degree.

So Avon is tinkering with its product mix and its methods of paying the "ladies." Stanley Gault, a director of Avon since the early 1980s, says that he was "astonished at Avon's lack of knowledge about its customer base" when he joined the board.

Avon is beginning to analyze and define its problem. It finally has begun investing in formal research. Avon's greatest problem as of the time of this writing is its continued dependence on the "ladies." But the company recognizes its problem and is facing it with the help of marketing research.

Fortunately, sales and profits are sufficient to allow further study of the problem and, perhaps, future action. An intense and comprehensive study of its marketing problem still is needed. Will the "ladies" be the way the company continues to go to market?

In every marketing problem—and in any corporate problem of importance—there is a need for a well-planned statement of the problem in writing. And there is need, before the problem is defined in writing, to consult others in the company who will be affected by the results of a study. Each must contribute his or her thoughts and data needs before a valid useful study of the problem can be initiated.

As we have stated in earlier chapters, it is important that marketing research be a part of the examination of any marketing problem that requires an intelligent and useful solution. Marketing research, as well as other phases of marketing and sales, must be used in a mutual effort to produce the best results. Defining the marketing problem must also be a mutual effort.

Another example from real life may be useful:

- Sales of our commercial dishwashers have been decreasing for several years.

- The dishwasher is no longer as profitable as before.
- Competitors appear to be getting a larger share of this market. The reason for this is not clear.
- The alternatives appear to be:
  —to drop the product from the line
  —to redesign it to better suit customer needs
  —to lower its price to a possibly more attractive level
  —to promote the line more vigorously
- To learn more about this market in order to make sound recommendations, a formal study appears needed. Such a study would determine the specific reasons for the decrease in sales and profits.

A statement of the problem would include the above points put into writing after extensive review of the matter with all company personnel involved. The easy way would be to hire a large, outside research agency and ask it to find out what is the matter. It would be better to work out a definition of the problem with the advice of the agency and company personnel. Then the problem could be put into writing, with copies for all concerned. With this would go statements of what contributions other areas of the company would make. These might include such departments as product engineering, legal, and sales. The result would be a much sounder study.

APPLICATIONS OF MARKETING RESEARCH

Marketing research can be particularly helpful in the following areas:

Marketing planning, where the aim is to devise a plan concerning product, advertising, and related matters, to help assure marketing success.

Problem solving, where there is a specific marketing problem.

Monitoring, to measure what is going on to ensure that all is well and to spot possible problems.

BROAD CATEGORIES OF APPLIED MARKETING RESEARCH

Preliminary Research (Situation Analysis)

Some preliminary research may be necessary even before the final statement and definition of the problem are agreed upon.

Assume, for example, that a product idea is posed by an experienced salesman in the construction field. He says that a long-handled heavy hammer is used in certain situations by the building trades, and he would like to have such a hammer to sell.

Some preliminary research may be indicated. Is the market for such a hammer regional or national? What trades would use the hammer? Does it appear to be really necessary for this trade, or could other hammers be used? The answers to these early questions can help define the nature and scope of more complete research.

A review of earlier research may also be useful. It is possible that this product suggestion has been studied before.

Perhaps there are secondary sources that can provide information. There may be government publications that mention this product, for example, or some trade publication may have mentioned such a hammer and discussed its use—in which case a prolonged search for secondary sources may be unnecessary.

From this preliminary work, perhaps involving a little time in the field and delving into secondary sources, a more accurate and useful definition of the marketing problem can be written.

Conclusive Research

Certain hypotheses were developed in the preliminary search and in the definition of the marketing problem. Conclusive research tests these hypotheses. This research is better organized and more thorough than in the preliminary search.

At this stage a more thorough search of secondary sources must be made. It may include the collection of data and information from the field. Field work (primary research) still is vital for many studies, but it will perhaps be used somewhat less in the future as databanks become more complete.

Methods of collecting information from the field are the subject of much of the rest of this book. They should be well-known to marketing managers, whether they direct their own studies or contract them out to a professional agency.

Performance Research

Performance research determines how well the recommended actions are being carried out and what benefits in sales and profits are being realized.

Performance research monitors how marketing management is doing. It questions the definition of the problem that has guided the work that has been done—and is being done. Have we made a mistake in our judgment of the market and of our idea of the marketing problem itself? Have consequences of our definition of the problem and subsequent marketing action shown that we made a mistake in our definition? Should some new study of the problem be made as a result of our questioning the soundness of our first definition and subsequent action?

It is always difficult to admit mistakes. How often has a product been kept alive long after it should have been buried because managers and executives could not bring themselves to admit they were wrong in the first place?

Poor results shown in performance research may require a new definition of the marketing problem—and a decision whether further study is needed.

DETERMINING WHEN MARKETING RESEARCH IS NEEDED

NEED FOR CONTINUOUS LISTING OF PROBLEMS

What are the problems that must be faced? On a list of problems, some will require considerable study because they are likely to produce good profits or, conversely, sizable losses.

Determining which marketing problems need early decisions is the function of marketing management and top management. Perhaps it is unnecessary to advocate a written, continuously updated list of such problems, but such a list in the hands of the marketing manager may help keep research studies on target and on time.

Some problems require no study at all. If the corporation president requires a new car for his official duties, it is highly unlikely that anyone will suggest a study to determine if he is right. But consider several other situations.

- We are a manufacturer of many food products for the consumer market. We believe our marmalade and jam line is of superior quality and taste, but it is not selling well. Is price the trouble? Is it the packaging? Should we drop out of the market entirely? What effect would this have on our other lines? What effect would dropping the unprofitable line have on our distribution channels? This is clearly an important problem that needs thorough study, even before writing the problem definition.

The definition will guide marketing research people. But it also will guide manufacturing people, the sales department, finance people, and others who will be affected by the findings and recommendations. All should have a hand in developing the problem definition.

- We are a manufacturer of fine china. Like other firms, we want to expand and become more profitable. Should we consider manufacturing and distributing a line of lower-quality, lower-price products? Do we have the manufacturing and marketing experience to make such a venture successful?

Again, solid thought must guide our definition of the problem. What do we need to know first? Certainly, we need complete knowledge of the present market. Who is selling competitive lines? Are these lines profitable? Is there room for another line? How strong are brand names? How strong would our brand name be in this lower-price line? Should we even use our brand name for this product? Can present distribution channels handle the new line? How strong are lines coming in from other countries?

The definition of the marketing problem would have to cover these important questions and additional questions posed by other involved corporation personnel. A definition does not have to be short. "Is there room for another lower-price line in the market?" would not be sufficient to guide subsequent action.

In some situations the financial strength of the company may be threatened, and this must be taken into account in devising the problem definition and subsequent research. In other situations there may be a problem of availability of competent personnel to guide whatever market action is to be taken. The problem definition, then, must take into account the situation of the company and its ability to take sound action.

Many corporate moves have been made because other firms' products and market fields looked exciting and, perhaps, profitable. In one case it has been reported that a major corporate move to another state came about because the chief executive officer thought his officers and he would be better and happier in their jobs in a suburb of New York City.

The problem, once defined and put onto paper, will lead to other questions before the best and most useful recommendations can be made to the company. We emphasize these first steps because they are so often neglected when upper management becomes gung ho and wants to get going rapidly in whatever project is being considered.

But early thinking often ensures that a new product, a new store location, or a reorganized sales force will produce the sales and profits hoped for. Poorly thought-out marketing decisions, on the other hand, can and do cause major ills—perhaps even the demise of the company itself.

We can all recall actions that could have done irreparable damage to a corporation. Think of products that appeared and quickly disappeared because they did not meet the needs of the market. Customers found the packages formidable and difficult to open. Because competitive products might not have been adequately considered, the new product did not offer something new and exciting. A thousand things can go wrong; a thousand opportunities can be missed. It is up to the marketing department, including marketing research, to anticipate and prevent as many of these as possible. But in each case first action should be a precise definition of the problem.

DEFINING THE MARKETING PROBLEM

We have already said that marketing research should no longer be considered a separate function. From the very beginning of awareness and consideration of a marketing problem, research should be a part of the marketing "team."

There is always need for a team to solve marketing problems. The team should have at least a semiofficial status. Brought together for the purpose, the team may officially disband after the problem is solved. Marketing research will be a part of the team, offering primary assistance in many studies and secondary assistance in others. Marketing research will play an important role in the formulation of the definition of a marketing problem.

EXAMPLES OF DECISIONS THAT MUST BE MADE

A New Product for a Manufacturer

- Is there an obvious need for the product?

- Does the company have sufficient financial means to design, manufacture, and push the product through the early sales growth years?

- What will be the best design?

- What will be the best price level for the market?

- How shall we choose between volume, price, and profit?

- What will be the probable market life for the product?
- What degree of quality will be necessary?
- Who are the competitors and how strong are they?
- What promotion will be needed? What will it cost?
- What will be the effect of this new product on present lines?

An example of a product that went wrong because all of the above were not sufficiently studied is the smokeless cigarette. It was called Premier. Here are a few facts about it:

- It contained less nicotine than almost all other brands.
- It was priced considerably higher than other brands.
- It was aimed at older smokers.
- It required explanation of how to use; it required more ad copy and less emotional appeal than ordinary cigarette advertising.
- Apparently it could be advertised as "cleaner" but could not be called "healthier."

Obviously, something went wrong during the research that preceded the introduction of the cigarette. The need for the product did not in fact exist. Perhaps the price was too high. And so on. Defining the marketing problem was not done well enough.

A New Unit of a Chain Store Company

Chain store companies have complex and sophisticated ways of choosing new store sites. Small chains, however, may not be so well organized in site selection. Following are some of the basic questions that need to be answered:

- What types of customers (income levels, education, life patterns, age) do we seek?
- What space is available for a new site?
- What shopping area will this site draw from?
- What zoning restrictions, taxes, and other legal problems will we face?

- What sales volume can be expected at this site? After one year? After three years?

- Will suitable employees be available?

An Established Store That Wants to Move

- Most of the questions in the example above.

- What will be the cost of losing some of our present customers?

- What new customers can we expect from the proposed site?

- Can we expect to be able to hire sufficient numbers of satisfactory employees?

- How long will it take to build up a new customer base?

- What quality and price levels will be needed for the new site?

- Do we have sufficient capital to see us through the move?

Marketing research, whether it is a separate function or a part of the marketing department and whether it is called marketing research or marketing planning, must have a part in answering most of the questions above. The small-store owner wishing to move will be wise to employ a local research company with site-selection experience. In any case, all of the above points must be thoroughly explored, and a definition of the marketing problem must be worked at.

BASIC POINTS

ALTERNATIVES

In any problem definition that the marketing department will make, it is important to understand the alternatives that can be reached. The research still has to be done. Much management thought will be required. The amount of time required before final recommendations are accepted and put into action must be clearly understood.

It is usually apparent from the beginning that there is more than one possibility for eventual action. A negative recommendation is just as important as a positive one. The child's toy will be made and marketed—or it will not. The store should be moved to a specific new location—or it should not. Research findings may support either action.

Another location not previously considered may turn out to be better. This point is so basic that it appears to be worth little thought. Be assured, however, that many studies will be more useful if all concerned persons and departments realize what the alternatives are and what effect each may have on the company.

Of equal importance, it is necessary in most cases for the various decision makers to agree that these *are* the alternatives. Each involved person or department will then have a clear understanding of what effect the study may have on him or her or on the department.

Before the final definition of the marketing problem is written, decision makers must agree on the nature and quality of the information needed to make a sound decision. Too many recommendations have been weakened by someone asking whether the latest census report had been consulted, or whether the research interviewers had been working in certain areas that the questioner considers important. There is always someone who, given the opportunity, wants to find fault with a study. His or her motives may be questioned; perhaps it is a bit of self-advertising. But it does happen and may be prevented or minimized by sound advance work with others in the organization.

THE PLACE OF MARKETING RESEARCH IN DECISION MAKING

It should be clear by now that marketing research can play a major role in certain areas of inquiry, and that it should play a minor role in others.

The place of marketing research in decision making will be determined by the marketing team or by the marketing manager. Advertising can say what is needed for the particular field. Engineering will have some questions. All should be considered in defining the problem and in making the study proposal.

We strongly advocate that marketing research play a greater role than it has up to now in many companies. It should be in at the beginning of discussion of a problem. It should take part in working with other functions in the company to determine the overall nature of the problems to be studied. It should play a major role in planning subsequent studies. It should competently carry out the research that is assigned to it, attempting to find answers to questions in the definition of the marketing problem. The research should be completed as needed, using the up-to-date methods described in this book.

SHOULD A RESEARCH STUDY BE DONE?

It is a given that decisions based on fact—on research in many cases—will be better than a judgment decision based on little or no solid information. Better research and better management judgment, for example, might have prevented the debacle when the new Coke was introduced some years ago. Better research and better management thinking might have prevented the introduction of the ill-fated Edsel automobile several decades ago.

New in our time is the speed with which products are introduced. Procter & Gamble has shortened its product development time significantly. Automobiles are being designed and produced more than a year faster than formerly. This speed and the apparent need for more new products certainly will tempt companies to shorten research time or even to depend too much on executive judgment.

But executive judgment is not infallible. Better judgment might have prevented some companies from entering the canned-soup market to compete with the very resourceful and entrenched Campbell Soup Co. Even Heinz, with its full purse, was not able to do so successfully a few years ago.

In all of these cases, however, marketing research alone would not have been enough. Management thinking and decision-making ability should have combined research results with thorough consideration by experienced upper managers.

But before reaching a marketing decision, there are other aspects that determine the extent of the study to be done.

DEGREE OF UNCERTAINTY

For a maker of military airplanes, the degree of uncertainty must be given early and prime consideration. Although there is always risk in this business, at the present time of great economic and political change, it is especially high. Marketing research in the usual sense thus would not be applicable. But careful thought by management, defense department officials, and economists clearly would be indicated.

A maker of gourmet foods, for example, would have to face considerable uncertainty when contemplating a new product containing large percentages of saturated fat and cholesterol. How strong is consumer awareness of these dangers to health? Will people be turning to a new health craze in a year or so? Recollection of the sudden birth of enthusiasm for oat bran and the equally sudden drop in interest will be a factor. Marketing research in the field and in the office definitely would be in order before launching this new product.

A manufacturer of a folding wood rule that had been popular up to 1941 brought the rule back into the market when World War II was over. The market had disappeared because of new building technology and the disappearance of older craftsmen. Sales were small and unprofitable. The rule was taken off the market in a short time. A small amount of field research might have prevented this experience.

A new banking office is planned for a site formerly occupied by a hotel. On the ground floor is a women's apparel shop that has a long lease. Planners for the new bank might easily assume that the shop owners could be bought out or be convinced to move. In actuality, the shop owners refused to move until the lease expired. The unoccupied building now stands as a symbol of a poorly thought-out plan. The definition of the bank's problem must now be reconsidered. Perhaps marketing research may reveal the appropriateness of this site for banking, or possibly the site was wrong in the first place.

PROBABLE PAYOFF OF EACH ALTERNATIVE

Consideration of the probable payoff of each new product, service, or other action must come early. The greatest potential profit, all else being equal, is the determining factor. Nonprofit organizations measure their "profit" by their ability to perform what they are organized to do.

Before the final problem definition is written, experienced financial people should estimate the probable payoff of each alternative. Past product successes or failures can give clues about what might happen. Observation of other stores that have moved, for example, can give some idea of what can be expected of a similar proposed move. This early judgment is extremely important in shaping the problem definition.

NATURE AND AMOUNT OF INFORMATION REQUIRED

The estimated cost of getting information must be weighed against the possible sales and profits that may result from the proposed action. Yet many actions have been taken without this early hard-nosed approach to decision making. The nature and amount of marketing research must be strictly controlled by cost and profit considerations. Here, the team will be invaluable.

In many market and product matters, there is usually one or a group of persons enthusiastic about a particular proposal. They say that the firm had better take action or Competitor A, or Competitor B, will beat it to the market. With the present-day compulsion to break out new products quickly, these enthusiasts may push a firm into ventures that more careful consideration would have rejected. The list of troubled companies that bought other companies during the 1980s is witness to this impulsive enthusiasm (and to the urging by brokerage firms specializing in such mergers).

Early deliberations should be devoted to whether the problem is nationwide or whether regional and local differences must be taken into account. Important regional differences in demand, for example, may dictate differences in the definition of the problem. If a brand of coffee has declining sales nationally, the problem may lie in one region. The definition of the problem will include the need for information indicating the reason for the poor regional sales and whether those slow regional sales might be a precursor of changes in other regions. Such information will affect the final definition of the problem.

ESTIMATED COSTS OF GETTING NEEDED INFORMATION

The name of the game is PROFIT. The determination of possible sales and profits for a new product or the realignment of a sales territory may not allow much money for research. Also, in some cases the need for action may be too pressing to delay a decision. But early on, based on the maximum or minimal profit projections, management should determine how much can be spent on planning and research.

A product with minimal sales potential but high profit percentage may raise a question about its future. How much time and money should be spent on planning and research? This is a management decision that must precede any planning and research. The team will decide on the importance of the product problem and the amount of time and money that can reasonably be spent upon it.

Finally, there must be an estimate of the time required to do adequate research. Most marketing research professionals have experienced a wrong marketing decision before completion of research. Usually this is a result of poor or inadequate planning at the beginning of the study.

Time is always a problem. Marketing research directors want enough time to do what they know is necessary to handle the marketing problem as defined. Knowing the importance of the problem to the company, they want to take no chances. Furthermore, they want to keep their reputations for accuracy and sound advice.

Management, including marketing management, is always eager to move ahead. A new product or a new service is exciting, particularly when the future of this product appears bright. New acquisitions also bring excitement. New lines, new markets, new faces—all stimulate the imagination. Perhaps, as problems arise, this mental state will not last, but for a while there is intense pressure to act.

Taking time for adequate planning and marketing research is difficult in such circumstances, but it is necessary. Often in the past, pressures to purchase or merge with other companies have led to acquisitions that have been deeply regretted in later years.

In one instance, a large company discussed purchasing a small Florida firm. Talks did not go smoothly. After some time spent in arguing and debating, the president of the small firm (a dramatic fellow) rose from his chair and announced his decision to fly home and forget the whole deal. The president of the larger company, by now enthusiastic about the proposed purchase, hopped into his car, chased the small company's president to the airport, and urged him to return. Of course, the deal was then consummated—to the advantage of the small company and to the later regret of the large company. These human, emotional things happen, but a coldly objective team approach and good marketing research might have prevented this small disaster.

Marketing, planning, and top management have the duty in such circumstances to consider whether adequate marketing and management ability exists in the newly merged company to handle long-range marketing needs. Marketing research can and should play a role in such an exploratory examination.

In many of the mergers and buyouts of the 1980s, this depth of research and planning was not done. Will we be smarter in the 1990s?

DEFINING THE PROBLEM FOR MARKETING RESEARCH

Now that problem definition has been considered, it is necessary to define the problem more specifically if marketing research is to be initiated.

- Others should be consulted. In manufacturing companies, depending on the nature of the situation, engineering, legal, packaging, and other personnel may have facts they need to know. Customer attitudes may affect their work. In nonmanufacturing firms, other types of personnel will need to be consulted. The important thing, when defining the research problem, is to get all needed input before finally stating the problem and beginning research.

- There should be an early forecast of the possible findings of the completed study to determine if they will be adequate. The definition of the research problem may need amplification or alteration if the research problem has not been defined broadly enough to cover the needs of all interested people and departments.

- These possible findings should be brought to the attention of all interested persons and departments. A great amount of time need not be spent on this, but it should be sufficient to alert all who are involved as to what might come out of the research study. Also, this step may alert the researchers to possible errors in their procedure.

- Probable and possible objections to the study findings should be forecasted. Managers, department heads, product development people, and others will inevitably have preconceived ideas of what actions should be taken. It requires no second sight to know who is likely to raise questions about the adequacy of the research and the reasonableness of the recommendations. To the extent possible, these objections should be aired ahead of time, for they may affect the definition of the problem and subsequent office and field work.

- A preliminary statement of the problems should be circulated to all departments and persons who will later participate in implementing the recommendations.

Although often these steps can be shortened and carried out rapidly, they may nevertheless seem tedious and unnecessary. But a marketing study that results in recommendations that raise strong objections may be stillborn. It is well to consider each of the above steps and to do those that seem most worthwhile for a particular study.

Our recommendations for laying this groundwork does not sanction any weakening of the hard-nosed search for truth and the fearless presentation of findings and recommendations. We are simply saying that marketing research (and any agency it employs) needs to recognize the human weaknesses and prejudices of the people it deals with and that it should conduct itself in a manner that will allow its findings and recommendations to be accepted and implemented.

STATEMENT OF THE PROBLEM

After all the thinking and discussion, the preliminary study, and the contacts with other departments and people who will be expected to implement recommendations, it is time to put the problem definition on paper in final form.

The head of a large research organization said recently: "The lack of a sound, accurate, and complete definition of the marketing problem has caused too many failures in marketing research." We have emphasized all through this chapter the need for taking time and exerting effort to construct such a definition. Unless the problem is defined well, subsequent actions may be useless, or possibly downright dangerous, for the firm.

Even with the smallest, shortest, and perhaps least important of studies, it is always wise to put the problem definition on paper. The person writing the definition should keep in mind the following points:

- In this day of computers, the ability to write clearly, succinctly, and to the point is rarer than it once was. Strong, convincing exposition follows clear thinking. A draft of the problem definition should be presented to several people to determine if it is as understandable and unambiguous to others as it is to the writer.

- A certain modesty is in order now. The study, it is hoped, will solve the research problem, but it will not solve any other problem of the company. Efforts in writing the definition to magnify expected benefits will be obvious to the experienced reader and will lessen his or her confidence in what is finally proposed.

ENDNOTE   [1] Adapted from "Avon Keeps Ringing But Wall Street Won't Answer." *New York Times*, July 15, 1990, p. F7.

5

PREPARING THE RESEARCH PLAN AND PROPOSAL

What's in This Chapter

In this chapter we emphasize the importance of thoroughness in preparing the research plan and the subsequent proposal. We also stess the role that the research study team plays in preparing the research plan and proposal. Once again, we show the need for consulting the people and department that will use the findings of the proposed research.

You now realize the critical importance of carefully defining the nature of the marketing problem. Far too many research studies go awry at this stage because marketing and top management people become impatient and want to "do something." A problem that has caused a drop in sales and profits will certainly lead many voices in the firm to call for action.

And here we must be cautious. These management voices calling for action are voices of experience. Management has solved many problems in the past and has learned how to face troubling situations. With declining sales of a profitable product, it is easy to understand why few managers will want a time-consuming study that they think can only tell them what they already know.

Any marketing research manager worth his or her salt knows that management is often right in its attitude. The question for research and for management is: When is it worthwhile to take the time to do a good market study? The idea of the *team* broached in early chapters will help answer this question. The team will decide when there is too little knowledge to reach a sound solution to a big problem.

Certainly, for any problem that will affect the firm adversely, it may be correct for the team to recommend research, even though other voices are raised for action "now." It is the duty of the marketing manager, working together with the team, to persuade other managers and the "caller-for-action-now" to back off while research attempts to find the best solution to the problem. This persuasion often will come from the research plan and proposal, which we shall now proceed to outline.

First, let us consider the case of a national baking company that finds one of its most profitable and popular crackers showing a sizable sales decline in the Northeast. The following questions arise:

- Is this the start of a national problem or is the problem confined to the Northeast? Is it a permanent problem?

- Are the lost sales possibly due to a large influx of ethnic groups with different tastes?

- Will the dispersion of these ethnic groups—if that is indeed the cause—bring continued sales decline? Management recently has become aware of a trend in other companies toward regional products for regional tastes.

- Have our competitors shown any sign of taking advantage of this new situation?

- If we find that a change in consumer taste is causing our problem, what shall we do? Change our formula? How?

- If not a change in consumer taste, what other reasons exist for this sales decline?

- How much time and money can be spent on this problem in view of present and future profit possibilities?

We present this case to show how the need for and nature of marketing research can grow and widen. At some point there must be an end to study and a beginning of action. All such decisions should be made by the marketing team that we have urged so strongly. In the case of a very large and potentially costly study, a proposal will be made to top management.

RECOGNIZING FAULTS IN THE MARKETER'S ORGANIZATION

We can all recall companies that stayed too long with older products and channels of distributions. In the past, many companies that were "loyal" to their distributors saw their competitors move vigorously to the supermarket or mass-market route. Today this problem has been largely solved, but many businesses suffered through such misplaced loyalty.

Is the problem, then, one of the company's own making? Is it unwillingness to recognize what should be plainly visible?

There is a story of a large national company whose sales reps continued to feel that they were "needed" by retailers and wholesalers. Being needed, they continued to dominate rather than help. The need disappeared and so would have the company, had it not seen the light in time.

Has the company fully recognized the vast changes in distribution? Where are the local hardware stores in many cities? Where are the wonderful grocery stores that took orders over the phone and delivered to the back door? What will happen to the chain restaurants that have married themselves to beef, when, for health reasons, great numbers of customers are turning to fish and chicken?

For all these reasons, any problem that at first appears simple may not be simple at all. All such situations must be recognized well ahead of preparing a research plan and proposal.

A growing problem, however, is management's need for speed in an increasingly competitive market. We speak in another chapter of how fast a new model car can now appear in showrooms. All manufacturers keep their inventories low. Speed of new-product introduction is high, and less time is available for marketing research. Meeting this challenge calls for the recognition of new research methods in the research plan and proposal.

SOME PRELIMINARY STEPS

At the risk of repeating some points made in Chapter 4, we would like to emphasize the importance of a few preliminary steps before even beginning to prepare a research plan. Failure to take these steps can lead to a research study that is less useful than it should be, or even useless.

Early discussion with others who need and will use the findings of a study can only lead to better research. If an outside supplier of information and figures on a continuous basis is being considered, such early discussion is mandatory if the resulting databank is to be used in a satisfactory way.

Talking with others in the company will bring into focus the specific needs of every department. Even before a marketing team begins its work, these early discussions will clarify the problem.

Early discussions will help determine the cost/benefit of research. Is the study needed at all? What can the organization afford to spend for research in light of the potential usefulness of the findings? If the use of an outside, continuing supplier of facts and figures for our databank is proposed, can this step be justified in light of how the information will probably be used?

We cannot say that a final decision for or against research will be made on the basis of these early steps. But we do say that the research will be better, more focused, and more useful to more departments—and to top management.

What has been learned from these early discussions should be organized and put into writing for the benefit of the team or management people who will make the decision to proceed or not to proceed with the study.

DEFINITION OF PLAN AND PROPOSAL

A *plan* amounts to a blueprint for the design, execution, and monitoring of a study. This plan is preliminary and subject to change, but it does put emphasis on the real problem, the real needs of the company. It should be carefully detailed and shown to the people who have been consulted.

The *proposal* is a statement of the plan encased in a discussion of the need for the study and what it will provide. Often the proposal is a selling document. Rarely will all decision makers in any firm agree immediately that a research study is needed, or that a continuing supply of pertinent facts and figures for a databank is really necessary at "that price."

Clearly all studies are not of equal importance. A proposed study of sales difficulties in the Midwest, for example, might not go all the way to the CEO. But how far up it should go is a matter of judgment and company policy.

MAJOR STEPS IN PREPARING A PLAN

We emphasize once more that one of the most important steps in preparing for a research study is to ensure that all possible interested persons are involved. Even though these persons have taken part in early discussions, it is good strategy and sound psychology to keep them informed as the plan and the proposal are formulated. Although this sounds more tedious and time-consuming than it usually is, there should be no chance that somewhere down the line some important person or department will be surprised at the way the study is going and register strong opposition.

Presented below are several matters to be considered in preparing a plan. Not all will apply to every study plan, but all must be given at least a little thought.

- The problem is clear by now, having been discussed with many people. The marketing department and others on the team plainly see the nature of the difficulty and why a study is needed. There may be disagreement about what the study findings will show, but all agree that the research is necessary.

  A research study does not solve a problem or provide decisions. It merely generates information that allows management people to make better decisions and take wiser actions. Information provided by outside suppliers of information can only help management. It will never take management's place.

- Time now spent in further defining and refining the marketing problem and putting the final version on paper is time well spent. Without a strict and mutually agreed-upon statement of the problem, even outside research firms or suppliers of continuing information may be misled and provide more or less information than is needed and useful.

  No steps should be taken by a research department or an outside research firm until there is such a clear statement of why this work should be done, and what benefit the employing firm can realize.

- It is often useful to hypothesize the findings likely to result from the study. A short statement of what these different findings may mean to the company can be useful. Such a statement alerts people and departments to begin thinking about the actions needed as a result of several possible findings. Too much should not be made of this suggestion, but it does indicate that the research findings can be contradictory (sometimes in surprising ways), and subsequent actions may differ in important ways.

INFORMATION TO BE OBTAINED

A determination of the type and amount of information should take into account the needs uncovered in early discussions in the company and in discussions with the team that will supervise the study.

If an outside research firm is to do the study or provide continuing information for a databank, it will be wise to draw on its knowledge and experience. The studies that this firm has done in the past have shown the kind of information that is readily obtainable and what is not. What is available from secondary sources, for example, may not be completely known by the employing firm.

One problem at this point is the large amount of information that certain departments in the organization would like to have. Product engineering wants something; traffic wants something else; product designers could use certain information about attitudes, and so on. A consequent sudden enlargement of a study can be fatal. The problem, as we have said, should be simplified as much as possible, as should be the list of the types and amounts of information wanted. A list of facts that are wanted but not immediately needed must be ruthlessly weeded out.

BASIC METHODS OF COLLECTING NEEDED INFORMATION

Detailed discussions of the basic methods of collecting information are found in other chapters of this book. Suffice it here to present a specific statement of how the study is to be done.

In Chapter 2 we showed that secondary information is much more readily available than in the past. For many studies, time spent in searching for information in secondary sources may well save a great amount of time and money that might have been spent for field research. An outside research firm can often find sources of secondary information unknown to a marketing department.

Also, primary research in the field is taking an increasingly smaller portion of the research dollar. Computers can put marketing people in touch with amounts and kinds of information undreamed of until the past decade.

The research plan must spell out exactly how the study is to be done: mail questionnaire, personal interview, focus groups, or other method (all covered in other chapters). The plan also must state why this method has been chosen. Perhaps the study will require the use of several types of research methods. Focus groups, for example, often are followed by quantitative studies. The plan should tell why this is necessary. It must be recognized that these methods may have to be changed to meet changing needs as the study progresses.

SAMPLING METHODS

Sampling methods have become far too complex to be included in detail in a research plan and proposal. Because of this complexity, if for no other reason, it may be wise at the very beginning of a research study to choose an outside supplier.

Two major types of sampling are probability and nonprobability:

Probability samples: Samples in which the elements being included have a known chance of being selected. The system of choosing participants in a survey permits no arbitrary selections. The system of choosing must be rigorously adhered to. A probability sample, if followed strictly, allows the determination of sampling error. This, in simple terms, is the difference between the sample value and the true value of the population being surveyed. A sampling error can be stated in mathematical terms—usually plus or minus a certain percentage. A larger sample usually will mean a smaller sampling error. A decision must be made by the buyer of a study about how much sampling error can be accepted for usable results.

Nonprobability samples: Samples in which participants are selected in a purposeful way. The selection may require certain percentages of the sample to be women or men, housewives under 30, or a similar criterion. This type of selection is an effort to reach a cross section of the elements being sampled. Because the sample is not rigorously chosen, however, it is statistically impossible to state a true sampling error.

Today, most samples chosen for applied research are nonprobability samples. If carefully done—with quotas, for example, of persons to be studied—the findings are generally valid (see Chapter 8). A true probability sample, because of the stringent requirements, is likely to be far too expensive and too time-consuming for most uses. The sampling method chosen for any particular study, therefore, must be explained carefully, with the reasons for its acceptability and likelihood of supplying accurate date.

The research plan may not require that the whole country be sampled. Cost and time factors may lead to the decision to cover only the Eastern states. Past experience for the products being studied may indicate that these states are indeed representative of the nation in this particular case. A larger sample in this group of states may be recommended.

In general, the more specific the description of those to be studied, the larger the sample must be. In some cases the sample may be the universe for a particular problem.

A study done by one of the authors found only seven qualified respondents. With a good questionnaire, which was very detailed, all seven responded. A study done in New York City subway stations among young working women at rush hour required thousands of questionnaires and produced a 10 percent return. But this small study appeared to give the research buyer what he wanted.

Sampling is complex. It is not a field for an untutored amateur. A proposal for a particular study must give management a very good notion of how well the sampling is to be done—and by whom.

QUESTIONS TO BE ASKED

Deciding what questions to ask is as difficult as choosing the sample and the sampling technique. Those who read and approve the plan and proposal should have sample questionnaires. Indeed, it will be of benefit for the research manager to solicit comments on the questions that have been prepared. It is often almost impossible to predict how respondents will interpret questions. Questions must be written so that they appeal to the respondents and encourage them to complete and return the questionnaire or to participate in the interview.

There is a real art to formulating questions (see Chapter 9). The questionnaire used in the proposal is almost certain to be altered as trial runs of it are made and weak points are discovered.

Of course, the first duty of the question writer is to translate information requirements into questions that will be easily understood and readily answered. The difficulty of preparing questions may be yet another reason to work with a professional research organization.

The questions presented in the plan must take into consideration the way they are to be presented to the respondents. For interviews in shopping malls, questions must be short, easy to understand, and start in an interesting way.

Questions to be addressed to technical people in a publishing house will be very different in style and content.

The proposal should explain why the questions shown were prepared as they were. Perhaps alternative questions can be prepared for the proposal receivers to judge. They may see difficulties that were not perceived by the question writer.

If there is an interesting and unusual way of preparing the questions and the questionnaire, it should be shown. This is a time for "selling" too. There is always interest in questions; there may be good discussion on how they will be received.

The questionnaire used in the study among young working women mentioned above was carefully geared to its respondents. The questionnaire and its envelope were a soft lavender, and on each envelope was pasted a little flower sticker. There was just a hint of perfume. The questionnaire was thus designed to appeal to the curiosity of young women.

PLANNING FOR ANALYSIS

In planning for the eventual analysis of the research data, a certain number of tables and other statistical treatments can be used. They arouse interest and can also explain a finding better than words in many cases. The development of questions for the questionnaire should consider how such mathematical presentations are to be made. Certainly, computers will often be used. Also, some questions can be constructed in a manner that will lend the responses to pictorial use.

How the questions are to be analyzed, however, must have first consideration. Today's use of computers allows tabulations and cross-tabulations that once were too tedious and time-consuming. A marketing researcher, if not completely at home in the computer world, would be smart to work with a computer specialist in designing questions and determining the order in which questions will be asked.

Some modern questionnaires require the respondent to follow a path through the document based on how he or she answers each question. The resulting questionnaire, with lines and arrows, gets too busy and too tedious—and frequently is not completed. Questionnaires that are too busy may not be answered by the equally busy respondent.

LIMITATIONS OF THE STUDY

No study can be perfect. In the proposal there should be a very careful explanation of what this proposed study can do and what it cannot do. Such an explanation may prevent acrimonious discussions at a later date. The proposal should tell why this study is limited and why other equally interesting matters cannot be covered at this time.

TIME SCHEDULE

As many researchers in the past have discovered, delayed research findings can reveal that, in effect, the decision has already been made by management. No researcher wants this to happen twice.

One of the authors, in his younger, inexperienced days, was asked to do a research study about a proposed new-product idea. In his preparation he planned to do certain things, to see certain people, to visit several sections of the country, to seek information on competition, and so on.

Meanwhile, various departments asked whether he would mind if they did "just a little work" while waiting for the study to be completed. Advertising wanted to prepare some early ads, product engineering wanted to refine its work, the sales department wanted to do some early planning. By the time the research had been completed, the momentum had built to a no-stopping point. Fortunately for the company, and the author, research results were positive—even if far too late. This was an experience that this researcher did not repeat.

The time schedule for research must be clearly set forth from the beginning. Timing should be a part of the proposal and covered in any meeting on the proposal.

If management wants to move more quickly, it must adopt a different research method. A more limited research method may offer more chance of error. If it is necessary to go to market more rapidly, the researcher must acquiesce but must also explain how and why the research techniques will differ. On the other hand, through the greater availability of usable secondary research, the use of outside data systems, and a little more hurry-up, the researcher can often meet the requirements for speed in today's competitive market.

The time schedule must result from an agreement among management, the outside research firm, if used, the internal research department, and the internal team, if it exists. Once it is worked out, the schedule must be followed as closely as possible. Other departments are waiting for and depending on the findings of the research, and a delayed study can be costly to them. Delays can prevent these departments from going ahead on other projects that may be even more important to the firm.

It is equally important, however, for all to realize that some schedules may have to be changed. New and unexpected findings may have to be followed, perhaps causing a change in research technique. A proposal should allow for such possibilities, even though the importance of staying with the original agreed-upon schedule is recognized.

We emphasize this need for close adherence to a time schedule because too many studies have been delayed beyond the promised time, causing trouble in many areas. If there is to be a delay, all concerned must be told immediately—with an explanation and a new date for completion.

COSTS

An outside agency usually quotes plus or minus a certain percentage in its price quotation. The agency's experience with similar studies usually makes its quotation fairly accurate. Internal cost estimates should be just as accurate. Plus or minus figures usually are not more than 5 percent. A study that has been well planned by marketing people should allow this degree of accuracy.

Costs may be quoted in terms of varying level of thoroughness. This may include geographic coverage (with the exclusion of areas too expensive to cover in terms of costs and benefits), variances in size of sample, methods of doing the research, and so on. This is a cost/benefit factor that management must agree upon.

WHO SHOULD DO THE RESEARCH?

We have earlier argued for the concept of the team that will conduct and monitor the study. Who will do what is a matter of discussion between an outside agency and internal personnel, a topic that is more thoroughly examined in Chapter 6. As we have pointed out, simply to dump a complex study onto an outside firm can be an invitation to disaster. On the other hand, allowing internal personnel to do too much may weaken the impact of the fresh thinking of the outsiders. Furthermore, outside research services usually prefer to control the study and do most of the work and presenting. The proposal should spell out who should do what.

In choosing an outside agency, there are important factors to consider: the degree to which in-depth knowledge of the employing company and its field is required; the agency's skill in the type of study to be done; whether results will be used for promotion; and so on. Often an outside agency will require some weeks of education before it can comprehend what is needed.

Another matter that should be included in the proposal (after some discussion among the team and with management) is whether company personnel can take some part in the actual research.

Here are the advantages of freeing up some company personnel to participate in the research, even though a competent agency has been hired:

1. Using people from departments that will be affected by the study will help "sell" the results. Sometimes there are a number of relatively young persons who can be freed up for a few weeks or months for this purpose. It can be good training for them, and it allows the department to feel that it had an important role in the research and the findings.

2. Using company personnel can also direct and redirect the progress of the study into the most useful and profitable areas.

3. Using people from departments other than marketing will educate these departments about the ways and benefits of marketing research.

However, because other departments may not be able to free people, they should not be pushed to do so.

THE PROPOSAL

The above discussion of the plan can be only a guide. Each individual firm and each study will require a different approach. But all of the above recommendations should be included in some way in the final plan and proposal.

The proposal and plan should also consider the following important matters as it is being prepared:

1. How are the findings and recommendations to be presented? To whom will they be presented? The answers to these questions can make a difference in collecting facts that will be best presented as charts, tables, slides, or in other ways. A study that will be presented solely to top management may require important differences in method of presentation and in the details presented.

2. As coldly logical and factual as research must be, some thought must be given to the types of personalities that will receive the proposal. To what extent will the proposal have to "prove itself" to certain management members? What will be needed to convince these people to accept the proposal?

3. What must be included to prepare for the known skeptics among top management and department heads? An experienced research person knows who these people are and how to work with them.

Some proposals may even go to the board of directors, although most will not. Regardless of who receives the proposal, it should always be treated with the dignity that the problem deserves. In most cases the proposal should be in writing, even when it is to be presented to a group for discussion.

Although the decision to go ahead with research will be made by the research team alone, the written proposal should be sufficiently serious and thorough to withstand scrutiny by others who will be affected by the research findings.

6

USING OUTSIDE ASSISTANCE

What's in This Chapter

In this chapter we explore the use of outside assistance for "one-time" special studies, for continuing information to be used in databases, or to meet changing needs in marketing. We discuss how the client company chooses, uses, and cooperates with an outside research firm. We also explore the need of the research firm to be aware of the pitfalls that may exist in agreeing to work with certain types of clients.

Not long ago, many companies, if they used marketing research at all, attempted to do it themselves. Often, of course, these research attempts were successful, and many marketing research departments are well-established in today's companies. This is especially true among the very largest corporations.

As an introduction to this chapter, we will spell out why this situation is changing. In view of these changes, clients seeking outside assistance and research firms seeking clients may need to consider new ways of working together.

This book advocates the idea of a team directing marketing research at the client level. It also urges giving serious thought to some sort of continuing partnership between research agency and client.

NEED FOR OUTSIDE ASSISTANCE

Probably the principal reason for the trend toward using outside suppliers of research is the more complex and sophisticated research techniques that have recently been developed. Computers have allowed ways of finding and analyzing information that could not have been dreamed of ten to fifteen years ago. Although computers have become almost universal, the use of computers for marketing research has become a specialized field of knowledge that few firms wish to develop themselves.

Furthermore, companies are slimming down their middle and top management staffs. For cost reasons, many companies have come to feel that a well-chosen, expert, outside research supplier can do the job of market research better, more completely, and at a lower cost than the companies' own departments.

The idea of partnership between client and agency has grown rapidly in recent years. Because of the wealth of information now available to clients on a continuing basis from agencies that specialize in gathering, analyzing, and reporting information, it is considered far too costly and time-consuming for any single company to attempt to collect such information itself.

For surveys, using outside research will be judicious when too much is at stake to depend on in-house research, and when too much employee time will be needed to complete a task.

Outside firms also are useful when there is an important question of confidentiality. Research firms can hide the name of the company sponsoring the study. This may be very important when knowledge of the company and its products may unduly influence survey responses.

Outside research firms can be used for specific problems if emotions are running high within a company. When two "sides" to an issue have developed, honest neutrality can be found only by employing outside experts.

However, in many firms there is still a blend of certain studies done internally and others contracted out. This book recognizes both circumstances. The marketing staff must have a sound basic knowledge of research methods and possibilities, both for surveys contracted out and for those done in-house. Indeed, top management itself should be able to judge the kind of research needed for a specific problem and whether the research is being done as thoroughly as possible.

DETERMINATION OF NEEDS

One mistake that many organizations—for-profit or not-for-profit—make is their unwillingness to think through their needs as precisely as possible before contacting or contracting with a research supplier. This is true whether the problem is a one-time problem or involves the need for a system for continuous input and analysis of information.

It is only fair for the potential client to approach the outside firm with a thoughtful analysis of its needs. The firm and the research supplier need to work together to define and refine the problem or the needs. The supplier knows his or her field just as the firm with a problem knows its business.

The employing firm may not even know in advance what research techniques are available. To the extent possible, however, the firm with a marketing research need should have that need carefully analyzed internally before seeking outside help. Then the skilled research firm can add its knowledge and expertise to the development of findings and recommendations for what is by now a well-defined need.

Dealing with an outside supplier of research should always be a two-way street, with the client firm and the research firm both contributing whatever knowledge is needed for the development of a research-based solution.

THE NATURE OF OUTSIDE RESEARCH SUPPLIERS

Larger firms with perhaps years of experience in dealing with suppliers of research already know how disparate the research field is.

Some research firms attempt to offer all types of help. It may be mail surveys, telephone surveys, or focus groups fully described in other chapters of this book). Many firms, on the other hand, specialize in the analysis of census and other information and the application of these data to the customer's needs. Research firms may be broadly categorized as having the following types of specialization: (1) special skills, (2) special facilities or equipment, or (3) special procedures. All of these specialized areas have been or will be covered in other chapters.

ADVANTAGES OF DOING RESEARCH IN-HOUSE AND WITH AN OUTSIDE SUPPLIER

The table below depicts the advantages of in-house and outside-supplier research:

	In-House	Outside Firm
Familiarity with company and with problem background	X	
Project control	X	
Contributions of specialists (psychologists, statisticians, etc.)		X
Objectivity, credibility		X
Cost savings (possible)		X
Ability to handle overflow demands		X
Political considerations		X

The difficulty in choosing a research supplier can be illustrated by what one city, Cincinnati, has to offer by way of marketing research help:

- Sixty listings under the heading of Market Research in the yellow pages.

- Twenty-one research firms showing head offices in other cities, mainly in Ohio.

- Forty-three local listings under Marketing Consultants; many of these offer to do marketing research.

- Twenty firms listed in *Quirk's Marketing Review*, May 1990. Listings for other types of research firms are published on a regular basis.

The above list describes a local situation in only one city. Many companies and organizations prefer to deal with large, nationwide (or even worldwide) research firms. Let us now consider the situation for a medium- to large-size firm that has had little experience with research suppliers. Having "noodled" the problem sufficiently, the company is ready to contact a research supplier.

DIRECTORIES OF RESEARCH SOURCES

The company looking for a marketing research supplier should start with directories of research sources. These provide a description of the

kinds of research facilities, services, and firms available. In each case
the publisher takes no responsibility for either the accuracy of the listing or the reputation of the firms listed or the quality of their services.

The most broadly useful research listing is the *GreenBook*, published annually by the New York chapter of the American Marketing
Association, and now past the quarter-century mark. It contains an alphabetical listing by company name that provides a brief description of
what each firm does, along with address, telephone number, and names
of one or more of the executives. There are also section listings by service
area (from advertising research to video), by market/industry specialists (from acquisitions to youth), by computer programs, by trademarks/
service marks (of the research firms), by geography, and by principal
personnel.

Annually, the national American Marketing Association (Chicago)
publishes its *International Membership Directory & Marketing Services
Guide*. It is basically the Marketing Services Guide that is useful to the
research buyer. This has both an alphabetical and a geographical index
indicating on which page or pages the specifics for the firm can be found.
There are also sections of listings such as advertising agencies, audiovi-
sual communications, computer hardware/software services, direct
marketing, health care marketing, marketing consultants, marketing
research, merchandising and public relations agencies, sales promotion, and trade show/exhibits. As the section headings indicate, this
guide covers a far broader range of listings than just research, and so it
is not surprising that the depth and range of coverage within the research category are far less than with the *GreenBook*. The Membership
Directory portion of the book is sometimes useful, but it is more difficult
to use. The index lists companies alphabetically and then lists members
by various office locations. But it is necessary to know the company
name, and then one has to go to the detailed alphabetical listing of members to locate the proper person in the proper office—a process that can
take quite a while.

The Best 100 Sources for Marketing Information, published in 1989,
is a supplement to *American Demographics*. This is a listing of the
"most useful" information suppliers; while most are private companies,
some are academic, government, and nonprofit sources. It begins with
an alphabetical list of the sources, each with a succinct statement of the
source's major service, then providing more detail for each under the
categories of demographics, psychographics/life-styles, buying behavior, media, direct marketing, the data game, and tools (mapping, software, PC systems, reference/publishing, custom research, consulting,
sampling, futures research, speakers, and modeling).

Several times annually, *Quirk's Marketing Research Review* publishes issues that provide lists of research services and facilities, including the firm's name, address, telephone number, name of contact person, and a brief description of the nature of the service. The Mall Research Facilities section, for instance, lists the number of permanent mall research facilities by state and location within the state; the estimated proportion of high, middle, and low incomes; the number of interviewing stations; and specific facilities (computer-aided interviewing, kitchen facilities, private display room, and one-way mirror for viewing of stations). The Focus Group listing is organized in much the same manner, with number of facilities by state, then specific listings for locations within each state, including identifying information for each, type of location (shopping mall, office building, freestanding, other), and specific facilities (conference-style room, living room-style room, observation room, test kitchen, test kitchen with observation room, and available video equipment).

In the Data Processing/Software list, there is first a section of companies listed alphabetically and providing identification material. Separate sections follow for data processing, statistical analysis, software for use with PCs, and software for use with mainframes. Each names the company and its services or products; the user then goes back to the first alphabetical listing for the identification material. The listing for Omnibus/Syndicated Research Studies has the usual alphabetical listing with address and telephone number and a list of its services or products, each one coded as either syndicated or omnibus. This is followed with a cross-index of study providers by category (from advertising to youth).

Quirk's publishes the *Researcher SourceBook* annually, a nationwide directory of over 4,500 listings of research services and products. It is claimed to be "the most complete directory of its kind." The first section contains listings by state and metropolitan area; the second is a cross-index by research and industry specialties; and, the third lists qualitative-research/focus-group moderators.

Once a year the *Marketing News* (American Marketing Association) publishes a *Directory of Software for Marketing and Marketing Research*. The firms are alphabetically listed with their addresses, telephone numbers, services, and products, and for each one a description is given (what it does, the industry or activity served, hardware and/or operating system needed, minimum memory required, and price). There is a cross-index by applications—what the program does—ranging from accounting to statistics. Of course, these listings are far broader than just marketing research, since the American Marketing Association covers all aspects of marketing as a discipline.

The National Directory of Focus Group Discussion Facilities is published annually by New Directions Consulting (White Plains, N.Y.). The facilities are listed alphabetically by city within state. Company names, addresses, and telephone numbers, along with (usually) the name or names of the people to contact, are listed. Description of facilities is limited to a few listings and is apparently provided in whatever dimensions given by the listed firm to the publisher.

Outside research companies often started by offering a special capability, a special service. Inevitably, in true American fashion, they felt the need to expand and become more profitable. This led, and continues to lead, to more techniques, more kinds of research that can attract more clients.

Specialized forms of research assistance are listed below. Certain research firms can do these jobs better than others, and few firms are able to use all these methods with equal expertise. Descriptions of these research approaches will be found in other chapters.

Mail surveys

Personal interview studies

Telephone studies

Panels

Omnibus studies

Sampling

Focus groups

Specialization in overall marketing measurements includes the following:

Single-source national data

Test marketing

Scanner test marketing

Controlled test marketing

Simulated test marketing

Specialized studies for specific marketing decisions might include copy testing and service research. In addition, there are research firms that specialize in problems of market segmentation, customer/prospect databases, advertising media studies, and audience studies.

OUTSIDE RESEARCH SUPPLIERS: AN OVERVIEW

In some ways, the marketing research industry has not fully matured. Research firms have come and gone. Especially in the late 1970s and the 1980s, new companies appeared and new techniques were proclaimed. It is difficult for any size organization seeking marketing research help to know where to turn. Even large companies with some past experience need to seek new suppliers occasionally. Some new suppliers offer techniques that are unavailable from older firms.

Furthermore, those in the industry have aggravated the problem by their continuous use of terms fully understood only by those already familiar with modern marketing research. A brochure that prides itself on offering statistical modeling and multivariate statistical procedures may be addressing peers rather than prospective customers. Research people in large companies may talk about statistical techniques over lunch. The many firms that should be using research in this decade may well be turned off by such jargon unless they become better educated in the marketing studies that they should be doing.

To choose firms of good, solid reputation and ability, careful study is required. Companies must do research to discover the kinds of research needed and the kinds of research firms capable of doing this work.

TYPES OF RESEARCH FIRMS AND WHAT THEY OFFER

Outlined below are the types of marketing research firms available and their areas of expertise:

1. *General description*

    A. *Firms offering custom-designed studies*. These firms offer studies designed to order to meet the specific needs of the buyer. The techniques and methods of such studies are described in other chapters of this book.

    B. *Firms offering syndicated studies*. These firms offer ongoing surveys conducted continuously or periodically, using the same basic data that are reported separately to multiple clients. Sometimes these reports take varying forms depending on the needs of the client. Examples are: Nielsen Scantrack and Nielsen National Television Index; special equipment is used in both cases.

C. *Firms offering standardized studies.* These firms offer research services centered on a method of doing things (usually a unique method) such as copy testing, simulated test marketing, or setting up a consumer panel or an omnibus study. Special equipment or facilities may be a built-in part of the service. For example, one part of the McCollum Spielman copy-testing service uses a special laptop computer keyboard for measuring instant and continuing reactions to advertisements being shown.

D. *Firms offering special facilities or equipment.* These firms sell (or rent) major tangible items such as premises (for group interviews, kitchen testing, etc.).

E. *Firms offering research tangibles.* These firms sell commodity-like items such as survey software, survey samples, and lists.

F. *Firms offering databases.* These firms offer banks of existing computer information on demographics, psychographics, buying habits, and the like. These can be used with data on individuals for use in a firm's own customer/prospect databank.

2. *Type and Location*

A. *Local firms offering special types of assistance.* These firms may specialize in interviewing, mall intercepts, telephone research, and the like. They may take on special local assignments for large, nationwide research companies. They often offer facilities for focus and other types of research groups. As focus groups have become more popular, these facilities have grown more sophisticated, as will be described in Chapter 10. These research firms also may handle research other than their specialties.

B. *Regional and national research firms.* These firms may be able to do almost all forms of marketing research. However, most still specialize and show their greatest strength in one form of research or another. These companies often offer consulting in marketing and even general management. They may offer marketing systems and marketing decisions systems. They also may offer computer-based information for use in databases, marketing strategy decisions, and the like.

C. *Consultants in various specialties.* These firms may consult and advise about packaging, advertising, personnel problems, and the like. They also may offer to do some research relating to their specialities. These firms may have a major field of interest, such as engineering or electronics. Their research, if it is done, can include necessary outside studies, both marketing and technical.

D. *Firms offering research tangibles.* These firms offer commodity-like items such as survey software and lists.

E. *Firms offering databases.* These firms offer banks of existing computer information such as statistics on demographics, psychographics, and buying habits. Data are provided for use in the client's own customer/prospect databank.

CHOOSING AN OUTSIDE RESEARCH FIRM

Before discussing the details of choosing the best research firm for a particular problem, we wish to stress a number of points.

First, the buyer of research should realize that the research contractor must make a profit. The contracting firm may shave its price a bit to try to obtain a new, large company as a client. But, in general, it is often too easy for the buyer of research to request just a little more and then a little more, and expect to get it for the original contract price. Too much persistence of this type can lead to a bad relationship between the buyer and seller of research. Some discussion about proper price may be necessary during early negotiations, but once the problem is defined and agreement has been reached on the kind and amount of work to be done and the price that will be charged, it is unfair to a research firm to expect added work without added cost.

The research buyer must realize that the research contractor probably will need counsel as the study progresses. This may mean a considerable amount of time for a company representative, but it can also mean the difference between a failed or a successful study. The time of the buying company's representative must be considered part of the total cost of the study.

Both the buyer and seller of research have a right to expect that an agreement reached will be complied with in a timely fashion. If operating problems arise that will delay the final report, the buyer should be notified as these problems arise. Further cost as well as more time may be involved.

There are two kinds of buyer–seller relationships. For a long-term continuing service, such as syndicated and ongoing ad hoc research, the interrelationships of people and technologies must be carefully considered.

For a short-term, ad hoc study, these interrelationships, while important, may be broken off at the end of the study, or even if things are going poorly. Careful choice of research contractors should obviate such problems, but poor choices are sometimes made. It sometimes happens that the top people in a research firm tend to disguise or hide a less capable backup staff.

Especially in selecting an ongoing research service, the buyer must think not only of dependability of the research method offered, but also whether the research firm is likely to stay in business. These are turbulent times in marketing research, and new marketing plans are going to require considerable capital. Commitment and resources are therefore crucial, as is the software offered. Once the buyer has made the choice of a research service, a long-term tie is probable.

For services with standardized procedures and/or a clear-cut philosophy, the crucial element is whether the *concept* of the procedure selected is acceptable to the purchasing company. To be sure, quality of work is important, but chances are that the research firm would not have been in business this long if the quality of its work were not good. So the choice often is made on the basis of the concept and the method of backing up that concept. After the choice has been made, the buyer is not likely to be shopping around very soon for similar types of work.

Now let us consider the specific steps to be followed in choosing a research firm:

1. The user firm, having checked all sources for finding names of research companies to contact (including other organizations that may have had similar research done), should decide on two or three that appear to be the most promising.

2. A first contact should probably be by letter. A written request allows the research supplier time and opportunity to consider what it can offer. The letter should give the proposed supplier as full a description as possible of the problem and why it is important to the firm. A copy of the firm's annual report might also be enclosed. Presumably the research contractor will do a little research on the company at this time.

3. An interview with the research firm should be suggested, preferably in its office. This allows the employing firm a first glimpse of how the research firm operates and the caliber of its personnel.

One of the authors remembers one such early interview; at lunch the door to the back office opened and out came a scruffy bunch of young men who looked like rebellious youth right out of the 1960s. The interview did not go smoothly.

4. The user firm should seek information about what companies it has worked for in similar studies. Where can references be sought?

5. In this early contact, the client firm should attempt to determine if the research personnel appear to have a quick understanding of the nature of the problem. Do they have some suggestions about how, in general, the research for this problem can be done? At this point, no final research methods can be decided—but some early comfort can come from hearing intelligent surmises.

6. The user firm should inquire about how the research firm likes to work with clients. Does it welcome supervision from time to time? How often would it suggest contacts between the buyer and seller of research be made? Will it issue interim reports? In the case of surveys, would the research firm welcome use of the buying firm's personnel to do some of the fieldwork?

7. The user firm should request a written proposal. This proposal should be in sufficient detail to prevent future misunderstandings and arguments: Who will actually do the work and who will supervise it? What kind of supervision will be needed? What kind of report will it suggest to meet the buyer's needs? Will there be interim reports to the buyer? What will be the geography of the study? What types of contact will be made? Should there be an agreement on secrecy?

Specifically for a survey, how will the research be done? In what areas will it be done? How will contacts be made? What is the nature of the sample, and what is the required percentage of fulfillment?

For continuing information, perhaps taken from the agency's databanks and contributing to the client's databank, what are the sources used? How are they analyzed? In what way does the agency think these continuing services can add to the client's ability to market effectively? What special services, such as mapping, can the agency offer the client? How does the agency keep up to date in a rapidly changing field? What is the background of the experts who will handle the figures and information for the client? Can they be counted on to work easily and effectively with the client's own experts?

The proposal must include price, plus or minus a standard percentage. The proposal should also state what kind and type of information, guidance, and help would be expected from the client company.

8. The client firm should be sure that each contacted research firm understands that other research firms are being asked to submit proposals.

9. Both the research firm and the buyer must understand that an extended study may change some of the proposed research methods, and that such agreed-upon changes might cause a change in price. But with adequate discussion and mutual planning, such changes should be minimal.

10. Both the client and research firms should understand that further discussions may change the proposal in some ways. A rush to agreement may actually be a rush to disaster.

11. Both the client and research firms should agree about who will be the prime contacts between client and researcher.

JUDGING THE PROPOSALS

In the case of a study involving a continuing relationship, where the research firm will be offering continuing, ongoing, perhaps largely mathematical information about the market, choosing a supplier is not a choice between "in-house" and "outside." It is a decision on *which* outside supplier.

The buyer might consider having the probably "winner" research firm consult various personnel of the client's firm. Relations between inside and outside people can be crucial to the study's success.

We stress once more the points that need to be considered carefully now, before it is too late.

1. Does the proposal show an understanding of the problem and its marketing implications? If the client firm has been as open as possible in the statement of the problem, then it has the right to expect a mature understanding of its needs.

2. Who will be assigned to this study? What is the nature of the organization that will back the research? Are statisticians, psychologists, field supervisors, and fieldworkers involved?

3. Is the total price acceptable? Large price differences among proposals signal a warning. They may reflect different assumptions

by different firms. It is the total cost that counts. Attention to the details of the component cost are of little value. The lowest cost proposal may only be a sign of poor planning or possibly poor work.

4. Has the proposal set forth a procedure for changes if they are required? Is this procedure acceptable to the client?

CHOOSING A CLIENT

It is always difficult for a seller to refuse a willing buyer, especially in a competitive environment. But there are times when the seller, aware of its own strengths and weaknesses, should do just that. Perhaps a research agency that has specialized in mail questionnaires is willing to do some mall intercepts. Or a seller who knows all about databanks might also be willing to do some other little job for a prospective buyer. Herein lies danger. A reputation built up with difficulty can easily be torn down by poor work. And older, successful firms simply may not know how to supervise kinds of research other than their own.

An example of this potential problem from another field of business is the trouble that many companies have had trying to break into another field. Well-trained personnel often were not available, and even top management was often in a quandary about what to do. The 1980s saw much of this, sometimes to the later great sorrow of the buying concerns. Research firms can be specially tempted when that "other" research appears to be so simple—and possibly profitable.

THE ACTUAL CONTRACT

The buyer and seller should sign an agreement in which all of the details of the research study are spelled out. Price, who will do the work, how the work will be done, the timing of the study and subsequent report—all should be included. Also, the payment and its method should be spelled out.

The supplier is almost certainly staffed with qualified people who want to do the best possible job. Once the research firm has been selected, its staff should work with the full cooperation of the buyer's staff. Points of possible contention have all been ironed out in the contract, and small, petty disagreements should not take place. Nevertheless, it is always important for the buyer to be aware that some things could go wrong. A strong, continuing relationship between buyer and agency will help prevent errors of understanding or judgment.

REFERENCES   Bogda, Peter, and Gilbert C. Meyers. "Grab a Partner for More Effective Research." *Marketing News*, Jan. 7, 1991, 2 ff.

Deutsch, Claudia H. "Avon Keeps Ringing but Wall Street Won't Answer." *New York Times*, July 15, 1990.

Guadagni, Peter M., and John D. C. Little. "A Logit Model of Brand Choice Calibrated on Scanner Data." *Marketing Science*, Summer 1983.

Kirchner, Russell J., and Richard K. Thomas. "Desktop Decisions." *American Demographics*, Aug. 1989, 34 ff.

Little, John D. C. "Information Technology in Marketing." Sloan School of Management brochure, Mar. 14, 1990.

Riche, Martha Farnsworth. "Seven Trends." *American Demographics*, July 1988.

Russell, David. "Let's Sort It Out." *American Demographics*, September 1989, 4 ff.

"The Winning Organization." *Fortune*, Sept. 26, 1988, 50 ff.

7

CHOOSING THE METHOD OF COLLECTING DATA

What's in This Chapter

In this chapter we explore the various methods of collecting primary data: mail surveys, personal interviews, telephone surveys, completely self-administered surveys, panels, omnibus studies, focus group interviews, interactive research, and observation. We discuss the importance of and criteria for selecting the data collection method best suited to the specific marketing research problem.

When firsthand (primary) data are required to help answer a marketing need or problem, the all-important consideration are relevance, accuracy, timeliness, and cost. While these points have been thoroughly discussed in Chapters 4 and 5, they bear repetition here. We start with an example.

A company producing shaving products was offered an electric vibrating shaver with a single-edged blade, to be used with lather. One of the authors took it home to try, as he typically did with proposed new products. When he cut himself badly, he concluded that this was a dangerous product. A testing organization was hired to have men try this at a washbasin while an observer watched through the two-way mirror. It *was* dangerous; every man in the small ten-person sample cut himself, some rather badly. Relevance this certainly showed. But accuracy, timeliness, and cost are at least equally important.

In this chapter we will provide guidelines on how the user of primary research should decide which of the available methods of data collection to use. There is no simple answer. Each method has its advantages and limitations. The user has to choose the most appropriate method.

Whatever the method, potential sources of error must be considered.[1] Though Deming, the famed researcher and probably the first advocate of area sampling in surveys, is talking mainly about surveys, his cautions apply fairly generally to all of the three methods of collecting primary data. Deming warns about errors in sampling (discussed in Chapter 8), questionnaire errors (discussed in Chapter 9), and interviewer error (discussed in this chapter). We would add respondent error, which can be reduced by certain detailed procedures of questionnaire preparation or observation as shown in this chapter.

We will now discuss the major techniques of obtaining firthand (primary) information: surveys (mail studies, personal interviews, telephone surveys, and self-administered surveys), panels, omnibus studies, focus groups, interactive research, and observation studies.

MAIL SURVEYS

Mail surveys are the ubiquitous form we are all so familiar with: A questionnaire is sent to a potential respondent, and if all goes well, the person writes in the replies and mails it back.

Of course, it is not all that easy, nor is it always a good technique, depending on the purpose and nature of its use.

OVERALL EVALUATION: ADVANTAGES

On the positive side, we present the chief advantages of mail surveys below.

Questionnaire Scope

Generally speaking, it is possible to ask about, and get answers to, a rather amazing breadth of topics. Since there is no one-on-one relationship, there seems to be little reticence to reveal personal habits and feelings. Women will freely respond to subjects such as personal hygiene and use of birth control methods and devices. Men, when assured of anonymity, will be willing to give details of their investments, net worth, and income.

Questionnaire Length

If the subject is of interest to the respondent, the amount of time the person is willing to spend on the questionnaire is almost incredible. The woman answering questions about her cosmetic needs and practices or the purchaser of a new car often is willing to spend an hour or more answering a detailed series of questions.

Respondent Interaction

There is an initial plus for the mail questionnaire: It is mighty convenient for the respondent. There is no interruption of activities to respond to the series of questions, and the person can reply at whatever time is convenient.

Furthermore, there is an opportunity for a more thoughtful response, since the person is not confronted with someone waiting for a reply. It is easy and inviting to jot down answers quickly.

The mail survey can be used wherever it is necessary to get responses that require the person to check out things, such as the make and model of the refrigerator, the number of packages of a particular brand and type on the pantry shelf, or the weight of one's dog or cat.

The mail survey also makes it easy to present exhibits, such as advertisements and product models.

Low Cost per Response

When we say that the costs of a mail questionnaire are low, we make the statement with qualifications. We assume that the user is an expert in mail surveys and knows how to get a high rate of return. On this basis, the costs per return are low compared with most other survey methods. But this also means that total cash outlays are not kept to a minimum. It costs money to take all the steps necessary for a well-conducted mail survey, as we will show.

Low Cost for Incremental Numbers

As with many production units, it is the going-in cost that is high; once the basic costs have ben paid, the additional cost per unit is minimal. Mail surveys are like that. Once the basic cost is paid for envelopes and paper, though postage costs rise proportionally with numbers, printing costs rise only minimally.

No Interviewer Bias or Cost

Since no interviewers are used in the mail survey, there is no chance for interviewer bias to creep into the responses. As we will show in the discussion of methods where interviewers are used, there is always the possibility of the investigator's unconsciously affecting the response through voice and body language. And lack of interviewers means that one of the largest segments of cost in the interviewer survey is eliminated.

OVERALL EVALUATION: LIMITATIONS

The mail survey, even at its best, has severe limitations. We discuss below the most important limitations.

Sampling Problems

Unlike many other survey methods, the sampling frame (the list of people to whom the mailing is going) is frozen, not flexible. It is either a good list or a not-so-good list, and there is only one (minor) self-correcting aspect: the return of nondeliverables (moved, died, out-of-business, or whatever). Thus the adequacy of the mail survey is dependent on how good the mailing list is.

Few sampling frames for mail surveys—telephone books, city directories, industrial directories, or purchased mailing lists—are complete or current.

Response Problems

As we have said, there is a low-response problem unless the researcher/ marketer knows how to conduct a mail study. And the problem is, with a low response rate, that those who respond are not necessarily typical of those who do not. Total results, therefore, may be misleading.

Studies have shown that often those who reply to a survey are those who are most interested, or those with extreme feeling pro or con the particular topic. So unless steps are taken to compare reactions of those who respond immediately and those who respond only on follow-up, it can be dangerous to depend on mail survey results.

There is still another response problem, depending on the market definition for the particular product or service. As we well know, there is a considerable functional illiteracy in our population. This is greater among households with lower incomes. So if the product or service is one whose market extends into the lower income levels, these kinds of people simply cannot or will not respond, leading to a nonmeasurement of that segment of the market.

Limited Amount of Questionnaire Subject Matter

While we have talked about the length advantages of the mail questionnaire when the topic is of high interest to the recipient, we must be realistic and admit that the content of many mail questionnaires is not all that interesting. Generally, the length of the mail questionnaire should be short.

Lack of Control over Respondent

The recipient of the mail questionnaire has the chance to examine all of the questions before answering any, or he or she can merely glance ahead at upcoming questions while filling in replies. There is no control over the sequence in which the questions are exposed. Respondents can "correct" replies as they proceed. There is no chance to explain questions or to probe for meanings of the replies.

This lack of control further limits the scope of questions in the mail questionnaire. It would not do to ask for unaided recall of advertising slogans for airlines and then ask about names of airlines recalled showing a list. The list would help a lot of people connect airline names with slogans.

Wrong Respondents, Wrong Information

Another limitation of the mail survey is that the questionnaire may be answered by someone other than the addressee. For the executive or professional, it might be the secretary. For a specific member of a household, it might be someone else in the household. These self-substitutions can rarely be detected. Also, the mail questionnaire recipient may consult others before responding to the questionnaire.

APPLICATIONS

With an understanding of the strengths and weaknesses of the mail survey approach, we can now consider its applications.

The mail survey often is used to get information from people who are difficult to interview in person: farmers and those insulated from personal contact by a "gatekeeper" (doorman, security guard, receptionist, secretary), including groups such as management, professionals (lawyers, physicians), and those living in exclusive quarters.

The mail survey may be able to handle difficult questionnaire content. If the topic concerns *delicate or personal topics* (such as birth control, sexual behavior, or personal finances), the mail questionnaire may be the way to go. Or if the topic is one where *the person needs to consult sources* to give an accurate reply, the mail questionnaire sometimes can provide a big assist. For instance, if a woman is asked to list several food product categories and the brands of each on hand, the only way for the woman to do that accurately is to look in the pantry, refrigerator, and freezer. Of course, there is no assurance that she will. In the case of an industrial survey, a question about sales or purchases of a particular item will almost surely require checking of records, if an accurate response is to be obtained. The mail questionnaire, once again, may be the way to go. But the rate of response is likely to drop if records must be consulted.

The mail questionnaire may be an ideal method when respondents have an *unusually high degree of interest in the topic*. Examples include buyers of new cars, users of cosmetics, and executives, professionals, and those in almost any sort of specialty work.

IMPROVING THE EFFICIENCY OF MAIL SURVEYS

Not too long ago it was unusual to obtain more than a 15 percent response in a mail survey. With the 1970 publication of *Professional Mail Surveys*, by Paul Erdos, all of that changed. Listed as a reference at the end of this chapter, this book should be on the bookshelf of anyone using mail surveys. Its main concern is with ensuring that mail survey results are made as dependable as possible.

Advance Notice to the Recipient

Advance notice increases the rate of return. Such notice should be in the hands of the recipient no sooner than five days ahead of the mail questionnaire.

The simplest, and least expensive, kind of notice is the advance postcard, which alerts the recipient that a questionnaire soon will be on the way. As Erdos points out, no such advance notice is going to help a great deal unless the name of the recipient can be part of the address; most of us tend to ignore mail sent to "occupant," or just to, say, "Market Research Director" or "Product Manager" at our place of business.

Sometimes an advance letter is used. If the recipient is of considerable importance—a chairman of the board, a senator, a news figure—it is far more appropriate to use a letter. Sometimes the nature of the survey is intended to be confidential, for the eyes of the recipient only. Occasionally, the reason for the study and other elements relating to it require a long explanation, making a postcard impossible to use. Local franchisees of a restaurant group, for example, may be informed by headquarters management that a survey research firm will be sending them a questionnaire, that the identity of the respondents will be kept within the walls of the research house, that they should feel free to reveal what would normally be highly confidential data (such as the most recently monthly sales figures), and so on.

Where a really long questionnaire is to be used, and there is doubt that the topic has enough interest to stimulate a high response, advance notice by telephone may be worth the additional cost.

The Outgoing Envelope

The first thing the recipient sees is the envelope containing the questionnaire and other survey materials. It should convey the unspoken message of importance and need to open.

The paper should be of high quality, of far better grade than that used for most junk mail. The name of the sender should be printed in the top left corner, and the name of the recipient should have a typed appearance (though it almost surely will have been computer-produced). It should be sent by stamped (not metered) first-class mail. A commemorative or special-issue stamp may help, since it draws favorable attention from some people. If advance notice has been sent, there should be—preferably in red, to get attention, and at a slant in a larger typeface than that for sender or recipient—the words: *Here Is the Survey We Wrote You About.*

The Cover Letter

Unless the letter is read, the sender strikes out without a chance. But the letter must also motivate the recipient to complete and return the questionnaire.

The letter, on the same high-quality paper as the envelope, must look interesting and important. It must appear short so that the recipient need spend little time in finding out what it is all about.

There are some "mechanical" methods of achieving these goals. One is a letter that provides a feeling of personal communication: what appears to be a personally typed letter (including the recipient's name and address, the name of the recipient in the salutation, his or her name at least once in the body of the letter), and what appears to be the personal signature of the sender.

The letter must motivate the recipient to respond. It doesn't hurt to start by asking a favor. Sometimes the importance of the project can be used in a persuasive way, but it is essential to avoid stressing importance to the sponsor; this sort of selfish appeal is self-defeating.

The purpose of the study should be described briefly. The importance of the recipient and his or her response should be stressed. Benefits to the recipient should be underlined (one possibility here is to promise to provide highlights of the total results to those who respond). Then the simplicity of the questionnaire and an estimate of the short time it takes to complete it also will help.

Incentives

Sometimes the recipient can be offered a small token for participation, and this is generally included in the mailed materials. Recently one researcher used a $1 bill "for a cup of coffee" or "to give to a kid." While the $1 bill did not cover the cost of a cup of coffee at most Manhattan eating places (most of the respondents worked in Manhattan), the incentive still worked pretty well.

Questionnaire Format

The art of questionnaire construction will be covered in Chapter 9. Here we discuss the more mechanical aspects—the ways of presenting the series of questions.

The questionnaire should have a simple, appealing appearance. Usually, the smaller the page size, the higher the return rate, assuming that the pages are not cluttered by small print and small margins.

Generally speaking, the fewer the pages, the higher the return rate, though if the subject is of high interest, this should be disregarded. The paper, as with letter, should be of high quality to get the questionnaire out of the junk mail category. Printing should be professional in appearance, and in these computer days typefaces and sizes can be varied to help make the questionnaire attractive and look easy to complete.

Layout should be uncrowded. It should be immediately clear where and how responses are to be provided, with boxes or brackets for checklist queries and lines for open-ended questions (where the respondent writes in, in longhand, the reply to the question).

Sometimes the use of small, relevant cartoons is effective for getting attention and stimulating response. While the hiring of someone to do this may be expensive, it is possible that the use of an in-house person or employee of the advertising agency who is experienced in this area may not be so costly.

Return Envelope and Postage

The impression of quality must be maintained. A high-quality envelope should be used to avoid the junk mail category. In addition, though we know of no evidence to substantiate this, it seems desirable to use postage-due envelopes, metered envelopes, or run-of-the-mill stamps. The first two are of no use to the recipient except for return of the questionnaire. And the stamp collector will have no incentive to keep the stamp, though the pinch-penny might.

Follow-ups

Follow-ups are aimed at increasing the proportion of respondents, thereby ensuring a more representative survey. But the researcher, whatever the technique used in the follow-up, must make sure that enthusiastic respondents do not reply twice. Most often this can be handled by keying, a method of identifying those who respond to the first mailing, and approaching only the nonrespondents in the follow-up procedure.

Sometimes a simple reminder postcard is sent to the entire original list within three to five days of the original mailing, but this is not a *real* follow-up. What we are talking about is a selective follow-up mailing that includes another copy of the questionnaire, a new letter appealing for a response, and another return envelope. While the bulk of response to a mail survey comes within two weeks after the mailing, the follow-up mailing should be sent out three to four weeks after the mailing. This way it may reach some who are just back from vacation or other extended trips, and a few additional responses that come in the prolonged time will reduce the number of required follow-ups.

The follow-up letter appealing for the response must meet all of the physical criteria of the first letter, though its content naturally has to be different. It might include a shortened version of the first letter. But it also must express appreciation to those who have returned the first questionnaire and to those who have not, it might offer some small incentive.

The letter generally must be phrased in such a way that the recipients do not get a clue that there has been keying; this could turn them off. There are many ways to manage this. For example, after reminding recipients that they had been sent the questionnaire and that their response is important, the follow-up letter might say that because the original mailing may have gone astray, a duplicate of the questionnaire and another return envelope are enclosed.

PERSONAL INTERVIEWS

In the personal interview, respondent and interviewer speak face to face. In the dawn of professional marketing research—around the middle 1930s—personal interviewing was *the* accepted way of collecting survey information. This meant personal interviewing in homes. In those days of a more peaceful and trusting social environment, interviewing in homes was relatively easy. There weren't too many adult women in the work force, so someone was generally at home during the day. And there was no problem with evening calls, if the man of the family had to be questioned.

Telephone surveys were not accepted as a good method. Because ownership was then 50 percent of the population, it was impossible to get a representative sample. Mail surveys, as we have pointed out, were generally downgraded since 15 percent was considered a good response rate.

Today things are different. The in-home personal interview is no longer a popular research method. It is costly and has a low response rate unless a great deal of time is spent in making callbacks to try to build up the completion rate. People are hesitant to open the door after dusk, and often even during daylight hours. Telephone ownership has hit new highs, and now researchers know how to get reasonable response rates with mail surveys.

Today personal interviews are still in the picture, but mainly in shopping malls. Shopping malls, nonexistent 50 years ago, are now a way of life in metropolitan America, and so is mall-located personal interviewing (often allied with in-mall research facilities). When we talk about personal interviewing today, it is chiefly mall interviewing (see Exhibit 7.1). But we are also talking about personal interviewing at business and professional locations, and, to a lesser extent, about in-home interviewing. Since space does not permit separate discussions of all of these, most of our comments concern mall interviewing.

THE ROLE OF THE INTERVIEWER

The interviewer in personal interviewing is the key to the face-to-face questioning. She (and it is most often a *she*) is the dominant factor in the value of the obtained data. Accuracy of the data is affected by the skill with which the questions are asked and the finesse with which follow-up and probing questions are handled. Unless the queries are handled in a neutral way, the interviewer's own biases may affect the replies she perceives and records. She is generally a part-time worker and underpaid, working at the lowest government-approved wage level. Not too surprisingly, she sometimes falsifies results, even to the level of complete interviews. But the cheating usually takes only the reduced form of her skipping some questions and filling these in later, to save time. Sometimes, it is easy to take shortcuts in filling quota sampling requirements.

Exhibit 7.1   A MALL-INTERCEPT INTERVIEW IN PROCESS

Photo courtesy of Elrick & Lavidge.

Desirable Characteristics of the Interviewer

It is relatively easy to spell out what characteristics a good interviewer ought to have (though it is a lot tougher to make sure that the interviewer has these). One is extroversion—a feeling of and ability to communicate rapport with others. It is a characteristic of the sort of person almost all of us enjoy on first exposure, even without any real knowledge about the person. The term literally means being pointed outward toward other people. It signifies a delightful personality.

Voice is important. Color that with proper ethnicity. In voice, accent, and appearance, the interviewer must be able to relate to the group she will be questioning.

Dress is relevant. Today's relaxed dress standards do not provide complete freedom for the personal interviewer. He or she should not be dressed in an overly casual style not fitted to the particular environment—mall or otherwise. Nor should the interviewer be overdressed.

Some research firms make the most of dress in mall situations, with young male interviewers dressed in identical sports jackets and wearing large buttons reading "Marketing Research—We Need Your Help." It seems to get that help.

Basic Training

Interviewers should be trained, and the better research firms do a pretty good job of this.

In the ideal program, there is a personalized training program for new recruits, who have been carefully screened. The participants are paid for their training time. Sessions are at a central location, ideally in the firm's research offices at the mall.

The introductory session, perhaps two hours long, consists of an interactive discussion covering the role and nature of marketing research, what surveys are and how they are conducted, and the role and importance of the interviewer. There is considerable use of slides and videotapes to help demonstrate the points made. A break in the middle of the sessions provides a chance for a talking tour of the research facilities. From its library, the research firm might lend copies of the *Interviewer's Manual,*[2] with assignments for reading (with payment for time spent) before the next session.

The second session, also two hours long, consists of interactive discussions of how to select potential respondents, make the initial contact, and secure cooperation. It discusses the procedures in following through on interviewing to be completed entirely within the framework of the intercept, and on interviewing requiring additional procedures within the research facility on premises. Specific materials prepared by the research firm are provided for "homework," (again with payment for time spent).

The third and final session, another two hours, is a series of practice sessions on a one-on-one basis, in which the number of research firm participants is equal to the number being trained. Each participant is taken through, by instruction, example, and self-practice, the major kinds of study handled by the firm.

Training for the Specific Study

Once the basic training is complete, interviewers are assembled for training for the specific study. The research firm will have available duplicated interviewer instructions for the study. This will include the following elements:

- Brief review of the general interviewing instructions covered in the second session of basic training.

- Introduction to the particular study.
  -Interviewer timing requirements (dates and hours of work assignments).
  -General purpose of the study (not too much detail here; occasionally the purpose must even be disguised to the interviewer).

- The process of interviewing.
  -Selection of prospective respondents (and meeting of quotas, if any).
  -Specific procedures for the initial contact and for securing cooperation (may include instructions about escorting the person into the research facilities and the procedures to be followed there).

The Need for Validation

In the mall situation, most forms of cheating are unlikely, because this is almost monitored. The research supervisor is never far from the scene, and there is no chance for the investigator to falsify an interview from start to finish, nor is there any profit in it. But there is the opportunity to force quotas.

When personal interviewing is done beyond the supervisor's view, however, there are simply tremendous opportunities for cheating. Who knows what goes on in the case of an in-home interview, or one done on business or professional premises? Only the interviewer—and that occasionally can be a sad story that contaminates the results of the study.

Falsifying interview data can be prevented to some degree by validation. The practice of validation involves a recall personal interview by a separate investigator who went through the identical questionnaire, getting all responses on the pretext that the first questionnaire had been lost.

One of the authors remembers his early professional days when he was personally directing field studies. He assiduously followed the practice of validating a sample of some 10 percent of respondents. One of his chief validating interviewers, who understood what she was doing and the need for it, turned in utterly unbelievable validation reports. She had been given a copy of the original questionnaire, with all of its responses and IDs. Her presumed follow-ups showed 100 percent agreement on responses to each question, an utterly impossible occurrence. When confronted, she admitted that her personal commitments made it impossible to do the personal follow-ups. So even the auditor may cheat, as we know so well from many stories from Wall Street.

In its report for guidelines in newspaper audience research, the Advertising Research Foundation, virtually the mentor of standards in marketing research, recommends that 20 percent of the interviews turned in by "new" interviewers be validated,[3] and we think that this should apply to any personal-interview study where direct monitoring of investigators is impossible. It also suggests regular and periodic validations on others.

ADVANTAGES OF MALL-INTERCEPT INTERVIEWING

The main advantages of the mall-intercept interview, and its possible follow-up with specialized interviewing within the on-mall premises of the research firm, center on its effectiveness, which takes several forms.

Convenience

The process is easy and fast. One of the most facile of research procedures, it can be set up and carried out in a hurry. The procedures can be designed to be carried out smoothly.

Monitoring of Mall Interviewers

While intercept interviewers are not directly monitored, they are never far from home base. They work under semimonitoring and for the most part perform well. If the study involves escorting respondents into the research facilities, monitoring is even closer at hand.

Mall Sampling

The mall approach makes it easy to spread the geographic distribution of respondents without having to take steps such as paying for interviewer travel (common in other forms of personal questioning) or toll telephone calls (as with telephone studies).

At low cost it is often possible to filter those qualified to participate in follow-up, on-premise, special research measurements. These may be measurements predicting sales for a new product, evaluation of a copy approach, evaluation of a new-product idea, or other sorts of measures, all of which are outlined in Part Three of this book.

Facilities

Some marketing research firms have made arrangements with mall management for the right to conduct intercept studies, where people within the mall can be questioned in the public areas. Many other research firms also have their own research facilities within the mall.

These facilities generally include one or more rooms for group interviewing, a method discussed in Chapter 10. Some have test kitchens, where food products can be kept and/or prepared for consumer trial. Many also have rooms that can be prepared for use as simulated stores, made complete with shelving and proper lighting for display purposes.

Low Cost

In comparison with most other methods, the mall approach is generally low-cost. Little of the investigator's time is wasted, procedures are standardized and specific, and there is monitoring. All of these spell efficiency and generally low cost.

Use of Exhibits

Whatever the form of personal interviewing—mall, in-home, or at-business—one major advantage of interview surveys is that it is possible to use illustrative materials, such as advertisements or illustrations of the product, during the course of the interview.

LIMITATIONS OF PERSONAL INTERVIEWING

Personal interviewing in the mall, in the home, and at the place of business differ according to the location.

Sampling Problems in Mall-Intercept Studies

The mall-intercept sample is not a probability sample; most often it is a quota sample, with the interviewer instructed as to the proportions she is expected to get by demographics (such as sex and age) and by apparent degree of affluence. There may be other quota controls, but the point is that this is quota sampling. While our discussion of sampling in the next chapter shows that we have no particular prejudice against quota sampling or many commercial surveys, we must state that this method of sampling does not permit projections of findings to a larger population or universe.

Sampling *within* a mall presents additional problems.[4] On weekdays there may be greater proportions of the elderly and of teenagers. If the mall has a number of entrances, those shoppers coming in from the parking lot will typically be of a higher income level than those entering from the bus-stop entrance.

Time Pressure of Mall Intercepts

There is time pressure on many mall interviews. With many mall shoppers, time is of the essence: They are there to shop and get back home or to the office. True, some are there on a leisurely basis and have lots of time. If the mall-intercept interviewer is like most of us, she will—consciously or not—choose the leisurely, those strolling around with apparently little on their minds, to stop and question, and avoid those persons seemingly rushing along.

Those in a hurry can be pretty tough people to question. They *don't* have time and it is not the right point in their activities to interrupt them. So even when the interviewer gets their attention, she is under pressure to speed up the questioning, and this does not make for high-quality interviewing.

High Cost of In-Home/At-Business Personal Interviewing

The per-interview cost of personal interviewing is the highest of any survey method. There is too much nonproductive time to be paid for. The refusal rate is high, running anywhere from 5 percent to 30 percent. The in-home interviewer is paid for nonproductive time going from one household to another. If a precision sample is being used, more nonproductive time is paid for returning for recall interviews.

As we have said, if the potential respondent is in a business or profession, the time spent on the interview is often excessive. If an appointment has not been arranged in advance, many hours may be spent in a waiting room hoping for a session. Even if appointments have been prearranged, since these are at the convenience of the respondent, they can rarely be geographically scheduled to minimize interviewer travel time.

APPLICATIONS

In general, the personal-interview study is chosen when it is necessary to show exhibits (such as advertising, product, or package).

The mall-intercept approach is useful in studies where there is an immediate need for answers to short-answer questions, or where the study requires the use of special research facilities and equipment. We will discuss some of the applications of the latter case in later chapters (simulated market tests in Chapter 13, copy testing and some forms of consumer product testing in Chapter 14).

TELEPHONE SURVEYS

Telephone surveys are studies based on one-on-one questioning and answering between an interviewer and respondent by means of the telephone. They involve the professional approach of a corps of interviewers working out of a central location, with workstations provided along with outgoing telephone lines for each, and a monitoring setup that provides cut-in listening with revealing clicks to provide ongoing supervision. Because most of these have outgoing 800 numbers, they can handle any survey from local to national. (Fortunately, the days of having interviewers telephone from their homes, with no sampling or interviewing control and with excessive time claims, are long gone.)

Today almost all telephone interviewing is computer-controlled. The interviewer, located in her unit with all of her needed materi-

Exhibit 7.2   TELEPHONE INTERVIEWERS WORKING WITH DISPLAY UNIT AND KEYBOARD

Photo courtesy of Elrick & Lavidge.

als in front of her, works with a computer monitor (display unit) in front of her and a keyboard at her fingertips, as shown in Exhibit 7.2. Note the presence of the supervisor in the foreground. The supervisor has facilities that permit listening in (without any click on the line or audible change in the interviewer's voice) to make sure that the questioning is proceeding as it should.

In a consumer survey, when the interviewer gets an answer to a dialing, he or she checks to make sure that it is a household and then asks to speak to the qualifying respondent in the household. It may be the male head of household, the adult female head, any adult male 18 or over, any adult female 18 or over, or a teenager, depending on the study.

Then the computer takes over. Each question is shown on the monitor in sequence, and the interviewer reads the question just as written. Since most questions designed for telephone surveys are short-answer questions, where the respondent's replies are limited to a choice of possibilities, these possibilities are also shown on the screen. The interviewer merely has to push the appropriate answer key, and two, maybe three, things happen. First, the answer is entered into the computer program for later analysis. Second, the monitor moves on to the next question.

But the third step covers important exceptions to this second step. These concern the handling of subsidiary questions and skip patterns. For example, in a study of women's use of cosmetics, a question asks which of each of a list of cosmetics is used. When the interviewer enters the replies in the keyboard, the computer automatically displays the series of questions about each, avoiding those that the respondent said she did not use.

Within any of these categories, one question may concern frequency of use. Based on preset standards, light users might be asked only a portion of the number of questions asked of heavy users.

All of the responses go immediately into the computer for later analysis.

THE ROLE OF THE INTERVIEWER

As in any one-on-one encounter, the interviewer role in telephone surveys is all-important. Almost all of the previously stated desirable characteristics for the good personal interviewer apply to the telephone questioner. The one exception is appearance, and the one additional emphasis is on personality, since the interviewer must be able to be personable while not visually present.

One big difference from personal interviewing is that the interviewer is under virtually complete control. The research firm, if it is a good one, carefully selects and trains its interviewers. When interviewers go on-line with respondents, their questioning is monitored by computer programming and by a supervisor.

ADVANTAGES OF THE TELEPHONE SURVEY

Since so much of the survey process is under the control of the research firm, there is little wonder that the telephone survey technique has so much going for it. But before going into these control-related aspects, we first must talk about a dominating aspect of the telephone method.

Imperative Nature of the Telephone

There is a compulsion to answer the telephone, regardless of what a person happens to be doing at the moment. Marshall McLuhan gives startling evidence of this in his quote from a *New York Times* news item about a mass murderer of some years back:

> . . . A psychotic war veteran [by the name of Howard Unruh] in a mad rampage on the streets of Camden, N.J., killed thirteen people and then re-

turned home. Emergency crews, bringing up machine guns, shotguns and tear gas bombs, opened fire. At this point an editor on the *Camden Evening Courier* looked up Unruh's name in the telephone directory and called him. Unruh stopped firing and answered.

"Hello."

"This Howard?"

"Yes . . ."

"Why are you killing people?"

"I don't know. I can't answer that yet. I'll have to talk to you later. I'm too busy now."

Interviewer Control

Perhaps the top advantage of the telephone method is interviewer control, which leads to most of the other advantages.

Almost total control of interviewers is feasible with centralized telephone interviewing, and with that control comes quality.

The Sample

Some 95 percent of households have telephones, and the business telephone coverage is just about 100 percent. With proper sampling techniques, then, the entire population is there for the calling.

Another sampling advantage is that with outgoing 800 lines, regional or even national studies can be handled economically.

Response Rate

In the telephone method, efficient callbacks are the rule; they are made at times when the desired respondent is more likely to be at home than at the time of the first attempt. A response rate of 80 percent is not out of normal range.

Speed and Interviewing Costs

No travel time is needed for the interviewer to make contact with the respondent. Telephoning is concentrated, both in the original and follow-up contacts, at those times of day when the desired family member or businessperson is most likely to be accessible. Repeated callbacks can be made at the more likely times. Because of more effective use of interviewing time and less extended periods of interviewing, the amount of time needed for the study and interviewing costs are reduced.

Questionnaire Advantages

With a computerized interviewing program, it is generally possible to modify the questions during the survey process. Certainly there is little to be said for changing horses in midstream. But as long as the sampling design has been set to permit it, the first day or two of interviewing can be used to straighten out the questions—a form of questionnaire pretesting, which will be described in Chapter 9. Special preparation for this streamlining is necessary, however, particularly through careful interviewer training for the process.

Sometimes, as we will show in Chapter 9, the order in which a list of possible answers is given respondents can affect responses. The first item in the list generally gets more responses than it should, and under some circumstances, all considered in Chapter 9, the last position in the list may also bias replies. The first and last positions in the list are the most likely to be affected. Computerized interviewing can be programmed to provide for equal average position, eliminating any such bias.

LIMITATIONS OF THE TELEPHONE SURVEY

The telephone survey approach, with all its strong points, has the following limitations.

Potential Sample Bias

Unless special steps are taken, the list of telephone numbers used in a survey will be a biased list. It is outdated the day of publication, with omissions of new listings and inclusion of the outdated ones. There are too many unlisted numbers. There is the additional problem of getting a good representative sample of the not-at-homes in the callback process. These issues and how to minimize their problems will be discussed in Chapter 8.

Negative Impact of Demanding Nature

We have mentioned the demanding nature of the telephone ring as an advantage for the telephone survey. Increasingly, however, that telephone ring all too often is an unwanted sales pitch. Too frequently it comes during our "quality time," meaning talking time, dinner time, and television time, all of which are important to us.

Increasing numbers of people have gone to unlisted telephones, whether to avoid sales calls or for other reasons. Details of the problem and how the surveyor can try to compensate will be discussed in Chapter 8.

Limited Interview Length

There is a limit to the length of the typical telephone interview. It generally cannot run for more than about 15 minutes, though the nature of the subject may extend the time considerably.

Inability to Show Display Materials

There is no way to provide visual aids, such as advertisements or other display materials. (A single firm offers an exception, as we show below.)

APPLICATIONS

The general usefulness of the telephone study is universally acknowledged. Moreover, there are a number of situations in which the approach offers special advantages.

Special Sampling Needs

If the study is one requiring a broad geographic sample, national or regional, the telephone survey may be the way to go. Telephone charges with an outgoing 800 line will be relatively low on a completed-interview basis versus costs by mail or personal interview. This applies not only to consumer studies in general, but also to geographically dispersed samples of specialized business, professional, industry, or other widely dispersed individuals.

Follow-up Studies

Often the telephone study can be used as an efficient follow-up method in connection with another basic method of data collection; this is discussed toward the end of this chapter.

SOME SPECIAL ADAPTATIONS OF THE TELEPHONE SURVEY

There are two modifications of the telephone survey that we want to talk about. One is a creative service that makes it possible to use displays in telephone studies; the other is a method of soliciting telephone respondents.

Using Displays

Interlok is a unique service of ASI Market Research, New York.[5] This research firm has contracted with a number of cable channels across the country to have its own local channel. Having this channel makes it possible to offer displays, with any needed audio instructions, on the television set while conducting a telephone survey. If questions are complex, they can be put on the screen too.

Target respondents are screened, qualified, and recruited by telephone. The individual respondent is instructed to turn the television to the particular channel at the appropriate time, the stimuli are shown on the screen, and the person responds by telephone.

This system, along with its uniqueness, has limitations. The sample is not a probability sample, and we have no way of knowing how representative its selection of communities may be. But it does seem to be a good way of handling a telephone survey when visualization is desirable.

Soliciting Telephone Respondents

Some firms use 800 telephone numbers (no charge to the user) to solicit telephone calls from consumers.[6] While the primary use of the technique is to get orders and handle complaints, an increasing secondary use is to measure consumer reaction.

Pillsbury's Best Sugar Cookie Dough, for example, was thickened after a number of users telephoned to complain that the thin-consistency product (made to spoon out and place on the baking pan) could not be used with a cookie cutter for holiday use.

Kool-Aid (Kraft–General Foods) offered premiums such as T-shirts and skateboards for turning in stated numbers of proofs-of-purchase printed on the package label. But complaints from mothers on the hot line showed that they disliked having their kids bring home the sticky packages to cut out the coupons. The company then made the coupons a part of the easily disposable cellophane wrapper.

The crunchy sound in the television advertising of Grape Nuts (Kraft–General Foods) irritated many viewers, who complained that it grated on their ears. The sound was softened.

One television advertiser modified a commercial showing a child unrolling toilet paper after parents complained that this was a bad example for their children.

We do not advocate this procedure as a basic, dependable research tool. But we do say that solicited negative comments and positive suggestions, as long as they do not harm the overall presentation (product, package, advertisement), may be worthwhile research input.

INCREASING THE EFFICIENCY OF THE TELEPHONE SURVEY

We live in a competitive business society, and competition produces new and better ways of doing things. This is happening in telephone surveys.

Voice Response

The automated-voice program can be tailored to ask standardized questions and to record responses that fall within predetermined limits. The voice is so lifelike that it cannot be differentiated from the voice of a real person. If the respondent replies with an answer out of the structured framework or asks a question of his own, the system automatically shifts to a live person.

Several sources offer such programs or services, among them the monthly *Current Employment Statistics Survey* of the Bureau of Labor Statistics, along with its *Current Population Survey*. Both of these surveys collect data on employment and unemployment, using a form of voice response coupled with use of 800 numbers to streamline their interviewing operation and reduce costs. Survey participants dial an 800 number. An automated voice requests each to enter his or her ID number on the telephone keyboard and reply to each of the six questions on the questionnaire. The automated voice repeats each answer to be sure it is correct, and the participant responds with a one to agree or presses # and then corrects the reply. The responses are entered directly into the database. To include those who do not have push-button telephones, there are plans to use voice-recognition technology, where the respondent speaks instead of pushing buttons on the telephone. Speech sounds are modeled to the patterns expected by the computer.[7]

Handling of Open-Ended Responses

An open-ended question is one where there are no response categories provided the respondent. People come up with their own replies. Such questions are sometimes used in "reason why" situations.

The Voice/CATI System[8] of Audits & Surveys (New York) is an example. This system stores the response in a computer file. But that is only the starting point. To be sure, analysts can listen to these and classify them into categories, the traditional way of analyzing open-ended replies. And these replies can be sorted by demographics or other classification methods used in the study. But voice analysis may follow: Inflection and intensity in the voice are used to measure how people feel.

Cutting Idle Time of Interviewers

Nielsen, largest of the U.S. marketing research firms, decided it had to reduce the spiraling costs of idle interviewer time in its local television measurement service.[9,10] The firm was aware that there was a lot of nonproductive interviewer time spent in busy signals, no-answers, and telephone company recordings.

Two computer firms developed a system that automatically dials out simultaneously on multiple lines for each investigator. Disconnected lines, busy signals, and no-answers are screened out. Only live voices are switched to the interviewer. The system can handle as few as 8 interviewer stations or as many as 80 stations with 120 trunk lines.

Results have been impressive. The system not only cut down nonproductive interviewer time, but also was welcomed by interviewers, who prefer talking to people instead of sitting around handling busy signals.

COMPLETELY SELF-ADMINISTERED SURVEYS

In a completely self-administered study, entire control is with the potential respondent. Such studies are often conducted by service firms such as restaurants, motels, or hotels, and occasionally by health and financial institutions or even retail stores, where questionnaires are left in convenient places for the potential respondent to pick up, fill in, and return either in a convenient depository or by a prepaid-postage return envelope. The important things about the method are that the respondent is entirely self-selected and the questionnaire is completely self-administered.

We spend little time on this method. It offers the advantages of low cost and a broad sample. Lacking any kind of control, however, it has little use other than in public relations. We will provide a few exceptions in Chapter 17.

PANELS

A panel is a continuing group that responds periodically to questioning. The panel may be composed of persons, households, or business firms. It is a rather common survey method, and the panel may exist, for questioning purposes, for as little as a week or as long as a year or more.

The panel may be set up by telephone, mail, or personal interview. Some research firms offer use of their ongoing panels to provide syndicated information available to all subscribers, while other research companies make their panels available for custom use. The user can specify the demographics or even require specific category or brand users.

To provide an overall picture of panels in marketing research, we will describe the various methods of collecting the information. The sellers of syndicated panel services—these measure such behavior as buying volume by brand and television viewing—may use consumer diaries or electronic devices to get the desired data. The consumer diary is just what it sounds like: a form for the consumer to keep track of purchasing or some other form of behavior. An electronic device attached to the television set may monitor television tuning. With retail store panels, the data collection method may be through the use of either scanners or physical audits (both described in Chapter 13).

There are also many research firms that offer the use of their continuing panels primarily for proprietary research, where the user makes use of the panel for a specific purpose. The client firm, with or without the aid of the research firm, develops its own questionnaire. Things are custom-tailored. Sometimes the research firm or the marketing firm will set up its own panel, to be used for a stated time period during the introduction of a new product.

With all of these types of panels, the constant is a fixed group of participants.

MAJOR TYPES OF PANELS

The major ongoing panels are divided into panels used for syndicated offerings and those used for custom studies.

Syndicated Panels

The major syndicated panels will be discussed in Part Three of this book, which examines the major ways of applying marketing research in marketing operation.

Nielsen provides a national measurement of television viewing

(NTI) using people meters to measure the television viewing of various household members. Arbitron's ScanAmerica combines people meters with in-home scanner devices (to read UPCs) to measure brand purchasing and to relate this to television exposure.

Nielson's Scantrack, a national panel of supermarkets, provides continuing measurement of the movement of products within these stores. There are other panels used to report similar product movements in drugstores and other store types. But many of these necessarily use means of measurement other than scanners, since scanners are still primarily in the larger food stores.

Custom Studies

Several major research firms offer custom studies. The leader, most likely, is NFO Research, headquartered in Greenwich, Conn. It has a mixed mail and telephone panel of over 1 million, and both by numbers and years of experience in the field, has to deserve the "grandfather" label.

Market Facts (Chicago) and the NPD Group[11] (Port Washington, N.Y.) each offer custom availability with panels of over 200,000, and M/A/R/C (Dallas) has a similar panel of 100,000 households. We mention these in order of size only because the greater the size of the panel, the greater the options in its use tend to be.

Insta-Vue,[12] a service of Home Testing Institute, one of the NPD group, has a panel of over 100,000 available for monthly mailings.

The Kapuler National TelePanel,[13] a demographically representative database, is an ongoing system of telephone screening. It is offered primarily as a low-cost, fast method of locating low-incidence users of categories and brands who can be questioned in detail at the time, telephoned later, or sent products for testing.

ADVANTAGES OF PANELS

The panel method has some great advantages, some of which are unique.

Longitudinal Analysis

The use of a custom panel—and a syndicated panel too, for that matter—makes it possible to track the reactions or behavior of the same person, household, or business respondent over a period of time. This may not sound impressive, but compared with the surveys that we have talked

**Exhibit 7.3   PURCHASE OF A BRAND BY EXPOSURE TO
EARLY ADVERTISING (Measured in First Wave)**

	End of First Month	End of Second Month
Total Panel Members	(5,000)	(5,000)
Total Exposed to Early Advertising	(500)	(500)
Purchases by total sample	10%	12%
Purchases by those exposed to early advertising	12%	16%
Purchases by those not exposed to early advertising	10%	11%

about up to now—the straight mail, personal interview, and telephone studies—it is. Those are snapshots, taken at a single point in time, whereas the panel approach makes it possible to get a continuing series of reports from the same people, thereby providing a motion picture or videotape type of record.

Suppose you wanted to check the impact of advertising on purchases. The introduction of a new product in a market might use an advertising blitz concentrated in the first month. On two successive one-shot surveys, done at the end of the first month and again a month later, questions about advertising recall and brand purchase could be asked, with results showing that brand advertising recall for the test product dropped from 10 percent to 5 percent in the two sweeps, while brand purchase went from 10 percent to 12 percent. By themselves, these figures wouldn't mean much. People would be unlikely to recall whether they were exposed to the blitz advertising, even though they could recall brand purchase within the week. But let's look at the panel results among 5,000 customers shown in Exhibit 7.3. The table shows clearly that the blitz advertising had a continued impact.

It is always possible, with one-shot studies, for the researcher to find people who have strayed from the brand in question and then to ask them why. But the panel method gives an opportunity to ask the question at the time the purchase behavior has changed, and to obtain a reply that is almost of the moment rather than dependent on memory.

Lower Costs

Panels of any sort cost less than a comparable series of parallel but separate samples. There is only a one-time basic sampling cost, be it households or stores, and the continuing cooperation, if well-done, is also high. Of course, there are replacement sampling costs to provide for turnover among panel members.

LIMITATIONS OF ALL PANELS

The Sample

The sample is the most serious limitation of the panel. No matter how carefully the originally designated sample was set up, there is no way that all sampling units are going to agree to participate. Even with a lot of work, it is difficult to reach a 50 percent level.

Turnover

With consumer panels, annual loss of members may run as high as 20 percent. Loss of interest happens early with some members. It will be much less with a store panel or with some other forms, but it is still a common occurrence.

Original Self-Consciousness of Panel Members

With consumer panels used on a continuing basis for measuring the same elements, such as brand purchasing, the members at first are sometimes so self-conscious about their participation that their behavior is affected. The problem is so serious that some firms offering such services have new members participate for several months before their results are put into the study findings.

EVALUATION OF A PANEL FOR A CUSTOM STUDY

Provision of Dependable Data

Consumer mail panels, when properly used, provide results comparable to one-shot interview studies. But the all-important term is *when properly used.*[14]

Since response to the mail panel is typically self-administered, the entire questionnaire is in the hands of the respondent and can be viewed in its entirety before any questions are answered. So where careful sequencing through the questioning steps is required for sound answers, the mail panel, like the mail questionnaire, may provide misleading results.

As with all mail questionnaires, it is unlikely that a person's response to an open-ended question will be very deep. There is no opportunity for an interviewer to probe to get a full and meaningful reply.

A former member of NFO reported that the results of a mail panel and of a one-shot telephone study were similar in terms of brand awareness, use, and attribute ratings in four product categories. There were close results between the two in travel behavior (meaning in this case the proportion who have traveled outside of the United States and within the United States to selected states such as Florida, California, and Hawaii. Beer drinking (incidence, amount drunk, and brands) was similar, as were concept tests (though we do not know their nature) and purchase interest.[15]

Specifying Small Segments of the Population

One of the most important advantages of the mail panel is that it can be specific for two types of small segments of the population: one is demographic and the other is behavioral.

Suppose the need is for a study among Hispanics or among widowers over 70 years of age. It would be expensive to do either study using most of the usual methods (though with recently developed specialized sampling methods in telephone interviewing, there are some ways).

The behavioral aspect is equally important. If the need is to survey people who have, within the past three months, bought a minor brand in a product category, or those who are considering a trip to Greece within the next six months, the mail panel may be the way to go.

In some cases the research firm may already have information in its files identifying such households of people. If not, most research firms offering custom panel use provide mail screening. If time does not permit this, most of these firms will make a fast telephone survey to locate those who qualify.

High Response Rates

Because most of these custom consumer panel firms work on a highly personalized basis with their households, their response rates to a mailing are typically high, rating 70 percent or better without follow-ups.

Delicate Subjects

For the same reason—that close personal relationship—there are virtually no holds barred on the nature of the subject. Questions about how women handle their feminine hygiene needs can be as easily asked as questions about the details of family financial affairs. Few topics are off-limits.

Follow-up Probes

Because of the flexibility of the panel method, those who respond in a particular way can be followed up with either another mailing or by telephone. Those reporting use of a coupon for a particular product can be asked about their reactions to the product. Those indicating that they are very favorable toward a brand may be asked why by a skilled investigator via telephone.

No Quick Results

A built-in disadvantage of the custom panel is the time it takes for results. It is at least as slow as the outgoing and returning mail, and, as we know, these days that can be mighty slow.

There are ways to speed up things, of course, but always at added cost. The research firm will handle the entire study by telephone, for instance.

Advance Review of Questionnaire

Another disadvantage is that the mail consumer panel member, as with the mail questionnaire, has the opportunity to look at all questions before answering any of them. We have already mentioned the limitations this places on questionnaire content.

No Way to Show TV Commercials

Still another disadvantage is that the typical custom panel has no way of showing its members television commercials, and so has no way of getting reactions to these. But Screen-Test,[16] a service offered by NFO Research, not only overcomes this problem but goes well beyond it. Panel members are sent a videotape, with instructions to play it on their VCRs. The respondents have questionnaires in hand, which are to be filled in during and after exposure.

In addition to television commercials, there are many other applications of Screen-Test. Children's television programs can be evaluated by both parents and children. Personalities on proposed pilot programs can be measured. But beyond these obvious broadcasting possibilities,

Screen-Test can be used for measuring reaction to some physical aspects of a proposed new product, such as design, color, or preparation, or to the operation of the product.

APPLICATIONS OF CONSUMER PANELS FOR PROPRIETARY STUDIES

Here we consider (1) a panel that is established for the specific use of the sponsor and (2) the existing consumer panel that may be used for a proprietary study.

We have already mentioned the use of an existing consumer panel to locate small segments of the population. Some existing consumer panels have so many members in each of the larger metropolitan areas that special samples can be used to track their behavior during introduction of a new product (typically termed *test-marketing* and described in Chapter 13). An existing consumer panel may be used for consumer product testing (trial of a new consumer product), as described in Chapter 14).

Consumer panels set up for a specific purpose are sometimes used in extended consumer product testing of a new, fast-moving item, where the same household or individual is checked to establish the product's holding power. In the offerings of some research firms in the field of simulated test marketing (described in Chapter 13), panels of triers are established for much the same kind of measurement of holding power.

OMNIBUS STUDIES

An omnibus study is an ongoing study in which a buyer can ask proprietary questions in the study. The number of questions available to the user is limited. If there were a great number, the buyer would be better off financially having his own complete study. But by buying into an ongoing service, the purchasing company gets results on a limited number of questions at bargain prices, because the general overhead costs of fielding the study are shared by a number of clients.

Omnibus studies, depending on the research firm, are scheduled on a weekly, monthly, or quarterly basis. Some are done through personal interviews, some by telephone. There is a different but parallel sample of people in each stage of the study.

SOME OMNIBUS SERVICES

We mention only a few of the leading, most frequently used general services—those dealing with a broad cross-section of the consumer population. There are some that survey specialized populations (such as executives), but we do not review them here.

Twice-Weekly

Excel[17] (International Communications Research Inc.) has a twice-weekly national telephone study of 1,000 interviews of adults age 18 and over, half of whom are from each sex. Interviewing is done with the use of computer monitors. Standard breakouts of data are provided, such as geographics and demographics (including sex, age, education, and race), with other breaks available at an extra charge.

Weekly

Omnitel[18] (Bruskin) is a weekly telephone service of 1,000 adults. Teenagers and children, at added cost, can be questioned. Follow-up questioning is available.

Gallup Overnight (The Gallup organization) also offers a weekly telephone sample of 1,000.

TeleNation[19] (Market Facts, Chicago) is another weekly telephone service, offering a 1,000 sample composed half of men, half of women.

Every-Other-Week

Telephone Caravan[20] (Opinion Research Corporation, Princeton, N.J.) conducts its 1,000 telephone interviews (500 men, 500 women) every other week. If questions are provided on a Wednesday, results are delivered a week from the following Friday.

Monthly

Limobus[21] (The Roper Organization, New York City) is a study among 2,000 individuals, using a personal in-home interview. It provides 16 demographic breaks in its results.

Quarterly

AIM[22] (Bruskin) provides 2,000 in-home personal interviews of persons age 15 and older. In addition to the usual advantages of the omnibus method, this service stresses its applications for questions requiring displays—impossible with the telephone omnibus—such as print advertisements, storyboards, packages, photos, and visual scales. The questionnaire actually starts with a deck of cards showing elements such as an ad slogan, a logo, or other symbol. Awareness and identification are checked.

EVALUATION OF OMNIBUS STUDIES

Low cost is the greatest advantage of the omnibus study. The overhead costs of conducting a massive national study are shared by numerous clients of the omnibus firm, and the direct costs encountered typically are low.

Because there are so many studies of high frequency, it is possible to get almost overnight results, especially with the telephone types.

As we will show in Chapter 8, omnibus studies are helpful in locating small segments of the population. Costs of locating a sufficient number of such respondents are low. Because it happens automatically in the process of questioning large number of people, there is no special overhead cost. If the incidence is so low that an insufficient number is found in a single sweep, it is simply a matter of using additional sweeps. But if the buyer of the study wants to locate a small segment, it may be wise to use a frequently offered service. Waiting for six months to build up a necessary base is seldom practical.

Most omnibus services offer follow-up probes of those giving specific replies. These probes generally are conducted on a follow-up basis rather than at the time of original questioning (unless there are only a few questions) so as not to delay completion of fieldwork for the standard service.

The omnibus study provides a low-cost method of measuring trends, as long as the buyer doesn't want to include too many kinds of measurements. But, for instance, it is possible to ask, "What brands of soft drink can you name?" and to report these data on a monthly or quarterly basis.

Since most omnibus services collect their data by telephone interviews, it is impossible to show display materials such as advertisements or products. Such displays are often a requisite for a sound solution of the marketing problem.

The user of the omnibus study can never see the total questionnaire that is used, for that would violate the confidentiality of the other clients. So buyers have to *assume* that the research firm has the guaranteed skill to avoid any order and content bias in the questionnaire.

Order bias, to be discussed in Chapter 9, is especially a risk. Suppose, for example, that both a soft drink and a cereal manufacturer wanted, in the same wave of the particular omnibus service, to ask questions about brand recall and recognition, with follow-up questions about advertising exposure and content recall for all brands known to the respondent. Once a respondent had gone through the first sequence, he or she would be well aware that showing awareness of a brand meant additional questions about it. The second time around, some or many people will cut down their true brand awareness list to avoid those additional questions.

FOCUS GROUP INTERVIEWS

In focus group interviews, a small number of respondents is interviewed as a group, in a situation and with a skilled moderator, both of which stimulate group interaction and get a broader range of response than is typically true in a one-on-one situation. And it really isn't an interview; it is a discussion. Chapter 10 is devoted entirely to group interviewing.

A basic use of the group interview is in the development of a questionnaire for later use in a quantitative study. There are two ways to accomplish this. One is an exploratory, interactive session to determine all of the aspects of the topic that may be important to consumers, whether the product be coffee, ice cream, or shaving cream. While what it learned in the group sessions will not dictate the information needed for the study, it may well come up with some additional important ideas. The second way is through questionnaire testing. Once a questionnaire draft has been developed, there are ways of trying it out with a group and questioning them about it. These are discussed in Chapter 9.

One of the most common uses of the group interview is in the new-product area. In an early stage of new-product development, occasionally the technique of determining consumer reactions and objections to existing products can help lead to new-product modifications. Early checking of reactions to a new-product idea (concept testing) through the group method may also be used in gauging reactions to a new product.

Another broad area of application is the testing of ads, either the concept and approach (in the early stages), or in draft form in a later stage. It is a good exploratory method for determining the acceptance of a particular personality for a commercial.

Specifically, too, the group method can be used with interactive devices (discussed below), to measure minute-by-minute qualitative reactions to a stimulus (usually, in marketing research, a proposed radio or television commercial). By reviewing the high and low points of response with the group, the moderator is able to determine the reasons for the reactions and come up with suggestions for improvement.

INTERACTIVE RESEARCH

In interactive research the participant interacts, via a computer connection, to questions or other stimuli presented on a screen or by some other means. The process may provide a response by means of a keyboard, a computer mouse, or a touch-sensitive screen. It is generally handled in the home or in a central location such as a mall.

IN-HOME

A few examples will bring the definition of interactive research to life. Nielsen, the national television measurement service, uses a people meter to track which members of the household are tuned to which television stations at various points of the day. The details of the system are covered in Chapter 18. Earlier in this chapter, we mentioned that Interlok (ASI Research), through use of its own local cable channels in selected markets, shows questionnaires and other items on the television set while an interviewer is right there—via the telephone—to get answers.

There is a system about to go national that has the consumer, at home, wave a scanner-wand over the UPC labels to record all UPC-labeled purchases in the home. This system is described in a later chapter.

Viewtel[23] (Viewfacts, Chicago), is an imaginative service that apparently is going to be available to only a limited number of basic subscribers. As we write this, the system has in its sample 1,000 Chicago homes where the viewer can see questions over the family television set. A wireless remote-control keypad is used both to get the display on the television screen and to provide a means of replying to the questions appearing there.

The Viewtel database for each family covers demographics. It also includes reading of print media, television viewing, and radio tuning and listening (including outside of home). Also in the database is recent purchase of various brands. Thus it is possible for the user to target families or people meeting specific requirements.

Viewtel can be used in locations other than the home, such as airports, places of business, and hospitals.[24] As of now, Viewtel will be used only for proprietary individual applications, and the panel of households will not be expanded for purchase as a syndicated service.

IN CENTRAL LOCATIONS

There are a number of interactive-research applications in central locations. One is designed to handle large numbers only, others are designed for small numbers only (as in group interviews), and still others are planned for both capabilities.

Max[25]—A System for Large Numbers of People

With this system, mall shoppers or those in other high-traffic locations are invited (personally or by signs) to vote their opinions on a computer unit consisting of a display (monitor) and a keyboard. Respondents are trained briefly on the use of the machine, which is made simple for the participant (see Exhibit 7.4).

If the respondent types a number not on the screen, MAX asks for a correction.

Filter questions can be programmed in, as when only a person who responds in one way, such as answering "1, yes, within the last 3 months" in Exhibit 7.4, is asked additional questions. The system can also be used for a numerical scale rating, and Max can ask open-ended questions, with the respondent typing in the replies on the keyboard.

One advantage of Max may be that it produces more truthful replies, since there is no face-to-face situation with an interviewer. It also gets results in a hurry. One 1,200-respondent survey required 4 days of questioning, ending on a Thursday. Results were delivered early in the following week. This included some 160 measures for each of 40 brands, with some advanced statistical analysis and recommendations.

Max is a self-selected sample, and subject to all the limitations of such a sample. Only those persons willing to use a computer will participate, and we suspect that this will exclude many older people and many of the less-educated.

We also have some doubts about the typing of the responses to the open-ended questions. First, how many respondents can give a good answer when it has to be typed? It will surely be a short reply. In addition, there are some people who cannot easily type.

Exhibit 7.4   EXAMPLE OF THE MAX COMPUTER DISPLAY FOR PARTICIPANTS

Screen: Have you ever tried this brand?
1. Yes, within the last 3 months
2. Yes, 3–12 months ago
3. Yes, more than a year ago
4. No, never

Quick Tally[26] (Quick Tally Systems)

This system can be used either in a large facility, handling just over 1,500 people, or with groups of as few as 12 or less in focus group interviews.

The keypad, shown in Exhibit 7.5, makes it possible for the participant to register reactions in one of three ways:

- Use of the full 12-button keypad for responses to a multiple-choice question

- Use of the first 2 buttons only for yes/no questions

- Use of the 11-point slider to respond continuously to an ongoing stimulus, such as a commercial

The system shows a changing line graph of the level of like/dislike

Exhibit 7.5   KEYPAD OF QUICK TALLY

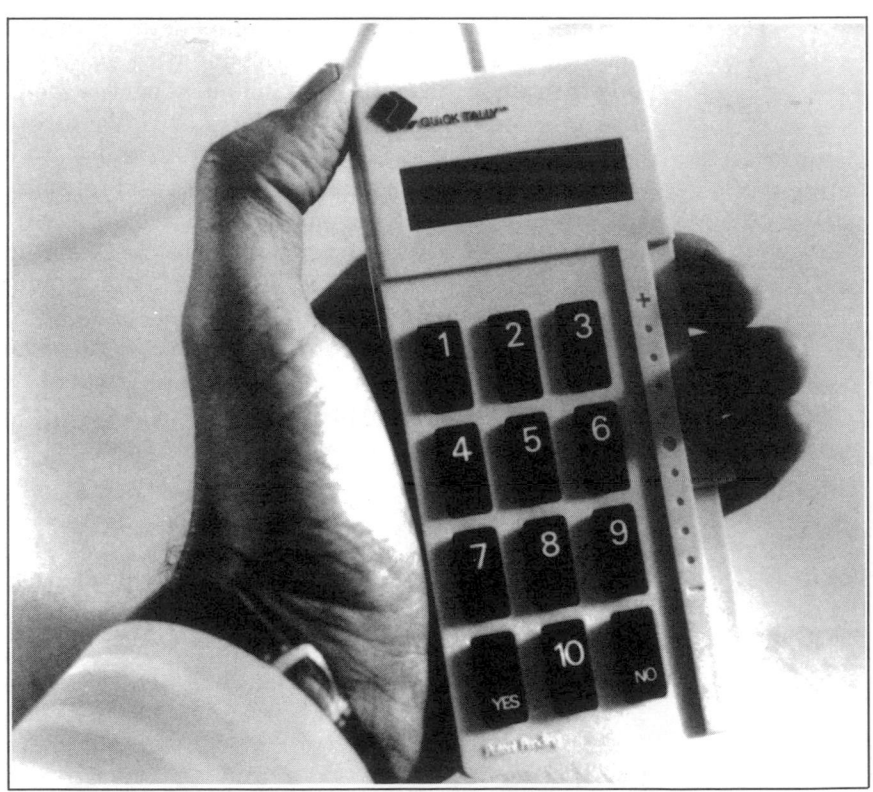

Photo courtesy of Quick Tally Systems.

superimposed on the playback of the stimulus material, most often a television commercial.

Results are instantly available on television monitors, even including breakouts by subgroups. Printouts are available, or the data can be provided on floppy disks.

PEAC[27]

This is a system similar to Quick Tally. Since it is most often offered as a continually available service, its details are presented in Chapter 14 as a copy-testing method. Participants in a theater-type setting push buttons, on a minute-by-minute basis, to show like/dislike reactions to group-presented materials.

Preference Analyzer II[28] (Ortek Data Systems)

This system is a kissing cousin of the systems discussed above. It provides a hand-held dial that comes in a choice of ranges: 0–100, 0–10, or 0–7, depending on the user's needs. Participants respond on a second-by-second basis to a sequential stimulus such as a commercial. It can be used by a single individual or by up to over 500 respondents, and superimposed averages are shown instantly on the changing stimulus in private locations. Exhibit 7.6 shows the physical units of the system.

EVALUATION OF INTERACTIVE RESEARCH METHODS

There is no interviewer with most interactive research systems. This obviates many problems: the cost of interviewers, the need for supervision, and potential biasing influence. There is no risk of the influence of inflection or accent, nor is there any limitation on delicate subject matter, often present with an interviewer.

Since replies are automatically entered into the system as the person responds, there is no need for the expensive process of individual coding of each answer. It is instantaneous, and the chance for error is less than when coding must be done manually by a third person.

All of these interactive systems ask the questions in the same form and order.

Most interactive research systems, if they are on a single-respondent basis, provide questionnaire skip patterns, so that subsidiary questions are always asked when they should be asked and skipped when they should not be asked. All of the programs provide continuous

**Exhibit 7.6   PHYSICAL UNITS OF THE PREFERENCE
ANALYZER**

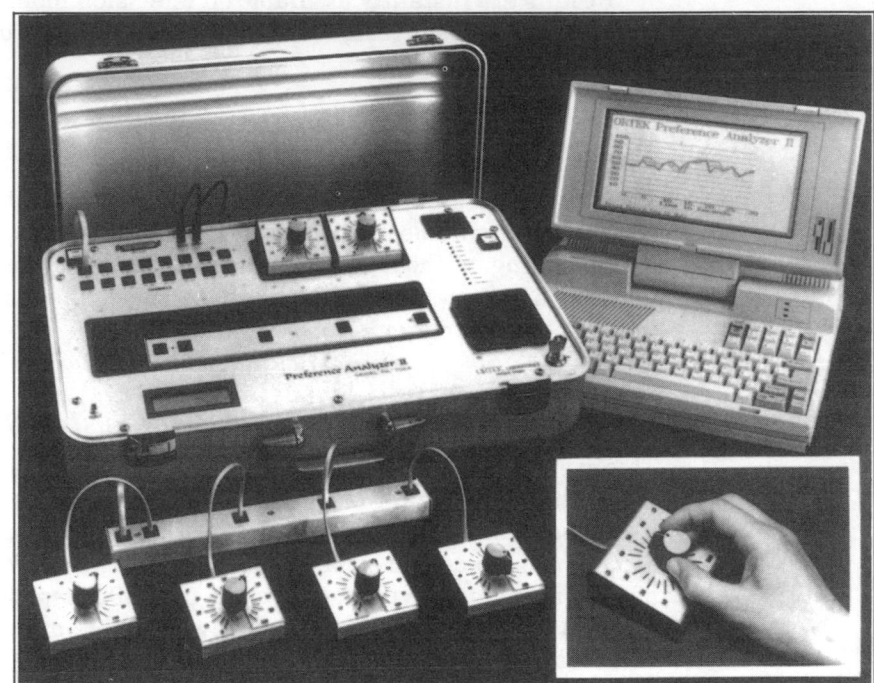

editing for consistency of responses, calling the respondent to task when
there is an inconsistent reply.

As all computer-based systems do, these interactive methods provide rapid reporting of results. The responses are barely in the system
before the summary tables come rolling out.

But no research method is perfect, and interactive methods have
their own limitations. First, because of the nature of the method, only a
reasonably straightforward series of questions can be asked. A complicated questionnaire, no matter how desirable, just cannot be used as a
self-administered questionnaire. It becomes too complex for the respondent to handle.

Since the method is virtually a self-administered project, there is no
opportunity for asking open-ended questions. They are unlikely to produce helpful responses, since there is no chance for them to be followed
up with probing questions that will define and refine their meaning.

OBSERVATION

Observation is a controlled recording either of events or, when applied to individuals, of people's behavior. It may be by personal observation or by mechanical means. It is not a survey method, since it does not involve the usual pattern of questions and answers. Observation nevertheless shares a common need with surveys: having a good sample.

PERSONAL OBSERVATION

For years personal observation, with hand counters, has been used in clocking pedestrian counts, mainly in and around retailing centers. In industrial surveys, observation has shown that many tools are used poorly and carelessly, and tools have been redesigned. Of course, personal observation is used in most surveys in a quite different way. Depending on whether the method is personal interview or telephone, the interviewer can record observations about sex, age, and apparent socio-economic level.

Auditing, which will be discussed in Chapter 13, is a method of measuring the amount of movement of merchandise, by category and brand, through a retail outlet. It requires an auditor to check the amount of goods on hand (both on-shelf and in the back room) at the start of the sales period, the addition to stock during the period (from checking receipts for goods delivered to the store), and the amount of goods on hand again at the end of the sales period.

There is another in-depth sort of personal observation in vogue in some places these days. Termed the "anthropological" approach by the few advertising agencies and other firms that use it, the method would seem to be almost totally subjective. It is an almost live-in approach within a few households or shopping places, used to arrive at generalizations about living styles relevant to the specific product.

Toyota, for example, "discreetly" observed car shoppers as they inspected cars in auto showrooms.[29] Observations included how shoppers were dressed, whether they appeared confident or timid, whether they kicked the tires, and what questions they asked.

An in-home observation study featuring breakfast eating concluded that although most people say they want a nutritious meal, they also want it to taste good. Enjoying it is a principal factor in deciding what to eat.

An in-home study may go further, perhaps even including videotaping. In one case (the topic and applications undefined) in which families and their friends were observed, they even talked about "delicate" subjects such as sex and death. The compensating factor was $40 for several hours, $300 for a week or more. In such cases, a consent form should be used to avoid legal problems.

Here are two examples of the application of personal observation. You be the judge of their value.

Toyota, which found that some consumers see its automobiles as art objects, always on display while in use, turned out ads for its new luxury Lexus describing the car as though it were a Henry Moore sculpture.

A gourmet ice cream maker learned, through similar techniques, that the eating of ice cream tends to be ritualized. It requires a special spoon and bowl, along with a favorite chair—all symbolizing the ultimate indulgence. The firm's ads have focused on the delights of feasting on a forbidden food.

MECHANICAL OBSERVATION

Mechanical observation is based on electronic devices such as scanners, which record consumer behavior in buying products at retail, and meters, which measure television or radio behavior in the home. Some of these mechanical devices are interactive, as we have said, and then they become more than a mere recorder of behavior, asking the participant for personal responses of one sort or another.

There is also the single-source study, generally involving use of one or more of these mechanical devices—sometimes also measuring question replies on a self-administered basis—from a continuing panel of people or households. This study is chiefly used to obtain data on purchasing, media exposure, and personal reactions. The intent is to provide data that can measure and explain the cause-and-effect relationship of advertising exposure and consumer purchases.

EVALUATION OF THE OBSERVATION METHODS

We must distinguish between the observation methods as concepts and the way these methods are used in practice. We admit to some bias in our judgment, for we think that the concept of observation is far superior to any other form of data collection. There the results are, and who can quarrel with them?

But it is not so simple as that in terms of the way observation is being used in marketing research. There are some major problems in this area.

One problem is the nature of the sample, whether households, individuals, or stores. Observation within both households and stores typically requires the setting up of a panel, making it subject to the sampling perils we earlier pointed out in getting and maintaining participation.

Another problem is the quality of the data going into the system. For example, there may be serious questions about the quality and completeness of store scanner data. Glitches may occur because of the nature of the system and the equipment: There may be package errors; large items may not readily scan and may be incompletely or inaccurately entered by hand; some items have UPCs that are easily marred; some brands with multiple forms are similarly labeled; and so on.

There may be errors of hardware, software, and transmission. Apparently only 87 percent of the store scanner data are usable.[30]

Some of the data recorded within households for media exposure and for purchasing are also highly questionable, as we will show in later chapters. The researcher must know the dependability of the observation data being entered into the system.

THE USE OF COMBINATION METHODS OF DATA COLLECTION

Often, more than a single data collection method is used within a single study. A mall-intercept approach may be followed with a product placement and a telephone follow-up for reaction. Consumer panel firms offering custom studies may make mail or telephone follow-up calls.

Some firms offering omnibus services will also make optional follow-up calls.

These are only a few of the more obvious possibilities. The ingenious researcher or marketing manager will see many other possibilities during the process of planning a study.

ENDNOTES   [1]W. E. Deming. "On Errors in Surveys." *American Sociological Review* 9, no. 4 (1950).

[2]*Interviewer's Manual.* Ann Arbor: Survey Research Center, Institute for Social Research, University of Michigan, 1976.

[3]*A.R.F. Guidelines for Newspaper Audience Studies.* New York: Advertising Research Foundation, 1990.

[4]Randall Rothenberg. "The Trouble with Mail Interviewing." *New York Times*, Aug. 16, 1989.

[5]*Interlok.* New York: ASI Market Research, 1989.

[6]Brent Bowers. "For Firms, 800 Is a Hot Number." *The Wall Street Journal*, Nov. 9, 1989.

[7]M. F. Riche. "A Bigger Role for Telephone Interviews." *American Demographics*, September 1990, 17.

[8]M. F. Riche. "A Wish List." *American Demographics*, September 1989, 8.

[9]Dorothy Goepel. "Nielsen Fine-Tunes Phone Interviews to Cut Time, Costs." *Marketing News*, Jan. 8, 1990, 30.

[10]"Predictive Dialing Eliminates 'Busy' and 'No Answers' from CATI Interviewing." *CMC News*, 1989 (first quarter), 2.

[11]*Beyond Linear Solutions.* Port Washington, N.Y.: The NPD Group, undated.

[12]*The Bigger the Better to Survey Your Market.* Port Washington, N.Y.: Home Testing Institute, undated.

[13]*National TelePanel.* Arlington Heights, Ill.: Kapuler Marketing Research, undated.

[14]V. B. Churchill. *How Good Is Mail Panel Research?* Address before Advertising Research Foundation Conference, 1988.

[15]V. B. Churchill. "Learning to Live with Continuing Household Panels." *Telenation Reports*, 1988 (Summer), 1–2.

[16]*Why America's Top Marketers Rely on NFO.* Greenwich, Conn.: NFO Research, undated.

[17]*Excel: National Telephone Omnibus Study.* Media, Penn.: International Communications Research, undated.

[18]*OmniTel.* New Brunswick, N.J.: Bruskin Associates, undated.

[19]*TeleNation.* Chicago: Market Facts, 1988.

[20]*ORC Telephone Caravan.* Princeton, N.J.: Opinion Research Corporation, 1989.

[21]*Limobus.* New York: The Roper Organization, 1989.

[22]*AIM.* New Brunswick, N.J.: Bruskin Associates, undated.

[23]*Viewtel: The Survey Research System of the Future.* Chicago: Viewfacts, 1988.

[24]*Viewtel: The Power of Contact for Marketers.* Chicago: Viewfacts, undated.

[25]Jeff Wiss. "Meet Max: Computerized Survey Taker." *Marketing News*, May 22, 1989, 16.

[26]*Quick Tally Systems.* New York: Quick Tally Systems, undated.

[27]*The PEAC System.* Chicago: Viewfacts, undated.

[28]*Preference Analyzer II.* Beaverton, Oreg.: Ortek, 1989.

[29]Kim Foltz. "New Species for Study: Consumers in Action." *New York Times*, Dec. 18, 1989.

[30]*More Valid Reasons: A Study of the Reliability and Validity of SAMI Scanner-Based Tracking Information*. Columbus, Ohio: SAMI/Burke, 1988.

REFERENCE   Erdos, P. L. *Professional Mail Surveys*. New York: McGraw-Hill, 1970.

8

SELECTING THE SAMPLING METHODS

What's in This Chapter

In this chapter we discuss the general concept of sampling, the basics of sampling, the application of sampling in a study, the choice of a sampling method, and the possible use of an outside source for sampling assistance. We also consider the important question of sample size.

Sampling is the process of selecting a relatively small section from the whole entity as an indication of the whole. It is a common occurrence in many aspects of life. It is also a well-accepted scientific tool. Your physician does not need to drain all of the blood from your body for a diagnosis—that would kill you. He draws a small amount of blood, from which the laboratory determines the characteristics of all of the blood in your body.

It can even be argued that sampling is a better way to go than a census. We all know about the many problems of the 1990 census (counting the homeless, the illegal immigrants, and other hard-to-reach people). World-famous statistician W. Edwards Deming says it even more strongly: "A sample is not a *last* resort, to be used when a complete investigation is impossible. Rather, it is the *first* resort. It is the answer to the question: 'What is the best way to do the job?' "

However, not all samples really represent the total well. That box of strawberries in the supermarket display may have the largest and most luscious berries on top. Your local weather station may be located at an airport, where the measurements are subject to more heat in warm-weather months, more cold in cold-weather months, and possibly always more wind because of open space.

This is what is discussed in this chapter. Sampling is fine as a concept. But it has to be carried out with considerable knowledge and care if it is to produce dependable results in a marketing study.

THE BASICS OF SAMPLING

The crucial aspects in understanding sampling basics are definition of the universe, determining the sampling frame, and probability versus nonprobability sampling.

DEFINITION OF THE UNIVERSE

The universe (population) is the total group to be studied, the target universe. It is the grand total of what is being measured: people, stores, homes, or whatever. But since most samples in marketing research are of people, homes, or stores, the term *universe,* as we use it here, typically refers to one of these.

If the purpose of the study has been well-defined, the universe is also well delineated. This is crucial if the study is to be significant and practical for the guidance of marketing management.

But we have to make a few points clear. We are talking, in marketing research terms, about a finite universe, not the statistician's indefinable infinite universe. We think in terms of such mundane and concrete things as the number of households, college students, stores, and physicians. And we think of a *parameter* as a known statistic of that universe, a number in that universe.

DETERMINING THE SAMPLING FRAME

The sampling frame is literally a list from which the sample is selected. Perhaps a parallel is in order. In photography the expert photographer frames the shot. It is all there. Minute study of the resultant photograph gives all the details; presumably the CIA expert photographer would *really* come up with dependable detail.

A sampling frame, then, is a list that represents those to be sampled. It may be a telephone book, a city directory, or a list of companies, as suggested in Chapter 2. It might be a database, as outlined in Chapter 16.

No frame is perfect. The residential listing in the telephone book not only omits unlisted numbers, it is also outdated on the day of publication because of moves in and out. A list of businesses of any category in any location is never either complete or perfect.

It is impossible to work from a perfect frame, but good research planning requires knowledge of the shortcomings of the frame so as make adjustments in the sampling design. If a cross section of all coin collectors is required, the subscribers to a numismatic publication are not suitable as a list; these will include mainly the more serious collectors. A better list for the purpose might be available from a list firm, though the nature of the list and its currency would need examination.

A database frame is more than just a mailing list, since it contains information over and above the name and address, such as frequency of purchase. The frame defines the sampling unit, the unit used in design of the sample. The frame, and therefore the sampling unit, may take the form of households, college students, retail stores of a particular defined type (nature and size, for instance), businesses, or transactions.

Sometimes there is no sampling frame available. As a rather extreme example, suppose that for some reason it is desirable to conduct a study of those who are overweight. No such list exists. But it is possible to use *screening* as a method of locating such people. A general frame of individuals can be used, and filter questions (with standards of overweight set up in advance) can be used, asking age, height, and weight, to determine those who qualify.

PROBABILITY VERSUS NONPROBABILITY SAMPLING

Now we get to the heart of the sampling method: the distinction between probability (random) and nonprobability sampling.

The Basic Distinction between Probability and Nonprobability Sampling

In probability (random) sampling, each sampling unit has an equal, known chance of coming into the sample.

Let's say you enjoy gambling and Las Vegas, and that you go for blackjack, where the odds favoring the house are least. If you know your game, you have a fair chance of winning. But you don't have a fair chance if the dealer stacks the cards, for then not every outstanding card has an equal chance of being dealt (or selected in the sample). The game and the draw are probability samples only if it is a fair deal.

In sampling, only a real probability sample can be expected to produce a defensible sample—a reasonably accurate sample where sampling error can be measured.

Nonprobability sampling in marketing research doesn't necessarily mean, as it does in the card game, that results are stacked. But it does mean that the accuracy of results is not measurable. Yet many of these methods of nonprobability sampling are used in marketing research. We take the view that this is not always bad, though the burden of proof is on the research source selling a service, or on the user who knowingly decides that the error risks for the particular study are not that great for the particular marketing decision.

The Forms of Probability Sampling

There are four forms of probability sampling: straight random, stratified random, cluster, and systematic.

The *straight random sampling method* is almost impossible to achieve in a typical marketing research study. It requires a near-perfect sampling frame, which is rarely available. Then it means that tables of random numbers (sometimes such pseudo tables are available from a computer program) must be used to select the units in the list to be chosen for the sample.

The greatest problem occurs when the universe is widely distributed (mail or telephone studies are exceptions), when the system would require excessive costs for interviewing. A relative minor risk is that through the laws of averages (call it probabilities) it is possible that some types of sampling units might just turn out to be over- or under-represented. But with a large universe and little knowledge of its detailed nature, this may be the way to go.

The *stratified random method* is generally a far better system, in cost and guarantee of accurate results. We first explain the method and then some of its alternative approaches.

We start with an analogy. Suppose a bank, for some reason, needed an estimate of the distribution of its coins received by date on the coin for each denomination: cents, nickels, quarters, and half-dollars. It would make little sense to get a total count, if all that is required is a reasonably good estimate. One way to arrive at such an estimate is to get the total count for each denomination from the sorting and wrapping machine, then to use every tenth roll of each to check and count the dates, and then to project the dates to the total count of each denomination.

Now let us get to the method as used in marketing research. The universe and the frame are defined and classified into homogeneous seg-

Exhibit 8.1   CELL DISTRIBUTION OF CIRCULATION SAMPLE OF 1,000 BASED ON STRATIFICATION OF TWO VARIABLES

	Architects	Developers	Contractors	Total
Eastern edition	150	100	100	350
Western edition	100	100	100	300
Southern edition	100	150	100	350
Total	350	350	300	1,000

ments. Then random samples are chosen from each segment. The method offers a sharpening of sampling, virtually guaranteeing that the use of these cells of units—done in two dimensions or more—will provide a cross section of each.

Exhibit 8.1 illustrates a real case, with fabricated identities and numbers. The publisher of a national architectural magazine, with a circulation of 100,000, produced three regional editions and offered either national or regional advertising. The publisher needed a survey of its circulation, describing subscribers' interests and activities to provide the sales reps with material to sell advertising space, both nationally and regionally, and in each case aimed at the three categories of circulation: architects, developers, and general contractors. On a straight stratified basis, using a 1,000 sample size, Exhibit 8.1 shows how the sample would be selected by cell.

Admittedly, Exhibit 8.1 is a contrived example, one designed for simplicity. But it shows how stratification works and how it is bound to improve the accuracy of the sampling results, since it takes steps to ensure a reasonable subsample within each cell.

The method has additional advantages. One is that disproportionate sampling can be used. If a particular cell in the same edition will produce too few cases for individual examination, when this is important, then oversampling within the cell can be used to beef up the number without overweighing that cell in total results for the study. Or if a particular cell produces more cases than needed for the sampling, the number within the cell can be reduced, with appropriate weighing in getting total results.

Exhibit 8.2 uses the same example as Exhibit 8.1, but with revised numbers—and these are far closer to the actual case. The sample distribution by cell is shown without any weighing.

All this, or at least most of it, looks pretty good. There should be a sufficient base to provide reliable results nationally for each group of readers and for each regional edition. And if you go by the rule-of-thumb

Exhibit 8.2 **REVISED CELL DISTRIBUTION OF CIRCULATION SAMPLE OF 1,000 BASED ON STRATIFICATION OF TWO VARIABLES**

	Architects	Developers	Contractors	Total
Eastern edition	100	150	50	300
Western edition	100	200	100	400
Southern edition	200	50	50	300
Total	400	400	200	1,000

bit on minimum sample size of 100 for specific groups, in all but 3 cells there will be the required sample size: architects in each of the 3 editions, developers in 2 of the 3, contractors in 1 of the 3. To have a sufficient base for separate reporting, the obvious solution is to oversample within the 3 cells showing only 50 cases.

The *cluster sampling method* is another random method. A cluster, or list of adjacent sampling units, is used as the basic sampling system. The most obvious example is neighborhood clustering of household units, something considered more thoroughly in Chapter 15, where market segmentation is discussed. But it is also used, for instance, in selecting clusters of names that are chiefly Hispanic, or indicating some other ethnic group, where this can be done readily by telephone exchange codes.

In the *systematic sampling method,* the sampling units are chosen from the sampling frame at a uniform interval at a specified rate.

Take the case of the residential telephone directory. Perhaps the book has 600 pages in it, with an average, after a check of perhaps 10 widely dispersed pages, of 400 listings per page, for an estimated total of 240,000 listings. The particular study requires a list of 2,000 for sampling purposes. (For simplicity at this point, we forget the number of completions required.) This means that every 120th listing should be drawn.

But it isn't *quite* that easy. For the method to be a true probability method, where every sampling unit has an equal chance of coming into the sample, there also must be a random starting point. So if we are using every 120th listing, we must select a random starting number of between 1 and 119.

If it is a long list from which choices must be made, there are some shortcuts. For the telephone book, for instance, while it is not desirable to cluster (it might result in overrepresentation of some ethnic groups), it *is* possible to use a template to fit over each selected page to spot the listing of choice.

Forms of Nonprobability Sampling

To begin our discussion of nonprobability sampling, we start with a simple example. Interviewers in a mall select certain kinds of people, such as women appearing to be in their 20s. They are asked several screening questions for use in determining which women will be used as subjects for follow-up questioning.

This example happens to be a quota sample. The other nonprobability methods are convenience and judgment sampling.

In *convenience sampling,* there is *no* sample design. It is almost like the reporter's questioning of people as he or she runs into them on the street, in malls, or somewhere else. Choice of the respondent is left entirely to the interviewer. As mentioned in Chapter 7, some methods allow potential respondents to decide for themselves whether or not to respond, and this is one of those methods.

This sort of sampling is sometimes useful, as we show later in this chapter. If it is necessary to locate bird owners, it would generally be very costly to do so on a straight probability basis. But it may be possible to use multiplicity sampling, where one bird owner provides names of other bird owners.

In *judgment sampling,* the researcher (or someone else) simply makes a judgment call about the units to be included in the study. The judgments are often handed down to the investigator or research firm. Here are a few examples:

- The mall interviewer is told to select chic young women for questioning. (What is "chic" and what is "young?")

- The research firm is asked to recruit leading family medical practitioners in a community for a group interview. (What is a "leading" practitioner?)

- The interviewer of a research firm is asked to question the owners or managers of the more successful retailers along a two-block stretch of a community. (What is a "more successful" retailer?)

Quota sampling appears to have a bit more going for it than the other nonprobability methods. Here the researcher starts with knowledge of how the universe is divided by strata, and investigators are instructed simply to fill the cells, so that the sample obtained is indeed representative in terms of the cells.

Exhibit 8.3 gives an example of such an assignment, and matching returns, all based on known statistics about the particular universe. This looks great. But let's take a deeper look. Suppose that the city is

Exhibit 8.3 INTERVIEW ASSIGNMENTS AND RETURNS BASED ON KNOWN STATISTICS

	Adult Men	Adult Women
To 50% of income	200	200
Bottom 50% of income	200	200

Chicago, and that each interviewer has simply been given a personal interview assignment of 20, with 5 falling in each cell. Interviewers can fill the quota from any distribution of ethnic group they see fit. Since most interviewers are white, the chances of interviewing the proper proportion of blacks or any other ethnic group are slim. The interviewers see no need to spend extra time or trouble to manage a control they have not been asked for.

This hole in quota sampling can be pretty broad. If a quota sample cannot properly provide a sample of ethnic groups, it cannot be taken for granted that it will automatically produce a good sample of owners of refrigerators by make.

Despite these reservations, we must admit that quota sampling has a place in marketing research. There are just too many studies where the cost of probability sampling would be prohibitive and the apparent risks of quota sampling not all that great.

But beware! In store sampling for scanner studies, to be outlined in Chapter 13, the typical national study selects stores doing a volume of $2 million or more annually and having scanners. One of the few studies ever undertaken to check the validity of a research method[1] had as its purpose the determination of the accuracy of the volume estimates made "across the board" (on a selected but representative list of grocery products) from scanner work. The criterion was actual warehouse shipments to the same group of 15,000 scanner groceries (in 24 areas). Results covered January through July 1987. The criterion had one shortcoming: It missed items delivered directly to the stores (by rack jobbers and direct trucking of such items as baked goods).

Here, in abbreviated form, are the significant findings in terms of accuracy:

- National and local volume and share trends are reasonably accurate.

- The finer the detail of measurement, the less the accuracy.

- In terms of products, accuracy was greatest with a particular commodity group, less by brand, least by type within brand.

- In terms of size of trading area, accuracy was greatest with national results and least with local results.

- In terms of time period of measurement, the shorter the time period (in this case a week was the shortest reported), the less the accuracy.

A real loss of even a tenth of a share point can, if the brand's volume is high, mean millions of dollars. So the method, as typically applied in a quota sample, just does not provide the precision measurement required. A particular major store in an area may have a policy of stocking only one brand of a commodity-type product, such as black pepper. This makes it likely that often the impact of a special promotion cannot be measured.

The study concludes that (1) while there are several sources of error that account for these results, the major one is sampling, and (2) no single set of sample stores can be adequate for all product categories.

One solution, applied many years ago by one firm, was to make a census annually, and then set up its panel of stores (then done by auditing, since this was in the days before scanning) for the year based on the outlets stocking the item. But this had the disadvantages of constant change within the stores and the need to revamp the sample every year. The answer arrived at by Arbitron's SamScan, as outlined in Chapter 13, is to have a national continuing census of scanner stores, which then provides constant adjustments in stocking of commodities and brands as these actually occur.

APPLYING SAMPLING IN A STUDY

In our preceding discussion of the sampling basics, we explained many of the factors in and methods of applying sampling in a study. We will now discuss the considerations in choosing a sampling method.

One factor is the precision required. Obtaining a clear-cut answer about the most likely effect of a proposed advertising approach on market share calls for a sampling design where precision of results is measurable—a probability sample of one sort or another. However, an exploratory study aimed at getting a rough idea about which of several advertising concepts is most promising for further development and testing can use a nonprobability sample. It would be wasteful to spend extra money on a more precise sample.

Another consideration is the availability of a frame. If a reasonable frame is available, that is most likely the way to go. It is generally neither easy nor inexpensive to draw a sample without a frame.

There may be factors about the study that virtually dictate the form of data collection to be used, such as mall intercept, mail questionnaire, or telephone study. If the study requires placement of a product with people for in-home trial, the telephone and mail methods (except in combination with other methods) are not feasible. These methods are also out for tests of television commercials.

However, if the study is aimed at measuring the number of people reached by a particular radio or television commercial, the telephone procedure, with its easy access and low unit cost, may be exactly the right method. If the study is aimed at measuring readership of a publication, then some sort of meeting between interviewer and respondent (in-home, in-office) to show and go through the publication is a requirement.

A final major consideration is cost. The cost of collecting the information has to be reasonably in line with the value of the study to the firm. This topic has been thoroughly covered in Chapter 5.

In the remainder of this discussion of applying sampling in a study, we talk about defining the universe, choosing the sampling frame and method, sampling small and rare populations, and controlling the sampling process.

DEFINING THE UNIVERSE

Defining the universe is not always an easy job. There may be alternative target populations. Suppose that a study is aimed at measuring the market for videocassettes in middle-income homes. The target population might be homes in such areas or it might be shoppers in shopping centers surrounded by such homes.

In one case, a manufacturer of cake mixes wanted to determine which of two alternative new mixes to place on the market. It decided to do an in-home product placement test in which people prepare a cake from each of the two mixes and provide their reactions. Michael Yesner, then-president of G. M. Feldman & Co. (Chicago advertising agency), talked about the possible choices. "You don't want all women," he said. "You don't even want all homemakers. Nor do you simply want all women who prepare foods at home. No, you start by wanting women who prepare cakes from mixes." But he warned, "Even that's not good enough. What you really want is *heavy users*. These are the heart of your market and the ones whose reactions mean the most."

A study of the market among college business majors for a hand-held calculator designed especially for business applications may appear to have a self-defined universe. Unfortunately, it is not so simple. Are we talking about four-year colleges only, or does this include either two-year schools or graduate schools as well? Do we include only institutions with a separate business school or college, or do we also want liberal arts institutions where a student can major in business?

CHOOSING THE SAMPLING FRAME AND METHOD

We start by taking a look at some of the more commonly used frames available.

One is the (residential) telephone directory, which may be used for a consumer study. Earlier in this chapter we described how the telephone book can be used with systematic sampling to produce a good sample of listings. But there are sampling problems, one of which is unlisted numbers. Despite 95 percent residential ownership of telephones, some 31 percent of these are unlisted.[2] The proportion has been increasing, as shown in Exhibit 8.4. SMAs run much higher than the national average, led by Las Vegas, where almost two-thirds of the residences are unlisted. Exhibit 8.5 shows the top 25 locations in this unlisted race.

All this would be of little concern except for one thing: unlisted residents are different from listed residents. The unlisted tend to be younger, nonwhite, and less educated. The differences by age group, shown in Exhibit 8.6, make the point. The majority of those under 25 are unlisted, but only a fifth of those 65 and over are.

There is a solution to the problem of unlisted numbers: random digit dialing. This is the selection of telephone numbers for a consumer survey in a randomized manner of dialing. There are several methods of going about this.

One such system is the randomizing of the last four digits, using only exchanges (first three digits) known to be in use. Another is to go through the typical procedure of pulling numbers from the residential directory, then adding or subtracting one or more digits from the selected numbers. For example, the number randomly selected from the alphabetical list is 428-0035. But it has been predetermined that +4 will

Exhibit 8.4   NATIONAL LEVELS OF UNLISTED TELEPHONES[2]

1984	21.8%
1985	23.5
1986	25.1
1987	25.3
1988	27.6
1989	31.1

be added, so that the number actually used in the frame is 428-0039. The logic seems reasonable. The number chosen for the list ought to include both listed *and* unlisted numbers.

Professional telephone sampling firms have even more refined ways of developing lists that include the unlisted; we talk about these later in this chapter.

Exhibit 8.5   **TOP 25 UNLISTED STATISTICAL METROPOLITAN AREAS (SMAs) 1989[3]**

Total U.S.	31.1%
Las Vegas	62.3
Los Angeles	61.2
Oakland	59.2
Fresno	57.4
San Jose	55.5
Sacramento	54.3
Anaheim–Santa Ana	53.9
Riverside–San Bernadino	53.9
San Francisco	53.2
Bakersfield	52.2
Jersey City	51.9
San Diego	50.9
Oxnard–Ventura	49.5
Miami–Hialeah	46.8
Tucson	46.5
Denver	45.5
Detroit	44.6
Chicago	44.4
Phoenix	43.4
Tacoma	41.7
Houston	41.4
El Paso	40.4
Newark	40.1
Portland, Oreg.	39.8
San Antonio	39.7

Exhibit 8.6   **PROPORTION OF UNLISTED TELEPHONES WITHIN EACH AGE GROUP[2]**

18–24	52%
25–34	48
35–44	41
45–54	35
55–64	28
65+	20

Another possible frame is the reverse, or criss-cross, directory, available for many communities. This book typically lists names, addresses, and telephone numbers, by block, along every street. For each, it lists all addresses and the nature of the occupants (residents, business, professional) and provides some useful demographics. Of course, like the usual telephone book, it is out of date on the day of publication. But it typically has few omissions, since there are no unlisteds. However, such books are not universally available, and smaller communities and rural areas are typically not included.

Another important possibility for a frame is the mailing list. Depending on the needs for the particular study, it is possible to obtain, on the consumer side, lists as varied as camera club members, computer owners, wealthy men, wealthy women, homeowners (by value of home), prime investors (by nature of interest), and magazine subscribers (for many magazines). On the business and professional side, one can find lists of small-town businessmen, broadcasting executives, attorneys in private practice, newspaper editors, personnel executives, hypnotists, T-shirt retailers, and steeplejacks.

Most lists, whether consumer or business, are available by geographic area, state, county, or SMA, often by ZIP code or mail carrier route. Most provide telephone numbers. On the business side, lists are commonly available by the Standard Industrial Code (SIC), and sometimes by business size (dollars or number of employees).

We must, however, warn about the use of a mailing list as a sampling frame. Too often the list is incomplete and outdated. Some firms offer a guarantee that their lists are 95 percent deliverable (meaning the list is current), but that doesn't confront the issue of incompleteness.

The American List Counsel (Princeton)[4] is virtually a list broker. The firm offers a catalog of almost every type of available list; it includes magazine and newsletter subscribers, book publishers, mail-order buyers, seminar attendees, and association members. It acts as a broker for major mailing list firms: D&B, American Business Lists, Polk, Donnelley. It also compiles its own specialized lists. The firm claims that it continuously updates information on virtually all mailing lists in the country (over 10,000).

An obvious sampling frame is the self-accumulated list, a list already in the hands of the marketing firm. It may include names and addresses of those who have made purchases, have had deliveries made, used credit cards, or registered at trade shows. There are many other possibilities, as will be discussed in Chapter 16, where the whole area of customer/prospect database marketing is considered.

One interesting offering for business lists is Instant Yellow Pages (Omaha, Neb.). This firm, a division of American Business Information

Inc., provides an on-line service where the user has access to a database of 9 million names.[5] For almost any city or state in the country, the user can specify the kind or kinds of businesses needed in the list, either by yellow pages categories or by SIC. For such firms the information available includes company name, address with ZIP code, telephone number, brand/specialty information, name and title of owner or manager, number of employees, and sales volume.

The user pays no subscription fee for the Instant Yellow Pages service, and there is no requirement of minimum usage. The user pays $1 per minute plus 15 cents per listing, and the charge can be put onto a credit card (Visa, MasterCard, or American Express). The user simply sits at a computer keyboard and follows three steps, after which program prompts come on to be followed to obtain the desired information.

SAMPLING SMALL OR RARE POPULATIONS

Up to this point, our discussion of possible sampling methods has been based on populations that occur reasonably often; it is not too difficult to find these "frequent" populations through the usual sampling methods. But occasionally the population needed is not that easy to locate; it is relatively infrequent or downright rare. There are some special sampling methods that may be relevant in these cases.

Much of this discussion is based on the thoughtful paper on the subject by Dutka and Frankel,[6] from whom we have even borrowed our title for this section.

Because of its very nature, the need for such sampling will not be faced often by most users. But chances are excellent that it will happen. A few business firms face the problem almost constantly. The brand manager of several minuscule prescription drug brands almost constantly faces the problem of locating users.

We are talking here about studies in which those who qualify for questioning or observation are like the proverbial needle in a haystack. There are not many of them, and without special sampling possibilities, it is too difficult and expensive to make a study among them.

Suppose it is necessary to survey users of a particular brand with a market share of 2.7 percent. That means that every 1,000 contacts will yield 27 cases. Without some shortcut method, that survey, to produce even 100 cases, will be long and expensive. Or suppose a bridal magazine, for promotion research, wants to do a study among engaged girls. The unknown incidence in the total population is probably low. Or the Florida Tourist Bureau wants to measure reactions of northern visitors to Florida within the past 12 months. How to find these people?

There are six techniques: direct screening, two-phase screening, stratification, multiframe sampling, selection of high-yield clusters, and multiplicity sampling. There is a seventh possibility: using data from an existing database.

Direct Screening

In direct screening, people are questioned to see whether they meet the requirements for being part of the sample, and if so, they are questioned. Let us say that the study requires a sample of adults who have purchased at least two books (other than textbooks) during the past three months. There might be a couple of ways to go at this through direct screening. One is through a telephone study, the other a mall intercept. Those who give the right answer are then asked the follow-up questions. But if the incidence is too low, this will mean a lot of nonproductive interview time, with both a slow survey and high costs.

Two-Phase Screening

In two-phase screening, one survey is followed by a second among those who quality. The first contact defines the qualifiers. The second produces the responses sought from those who qualify.

Time permitting, there are several ways of tackling this technique. One is by cluster sampling. For example, where users of outdoor gas grills are to be questioned, clusters of neighborhoods where outdoor grilling is likely to be common can be spotted. Either by telephone interviewing (using clusters by ZIP code, perhaps) or by personal interviewing within clusters, those having gas grills can be located efficiently.

Another tool in two-phase screening is the omnibus study, described in Chapter 7. This sort of study, you will remember, is a continuing study done either personally or by telephone, depending on the choice of sponsoring research firm. Users can buy into the continuing effort with their own proprietary questions at a far lower cost than if they attempted anything like this on their own. This makes it possible to ask a screening question and have the research firm follow up with those who qualify. It is an inexpensive way to accumulate lists of those who qualify. But there are limitations. If the study requires follow-ups, in-home placement of a product, exposure of a television commercial, or the like, the research firm may not be able to provide that aspect at reasonable cost, if at all.

Panels are still another possibility in two-phase screening. These too have been discussed in Chapter 7, but we want to refresh your memory. Like the omnibus studies, these are offered for proprietary studies on behalf of individual buyers. The panel typically is a national list of families that have agreed to participate in mail and telephone studies, and the sponsoring research firm tries to make sure that the total panel represents national and regional—sometimes even local—demographics.

With panels, the screening can be by telephone or, if there is no great time pressure, by mailings. The follow-up, again depending on the needs of the particular study, may be handled by mail or telephone. NFO, as explained in Chapter 7, even has a system for exposing a videotape to panel members who qualify—clearly a sound way of testing television commercials, product concepts, and the like.

Stratification

Stratification is sorting out those with specific demographic characteristics from selected small geographic areas where there seem to be concentrations of specific groups such as Hispanic women in their 30s. Some specialized sampling firms can provide listings for households that seem to qualify. From census data it is possible to do this for areas as small as ZIP code areas.

Multiframe Sampling

Seldom is a list of the desired rare population available, even more seldom are such lists complete or current. Dutka and Frankel[6] give the example of a proposed study of golfers in a particular county. Some golfers are members of country clubs or are registered at public courses. Others are simply members of the general population. So the answer, both in terms of costs and a good sample, is to work with two frames. One is the list of country club and public course golfers, and the other is some sort of probability sample of the general population. Of course, there are low-cost means of doing this. The two segments of the sample can then be weighted properly according to the proportions of country club and public-course golfers, on the one hand, and of the remainder, on the other hand.

High-Yield Clusters

The concept in selecting high-yield clusters is almost trial-and-error, and it is particularly applicable to residential telephone surveys where the costs of an initial qualifying call are not too high.

Let us say that a random-digit dialing system is intended to produce a sample of residences only. Yet a random-digit system is almost surely going to produce nonresidence numbers. To minimize the proportion of nonresidence numbers, clusters of perhaps 100 numbers are set up. Within each cluster, a 10-digit number is randomly chosen. It is like looking for the *school* of fish.

Although we are not sure how this technique affects overall sampling accuracy, there is little question that it cuts costs and produces qualifiers.

Multiplicity Sampling (Snowballing)

Multiplicity sampling is a form of networking. Members of the rare universe are located by screening within each individually designated enumeration unit. A respondent who qualifies for the sample is asked to provide the names of others who also presumably qualify. A network might include all households containing parents or their children. Each network of households then becomes the sampling unit from which information about the other members of the network, such as diabetics, can be obtained.

This system is useful where those qualifying are literally few and far between (perhaps widely scattered geographically), without a known list. Some other examples might be freshwater bass fishermen, or those with highly specialized knowledge (concerning, for example, automatic machines to apply plastic coating to metal surfaces).

The big drawback is that there is no way of checking to be sure that the sample is representative; this is certainly far removed from probability sampling. Also, it is certainly an inferior way of sampling if incidence is reasonably high (cat owners) or if a list is available (cat owners).

Using Data from an Existing Database

There is at least one database, updated annually, that can provide information about the likely incidence of product users. Mediamark, based on its annual studies, has such data available on some 400 products, nationally and regionally. Survey Sampling, a subscriber to the annual Mediamark magazine audience studies, makes these data available to its clients,[7] and to a limited extent these are also directly available without charge from Mediamark.

CONTROLLING THE SAMPLING PROCESS

In considering control of the sampling process, we will talk about getting the right respondent, the general problem of respondent cooperation, the completion rate, and handling busies and no answers (in telephone surveys).

Getting the Right Respondent

Qualifications for being a respondent must be carefully and thoroughly spelled out. If the study is to be among new mothers, what is the definition of "new"? What is the permissible age of the infant for the mother to qualify? Of course, this will depend on the purpose of the study. Does it concern diapers, milk preparations, liquid foods, or solid foods?

If a telephone survey requires the adult male household head, the questioning procedure must establish the role of the person answering the call, and not permit the interviewer to assume that any male voice on the phone belongs to the male household head. If a heavy user of cake mixes is required, the questions and questioning procedures must be objective and thorough. "Heavy" is not a term to be interpreted by either interviewer or respondent. There should be information from some recent study that shows, perhaps, that 30 percent of women preparing cake mixes prepared two or more in the past month, and so this objective definition could well be used in deciding who qualifies for questioning.

A survey among shoppers within a large retail establishment required tight controls to provide a tight sample. The store had three main exits. To set up the sample design, exit traffic counts were made by day and hour. Then interview quota numbers were set at each exit by day and hour so that proportions would parallel the original counts.

In a mall study where interviewers intercept shoppers to question them, investigators can be given instructions about the ratio of men and women to interview. If the study calls for tall men to be queried about their clothes-buying habits (on behalf of a tall men's store), it is a matter of simple judgment for the interviewer to select those men over 6 feet tall. The interviewer won't be making many errors in selection. While it will be a judgment sample, it will be practical and effective.

But there may be special problems in shopping mall interviews. The typical Monday customer is likely to be different from the Saturday shopper. The morning customer is different from the afternoon or evening customer.[8] The interviewing should be scheduled so as to represent all of the varying categories of shoppers.

Consider the reasons for these differences. More than half of all young married women are working. When a young woman adds her own salary to her husband's, a family income of close to $50,000 may result. That young couple should have a pretty good disposable income, even with today's prices. These couples are in the "accumulating" period of life, busy stocking their homes with all the fine things they have decided they need or want. On evenings and weekends, young husbands and wives will form a shopping team, even when buying groceries.

The lone woman who drives into the parking lot in a large car is important because she will have more money to spend. But for every such woman, there are several working women whose total business is even more important.

In consumer telephone surveys, the use of a recording form to make sure that the prescribed steps are properly carried out is crucial (see Exhibit 8.7). Properly administered, it will ensure that the consumer telephone sample is carried out according to specifications.

No less rigor is required with the business sample. In a telephone survey where executives are the target sample, it is often difficult to get past the secretary of the executive. A personal visit to the office often presents the same problem.

What about a telephone call or a letter ahead of time, to see if a specific time can be set for that telephone call or personal visit? The nature of the questioning can, without details, be stated. This not only gives the secretary a chance to clear it with the boss, but gives the executive, if necessary, a chance to get materials and documents ready for the interview, so that greater accuracy may result.

However, the advance call may also cause problems. It is often difficult for the potential respondent to arrange time ahead. The advance call may provide the person with an easy "out," either of postponing or refusing the interview outright. There is no chance to discuss the matter at all, since the interviewer is working through an intermediary.

Respondent Cooperation

Thirty percent of the U.S. public refuses to participate in market surveys, according to a 1988 study.[9] Nonparticipation rises with interview length and varies with subject matter. Such data present the possibility of a serious sampling problem.

Respondent cooperation in telephone interviews varies by geographic area,[10] as shown in Exhibit 8.8 on page 186.

The Completion Rate

The completion rate is the proportion of those in the potential sample who actually participate by becoming respondents. No matter how precise the sampling system, it just isn't working if too few of the candidates end up being questioned or observed.

Exhibit 8.7   **A CALL REPORT FORM FOR USE IN CONTROLLING CONSUMER TELEPHONE SURVEYS**

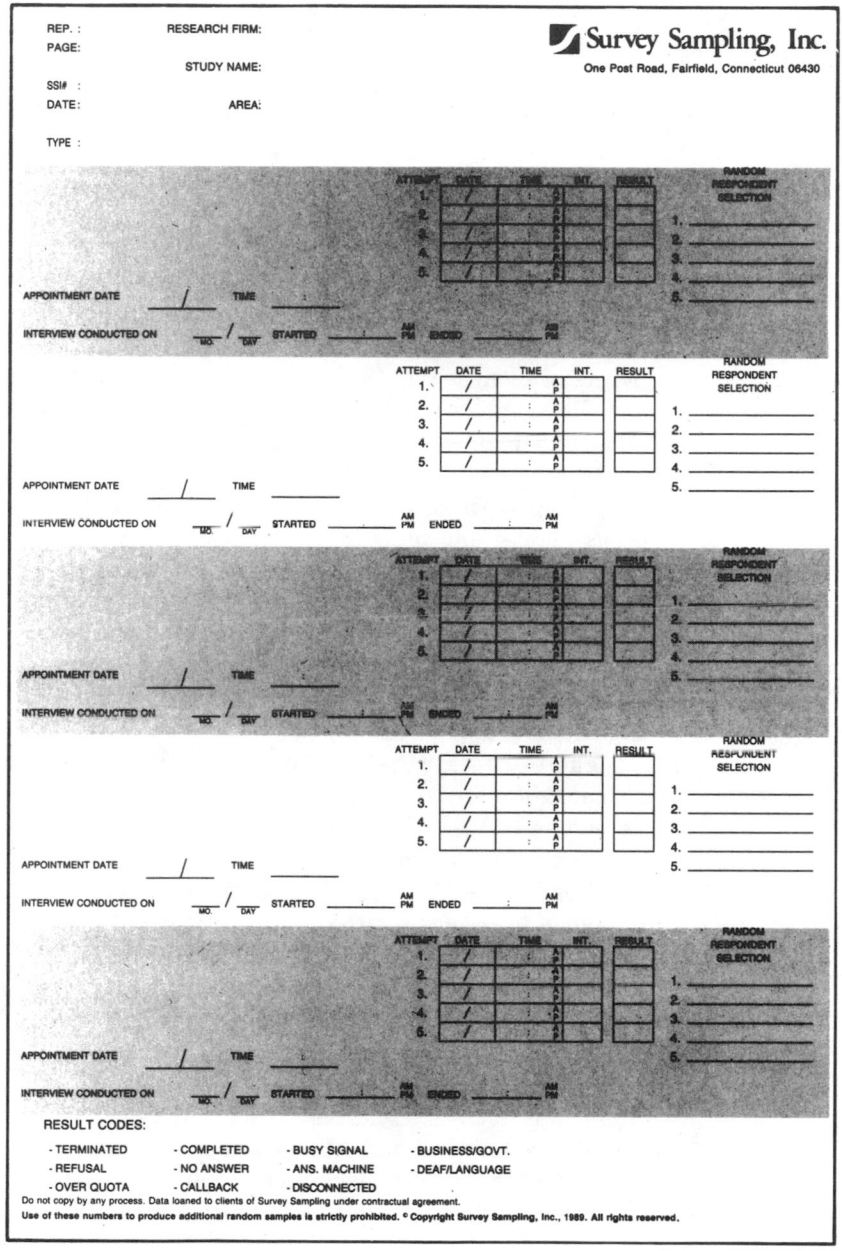

Exhibit 8.8   COOPERATION RATES ON TELEPHONE SURVEYS IN TWO AREAS[11] (BASED ON 600,000 THREE-ATTEMPT DIALINGS DURING A 12-MONTH PERIOD)

	New York SMA	Syracuse SMA
Desired number of interviews	5,000	5,000
Contacts completed	2,600	3,100
	(52%)	(62%)
Cooperation rate	936	1,860
	(36%)	(60%)
Total sample needed	26,709	13,441

Here we are talking basically about probability sampling, where firm standards of performance must be set up and achieved if measurements of accuracy are to be used. But we feel that the same standards should be followed even with nonprobability methods, so that even within their basic limitations there are some guiding rules.

It is generally accepted that for minimal dependability of results, at least 50 percent to 60 percent of those designated as potential respondents should end up being questioned. The shortcut artist may try to reach this goal by completing interviews with alternative or substitute listings. This doesn't achieve the desired completion rate.

The problem is that nonrespondents are typically different from those who do respond. Simply maintaining the same low ratio of completions to attempts while building sample size doesn't change the bias being accumulated in the sample.

There are steps that can be taken to try to reach that 50 percent to 60 percent completion level. They center on both the first contact with the person and on the follow-up contacts.

On the first contact, as we have said in Chapter 7, an old trick in mail surveys is to use an attractive commemorative stamp on the outgoing envelope to induce recipients to take interest, open the envelope, and perhaps save the stamp. The return envelope should have a run-of-the-mill stamp that no one will particularly want to save. There are other methods of making a strong appeal to the recipient of the mail questionnaire. These have been discussed in Chapter 7.

In consumer telephone surveys, the timing of the call may be all-important. If the study is being done with working mothers, the hours of dinner preparation and serving must be avoided if cooperation is to be secured. If the male household head is to be questioned, weekday working hours should be avoided. Evenings and weekends provide a much better chance. But evening calls to retired people can be risky. Some senior citizens retire early and will not be pleased if prevented from doing so or if awakened from their sleep.

Even with excellent planning, the first contact is most unlikely to achieve that 50 percent to 60 percent completion rate. Callbacks are crucial. So are specific plans and record keeping to ensure that the callback plan is properly carried through.

In the case of mail survey follow-ups, the procedures are fairly cut and dried. Records are kept for each individual showing date of original mailout. After a predetermined number of days without a response (usually no more than ten days), a second mailing or even a telephone call is made, and the date is recorded.

With telephone and personal interview studies, the procedure is different. First, it is necessary to have some ideas as to *why* there is a nonresponse. It may be that there is no one at home (or no answer to the telephone), or the qualified respondent is not available. In the former case, the callback is made on a random basis, following a predetermined plan that may schedule the follow-up attempt at a time when someone is there. It may be a different day, a different hour. If the nonresponse is due to the qualified person's not being available, there should be a procedure in which the individual who is at home can suggest a good time to make the call.

Handling Busies and No-Answers

In consumer telephone surveys, there are many busy signals and no-answers. To the researcher or marketing manager wanting acceptably reliable results, these must be regarded as part of the base and therefore as a reduction of that all-important completion rate.

The key to solving these two problems is understanding them. On a societal basis, one of the major reasons for no-answers is the increasing proportion of couples who both work, and the proportion is greater with urbanization and with income. On evenings and weekends young couples may form a dining-out or a shopping team.

But weather is also a consideration. In the good weather during the summer months, people spend less time in the house and more outdoors. In the cold season, the reverse is true.

While callbacks are the basic answer, these will not work well unless planned diagnostically and systematically.

One solution is to reduce the need for callbacks. Predictive dialing is one method of doing this. On completion of one interview, the interviewer presses a key and the next respondent is on line. Interviewers need not listen for the ring. The system provides only a human voice for the interviewer to talk with.

As described in Chapter 7, Nielsen Media Research[11,12] cut its interviewing staff by almost 50 percent through elimination of time wasted on busies and no-answers. The system has a voice-recognition capacity that switches only "live" respondents to a waiting interviewer within 1/50th of a second from the time it identifies a live voice.

The system can be adjusted to increase the number of dialings made if interviewers have to wait too long between calls. The system calls back on busies and no-answers at predetermined intervals. The method is especially useful where calls are frequent and interview length is not long.

Other steps can be taken to increase the completion rate in telephone studies. Interviews should be conducted only between 9 a.m. and 9 p.m. Interviewers should be thoroughly trained, and an emphasis should be put on making the interviewing experience pleasant and appealing to the respondent so that further cooperation is encouraged. The respondent should be told the topic at the start of the questioning, and the questionnaire should be held to a reasonable length. (Many of these topics have been discussed in Chapter 7.)

USE OF AN OUTSIDE SOURCE FOR SAMPLING ASSISTANCE

In the case of a consumer survey, should the user firm opt to do its own sample design or should it go outside for special assistance? We will now take a look at the considerations and at the types of outside assistance available.

CONSIDERATIONS

It is usually more efficient—in terms of having a better sample and saving on internal costs—to buy the sample from an outside source. The exceptions are the cases where the sample size is small and simple or where the sample requires in-house attention because of its extremely specialized nature.

TYPES OF OUTSIDE ASSISTANCE

There are three types of outside assistance: the sampling consultant, the list provider, and the specialist sampling firm.

The Sampling Consultant

The sampling consultant is an individual or firm that has considerable know-how in designing samples, though an individual may lack the staff and data to develop the particular sample. In a few large metropolitan areas, there are specialists who do little else. In smaller areas, the sampling consultant is more likely to be an instructor at a local college. Generally, we have found it more efficient to use a marketing or social science instructor with sampling skills than to consult a straight statistician whose theoretical approach may sometimes make it difficult to arrive at a practical plan for use in marketing research.

The sampling consultant, after coming to an understanding of the applied problem, can provide strong assistance in defining the universe. Then the consultant can select the sampling frame (or suggest how to proceed if there is no frame) and develop the specifics of the sampling method.

The List Provider

Mailing lists and some of the firms offering these have already been generally discussed. Now we need to get down to some specifics.

Those who use mailing lists as sampling frames should understand that this is a buyer-beware situation. We have mentioned certain shortcomings of some of the lists. A warranty that 95 percent of the provided names are "deliverable" doesn't solve the basic problem. The typical mailing list company is not a good source for assistance in defining the universe or for recommendations on sample design. The user needs the skills to make the sampling decisions guiding the purchase of what is virtually a commodity.

With these caveats, we now describe more fully two services of one of the leading firms in the field of marketing research lists—R. L. Polk.

One of Polk's offerings is the *Polk X-1 List,*[13] a most impressive consumer list. It is a list of over 78 million households addressable by name and 87 million addressable by "resident" (93.5 percent of total U.S. households). The list has been compiled from 22 different sources, with duplicates removed. Some 23 descriptive elements are included (such as sex of household head, household income, home ownership, ethnicity and religion, credit card use, and mail responsiveness), though not all of these are available for each name.

Polk has other specific consumer lists.[14] It can provide households by income, new movers, those with children, credit card users, mail-order buyers, do-it-yourselfers, blue-collar workers, senior citizens, and auto owners (60 million, by make). A key factor in deciding whether to use one of these lists, of course, is the requirement, if any, for the method of data collection (mail, telephone, personal), and the resultant costs of using a Polk list rather than probability sampling.

Polk also offers business lists by SIC, bank lists, and physician lists.

The firm promotes use of its lists on an ongoing basis for marketing research, and to facilitate this, it has an Online Information Network. Online lists and marketing information are available 24 hours a day. It's a dial-up database service for which the user pays an annual subscription fee. The user needs a PC and, of course, a modem.

Within this program there are three different databases:

- 14 million business listings from every yellow page directory in the country

- 551,000 U.S. manufacturers (including the name of the owner or manager, sales volume, and number of employees)

- The top 4.3 million "high-income" consumers (selected on the basis of information from census, real estate valuation data, and various other indicators of wealth and purchasing power)

The business list can be provided by SIC, the manufacturer list by sales volume or number of employees, and the consumer list by age group, ZIP code, county, or state.

The Specialist Sampling Firm

The specialist sampling firm typically has a staff consisting of top experts on sampling design and those who constantly obtain and update their databank of statistics about the particular universe. While we cannot mention all of them, the description of three in some detail will give an idea of their capabilities and how they work.

Probably the top specialist firm is *Survey Sampling Inc.* (Fairfield, Conn.).[15] For telephone studies among either consumers or business firms, the firm provides telephone numbers, on a highly sophisticated basis. Names and addresses of consumers are available both for mail surveys and door-to-door consumer surveys.

For telephone consumer samples, Survey Sampling works from residential telephone directories throughout the country. Four steps are followed:

1. All working exchanges and working blocks of numbers (the first two digits following the exchange) are identified.

2. Each exchange is identified by county.

3. The sampling frame is stratified by county (and within county by working telephone block) proportionate to estimated telephone households.

4. The sample is selected systematically as required.

Business listings are generated from the firm's yellow pages database, with additions from its own business list (duplicates are eliminated).

Survey Sampling also offers a system where the numbers provided in a specific list will not be duplicated in any other list. This helps to minimize the problem of respondents being overworked in surveys.

The telephone list of residences is available by target markets such as income, ethnicity (blacks, Hispanics, and others), and age. Other special segmentation is possible, such as occupation and nature of dwelling unit. But now we are down to some assumption-statistics that are not too reliable, being based on the concept that we can assign individuals to specific groups by knowing the type of neighborhood, the type of name, and the like.

The strength of the consumer list for mail surveys is dubious, because there is no explanation of its source. The list is huge, with a database of over 78 million names and addresses representing 88 percent of all U.S. households. It is possible to select a particular list to focus on a specific segment such as income or ethnicity.

Survey Sampling also offers samples for in-home personal interviewing, but this form of study is now so rare that we do not review this offering here. But we should take a look at the firm's telephone sampling database for business lists. The lists are basically assembled from the yellow pages, with additional input from trade directories, credit-reporting agencies, and self-reporting measures. There are two basic lists, one by yellow pages groupings and the other by SICs.

M/A/R/C, one of the country's largest marketing research firms, also offers samples of telephone households.[16] The firm claims to provide both unlisted numbers and new connections. Two databases produce samples: a county database and a telephone number database. The county database provides data on population, with breakouts geographically by Nielsen regions, SMAs, Areas of Dominant Influence (ADIs), county sizes, and client needs. You'll remember from Chapter 2 that ADIs are comprised of all counties where the dominant share of TV viewing is spent with home stations, though it is now used as a base for many kinds of statistical data.

The telephone database has been set up to provide (through a process of random digit generation) a list including virtually all operating numbers while still producing some 70 percent of actual working numbers. The starting point is a continuing random sampling of numbers within published telephone directories. Each selected number is used as an indicator of the range of numbers that are likely to be working numbers. From a file of telephone prefixes the firm has on hand, a county code is assigned to each telephone number.

A set of on-line computer programs enables M/A/R/C personnel to access the databases and pull samples from them.

The third specialist sampling firm is *Sophisticated Data Research* (Atlanta). Unlike Survey Sampling, Sophisticated Data Research provides sampling lists not only for consumer telephone surveys (telephone numbers) but also for mail surveys (names and addresses).

The firm's Genesys[17] System produces random digit dialing samples where a number of predefined, independent, geographic and demographic sampling strata are used. Geographic strata possibilities include region, state, country, ZIP code, SMA, and ADI. The 20 possible demographic variables include household income, owning versus renting, specific age groups, race, home value, education, and college graduation. The buyer has the option of purging business listings.

The telephone numbers in the selected sample can be delivered in the form of hard copy, on-line, or floppy disk.

The second offering of Sophisticated Data Research is listed household samples.[18] These lists can be used for both telephone and mail research, since they include names and addresses as well as telephone numbers. The database comprises over 80 million households, nearly 70 million of which are available with telephone numbers. The lists are available by demographics (age, household income, household composition, presence of children) and by geography (ZIP code, census tract, street address).

THE SIZE OF THE SAMPLE

How large should the sample be? To start this discussion, we first give three definitions. Then we consider the two major factors in arriving at sample size.

SOME DEFINITIONS

Precision of the Study

The precision of the survey result is a function of the sample size. Precision is related to the square of the number in the sample. That is, the accuracy of results increases proportionately to the square of the sample size. If the sample size is doubled, let us say from 500 to 1,000, accuracy rises only to the square root of the doubled sample size (2), or a bit less than half (1.4). This is based on probabilities, and while technically the rationale applies only to probability sampling, it is commonly used as a guide in planning the size of nonprobability samples as well.

The relationship between sample size and accuracy (reliability) is presented beautifully in Exhibit 8.9, reproduced with the permission of Nielsen Media Research.[19] The first illustration (on the left), a photograph, is made up of several hundred thousand dots. The dots are so dense that they can be detected only with the aid of a magnifying glass. Think of these dots as the universe from which several samples will be drawn.

The second illustration is made up of a sample of 250 dots, the third 1,000 dots, the fourth 4,000 dots. All the samples are proportionate sampling, since the sample dots are distributed proportionately to their distribution in the original photograph (the universe).

Now prop the book up and step back a foot. You will find that the 250-dot sample gives a recognizable picture but little detail. But if all that is needed is reliable identification of the person, the 250-dot sample would be sufficient. The 1,000-dot sample is much sharper at this same range; it is now possible to make out details of the features. The 1,000-dot picture is roughly twice as sharp as the 250-dot reproduction because it has four times as many dots. The 4,000-dot sample is almost as sharp as the original. Survey sampling reliability follows this same pattern: the sample size must be quadrupled to double the accuracy (reliability).

Exhibit 8.9 PHOTOGRAPH AND THREE REPRODUCTIONS BY DENSITY LEVEL

Original	Reproductions		
Photo	250-dot	1000-dot	4000-dot

Source: Nielsen Media Research

194 BUILDING THE RESEARCH STUDY

We must define what we mean by sampling precision. We do *not* mean how *accurate* the results are, for accuracy depends on too many factors: how good the questions are, whether or not the interviewer (if there is one) affects the results, respondent error (memory inaccuracy, for example), and other elements. All we are talking about here is the degree to which data on a simultaneously replicated study parallel those of another study, or how similar the results of two simultaneous studies are.

Sampling Error

Sampling error is the difference between a survey result and its parameter (a known statistic of the universe). In Exhibit 8.10 note first that the census estimate is a parameter rather than an absolute figure. All census data are parameters, since none is really complete. Also, the differences between the percentages in the survey and the estimate are all within the sampling error range that make it possible to report that all differences are within the two standard error range (with the likelihood that better than 9 times out of 10, the results will stand up). Later in the chapter we will explain how to determine whether percentage differences are statistically reliable.

The Confidence Interval

The confidence interval is an estimate, plus or minus, of the value of the population parameter. It makes it possible to determine how likely (probable) it is that the mean of the population will fall within stated statistical limits. Generally, the professional research firm or the marketing executive settles for a 95 percent probability—meaning that

Exhibit 8.10   DIFFERENCES BETWEEN A NATIONAL SURVEY AND CENSUS ESTIMATES

Race	Results of National Survey		1987 Bureau of Census Estimate (thousands)		Difference between Percentage in Survey and Percentage in Census Estimate
Total	3,000	100%	243,400	100%	
White	2,499	83.3	205,820	84.6	1.3%
Black	327	10.9	29,736	12.2	1.3
Other	174	.6	7,844	3.2	2.6

there are 95 or more chances in 100 that the reported survey figure falls within the range of a stated numerical value from the parameter.

For simplicity and because it answers almost all needs, our discussion here is limited to a discussion of percentages. But another measure of the confidence interval might be in terms of means.

We intentionally avoid discussion of the theory of probability, on which the concept of confidence interval is based. Understanding the theory is not necessary for the applied research user, any more than it is necessary for the dieter to understand how the body metabolizes food.

The confidence interval can be calculated only when the study has used probability sampling to obtain the results.

OVERALL PRECISION REQUIRED

Once the overall precision (range of the confidence interval) has been defined for the particular study, it is possible to make some tentative decisions on sample size. We say *tentative* only because there are still other aspects to be considered. But let us get to the overall requirements.

To keep things simple, we present a table (Exhibit 8.11) showing the confidence interval for varying sample sizes and the expected results, in terms of the percentage giving a particular reply. Note that technically this can be used only with probability sampling, since there is no way of

Exhibit 8.11   CONFIDENCE INTERVAL FOR VARYING SAMPLE SIZES AND EXPECTED RESULTS

Expected Results

Sample Size	50%	45% or 55%	40% or 60%	35% or 65%	30% or 70%	25% or 75%	20% or 80%	15% or 85%	10% or 90%	5% or 95%
100	10.0	8.9	9.8	9.5	9.2	8.7	8.0	7.1	6.0	4.4
200	7.2	7.0	6.9	6.7	6.5	6.1	5.7	5.0	4.7	3.1
300	5.8	5.7	5.7	5.5	5.3	5.0	4.6	4.2	3.5	2.5
400	5.0	5.0	4.9	4.8	4.6	4.3	4.0	3.6	3.0	2.2
500	4.5	4.5	4.4	4.3	4.1	3.9	3.6	3.2	3.0	1.9
600	4.1	4.0	4.0	3.9	3.7	3.5	3.3	2.9	2.5	1.8
700	3.8	3.8	3.7	3.6	3.5	3.3	3.0	2.7	2.3	1.6
800	3.5	3.5	3.5	3.4	3.2	3.1	2.8	2.5	2.2	1.5
900	3.3	3.3	3.3	3.2	3.1	2.9	2.7	2.4	2.0	1.4
1,000	3.2	3.1	3.1	3.0	2.9	2.7	2.5	2.3	1.9	1.4
1,500	2.6	2.6	2.5	2.5	2.4	2.2	2.0	1.8	1.5	1.1
2,000	2.2	2.2	2.2	2.1	2.0	1.9	1.8	1.6	1.3	1.0
2,500	2.0	2.0	2.0	1.9	1.9	1.7	1.6	1.4	1.2	.8
3,000	1.8	1.8	1.8	1.7	1.7	1.6	1.5	1.3	1.1	.8
4,000	1.6	1.6	1.5	1.5	1.4	1.4	1.3	1.1	.9	.7
5,000	1.4	1.4	1.4	1.3	1.3	1.2	1.1	1.0	.8	.6

knowing whether a nonprobability sample produces a sample similar to one based on selection probabilities. Practically, however, as we have stated, it is often used as a guide in determining the sample size of non-probability samples.

In Exhibit 8.11, the figures are rounded to tenths and thus are approximations, which is all that is needed. The formula on which this table is based contains a radical (square root) sign; as the sample size is quadrupled, therefore, the confidence interval is cut in two. Try looking at 2,000 versus 500, or 4,000 versus 1,000.

The confidence interval decreases as the expected percentage of results moves away from 50 percent (either plus or minus). This has some practical implications. For one thing, increasing the required accuracy places a heavy premium on the price of the survey because of the effect it has on sample size requirements.

Another implication is that if the expected result cannot be predicted, 50 percent is the correct percentage to use. That is where the greatest error margin is experienced. So if results cannot be predicted in advance, sample size planning should be on the conservative side—in this case, the larger, more expensive side.

OTHER STATISTICAL CONSIDERATIONS

It is often crucial to examine results for some subgroups of the universe separately. An example will demonstrate this point.

A cross section of users of underarm deodorants is being questioned about their reaction, after trial, to a new product that is not identified in the test procedure. But the manufacturer wants to be sure that the reactions of current brand users can be considered separately. If the market share of that brand is low, a "standard" overall sample size may not provide a sufficient number to provide the required subgroup reactions.

As a rough rule of thumb, subject to many exceptions, the practical researcher thinks of no group of under 100 as large enough to look at. Depending on the importance of the group, this number may be far too small. However, there are methods of beefing up the sample number in one or more cells. The general approach is disproportionate sampling, outlined earlier in this chapter.

FINAL DECISION: A MARKETING DECISION

For all of our talk about sample size and statistics, deciding on sample size is not a matter for sampling statisticians. Their input can contribute to the decision, but the actual decision is a judgment call by marketing management or top management, depending on the importance of the particular problem. In any case, the decision will not be based on such points as sampling size anyway. It will center on costs versus value, and while the sample size may be a major factor determining cost, it is unlikely to be a subject of discussion if the marketing researcher's proposal for the study is carefully prepared and effectively presented.

ENDNOTES

[1] *More Valid Reasons: A Study of the Reliability and Validity of SAMI Scanner-Based Tracking Information.* SAMI/Burke, 1988.

[2] L. B. Piekarski. "Choosing Between Directory Listed and Random Digit Dialing in Light of New Demographic Findings." Address before American Association for Public Opinion Research, May 19, 1989.

[3] Untitled booklet. Fairfield, Conn.: Survey Sampling, undated.

[4] *The Only Mailing List Catalog You Need.* Princeton, N.J.: American List Counsel, vol. VI, undated.

[5] *When I Need Business Information or Lists Fast.* Omaha, Neb.: Instant Yellow Pages, 1990.

[6] Solomon Dutka and L. R. Frankel. *Techniques for the Cost Efficient Sampling of Small or Rare Populations.* New York: Audits & Surveys, 1988.

[7] Thomas Danbury. "Tech Tips: How Market Researchers Can Independently Estimate the Incidence of Product Usage When Planning Surveys." *The Frame* 14, no.1 (1991), 3.

[8] Randall Rothenberg. "The Trouble with Mall Interviewing." *New York Times,* Aug. 16, 1989.

[9] "Research Industry Faces Uncooperative Respondents." *The Frame,* Spring 1989.

[10] "New Product Adjusts for Refusals," *The Frame,* Spring 1989.

[11] Dorothy Goepel. "Nielsen Fine-Tunes Phone Interviews to Cut Time, Costs." *Marketing News,* Jan. 8, 1990, 30.

[12] "Predictive Dialing Eliminates 'Busy' and 'No Answers' from CATI Interviewing." *CMC News,* 1989 (1st quarter), 2.

[13] *X-1 1990.* Detroit: Polk, 1990.

[14] *Mailing List Catalog.* Taylor, Mich.: R. L. Polk & Co., undated.

[15] *Survey Sampling, Inc.* Fairfield, Conn., undated.

[16] *M/A/R/Cs Telno System.* Irving, Tex.: M/A/R/C Inc., 1987.

[17] *How the GENESYS System Provides a Diversity of Custom RDD Samples.* Atlanta: SDR Sampling Services, undated; *Fact Sheet.* Atlanta: Sophisticated Data Research, undated.

[18]*Listed Samples Now Offered by SDR Sampling Services.* Atlanta: SDR Sampling Services, undated.

[19]*What TV Ratings Really Mean.* Nielsen Media Research, 1987.

REFERENCE   Deming, W. E. *A Chapter in Population Sampling.* Washington, D.C.: Bureau of the Census, 1947.

9

DEVELOPING THE QUESIONNAIRE

What's in This Chapter

In this chapter we consider the format of the marketing research questionnaire and the mechanics of its preparation. We discuss the parts of the questionnaire, the types of questions and the merits of each, and the functional details and procedures of questionnaire construction. We conclude with a look at computer-assisted questionnaire construction and at questionnaire testing.

George Gallup once said that nothing is so difficult or so important as the selection and wording of questions.[1] If questions are not selected to cover topics that will contribute to getting the information needed for the solution of the marketing problem, or if some vital information is missed, the problem will not be completely solved, or at worst, it will produce information that may be wrong or misleading.

The inexperienced researcher or marketing person may attack the marketing research problem by first drafting a questionnaire. That is not the way to go. As pointed out in Chapter 5, the beginning point, once the marketing problem has been stated and agreed upon, is to list the aspects of information to be obtained from those being surveyed. Only at that point can even the most experienced researcher or marketer begin to think about the phrasing and sequence of questions.

Building a questionnaire is not easy. It is a bit like building a house, which can be started only after the architect has visualized the needs and cost constraints of the family, including planning the construction and layout to meet the size and nature of the proposed lot.

There are strong caveats about preparing a questionnaire. First, there are limitations to what a questionnaire can measure. Some events simply are not important enough for a person to keep in mind very long. Any woman can tell you her wedding date—but her bridesmaids can't. For quite a while, a woman can accurately report the make or brand of a fashion item or cosmetic. If it is a canned or frozen-food item, her memory span will be considerably shorter, and if it is a commodity-type product such as salt or sugar, where the brands are pretty much indistinguishable, she will have forgotten it altogether. A man will remember his make of car as long as he owns it, but he will rarely remember the make of a shirt or when or perhaps even where he bought it.

But both the man and woman are likely to remember the brand name of a major appliance for the period of time that it remains in the home.

Depending on the subject, there may be déjà vu. As we will show in Chapter 14, recall of print advertising in magazines may be artificially high, because some respondents *think* they have seen an ad when they really have not. When dummy ads that had never been used were inserted into a publication which was then used to check ad recall, there were always some persons who claimed such recall when it just could not have occurred.

The respondent may not have the information needed to handle the question, and the person designing the questionnaire must avoid presumptions that will produce incorrect replies. Many years ago Gill[2] reported the results of a question asked, without explanation, about reaction to the (fictitious) Metallics Metals Act. Seventy percent of respondents made judgments about it in terms of whether it should be left to the states or passed as national legislation.

Nor is a questionnaire a good way to predict make or brand purchase from an intent-to-buy query. "At one time the question 'What brand of refrigerator will you buy next?' produced more votes for General Electric than for Frigidaire, although Frigidaire [later] sold more than General Electric."[3] At the time of the questioning, people were telling the truth. However, when time for making the purchase approached, the buyers looked and shopped around; they consulted ads, looked at window displays, and talked with salesmen. They changed their minds during the shopping process.

If the completion of a question causes inconvenience for the respondent, the question may be poorly handled. The researcher may want to get the model number of an appliance in order to analyze subsequent questions about experience and satisfaction by each major type within a line. The question would require precise phrasing and also use of the right medium of questioning. A telephone survey would generally be a wrong way to go at it; most people are unlikely to be agreeable enough to take the time then and there to check out the matter. It would work, however, with a self-administered questionnaire using a panel for a custom study.

We have much more to say about constructing a questionnaire. But first we want to provide some additional background. The remaining portions of the chapter cover the structure of the questionnaire (its parts and the types of questions), constructing a questionnaire, computer-assisted questionnaire construction, and questionnaire testing.

PARTS OF THE QUESTIONNAIRE

The three major parts of the questionnaire are the introduction, the body of the questionnaire, and basic data.

THE INTRODUCTION

To be successful, the introduction must achieve two things: (1) It must be persuasive, and (2) it usually must qualify the respondent as someone who belongs in the sample.

Generally, the starting point of the questionnaire is self-identification. If this is any form of a one-on-one interview situation, the investigator has to explain who he or she is, often giving a personal name, and the firm doing the study. Usually this is the name of a research firm, for often the name of the particular marketing firm would have a biasing effect on many responses. People generally want to please. If they know the name of the marketing firm, their replies about the firm, its product(s), or its advertising might be phrased more favorably than they should be. With mail questionnaires, as explained in Chapter 7, the identification is provided in a cover letter.

The introduction states the topic of the study; if it is a one-on-one survey, perhaps it will also state how long it will take. (It is dangerous to understate the length, for the participant may resent this after finding out about the deception and terminate the interview.) The importance of the family or the individual being a part of the study should be warmly and firmly stated in the introduction. Respondent cooperation is voluntary but crucial. We have already seen how low rates of cooperation can damage dependability of results. Even the census has trouble getting cooperation these days, and there the respondent is required to reply.

Then the person may have to be qualified to ensure that he or she really belongs in the sample. To be sure, this is sometimes not necessary; the sampling frame may already have provided that assurance. A list for a mail survey may have been so well developed that it is almost certain to be 99 percent correct. (Of course, someone other than the addressee sometimes replies.)

Particularly in one-on-one studies, there may be some qualification needed. A sampling unit may be only a filtering device along the way to the sample. Possibly only users of a particular type of cosmetic are wanted. There may be a need (mainly in telephone studies) to select the person within the household who meets probability requirements. So here an inventory of household members—perhaps those age 18 and over, listed by sex—is obtained from the person on the other end of the line. Then, by reference to a table provided by the research firm (with firms using more sophisticated methods, there may be successively varied questionnaire forms), if the respondent is the one qualified, the interview is continued. Otherwise the qualified person is asked for; if necessary, tentative arrangements are made for a callback time.

THE BODY OR CONTENT

Now we are at the heart of the questionnaire. This is what the survey is all about. The content is composed of questions that cover information needed to solve the marketing problem. It is especially in this section that the person drafting the questionnaire must understand the topics that cannot be measured at all and those that can be well measured only with considerable care and forethought.

The range of topics covers facts, knowledge, opinions and attitudes, motives, and possible future behavior.

Factual questions include such things as ownership (the make of microwave or VCR owned) and behavior (shopping, buying, and media exposure). Our earlier discussion within the chapter has shown that these are not all equally easy to measure.

Measurement of *knowledge* is typically more difficult. An advertising study about airlines may ask:

> Will you please tell me, if you can, what airline advertises:

- We love to fly and it shows
- We've got your ticket
- We give you more
- The world's favorite airline

We observed above that measuring knowledge may be more difficult than measuring behavior. We will say more about this later in the chapter.

Question phrasing gets even more difficult when attempting to measure *opinions and attitudes*—feelings about products, firms, advertising, and so on. This sort of question requires not only a clear statement of the concept, but also an entirely unbiased phrasing that does not "lead" the person to a particular reply.

There is also the measurement of *motives*, still more difficult and uncertain in dependability of results. This is perhaps the weakest area of consumer questioning in market research. We will shortly talk about the open-ended question—in our opinion not a sound method for measuring motives or even the simpler reason-whys. We have already talked about the "anthropological" observation approach in Chapter 7, and we have expressed our strong reservations about "motivation research."

Finally, there is *possible future behavior*. Questioning in this area is fine as long as the user recognizes that results are an expression of attitude and not an accurate prediction of behavior. People are often willing to tell about their plans, but often these plans are not carried out. "There's many a slip twixt the cup and the lip" is not only a well-known aphorism, but sound observation as well. When you went to work or school yesterday, you likely had many definite plans for the day. Many of these probably did not come off. You may have had plans to visit Europe this year, but with the tremendous increase in air fares, you thought better of it. Life is dynamic. Situations change, and these affect plans.

BASIC DATA

The last section of the questionnaire, which consists of basic data, is mainly information—in addition to the qualifying material in the introduction—about the household and the individual. It almost always includes demographics about the household (if not already covered in the introduction), aspects such as family size and nature, income, and many other topics discussed in Chapter 8, when we talked about sampling. It typically covers demographics about the respondent as well, and it may get into questions about life-style and psychographics.

This section of the questionnaire has three purposes. First, where there are known and dependable statistics about the population from which the sample has been selected, such data provide a rough sort of check on how well the study has done its sampling job. Second, it provides a method, through analysis of subgroups, for spotting differences of key results in response by subgroups such as sex and age. It can therefore provide a honing of results to make possible more specific marketing recommendations. Third, there is identification material such as respondent's name, address, and telephone number. It also includes some descriptive aspects of the interviewing situation—date, time of day, and name or initials of the investigator when there has been a one-on-one interview.

TYPES OF QUESTIONS

The basic types of question in a survey questionnaire include two-choice, multiple-choice, rating, and open-ended questions.

TWO-CHOICE QUESTIONS

Two-choice questions (sometimes more esoterically termed *dichotomous* or *binary*) give the participant two choices from which to make a response: this or that, for or against. Sometimes, depending on the need, categories of "no choice" or "no opinion" or "don't know" may be added (with or without these alternatives being named by the interviewer, if it is a one-on-one interview).

Some examples are provided in Exhibit 9.1.

Exhibit 9.1   EXAMPLES OF TWO-CHOICE QUESTIONS

Do you *own* or *rent* this home?

Did you read a newspaper yesterday?

Of the two local newspapers, which one is your overall preference:

- the *Times-Star*
- the *Herald*

This sort of question is easy for the respondent: It is quickly grasped and can be rapidly answered. With some care in phrasing, it is not likely to be biased, though, of course, with opinion questions it may take considerable thought to work out unbiased, neutral alternatives. Where the type of question is applicable, it has the added advantage of sorting out respondents into skip-patterns for further questioning.

But unless care is taken, the two-choice question may produce unreliable results. The respondent must be able to make what seems a rational choice. A brand-preference question between two brands, for example, generally should not be asked unless it has been established that the person has tried both brands.

Also, two-choice questions should not be used as an easy substitute for more structured questioning. It would not do to use a question of "Yesterday, was your television set on for more than two hours?" to classify users into light and heavy viewers. Such a question, unless recent and reliable spreads of hours of television watching are known for the particular kind of population, should be more accurately asked by finding out how long the set was on, dividing the total respondents into the top and bottom halves, and going on from there.

MULTIPLE-CHOICE QUESTIONS

In the multiple-choice question (sometimes termed the *list* or *cafeteria* question), the question is followed with a list of choices from which the respondent selects a reply. The choice may be a single item from the list or it may be more than one item. The question form can be applied to almost any of the types of information that the questionnaire is designed to measure: facts, knowledge, opinions and attitudes, motives, or possible future behavior. If there is an interviewer in the method of data collection, the list may be either stated or simply listed on the questionnaire, which is used by the interviewer to check off the reply or replies.

Since the basic nature of the list in this type of question can vary so much, we must talk about its three basic forms or uses: the name list, the quantitative list, and the qualitative list.

The *name list* may be a list of product categories, brand names, companies, television stations or channels, or whatever. It may provide a list of automobile makes for the respondent to check off for ownership. It may be a list of electronic devices within the household, including items such as VCR and computer. It is a finite sort of list, and the major alternatives can all be listed in advance.

The advantages of a name list are that, like the two-choice question, it is easy for the respondent (and for the interviewer, where there is one), and it facilitates data processing.

With the *quantitative list*, the respondent is offered a number of numerical categories from which to select the reply. A question might be asked, for example, about the number of miles the person has traveled in his car in the past 12 months, listing several numerical ranges. The problem is that the categories must be representative so that the results will not be distorted; some guidelines are provided later in this chapter.

With a *qualitative list*, the participant responds to questions about reasons and motives or about recall. A list of reply options is provided.

The multiple-choice question has several advantages: It is fast and easy for respondents. It simplifies the procedure of data processing, since there is no need for coders to translate replies for entry into the computer system.

The multiple-choice question also has limitations. We are skeptical of its use with qualitative lists designed to measure reasons and motives. It is hard to believe that the questionnaire designer can come up with all of the major appropriate answer categories, or that the respondent can simply look at a list of possible replies and tell just what it was that made him or her act that way. Motives and reasons-why are a lot more subtle than that, and they cannot be accurately measured through use of a multiple-choice list of canned possibilities.

All three types of multiple-choice question share common shortcomings. If the list is incomplete, even allowing respondents to come up with their own additions will not correct the findings. If an important brand name is omitted from a recognition list, that brand will be grossly understated.

If the list is too long, people will become bored or distracted, and the last items in the list will be understated in the proportion of replies.

One of the biggest problems with the multiple-choice question is the influence of position of a particular item in the list. The psychological laws of primacy and recency apply. If the multiple-choice question is an option question, where people are asked to choose the company, brand, or advertisement they like best in a series, the first-listed one has a preferred position and is the one against which all of the others are rated. The last item in the list also gets a psychologically preferred position, though at a lower level.

There are ways around this. With duplicated questionnaires, the order of items can be rotated successively on each questionnaire. With computer-assisted telephone systems, such rotation can be built in. More about this later.

RATING QUESTIONS

Rating questions measure the degree of feeling about something—be it a brand, a company, or advertising—on some numerical system provided to the respondent. There are two types: ranking questions and scaling questions.

In the *ranking question*, the participant ranks each item in the list from top to bottom. This is what the sportswriters or coaches do weekly during football season when we read about the top 20. But sometimes these rankings in marketing research take the form of paired comparisons, where only two brands are compared. For most purposes, this is an unrealistic basis of ranking—it is not the way decisions typically are made in the marketplace.

A longer list of items to be ranked seems to make more sense, although this doesn't mean that the system is perfect; we have grave doubts about it.

True, it is easy for people to use. But we do not think it is safe to average rankings, and that is about the only way to summarize them. The problem in averaging rankings is that Respondent A has a really tough time making a decision between Abcissus and Betram; they are in a virtual tie. But Abcissus is ranked slightly higher, so gets the Number 1 rating. Respondent B ranks Betram as Number 1, liking it far better than Abcissus, assigned the Number 2 rating. On an average basis (with our supersmall sample of two respondents), the ratings are 1.5 for each, clearly not a fair representation of the voting.

Scaling questions provide a more accurate measurement. In a scaling question, the person rates each item on a numerical or qualitative basis. It is rather like the way you are graded academically. Some professors give examinations consisting of short-answer questions (true-or-false and multiple-choice) and are able, with computer assistance, to come up with numerical scores for everyone. Other professors use essay examinations and give letter grades (qualitative) to each student. In the case of scaling questions, the choice responses may be either on a quantitative scale or on a qualitative scale.

The *Likert scale* is qualitative. It offers statements about the particular attitude being measured, and the replies are then converted to numerical values. The number of items in the scale is pretty much up to the user, generally running between 5 and 7. The first step is to put together a number of statements—maybe about 50—representing a series of favorable and unfavorable statements about the issue. These should be attitude-revealing statements. Then a sample of people resembling those to be included in the final study review the list of possible attitude statements, eliminating those they feel contribute little to the possible final attitude measurement. The idea is that the remaining statements discriminate well between very favorable and very unfavorable attitudes. For each statement, the sample of people respond to each statement (we assume in this case that a 5-point scale is being used) on the following basis:

Strongly agree

Agree

Neutral

Disagree

Strongly disagree

Values assigned to each statement range from +2 to –2. If there were 25 statements at this stage, the range of the sum of any one person's total scores would be from the best-possible attitude, a +50 (25 × +2), to the poorest, a –50 (25 × –2).

Refinements are made by eliminating statements where most respondents agree on the answer, and statements not discriminating between those who are generally favorable and those who are generally unfavorable.

The scale is then ready for use. The values for each person are calculated by using the same categories shown above (from *strongly agree* to *strongly disagree*) and showing the statements down the page. Numerical values for each person are summarized to get a score for the respondent's overall, total attitude.

Although a Likert scale takes time and money to develop, it is generally regarded as a simple scale both for the participant to use and for analysis. Because of the time and costs involved, however, it is not a widely used method of measuring attitude in commercial studies.

The *semantic-differential scale* is far more popular, mainly because the researcher or marketer can develop it easily on a judgment basis, and it is as easily understood by the participant as the Likert scale. Developed by three University of Illinois psychologists,[4] the scale provides a 5- or 7-point listing with qualitative descriptions at each extremity for each attribute of an item. Exhibit 9.2 provides an example of how the scale might appear.

The semantic differential has considerable versatility. It can be used not only for media, as in Exhibit 9.2, but also for ratings of retailers or service establishments, brands, or other kinds of units. Its versatility also means that within the same study it can be used to obtain similar measurement for a competitor or against an "ideal." A resultant profile can instantly show the comparisons.

The Smiley scale, shown in Exhibit 9.3, is a visual scale. This scale is particularly versatile in that it can be used across age lines (from young children on up) and language lines.

For children, the Snoopy scale, shown in Exhibit 9.4, seems particularly appealing. Moskowitz[5] mentions it in connection with sensory testing of chocolate bars among children, but it should have equally useful applications in getting reactions to other juvenile products and for commercials aimed at children. The thermometer scale, shown in Exhibit 9.5 on page 210, is almost as effective.[5]

OPEN-ENDED QUESTIONS

The open-ended question is the counterpart of the multiple-choice question, with a major difference: No list of answers from which to make a choice is presented to participants. They are on their own. Most often this sort of question is used to ask for reasons-why on some sort of a choice or reaction. Less often a similar question is asked about aware-

Exhibit 9.2   USE OF THE SEMANTIC DIFFERENTIAL IN MEASURING IMAGERY OF A MAGAZINE

	1	2	3	4	5	6	7	
Modern	[ ]	[ ]	[ ]	[ ]	[ ]	[ ]	[ ]	Old-fashioned
Interesting	[ ]	[ ]	[ ]	[ ]	[ ]	[ ]	[ ]	Dull
Well-written	[ ]	[ ]	[ ]	[ ]	[ ]	[ ]	[ ]	Poorly written
Leader	[ ]	[ ]	[ ]	[ ]	[ ]	[ ]	[ ]	Follower
Popular	[ ]	[ ]	[ ]	[ ]	[ ]	[ ]	[ ]	Unpopular
Classy	[ ]	[ ]	[ ]	[ ]	[ ]	[ ]	[ ]	Cheap
Good illustrations	[ ]	[ ]	[ ]	[ ]	[ ]	[ ]	[ ]	Poor illustrations
For men	[ ]	[ ]	[ ]	[ ]	[ ]	[ ]	[ ]	For women
Friendly	[ ]	[ ]	[ ]	[ ]	[ ]	[ ]	[ ]	Unfriendly
Reliable	[ ]	[ ]	[ ]	[ ]	[ ]	[ ]	[ ]	Unreliable

Exhibit 9.3   EXAMPLE OF A SMILEY SCALE[5]

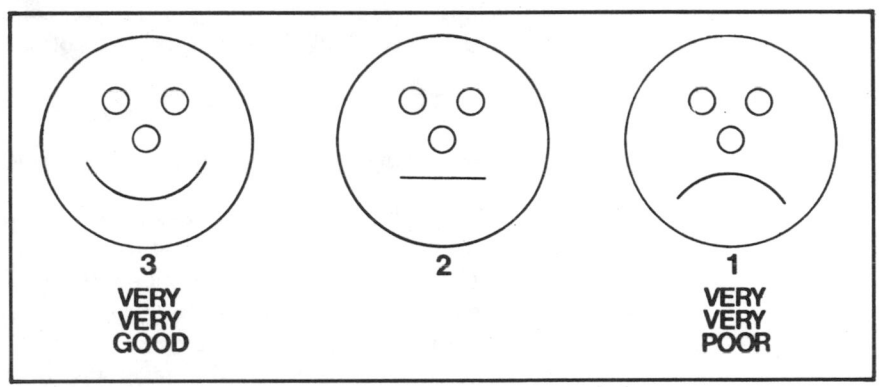

Exhibit 9.4   THE SNOOPY SCALE[5]

Exhibit 9.5　　EXAMPLE OF A THERMOMETER SCALE[6]

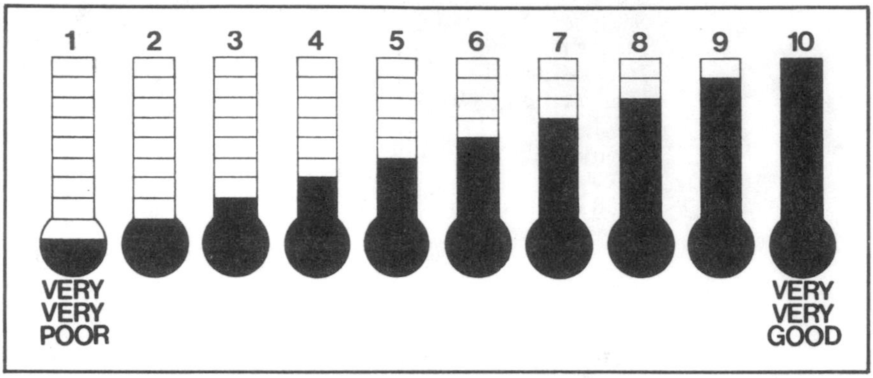

ness or knowledge (such as "What brand or company advertises 'the man with the pink eye'?"). But since the range of response is very limited, we exclude this sort of query.

Here is the sort of question we are talking about:

When you bought your car, what were the reasons for selecting that make?

The sky is the limit to the answer possibilities, and therein lies a weakness. Various people will answer within different boundaries. Typically, there will be a tremendous variety of responses that perhaps can be classified under *dealer, advertising, salesperson, price, financing arrangements,* ad infinitum. This makes it difficult both to classify and to interpret results. In a study where interviewers are being used, it is difficult to train interviewers to ask skilled questions for probing that will not lead responses. But there is an even more serious objection: Most replies people give to open-ended questions relating to reasons-why are of little value. We have explained before that measuring motives by direct question is not possible, since so much of the explanation is on the subconscious level.

An open-ended question, then, should not be used to measure motives. In a survey, for example, some screening questions might be used to locate two groups of those who have tried Sam's Potato Chips: those currently using them and former users. Then two questions may be asked:

What do you like about Sam's Potato Chips?
What do you dislike about Sam's Potato Chips?

Some people will simply respond "flavor," others "saltiness," still others "crispness," and so on. These are vague responses and not really very helpful. In short, complete avoidance of the open-ended question is in order. If it is to be used at all, it should be used only when boundaries are placed upon it, so that replies cannot float all over the place. In the case of Sam's Potato Chips, it might be relevant to ask separate open-ended questions such as these:

What do you like (dislike) about
- the flavor?
- the crispness?
- the color?
- the amount of salt?

CONSTRUCTING A QUESTIONNAIRE

A questionnaire must provide respondents with a means of communicating and must persuade them not only to reply but to reply correctly and accurately. There are often some topics about which they may want to be a little less than honest. Constructing a questionnaire, therefore, is not a simple task. It is a skill acquired over years of experience. (But like so many of life's skills, this doesn't mean that all with experience actually acquire the skill.)

Constructing a questionnaire is definitely an art. If twenty seasoned research experts were each given an outline of questionnaire content and asked to put together a questionnaire, you could win a bet with odds of 1,000 to 1 that there would not be two questionnaires that were identical.

It would be nice to provide a concise list of rules for constructing a questionnaire; then even a computer could handle the entire task. But the saying, "Any fool can make a rule" is particularly appropriate in questionnaire construction. So all we can do is provide some guidelines.

PHRASING OF QUESTIONS

Clarity

There are many aspects of clarity, all of them important in the phrasing of survey questions.

Each question must be understandable to all those participating in the study. The words must match the vocabulary level of the most poorly educated respondent. They must have a common meaning to all. An early national Gallup Poll study on securities, for example, found that stock ownership was surprisingly high in the Southwestern states. Some follow-up work showed that many of those responding were talking cattle rather than equities. As another example, this one from Blankenkamp,[6] a firm wanted to determine the extent to which people prepared food at home using a barbecue-style sauce. Two questions were phrased:

> In just the past two months, how many times have you eaten any barbe-cued food which was prepared at home?

> In just the past two months, what types of barbecued food have you eaten which were prepared at home?

Pretesting (discussed later in this chapter) soon showed that people defined barbecued food as anything cooked outside on a charcoal grill. Consequently, the questions were rephrased as follows:

> In just the past two months, how many times have you eaten any food that was prepared at home using a barbecue sauce?

> In just the past two months, what types of food have you eaten which were prepared at home using a barbecue sauce?

Another, and surprising, example shows that even the term *department store* means different things to different people. Some 47 percent of shoppers consider J. C. Penney a department store, 33 percent put Sears into that category, and 13 percent put K mart there.[7] So when 41 percent of respondents said, in a poll, that they would do most of their Christmas shopping in department stores, the figure cannot be interpreted.

An important aspect of clarity is that questions must provide a framework for answering—an anchor, if you will. They cannot be vague, for most respondents *will* try to give a response, if only to please the questioner. For example, the purpose of a question in one study was to measure consumer opinion about the food value of whole milk (not skim or low-fat milk). It was realized that most people could not answer in terms of calories, for as much interest as there is in calories today, few could respond in caloric terms about a pint of milk. So instead, this question was devised:

> Which do you consider more nourishing—a pint of whole milk, one-half pound of beefsteak, a half-pound of potatoes, two eggs, or two pounds of green beans?

The respondent was choosing on the basis of opinion rather than knowledge. But there was a *basis* for answering; the person was able to make the call in terms that could be interpreted in results of the study.

A study for DeBeers, designed by one of the authors, was aimed at, among other things, determining the size of diamond the public preferred for certain uses. From previous experience, we knew that consumers in general cannot define a given stone as being of 1-, 2-, or 3-carat size. So each respondent was shown five stones of different sizes and asked to make a choice for each of the uses. In this way the issue was not confused. We knew precisely what size stone was preferred and did not have to depend on respondent knowledge of carat size.

Using Terms of Specialized Groups

Jargon, according to one of the definitions provided in our desktop dictionary, is the specialized vocabulary and idioms used by those in the same line of work. Engineers, physicians, and restaurateurs have their own vocabularies. Each group can talk in its own shorthand, and this saves considerable time within the group. As laypersons, we may resent jargon in another field, but that is not going to change its use.

The implication for questionnaires is that marketers and marketing researchers should use the jargon when dealing with a single group in the same line of work. It shows that the questioner understands the field. It saves time. One word of jargon may be equal to twenty nonjargon words. Want to test it? Explain a standard deviation in a sentence.

There is also the simple issue of understanding. Sometimes a question may make no sense because of its terms. This example, while not from an actual questionnaire, is not too far off the track:

Do you think that people should cut down on foods with high cholesterol, such as roast beef and bacon?

The point is that the examples given in the questions may destroy the value of the results. Substitute goat meat and see how far you get.

Neutral Questions

While the chances of influencing responses through poor choice of words are greater in opinion surveys than in commercial surveys, the way that questions are phrased, and even the words used, can influence responses and thereby distort results. Certain terms are "danger words," among them *premium brand, price brand*, and *hit show*. Even adjectives alone can influence. It would not do to ask:

Do you like the easy return policy of Store X?

The word easy, even if used in advertising, suggests which way the person should be replying. (Of course, it is a poor choice in another way as well, since it assumes that the person knows about the policy. Filter questions should be used.)

The intensity of the phrasing also affects replies. The question "Is the service at _____ [store] all you could expect?" will get a distinctly greater negative response than if it were phrased "Is the service . . . reasonably good?" Better than either, to be sure, is use of some sort of a rating scale.

Behavior Questions

Behavior questions must be specific, not generalized. Because most people cannot easily generalize their behavior, generalized questions used to measure behavior are typically poor and inaccurate. A good behavior question is specific. It avoids asking about how often the person shops at a supermarket, asking instead about when the last time was.

Personal or Private Questions

In general, questions relating to respondents' private lives probably should be phrased in a direct, businesslike approach, in a way that suggests this is simply another matter-of-fact question. Many years ago we were assigned an interview with the wife of the senior member of a major Manhattan law firm. She responded, among other things, with detailed information on the family's finances. Her husband later telephoned to demand that we not disclose any of this, and it was easy to agree since it was only classification data we had been gathering. If the interviewing is personal, then handing the respondent an answer card with categories when only a code (letter or number) is to be used to represent the reply can also make things easier. We offer some additional ideas in our later discussion of the psychological flow of questions.

But direct questioning may not always obtain the right answer. In one study[8] it was necessary to determine the amount of beer that each person consumed so that consumption level could be analyzed by demographics (such as sex, age, and income level) and imagery about each major brand. It was soon evident that two classes of people often were unwilling to give accurate replies: Some users did not want to admit to any use, and many heavier beer drinkers were unwilling to admit just how much they put away. So the following pattern of questioning was developed. First, in almost staccato fashion, each respondent in a general population survey (men and women age 18 and older) was asked:

"What is your favorite brand of personal bath soap? Toothpaste? Beer?" The nonuser does not name a brand, but the beer drinker is committed without even thinking about it.

Then came a second rapid-fire query:

> Now let's talk about the amount of beer you drink. Into which of these groups do you fall? Just give me the letter of the group.

The respondent was then handed the card shown in Exhibit 9.6. The group category descriptions were intended to lead participants into believing that no matter how much beer they drank, there were those who drank more. Even a person drinking as many as 36 bottles or cans weekly is labeled only a "moderate" beer drinker. Also, the person could merely use a letter, not a numerical figure, to indicate level of consumption. This questioning method produced results paralleling tax data for the area.

It is also helpful to tell the participant that "the information is needed just to help us understand how different kinds of people respond. It will be used only for statistical purposes and no one will be told about this or any of your other replies."

Exhibit 9.6   AMOUNT OF BEER CONSUMED WEEKLY

A. HEAVY BEER DRINKER
   (over 60 bottles or cans)
B. MEDIUM-HEAVY BEER DRINKER
   (49–60 bottles or cans)
C. MEDIUM BEER DRINKER
   (37–48 bottles or cans)
D. MODERATE BEER DRINKER
   (25–36 bottles or cans)
E. FAIRLY LIGHT BEER DRINKER
   (13–24 bottles or cans)
F. LIGHT BEER DRINKER
   (7–12 bottles or cans)
G. VERY LIGHT BEER DRINKER
   (6 or fewer bottles or cans)

Questions Involving Pride

Questions that involve the respondent's pride must be handled with considerable care so as to avoid incorrect replies. Sometimes, as we have shown, the method of handling is to stick to behavior questions. But even that has to be done carefully. Thus you wouldn't ask a straight question about the newspapers read yesterday, for certainly in the major areas served by the *New York Times* there would be a gross overstatement of readership of that prestigious publication. Instead, as the major newspaper audience measurement services do, filter questions would be asked, leading up to the *yesterday* question, and even then there would be some check on readership of selected items in that day's editions among those claiming yesterday readership.

Food survey respondents often tell researchers what they wish they were eating rather than what they are actually eating.[9] More than 50 percent of consumers in a survey told Del Monte Corp. that they liked the idea of low-salt canned foods. When Del Monte introduced a line of low-salt canned goods (without a market test), the results were disappointing.

The answer again is one of using behavior as the measurement. NPD, using a diary technique to have participants record their eating behavior, followed this with a measurement of attitudes, then related behavior to attitudes. The "nutritionally fit" (those who claim to know more about nutrition than others, try to eat healthy foods and avoid harmful ingredients, and enjoy exercise) consume more pancakes with syrup, peanut butter, and pretzels than any other group. "Restrictive dieters" (those who worry about calories and avoid additives) eat as much candy, ice cream, cake, cookies, pies, and pastries combined as they do fresh fruit.

But sometimes even the right series of behavior questions cannot get the right answer where pride is involved. Some years back, Dr. George Gallup wanted to determine how many people had read a bestselling novel. Sales data for the book would not provide the right answer, since some copies, especially those in libraries, are read by more than one person. On the other hand, if a direct question were asked about whether or not the person had read the novel, pride would make some say yes when they had not. So Gallup asked simply:

Do you intend to read _____?

Those who had read it almost automatically reported the fact, and all nonreaders were able to salvage their pride by saying that they intended to do so. Berry[10] tells of a case where, because of pride, it was impossible to ask a question that would get a truthful response. A multiple-housing development was being planned. A survey showed conflicting results. Prospects said they *wanted* three bedrooms, two baths, living room, dining room, and kitchen. What they said they were *willing to pay for* was two bedrooms, one bath, living–dining area, and kitchen. The sponsor didn't know how to plan. A psychologist told the firm how to proceed. Only four model units were built to make the sales. Two were of the size prospects said they wanted, and two were units of the size they said they would pay for. The resident manager was put in one of the larger units, but prospects were always shown the larger unit first; when they declined that unit, they were then shown the smaller units, the ones they could afford. The project was successful.

ORDER OF THE QUESTIONS

The structure of the questionnaire must be logical and psychological. Logical means that one question should reasonably lead to another. Psychological means that where the participant's personal reactions may make it difficult to get an accurate response, sequence sometimes can assist.

Logical Flow

Things should flow logically from one question to another. Each question should lead to the next, as far as possible following a train of thought. It is usually best to lead from the general to the specific, since that is the way most of us seem to think.

A retailer wanting to find out what potential customers think of the store must generally start by locating people who shop in the area. Then it is usually necessary to determine frequency of shopping in that general location, and to further qualify the person as to whether he or she knows the store is there. Only then is it reasonable to ask about attitudes toward the particular store.

Logic also dictates branching or forking patterns, where responses dictate which of a series of questions should follow a given response. Users of a product category or of one or more specific brands may be filtered off into a group of subsidiary questions.

Psychological Flow

Pride and personal questions should appear well along in the questioning. If a question may make a person feel "ignorant," "uninformed," "unintelligent," or otherwise threatened, the series of responses may be abruptly cut off. These should be well along in the questionnaire, after a great deal of rapport between questioner and respondent has been established.

Sometimes personal or private questions can be asked more easily when they are asked in a context of other easy-to-answer questions; they seem to stand less on their own in such an environment.

Occasionally the forking question may help. Many people are unwilling to respond directly to a question about age or income, for instance. On the age question, it is possible to start with a broad query: "Are you yourself under 40, or are you 40 or more?" Most people, even women, will respond. Then, depending on the reply, the person can be asked:

If under 40	*If 40 or over*
"Are you under 20?"	"Are you under 50?"
"Are you 30 or older?"	"Are you 60 or older?"

With use of three questions at most, in which the person has not had to answer directly about age, it is then possible to classify each person in one of six age groups:

- Under 20
- 21–29
- 30–39
- 40–49
- 50–59
- 60 or over

In a similar vein, it is often possible to ask knowledge questions—which may be ego-threatening if the person too often cannot reply—within a framework of easy-to-answer questions.

Memory questions must be asked in the right order, for the question sequence may possibly lead to biased replies. In the case of measuring the specifics of advertising recall, it is necessary first to establish that the person has been exposed to advertising for the category, then to mention the brands recalled for the advertising, and only then to ask for memory details of each brand's advertising. Any reversal of the order will stimulate the level of response about advertising details.

On the other hand, when the nature of the study requires it, question sequence can help stimulate past memory. Time may blur memory, especially if the event was not that important to the person. Measurement of radio or television audiences—when done with a recall sort of measurement—must start with a series of questions to jog memory—questions such as whether the radio or television was on yesterday. At what time? Then on into the stations, channels, and programs. And then into whether the specific program was seen and recall of advertising. There will be more about all of this in Chapter 18.

Questions of low interest should come along later in the questioning. By that time the respondent is well into the thing and likely to continue, even if a bit bored.

COMPUTER-ASSISTED QUESTIONNAIRE CONSTRUCTION

The computer cannot construct a questionnaire. It cannot evaluate the strengths and weaknesses of a questionnaire. But it can be extremely helpful. It can help the questionnaire designer put together the questionnaire in a form that works for the interviewer during use, in management control of the interviewing process, and in computer summary of results.

ADVANTAGES

One advantage of computer-assisted questionnaire construction is that the program builds, if that is what is needed, an on-screen questionnaire that can be used in telephone computer-assisted surveys or in central location studies.

It can be of great assistance to the telephone interviewer, or to the respondent in the case of a central location study. In either case it can prevent actual or interviewer-provided response error, since it immediately spots inconsistencies and demands corrections before the next question is asked. (Of course, all this is a part of the input into the particular program for the study.) Later editing and entry of data input into the computer are eliminated.

Such a program also helps solve the important and annoying problems of rotation of questions or answers, previously discussed. Most of these programs also provide for the entering of open-ended responses (with classification to come later).

For the firm conducting the study (the marketer or the research firm), the program can also provide assistance in project management. It can give running and final reports on such aspects as time and costs per interview and locations and categories of completions (and follow-up needs).

Moreover, most programs are easy to learn and run.

THE ACRS PROGRAM (M/A/R/C Inc., Dallas)

ACRS[11] (Automated Custom Research System), a division of one of the country's largest research firms, also seems to have one of the best computer programs for questionnaire building. It may be superior because it was developed by people in marketing research rather than by computer whizzes. In fairness, there are other computer programs—and good ones—that offer a similar questionnaire-building capacity.

This program has several applications such as questionnaire-building (for the researcher or marketer) and interviewing (particularly telephone CRT).

Unique Advantages

One unique advantage of a computer-assisted program is its *capacity*: It can handle not only the simplest of questionnaires, but the longest and most complicated as well. It can take care of questionnaires ranging from 2 to 12,000 questions. Of course, who is ever going to have a questionnaire of the latter size? It can also accommodate samples ranging from 100 to 60,000. But again, who will ever need a sample of the latter size?

It offers advantages in questionnaire *mechanics*. Answers from previous questions can be inserted automatically into the text of later questions. If a questionnaire about automobiles has asked about whether the person has test-driven any makes within the past six months, and a later portion of the questionnaire probes into each such test drive, the program can be structured so that the name of each car tried is inserted automatically into the questionnaire at the right point.

The replies to an open-ended question are available to an interviewer for later access, if required. Any interview temporarily terminated at the respondent's request—this applies specifically to telephone interviewing—can be rescheduled for completion, with the telephone number being provided to a follow-up interviewer for dialing and the interview being displayed at the break-off point.

The computer-assisted program aids in *interviewer control*. The system provides for monitoring of video and audio aspects of the interviewing process with no awareness on the part of either interviewer or respondent. Supervision—like the idea or not, it is important for quality interviewing—cannot be better performed than that. Also, a running record of each worker's productivity is provided.

In the area of *project management*, there are ongoing, long-range advantages. In terms of field management, the program can clock the time of each interview, assign numbers to respondents by sequence or any other pattern (such as type), and record interviewer number. All of this information can be integrated into a master file for overall control.

These ongoing records can be monitored to determine dialings and completion rates by significant elements such as type of respondent (sex, age, income level), specific markets, and community size or time zone, up to a choice of 159 specifications. The programming can be restructured as monitoring of incoming results may suggest.

The evaluations are helpful in future *project planning*, since they can be entered into the firm's database to help establish time and cost estimates and controls.

How the Program Works

This program, complex as it sounds, is surprisingly user-friendly. It is a do-it-yourself program that moves easily and simply from one menu to another. It asks for ongoing input from the user (the researcher or marketing manager, the interviewer or the respondent, depending on the nature of the particular use).

The computer requirements, unless the user is planning some of the more advanced applications, requires only a desktop PC.

QUESTIONNAIRE TESTING

All the way through this chapter, we have stressed that there is no set of rules, no list of principles for building a questionnaire. It is an art, not a science. And the best-planned questionnaire may fail unless tested. The questionnaire should be tried out to find out how well it works and how it might be improved. It's a bit like trying out a stain on a piece of wood to make sure that it is giving the color wanted. Without testing, a researcher can never can ever be sure that a questionnaire will obtain the information in a valid and useful way.

In questionnaire testing, the major aim is to find out whether the series of questions is working.

THE TESTING PROCEDURE

Whether the questionnaire is to be used in a mail study or in a telephone survey or some other form of one-on-one interview, there is one basic that applies in testing it. The test should always be on a personal basis. It is the *only* way to learn about any underlying weaknesses of the questioning and to determine how to go about correcting them.

We first discuss three aspects of testing: the method, the process, and the number of people to involve.

The Method

There are several methods of testing: the informal method, the one-on-one method, and the group procedure.

The *informal method* is just that. It includes getting the feel of how things are going as the questionnaire goes into use. This is particularly common in telephone surveys, where the rationale is that misunderstood or leading questions will become evident. But the question is: to whom and by what standards? Also, while most gross questionnaire errors will become clear, some others that are subtle but important may be completely missed.

For one-on-one personal interviewing (malls or in-home), the same trial-and-error approach is used as a test. The first day's results are examined, but in this case there isn't the possibility of much or any supervision.

The *one-on-one* method is an improvement. In this case the interviewer usually goes through the questionnaire as a typical interviewer, following written instructions. But for testing purposes, these interviewers are specially trained. On conclusion of the interview, they go back over each question with the respondent, exchanging ideas about the response to determine whether the question really did represent the truth of the person's opinion, memory, or behavior.

The best method may well be the *group interview*. The procedure to be followed in the final study should be used. If a mail questionnaire is being tested, each person in the group should be given a copy and asked to complete it. If the method will be some form of one-on-one approach, then an interviewer should question each person individually and separately before they are all called together. But the point is, as we will show in Chapter 10, that through the interaction of the group any major weaknesses of the questionnaire will quickly be uncovered. Each question and its understanding (or misunderstanding) are reviewed. The discussion among the group members brings out fine points that might not be otherwise uncovered.

In the group-interviewing method, only ordinary but competent interviewers should be used; the idea is to keep things at the real level of what happens in the field. An elite corps of interviewers is to be avoided.

The Process

Good testing processes are interactive. In the one-on-one method, the individuals present their interpretations of each question, along with an explanation of the reaction they gave to each question. But the interactive process is even better when the group interview is used. For then the interaction is not only between questioner and respondent, but also among respondents, with little chance of missing any minor points that some may have thought of. The test participants should be asked what, if anything, gave them trouble. Testers often come up with sound suggestions that the researcher or marketer would never have thought of, and their thoughtful perceptions should always be taken into account.

The People to Include in the Test

Unlike the sample for a survey, discussed in Chapter 8, those persons used for testing questionnaires need not be a group large enough to pass sampling error standards. The number of people used for questionnaire testing depends more on the range of the kinds of people than on the accuracy of the results.

If there is to be a wide variety of people in the study, then that variety should be represented, at least at the extremes. If the extremes are broad, several different groups may be required. Numbers are much less important than variety. The purpose of the exercise is to refine the questionnaire to a good measuring instrument, not to get precision results.

ENDNOTES   [1]G. H. Gallup. *The Sophisticated Poll Watcher's Guide.* Princeton, N.J.: Princeton University Press, 1976.

[2]Sam Gill. "How Do You Stand on Sin?" *Tide*, Mar. 14, 1947, 72 ff.

[3]H. S. Hardy, et al. *The Politz Papers.* Chicago: American Marketing Association, 1991, 68.

[4]C. E. Osgood, G. J. Suci, and P. H. Tannenbaum. *The Measurement of Meaning.* Urbana, Ill.: University of Illinois Press, 1957.

[5]H. R. Moskowitz. *New Directions for Product Testing and Sensory Analysis of Foods.* Westport, Conn.: Food & Nutrition Press, 1985, 150.

[6]A. B. Blankenship. *Professional Telephone Surveys.* New York: McGraw-Hill, 1977, 105.

[7]Susan Small-Weil. "What's a Department Store?" *Advertising Age*, Oct. 8, 1990, 50.

[8]A. B. Blankenship. "Creativity in Consumer Research." *Journal of Marketing* 25 (1961):34–38.

[9]"Why Food That's Good for You Can Be Bad for Sales." *Ad Forum*, April 1984.

[10]Lionel Berry. "Unhealthcare: Marketing Lessons and War Stories That Help You Develop Strategies That Work." *VISION 2000*, Academy for Health Services Marketing, 1990, 77–78.

[11]*Automated Custom Research System*. Dallas: ACRS, a division of M/A/R/C Inc., undated.

REFERENCE   Payne, S. L. *The Art of Asking Questions*. Princeton, N.J.: Princeton University Press, 1951.

10

USING FOCUS GROUPS

What's in This Chapter

In this chapter we discuss the nature and uses of focus groups, describing how this method of collecting data can elicit information that is largely unavailable through other types of marketing research. We caution about the possible misuse of focus groups, detail the techniques used in moderating group discussions, and distinguish between focus groups used for consumer product research and those used for industrial research.

BASIC CONCEPTS

Focus groups, when used correctly, provide information and guidance about a particular problem through the use of group dynamics.

Group dynamics simply means what we all have known for most of our lives: A relatively small group of interested people can, by talking among themselves and with a moderator, produce more valuable thoughts and ideas than if each participant were interviewed separately.

Groups can be used for information on attitudes, buying habits, new-product ideas, and a hundred other things.

Used correctly, focus groups are an invaluable tool for marketing researchers and the sponsors that use them. For many purposes, nothing duplicates what can happen when a group of persons interested in a topic or a product sit around a table for one to two hours discussing how they feel about that topic and what product ideas or changes they can offer. An experienced moderator can develop a spirit of cooperation that will bring forth ideas that go beyond what has been believed. Or the group can enthusiastically choose a course of action for a sponsor, helping to clear up the organization's concerns about what action should be taken.

It must be said here, and will be said again later in this chapter, that a focus group, invaluable as it can be, is not a true sample of the population. For the most part, the focus group or groups should lead to further analytical research and further management consideration of the problem.

Groups can break up with strong opposing opinions. And this may be just as valuable for a client firm in planning for its marketing strategies.

Unlike other marketing research, focus groups can dig deeply into mind-sets, customary ways of action or belief, and possible reactions to something new (rational or irrational). They can try to determine why such conditions and reactions exist and what can possibly be done to change them.

Focus groups will be only as valuable as the forethought and preparation that go into them. Also, with a well-conducted focus group, the "sum is greater than the parts." Participants stimulate each other into thoughts and reactions that might not occur in a normal one-on-one interview or when filling out a questionnaire.

Focus groups, therefore, present a valuable means of marketing research. The danger lies in rushing into this form of research, which on the surface appears to be both quick and inexpensive. In truth, focus groups are neither.

WHAT IS A FOCUS GROUP?

Greenbaum says that "a focus group consists of a decision about a topic of particular interest to a client organization among eight to ten people led by a trained moderator. The participants in the group have some common characteristics that relate to the topic discussed in the group."[1]

The great strength of the focus group for marketing research is its facility to allow free discussion and thought about the problem under discussion. Under the guidance of the moderator, who keeps the talk limited to the topic, minds can range freely. Interaction with each other can produce ideas and suggestions that are truly the "sum that is greater than the parts."

A trained and experienced moderator keeps discussion in line and guides it toward a conclusion that all can agree upon. The moderator is not a leader who directs all discussion, sometimes with a list of questions to be given to the group; this can be a very wrong approach indeed. Guiding, not leading, is what makes a good moderator.

Discussion must be kept centered, however, on a topic of interest to the sponsor. The sponsoring firm is paying for the group and expects to be educated and guided by what it learns. The moderator must draw the group away from too much free discussion that is not helpful to the firm, and still leave it free to bring out new and valuable ideas that neither the moderator nor the sponsor had expected.

But focus group findings and ideas are not projectable. It would be a mistake to assume that what two or three focus groups say is true of all similar people in the market. The focus group can guide and "focus" further research, but that is all it can do. But we must realize that this function of research groups is in itself very useful, sometimes vital.

Focus groups can be used for both consumer and industrial problems. Industry focus groups have special requirements that will be described at the end of this chapter.

WHAT FOCUS GROUPS CAN DO

GENERATING NEW-PRODUCT IDEAS

Focus groups can lead the client firm to ideas for new products. These certainly will be unfocused; for the most part they will not be much more than "Wouldn't it be nice if you could make 'something' that would help me to do this or that?" A hole in the market's offering may be disclosed. If further research shows that a sufficient number of consumers have similar difficulties and would like that "something," the firm has the option of making the product.

Several problems arise. For example, will there be protection for the firm against suits for "stealing" the product idea? The legal department will have a say in this.

The idea may have come up before and been rejected. Perhaps it was impossible to make the product and sell it at a profit in today's market. Perhaps it would interfere with the sale of a similar product now in the sponsor's line. These are matters for management to decide. The focus group has done its job by bringing forward an idea that, at least at first, appears to be worthy of further consideration.

If several focus groups should come up with this "something," it may well be worth more serious thought. Even though it may have been considered before, perhaps it is timely to put it in the line now. Perhaps costs can be adjusted so that a profit becomes visible. All we are saying is that focus groups can be a valuable source of new ideas, but then these ideas must undergo further marketing research study and management consideration.

PREDICTING NEW-PRODUCT SUCCESS

Focus groups can indicate the likelihood of success with a new product. It would be possible, for example, to test the concept of electric automobiles for the current market. What would be the advantages? Would people accept the drawbacks of electric power in a time of very high gasoline prices? How would electric cars be used, as compared with gasoline models? What would be the reaction from the group if electric cars could do this or that? Distance on one charge of the battery, speed, and acceleration would certainly come up for discussion. In a changeover period from gas to electric, how could this be handled?

DETERMINING REASON FOR DECREASING SALES

When sales have slumped on certain products, focus groups can help uncover the reasons. The products might, for example, seem to be doing the job they were intended to do, but are there little annoyances that are hurting the sale? Very small matters can hurt subsequent sales. A plastic wrap can be so efficient that it not only keeps out dirt and bugs, it keeps out customers. A focus group might be allowed to handle several competitors' products (without identification) and praise and complaints noted. Is ease of opening and closing a problem? Does the product have an odor when first opened? Is it hard to find the product due to poor distribution? A thousand other matters might come up, including unexpected sales success by a new competitor.

SPOTTING PRODUCT GAPS

Identifying gaps in a product line is a frequent outcome of focus group discussion. Perhaps a group talking about tableware may have ideas about silver versus stainless steel. Nothing will probably change in this dichotomy, but the group might voice a desire for the return of the large-bowled soup spoon or a slotted serving spoon.

DETERMINING HOW PRODUCTS ARE USED

New approaches to product use can be discovered through focus group discussion. For example, a manufacturer of tools found that the reason contractors were buying such inexpensive tools was to prevent theft. It seemed less costly to let the workers steal cheap tools than better ones. Is that attitude common? What can be done about it? Are less-expensive tools good enough for the work required? Can the manufacturers do anything to help contractors diminish theft? A focus group among contractors and another group among workers might unearth some new ideas.

EVALUATING COMPETITIVE PRODUCTS

Focus group discussion can lead to an awareness of consumer thinking on product quality. A competing product that seems so poor to your engineers, for example, may be good enough for most people and most jobs. Is the quality more than most people want or are willing to pay for? A manufacturer of a beautiful product for home ornamentation had used an expensive Brazilian wood. Survey research found that almost no one knew or cared what the wood was. Domestic wood was cheaper and just as salable; moreover, competing products used domestic wood. The change was made; sales remained about the same, but profit was greater. A few focus groups could have uncovered this attitude much sooner.

EVALUATING PACKAGING

In an effort to put absolutely sanitary and meddleproof products on store shelves, there has been a move to better and tighter packaging. A few focus groups can find whether the sponsor's packaging is too difficult to handle—perhaps especially by older people. Are competitors' products easier to handle? Are there any suggestions from the group for improving the packaging?

EVALUATING PRICE

The qualities that lead to higher market prices may well be qualities for which customers feel no need. In a time of inflation, the manufacturer may be looking for ways to cut costs and lower retail prices. Unnecessary product features may need discovering. For example, a "pound" of coffee is now 13 ounces in the market. Research must have preceded this move. Focus groups might have been used to measure the reaction to this proposed change. Apparently, the retail price for this "pound" is more important to the customer at the moment of sale than the lost ounces.

JUDGING ADVERTISING STRATEGY

Chapter 1 mentioned Burger King's Herb the Nerd. Certainly, a large campaign such as this was researched at the customer level—but apparently not thoroughly enough. This advertising postponed the chain's discovery of its competitive place on the market. In fact, the chain was seeking younger, brighter customers. Few companies can be all things to all people. Finding a viable and profitable niche can be a matter of life or death. A few minutes' reflection will bring to mind other chains that have not yet found their niche.

Focus groups can be used to lead to further and more accurate and usable findings for action. Big and expensive mistakes can be avoided. Some years ago, for example, a water-purifying company advertised that "the water you are drinking now might have been drunk by Julius Caesar." Perhaps this was a fact, but not one to lead to a happier sales situation.

PINPOINTING WHAT CUSTOMERS/PROSPECTS THINK

Focus groups can discover consumer attitudes toward the sponsoring firm. We all know firms that live with an apparent public opinion that they are "losers," or at least permanent second-placers. What is the attitude toward the client company, especially among those who are or should be customers? Focus groups can help identify these attitudes sufficiently to warrant further research that can lead to beneficial and remedial action.

Our discussion here by no means covers all of the possibilities for focus groups. New uses are constantly being found. Furthermore, there are interesting variations of group research.

CHOOSING FOCUS GROUPS AS A RESEARCH METHOD

Focus groups are best used to discover attitudes, prejudices, changing ways of using products, and changing ways of viewing pricing and distribution. Because they have become popular in the minds of researchers and businesspeople, experiments constantly are being proposed for new uses for group research or new methods of conducting it.

Focus group research in the past was sometimes used by companies on their own premises or in convenient church or school buildings. The moderator was on the company's staff, often the marketing research director or one of his or her staff. Satisfactory research could be performed under these circumstances if the moderator was able to remain strictly neutral in attitude and to listen to opinions and attitudes that did not fit with his or her prejudgments and the policy of the firm. In practice, this neutrality was very difficult to reach. Embued with the company's policies and thought patterns, the staff moderator would have to be a strong person to listen to other ways and other opinions.

Furthermore, as the science of focus group research advanced, it became increasingly necessary to turn to professionals to perform the actual research—though still under the watchful eye and guidance of the sponsor. Many times, if the advertising or research agency hired a professional moderator, both the sponsor and the agency helped to prepare the moderator for this particular assignment, and both the sponsor and the agency would carefully oversee his or her work.

The moderator from "outside," having a less than complete knowledge of the sponsor's product or problem, will certainly need this guidance. No matter how neutral he or she will claim to be, there will be a degree of negative or positive thinking on the subject in question. That is the reason for the carefully prepared agenda for the moderator, discussed later in this chapter.

New and expensive focus group techniques have been introduced in the last decade. One-way mirrors allow the sponsor to see and hear without being seen or heard. Ways of communicating between sponsor and moderator have been devised. It is now possible, during the session, for the sponsor or the agency to offer advice to the moderator on directions that the discussions should be taking.

In some cases, there will be a need for a closed-circuit television camera located where the participants can be viewed as a group or individually. It is possible, as we will describe later in this chapter, to have groups in several cities being watched by television in the sponsor's offices.

The "science" of focus group research has reached a point where special rooms are dedicated to this activity. The daily cost of using such a room and its equipment may range from $300 to $700 or more, not including the moderator's fee, the cost of recruiting and paying the participants, furnishing snacks or even dinner, the cost of preparing and presenting the report, and so on. Focus groups are not by any means a "cheap and easy" form of marketing research, compared with other methods. But focus groups in many cases can do what no other research method can do. And in these cases, focus groups are vital.

Because focus group research is quite expensive, firms are tempted to go one of two ways, both of which are wrong. First, there is the strong temptation to look upon the "findings" of two or three focus groups as valid answers to the problem in question. The "truth" appears to be so clear that no one could doubt its validity. So what perhaps 20 paid participants said becomes gospel, requiring no further research.

The second error is to look at the cost of focus group research, forgo it, and depend entirely on some other type of research. In many cases, this would be adequate. But in many other cases, the possibility of new thinking about products, their pricing and distribution, and the attitudes and prejudices of consumers would be lost. Those 20 participants could well have guided the sponsoring firm into new ways of looking at its business, its products, and its distribution.

The 1990s will be a decade of consolidation of work forces and a time of continued cost cutting. There will always be the temptation to cut such "frills" as focus groups (or even marketing research itself). The need to produce a product as quickly and cheaply as possible may lead decision makers to depend more than they should on the infallibility of their own judgment. The history of new products that fail within the first or third year makes this thinking questionable. There are many times when focus groups and other research could have prevented subsequent large losses.

Large firms know the value of good focus group research. They need no education about what these groups can do. But even though this type of research has had extensive publicity in business publications in recent years, its strengths and weaknesses remain largely untested by most other organizations. Or, quite likely, some focus group research has been done poorly and led to findings of no particular merit.

For many marketing problems of importance, the idea of expensive focus group research needs to be sold. A group that can cost up to $2,000 or more—a group that cannot be expected to produce actionable recommendations—must be looked upon with some suspicion. This is especially true when the market appears to require even faster action than was needed during the 1980s.

Whoever is in charge of this "selling" should start with broad knowledge of what focus groups can offer. For more detail than is possible in this chapter, we recommend *The Practical Handbook and Guide to Focus Group Research*.[1] If a marketing research firm is recommended by an advertising agency, that agency will (or should) have a broad, basic knowledge about why and how focus group research can be sold to marketing and upper management. The benefits and weaknesses of this group research should be kept fully in mind. A management that is oversold and then disappointed will be less likely to accept research proposals in the future.

Even though the advertising agency or marketing research firm supports the idea of using focus groups and is in a position to recommend someone to moderate the group, the research sponsor should still carefully examine the credentials and the background of this person. If this is the first time a focus group has been used, it is especially important that the job be done correctly.

It is also important that people and departments that must use the recommendations of the focus group and subsequent marketing research should be satisfied in advance that the proper course of action is being taken. Of equal importance, the definition of the problem to be given to the moderator must be broad and specific enough to satisfy the concerns of each department involved. This is especially true if a recorded or written version of the focus group action is to be made available to these departments. Of all departments in a firm, the marketing research department is often the most vulnerable to a "Why didn't you?" response from others.

There must be early decisions and agreement about coverage of focus group sessions. This will include geographic coverage (often a bone of contention), coverage of ethnic groups, groups known to have similar and pertinent interests, and groups with similar educational backgrounds.

NEWER TECHNIQUES OF GROUP RESEARCH

While the typical focus group still involves seven to twelve or thirteen participants, a moderator, an agenda for discussion, a room equipped with a one-way mirror in which sponsors listen and watch, suitable electronic equipment, and chalkboards, there have been recent new ideas and new techniques.

INTERACTIVE DEVICES

Market Opinion Research (MOR) offers the "Interactive Group Research System" that "can be customized to virtually any client's need, whether it is testing new television ads, testing advertising or product concepts, or observing consumer reactions to words, phrases, or visuals. Furthermore, the system can be modified midstream, that is, while the research is being conducted, to address new issues and unanticipated alternatives."

The MOR system incorporates a large group session during which rating of various stimuli are obtained, followed by focus group sessions.

Twenty-five to fifty participants are prerecruited to come to a central location for a session. Frequently several sessions are held to raise the ultimate sample size to a number suitable for statistical analysis.

During the structured session, participants are led through a series of ratings by a trained moderator. The ratings are obtained using hand-held dials that are calibrated to a zero to 100 scale. The dials can be used to respond to forced-choice questions or used to obtain continuous feedback as the participants view a videotape or listen to a soundtrack. There is no limit to the types of data that can be obtained through this measurement system. All ratings are automatically fed into a computer, which affords immediate access to the results.

Following the structured rating session, focus group discussions are held with a subset of the group participants to enhance understanding of the ratings given in earlier sessions.[2]

We give the above description in some detail because it is an example of the kinds of changes that can be made to the typical focus group session. It is called an "interactive group session." Participants have the opportunity to react quickly to various stimuli, and then focus groups support the findings with qualitative reactions.

Option Technologies Inc. offers a system incorporating the following steps:

- A group of people, perhaps a focus group, generates a list of items relevant to the topic under discussion.

- The list is entered into a computer. The system generates a systematic set of questions about the list that is projected onto a large-screen monitor, providing a visual stimulus for group members to register their opinions.

- Participants vote on individual, hand-held keypads linked to the computer, which organizes the votes into graphics that are fed back to the group by a projection system.

- Participants verbally interpret the meaning of their opinions as projected on the monitor. Group discussion clarifies the issues under research and leads to a systematic and organized basis for further research.[3]

TELEPHONE GROUPS

The Teleconference Network runs telephone focus groups. George Silverman, president, says:

Respondents are invited from your list or ours to participate in a nationwide group telephone discussion at a specific day and time. At that time we call them at their office or home anywhere in the country from our telephone conference system. Our moderator guides the discussion using techniques designed to create maximum interaction between the participants. You (the sponsor) and your colleagues can be given inputs to the moderator's assistant without being heard by the participants, as if you were behind a one-way mirror. The session lasts for about an hour and a half and provides about as much information as a two-hour face-to-face session.[4]

Those who advocate telephone groups say the advantages outweigh possible loss from inability to see the participants. People are said to be less inhibited because they are not seen. There are means available to lessen the problems that arise from two or more people trying to talk at once. No expensive equipment is needed. People's reactions can be heard in the background as one speaker holds forth. The Teleconference Network offers Instant Participant Polling, where the moderator can ask for votes and ratings without the participants hearing each other's responses and without interrupting the flow of the session.

It is said that this type of focus group can deliver:

- Difficult-to-recruit people
- Higher-quality respondents
- Lower costs
- Greater openness, interaction, focus, and intensity

TeleSession offers telephone-based focus groups. This firm, according to Lincoln G. Clark, vice president of market development, "unlocks a powerful approach to group discussion for busy, hard-to-reach, or geographically separated participants."

TeleSession began conducting focus groups over the phone in 1970, when it began recruiting doctors for a study. After over ten thousand groups later, people continue to agree to take part. They view the sessions as an opportunity to learn from their fellows, and partly because they enjoy the experience.

The system allows only one person at a time to speak, but indicates who is waiting to talk so that everyone gets his chance. The sponsor can telephone by a special number and hear the whole session.

"Sometimes," Clark says, "in face-to-face groups a problem arises when a question is asked and the first person's answer unduly influences everybody else's response." TeleSession, it is claimed, has the key to this difficulty. An assistant will go to each person's line privately (after a question has been asked), get the answer, log it by name, and hand the complete list to the moderator. This person will then share the answers and ask the group to comment.[5]

LONG-DISTANCE OBSERVATION

FocusVision Network Inc. offers a videoconferencing system. In different parts of the country, for example, groups gathered around tables are asked to sample new or improved products. Three major advertising agencies, geographically far apart, have set up video cameras as well as microphones. Executives are able to watch these groups and hear them, even though they are a thousand miles away. These executives can speak to the moderator, sharpening up the direction the group discussion is taking.

Using this system, it is possible for executives of the sponsoring firm to view focus groups in action in various parts of the country without leaving their offices.[6]

All these systems have their strengths. Perhaps some have certain weaknesses. Using the telephone obviously allows hard-to-reach experts to be enrolled, since they do not have to leave their homes or offices. Each participant can hear all the others and each has a chance to contribute without being identified. The sponsor can listen in on the actual session or later via a tape recording.

Face-to-face groups offer the opportunity for more personal contact. Perhaps the group dynamic works better when all participants are seated around the table and can see each other. Facial reactions and visible muscular reactions often tell more than words what the participant is thinking, and other participants can and do react to these signs.

Televised or telephone groups, with both researcher and sponsor listening, offer obvious two-way advantages.

The research client must therefore do a little research to find what is the best way to approach a problem. The benefits of good focus research are too great to allow the use of a system that is not in tune with the needs of the client in any particular problem.

THE PARTICIPANTS

First, it should be said that professional research firms, especially those that do a large amount of focus group research, have tried and proven ways of locating good group participants. A sponsor, having chosen a research firm, would do well to let that agency guide and carry out the participant search. The agency will, of course, vary its procedure to fit the requirements of the sponsor's particular problem. However, it is still the responsibility of the sponsor to oversee the selection of participants—at least the method by which this is done.

There are several standards that should be followed in the selection of focus group participants if the far more prevalent face-to-face technique is to be used:

1. The group ordinarily should not have less than seven or more than ten to twelve participants. This is because of the known and observed behavior of human beings put together in a room and faced with a problem of mutual interest. With less than seven, there is not enough interplay to provide worthwhile information. If all participants were equally vocal, equally outgoing, and equally informed, it might be possible to use fifteen participants or even more. But people do not come like that.

   It is difficult to work with larger groups. At this level, one or two persons tend to dominate the flow of conversation and the discussion proves difficult to control. It becomes harder for the moderator to restrain side conversations and remarks that add nothing to the goal of the meeting.

2. The group of participants should have enough knowledge of and experience with the type of problem to be discussed to advance meaningful ideas and reactions. To ask a group of secretaries to discuss nuclear power would bring forth a number of loud prejudices, but probably no meaningful thoughts. A group of nuclear scientists likely would be lost talking about word processors. It is easy to fill a room with warm bodies and vacant minds on particular problems.

3. In this day of presumed sex equality, a group perhaps should include both men and women. In practice, it is hard to control such a group and achieve meaningful ideas. There are exceptions, of course. If the problem requires information on how men and women react to certain products or subjects, clearly we can contemplate a mixed group. But even here it may be better to have one group of men and another of women—both discussing the same agenda with the same moderator.

4. It is not a rule for all sessions, but often it is not wise to include a great disparity of ages. The young may defer to the older members. The older members may protest the "new" ideas of the young. Group dynamics may never get off the ground as emotions dominate.

   The screening of participants must be carefully done. Sponsors may set criteria for screening the participants. Sponsors know (or believe they know) the kinds of people who will be important to them and their products. People who have been used frequently or in recent months may not be chosen. It is too easy to become a "professional" focus group person. Even with the best screening methods, the loud talkers, the silent ones, and the know-everythings still may show up, for the world is full of these. Telephone screening usually is used. Perhaps a prospect who cannot take part may be able to recommend someone. Agencies can keep lists of possible future participants. The research agency can only do its best to find the people who will make the most effective participants for a particular study.

Participants must feel that they are taking part in a creative discovery that is both worthwhile and interesting. They must feel that they are important in helping to solve the sponsor's problem. This is easier to accomplish than might be thought. Participants want to be paid, but running a close second to money is the emotional interest in the topic being researched. This has been shown in innumerable sessions over the years.

Paying participants is an almost universal practice. Even though the participants can become interested in what will go on in the session, they feel that they should be compensated for their time and trouble. The time may include a journey to and from the focus group room. The trouble may be arranging for a babysitter. Payment of the respondent is perfectly in order and, in fact, necessary to get a good representative group together. Even though the income of the participants apparently would not require this payment, they will expect it.

Payment will be in line with local custom and with the nature of the people chosen. It should be spoken of, and hopefully viewed as, a "bonus" rather than a salary. As a bonus, it can appear to be an extra payment, almost as a welcome "extra" for being so helpful.

Payment in kind is seldom acceptable. But when offered, it should be intrinsically valuable *to the participant* as well as valuable in itself. Packages of corn flakes will not get many people very excited or willing to cooperate, whereas a short-wave radio might.

THE MODERATOR

The role of the moderator in a focus session is to draw from his or her group the best and most innovative ideas about the assigned problem. Trained to seek the best ideas from each member and to foster interplay and discussion, the moderator must bring the session to a close with suggestions that will be of value to the sponsor in guiding further research or further rethinking about the problem. The moderator should have the following characteristics:

1. Be acceptable to the group as a person they can work with easily. This does not mean that the moderator should be "one of the boys" or "one of the girls." He or she may be better educated, more experienced, more "worldly," but a comfortable association still can be achieved. A false letting down to become "one of the fellows" is easily spotted and is often resented.

2. Have a quick mind capable of noting new ideas that come from the group and pressing for further discussion, even though it means leaving the fixed agenda. The new ideas, obviously, must pertain in an important way to the problem under discussion. A fast talker may not be a fast thinker. Sometimes the relatively quiet person who listens well can spot these new ideas readily when they arise.

3. Have a good memory for names. Group dynamics will flourish if each participant can feel the importance of what he or she is saying and thinking. A forgotten name throws cold water on the status and self-worth of that person. Place cards with names clearly visible are almost always used.

4. Have the prestige and ability to control a group if it wanders, bringing it back to the topic under discussion without appearing to dominate unduly. The moderator must also be able to recognize important new ideas that were not on the agenda but suddenly loom as significant. This sometimes means swinging a free-talking group from one subject to another without causing sudden and continuing silence in the room.

5. Be as neutral as possible. This is difficult, as any judge knows. We all have ideas about almost everything. Most of our ideas are by nature uninformed. Generally, the participant who seems not to have strong opinions or feelings about the problem under discussion is the best person. Not ideal—but the best. One caveat: The person without strong opinions also may be a person of less than ideal intelligence, one who is unwilling to take the trouble to follow the discussion.

6. Have a strong belief in the purpose of the study. Without taking sides, the moderator must have a real desire to see the research problem solved.

7. Be able to moderate both men's and women's groups. Men can moderate women's groups on almost any topic (often even personal matters), and vice versa.

POSSIBLE SOURCES FOR A MODERATOR

Professional moderators are available in most large cities. They work for marketing research agencies and advertising agencies. Being professional, they are more likely to be neutral toward any particular problem. Good moderators are used often. They are expensive; their fee can run up to $1,000 or more. In many instances this is not too much to pay for the professional results that are produced. This is entirely the sponsor's problem; he or she must weigh this fee against the importance of the problem under discussion. Choosing the name of a new product that can bring millions of dollars of profit to the sponsor clearly can position itself above the cost of a few highly trained moderators.

A second source for moderators is, of course, a person from the sponsoring firm. It is very difficult, almost impossible, for in-house moderators to remain as neutral as outside moderators. In-house moderators will be affected by all that has gone before in the firm and by their knowledge of how executives of the firm think and what their reactions to the focus group findings will be.

The moderator should be chosen with the particular problem in mind. Yet this is sometimes ignored in the pressure of getting started on a research project. To choose a moderator with no interest in or knowledge of sports to conduct a group about athletic problems would be self-defeating. Such a moderator might easily miss some good ideas that arise unexpectedly from the group.

PREPARING FOR A SESSION

NATURE OF THE GROUP

We want to reemphasize the importance of several points made earlier in this chapter:

- Although the group is not a "sample," every effort should be made to keep it representative for the specific problem. A person who never gardens would be a poor group member of a group discussing garden tools.

- Groups should be carefully screened to get the best persons for the problem under discussion. Homeowners? Income level? Age bracket? This point is sometimes ignored in the rush for decision. Time spent in gathering the most representative group is time well-spent.

- The moderator and the sponsor should oversee the choice of participants in the group. But the sponsor must resist a tendency to "pack the house" to favor a finding he wishes.

- The most valuable thoughts and ideas surface when a group is fairly homogeneous. Knowledgeable group members are likely to grow silent in the face of obvious ignorance of the subject in question.

- Usually, more than three groups discussing the same problem will add very little, though if there are known or suspected regional differences, for example, more than three may be necessary. Often it may be advisable to form the different groups by age and sex.

- Seven to twelve participants is usually the size limit for an effective group.

PREPARING THE MODERATOR'S GUIDE

Preparation of the moderator's guide should be a joint effort of the sponsor, the ad agency, if one is involved, and the moderator. This guide must not be just a list of questions to be answered by the participants. Use of such a list leads to a classroom atmosphere that banishes free-flowing discussion. An experienced moderator knows how to bring out the silent, restrain the overtalkative, and search for the best and brightest ideas for the sponsor.

The guide should contain open, nonleading questions designed to stimulate thinking and discussion. Such questions might not be used verbally at all; rather, they may serve as a reminder to the moderator of matters that the sponsor wants covered. The moderator knows how he or she likes to operate and will guide the agency and sponsor in how to approach sensitive and crucial areas.

The moderator's guide should consider the types of participants in the group—their knowledge and experience. (See the discussion on industrial focus groups later in this chapter.)

The guide should not show bias or reflect already formed opinions. This may be difficult for the sponsor (or even the ad agency), for some matters that appear to be "true" to them tend to be taken for granted by them.

The moderator's guide should be developed, as far as possible, with the counsel of those people and departments that will have an ultimate interest in carrying out the findings of the research study. Corporate staff departments have sometimes overlooked ideas from others in the interest of retaining the importance of their own fiefdoms.

All interested persons and departments have the responsibility to make sure that everything pertinent is included in the guide. But restrictions of time will require selection of the most useful matters for the group to discuss.

The moderator's guide should contain suggestions on timing of the session. Although some phase of the discussion may be interesting enough to take up the full hour or more, the sponsor probably wants more coverage. And he is paying the bill.

BRIEFING THE MODERATOR

It is the client firm's responsibility to see that the moderator understands the problem and the importance of the findings of each session. The firm's marketing department and perhaps the research agency should prepare the moderator for the kinds of ideas and thoughts that may arise during the session. The moderator should be given the opportunity to prepare for the various directions that the discussion may go.

This definitely does not mean that the moderator should prejudge how the discussion should or should not go. He or she must be able to distinguish between real issues, side issues that would be of no importance in the problem, and side issues that may give a new and potent view of the problem.

Thus the moderator, while being as neutral as possible during the discussion, must still know enough about the industry and the problem to recognize unexpected and valuable points that may be brought up. One of several possible actions may then be taken by the sponsor.

If communication between the sponsor (perhaps sitting behind a one-way mirror) and moderator through wireless microphone and pocket receiver may take place, the moderator must know how to handle this process without disturbing the group.

The moderator must know what equipment and supplies will be present. Some focus group facilities use television monitors to allow sponsors to view in their offices what is going on. Some television monitors may be used to tape the session for later viewing. Apparatus allowing the moderator to hear the sponsor must be used without causing sudden quiet among the participants or arousing their interest in what is going on.

Some moderators refuse to allow any disruptions such as these. The sponsor's questions may be allowed when the taped session is being reviewed right after the session or at a later date.

The moderator must be prepared to give his or her views about the session's results. For example, he or she may have noted some movements, head shaking, or whispered asides that were meaningful but not noticed by the sponsor or ad agency.

The moderator must understand why participants have to feel the need of their contribution to the discussion. This feeling of importance, in the long run, outweighs any interest in payment for participation.

A professional moderator has had experience in "waking up the crowd." He or she knows how to get a session off to a good start, with members of the group eager to participate and share their ideas. The first moments are crucial.

THE PHYSICAL LOCATION OF THE GROUP SESSION

Most professional research firms that offer focus group sessions will already have a proper room set up for the session. The room will include one-way mirrors so that the client may watch and hear without being seen. It will have ready such things as chalkboards, a table of sufficient size, proper television equipment as needed, projection equipment, and pads and pencils for taking notes.

Only rarely today is a focus group conducted in locations such as church parlors, private homes, or schoolrooms. The locations may be used if it is necessary for the moderator to go to a group that would otherwise be impossible to reach. If this happens, as much as possible of the equipment listed above should be taken along.

If it is necessary to use a location other than a room provided by the research firm, the focus group session always should be held in a room without outside distractions. It should be large enough for the participants to feel uncrowded, but not be so large as to make them feel "lost" in it. Groupings of plants or movable screens may help. Other factors that should be considered: The possible need to control noise from an adjoining room, and the facts that older groups may not hear so well and that younger groups may talk too much and too loud.

THE FOCUS GROUP ITSELF

GETTING UNDERWAY

Name cards are a necessity for almost every session, if only for the moderator. If name cards have not been prepared in advance, participants should be instructed to write their first names—in large letters—on the cards.

There should be a brief discussion of the ground rules for the session. Only one person should speak at a time (this is difficult to enforce if the discussion becomes lively and also worthwhile). Titles should be avoided. The moderator tells the purpose of the session, stating that the sponsoring firm looks forward to the group's discussion on this topic as an aid in deciding on a crucial matter. If necessary, there may be a brief account of what the sponsoring firm is, what it does, and why problems such as this make so much difference. Some mention of what will be done with the results of the session is in order.

Usually, the participants introduce themselves with a few short remarks.

The one-way mirror should be explained to the participants, who will quickly forget about it. Other equipment can be mentioned, and this too will be quickly ignored by the participants. Exhibit 10.1 shows clients observing a group session.

Refreshments, if any, should be offered before or after the session. One of the authors, in early innocence, offered cans of beer to a group of contractors. The resulting tape sounded like the War of 1812. Even dishes and cups can be noisy.

Exhibit 10.1   CLIENTS OBSERVING GROUP SESSION

Source: Courtesy Elrick & Lavidge.

CONDUCTING THE SESSION

The moderator's guide should include coverage of all phases of the research problem. This guide should be used to steer participants into discussion of the areas the sponsor wants covered.

If there is good rapport between the moderator and the group, it should not be necessary for the moderator to spend time merely asking questions and receiving answers. With good rapport, participants should quickly find themselves eagerly voicing their thoughts without prodding.

But there will always be those who talk too much and those who talk hardly at all. The quiet ones do not necessarily have golden thoughts to voice, but they should be given their chance. The louder members may be dominating simply to hide their fears and ignorance. Not being psychiatrists, we can only point out that these types of people do show up and must be dealt with. A well-chosen moderator will be experienced enough to draw out the quiet ones and to quiet the talkative ones.

The discussion must be serious but never boring. Lighter moments can be built into the guide. A deadly serious one and a half hours can be just that: deadly and not productive. Lighter moments do not come from telling prepared jokes. They come from the moderator's own humor, which in turn ignites humor among the group. Some fear that lighter moments and humor will lessen the success of the session itself. We can only say that our experience tells us that a session conducted with lighter moments and a few good laughs is likely to be more productive and beneficial in the long run.

CLOSING THE SESSION

At the end of the discussion, it is up to the moderator to summarize the suggestions made, the ideas expressed, and the attitudes that became apparent. The group will now want to feel the importance of what it has just said. The moderator need not overdo this praise. The group will quickly see through too lavish commendation. What the participants really want is an explanation of how their thoughts can be turned into action. Perhaps a new-product idea will be passed along to the sponsor, or a difficult-to-open package will be modified.

WRAP-UP AND REPORT

Debriefing and wrap-up should be done immediately after the session, if the client's representatives are present. They have heard all the talk and now need to know how their impressions accord with the moderator's. Strong points can be emphasized and errors noted while they are fresh in everyone's minds. What major ideas and suggestions came from the session? If other groups are to be used, what lessons about running the sessions can be learned from this experience?

Debriefing and wrap-up can also come after the conclusion of a number of sessions on the same research problem. Here the emphasis will be on those ideas and attitudes that were common to all groups.

There may be a written or video screen report. This should emphasize all the important attitudes and issues expressed by one or more of the groups. The needs of the sponsor can begin to mesh with the ideas and thoughts of the group.

When the findings are presented to the client and/or the advertising agency, they will be succinct and clearly worded so that the client can quickly see how this research will help the firm achieve its goals in the market.

The report should also recommend further research necessary to put quantitative meaning behind the qualitative determinations of the group.

INDUSTRIAL FOCUS GROUPS

Focus groups that deal with industrial research problems are much like those covering consumer products, but with several important differences.

First, the moderator must be quite knowledgeable in the field being discussed. All moderators may know about corn flakes or shopping in supermarkets, but not all know enough about printing presses to conduct a discussion with a group of technicians from newspapers. Thus the screening of possible moderators in industrial areas must be even more thorough than for those in consumer product areas.

Preparing the moderator and the moderator's guide about the industrial problem must also be very thorough. It may be advisable to have an in-house moderator lead the discussion, or to at least have one in the room to help the moderator over difficult technical points. Also, participants in industrial focus groups must be carefully chosen to make sure that each can speak to the problem.

Time considerations are important. More so than a consumer product group, a group of technical people will become impatient if a session runs too long or becomes too wordy and repetitive. However, if interest becomes keen, participants may wish to continue the discussion. Cutting off such discussion in this circumstance would be a mistake.

To maintain a true focus group atmosphere, a company representative, if one is in the focus group room, should never be allowed to turn the discussion into a sales event.

The great value of focus groups is their ability to delve into motivations, rational or irrational, for the way people act in the market. A group discussion allows a few people to let their minds range freely into the reasons why they act the way they do in the market, or why they think they will act in certain ways in the future.

Focus groups seek new ideas for their sponsors by finding answers to such questions as: What if the firm does do this or that in the market? What are consumers likely to do? What do you really think about our product and its distribution? Are there any changes, big or little, that would make our product more acceptable to you?

Focus groups are likely to remain with us far into the future. Their value is too great to ignore. What we must all do when using focus groups, however, is make sure that our groups are being planned carefully and carried out properly. A poor presentation may weaken or kill the results of many months of work. It is the duty of the marketing research agency and its clients to keep abreast of new developments for presentation.

ENDNOTES

[1]Thomas L. Greenbaum. *The Practical Handbook and Guide to Focus Group Research*. Lexington, Mass.: Heath, 1988.

[2]"Marketing." *News from Market Opinion Research*, Fall 1988.

[3]Kimball Wheatley and William A. Flexmer. "Option Technologies, Inc." *Marketing News*, Feb. 27, 1987, 23.

[4]"The Teleconference Network.™" *The Market Navigator*, Orangeburg, N.Y., 1990.

[5]Brochure, TeleSession Corp. New York, 1990.

[6]News release from FocusVision Network Inc., Newport Beach, Calif., 1990.

REFERENCES

Blum, Anthony G., and Kathy Law. "Making Focus Groups Even More Effective." *Agri Marketing*, March 1984, 24 f.

Clark, Lincoln G. "Focus Groups Are a Phone Call Away." *Marketing News*, American Marketing Association, Jan. 3, 1986.

Ferber, Robert. *Handbook of Marketing Research*. New York: McGraw-Hill, 1974.

Greenbaum, Thomas L. "Keys to Improving the Effectiveness of Focus Group Research." *Marketing Review*, June–July 1984, 23.

Hammond, Meryl. "Creative Focus Groups: Uses and Misuses." *Marketing and Media Decisions*, July 1986, 154–156.

Levy, Sandra. "Listening to America Behind See-Through Mirrors." *Adweek*, Jan. 24, 1984, 24 f.

Miskovic, Darlene. "Behind the Mirror: Here Are Some Rules That Can Help Sharpen the Value of Focus Groups." *Advertising Age*, Nov. 17, 1980, 55.

"1991 Focus Group Facilities Directory." *Quirk's Marketing Research Review*, December 1990.

Rydholm, Joseph. "Regaining a Foothold." *Quirk's Marketing Research Review*, December 1990, 8 ff.

Schwartz, Joe. "Why They Buy." *American Demographics*, March 1989, 40 f.

Silverman, George R. *The Teleconference Network*. Division of Market Navigation Inc. Various publications on focus groups appearing from time to time.

11

SUMMARIZING RESULTS

What's in This Chapter

In this chapter we show how research results are put into meaningful patterns. We discuss the procedures involved in converting completed questionnaires into tables, the importance of coding, and the statistical treatment of survey data. Finally, we emphasize the significance of the computer in transforming and facilitating the interpretation of research information.

The two major tools used in summarizing results of marketing research are tabulation and statistical treatment. Computers have brought a tremendous assist to both.

Tabulation is patterning data into summary tables. Basically, that is what marketing research is all about. Whether we are talking about scanner data from retail stores or responses to a survey, tables are the basic way of presenting the summary of the data. For consistency and simplicity, our major emphasis is on survey data.

Tabulation is the preparation of tables showing the frequency distribution of particular events. Depending on how the data were collected, it may be the number of people who respond to a question in a particular way, the number passing a given point (for a location or a billboard study), or the number behaving in some manner (such as purchasing a particular product category or brand).

We start with an example of a simple table, computer-produced, in Exhibit 11.1, virtually self-explanatory. It shows the distribution by age in a survey of 675, by ownership of the product, by income, by sex, and by each of the nine communities within which the study was done.

Exhibit 11.1   **DISTRIBUTION OF SELECTED DEMOGRAPHICS BY AGE**

	OWNERS			INCOME		SEX		CITY COMMUNITY								
	NOW	NON	FOR-MER	UNDER 25000	25000 &OVER	MALE	FE-MALE	KETT-ERING	CEN-TER-VILE	MIAMI TWP.	WEST CAR-ROL-LTON	MIA-MIS-BURG	MOR-AINE	OAK-WOOD	WASH-ING-TON TWP.	BEA-VER-CREEK
SAMPLE SIZE NO ANSWER	300	300	75	236	233	195	397	109	109	109	58	58	58	58	58	58
PERCENT BASE	300 100%	300 100%	75 100%	236 100%	233 100%	195 100%	397 100%	109 100%	109 100%	109 100%	58 100%	58 100%	58 100%	58 100%	58 100%	58 100%
DEMOGRAPHICS--AGE																
24 YEARS & UNDER	32 10.7	10 3.3	9 12.0	20 8.5	13 5.6	17 8.7	28 7.1	12 11.0	7 6.4	11 10.1	6 6.9	4 6.9	6 10.3	4 6.9	2 3.4	1 1.7
25 TO 34 YEARS	73 24.3	48 16.0	24 32.0	61 25.9	58 24.9	38 19.5	85 21.4	12 11.0	23 21.1	27 24.8	15 25.8	18 31.1	15 25.9	12 20.7	9 15.5	14 24.1
35 TO 44 YEARS	91 30.3	42 14.0	19 25.3	34 16.1	80 34.3	48 24.7	93 23.4	18 16.5	31 28.4	31 28.4	9 15.5	11 19.0	9 15.5	8 13.8	18 31.1	17 29.3
45 TO 54 YEARS	65 21.7	54 18.0	11 14.7	29 12.3	48 20.6	40 20.5	75 18.9	15 13.8	26 23.9	14 12.8	11 19.0	14 24.1	9 15.5	19 32.7	10 17.2	13 20.7
55 TO 64 YEARS	28 9.3	80 26.7	7 9.3	48 20.3	25 10.7	34 17.4	66 16.6	32 29.4	16 14.7	17 15.6	8 13.8	6 10.3	12 20.7	4 6.9	13 22.5	7 12.1
65 YEARS & OLDER	11 3.7	66 22.0	5 6.7	40 16.9	9 3.9	18 9.2	50 12.6	20 18.3	6 5.5	9 8.3	11 19.0	5 8.6	7 12.1	11 19.0	6 10.3	7 12.1
MEDIAN	40	54	37	45	41	44	44	53	43	40	46	41	44	48	45	43

Mere summaries may be misleading. Sometimes additional sense can be deducted from results by treating them statistically. Take another look at Exhibit 11.1. There are two basic statistical treatments there—we call them "statistics" for short—that make it easier to get a handle on the meaning of the table. One is the percentage given below each number of cases in a column. The other is the median given at the bottom of each column. It is a lot simpler to compare those percentages from one column to another than it is to compare cases. It is easy to spot that there are relatively more people in the "higher" income group than in the "lower" group falling within the 35–54-year bracket. The medians make it clear that there are sharp age differences by ownership. Both generalizations would have been difficult to observe from a table showing number of cases only.

TABULATION

INTRODUCTION

The Process of Tabulation

There are three steps in converting completed questionnaires to tables: editing, coding, and counting. However, today, when almost no tabulating is done other than by computer, the order of the actual process is somewhat reversed. We will explain this later in the chapter.

The Need for Early Planning of Tabulation

Data processing, as it is commonly termed today, should be planned at the time of the study design. There are at least three good reasons why this is so.

First, the researcher or marketer must think about specific potential results. If thinking and planning are well done, this means plans for specific tables are made as part of the basic study plan. Forgive a homely analogy: When you buy a side of beef for home use, you don't just haul away the whole thing. You have it cut up into freezer-storable and meal-usable pieces. So also in marketing research. The tabulation planning should also be done in advance. The carving up of the returns should be thoroughly planned in advance so as to meet the marketing needs of the study.

Second, the data collection method should be tailored to provide efficient data processing. We are talking mainly about precoding of questionnaires. Precoding is the printing of assigned codes to various answers listed on the questionnaire. As mentioned in Chapter 9, whenever possible and reasonable, alternative replies to a question should be listed on the questionnaire. More about this shortly.

Third, only if data processing is thoroughly planned is table production inexpensive. The going-in time, the setup time is costly. If an outside firm is being used, poor advance thinking about tables will be costly. Additional runs really chew up the dollars.

EDITING

Editing is the inspection of questionnaires (or other data form), with modification or correction of replies. At first blush, this sounds as though the sponsor of the study is acting as a censor, making sure that results come out as hoped. This is not the case at all. Editing is not editorializing. The function of an editor of a publication is to make the best sense out of what is in hand, and that is exactly the purpose in editing marketing research data.

A specific intent is to eliminate or minimize errors in the raw data. There are two basic forms of error: interviewer error and respondent error.

Interviewers make mistakes. They may check wrong response categories, for example, or they may fail to ask the proper flow-through questions. They may be poor at recording open-ended responses. Of course, with a computer-assisted program, many of these errors can be minimized or eliminated during the interviewing process.

Respondents also make errors. They may be inconsistent in their replies. They may say at one point that they do not smoke, yet later talk confidently as regular smokers.

Editing blows away some of the smoke. Through checks of consistency within a single questionnaire, it improves the quality of the raw data.

The Process of Editing

Editing is done in one or both of two ways: personal editing and computer editing.

In the personal-editing process (where the computer is not a part of the process), there can be as many as three steps: the interviewer, the field editor, and the central research office. While personal editing still serves its purposes, in this computer age it has been largely superseded.

The computer-editing process starts at the point of data collection. Here, if the method is by telephone or one of the interactive systems, the editing process is computerized. If the respondent or the interviewer enters an inconsistent response, the computer will not let it pass. The error must be corrected before the next question appears on the screen.

Computer checking is simple and efficient. The computer is told the acceptable patterns for sequential questions, what to look for in contingent questions and inconsistent replies, and how to handle no-replies. If hard-and-fast rules for the particular correction can be set up, the computer performs automatically. If a particular response becomes a judgment call or requires going back to the original questionaire for checking, the computer can be instructed to buck it back to the editor for handling.

CODING: AN INTRODUCTION

Coding is the assignment of a number (occasionally some symbol such as a letter) to represent each reply to a question on a questionnaire. The code is merely an ID, if you will, and is used to identify both nonquantified material as well as actual numerical data, as each appears in answers.

Coding translates the raw materials (answers) into simpler and more readily countable form. In these days of general computer use in summarizing data, it is a definite requirement; the computer can deal only with numbers. So the marketing researcher has to know what coding is all about.

It is true that GIGO (garbage in, garbage out) applies to the computerized era of marketing research.[1] Nicely arranged data tables are produced for the analyst. From that point on, marketing decisions are made. But without considerable care about the input, these lovely tables may be dangerously acceptable and misleading. Coding is not a function to be left to the inept. The coding of open-ended question responses, in particular, requires skilled researchers and should never be left to an individual field investigator.

To understand how numerical coding works, think of a coding structure that provides 80 or more basic locations (columns) numbered 1 through 80. Many computer experts compare these 80 locations to lines of identical houses in a development. But that is only half of the concept. Each house needs its own specific mailbox, and there are up to 25 of these available in each column, for a total of 2,000, but deduct 1 space because computers start at 0 instead of 1. So there are 1,999 mailboxes or addresses. Any single complete code for a question has to either be incorporated into this space or extend over into a new space.

Exhibit 11.2 shows a prelisted-categories question with codes included.

We have used three columns (7 through 9) in this code structure, along with code positions running from 1 through 0 in Columns 7 and 8 and the first two positions in Column 9.

It would have been possible to provide coders with the list of answers and codes and have them enter the codes (either directly into the computer or onto the questionnaire, with machine entry a separate step). But as often as possible these days, the codes are part of the questionnaire, since this minimizes error and saves time and money. When the codes are entered on the questionnaire, the term is *precoding*.

Exhibit 11.2   QUESTIONS WITH CODES

To which of these types of groups, if any, do you belong? As I mention each one, please tell me whether you are currently a member.

Church group	Yes [ ] 7–1	No [ ] 7–2
PTA	Yes [ ] 7–3	No [ ] 7–4
Fraternal group	Yes [ ] 7–5	No [ ] 7–6
Civic club	Yes [ ] 7–7	No [ ] 7–8
Charitable or fund-raising group	Yes [ ] 7–9	No [ ] 7–0
Musical group (other than church)	Yes [ ] 8–1	No [ ] 8–2
Sports club	Yes [ ] 8–3	No [ ] 8–4
Political club or group	Yes [ ] 8–5	No [ ] 8–6
Card club	Yes [ ] 8–7	No [ ] 8–8
Volunteer group (where you provide time and service without pay)	Yes [ ] 8–9	No [ ] 8–0
Other social group	Yes [ ] 9–1	No [ ] 9–2

CODING: THE THREE BASIC TYPES

Three types of coding are required to handle the three basic kinds of data collected in surveys: names, quantitative data, and qualitative data.

Name Codes

Name codes apply to brands or makes, firms, or other things such as television show names or personalities. The names in the list are almost always known in advance and are finite. If it is a product study, it is simple enough to prelist the brand names that will account for the majority of replies, and the same applies to a prelisting of retailers or manufacturers. (There is some risk in providing such lists on self-administered questionnaires, where respondent error may result.)

Quantitative Codes

Quantitative codes are used with questions that request replies in terms of numbers.

Whatever the nature of the quantitative question, categories should be mutually exclusive. For example, too often the question about household income shows categories such as:

$30,000–$35,000
$35,000–$40,000

There is no single place to list a $35,000 income.

Quantitative questions come in two forms for coding. One is the closed-end list, and the other has categories that can be set up only after the answers are in hand. Here are three examples of the closed-end type of quantitative question:

How many times have you eaten dinner at home in the past seven days, not including today?

What size and width of shoe do you, yourself, wear?

Do you, yourself, own a car? If so, what model year is it?

In each case, answer categories can be set up in advance. The range is known.

With open-ended quantitative questions, there are definite problems, even though there may be a rough idea of the range of answers. The likely distribution of answers is not known in advance. Setting up categories in advance may produce data that destroy the chances to analyze data, or, worse, actually distort results. Here are three questions that illustrate what we mean:

At what time did you first turn on your television yesterday?

What price did you pay when you last bought a can of Campbell's soup? [This is a poor question; it is used only to help illustrate our point.]

When did you last buy fresh beef in any form?

Consider the television question. Beyond its assumption that the person *did* look at television yesterday, since most viewers tune in on the hour or half-hour, answer categories should—depending on the marketing purposes of the study—be by half-hour period to tie in with behavior.

In the soup question, there is a similar problem for a completely different reason. Retailers commonly use "psychological" pricing, believing a price of 49 cents is far more appealing than 50 cents, or 99 cents more appealing than $1. Though this assumption has never been tested, it does mean that in the soup illustration a category of 40 cents–49 cents would almost certainly not be representative of the array of replies. Too many of the replies in the category would be at the upper end.

The question about beef demonstrates another point. To start with, it is almost impossible to predict the range of answers. People who buy fresh meat may store it in the freezer section of the refrigerator, and some, despite health warnings, keep it there for months. More important, even if it were known in advance that most such purchases were made within the past seven days, with a clustering of replies around three days, this is not an indication that only two categories—within the past seven days and more than seven days ago—are the right ones to use. The categories would not be sufficiently sensitive (discriminatory, in statistical terms).

To give another example, a study of beer drinkers asked about beer-drinking preferences and occasions. The brewer wanted to analyze results by heaviness of beer drinking (heavy, medium, light) and wanted the groups to be numerically equal for data analysis. It was necessary, then, to know the amounts of beer consumed by each person in the survey, so that the three groups could be defined before the production of the "final" tables.

If the question is aimed at producing results that can be compared with known data, such as census figures on household income, it makes sense to start with a quantitative list paralleling the reported categories. If the results of the study are to be compared with previous studies, where applicable the quantitative categories should be the same.

In summary, here are the guidelines to setting up categories for quantitative codes:

1. They should be mutually exclusive.
2. Where feasible, they should be of equal size.
3. They should be representative of the particular series.
4. They should tie in with the marketing purposes of the particular study.
5. (Where applicable) They should parallel categories of existing data.

Today the computer takes over much of the work in establishing quantitative categories. Each specific response can be entered into the system and totaled for each specific category. These preliminary runs give the researcher or marketer the information needed to set up the quantitative categories that meet all requirements. Then appropriate class intervals can be set up and the computer instructed to enter this information for each questionnaire.

Qualitative Codes

The qualitative question typically produces a conversational type of reply having to do with descriptions, explanations, and reasons. There is no list of answers from which the respondent makes a choice. The question is open-ended. The answers can range widely, and it may be difficult to make sense of them. Setting up codes for qualitative answers—if the analysis is to be useful—calls for much thought in terms of what the particular question is intended to contribute by way of information for the specific study. As we will show in Chapter 14, for instance, the DAR (Day After Recall) measurement of broadcast advertising asks open-ended questions about recall of program content to establish whether the person really was exposed to the program.

Setting up codes for such open-ended questions is often much more difficult than this. People drink beer. They comment on their reasons for doing so. If these comments are simply listed in the report, replies will vary and make little sense. People drink beer because it makes them feel good. People drink beer because it makes them more sociable. Some regard it almost as a reward after mowing the lawn or spending time on some other chore. Some drink beer because they find it is refreshing or has a flavor they enjoy. Some report they drink it because it is relatively inexpensive. Some say they drink it because that's what their friends drink when they get together. All this sounds confusing. But if the reasons are classified under only a few headings, they begin to make sense.

Categories such as *social reasons, physical effects, flavor, a reward for effort, refreshing,* and *economy* might do it.

The respondent's viewpoint must also be considered in setting up categories of these qualitative answers. In a restaurant study asking why patrons come there, an open-ended question might produce answers covering a broad range: "to save money," "there's lots of parking space," "no reservations are needed," "the food is good," "you never have to wait for a table," "the servers are friendly," "there's a broad menu selection," "it's near where I work," or "it's the best steak place in town." With answers strung out like this, it is difficult to see a pattern. But categories such as *good food, reasonable prices, convenience,* and *service* bring some semblance of order.

As with quantitative questions, the computer provides an easy way of setting up these categories in advance of final tables. As we show later in this chapter, the more sophisticated computer tabulating programs provide the opportunity to enter each qualitative response from questionnaires and print them out. The researcher or marketer can then review them, set up appropriate categories, and have the computer enter the category for each response before running the final tables.

STATISTICAL TREATMENT: GIVING MEANING TO SURVEY NUMBERS

Few single numbers coming out of surveys provide much marketing meaning by themselves. A study shows that 250 people bought a particular brand of a product over a specified period of time. By itself that figure has no meaning. We have to know much more than that to make any sense of the figure. The nature and size of the sample must be known, though these are not the concern of this chapter. Using percentages makes things a lot easier to grasp but also requires thorough understanding. Percentages don't always mean what they seem to. They can be, and often are, mistreated and misinterpreted.

RAW NUMBERS AND PERCENTAGES

What is that 250 a part of? The 250 brand purchaser figure begins to assume some meaning if we are told that this is a sample of 1,000, and therefore 25 percent had bought it within the measured period. We understand still more if we know that this 25 percent is among a sample of people provided with a cents-off coupon for the brand and that the usual level of purchase is 10 percent. Now we can start to make some marketing sense of the figures. We are beginning to use percentages, and these make the data a lot easier to understand.

There are caveats in the use of percentages, however. Just because they are in an easy-to-understand form doesn't make them the answer to everything. Their simplicity will not eliminate the rule of thumb that a sample or subsample of under 100 has little dependability.

Another warning: Percentages from different groups of people should not be averaged. Take a look at Exhibit 11.3, which shows the percentage of brand users for three age groups. Let us say that we want to determine the percentage of users in the first two groups to arrive at a figure showing usage among those age 18 to 49. Averaging the two percentages gives a figure of 7.4 percent.

Exhibit 11.3　PERCENTAGE OF BRAND USERS AMONG THREE AGE GROUPS

	18–29	30–49	50 and Over
Total interviews	100.0%	100.0%	100.0%
Brand users	14.0	.8	.4

7.4%

But now we let the numbers as well as the percentages tell the story, and put in a third column as well, to show the total for the combined 18–49 group, as shown in Exhibit 11.4.

When the two age groups are combined in terms of their real weights in the study, the resultant *correct* brand usage figure for the 18–49 group turns out to be 5.8 percent. While the difference from the average percentage may not appear all that great, the two figures might be of rather different marketing significance in terms of the particular problem. And the difference between an *averaged* percentage and a *weighted* one might be far greater.

There is yet another caution in the use of percentages. A 50 percent rise followed by a 50 percent drop in volume or replies (or whatever is being measured) does not mean a net change of 0. If the volume starts at 100 units, rises 50 percent to 150 units, then drops 50 percent to 75 units, the net change is clearly a drop. The problem is the changing base on which each percentage was calculated. The higher the base, the greater the numbers implicit in a percentage.

The percentage must be stated proportionately to some norm and examined in relationship to other numbers, all related to the marketing purposes of the study. So we discuss raw numbers and percentages, the difference between numbers, and the similarities between numbers.

Exhibit 11.4   NUMBER AND PERCENTAGE OF BRAND USERS AMONG TWO AGE GROUPS

	18–29		30–49		Total 18–49	
	No.	%	No.	%	No.	%
Total interviews	150	100.0%	250	100.0%	400	100.0%
Brand users	21	14.0	2	.8	23	5.8

AVERAGES

Averages (what statisticians call *measures of central tendency*) come in three forms: the mode, the mean, and the median.

The Mode

Fashion-wise, we all understand the meaning of the term *mode*: Everybody's wearing it or doing it. Statistically, the term has almost the identical definition: It represents the point in the array showing the greatest response level. It is not an average used often in marketing research.

The Mean

The *mean* is a commonly used average in marketing research. It is readily understood as the sum total of values divided by the number of cases. However, it has one shortcoming. It is affected by a few large or small numbers (skewing), since it is based on all the values in the array. In terms of household income, for instance, the presence of a small number of very wealthy families in the study could produce mean income results not truly representative of the typical family in the sample. The mean income is too large to be descriptive of the typical family.

The Median

The median is the value of the middle case in a series. There are as many cases on the higher side as on the lower side. The measure offers the advantage of being unaffected by extreme cases at one end or the other.

An Example

Exhibit 11.5 demonstrates the case. It shows that the starting point in choosing the measure of central tendency to be used is to calculate and examine all three types of averages. If the mean and median are about the same, the mean should be used. It is the most common and generally the most understood. But if the mean and median are greatly different, the median probably should be used as more representative.

Exhibit 11.5   INCOME OF 25 SURVEY HOUSEHOLDS

$95,000	$83,500	$64,000	$36,000	$29,500
90,000	70,000	63,500	34,000	29,000
89,000	68,000	61,000	32,500	28,000
87,500	65,000	40,000	31,500	27,000
86,000	64,000	38,000	30,000	26,000

Mean	$54,720
Median	61,000
Mode	64,000

The Answer on Averages

For marketing research, the answer on averages is use of either the mean or the median or both. Depending on the nature of the numerical distribution, these may or may not be close. Together they provide a good indication of what the average really is.

DIFFERENCES BETWEEN NUMBERS

Understanding the marketing significance of survey numbers takes a lot of doing. It means understanding whether the difference between two or more numbers, or sets of numbers, is probably real, and whether the relationship of two numbers may be causal.

Difference between Numbers in a Single Array

Suppose that in a survey of 1,500, results showed that 64 percent chose Brand X, 24 percent chose Brand Y, and the remainder made no choice. Are these real differences?

Assuming that this was a probability sample, as described in Chapter 8, the answer is *yes*. If you turn back to Exhibit 8.9 (page 193), you will see that with a 1,500 sample, the sampling error for 64 percent is some 2.5 percent, and for 25 percent it is some 2.2 percent.

Difference between Numbers in Sets of Numbers

By sets of numbers we mean a series of arrays. An example is a comparison of results on a question shown by men and women.

Cross-tabulation is the starting point. A cross-tabulation shows, for instance, the use of beer by sex, or the number of miles driven by car owners in several age groups, or how many in one group versus another group enter into various kinds of community activity. The differences, if they hold up statistically, may have tremendous marketing significance. We do not get into the sampling statistics here. They are discussed in Chapter 8.

The selection of aspects to be cross-tabulated is crucial. The basic need is to spot cross-tabulations that might lead to marketing decisions.

There are two distinct types of cross-tabulations. One is so-called "typical" breaks, including demographics (such as geography, household size, presence of children, income, sex, and age). The other is "special" breaks determined by the specific needs of the study (such as awareness or use of a product category or brand and purchase intent). Differences by age groups or frequency of exposure to advertising could be crucial to a marketing campaign.

Are the differences between such figures real enough for marketing decisions to be based on them?

The first thing to do is look at the specific differences in percentages. The statistical method already outlined for comparing numbers in a single array applies. But in the case of sets of numbers, things are a bit more complex. We purposely avoid describing the statistical procedure for measuring the statistical significance (reality) of differences between two percentages from different arrays of data, but, in brief, the dependability of such differences—again assuming probability sampling—rests on the number of cases in each category and the proportion of those giving the particular answer or answers being compared.

A study of users of a brand of roll-on deodorant shows that 59 percent find it "highly acceptable." A study a year ago produced a 50 percent figure. In each case, the sample size was 1,000. Is this a real difference? Exhibit 11.6 shows that based on a probability of 93 percent, it is a real difference. This is a greatly abbreviated table, shown mainly to demonstrate the point. We have used the maximum error range (at the 50 percent category reply level). It would be possible to produce tables showing cross-hatched details by the percentage of respondents replying in each case and the sample size in each case.

Chi-square is another statistical tool to evaluate the statistical significance of differences between sets of data. It basically compares one or more frequency distributions of data to indicate whether there is a real difference. It compares an actual set of data against a theoretical one to show what would be expected by chance alone.

To show how chi-square works, a hypothetical set of results is given in Exhibit 11.7. This shows the results for a question versus statistically

Exhibit 11.6   **SIGNIFICANT DIFFERENCES BETWEEN PERCENTAGES WITH DIFFERENT SAMPLES OF CONSTANT SIZE**

Sample Size	Significant Difference
100	5.00
500	4.48
1,000	3.16
1,500	2.58

Note: These are gross measurements where the category reply level is figured at 50 percent, the maximum sampling error range.

Exhibit 11.7   **HYPOTHETICAL RESULTS FOR A DICHOTOMOUS QUESTION**

Q: **Did you, personally, happen to drive a car within the past 24 hours?**

	Real or Observed Distribution		Expected or Chance Distribution
	Men	*Women*	*Men or Women*
Yes	60%	40%	50%
No	40	60	50

expected results. The statistical analysis uses the sum of the differences between the real and the expected values as the key. The calculation is somewhat more involved than this, but there is no need to outline the details, since all we want to do is to acquaint you with the nature of the measurement.

USE OF SIMILARITIES BETWEEN NUMBERS TO SHOW CAUSE AND EFFECT

Another major use and application of numbers in marketing research is analysis and understanding of the similarities between numbers. Since this is essentially a discussion of the possible causality of some numbers, we start right there.

Columnist James Kilpatrick gives an interesting example.[2] In 1987 Congress amended the law to allow states to raise the speed limit from 55 to 65 miles per hour on rural segments of interstate highways. During the first year of change, fatalities on these segments rose 14 percent.

This looks like a solid case against the increased limit. One of the most detailed reports came from Maine, where on one stretch of rural interstate fatalities jumped from 1 to 13. But let's look at the nature of the cases. The single case in 1987 came from intoxication. In 1988 here is how the causes were distributed for the 13 cases:

- 6 drivers fell asleep.
- 2 drivers were drunk.
- 1 driver took ill at the wheel.
- 1 driver swerved to avoid an animal.
- 1 driver tried to make a U-turn and was hit by a truck.
- 1 driver lost control when he tried to pick up a can from the floor.
- 1 driver swerved into the median, reentered the road, and rolled over several times; it was raining and the driver was speeding.

So while the speed limit had been raised, speed had nothing to do with the increased fatality rate.

We rather like an illustration from another culture. Body lice in the New Hebrides Islands was considered a cause of good health. Why? When people became ill they developed fevers, and the body lice left to find more comfortable hosts. So no body lice and illness occurred together and made it easy to conclude that the first led to the second.[3]

A medical intern earns far less—his or her income being almost at poverty level—than a person with only a bachelor's degree who enters business or industry at the same time. But, of course, the advanced degree is not the cause of the lower income. Income adjustments will occur shortly.

In general, the greater the church attendance in a community, the greater the number of bars. Thus it looks as though setting up a number of bars will increase church attendance. Not true, of course. All the generalization indicates is that larger communities have both more bars and greater numbers of people attending church.

The next example, from marketing research, is closer to home. Many surveys try to measure the sales impact of advertising (or other marketing efforts). One often used procedure compares the proportion of purchasers among two groups: those who remember seeing or hearing the advertising and those who do not. Exhibit 11.8 shows brand purchase by those who recall the brand's advertising and those who do not. The obvious but incorrect conclusion from the exhibit is that advertising accounted for the 15 percent difference in purchase level. But the results actually show only that there is a correlation between advertising awareness and purchase. The correlation may be due to people who purchase the brand and then become more aware of its advertising. Particu-

Exhibit 11.8   BRAND BUYING AND ADVERTISING RECALL

	Those Remembering Advertising	Those Not Remembering Advertising
Total Group	100%	100%
Purchased Brand	20	5
Did not Purchase	80	95

larly in the case of higher-priced items, psychologists have found that people "shop" the ads after purchase to help reinforce their purchase choice.

These examples (statisticans refer to them as showing "spurious correlation") do not mean that correlation, as a statistical tool, is of no use. It *is* useful. One simply has to know how to use it and interpret its results.

Measuring Relationships by Cross-Tabulation

The example given in Exhibit 11.8 illustrates the use of cross-tabulation to determine the amount of similarity in two sets or subsets of data in one or more surveys.

If marketing research is to be useful in marketing decisions, the cross-tabulation that might assist in leading to marketing decisions must be spotted. Differences by age groups, or even concentration on a single age segment, might suggest different approaches for each target market by age.

Measuring Relationships by Statistical Formulas

Cross-tabulations in surveys are helpful when they are planned with insight. But they lack the precision of statistical treatment, and so we must take a look at such measures. Remember, though, that correlation does not prove causality, and that even the refinements of statistical treatment cannot alter that fact.

There are two major categories of correlation analysis: bivariate and multivariate. *Bivariate analysis* measures the relationship between two variables. *Multivariate analysis* measures the relationship among three or more variables. We start with bivariate analysis.

Take a look at Exhibit 11.9, a scatter diagram. Based on a sample survey of 1,000 cases, it shows for each household in the sample, when

Exhibit 11.9   SEVEN-DAY SPENDING FOR PRODUCT CATEGORY BY COMMUNITY SIZE

Community Size

A   B   C   D   E   F
(where A is smallest, F is largest)

Spending	A	B	C	D	E	F	
$20.00 or more			•	••	••	••••• ••	12
19.50–19.99	•			••	•••••	•	9
19.00–19.49			•••	•••••	•		9
18.50–18.99	•	•	•••	•••			8
18.00–18.49	•	••	•••••	•••			11
17.50–17.99			••••• •••••		•		11
17.00–17.49		•••	••••• •	•			9
16.50–16.99	•••	••••	•••	•			11
16.00–16.49	••••• •	•••	•				10
15.50–15.99	••••• •••		•	•			10
	21	13	31	18	9	8	

classified by community size, how much was spent for the product category in the past seven days. We see that there is indeed a positive relationship between amount of spending and community size. It is linear, though far from perfect.

Once such data are entered into the proper formula, the possible extremes of results are from +1.00 to −1.00. The +1.00 means hat it is a perfect positive correlation, that in every case all the dots will fall on a straight line and size will be a perfect predictor of spending. The −1.00 means that there is a perfect negative relationship, and in Exhibit 11.9 all dots would have to be in a straight line running from the lower right corner to the upper-left corner. A zero figure means that there is simply no relationship whatever between the two variables, but that the dots are scattered throughout the diagram in an utterly random fashion.

In the scatter diagram as shown in Exhibit 11.9, there is a positive correlation because there is a general tendency for dollar spending to rise with community size. But it would be something less than +1.00.

To arrive at the straight correlation coefficient, it is necessary to enter, for each case in our example, the specific population and sales (not the class intervals) and run through some calculations.

Multivariate analysis may improve the understanding of how one variable is interrelated with two or more other variables. For example, a restaurant chain's sales by individual locations showed that the more dollars spent on advertising, the greater the sales. It made it appear that the right choice was to have the local restaurants spend more advertising dollars.

More careful analysis, as shown in Exhibit 11.10, showed that this marketing decision might have been wrong. Suddenly the pattern of results has shifted. Look at the results separately for the largest restaurants, the middle-sized restaurants, and the small restaurants. In the largest ones, there is indeed more business associated with heavier advertising dollars. But the pattern is fuzzy in the middle-sized restaurants, and even more so in the smaller restaurants.

The total picture, then, was misleading. The heavy weighting of the largest restaurants in overall results hid the results in the medium-sized and smaller outlets. Clearly, there were other undefined marketing policies and actions to be considered.

While the example is shown in terms of cross-tabulations, statistical multivariate analysis expresses such relationships more precisely and in fewer numbers.

In straight problem-solving survey results, it is often difficult, and sometimes impossible, to determine causality. The person planning the study has to have the foresight to include all aspects of measurement that might help determine causality. In monitoring studies, especially of those of the single-source method (see Chapter 13), causality is far more readily determined. And in marketing-planning studies, the designs are generally so limited and controlled in scope and stimulus (product, advertising, packaging, and so on) that cause and effect are virtually self-evident.

Now we want to talk briefly about three statistical tools, each somewhat different in how it works, each useful in reducing a large number of qualitative or quantitative responses to a smaller, more workable series of elements. These tools are factor analysis, cluster analysis, and discriminant analysis.

Factor analysis examines the relationship of each of a large series of variables with every other one to determine which are highly correlated with other ones. The process ends with a reduced number of packages of variables. For instance, in a consumer product test, overall ratings for the test brand are on a scale of 1 to 10, with 10 being the top rating. Rat-

Exhibit 11.10   SALES VOLUME INDEX OF RESTAURANTS
BY THEIR SEATING CAPACITY AND BY
ADVERTISING DOLLARS

	Seating Capacity		
	Largest Third	Middle Third	Smallest Third
Top half of advertising spenders	110	100	90
Bottom half of advertising spenders	90	105	91

ings of 30 aspects of the product are also each on a 1 to 10 scale. But 30
separate characteristic ratings are difficult to summarize when looking
at each cross-classified by 10 overall ratings. Factor analysis, using in-
tercorrelations as its key, may now be able to establish 5 (or some other
number) groups of factors, each group appearing to measure a unique
bundle of ratings. The researcher provides a creative name for each category after examining the elements that comprise it.

Cluster analysis is a special form of factor analysis that is applied to
people rather than objects. Its primary use in marketing research is
placing people into clusters based on demographic and psychological
profiles, as will be explained in Chapter 15.

Discriminant analysis, as Barker points out,[4] combines many features and objectives of cross-classification and regression (the use of correlation data to make predictions of an element when other variables
are known). A major application in marketing research has been to assign people to a single group, given certain information about them. It is
a common method of how marketers categorize prospects and customers. Your life insurance premium, for example, is based on the risk
category in which the firm puts you. Factors such as age, height and
weight, and medical history are typically taken into account. A man
seeking to buy beer in a particular state may be asked for an ID if his
appearance suggests that he may not be of a legal age to purchase alcohol. In marketing research, the tool is frequently used to add new names
to the customer/prospect database (see Chapter 16).

DATA PROCESSING OF SURVEYS
BY DESKTOP COMPUTER

INTRODUCTION

Today many computer programs produce survey tables. These are programs for the PC. Individual researchers or marketers can handle the

analysis and table production on their own. If after their careful advance planning of tables, they see some data they feel need further analysis, all is there at their fingertips. The individual data (for each questionnaire) may well be entered by someone else.

The basic end product is a table similar to Exhibit 11.1, early in the chapter, showing the base number of interviews and the number and percentage falling into each category.

Most programs go much further. With a numerical question, they will produce measures of central tendency: mean, median, or mode. Some produce measurements of the statistical significance of differences between means or percentages.

General Advantages

Such programs have five main advantages:

1. Speed

2. Thoroughness of analysis

3. Simplicity of use

4. Production of hard copies of standard tables

5. Production of hard copies of custom tables

Only the last of these requires any explanation. Despite everything we have said about planning the tables before the study goes to the field, we well know that there will almost *always* be additional tables the researcher or marketer sees necessary before the study has been completely finalized. Unexpected results to a question or to a cross-tabulation require additional special tables here and there. That is one of the major reasons why the PC is such a useful device for the researcher or marketer.

Canned Programs

There are many types of analyses provided by numerous software firms: survey analysis, statistical analysis, sales analysis, and graphics. Some offer controlled interviewing programs (already discussed in Chapter 7) and drawing of a sample (discussed in Chapter 8). But, with only a few exceptions, here we will discuss only programs aimed at survey analysis.

One is SPSS (SPSS Inc., Chicago). This venerable firm began providing computer software for mainframe tabulation of surveys staring in

1968,[5] long before the PC. So it has had a lot of experience. SPSS claims that its SPSS/PC+ package for microcomputers, introduced in 1984, is the world's most popular.

Like most programs, SPSS is menu-driven. The program provides summary statistics on one or more variables, including frequency counts and percentages. It provides cross-tabulations or cross-classificaitons handling up to 10-way contingency tables (including measures of association). It offers group means and standard deviations.

If the user orders the entire package there are additional possibilities, a few of which are various forms of graphs, and factor, cluster, and discriminant analysis.

QPS (Questionnaire Processing System) (DATAN, Princeton, N.J.) offers a program that permits the nontechnical user to enter and clean survey data and create tables showing frequencies. The program also can be used to create questionnaires and help carry out single-station interviews.

The Survey System[6] (Creative Research Systems, Petaluma, Calif.) is the most sophisticated survey tabulation software system we have personally examined. It has broad capabilities. While user-friendly, it distinctly requires more self-training than most desktop computer systems. Exhibits 11.11, 11.12, and 11.13 on the following pages are examples of what this program can produce. Although our review here stresses tabulation with displays showing statistical analysis of results (such as the mean, median, chi-square, standard deviation, standard error), the table in Exhibit 11.11 happens to use only the median and mode, both of which seem appropriate in this particular case. Exhibits 11.12 and 11.13 show the versatility of the program, and how it can produce camera-ready material for use in either hard-copy reports or visual presentations. The program can handle data entry through keypunching from written questionnaires or in programmed telephone interviewing. It also handles direct input from respondents, such as when respondents are in front of a display screen with instructions telling them how to respond on a keyboard. It has a tremendous capacity: 32,000 questionnaires where each may handle up to 3,000 columns each of numerical and text material.

Tabulyzer[7] (Business Research & Surveys, West Orange, N.J.) is another thorough program. It does all one could expect and turns out tables that show what they should and are easily understandable. Starting from completed, coded questionnaires, it handles up to 32,000 questionnaires with 500 questions.

Following easy steps, the user can construct camera-ready tables and print them in finished form. Exhibit 11.14 on page 273 shows a sample table, including cross-tabulation and statistical measures.

The Quik-Poll program[8] (TBX, Rome, Ga.) is another impressive program. This is for the user with minimal needs: small samples, short questionnaires, simple data analysis. Questionnaire data are easy to enter into the system, which can handle both straightforward queries (dichotomous, multiple-choice, and ranking questions) and open-ended questions, up to a total of 100 questions. The program provides straight tabulations showing numbers and percentages, plus standard deviations. The breaks and cross-tabulations are somewhat difficult to handle, however.

Exhibit 11.11   NUMERICAL PRINTOUT FROM SURVEY SYSTEM SOFTWARE PROGRAM

RESTAURANT PREFERENCE STUDY

TABLE 7:   THINKING ABOUT YOUR LAST TRIP TO A RESTAURANT, HOW MANY MILES DID YOU TRAVEL TO GET TO IT?

Base: Those who eat out 1+ times/week

| | | SEX | | AGE | | | NEIGHBORHOOD | | | |
| | | | | | | | CITY | | SUBURBS | |
	TOTAL	Male	Fe-male	25-34	35-49	50-64	East	West	East	West
BASE	491	255	236	184	165	142	70	109	183	129
1-5 Miles	191	86	105	64	67	60	34	52	70	35
	39%	34%	44%	35%	41%	42%	49%	48%	38%	27%
6-10 Miles	270	149	121	108	89	73	29	53	104	84
	55%	58%	51%	59%	54%	51%	41%	49%	57%	65%
11-15 Miles	26	17	9	9	8	9	7	3	9	7
	5%	7%	4%	5%	5%	6%	10%	3%	5%	5%
16 or more Miles	2	2		2						2
	0%	1%		1%						2%
Don't Know	2	1	1	1	1			1		1
	0%	0%	0%	1%	1%			1%		1%
MEAN	6.4	6.7	6.0	6.6	6.2	6.2	6.1	5.7	6.3	7.1
MEDIAN	6.5	6.9	6.0	6.8	6.3	6.3	5.7	5.7	6.5	7.2

Source: Reproduced with the permission of Creative Research Systems.

**Exhibit 11.12   EXAMPLE OF PIE CHART FROM SURVEY
                   SYSTEM SOFTWARE PROGRAM**

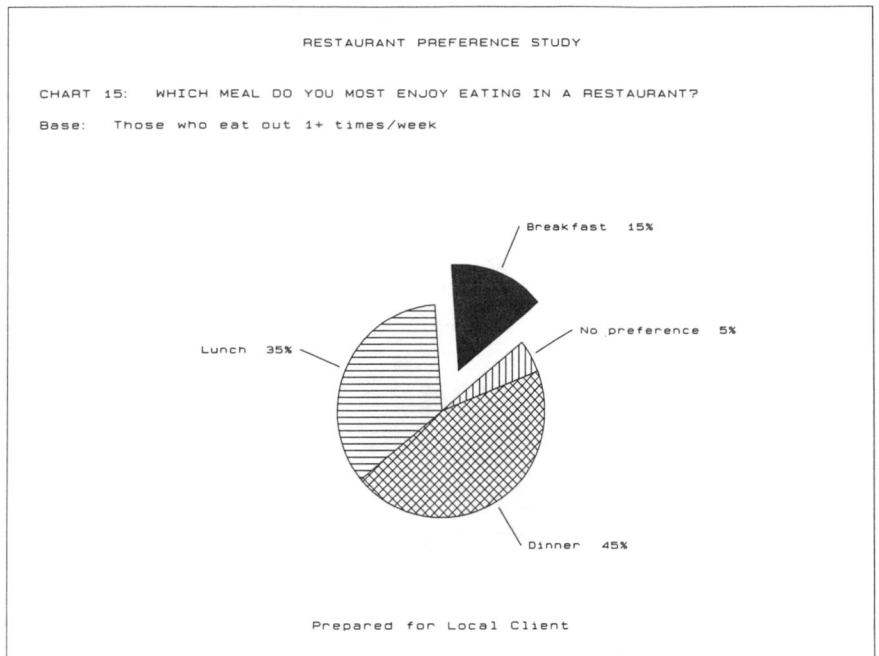

Source: Reproduced with the permission of Creative Research Systems.

Finding an Acceptable Canned Program

The starting point in finding a suitable canned program, like everything else in marketing research, is a clear definition of needs. How
large and complex are the studies likely to be? What are the demands for
statistical analysis? How important are related aspects such as questionnaire construction, sample selection, and use in controlled interviewing situations such as telephone surveys and direct respondent input?

The second step is to start listing the possible software suppliers that
might fill those needs. The annual directory of Software for Marketing
published in *Marketing News* (American Marketing Association) should
be consulted. However, the descriptions in this publication are provided
by the software manufacturers and are sometimes more advertisements
than descriptions of specifics. Also, checking with a few peers and users
helps whittle down the possibilities.

The third step is the real test of whether the particular program

Exhibit 11.13 **EXAMPLE OF BAR CHART FROM SURVEY SYSTEM SOFTWARE PROGRAM**

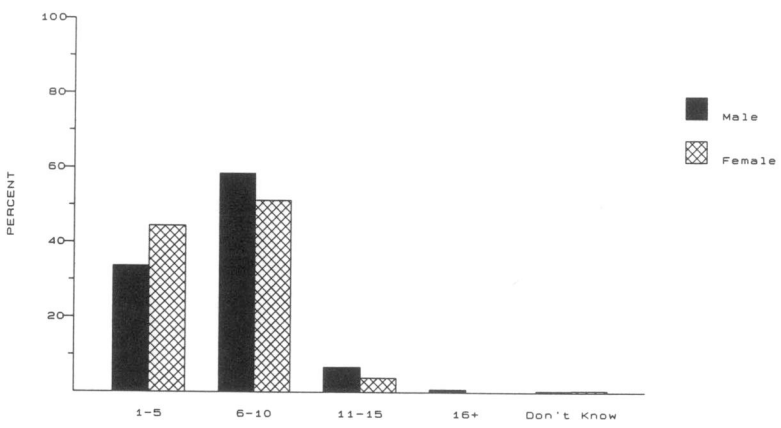

RESTAURANT PREFERENCE STUDY
CHART 7: THINKING ABOUT YOUR LAST TRIP TO A RESTAURANT, HOW MANY MILES DID YOU TRAVEL TO GET TO IT?
Base: Those who eat out 1+ times/week
PERCENT
100
80
60
40
20
Male
Female
1-5
6-10
11-15
16+
Don't Know

Source: Reproduced with the permission of Creative Research Systems.

meets the needs. It includes review of a demonstration disk and an operating manual (the hard-liners of computerization still call them "documentation"). The Information Center of the American Marketing Association (Chicago) has some of these available. Also, most software producers are willing to provide them if a sale seems likely.

THE DESKTOP COMPUTER IN SUMMARY AND ANALYSIS OF OBSERVATION DATA

INTRODUCTION

Now we move from the summarizing of *survey* results and consider other kinds of data, mainly those obtained from observation. These cover a broad range of informaiton and specific methods of collecting it. One basic distinction we will start with is between external and internal information.

External information is information that comes from sources outside

Exhibit 11.14 PRINTOUT FROM TABULYZER SOFTWARE PROGRAM

```
WHAT PERCENT OF YOUR WIDGET PURCHASES ARE
ORDERED DIRECT FROM THE MANUFACTURER?
```

	TOTAL	SIZE OF FIRM		BUSINESS CLASSIFICATION			TYPE OF WIDGET USED	
		SMALL	LARGE	BUTCH-ER	BAKER	CANDLE STICK MAKER	COPPER	ALUM-INUM
(15) Percent	2	1	1	1	0	1	1	1
	9.1%	8.3	10.0	11.1		16.7	8.3	10.0
(25)	5	2	3	2	2	1	2	3
	22.7%	16.7	30.0	22.2	28.6	16.7	16.7	30.0
(50)	4	2	2	2	1	1	2	2
	18.2%	16.7	20.0	22.2	14.3	16.7	16.7	20.0
(75)	3	2	1	1	2	0	2	1
	13.6%	16.7	10.0	11.1	28.6		16.7	10.0
(85)	4	3	1	1	1	2	1	3
	18.2%	25.0	10.0	11.1	14.3	33.3	8.3	30.0
(90)	2	1	1	2	0	0	2	0
	9.1%	8.3	10.0	22.2			16.7	
(100)	2	1	1	0	1	1	2	0
	9.1%	8.3	10.0		14.3	16.7	16.7	
TOTAL RESPONSES	22	12	10	9	7	6	12	10
BASE=NET RESPONDENTS	100.0%	100.0	100.0	100.0	100.0	100.0	100.0	100.0
MEAN	59.09	63.33	54.00	56.11	62.14	60.00	65.00	52.00
VARIANCE	851.45	780.56	889.00	798.77	741.84	1033.33	870.83	736.00
STD. DEV.	29.18	27.94	29.82	28.26	27.24	32.15	29.51	27.13
STD. ERROR	6.22	8.07	9.43	9.42	10.29	13.12	8.52	8.58
MEDIAN	74.50	75.00	50.00	50.25	74.75	84.50	75.00	50.00
CHI SQ (DF)		1.36 (6)		8.77 (12)			5.40 (6)	
T-Value		0.75		-0.43	0.13		1.08	

Source: Reproduced with the permission of Business Research Surveys.

of the marketing firm. These include product movement data typically collected on a syndicated basis, as will be described in Chapter 13, and generally using the store scanner technique of collecting the data. They also include single-source data, where the information, as described in Chapter 7, comes from the same group of households and typically uses more than a single method of collecting the data. Also included are audience data. Television measurement, as will be shown in Chapter 18, now uses a so-called people meter attached to sets in households to measure tuning and presumably viewing by individual family members.

Internal information is generally proprietary information within the files of the firm: sales of the firm's own brand(s) and those of the competition, with appropriate details of time, geography, and product nature. It may also include demographic and psychographic descriptions of its brand users and, for a particular marketing campaign, demographic and psychographic descriptions of its audience.

The purpose of a computer summary is to analyze and meld external data with internal data to provide a new understanding that will assist in the planning of marketing strategy and tactics.

The benefits depend on how well the blending and analysis are carried out.

One benefit is the solution of specific problems. This can be achieved through *custom analysis,* but this is a less-used application than *use within a system.* Such a system may have a broad base and be part of a virtual marketing information system, as described in Chapter 3. It is more likely to have a somewhat more limited base, and perhaps be part of a competitive marketing intelligence system, as described in Chapter 3. Or it may be essentially a customer/prospect databank (where continuous information is collected about customers and prospects so as to be able to market to them more effectively, as will be described in Chapter 16.

SYSTEM REQUIREMENTS

If all of the appropriate data are to be stored within the user company's computer, the memory needs will likely be so great as to require a mainframe, with selective data being requested by the individual user at a workstation with a PC. Even if only internal data are stored within the user's computer, the size of the files will almost surely require a mainframe.

One means for putting external data in the system is a direct computer connection from the database source (usually a research supplier) making use of telephone lines. This on-line procedure requires use of a modem. Some database sources have 24-hour availability.

Another method for entering external data into the system is the insertion of source-provided disks into the PC of the user. Sometimes a magnetic tape is provided by the source; when this form is used, it is primarily to place the data into a mainframe computer.

Increasingly, suppliers are providing systems, which are aimed not only at making the suppliers' data easily available, but also frequently making it compatible with other suppliers' systems. These systems can be modified to access internal data as well.

THE USE OF COMPUTER SYSTEMS

Computer systems simplify getting answers of marketing significance. Before the advent of computers, the researcher or marketer had to examine many, many tables of numbers to see what was going on. Today, there are even more tables and numbers to cope with. It would be almost impossible to get any understanding of the significant changes occurring without the kinds of systems mentioned here.

The use of a good program can locate these changes with relative ease. As we will show in Chapter 13, the program can locate significant brand and market share changes from the last time period, starting at a selected macro level (say geographic areas) and working right down to a micro level (such as major markets). Moreover, it can do this not only for the company's own brand but for the major competing brands. It can establish a baseline and spot what significant ups and downs there are in market share. Fancy statistical tools are no longer necessary for the analyst; they are necessary only as a component part of the program.

A good program can also spot reasons for a change. It will show, for example, that a competitor's share increase of .5 in one market, while all other markets were virtually flat compared with the last measurement, is associated with a sharp increase in couponing or in advertising in that single market.

ENDNOTES

[1] J. L. Pope. *Practical Marketing Research.* New York: AMACOM, 1981.

[2] James Kilpatrick. Syndicated newspaper column, Nov. 16, 1989.

[3] J. A. Paulos. *Innumeracy.* New York: Hill and Wang, 1988.

[4] R. F. Barker. *Marketing Research.* Reston, Va.: Reston Publishing, 1983.

[5] *Serious Data Analysis Software.* Chicago: SPSS, 1989.

[6] *The Survey System.* Petaluma, Calif.: Creative Research Systems, 1989.

[7] *Tabulyzer III.* West Orange, N.J.: Business Research & Surveys, undated.

[8] *Surveys for Success.* Rome, Ga.: TBX Inc., 1989.

REFERENCES

Paulos, J. A. *Innumeracy: Mathematical Illiteracy and Its Consequences.* New York: Hill and Wang, 1988.

Zeisel, Hans. *Say It with Figures.* New York: Harper, 1985.

12

PRESENTING RESEARCH RESULTS

What's in This Chapter

In this chapter we stress the importance of the presentation to the over-all success of any research study. We detail the preparation of the several parts of the presentation, differentiating where necessary between the written and the oral report. We conclude with a discussion of some of the visual and electronic aids that are available to the presenter.

THE BASIC NEED

The crucial moment has come. Research is complete and a report has been written. If the presentation of the findings and recommendations is not done well, the whole study may be gone with the wind.

The basic need for all marketing research is a report and presentation that can be believed and trusted by upper management and by all the department personnel and managers who will be affected by the research.

For nonprofit institutions, the research recommendations must show how making a particular decision or taking a certain action can help the institution do its work more efficiently and with lower cost.

No matter how relatively unimportant a particular research problem may be, its solution should clearly lead to greater efficiency, lower costs, and more short- and long-term benefits for the organization.

Somehow the presenter must quickly convince the audience, orally, in writing, or by both means, that what they are hearing is "good stuff" worthy of attention and probably something they can act upon for their own benefit.

All of us have had to sit through talks that were dull, dull, dull—talks that wandered around the subject, talks that appeared to have no point that was not drowning in an ocean of words. We have been the victims of speakers who did not know how to "work an audience," to bring them to the point where they are quite ready to accept what is being recommended. "Working an audience" is also required in a written report, which must be so planned that interest and belief build up paragraph by paragraph, illustration by illustration, to the point where the recommended action appears almost inevitable.

Marketing people should certainly know how to do this. Their jobs center on selling something. But not all of them, by any means, can present a research report with the same enthusiasm as they might have in selling a carload of soap.

So many matters in business and personal life are both well-known and unfortunately ignored. The preparation of a research report and its verbal counterpart can be of the greatest importance. Yet too often, little time has been devoted to the effect that this report will have on a particular group at a particular time.

A research report can succeed in its purpose even though it is poorly presented. But this is the hard way to go. If the subject and study are of vital importance, the recommendations and subsequent action will be remembered. And so, unhappily, will be the presenter.

Even if the report is to be presented by an outside group that performed the study under supervision, company and research people must work together to prepare a convincing presentation. If the bulk of the presentation is given by an outside research firm, the onus of success or failure lies with the firm's own marketing people, who employed the agency and supervised its work.

Preparation and practice are basic to a convincing presentation. One of the authors remembers too well a moment in his early life when he was called on to speak to an audience at a national convention in New York City. Quite unprepared, he stepped up to the podium with a brainful of treasured thoughts on the subject of his speech. He started (and should not have) with the mind-deadening "Good morning, I am delighted to be here today, etc." At that moment, great waves of hysterical fear shook his body. A thousand faces stared at him. Within seconds he was pondering escape: "I just got a message that my mother is very sick and I must leave." Good sense prevailed and the talk went well enough.

There were no major audience withdrawals to a nearby bar. The speaker no longer remembers what he said. Almost certainly, the listeners do not remember. What they had heard was a poor, underprepared talk by a speaker who really did have something worthwhile to say, but did not know how.

From the very start of a marketing research project, some thought must be given to how the report is to be presented. This may well mean the shedding of less important questions to emphasize the basic problem. Constant attention to this basic problem and its recommendations will make the study and its presentation much more usable and interesting in the minds of the listeners and/or the readers of the final presentation.

The only reason that the research presentation has its audience is the selfish desire to learn something that will help them. We all know that, but sometimes forget. The advertising manager wants to know how to put together an ad or a television spot—one that will sell more product. The product design engineer wants to be able to produce better products—products that will sell. The sales manager lives and thrives on sales; how can the research report help him now and in the near future?

Presenters will succeed if they have planned their research well and speak to these desires of their listeners. Presenters who forget that they are talking to Joe the package designer, to Mary who writes ad copy, and to the company president who is measured by the rise and fall of sales and profits have failed to do their job. A good presentation should be a mutual interplay of interest between the speaker and audience. As was suggested in Chapter 1, the development of a research study should be a mutual effort of researchers and users of research.

All of this has been said many times, we are sure. And almost as many times ignored or overlooked in the haste of a business moment. Tom Lehrer, an accomplished "audience worker," is reported to have said, "I wish people who have trouble communicating would just shut up." But most people in line and staff cannot just shut up. They must learn how to put a point across. And, of course, to do or supervise the research that has led up to that point.

One more matter: A research presentation must be like the story of the Southern preacher who told why his sermons were so successful. "First I tells 'em what I am going to tell 'em. Then I tells 'em. And finally I tells 'em what I just told 'em." Almost all good research presentations require follow-up. These may be in the form of visits to important people in the group to see what they got out of the presentation and what they intend to do about it. During these follow-up visits, it may be necessary to do some further selling. Perhaps a point was misunderstood. Perhaps the listener liked everything except one matter that was "inappropriate." Clearly, such things need attention. Perhaps a little more of "I tells 'em what I just told 'em" is in order. It is even possible that more research appears to be needed on one or two minor points. Often these follow-up visits are just as important as the original presentation, especially if the confused one happens to be the president of the company.

We make no apology for this lengthy sermon. Good research requires a good presentation. Good presentations do not have to be dull and wordy. A research study that took perhaps a few weeks to several months to complete deserves the best possible presentation. And the best possible presentation can come only after thorough preparation and practice.

BASIC FORMS

As we said above, from the very beginning of a research study, attention should be given to how the final report will be presented. Once this decision has been made, consideration can be given to the charts and illustrative material that may be needed, and to how charts and graphs and illustrations can be shown to the listening group. These decisions will have to be tailored to the size of the prospective group, which is why, early on, some thought must be given to the people who will be at the presentation meeting, or the people who will get copies of the final report.

A written report is by far the most prevalent presentation form. Even if an oral presentation is also made, the written report can be used for further study after the meeting.

Both written and oral reporting will be covered in greater detail later in this chapter.

THE WRITTEN REPORT

BACKGROUND

Virtually all marketing research reports are prepared in written form. This written report becomes a base of subsequent action: an oral report, a suggestion for further research on subtopics, and so on. Also, this written report may be needed for the databank.

Now let us consider who makes up the typical group that receives a report. In business, it may include top management, middle management, or a mixture of both. In some situations, a version of a report may be given to the lower ranks.

The nature of the audience will determine how a report is to be written or how an oral presentation is to be made. This does not imply talking down to some groups, but it does mean talking in their language. Also, different audiences may require that some attention be given to the length of the written or oral report.

KNOWLEDGE OF THE AUDIENCE

Knowing the audience is essential for good reporting. The presenter of a report should know in advance who will receive copies of the written report or who will be at an oral presentation. The report should address itself directly to these people and their needs.

This is a good policy for the presenter and the company. There is rarely a company these days where everyone is in agreement. No questions, no objections—this is a dream world. Perhaps it was true in years gone by when Mr. Altman owned the B. Altman store on Fifth Avenue, or Mr. Carnegie ruled the Pittsburgh steel mill. But business does not operate like this today. There will be objections, and there will be open skepticism. But no one would want to return to the old days of bosses that were feared and obeyed.

It is good, even early in the research, to consider the possible objections and questions from the report readers or audience. Anticipating objections from people with known mindsets may alter how a report is written (or even how the research is done).

An outside presenter also must know the audience and will need special guidance to acquire that knowledge. The in-house marketing manager may know what troubles a report might encounter, what objections may be raised. The marketing staff should educate the outside presenter so that he or she can effectively sell the report to a known audience.

PREPARING THE FIRST DRAFT

GO BACK TO THE PROPOSAL

What was the exact definition of the problem to be studied? Research studies sometimes tend to wander from the original problem and proposal. Interesting side matters come up. But no matter how fascinating they may be, this study is to be directed toward the solution of the stated problem. If research has uncovered another problem that needs looking at, then this will be the basis of another study.

After all the work and thought that has gone into the research study, do these recommendations still appear sound? Will they affect the needs of the company in the way first intended? Look over the findings, and particularly the recommendations, with the eyes of upper and middle management. Will the whole study now make sense in the light of conditions when the study was begun?

The written or oral presentation must address itself precisely to the above questions. Writing the presentation report should begin only when it is absolutely clear that it will speak in a helpful way to those who requested and approved the study. Then the written and/or oral report will be much more meaningful and acceptable to the receiving group.

THE SEQUENCE OF SECTIONS

REPORT DIGEST

A report digest is almost always placed at the beginning of the report. This is to allow the marketing manager and other executives to quickly and easily grasp what has been learned and what is being recommended.

Sometimes the digest is bound separately for executives who will not want to read all the details. Experienced presenters frequently make use of this technique of the separate executive summary. Sometimes, of course, managers and executives want the long form too, and they must understand that it is available at their request.

This executive summary will include:

- Action implications buttressed by key findings

- Discussion of findings for product, advertising, or other interested middle management

- A short appendix with a few details of procedures, a sample of appropriate materials, a few detailed tabulations, and statistics

Two matters should be thought about in preparing this executive report. One is that middle management, and even upper management, has become leaner in the past decade, with fewer people being hired to do the same or more jobs. Another matter is that some companies are pushing management jobs down into divisions or branches. Of course, this means that the branch and divisional people have more decisions to make, more papers to read. They will therefore welcome brief, succinct, useful research reports.

THE OUTLINE

Next in the order of tackling the report is the preparation of the outline.

Time should be taken to make this outline as complete as possible, for it will greatly facilitate the writing of the final report. In a sense, actually, this outline becomes almost a first draft of the final report.

All sources of information should be named. If an important figure is to be used, it is astonishing how quickly a source can be forgotten when attribution must be made. If the presenter may have to answer questions about sources, he or she will be delighted if the source can be readily named. Also, details that might seem so obvious that they need not be put on paper should now be recorded. It is easy for important details to get lost if they are not written down.

THE FINDINGS

Findings pertaining to the problem should be stated and arranged relative to the basic purposes of the study. This can be a difficult exercise. Findings can be applied to several basic questions asked of the study. Some findings, while interesting and perhaps valuable for some other research problem, may be temporarily discarded. Some guidance from the committee that oversaw the research procedure will be useful in separating the wheat from the chaff. For example, if it is found that men in the Southwest prefer a somewhat deeper yellow label on a bottle of mouthwash, this is probably a finding about which nothing at all will be done. It is interesting but not actionable. On the other hand, if it were found that Southwestern men preferred a wholly different color for a particular mouthwash, possibly something might at least be considered. These matters are the chaff separated from the wheat of actionable findings.

Certain key findings can be spotted quickly. Some stand out as possibly *the* answer. These can be separated out for special handling. Perhaps they require a table, a chart, a visual of some kind (to be decided later).

These key findings may be the basis of a separate executive report described earlier in this chapter.

KEY ACTION RECOMMENDATIONS

Key action recommendations largely stem from the key findings noted above. As we said, these key findings and recommendations may serve, after some further thought and rewriting, as the basis for a separate executive report. If a separate executive report is not wanted, then these key items may be featured early in the final report.

DESCRIPTION OF PROCEDURE

The details of procedure will include such facts about the study as the questionnaires used, storyboards, sampling methods, response rate for questionnaires, and the like. Not many will read all this in the final report, but these details must be ready for questioning minds.

Moreover, the procedure facts must be outlined and put into the final report in sufficient detail to protect both the validity of the recommendations and the validity of the procedures. A second study might wish to follow the same procedures so that it can be compared with the first study.

When the procedural outline is in almost final form, the appropriate people should review it and make comments and suggestions. The outline will allow interested people to make final comments before the report "goes to press," and it will allow the research committee to have its last say before the study is published.

All reports, as we have stressed, should first appear in written form. Writing reduces excessive verbiage and helps keep the report and recommendations on target. Writing tells us when to "sit down and shut up." It insists on a logical march from question to answer, without going down side roads that lead nowhere.

When the report has been organized and correctly packaged, it may be turned into an oral presentation or a video presentation, or it may become the basis for a small group seminar. Thinking is sharpened in writing, facts and figures become organized, and more opportunities for action open up.

THE BODY OF THE REPORT

The body of the report will follow the description of procedure. It might include the following:

- A statement of the problem, perhaps modified somewhat to allow for changes in instructions and changes due to early findings in the research. This restatement should nevertheless remain as close as possible to the problem statement that initiated the research.

- A short description of how the research was done. However, if the research technique was complex, the description probably should be in an appendix.

- A presentation of the findings in some detail, but only what is necessary for backing up the recommendations or, perhaps, for meeting the special needs of some departments or persons.

- A list of the major recommendations. These should be definitely and enthusiastically stated where possible. Wishy-washy statements such as "It looks like . . ." or "Perhaps it can be understood that . . ." should be avoided. If the research has been done well and thoroughly, most recommendations should be presented, in a firm, positive way, as sound and actionable.

- Some research presenters prefer to put the recommendations right after the restatement of the problem. Our experience is that interest quickly dies down after the recommendations are made. By first describing the techniques, then presenting the findings, and then stating the recommendations, some excitement can be built up and interest sustained and quicked by a building-block method of presentation.

- A statement of the implications of the findings and recommendations for specific departments of the sponsoring company.

Objectivity in report writing must be clearly visible. Newspaper, magazine, and special-interest publicity are often suspect. For a marketing research report, there must be no suspicion of weakness of method or self-serving ways of making recommendations. This is always difficult, since the research agency almost inevitably reaches its own early solution to the problem. It is then hard, but not impossible, for the research presenter to stick coldly to the facts and their implications.

It is good psychology to admit early in the report that the study had some shortcomings, if indeed it did. Statements such as "Some sections of the country were not covered, and here is why," or "We did not question as many older people as we should, and here is why" will help to win over the skeptics.

STYLE

A research report needs sharpness, clarity, and color. The first two needs we have discussed. Color is also important. How to capture and use color? We do not have words to describe color, but we all know it when we see it or read it. One thing that a report writer can do is to wait for an hour, a day, or a week, and then reread what has been written. Is it colorless, dull, wordy? If the answer is yes, then back to the word processor, or even the old-fashioned typewriter.

Mark Twain once said that "the difference between the almost right word and the right word is really a large matter—'tis the difference between the lightning bug and lightning." There are words that have an emotional implication, no matter how innocently they are used in a report. The word *liberal,* describing a person or firm, puts an immediate spotlight on that person or firm. The word *international* used instead of *American* to describe a company causes patriotic emotions to rise. You can think of other words that should not be used if a more neutral word can be found without making the sentence colorless.

Simple words usually are best. Avoid at all costs a pretentious style calculated to impress top and middle management. For example:

Complex	Simple
currently	now
time frame	time
optimum	best
redundant	unnecessary
cognitive	perceiving
evoke	cause
endeavor	try
parameter	limit

A recent presentation at a scholarly meeting was called: *E Pluribus Unum: The Ideological Imperative of Revolutionary America.* Scholars feel the need to impress each other. Any title like that would kill a business presentation.

Avoid using research jargon. Ordinary English is best. Marketing language is expected: It makes the marketing people feel at home and leads them to regard the presenter as a team member. The presenter's use of slang or vulgarisms, to appear to be just a regular marketing person, will appear false and demean the importance of the study and its recommendations.

Some years ago the *New York Times* pointed out that the Lord's Prayer has 56 words; the Twenty-Third Psalm has 118 words; the Gettysburg Address has 225 words; the Ten Commandments have 297 words. Then the *Times* counted the words in an agriculture directive on pricing cabbage: 15,629 words.

But—and this is a big but—you must use enough words to prevent any later misunderstanding of your meaning. Ordinary life is full of times when we do not understand each other because of different interpretations of word meaning. A research report must avoid such problems.

THE ORAL RESEARCH REPORT

We speak here as sorry victims of many poorly prepared oral reports and speeches. We must admit that we ourselves have been guilty of committing some offenses in this area in the past.

We will now discuss some of the things we have learned, sometimes painfully. On the surface, many appear obvious. But the obvious things are often overlooked, and that can ruin an otherwise good presentation.

SPEAKING DIRECTLY TO THE AUDIENCE

A well-presented research report will speak directly to those who need its assistance. The sales manager wants to know what the chances are that a new line of herbal teas will sell; his or her success in the firm may depend on the answer. The ad agency needs to know who will probably buy this tea, and why. The packaging people want to know what will really pull the tea onto a supermarket shelf. And so on. The presentation must be addressed straight to those people wanting help and advice.

AVOIDING DULLNESS

Rarely will top executives be interested in the minute details of the recommendations at this early point. Later they will want to know almost everything that will affect their firm, if action is to be taken on the recommendations, but for now top management will usually want just the highlights of both findings and recommendations. It would be a serious error to make these executives sit through a long, boring meeting. Tailoring a presentation to these executives means a quick but thorough coverage of the study and its recommendations. If the executives wish to learn the details, that is their privilege. But good judgment usually means that the top managers will be spared a long session.

Why, it must be asked, are business meetings so often dull? People dealing with other people can lighten the contacts without destroying the serious purpose of a meeting. Often, serious business moves better on a greased runway of humor. This is definitely not meant to urge the inclusion of ready-made jokes. A light touch is good enough. A trained presenter will know how to get a few smiles and laughs without turning the session into a vaudeville act. Top executives, for the most part, will be grateful for a few light moments in the course of a presentation.

If it is known that top management will sit in on a research study presentation, serious thought must be given in advance to how such managers can be "captured," to how their interest and attention can be fully aroused. This will not come naturally, without planning, except in a few instances. Even though top management knows all about the study, it is still incumbent on the presenter and the marketing team to think about what the executives really want to know.

If you want examples of what is subconsciously wanted in both written and oral reports, pick up a few of the popular new books written for businesspeople. Short paragraphs and short sentences characterize the writing. There are multiple headings that "tells 'em" what the report and its subsections are going to "tell 'em." Management people are not ignorant: A preponderance have gone to college, and many have MBAs. But still they treasure writing and oral presentations that make their job a little easier. So eschew words like *eschew*. No prizes are given for multisyllabic intercommunications.

WHAT CAN GO WRONG?

Any presenter with long experience can tell you that anything that *can* go wrong at a meeting probably *will* go wrong. Often enough anyway. No matter how well the main report has been written, no matter how well an outline has been prepared to guide the meeting, something or somebody may well gum up the works. The best advice for any meeting, especially one with top management in attendance, is to practice, practice, practice. Thousands of dollars may have been spent on doing the study. A few hours of practice is of no importance in comparison. And let the experienced presenter tell you what it feels like to have a projector refuse to work while the president is sitting in the audience waiting for the show to start.

Three real-world anecdotes will show the kinds of things that can go wrong in an oral presentation. All were unusual, but all could have been anticipated to some extent.

Results of a major study were being presented to the management of one of Canada's largest corporations. The presentation was badly marred by two things. First, the punch bowl in which the research director was serving a new hot punch decided to break just as the firm's president was serving himself. Second, the president had just received word about how bad the final quarter's profit was.

An uninformed marketing research person had just completed his first major study for his company. A break was scheduled in the presentation for coffee and Danish. At that time the president was heard to say, loudly, that "our research department wants to make big things of our studies." The coffee break was never repeated.

A woman's club in a suburb of a large city asked an important person in Washington to deliver a talk on world affairs. The club members and their husbands had enough influence to bring a positive response. In came the well-known man on a government plane. Audience assembled, lights lowered, high anticipation of hearing behind-the-scene news—

and the sound system did not work. After a futile effort to make his voice heard, the speaker gave up and flew home. An unusual event perhaps, but things like this do happen, though they can be avoided.

The eleventh commandment for oral presenters might be: practice, practice, practice. Anticipate the worst and try to prevent it.

The Physical Facilities

The room must be ready with proper lighting, air-conditioning, and a sound system that enables all to hear. All possibly distracting noises from outside sources must have been eliminated.

The correct number of chairs and tables must be ready. No one will go after chairs as a few extra people show up.

Advance Preparation of Presentation

The presentation must have been well-prepared, and all possible interruptions considered. Perhaps several persons should participate in the presentation, to relieve possible boredom with just one voice and face.

Advance Announcement of Length of Presentation

Stating how long the presentation will be is good psychology. It eliminates some shuffling and watch checking.

VISUAL AIDS AND THEIR USE

All visual aids—chalkboards, flip boards, overhead transparencies, and the like—*must* be ready ahead of time.

Charts and graphs should be checked and double-checked before the time of presentation. Even a U.S. president has been seen on television searching for a wandering note. Probably this did not hurt the president's speech, but it might hurt your presentation if the enthusiasm built up in the audience is allowed to simmer down during the search for a misplaced item.

Illustrations used in the written report, of course, also can be used in the oral report. When the charts and graphs are prepared, however, it is essential that their dual use be recognized ahead of time and prepared accordingly.

A warning is necessary about visual aids of all kinds. Too many visuals can become distracting, frequently boring. They should be used solely to clarify or reinforce a point. Visuals, if used incorrectly or too profusely, can diminish the power and effectiveness of what the presenter has been saying. Too often the presenter believes that pictures are better than words. Visual aids should be used only if they serve a real and necessary purpose.

SOME ELECTRONIC REPORTING AIDS

We cannot in this book name and describe every reporting aid now on the market. New ones appear frequently. Marketing researchers, particularly those whose duty it is to make presentations, should search for and be aware of what is available.

Presented below are short descriptions representative of the kinds of electronic aids now available. These descriptions were taken from advertising brochures issued by the specified firms.

OVERHEAD PROJECTORS

Present It is a software program for PCs that uses a dot-matrix printer to produce charts, title pages, and text pages, with varying typefaces.

Another program is *PC Presenter*, which eliminates the need for transparencies and is available for either PCs or Apple/Macintosh. It performs smooth transitions from screen to screen, blends texts and graphics, fades in and out, and shows split screens.

GRAPHICS

In the preparation of graphics, computer-generated text and numerical charts can be produced by the PC. A simple example of this is *Graph-in-the-Box*. Data and text can be highlighted directly on your screen, and the program automatically produces the line, bar, column, pie, or mixed graphs. Data can also be entered using the keyboard. The graphs can be saved, printed on a printer, or input to a document created with a *Ventura* or *Pagemaker* desktop publishing program.

MAPS

GraphicProfile, according to Donnelly Marketing Information Services, "makes demographic data easy to understand and use. AmericanProfile offers the most current demographic data available, and Graphic Profile offers a whole new way to view the data." GraphicProfile produces color-keyed maps that can be produced in several forms, including six-color computer-printed maps, 35mm slides, and transparencies. Data can be mapped for various geographic units—states, counties, tracts within SMSA counties—using demographic data and the company's own data.

It would not be feasible to name and describe all the aids now available to presenters. The above are meant only to show a few techniques and the firms offering them. The research and/or the client firm must brief itself on what aids for presentation are available and which are most suitable for a particular study.

REFERENCES   Carnes, William T. *Effective Meetings for Busy People*. New York: McGraw-Hill, 1980.

Fletcher, Winston. *Meetings, Meetings*. New York: Morrow, 1984.

Haynes, Marion E. *Effective Meeting Skills*. Los Altos, Calif.: Crisp Publications, 1988.

Snell, Frank. *How to Win the Meeting*. New York: Hawthorn Books, 1979.

Thomsett, Michael C. *The Little Black Book of Business Meetings*. New York: American Management Association, 1989.

PART THREE

APPLYING MARKETING RESEARCH TO MARKETING PROBLEMS

13

THE USE OF OVERALL MARKETING MEASUREMENTS:

Decision Making About the Marketing Mix

What's in This Chapter

Our primary concern in this chapter is the measurement of the success of a firm's marketing efforts. We describe how the marketing manager and researcher, through continual monitoring, are able to make reactive marketing moves and plan future marketing. We discuss syndicated national measurement services and the management of vast quantities of data. The three types of test marketing—traditional, controlled, and simulated—are also explained.

MARKETING MEASUREMENTS

The major emphasis on products here is on packaged goods: groceries, household products, and toiletries—products retailed primarily in food and drugstores. Measurement of other types of products will be covered in Chapter 17.

MOVEMENT OF GOODS AT RETAIL

Some of the key terms used in the measurement of goods at retail are presented in Exhibit 13.1.

There are several ways of measuring the success of the total marketing operation, whether the operation has been continuing one or is experimental. One is to measure sales dollars. This alone is not a sound measure, however. If the firm's product is in a rising market, its sales may rise, but it may be losing share of the market. If the product is in a falling market, the firm's dollars of sales may drop but it may still be in the top portion of marketers as expressed in terms of market share. Sales dollars alone, whether monitored at the factory door or at the retail store, mean little as a sole measure of the marketing effort's success. The real key is market share.

The measurements discussed in this chapter include gross measurements of brand movement (volume and shares), consumer-tracking studies (measuring consumer awareness of such elements as brand and advertising), and test marketing (where the marketer tries out a proposed marketing campaign for either a new product or a revision of present marketing efforts).

We discussed in Chapter 11 the many forms of recording devices used in marketing research studies. The major one is the scanner, which

---

Exhibit 13.1   **SOME TERMS USED IN MEASUREMENT OF GOODS AT RETAIL**

Market share: Proportion of retail dollars (sometimes unit sales) of a product category held by a particular brand.

Distribution: Proportion of stores stocking a brand or item at the time of the check.

Percent stores stocking: Proportion of stores having a particular brand or item on the shelf.

Dollars: Sales expressed in retail dollars.

Volume: Retail sales expressed in terms of cases, units, pounds, etc.

Price: Retail price expressed in terms of average, promoted, and nonpromoted price.

Display: Special display featuring a brand or item in retail stores.

Facings: Number of units of item displayed on the shelf.

makes use of the UPC (Universal Product Code), now so common on many consumer products, particularly those sold in grocery outlets.

The UPC was introduced in the early 1970s. The one used for this book appears on the back cover.

Almost all products now sold in food and drug outlets carry their own UPCs, and the system is spreading rapidly to products sold in other types of outlet, such as discount stores, convenience stores, book outlets, and even hardware stores. Each brand has a different coding for variety and for size. The basic idea of the UPC is to make it easier for the retailer to ring up and keep track of sales at the checkout counter. To use the scanner—that busy electronic device at the checkout counter—all the checker has to do is to pass the UPC over the scanner's light, and both price and item are recorded.

SCANNERS AS A MARKETING MEASUREMENT DEVICE

Although the scanning system was designed for other reasons, it has revolutionized much of marketing research. Scanners now provide virtually instantaneous measurements of customer purchasing behavior. Combined with other measurements, they give an amazingly rapid evaluation of marketing performance. As we will show, they can also give a good idea of the effectiveness of a given promotion (such as a price offer or a particular advertising campaign).

The emphasis on this chapter, in discussing the measurement of total marketing performance, is largely on items sold almost entirely in supermarkets, such as dry grocery goods, canned goods, frozen foods, branded meats, branded dairy goods, and household supplies. The UPC describes the brand, the nature of the item, the size and nature of the container, and price.

AUDITS AS A MEASURING DEVICE

Store audits, introduced many years ago by the A. C. Nielsen Co., are a simple concept. Taking inventory at the start of a period, adding stock deliveries for the period, and subtracting the inventory at the end of the period results in a measure of sales for the period. In simple formula terms, here is the way it works:

Starting inventory (made at start of period)	_____
Additions to stock during period	+_____
Closing inventory (made at end of period)	−_____
Sales during period	=_____

Periodic checks are made by trained auditors, who have access to store shelves and backrooms where goods are stored and to stock deliveries made during the period. These measurements are typically reported in terms of both units and retail dollars. They include reports about such items as the number of shelf facings and promotional offerings, which help the subscribing firm get an understanding of what is happening in the marketplace.

Until a few years ago, store audits were the measuring method used by Nielsen for determining retail movement in food outlets, drugstores, and mass merchandisers. But today, most retail sales data are obtained by scanner. Information Resources Inc. (IRI) measures food stores by scanning, as does Nielsen, but IRI is well along in its scanner-expansion program to provide considerable drugstore and mass-merchandiser data by mid-1991. More about this later in the chapter.

One national syndicated retail reporting service covers a variety of outlets not yet completely equipped with scanners. The National Total-Market Audit (Audits & Surveys) provides bimonthly retail store data for some 32 store types, ranging from appliance stores to video stores.[1] Where scanners are available (in more than half of the stores), these are used, but otherwise audits are conducted.

SINGLE-SOURCE DATA AND THEIR MARKETING SIGNIFICANCE

The movement of goods at retail is a significant measurement, but it is not a complete measurement. It concerns only merchandise, not people. The purchasing behavior (and other types of behavior too) offers a chance to understand the dynamics underlying the movement of goods at retail. This is especially true when consumers can report both buying and other behavior simultaneously. This is what is now commonly referred to as single-source data.

So the marketer need not depend on inference on purchase data from one source and advertising data from another. Instead, all the data come from a single source. These single-source data then paint a total picture of what is bought and of the impact of television, coupons, retail features, displays, and other marketing features on product sales.

But we have to pause for a moment to provide a definition for the term *single source*. Gold[2] mentions that the term probably was first used by John Downham (Unilever) in 1979 to describe frequency measurement. In 1983 Mike Naples, in a talk, used it as an electronic measurement of buying and media exposure from the same individuals. Starting in 1986, there was less emphasis on media evaluation as the major application. Walker Smith of DowBrands, reports Gold, seems to have the best current definition, when he proposes that ". . . single source is an idea about what to do with data and not necessarily a type of data, such as scanning or commercial delivery. . . . The nature of the data believed capable of supporting single-source work . . . is a single database . . . with all relevant data on all marketing support and marketing response variables . . . on a common unit of analysis at the individual consumer or consuming household level of aggregation."

When sales data are scanner-provided for total store sales only (that is, no breakout for family members), this is essentially only a special case of a controlled store audit, where the research firm simply makes sure that the store is kept stocked with the merchandise.

Purchase data are sometimes obtained by use of hand-held scanners in a panel of homes, where the purchaser records purchases through use of a wand that is run over the UPC of all purchased products. The panel homes may be individually wired to provide measured viewing of television channels, programs, and commercials.

There is usually in-store observation on price, facings, displays, and the like, and related retail advertising is recorded.

The marketing implication of gathering and correlating all of these data is the relating of cause and effect, as in coupon redemption: percentage of sales related to coupons, source of coupon purchasers (loyal purchasers, switchers, heavy/light users), distribution means (newspaper, magazines, free-standing insert); short-term sales response to coupons, ad features, shelf-price reductions. In other words: bottom-line implication. Such data provide an in-depth examination of the product, its market, its promotional mix, and its consumers, to arrive at decision-leading information.

NATIONAL SYNDICATED SINGLE-SOURCE SERVICES

Two research firms offer national single-source measurements of the total movement of goods at retail, where there is a combination of store sales data and promotional efforts with purchasing and other behavioral aspects of the consumers making these purchases. These two services are the Nielsen ScanTrack service and the IRI InfoScan service. Other services will be mentioned in Chapter 17. The two services discussed here are those either completely into scanner technology or rapidly moving there, and they are the most important in the field.

NIELSEN'S SCANTRACK

ScanTrack is a national service in the country's 54 largest markets offering continuing measurements of product movement in more than 3,000 scanner-equipped groceries nationally.[3]

Information is available for national totals and for each of the 54 markets, if this is what the user requires. The results can also be reported by market or combination of markets needed, and thus can be used by regional marketers as well as national.

Results can be reported on an item-by-item basis for any product carrying the UPC. Currently, over 900 individual product categories are reported. Within the desired category of merchandise, the results show elements such as the amount of each brand's sales, sizes and flavors, and price paid (regular or special). Product penetration among retailers is reported.

Each ScanTrack report also provides a statement of three kinds of retailer activity related to sales: retailer local advertising support (and the importance of the ad), display activity (displays separate from the usual stocking location of the brand), and retailer coupon ads (store coupons in the retailer's advertising).

Nielsen obtains its consumer buying measurements through its ScanTrack National Panel, a separate service. This is a representative sample of 15,000 participating households throughout the country. Each household has been selected by location and demographics to provide a nationally balanced and projectable sample.

Participants use a hand-held scanner at home to record, by passing the scanner over the UPC, all purchases made regardless of the store in which the item was bought. The store might have been a supermarket, a drugstore, a discount store, a department store, or some other type of outlet. Results are recorded in a miniaturized in-home computer provided by the research firm, and results are transmitted to Nielsen by telephone line.

Nielsen also measures television viewing and magazine readership in a portion of the panel homes, making it possible for panel members to have their television viewing monitored through people meters, a system that will be described in Chapter 18. A person viewing television pushes his or her identifying button on the meter resting on top of the television set, as shown in Exhibit 13.2.

Individual commercials are identified through a system Nielsen calls Monitor Plus, to be described in Chapter 18. Individual programs people watch are matched to the commercials they are exposed to. The intent is to get an accurate measurement of commercial exposure.

Exhibit 13.2   USING THE NIELSEN PEOPLE METER

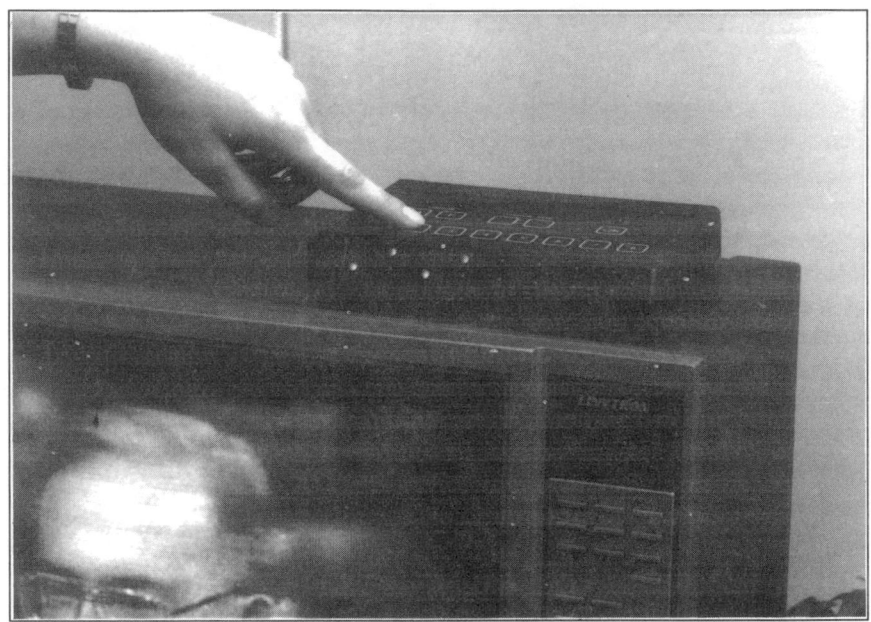

Source: Courtesy of A. C. Nielsen Co.

Nielsen provides a single-source measurement in a somewhat different form in key major markets throughout the country. In these locations, there are local panels of households, large enough to provide a reasonable basis for measurement by individual markets.

ScanTrack results are delivered to the subscriber in whatever format is selected. Hard copy, computer tapes, or floppy disks are available. Alternatively, the data are available to the subscriber's own computer system with direct access to the on-line facilities of the Nielsen mainframe computer. All this can be combined in the user's own marketing information system through the use of METAPHOR, a program described in Chapter 2.

NIELSEN/NPD RESEARCH

Nielsen/NPD Research provides a national panel of 15,000 families in the 50 markets in which Nielsen has store scanners. Panel members use a hand-held scanner wand at home to record every item with a UPC code that they have purchased from any type of store. Then they simply move the wand over the television set, which has been specially wired to receive the message. One-third of the households are metered for television viewing. The viewing information is matched with the commercials aired on these shows to obtain a measure of total commercial exposures. By mid-1990, 7,500 of the 15,000 households will be metered, and Monitor Plus will be associated with these 7,500 households in 23 markets (representing 50 percent of U.S. households).[4] Of course, the national sample size permits individual market breakouts only for the three or four largest markets.

IRI's InfoScan[5-9]

InfoScan comes in two parts: a national consumer panel and a panel of stores.

InfoScan provides each of its 60,000 national consumer panel members with a card that is presented to the drugstore or supermarket cashier in the panelist's neighborhood at time of checkout. The process makes it possible to identify product purchases with household and to match purchases with in-store price and promotional condition. Coupons are matched to UPC. Information is transmitted electronically to the research firm's computer.

Six thousand of these panel homes are television-metered to measure household television tuning. The data are reported every four weeks. With the recent closing of SAMI and the new availability of Arbitron's television ratings to IRI, it appears that further development of IRI's national movement into single-source data is at an end. The television ratings will be tied into product movement by area, but not on a single-source basis.

Results are available for the entire United States by region, and, for some categories, by market (though not on a projected basis).

How are these panel members recruited? Twenty-six metro markets are the sample base, and within each of these, neighborhoods are selected to represent the market. Census data are used to set up quotas, and participants are recruited in supermarkets. The sampling procedure, in our opinion, seems not to meet the rigorous requirements of good sampling.

For the panel of stores, each of the 2,700 stores covered in 64 geographic markets has annual sales of $2 million or more. Field personnel visually survey stores and all print media to record retailer merchandising efforts, displays, and ad features.

Stratified random sampling is used to select stores from the $2 million supermarket universe to project to national results, custom-defined regions, local chains, and individual markets.

Store results measure product movement (dollars and units) and market share, and they also report store promotion activity.

InfoScan is now expanding its measurement of merchandise movement by scanner to drugstores and mass merchandisers. The firm had such coverage in 350 drugstores in February 1991, with 500 due by July. Scanner data from 150 mass merchandisers were due to be available by mid–1991.

Both aspects of InfoScan are available in a choice of formats: hard-copy reports, floppy disks, or magnetic tape. They can also be accessed through a PC equipped with IRI's Express software.

MULTI-MEDIA CONSUMER PROFILE

Multi-Media Consumer Profile (Birch Scarborough) is a single-source measurement conducted annually in selected local markets. It provides data about media, retail shopping, and product consumption.[10] A minimum of 2,000 interviews is obtained in each selected area of dominant influence (ADI). As of this writing, 30 markets are available and others will be added on demand.

Three questionnaires are completed with adults 18 and over in telephone households. Two of these are telephone interviews, and the other is a self-administered Consumer Product Booklet and TV Diary.

The initial interview, by telephone, includes questions about newspaper reading, radio listening, magazine reading, demographics, and product/service use. Following completion of this first interview, each participant is mailed a self-completion Consumer Product Booklet and seven-day television diary. The product booklet contains numerous questions about entertainment and recreation, travel, retail shopping, and household expenditures.

A second telephone interview, conducted within eight days after the first, repeats the newspaper and magazine-reading questions. This second interview, conducted by a different interview team, not only helps validate the first interview, but also extends the time period of interviewing to provide estimates of reach and frequency in addition to audience size. (These terms will be explained in Chapter 18.)

These data make it possible to relate buying behavior with the combination of media to which the particular household has been exposed, and by frequency of exposure.

OBSERVATION OF THE IN-STORE ENVIRONMENT

Typically, the observations made by trained fieldworkers include:

- Distribution (and out-of-stock)

- Shelf price
- Shelf facings (reported in number and share)
- Shelf location
- Display activity
- Presence of point-of-purchase material

Sales volume is not measured.

While several research firms handle such studies on a custom basis, Ehrhart-Babic offers its *National Retail Tracking Index* (NRTI) on a syndicated basis.[11] Though syndicated, it is available on a highly flexible basis.

On a regular schedule, the observations are made in five major store types: supermarkets (every four weeks), drugstores, mass merchandisers, convenience stores, and hardware/home centers (all quarterly). Fifty-four metro areas are covered. The buyer can select panels reflecting InfoScan and ScanTrack geography.

Results, depending on user needs, can be shown by category, brand, and types/sizes. These are reported by total (U.S. or total markets surveyed), by individual markets, and by major chains. Breaks by sales regions and other special analyses can be provided on order.

But crucial to the user of ScanTrack, InfoScan, and CensusScan, NRTI offers syndicated panels to apply results specifically to their single-source data.

SOME COMMENTS ON SYNDICATED NATIONAL MEASUREMENTS

THE USERS OF SUCH SERVICES

The large firm is the major user of syndicated national measurements, according to a survey of 43 U.S. consumer product firms.[12] Over three-fourths of the firms purchasing scanner data do over $300 million in business annually—chiefly food manufacturers (80 percent), followed by health and beauty aid manufacturers (13 percent), and then other firms in varying fields. This is not too surprising, since these kinds of products tend to be sold almost entirely in scanner stores.

These firms spend an average of over $1 million annually for scanner data. Many purchase scanner data from more than one of the three major suppliers, and typically the purchasing firm has been buying scanner data for nearly three years. Most users also purchase data on in-store displays, pricing, local advertising, distribution, and couponing. About half buy panel data providing purchaser demographics.

The scanner results are used mainly for basic tracking (keeping an eye on category and company trends), tracking or testing marketing variables (promotions, in-store displays), planning (goal setting and forecasting), new-product and test-market tracking, and competitive tracking. Some 70 percent of user firms use scanner data as a look-up (reference) tool with only 30 percent using them as a discovery tool (to discover activity in the market).

On a scale of 1 (low) to 5 (high), the typical overall satisfaction rating is a surprisingly low 3.5. With a new technique seeming to promise the moon, why so low? Let us see.

THE INCREDIBLE AMOUNT OF DATA

Each month, according to the survey, a mass of new data arrives to be analyzed. And too many firms have assigned too few people to analyze too much data. On the average, firms assign the equivalent of one person to analysis, apart from those maintaining the system and those within the firm making independent analyses.

Comments made by a user in American Chicle (a Division of Warner-Lambert), a producer of mostly small, low-price items (chewing gums, breath mints, convenience antacid tablets, cough drops, and confections) agree with this assessment.[13] The major problem is the difficulty of successfully switching from a traditional data service of the past to a radically different service. Beyond the cost of the service are the many demands placed on the user. The costs in people and in time are far beyond the original concept. Single-source data affect so many areas of the organization that the service forces the organization, through much new learning, to develop many new ways of operating. In a real sense, it is a revolution in dealing with marketing information.

It is difficult to tie in these new types of results with other systems of information input within the company. For example, data relating to market size and the firm's relative position in it had been a part of bimonthly reporting to management. Suddenly there were four-week reports. Since top management was involved, this time shift presented major problems.

The increasing bottom-line emphasis also means that it is difficult to get existing personnel to take on the additional time commitment for implementation of a new service.[13]

There are several pertinent suggestions for the new national user. To ease the conversion process, the user firm should tackle it one product category at a time. A mistake could be corrected in each situation in a single category, rather than making the mistake in multiple categories simultaneously. In addition, thorough training of those to receive and implement the findings is essential.

QUALITY OF THE DATA

The state-of-the-art methods of gathering and analyzing the data of most of the national syndicated services are appealing. However, the user or potential user has to look behind the glitter of the methods to understand what is really there.

All might not be well in this brave new world. Nearly 50 percent of users raised questions, without prompting, about the quality of the data. We suspect that it was largely quality concerns that prompted a late 1990 proposal that CASRO (Council of American Survey Research Organizations) offer an auditing program where survey firms could choose to allow back-room inspections of projects to determine whether various procedures were up to snuff.[14] The proposal was referred to a committee, with little likelihood of further action.

The user should check to make sure that volume reported bears some relationship to shipments. With automation there is a chance, for instance, that a product might have been placed into an incorrect category, thereby throwing off results.

The Sampling of Stores

Can a sample of stores be representative of the universe of stores? A major, massive study by SAMI (a firm then offering a scanner-based retail sales service) showed that while a sample of stores did indeed produce sales results parallel to those of total stores, results became less accurate as the analysis moved from broad to narrow bases in terms of trading area (from national to regional to local), product (from category, to brand, to item), and time (from longer to shorter periods).[15] For some product volumes, the discrepancies ran as high as 20 percent.

Brian Shea, marketing research manager of Ore-Ida, whose company has used both ScanTrack and Nielsen, has much to say about their sampling methods.[16] One of the big problems, he says, is that neither source right now projects data to total U.S. retail grocers because they're getting it only from the larger scanner stores. Right now they are projecting only to retail grocers doing more than $2 million annual volume. That means that if you are selling to grocery stores that don't have that volume or that don't have a scanner, you are not being fully covered. In the case of Ore-Ida, the coverage of volume ranges from only 70 percent on up to about 95 percent or 96 percent, depending on the product. The firm has had little success in getting suppliers to project to that larger universe; their argument is that they really don't have much information on what those stores are doing.

Within this basic sampling limitation, Shea argues that the Nielsen store sample is superior to that of IRI. "They cover a lot more geography with a lot more stores," he says. "They draw a more representative and valid sample both at the local market level and at the total U.S. market level." IRI, he comments, is far more metro-market-based, covering much less geography. So IRI particularly understates sales for products doing well in nonmetro areas.

Shea sees both services facing a lack of comparability of the stores sampled from one year to the next. As smaller stores close and more stores convert to scanners each year, the universe of larger stores increases. He points out that this creates a comparability problem for the user, who really can't make good comparisons from one year to the next. Shea thinks that the increase is about 1 percent annually. That may not sound like much but, as he puts it, ". . . at the level of our business that difference may be a 'make or break' kind of thing. It's an even bigger problem at the individual market level, where there may be several major chains. If a new chain enters the sampling picture, you may have real problems. Right now neither service is addressing the issue at all."

The Sampling of Consumers

Both national services use consumer panels. Results are not projectable. Participants are a most select group, willing to be analyzed.

This is far from the random sample necessary when precision results—such as those presumably reported by the syndicated services—are required.[17] Further, there is a clustering of panel households around one or two participating stores, and where panel homes are asked to use ID cards in-store, participation is below acceptable levels for some groups of households.[17]

There may also be a serious question about the adequacy of fieldwork with the participating families, such as explaining the task and gathering of data.[18] The use of these in-home scanners may not be much better than the former diaries; there may be gaps in the recording of purchases, as well as poor cooperation and participation by panelists.[19]

Scanner Data: System Problems

Quality of the data going into the system and quality of the system data are the basis for problems that can occur at both stages of scanner data collection:

Some items don't carry UPC labels, for example, even though they may be part of the total marketing offerings against which the manufacturer is competing. Bakery and deli items are typically keyed only for the department and the price.[16] Giant packs, such as for dog foods, may not be coded with a UPC label at all.

Some items are not differentiated by scanning.[15] Different flavors of the same brand may carry the same UPC. A particular item may be discontinued by the supplier and the same UPC used on a new item several months later.

Some symbols are easily marred.[15] A symbol may be placed in a vulnerable spot on the package, where continued human or package contact will blur it.

It is almost impossible to keep current with new products entering the scanner system and with the frequent use of a former UPC code for a different product, size, or type. "When those new UPCs start showing up," Shea points out, "someone has to identify the items they cover and enter them into the system, so as to get them into the sales output." As Shea mentions, the producer can identify his own new products but has no way of doing it for the competition's products.

Because getting a new UPC and slotting it correctly for the trade can cost the producer a great deal of money, the step may be skipped. This causes more confusion. The item may be changed, but the same UPC may be used for it. Or an item may be removed from the marketplace, and a new item later on may be introduced under the same number. This causes problems because even when the change has been identified, the date of the change may not be known.

Special packs sometimes are another source of UPC contamination, says Shea. A manufacturer may offer a bonus pack—say, a pack with 15 percent more volume—under the same UPC. A yogurt producer may offer a banded pack of four under a particular UPC that normally covered only a single package. Where the category has heavy turnover, this can cause serious volume error. "I've seen contamination as high as 30 percent on this sort of error," says Shea.[16]

On the output side, there are errors of hardware, software, and transmission. Apparently only 87 percent of the data are usable.[15]

Scanner Data: Recording Errors at Retail

Some items may be inaccurately recorded by the checkout clerk. Baby foods are an example. A mother buys 20 jars of the same brand of baby food in many different flavors. The checkout clerk scans the chicken noodle dinner jar, then hits the quantity button for the total number of jars, missing the content detail. In some stores this may be a matter of checker discipline, but other stores don't really care that much. Unless the store is using the data for tight inventory control, all it wants to do is to move the customer through the checkout line as quickly as possible.[16]

Category Definition

Product and brand categories in these syndicated national studies are based on the way that the manufacturer and retailer specify. The difficulty, says Shea, is that other manufacturers (the users) often define a category differently for their particular marketing purposes. One of Ore-Ida's brands is Weight-Watchers. The technically correct category might be only diet-type entrees. But Ore-Ida may specify other products for inclusion, and Lean Cuisine, a competitor, may use a different method of classifying. A retail chain may have yet another category definition. So the same basic counting method may produce three different sets of figures.

In-depth coding is necessary, too, according to Shea.[16] And there is a difference in the amount of coding depth provided by the two major in-store scanning suppliers. "IRI has not done a lot of in-depth coding on an item-by-item basis," he reports. "If you want to look at class or subclass information, you may have trouble. Maybe within frozen desserts you have cakes, and perhaps within cakes you want to look at cakes with frosting and those without. Or maybe you want to look at vanilla, chocolate, and strawberry frosting subcategories. You have to be able to spot trends that are important to know for your marketing."

There is a difference in the degree to which each of the two services is willing to provide customizing of categories. "IRI started by saying, 'Here's your service; take it or leave it,' " according to Shea. "Nielsen went the customized route, but underestimated our demands." Nielsen apparently expected Ore-Ida to ask for a small number of subcategories, but frequently the company needed 200, 300, or 400 special subbreaks. There is a real problem, says Shea, in a supplier's being willing and able to supply customized requests at reasonable cost and within a reasonable time.

Both Nielsen and IRI offer these services, and as we have pointed out, so do other firms. Specifically, these measurements cover checks on newspaper advertising, in-store displays and other promotions, and promotions to the trade. The problem for the user, says Shea, is that these measurements are seldom at a finer level than by brand. Banquet, a Con-Agra brand, applies to many categories. Let's say a Banquet 25-

cent coupon runs in the Sunday paper. On what product is that coupon used?

"Ore-Ida," comments Shea, "is in the corn cob business. Green Giant is a competitor. Green Giant is a blanket brand encompassing many different vegetables. When we get a measurement of trade or consumer promotion by Green Giant brand, we have no way of allocating it to their several corn cob items which are competitive to us. This is mainly a problem at the consumer promotion level, and Ore-Ida is just as likely to have its own consumer coupon read 'Good on any Ore-Ida product.' "

The Manufacturing of Data

National syndicated services of scanner data cannot report that they have missing data. Yet they do; not all of their stores and consumer panels produce figures for each time period. So the syndicated reporting services re-create these data by various methods of projection and estimate. If there are many of these superficial data, there is a real question about the validity of the material. Suppose, says Gold, there happens to be an unusually high proportion of artificial data over the Christmas shopping period. Projections or estimates for such a period would be extra difficult, probably extra poor.[17]

This building of missing data seems unique in marketing research.[17]

HANDLING THE MASS OF DATA

National Scanner Data

The overwhelming quantity of these data requires a great amount of time for even an astute analyst to come up with simple summaries that show the major trends. For the first time, there is now a program, Cover-Story (IRI)[20] that plows through all the mass of data and in short order produces the kinds of results that marketers and researchers can quickly grasp.

The program, operating from on-line data, can provide within minutes highlights of performance of a brand and its competition. Specifically, it can sort through all the data and quickly provide a comparison of current results with past results, by category and brand. And it can do this by markets, regions, or key accounts. It can even produce a memo highlighting the major findings, as shown in Exhibit 13.3. It is compatible with not only InfoScan but ScanTrack as well.

User comments are enthusiastic. The director of decision support services of Quaker Oats says there is no other program offering what it does.[21] The same source quotes Gary Overhultz, IRI executive vice presi-

Exhibit 13.3   A COVERSTORY COMPUTERIZED REPORT

To: Director of Marketing

From: CoverStory

Date: 01/18/90

Subject: XYZ Cereal Brand Summary for Four Weeks Ending December 29, 1989

XYZ Cereal's volume share in Total United States was 16.6 in the Total Cereal category for the four weeks ending 12/28/89.This is a decrease of 1.3 share points from a year earlier up by .4 from last period, (4 week ending Nov. 30, 1989). This reflects volume sales of 8.1 million equiv. ounces - down 6.2 percent since last year.

Category volume (currently 48.8 million equiv. ounces) rose 1.4% from a year earlier. Display activity and unsupported price cuts rose over the past year - unsupported price cuts from 31 points to 47. Price fell during the year by .16 dollars to 2.20. Featuring (30 ACV points) and distribution (100 percent of ACV) remained about the same level as a year earlier.

Components of XYZ Cereal Volume

Within the XYZ Cereal line, share decreases have been sustained by:

- 9 oz. off 1.1 share points from last year to 8.2
- 13 oz off .3 share points to 5.4
- Variety pak off .2 to 3.0

XYZ Cereal 9 oz. share decrease may be partly attributed to 6.6 pts of ACV decrease in distribution versus year ago.

Geographic Highlights

XYZ Cereal posted significant gains relative to a year ago in:

- **Philadelphia:** up 2.6 share points from last year to 18.9. This may be attributed to 6.5 pts of ACV distribution vs. year ago and 13.4 points increase in displays since last year.

but posted losses in:

- **Atlanta:** down 1.8 to 13.2 This may be partly attributed to 20.5 ACV points decrease in featuring versus a year ago and 9.1 points decrease in displays versus year ago.

Competitor Summary

Among XYZ Cereal's major competitors, the principal gainers are:

- **Corn Krunch:** up .3 share points from last year to 8.5 (but down .2 since last period).
- **Sun Cereal:** up 2.6 share points from year ago to 6.8.

and loser:
- **Oats Plus:** down .7 to 4.8

XYZ Cereal's share is 16.6 - down 1.3 points from the same period last year.

Corn Krunch share increase may be partly attributed to supported price cuts (up 10 points to 28). Sun Cereal share increase may be partly attributed to 8.0 pts of ACV increase in distribution versus year ago.

Source: Courtesy of Information Resources Inc.

dent, as saying that CoverStory in 15 minutes can cull detailed information from the mass data that would take an analyst 3 days.

CoverStory has helped Ocean Spray, a company marketing bottled cranberry, cran-apple, and cran-raspberry juices.[22] Tracking the sales of each line in thousands of stores with scanner data is a gargantuan task. CoverStory sorts through these data and prepares reports describing each product's market, showing whether total sales are up or down, and it can separate out results for each one of the products. The program makes still further analyses to arrive at possible explanations. Gordon Armstrong of Ocean Spray comments that such analyses don't provide decision making for the user, but they do show what is happening.

Scan*Fact PC, offered by Nielsen, is a similar software service.[23] A menu-driven program, it enables the user to pull from its company database whatever specific data are needed for the analysis of marketplace activity concerning the firm's products and categories. The product breadth can be as wide as industry totals, as narrow as individual UPCs. The geographic breadth may range from national sales areas or territories of the user firm to local markets. It is flexible enough to be operated with a Microsoft mouse. Graphs can be produced.

The program can also produce a Topline Trend Report. The report can take the form of comparing the performance of one product in several markets or the performance of several products in one market.

Reports and charts can be produced showing the relationship of price and share in a given market. Ranking Reports show the current and prior ranks of products, their share and change in share, and their volume and change in volume. Another type of report is the Exception Report, which, based on brand totals, singles out products with unusually good or bad performance (against the performance of comparable products) in a market over a period of time.

In-Store Tracking Services

The On-Line Report System[24] (Ehrhart-Babic) is a parallel, but not identical, system to Scan*Fact PC. The input is the in-store data produced by the firm's National Retail Tracking Index, outlined earlier in this chapter. Results can be checked by product categories and brands. Through a user-friendly program, these data can be produced quickly by regions and markets. All this can be merged with either scanner or traditional retail movement data.

TEST MARKETING: AN INTRODUCTION

If you are like most of us, you like to try out things before you make a big commitment. Test marketing is the same sort of process. It gives the marketing firm some idea of what is likely to happen should it decide to go ahead with a broader expansion (termed a *rollout*) on a regional or national basis.

Test marketing aims at providing estimates of sales volume and market share for a new product, a product extension, or a new marketing device such as a modified advertising campaign, varying media mixes, or change in advertising dollars.

The concept is that of running an experiment. The idea is literally to conduct a test or experiment to arrive at a sales prediction. There are several ways of tackling this. One is to try things out in a series of presumably balanced markets under normal conditions. This is the traditional test market. Then there is the scanner test market, run in specified areas where the research firm has set up relationships with scanner stores. In the controlled test marketing, the research firm forces distribution of the brand, making sure that it is stocked in all selected stores and that stocks are maintained. Then there is simulated test marketing (STM), virtually a laboratory situation, in which real stores are rarely used.

TRADITIONAL TEST MARKETING

THE BASIC STUDY

Many years ago there was a motion picture called *Magic Town*. Its basic theme was that someone had discovered a town in the United States that was so typical of the entire country that whatever happened there was sure to be followed by a parallel national pattern. It wasn't long before someone who observed this moved in to manage national manipulation based on concentrated local effort. Of course, it wasn't that simple. But the concept of traditional test marketing is not too different.

Before getting to the question of the market or markets to be used in traditional test marketing, we must make a basic point. Traditional test marketing is marketing under "normal" conditions. The company's own sales force handles the "sell-in" (meaning getting retailers to stock the product, give it good shelf position, provide in-store promotion and cooperative advertising, as required). The sales staff also makes sure that the shelves remain stocked.

Traditional test marketing is built on the idea that if a small number of reasonably typical communities throughout the country are selected, and the product or marketing method tried there, results will pretty well predict what will happen when there is a rollout on a regional or national basis, and that if a simultaneous series of parallel markets are set up, it will be possible to predict which of two or more product variations, copy approaches, or the like will work better.

We start with an elegant example of how *not* to test market.[25] Phonovision was a service enabling telephone users to dial, hear, and see one another (the image is snapshot size, divided into two half-segments, one of the sender, the other of the receiver). It was aimed, the manufacturer says, for use in hotel lobbies, airports, shopping centers, and other high-traffic indoor locations. It was to appeal to those on expense accounts.

One test telephone was located in the student union of the University of California (Berkeley), the other in the student union at the University of California (Los Angeles). Cost to the user was about $10 for three minutes between Berkeley and Los Angeles.

The test could scarcely have been more poorly designed. It was in the wrong locations, and though some parents of college students may not agree, it did not reach those on expense accounts.

One of the greatest problems is the selection of test areas. For packaged goods, the most important criteria are category development and brand development. The category development index (CDI) and the brand development index (BDI) measure the extent of variation of consumption of category and brand in the proposed test areas and the country as a whole. The idea is to select test markets not too far different from the country in these respects.

Matching (in this case local markets with national data) on sales may not assure comparability.[26] Change may creep in even without the introduction of any known marketing variables. Matching test cities with one another on the basis of causal variables (regular price, national advertising, couponing, displays, in-store fliers, and the like) could help. While the test markets might then deviate from national figures, they appear more likely to remain the same, in a marketing sense, through the test period.

Also important are demographics. As a quick check, per capita income and racial composition are looked at for demographics. On the market profile side, the retail composition (chain and independent grocery stores and drugstores) versus the United States does not match.

In addition, the business nature of the community must be considered. The area should roughly parallel the business composition nationally, by type of business.

Usually, medium-sized cities are selected. They are considered more representative than the larger cities, and the expense of test marketing (media and auditing costs) in larger cities is excessive. Of course, a test for ice cream should not be done in Alaska, nor orange juice in Florida. Certainly, the soap or detergent manufacturers should not think about testing a product in Cincinnati, home of Procter & Gamble.

Distribution channels must be considered. It would not be wise to test a furniture design in North Carolina, which has mainly manufacturers and wholesale outlets but few retail furniture outlets. The general competitive situation should be roughly comparable to what the marketer faces, in terms of outlets such as Sears, Wal-Mart, and Walgreens. Distribution channels should be reasonably similar to the national patterns of the marketer.

The advertising media should be representative. Usually this means that there should be one or two newspapers, one or two television stations, and one or more radio stations. The media should be self-contained, that is, they should not have much coverage beyond the test market. If they do, the marketing firm is not only spending more money for its test than is required, but it cannot relate costs to sales results.

With all of these problems, are there any cities that are commonly chosen for test market? Surprisingly, marketers and research firms seem to think so. Exhibit 13.4 shows a list based on a report of markets typically used by some nine major research firms and advertising agencies, with one added count for each mention in an *Ad Week* count.

The duration of a traditional market test depends on the nature of the product and the consumers' buying habits. The rule of thumb for packaged goods is an average of three purchases (trial and two repeats). If the product is one with a slow but continuing purchase pattern, the test period must be long. In one case of a ready-to-eat cereal, the original buying level was high. But repurchase did not continue, an important requirement for such a product.

It took six months of market testing to determine this. But with an infrequently bought product, such as a laundry detergent, a sound market test might take a year or more. With a durable item such as a refrigerator, test marketing simply is not applicable. Chapter 14 tells how marketers test such products.

Competitive pressure also affects the length of the test. A strong competitor means that the marketer must stay in there longer to find out whether it is possible to make inroads.

This possible competitive action is one of the great risks and uncer-

Exhibit 13.4   A SUMMARY OF THE MOST FREQUENTLY USED TEST MARKETS[27,28]

On eight lists
Erie, Pa.
Ft. Wayne, Ind.
Grand Rapids, Mich.

On seven lists
South Bend, Ind.
Spokane, Wash.
Syracuse, N.Y.

On six lists
Des Moines, Iowa
Lexington, Ky.
Omaha, Nebr.

On five lists
Albany, N.Y.
Albuquerque, N.M.
Binghamton, N.Y.
Boise, Idaho
Evansville, Ind.
Fresno, Calif.
Portland, Maine
Roanoke, Va.
San Antonio, Tex.
Tucson, Ariz.
Wichita, Kans.
Green Bay, Wis.

On four lists
Charleston, S.C.
Corpus Christi, Tex.
Peoria, Ill.
Rockford, Ill.

tainties of the traditional test market. Once a major competitor gets wind of what is going on, it may decide to make an effort to kill the test by spending heavy marketing funds on advertising and coupons to throw off the test results.

This lack of secrecy is a real problem in itself, and with traditional test marketing there is no way of solving it.

The final problem of traditional test marketing is the possibility of economic problems arising in one or more of the selected communities during the course of the test. Regardless of how carefully the various communities have been selected, there is always the chance that local economic conditions may mean that the community is temporarily no longer typical.

Several commercial research firms provide test marketing research.

CONSUMER TRACKING STUDIES

Generally associated with traditional test marketing, consumer tracking studies are diagnostic aids. At this point, it is time to distinguish between evaluation measures and diagnostic aids.

A quantitative or qualitative evaluation says how well the marketing effort is going. A diagnostic measure helps to provide an idea of why it is going well or not going so well. The consumer tracking study helps diagnose why the test marketing program is or is not a success.

These studies track what is, or is not, happening as a result of the marketing campaign. They do this by continuing contact with consumers, doing "waves" of studies, as they are sometimes called, to measure such things as:

- Brand awareness

- Recall of advertising

- Purchase behavior

- Product satisfaction

- Intent to repurchase

Questions about recall of advertising must be on a neutral basis, so as not to suggest the test product or any other product. They have to probe for "unaided advertising recall," which means using an innocuous question such as: "What makes of pizza have you seen or heard advertised within the past week?" No brand is suggested. There are usually follow-up questions without brand suggestion, such as: "Are there any others?"

Typically, the person is first questioned about what brands of pizza he or she is aware of. Brand names are recorded in order of mention. When the respondent stops, a probing question is asked, such as: "Can you think of any others?"

The first two brands named are "top of mind awareness," and often are regarded by marketers as an indication of probable buying. One study offers evidence that the probability of switching to a brand is higher if it is mentioned first or second instead of not being named at all.[29] When all brand mentions are totaled, the proportion each gets is "share of mind."

To determine brand recognition, in some studies an aided-recall question on brands is also asked. Such a question does not really add much to the marketer's knowledge, however.

Purchase and repurchase behavior are particularly significant. Overall audit figures report only total sales and market shares. Such reports may show that market share has risen from 2 percent to 4 percent over the period of a month. They do not show that first-time buyers in the first months were 2 percent (with only half of these rebuying during the second month), and another 3 percent of new buyers during the second month. Such information about the individual consumer is critical.

Determining satisfaction level with the product can often produce extremely helpful information, as will be described in Chapter 14.

Finally, it is helpful to ask about intention to repurchase the product. However, this sort of question is an attitude question only; it cannot be used as a predictor of buying behavior.

These consumer tracking studies can take one of two forms: the "one-shot" study or the panel. While both are done in waves, as described, the one-shot study is conducted with a separate, but comparable, sample of respondents each time. The panel study is conducted with the identical group of people on each wave. Both approaches most often use the telephone interview method, described in Chapter 7.

The one-shot study is nothing more than a continuing study of different samples of the population, as described in Chapter 7. Whether one-shot or panel study, the crucial starting point is definition of the target group. Then exactly what is to be measured is determined, to assist in diagnostics of the test marketing effort. The one-shot approach offers the advantage of getting true measures of advertising recall and brand awareness.

The panel approach (going back to the same people over the time of the market test) cannot handle either of these, since participants, following the first contact, are well aware of what the game is all about.

But the panel approach offers special advantages. Since the same people are questioned over the period of the test, the marketer is provided with a series of snapshots. An internal analysis of this identical group of people can provide considerable information about people's repeat buying.

If the particular test is one of advertising approach or of advertising pressure, where different markets are used for varying marketing approaches, specific questions may be helpful to the marketer.

Panels are available on a standard basis by some research firms and may be established by other research firms as required. Some are mail panels, others are by telephone. By mail, the cooperation level may be as low as 10 percent; it may be 50 percent by telephone. With a continuing panel, the annual dropout rate may approach 20 percent.

There are other problems with panels. Most consist primarily of women. This is fine as long as the product is one bought mainly by women, such as breakfast cereals. It is not so good for a product purchased chiefly by men, such as beer.

In addition, panels include response bias. The respondent does not always provide unbiased information. New panel members are likely to report unusually high purchase levels, simply because of the novelty of the measurement. Sometimes the marketing firm discards the first measurement, waiting until respondents settle down.

Tracking studies must meet rigorous requirements if they are to be useful.[30] They must be able to measure small differences. Large shifts are rare in tracking studies. Thus the sample design has to include a large and random sample with rigorous controls in execution. It has to be spelled out in a manner that allows each sampling wave to be completely comparable.

The questionnaire should include items that are purchase-predictive. The sequence should minimize bias and should include queries about competitor performance so that marketing management can avoid the same errors and learn from the same successes. A major gasoline producer, for example, planned advertising that would emphasize quality of service at its stations. But tracking studies showed that a competitor following this strategy for years had failed to improve attitudes toward its service. Advertising alone could not achieve the goal, since individual dealers were not perceived as providing it.

CONTROLLED TEST MARKETING

Controlled test marketing is rather like the pharmaceutical research procedure in which selected markets are given a "shot in the arm" to see what happens. The concept is: Let's not wait for the long-term case study method of traditional test marketing, but let's push things to get a fast reading.

Sometimes termed minimarket testing, controlled test marketing parallels the minimarket testing of scanners. Depending on the nature of the stores, it uses either scanner measurements, "old-fashioned" in-store auditing, or a combination of both.

It is a test where sales are measured within a controlled store environment. The manufacturer generally chooses the markets. The length and frequency of the checks are set to parallel the real-life elements of expected product movement, repurchase cycle of the category, and purchase seasonality.

The research firm conducting the controlled market test obtains distribution of the product in a representative sample of stores within each market selected for the test. It handles "sell-in" and guarantees that this will be 100 percent. (Retailers are paid for shelf space.) It stocks the product in the stores, handling both warehousing and distribution. The research firm maintains retail inventory levels, handles pricing, shelf conditions, and building and placement of displays. The research firm even handles the billing function. It literally acts both as a wholesaler and a very busy, attentive sales force.

Measurements of product and brand movement parallel to those of the national services are reported for the test period.

The method offers several advantages over traditional test marketing. Costs are far lower. The forced test requires only about six months, as against the much longer time of the traditional test market. The whole process is accelerated. The sell-in period is far less than the usual 60 to 90 days. The method also makes it more difficult for competitors to know what is going on, so there is less chance that a competitor will jam the market.

However, this is not normal marketing. Distribution is abnormally high and is kept that way; preferred shelf position at eye level in the appropriate aisle is provided, along with a high number of facings; and there may be in-store promotion. These are scarcely normal marketing conditions, and they are most unlikely to be attained in national distribution. The results may thus provide highly optimistic results.

The usual form of controlled market test may be declining. The problem today is getting retailer cooperation. As will be shown in Chapter 17, the retailer today knows, largely through scanner results, just what shelf space is worth, and a declining number of retailers are now willing to sell space for controlled tests.

Many chain stores will sell, for a fee, their scanner information.

But "promotion testing just has to produce less costly answers than before," says Fitzhugh H. Corr, chairman of Burgoyne Information Services, "and the single-source facilities have become excessively expensive and allow little freedom in the choice of cities and store types to include in the test." It is therefore hardly surprising that SPAR/Burgoyne is one of four of the larger research firms still offering the common form of controlled market tests. The other three are Audits & Surveys; Ehrhart-Babic; and PAR (Product Acceptance & Research).

An example of the usefulness of controlled market tests is given by PAR.[31] A manufacturer of a flavored laxative wanted to determine the impact of an additional flavor on its total sales and the degree to which it would cannibalize the existing flavors in the line. A controlled store test in Peoria, Ill., showed that the product would increase sales with little impact on the firm's existing flavors.

IRI's BehaviorScan[32] is a state-of-the-art controlled market test. The locations include Pittsfield, Mass.; Marion, Ind.; Eau Claire, Wis.; Midland, Tex.; Grand Junction, Colo.; and Cedar Rapids, Iowa. The single-source approach is used in a creative way to produce a measurement system covering both individual purchasing behavior and exposure to television advertising.

IRI-installed scanners in supermarkets account for some 95 percent of total all-commodity sales volume in each area. In several markets, these scanners have also been installed in drug outlets to permit broader coverage of product types. Through the presentation of special ID cards at the store checkout, these scanners keep track of purchases by individual panel families.

There are up to 3,000 panel households in each area, with representative demographics in terms of household size, household income, and age of household head. In some of the households, there is an electronic device on the television set that makes it possible to cut into the regularly scheduled broadcast to substitute a test commercial, and arrangements have been made with local newspapers and some national magazines to print special editions of their publications for the panel households. The morning newspaper of one household may contain a cents-off coupon for the test product; the household next door may get a newspaper without such a coupon.[33]

This process offers some interesting test marketing possibilities. It can be designed to measure the introduction of a product with typical marketing support (advertising, store promotions, etc.). Or it can be designed, under very real conditions, to test two or more varying prices, advertising approaches, or store promotion approaches.

As appealing as this concept appears, it is not a panacea. R. J. Reynolds has major company entries in several very different broad areas. In some product areas, the approach simply is not appropriate.[34] Kentucky Fried Chicken, for instance, is not sold through grocery stores.

Tobacco and wines and spirits (Hublein) do less than half their sales in grocery and drug outlets. And store-scanner data cannot pinpoint individual behavior, only household behavior. These products are individualist products. Further, the electronic test market is concentrated in smaller counties, while consumption of cigarettes, spirits, and many other products follow a different pattern. Also, for both groups of products, various state laws govern permissible marketing. In the case of spirits, this means that in some states the products are sold only through state stores, so that the sample of the electronic test markets is meaningless.

Nevertheless, the food end of R. J. Reynolds (Del Monte) has profitably used electronic test marketing for media-weight tests, new-product evaluations, and pricing and promotion tests. But even within the environment of success, Del Monte has learned that the test market results (and this would apply to *any* test market results, regardless of the method) do not predict trade reaction.

SIMULATED TEST MARKETING

Our limited view of simulated test marketing (STM) is that it is really test marketing in a test tube situation. To parallel traditional test marketing, it applies only to a situation where the product and its packaging, pricing, and advertising and promotion have been developed in finished form. While many of the research firms offering STMs offer them, in their terms, as concept tests or other less developed forms, our review here is on the well-rounded form that includes all the marketing variables having the greatest chance of producing dependable estimates of sales dollars and market shares.

Although there are variations, as we will show, typically consumers are invited into a central location facility, such as a research center in a shopping mall (in the case of one service, a real store). They are given information (generally in the form of advertising) about the test product, then invited to shop stocked shelves (including the test product) with provided funds.

Following the first purchase, or lack of it, the consumer is later interviewed to determine repeat buying and frequency of purchase of the test product. Then, generally, a computer model of behavior provides an estimate of sales volume for the new product or line extension.

In 1987, 53 percent of STMs were conducted for foods, 24 percent for health and beauty aids, 16 percent for household products, and 7 percent for other products (such as pet foods and beverages).[35]

SOME ISSUES

The basic idea of STMs is that they can replace market tests, with all of their high costs, long duration, and risk of discovery by competitors. Many marketers consider simulated test marketing as a kind of pretest, to be used as a fairly good measuring instrument to predict sales volume and market share. Gold[17] says that "more and more marketers are forgoing marketplace testing by going directly from STMs to national/regional rollouts. The risks," he says, "are higher this way, but they can't afford the time or the competitive reaction that market testing poses."

But while STMs, as we will show, seem to produce reasonably good results, not all is right with their world. There are some issues, some problems.

Artificiality

As with controlled store tests, STMs have many aspects of artificiality, perhaps even more so. With almost all STMs, there is forced advertising exposure. The shopping environment is often forced and artificial. Sometimes the sales prediction has no provision for competitive action.

On the positive side, STMs emphasize measurement of behavior, which is more dependable than measurement of attitude.

Validity

According to the 1987 survey mentioned above,[35] 40 percent questioned validity (we assume this refers to services competitive with their own). It is certainly true that we received little useful material other than broad claims when we asked suppliers for substantiating data. There was only one that produced results worth showing.

Reliability

Lipton used two different STM sources for a particular product, where testing controls were held constant. Qualifications for respondents were the same. The test conditions in the simulated store setting were identical: The competitive set, including pricing, and the number of items and facings for each product, were identical. Advertising for the test product was the same in each test, and in each test the advertising was presented in a cluttered environment. The in-home use periods were the same. Each supplier was given identical marketing inputs to help drive their respective models.

But there were some basic differences in the two methods. Supplier A used a 500 sample, Supplier B, a 300 sample. Supplier A motivated trial buying by offering a 25 percent discount on all varieties/sizes in the simulated store, while Supplier B provided a flat sum in the form of a coupon to be applied to all purchases.

Lipton was amazed that the basic results of the two services were so close. One estimated the new product's share at 3.0 percent, the other at 3.4 percent. Each predicted that cannibalization from the Lipton parent brand would account for some 40 percent of its volume. But the test provided more than reliability. After the first year in the market, the test product had achieved a 3.2 percent share.[36]

Use of a Simulation Model

Using a simulation model means only that through a trial-and-error process, various inputs are incorporated into the system until a particular weighting of factors comes up with an estimate (in this case chiefly sales) that is reasonably close and provides reasonably good continuing estimates. But constant checks are made on an ongoing basis to provide adjustment of weights as required.

Dependability of Predictions from the Model

What the simulation model generates in the way of predictions depends on the elements of the information produced by the specific research, the accuracy of the statement of the marketing program, and the dependability of the particular modeling program. We cannot comment on the latter, since we lack real validity results, but we can on the other two aspects.

We will show the inputs going into the system for each of the suppliers whose services we report. Less often seriously considered is the important input of the marketing plan.

The specific inputs of the client's marketing plan are an important building block in the predictions of any of the modeling programs, but they may often be the weakest. Moult, then with a major STM firm, commented: "... We've learned to adjust for overstatements that consumers make in survey research, but not yet how to adjust for overly optimistic marketing plan assumptions from clients, such as awareness or advertising impact, distribution, trade deal response, and coupon redemption rates.[37]

Eskin, then a vice chairman of Information Resources Inc.[38], was candid enough to say that many suppliers (he excludes his own firm) do not take seriously the importance of the correctness of the submitted marketing plan. Too often, says Eskin, the research firm accepts the plan on faith, only to learn later that there was an erroneous forecast of distribution.

Malhotra[39] brings these warnings to life. In one case, actual redemptions were far lower than the marketing plan called for. In another case, while the media dollars actually spent were according to the plan, GRPs (gross rating points), because of poor copy, were far less than the plan called for. The result was a significant drop in predicted volume for the first year of sales.

The prediction of and reaction to competitive effort within the marketing plan, says Malhotra, is ". . . a factor most difficult to account for."[39] Lix and Clancy go on to say that "competitive response to new products and new campaigns is both swift and sure. Soon after launch the new brand (or new campaign . . .) is hammered by the very products it was designed to dislodge."[40]

Procter & Gamble, based on a strong rating in such a test of its Wondra Hand Cream, went to a full rollout. But Cheseborough-Pond, with its Vaseline Intensive Care Lotion, quickly knocked out the new entry with a two-for-one promotion.[41]

Colgate, with its Fab 1 Shot, a laundry detergent–fabric softener, made a different kind of mistake.[42] It went ahead on the incorrect premise that the product's primary market would be largely families. But since the product was packaged in small, individual envelopes, 1 Shot had its greatest appeal among convenience-minded singles. Today, its market share is only .1 percent. Although the simulation may have been accurate, the assumed audience was not.

THE MAJOR SYNDICATED SERVICES AND THEIR OFFERINGS

Our review covers five major services:

- Bases (Burke Marketing Research, Cincinnatti)
- Macro Assessor (M/A/R/C, Irving, Tex.)
- Litmus (Yankelovich, Clancy, Shulman, Newton, Mass.)
- STM System (Market Simulations, Westport, Conn.)
- Comp/Comp Plus (Elrick & Lavidge, Downers Grove, Ill.)

Bases and Macro Assessor are included because of an estimate[43] that the former accounts for 60 percent of the market, the latter for 20 percent. Each of the others is included because of our opinion that they have one or more innovative aspects.

The Typical Test

An outline of the characteristics of the typical simulated marketing test is shown in Exhibit 13.5.

We look first at the testing by *the nature and stage of the product* offered by these services. Most of the five major services offer what they term simulated test marketing for line extensions and restaging (repositioning) of current products. But our purposely restricted definition of STMs means that only those products going through the rigorous degree of testing required for new products, including availability of the finished product (also covering packaging and pricing) and specific marketing plans, are included in our summary. We are simply saying that a simulated marketing test (SMT), from our perspective, should parallel all the elements of a real market test.

Then there is *the testing process*. While *the recruiting process* varies

Exhibit 13.5   THE TYPICAL SIMULATED MARKETING TEST

Nature and Stage of the Product
1. Place of product within the firm's product line
   - New product
   - Line extension
   - Restaging
2. By degree of product and marketing tangibility
   - Concept
   - Prototype
   - Finished product (product, packaging, and pricing) and marketing tangibility (specific advertising and promotion plan)

The Testing Process
1. Recruiting and screening
2. Presentation of stimuli (product, advertising)
3. Product placement or purchase
4. Product trial/usage
5. Measurement of repeat buying

Modeling Input
1. Test data on trial and repeat buying
2. Marketing plan
3. Probable competitive reaction

Modeling Output
1. Volume
2. Share

somewhat among the five services we review, all share the common *security screening*. In their recruiting questioning, they screen out those who are possible communication "leaks," such as those working for a marketer, advertising agency, advertising medium, or marketing research firm.

All the services *display advertising of the product and the product itself*, though the nature of each display varies from one service to another. In each service, there is *product placement in the home*, either through purchase by or gift to the test participant. The specific method for each service will be discussed shortly.

And finally there are measurements of *product trial* and, generally only on client demand, *repeat buying*.

The *modeling input* refers to the detailed marketing plan that the research firm obtains from the client firm, so that it can have specifics to program into its simulation model. Exhibit 13.5 shows the three main elements for which each service wants input. Most have far more demands, as we will later be reviewing.

The two common elements of *modeling output* from all of these services are volume and share. But each service has its own additional specifics.

While all of the services have some things in common, they also have many differences. (Where a particular service has more than one offering, we will consider the one we think is more realistic and predictive.) Exhibit 13.6 outlines the major characteristics of each of the five.

There are some procedural points common to all of the services: All are prepared to select a sample of potential purchasers, and all conduct follow-up in-home checks to measure continuing response. There are common areas of forecast, including percentage of triers, repeat rate, cannibalization, attracting customers of competing brands, and measurement of consumer profiles.

BASES AND RELATED MODELING

Bases III (Bases Burke Institute)[44,45] tests products in a controlled store situation, as described earlier in this chapter, generally four to five stores in as many markets. After being qualified as in Bases I or II, participants are given print ads or shown commercials for the test product. They are then provided with purchase coupons.

The after-use interview, usually by WATS-line questioning, covers a wide range of topics, including purchase intent (intensity of feeling, reasons, quantity, frequency, and size), attitude (like/dislike, price/value, uniqueness and attribute ratings), other brands that would be reduced or eliminated, and additional questions by client request.

Exhibit 13.6 MAJOR CHARACTERISTICS OF FIVE OF THE SYNDICATED STM SERVICES

	Bases	Macro Assessor	Litmus	Market Simulations	Comp/ Comp Plus
Market Locations					
Marketer's choice	X	X		X*	X
Specified standard markets				X	
Choice based on brand/category dominance	X		X		
Choice based on marketing plans			X		
Participant Sampling					
Recruiting medium:					
At central location	X	X		X	X
By telephone		X	X	X*	X
Character of sample:					
Household purchaser of category	X*		X	X	
Category usage	X*	X		X	X
Brand purchasers	X*		X	X*	
Potential purchasers	X*	X		X*	
Demographics	X*	X		X*	
Sampling method:					
Quota intercepts	X*	X		X	X
Probability	X*		X		
Sample size per test	300–600	300–400	300–600	250–500	300–600
Location of Test Procedure					
Simulated store		X	X	X*	X
Actual store	X				
Questioning at Test Location					
Method:					
Interviewer	X	X	X		X
Interactive		X		X	
Questioning before exposure*		X		X	
Questioning after exposure				X*	
Follow-up at Home Questioning	X	X	X	X	
Input for Modeling					
Details of client marketing plan*	X	X	X	X	

Forecasts*

Percent triers	X	X	X	X	X
Repeat rate	X	X	X	X	X
Cannibalization	X	X	X	X	X
Attracting customers of competing brands	X	X	X	X	X
Consumer profiles	X	X	X	X*	X
Sensitivity analysis			X	X*	
Optimization	X	X*	X		

Post-Test Check

Direct mail*					X

---

*See text discussion of particular service.

A top-line estimate (termed *volumetrics*) is provided about six weeks following start of fieldwork. An empirically based model using actual in-market data, the report also includes a comparison of key measures from other products tested.

MACRO ASSESSOR

This simulated test-marketing system is a combination of Entro, a system devised and introduced by M/A/R/C in early 1986, and the Assessor system, acquired by the firm in the summer of 1989. As with all other forms of STMs, we review only their specific techniques connected with final product and packaging, pricing, and marketing plans (advertising and promotion).

The system (the firm terms it *Phase 4: Total Proposition Evaluation*) uses research testing facilities in malls and office locations. Along with personal interviewers in the questioning process, PCs are used, so that with a separate interviewer and participant for each, a number of interviews can be conducted separately but simultaneously.

Once recruited, the participant is asked about purchasing of the product category (frequency and type of store). He or she is then asked questions about the evoked product set (the products the participant considers acceptable, including the most often purchased product, the next-choice product, products bought on the last buying occasion, other products bought within the last three months, other products bought within the past year, and a single product the buyer would not purchase). Somewhat similar (not identical) questions are then asked about the products within the evoked set.

Advertising is displayed to consumers in a cluttered format through either a portfolio of print ads or a reel of television commercials. One of the advertisements is for the product being tested. Immediate recall is checked, along with details of recall and believability and meaningfulness.

Following advertising in the cluttered format, consumers are asked to shop in a simulated retail store. Consumers have the opportunity of purchasing any of the brands, including the test product, on display. Nonpurchasers of the test brand are given either a sample of or a coupon for the test product, and they are asked about their reasons for not buying.

After home use of the product, a telephone interview covers the purchase opportunity for the test product and other products in the lab/store shopping list, preference for test product or other products, expected purchase behavior for test products or other products, and evaluation of post-usage appeal for the test product (purchase intent, livability, price–value rating, uniqueness versus other products, overall acceptance, rating versus pretrial expectation, product likes and dislikes, reasons for not reordering, perceptions of test product (same product/user attributes as in central location interview), and custom questions by client request.

But there is still a crucial missing ingredient: moving from the test results to a prediction of sales. The attitudinal measures of appeal, the behavioral decision process within the competitive environment, and the preference for the new product relative to other products are used either singly or in combination within the marketing model of the system. If the particular product is one sold through scanner outlets, M/A/R/C access to InfoScan data (described earlier in this chapter) can provide calibration of forecasts.

THE LITMUS MODEL

In the Litmus model (Yankelovich, Clancy, Shulman),[46,47] once the qualified person has entered the mall research facility, he or she is taken through a brief interview covering attitudes, beliefs, and behavior relating to the product category. Then the participant watches a half-hour television program, including advertising for the new product and up to four additional commercials (competitive and control). When print is to be the major form of advertising, a print portfolio is used.

In the final stage, participants visit a simulated store, where they can spend their own money to buy any product they wish, at a discount. The proportion of those buying the test product gives the estimate of new product trial.

In an exit interview, participants are questioned about new-product and competitive-product perceptions and attitudes, advertising recall, and anticipated purchases. As they leave, they take with them whatever products they bought, and it is assumed they will use these in the normal way.

Two to six weeks later (depending on the purchase cycle), the participants are contacted by telephone to check product attitudes and repeat purchases. If product "wear-in" or "wear-out" is a possibility, potential repeaters are provided with more product and again interviewed by telephone for additional diagnostic information.

The marketer moving into a test market or a regional rollout, as shown earlier in this chapter, needs much more than sales data. The Litmus model seems to provide an amalgam of simulated test marketing and models. As with some of the other systems, Litmus, using both market-response data and detailed monthly marketing plan data provided by the client for itself and the major competition, turns out forecasts of consumer awareness, dollar and unit sales, sensitivity of sales to changes in the various inputs of the marketing plan (such aspects as media weight or share of voice, distribution, promotions, couponing, and sampling) to obtain greater share without raising spending. But its unique contribution is that it also can seek out the optimal marketing plan combination to generate the highest sales level within the spending constraints.

STM System

The STM system (Market Simulations Inc.) has a unique feature—its kiosk.[48] This furniture cabinet encloses a computer, a VCR, and a touchscreen-equipped TV/computer monitor.[49] The touchscreen interface is the heart of the system: It enables respondents to interact naturally and easily. Since the kiosk can be programmed to foresee and react to all of the possible interactions between the stimuli presented to the participant and his or her response, full shopping trips, respondent-controlled, can be naturally planned and presented.

The kiosk can computerize pictures, written words, and other visual materials. Images of packages can be displayed on store shelves, with prices immediately below on the shelf edge. For a new product without packaging, an artist's rendition can be computerized and touched up, or the packaging can be created from scratch.

Since the kiosk can computerize sounds (spoken words, music, or other audio material), both words and music can be easily built into the concept presentation. Oral instructions can be provided to participants as required.

Finally, the kiosk records all interactions between respondent and machine.

There are now 18 mall locations in 13 large cities with STM kiosks. Most tests use between five and ten kiosks. So there is some choice for the marketer in terms of category or brand dominance. Typically, five to ten markets per test are included. Qualified respondents are recruited within malls, and low incidence samples are recruited by telephone.

The procedure with the STM system is as follows: The participants are offered a cash-value certificate, redeemable at the end of the interview, for their participation. They are then taken into a private room and seated before the screen. The screen displays a question about how the respondent heard about the last new product in the category, and the touchscreen provides four answer categories: *advertising, coupon, both* and *just saw it on the shelf.*

Those responding "advertising" then see an executed television ad concept, shown in a real-life situation with visualized copy points as demonstrated in Exhibit 13.7, but including a sound track. Competing ad concepts are also shown. In each case, the voice-over is provided by a professional announcer. Sequential visuals contain the basics of the executional idea. The consumer both sees the copy points and hears them.

A "coupon" response is followed with an inquiry about "casual" or "committed" use. Those in the first group are handed a cents-off coupon for the test brand; those in the second group are given three cents-off coupons (one for the test brand and two for competitive brands most heavily couponing in the marketplace).

Those responding "both advertising and coupon" see and hear the advertising and get the appropriate coupon(s).

Exhibit 13.7 **SIMULATED ADVERTISING EXAMPLE FROM MARKET SIMULTATIONS**

Source: Courtesy of Market Simulations.

Exhibit 13.8   **SIMULATED SHELF EXAMPLE FROM MARKET SIMULATIONS**

Source: Courtesy of Market Simulations.

Participants responding "saw it on the shelf" are immediately taken visually (via the screen) to a simulated shelf showing realistic computerized packages (where there can be as many computerized packages as needed for the display). An example is shown in Exhibit 13.8. Now the shopper can select a particular package for a close-up look, and on comes the back panel of the individual package, as shown in Exhibit 13.9. Another screen-touch provides a look at the side panel for more information, and another touch enlarges the partly exposed side of the package, bringing the whole side into focus for reading or examination, as shown in Exhibit 13.10.

Immediately following the trial shopping trip, the participant answers a paper-and-pencil series of questions. First among these ques-

Exhibit 13.9　　**SIMULATED PACKAGE BACK FROM MARKET SIMULATIONS**

Source: Courtesy of Market Simulations.

Exhibit 13.10　　**SIMULATED PACKAGE SIDE PANEL FROM MARKET SIMULATIONS**

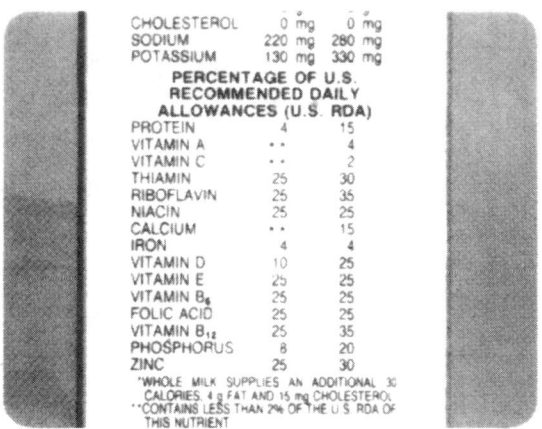

CHOLESTEROL	0 mg	0 mg
SODIUM	220 mg	280 mg
POTASSIUM	130 mg	330 mg

PERCENTAGE OF U.S.
RECOMMENDED DAILY
ALLOWANCES (U.S. RDA)

PROTEIN	4	15
VITAMIN A	* *	4
VITAMIN C	* *	2
THIAMIN	25	30
RIBOFLAVIN	25	35
NIACIN	25	25
CALCIUM	* *	15
IRON	4	4
VITAMIN D	10	25
VITAMIN E	25	25
VITAMIN B$_6$	25	25
FOLIC ACID	25	25
VITAMIN B$_{12}$	25	35
PHOSPHORUS	8	20
ZINC	25	30

*WHOLE MILK SUPPLIES AN ADDITIONAL 30
CALORIES, 4 g FAT AND 15 mg CHOLESTEROL
**CONTAINS LESS THAN 2% OF THE U.S. RDA OF
THIS NUTRIENT

Source: Courtesy of Market Simulations.

tions is purchase intent, included mainly for cathartic reasons. Optional diagnostic questions may include open-ended likes and dislikes, performance and/or image ratings, and other specifics of particular interest to the particular manufacturer.

　　Following an in-home trial of a sample of the new item, a telephone interview offers the person a chance to repurchase the item at the same original price without delivery cost. After this questioning, the respon-

**Exhibit 13.11   THREE-MONTH BRAND SHARES AMONG
KIOSK RESPONDENTS AND NATIONAL
SALES DATA**

	Kiosk Respondents	National Sales Data
Peanut Butter		
Jif	41%	44%
Skippy	33	31
Peter Pan	27	25
Refrigerated Juices		
Tropicana	45	45
Minute Maid	38	38
Citrus Hill	8	10
Dole	5	6
Chiquita	3	1
Fresh 'n Natural	1	3
Lo-Cal Frozen		
Lean Cuisine	39	37
Weight Watchers	34	38
Budget Gourmet SlimLine	26	25

dent is queried about product usage patterns and reactions and about buying plans (frequency and quantities).

Market Simulations has provided some validation data that seem worth reporting. While the data are limited in numbers, they are specific and cover both simulation and modeling.

The simulation side is the shopping trip. The validation thus far has covered, in each of three product categories, some 200 purchasing respondents (three-month purchasing) in five locations. Kiosk store brand shares and syndicated share data for the same quarter are shown in Exhibit 13.11. This has to be a pretty good record.

The validation score for the forecasting model is a little less impressive. The first step was to locate other STMs that generated correct predictions against actual sales (and, of course, this required considerable input from cooperative manufacturers). Then the MSI prediction was compared with these others. In total, the 228 projections covered 98 projects in 28 categories, and results showed the MSI model to be "equally accurate." So the validation says, in effect, that "we are as good as you are."

COMP AND COMP PLUS

These STM procedures are offered by Elrick & Lavidge, one of the larger marketing research firms in the United States. In the Comp procedure,[50] when qualified respondents are taken into the mall research facility, they are asked about their use of related products and awareness and perceptions of those products, how they rate the importance of product benefits and attributes in the purchase decision, past purchase and use behavior, future purchase intentions, and demographics.

Television or print advertising is then exposed for the test product and related products, with recall. Next, in a simulated store, respondents are given a chance to buy test products or related products from displays on shelves or in cabinets. Prices are included. The participants then rate the test product and each of several other familiar products.

Following an at-home trial, a personal in-home interview covers likes, dislikes, and perceptions. If there are repurchase waves after the final wave, there is a remeasurement of product perceptions to determine change and to measure any change in usage rate. The data are collected by telephone interviews.

The Comp Plus procedure offers a degree of uniqueness.[51] Firms using the service are provided an opportunity to develop their own direct mail lists of potential triers of the test product. This can lead to a more thorough understanding of the characteristics of the trier pool.

In the Comp test, a trier profile is developed from the profile of those who "purchased" the product in the simulated store. This is enriched (through overlays), with further demographics and psychographics, from the database of the parent company. An important side benefit is that the marketer wishing to build a customer/prospect database has the means of doing so.

OBSERVATIONS AND COMMENTS ABOUT TEST MARKETING

There is no single correct method for running a market test. Each product requires individual consideration of whether a market test is required, and if so, what type is best. One obvious risk is the possibility of a competitor's discovery of and intervention in the test. Another concern is the question of how predictive the test is.

Test marketing, with all of its limitations, is still in good fashion. According to a 1987 study[52] of 140 consumer-product firms conducted by Market Facts, 51 percent had conducted marketing within the preceding year. The study also showed that:

- 31 percent used the traditional method.

- 47 percent used a scanner panel.

- 76 percent used a simulated situation.

- 47 percent used a controlled test.

These figures total more than 100 percent because many companies used more than one method.

SPECIALIZED ANALYTIC TOOLS TO EXAMINE AND TEST ASPECTS OF THE MARKETING MIX

Because of the availability of purchasing and media exposure through single-source data, specialized electronic methods of data analysis have been developed. Some are as simple as tracking. Others are more sophisticated, aimed at spotting significant variations in buying and the reasons for these, and analyses aimed at evaluating various aspects of a marketing program.

EVALUATION OF VARIOUS MARKETING STRATEGIES

There are a number of systems that provide ways to analyze causes of particular events in the marketing mix: to determine, for instance, through analysis of existing data, the impact of trade promotions, pricing, and the like.

Adpro (Nielsen) is one such system.[53] Marketing mix management, as Nielsen terms it, integrates the key elements of television and promotion to help the user evaluate marketing strategy and compare it with that of the competition. The television portion provides gross rating points (GRPs) and share of voice for network and local television, based on the Nielsen Monitor-Plus service and the Nielsen Station Index, both described in Chapter 18.

Consumer promotion is measured by a continuous tracking of coupons, sweepstakes, and refunds in newspapers, free-standing inserts (FSIs), magazines, and direct mail. It is reported on a 100-household-impression basis derived from an event's circulation and the number of households in a given market.

Trade promotion is monitored weekly by brand and market and covers retail feature and display support. It is translated into impressions per 100 households by a calculation using retail transaction counts and number of households in a particular market.

Adpro enables the user to understand the relationships between sales and the many aspects of advertising and promotion.[54] It can be used to monitor how well the advertising and promotion aspects of the marketing plan have been executed. There are many capabilities provided through analysis of some of the aspects by consumer groups such as identifying the target group(s) for a brand based on household purchase behavior, and profiling the target groups' television preferences by time of day and type of program.

ScanPro Promotion Analysis Services (Nielsen) provides an analysis of what happens in the retail store and why.[55] There is on-line access to sales in scanner stores, as well as to user-selected promotion activity (nearly 100 retail conditions covering price cuts, feature ads, and displays) by markets, brands, and time periods. Even incremental profit from specific promotion events can be calculated, given the users' specifying of margins and spending levels. A simulator program offers a prediction of what various promotion strategies will produce in terms of impact and profitability.

Also available is a ScanPro Monitor, an on-line database of weekly data from over 2,300 ScanTrack stores accounting for 70 percent of national grocery volume. The user firm can select a report from either a menu of standard formats or menu of customized formats, or it can construct its own analysis of specific issues or events. Consulting services are also available.

ScanFact (Nielsen) is a software system for the PC user aimed at facilitating access to and analysis of Nielsen data.[56] The marketing executive or researcher can use the database to aggregate for products, markets, or time periods. Reports can be generated, and it is possible to create an automated production system that automatically calls the Nielsen mainframe computer, which then updates the information and produces the desired reports and graphics.

DataServer (IRI)[57] utilizes the scanner database of the particular user. From there it is possible to go from the simple matter of retrieving required data to a complicated analysis leading to forecasting and promotion planning. It makes these analyses to the PC user, tied into a mainframe containing the database.

This software can be used to make competitive analyses over a period of time and by area. It can track new product introductions, indicating adjustment of marketing strategies as required. It can make market-by-market comparisons and flag trouble spots.

The Analyst WorkStation (Management Science Associates) is perhaps the most sophisticated of the systems. It allows the user at a PC or PC-compatible workstation to pull data stored and updated in the mainframe of the leasing firm (Management Science Associates), and to massage and format these in many different ways.[58,59] It comes close to meeting the definition of a marketing information system given in Chapter 3.

To give some idea of the variety of information that may be stored, we mention client sales/shipments, in-store scanner data, scanner/diary panel, media expenditures and causal types of data, whether produced by the client firm or purchased from a third-party supplier.

The system can be used to track new products, evaluate promotion and pricing policies, analyze advertising effectiveness, relate product movement to retail aspects (distribution, shelf facings, and in-store merchandising), and prepare sales reports for the field.

The system permits the user to examine, analyze, and graph the data. Its flexibility is so great that the user can put together the analysis in many different time segments (weekly, four-week, monthly, quarterly, etc.), compare the current period with some selected base; compare the firm's product with a selected list of brands; calculate share on one or more bases (category, segment, competitive set, etc.). The user can create or modify any of these.

ENDNOTES

[1] *The National Total Market Audit.* New York: Audits & Surveys, undated.

[2] L. N. Gold. "Introduction to the Workshop: a Proper Definition of Terms," in *Fulfilling the Promise of Electronic Single Source Data.* New York: Advertising Research Foundation, 1989, 5–9.

[3] *Tomorrow's Standard . . . Today!* Northbrook, Ill.: Nielsen Marketing Research, 1989.

[4] L. C. Winters. "Home Scan vs. Store Scan Panels: Single Source Options for the 1990s." *Marketing Research*, December 1989, 62–63.

[5] *InfoScan.* Chicago: Information Resources, Inc., 1990.

[6] Magid Abraham. *Letter*, July 20, 1990.

[7] Barbara Jarzab. Telephone conversation, Aug. 1, 1990.

[8] Nancy Millman. "2 Product-Tracking Firms Join to Tackle Rival A. C. Nielsen." *Chicago Sun-Times*, Oct. 2, 1990, 31.

[9] Bob Bregenzer. Letter, Mar. 19, 1991.

[10] *Multi-Media Consumer Profile.* Coral Springs, Fla.: Birch Scarborough, undated.

[11] *National Retail Tracking Index.* Englewood Cliffs, N.J.: Ehrhart-Babic, 1989.

[12] *Scanner Data in Practice.* Lexington, Mass.: Temple, Barker & Sloane, 1989.

[13] M. A. Abate. "Applications and Analyses in Single-Source Data: Experiences of the American Chicle Group, Warner-Lambert." *Journal of Advertising Research* 29, no. 6 (1989):RC3–6.

[14]"The Best-Laid Plans." *Inside Research*, Oct. 1990, 1.

[15]*More Valid Reasons: A Study of the Reliability and Validity of SAMI Scanner-Based Tracking Information*. Columbus, Ohio: SAMI/Burke, 1988.

[16]B. M. Shea. Interview, Nov. 25, 1990.

[17]L. N. Gold. "High-Tech Research Systems: Look Before You Leap." *American Marketing Association, 10th Annual Marketing Research Conference, 1989*.

[18]G. D. Metzger. "Single Source: Yes and No." *Media Research Workshop*. New York: Advertising Research Foundation, 1989.

[19]M. F. Riche. "Scanning for Dollars." *American Demographics*, Nov. 1989, 8.

[20]*CoverStory*. Chicago: Information Resources Inc., 1990.

[21]Betsy Spethmann. "Software Softens Scanner Data Deluge." *Advertising Age*, May 14, 1990, 44.

[22]Jan Larson. "Expert Systems Save Time." *American Demographics* 12, no. 7 (July 1990): 23.

[23]*SCAN*FACT PC User Guide*. Northbrook, Ill.: A. C. Nielsen Co., 1988.

[24]*On-Line Report System*. Englewood Cliffs, N.J.: Ehrhart-Babic, undated.

[25]"Videophone Connects Two Campuses in California." *New York Times*, Oct. 16, 1989, B16.

[26]R. I. Haley. "The Matched Checkerboard Revisited." *Advertising Heavy Spending Tests*. New York: Advertising Research Foundation, 1985, 103–109.

[27]"A Telling Look at the Most Frequently Used Test Markets. Times Publishing Company." *Advertising Week*. Oct. 3, 1983.

[28]"Test Markets: Winners *and* Losers." *Advertising Week*, Oct. 3, 1983.

[29]Joel Axelrod. "Attitude Measures That Predict Purchase." *Journal of Advertising Research* 8, no. 1 (March 1968): 3–16.

[30]Fred Cuba. "Fourteen Things That Make or Break Tracking Studies." *Journal of Advertising Research* 25, no. 1 (1985): 21–23.

[31]*Case History: Flavored Laxative*. Evansville, Ind.: Product Acceptance & Research, undated.

[32]*BehaviorScan*. Chicago: Information Resources Inc., 1989.

[33]Richard Kreisman. "Buy the Numbers." *Inc. Magazine*, March 1985.

[34]Jacob Kandathil. "The Advantages of Electronic Test Markets: An Advertiser View Based on Experience." *Journal of Advertising Research* 25, no. 6 (1985): RC11–12.

[35]A. L. Baldinger. "Trends and Issues in STM's: Results of an ARF Pilot Project." *Pre-Test Market Research*. Chicago: American Marketing Association, 1988, 24.

[36]Joe Russo. "Simulated Test Markets in the Real World." *Pre-Test Market Research*. New York: Advertising Research Foundation, 1988, 118–119.

[37]W. M. Moult. *The Role of Simulated Test Markets and Test Markets*. New York: Advertising Research Foundation, 1988, 140.

[38]Gerald Eskin. *Setting a Forward Agenda for Test Market Modeling*. New York: Advertising Research Foundation, 1988, 14–15.

[39]Rakesh Malhotra. *Some Issues and Perspectives on Use of Simulated Test Markets*. New York: Advertising Research Foundation, 1988, 57.

[40]Thomas Lix and K. J. Clancy. *The Growing Problem of Competitive Response*. New York: Advertising Research Foundation, 1988, 123.

[41]Judith Rosenfeld. "Speeding Up Test Marketing." *Marketing Communications*, June 1985.

[42]"The 'bloodbath' in market research." *Business Week*, Feb. 11, 1991, 13 f.

[43]A. L. Baldinger, senior VP and director of marketing research of the Advertising Research Foundation. Letter, May 21, 1990.

[44]*Your Guide to Better Product Decisions*. Cincinnati: Bases Group, undated.

[45]Esther Brock, manager of marketing support, the BASES Group. Letter, Aug. 14, 1990.

[46]*Market Response Research and the Litmus System*. Westport, Conn.: Yankelovich, Clancy, Shulman, undated.

[47]K. L. Clancy. Letter.

[48]*Introducing the Real World*. Westport, Conn.: Market Simulations, undated.

[49]K. L. Sobel. Letters, May and June 1990.

[50]*COMP*. Downers Grove, Ill.: Elrick & Lavidge, 1988.

[51]G. S. Dispensa, director of quantitative information services, Elrick & Lavidge. Memo on Comp Plus, June 12, 1990.

[52]*Practices, Trends and Expectations for the Market Research Industry 1988/1989*. Chicago: Market Facts, Oct. 1988.

[53]Nielsen Marketing Mix Management. Northbrook, Ill.: Nielsen, undated.

[54]AdPro Applications and Delivery. Northbrook, Ill.: Nielsen, undated.

[55]ScanPro Promotion Analysis Services. Northbrook, Ill.: Nielsen, 1988.

[56]ScanFact PC Software. Northbrook, Ill.: Nielsen, undated.

[57]*DataServer*. Chicago: Information Resources Inc., 1989.

[58]*Analyst Workstation User's Guide*. Pittsburgh: Management Science Associates, 1990.

[59]*Welcome to the Analyst WorkStation*. Pittsburgh: Management Science Associates, 1989.

14

SPECIFIC STUDIES FOR SPECIFIC MARKETING DECISIONS

What's in This Chapter

In this chapter we show how to determine in advance the specific steps to be taken in monitoring the marketplace, identifying and correcting marketing problems, and planning for the future. We examine the evaluation and testing of new products, and we discuss the development, evaluation, and effectiveness measurement of advertising and promotion. Finally, we look at the various aspects of product delivery.

In late 1989 Farberware made a successful national rollout of the Microbrew, the first coffee brewer that makes coffee in a microwave. The product is shown in Exhibit 14.1. Just 6½ inches high, the product combines percolator and drip. A paper cone filter is situated just below a chamber that holds two cups of water. In the middle of the chamber is a small cylinder that operates as a pump when heated by the microwaves; this delivers hot water to the cone below. The user places ground coffee in the cone and water in the chamber above it. Making two cups of coffee takes about four minutes.

Microbrew was rolled out in October, with television advertising

Exhibit 14.1   THE MICROBREW*

Source: Photo courtesy of Farberware.

and shipments concentrated in the 10 largest U.S. markets.[1] The television commercial had been tested in advance by a research firm using the DAR (Day after Recall) technique, described later in this chapter. It scored 75 percent better than average commercials of similar length.

Shipments were just a bit later than had been hoped for to meet the demands of the Christmas shopping trade. And only two of the "big boys" as Farberware termed them—Wal-Mart and K mart—stocked them. Despite these drawbacks, there was a 70 percent sale-through in the 10 top markets, and Farberware deemed the rollout highly successful. At least one competitor did too, for it is planning introduction of a cut-rate copy of the $30 item.

The development and introduction of Microbrew didn't just happen. It was planned,[2] and virtually all of the planning, starting with the development of the product, was based on marketing research.

It all began when the marketing people started thinking about some secondary data:

- About 80 percent of households had microwaves. But most owners expressed disappointment in the microwave's limited uses and were looking for more applications.

- Fifty-four percent of coffee maker purchases are made by households of one or two people, usually older people, students, or young couples.

- Although coffee drinking is on the decline (52 percent drank coffee in 1987, only 50 percent a year later), consumption of high-priced, home-ground coffee is increasing some 20 percent annually.

This interesting information led to the creative idea that there could be a market for a coffee maker that could make better coffee in a microwave for those wanting to brew only a cup or two at a time.

A study of consumer desires about coffee makers showed that a throwaway filter was preferred to a permanent one requiring cleaning, and that a plastic pot was preferred to a glass pot, which tended to chip and crack. A concept test followed in which various ideas about microwave coffee makers were presented to consumers. The results indicated interest in such a product, but with greater acceptance of a two-cup than a six-cup size. On the basis of these studies, the company's chief engineer was asked to design a product that would brew better coffee in a microwave, in one- or two-cup quantities, using a paper filter. He came up with a product within a few months.

When the time came to have some consumers try the product, enough units of the coffeemaker were made to allow a small number to try it at home. Two different research firms ran these consumer product tests, and each firm reported that the test product had received some of the highest consumer ratings it had obtained in their testing work over the years.

Advertising research uncovered the product attributes that could be the basis for advertising campaigns. It would be a good gift item. It made fast but good coffee. It made exactly two cups, with no waste.

The case of this coffee brewer is a good example of what we will discuss in this chapter. We will take you through the use of marketing research to make specific marketing decisions, in the sequential steps of offering the right product, the right advertising and promotion, and delivery.

A MULTIPURPOSE FACILITY

Impact Resources (Columbus, Ohio) offers MA.RT (Market Audience . Readership Traffic),[3] a unique approach that can be used in marketing planning. It seems to offer many potential applications to marketing decision making. However, it does not offer applications to *all* decision areas, and it is *not* a complete research facility—unlike most of the services described in Chapter 13—in that it does not provide a continuing monitoring of what is happening in the marketplace as marketing changes are made.

This database is a pool of information about a large number of anonymous families in each of the top 50 markets in the United States, available primarily to user firms wanting to use it primarily to solve marketing problems within specific markets. A single market report, updated annually, contains information about 5,000 to 18,000 families.

Its 115 items cover 145 demographics (from characteristics of the respondent to family members and income); 18 life-style aspects (from leisure activities to ownership of various electronic, communications, and entertainment equipment); retail store preferences and motivations (store types preferred for each of 13 classes of merchandise, and a checklist of 5 reasons for each preference); 10 shopping items (4 types of shopping, assorted other items); 14 media measurements (including television and cable, radio, newspapers, local magazines, and other publications); 4 health care aspects; 7 measurements of auto ownership (including year, make, and model); 3 restaurant aspects (for fast food, full-service, and fine dining); and major purchase intentions for 12 items.

Sampling is a mix of judgment and quota sampling (see Chapter 8 for definitions of these terms). In each market, between 20 and 100 high-traffic locations (including shopping malls, strip centers, and downtowns) are chosen on the basis of knowledge of the population and demographics. The larger and more complex the market, the more sites used.

Consumers at these sites are chosen on a quota basis, tied to known population data. Separately by gender, quotas are assigned for each of seven age groups, starting at age 14. The sample returns are adjusted to provide close adherence to the known data for the market.

Data are collected through self-administered questionnaires. The respondents are comfortably seated while completing the questionnaire. The procedure is said to take 10 to 20 minutes and is sufficiently easy and enjoyable so that no incentive need be offered.

The database of names is available for any one or a number of the market areas. It is offered for sale to any user in computerized form.

Let us consider some applications. Most come, logically enough, from Impact Resources.

A national grocery chain long had been second in market share in a particular market. A new chain entered the market, and eighteen months and three stores later it had cornered a significant proportion of the limited market.

After purchasing the 5,000 database for the market, the client chain found that shopper profiles of the first chain and its own were remarkably similar: older, with higher incomes, who chose a grocer on the basis of store location and product selection. Since the analysis showed that the first and second chains were competing for the same customers, the potential of each was limited. The third chain had made its rapid inroads because it was targeting the younger and less well-to-do consumers, who were choosing their grocer primarily for price.

The solution was clear. The client chain began to match the competition's advertised prices. Television and radio ad budgets were increased, since the database showed this was the way to reach the target group. "At last report," says Impact Resources, " 'Number 2' was gaining on 'Number 1' and no longer losing ground to 'Number 3.' "

A little imagination will indicate other possibilities. In making advertising dollars work harder, a drug discount chain could go through several analyses with the MA.RT database. It could profile its own customers and those of the largest competitor in terms of demographics, psychographics, shopping preferences, and media choices. So it would be possible to pinpoint these advertising dollars to take advantage of all of the knowledge about the firm's own customers and those of its competition, and to use the right media and the right appeals with considerable effectiveness.

We give just one other example in the potential use of these data, this time for the location of stores in a market that a chain had not yet entered. It might be any of the store types covered in the questionnaire (there are 12 of them), but we'll use supermarkets. A demographic picture of consumers and grocery preferences could be constructed for each geographic area of the market. A dozen locations with the lowest ratio of competitors to potential consumers might be selected. Then customers of the competitors could be profiled. The weaknesses in the profiles could be exploited, and use made of the life-style and media information to aid further development of the new locations.

Just one brief judgment statement: While the sampling design may leave some room for improvement, we have already said that we believe quota sampling is acceptable for studies that do not require precision measurement of small differences. MA.RT does not claim such precision measurement, and in our opinion provides a sound base for the typical uses to which it is put.

PRODUCT GENERATION AND TESTING

Let us now move on to some of the specific research tools that may be helpful in the various stages of marketing.

The first of these is product generation and testing. Although it has been repeatedly said that more than 80 percent of all new products fail, we know of no proof to back up such a figure. But its common acceptance must mean something. Most new products fail. So the use of research in developing and evaluating products is important. It reduces the risk of failure.

Product research—the blanket term covers the several different kinds of research in this process—is especially important with fast-turnover items, such as packaged foods, drugs, cosmetics, and household goods. It is less important with durable goods (such as televisions, dishwashers, refrigerators) where the product should last ten years or more.

The aim of product research is to provide company management with information about the likely acceptance of a new product, a modified product, or an existing product. Product research has three successive roles to play in this aspect of marketing:

1. Getting ideas for new products (concept generation)

2. Evaluating new-product ideas (concept testing)

3. Evaluating the product (consumer product testing)

Here is an example of how these three successive steps occurred in the case of dry beer, first introduced in Japan.[4] As a result of consumer research, Agahi Super Dry was introduced in March 1987. It soon had 20 percent market share, a high level in a competitive market. Three other Japanese breweries entered the dry market, and dry beer in 1989 had 40 percent of the Japanese market.

American breweries took notice. Michelob asked beer drinkers what they thought dry beer would be and should be like. Consumers wanted the taste of beer and the refreshment, but no aftertaste. Michelob Dry was introduced in 1988. Pabst Blue Ribbon Dry and Olympic Dry were introduced in much the same way. There are now at least 11 dry beers, accounting for 1 percent of sales, so judgment is still out as to whether dry beer will become a significant segment of the American market.

GETTING IDEAS FOR NEW PRODUCTS

Consumers did not invent the airplane, the computer, or the space shuttle. They cannot invent technology for new products, or even come up with ideas for new products entirely outside of their experience. But in the field of products they use, the public *can* provide ideas for product improvements and even occasionally define a new product that is needed.

When the focus group interview approach is used to generate product ideas, it is generally moderated to direct consideration to the nature
of consumer needs within the given product category. If there has been a
market segmentation defining the characteristics and psychological
needs of the target group (such research will be specifically discussed in
Chapter 15), this will make it easier in the group session to ensure that
the group is sufficiently homogeneous to come up with a definitive statement of needs.

Consider bacon, for example. A popular choice for many years, it lost
favor as medical studies showed the risks of fat. Based on focus group
interviews, a major meat packer decided to reduce the amount of fat in
its sliced bacon.

The focus group interview may be a productive way to develop consumer ideas for new or modified products. As in all focus groups, it required a highly skilled moderator to make these focus groups on bacon
successful. The moderator moved gradually into a discussion of bacon by
first getting participants to talk about their breakfast habits, then examining the area of bacon preparation and serving. The moderator then
probed, and continued to probe, into the problems of preparation and
serving of the product.

Careful examination of what participants reported about the preparation, serving, and use showed that the major objections were the time
and messiness of handling and preparation (spattering of grease, pour-
ing off of grease, and so on) and the greasiness of the final product.
Cleanup mess and time were also factors, as was the unhealthiness of a
product having that amount of saturated fat.

When the group moderator summarized all these objections to the
group, and participants were asked for their suggestions to improve the
product, it was no surprise that a less fatty bacon was the unanimous idea.

Alford and Mason[5] came up with an interesting formalized approach
to the generating of new-product ideas. The product area is household
cleaners, very broadly defined. On a rationalization basis, 25 possible
viable new-product ideas were developed. To get to this number, factors
such as the cleaning instrument (from broom to wet mop), ingredients
(from alcohol to scenting agents), objects to be cleaned (from air-
conditioning filters to wool), packaging (from aerosol to unspillable),
substance to be removed (from blood to tar), and texture, (from cream to
wax) were taken into account, in all combinations.

A focus group session with housewives was conducted and came up
with three areas of findings. The women were generally dissatisfied
with all aspects of household cleaning products and the way these were
presented in advertising. But they failed to come up with any new-
product ideas. When five specific product ideas (that had survived out of

screening of the 25 ideas mentioned above), the women reacted favorably to two.

EVALUATING NEW-PRODUCT IDEAS

Concept testing, as we have said, means getting reactions to a new-product idea or concept. There may well be more than one idea; if so, are *any* of the ideas any good? Which one or ones?

The concept test certainly can kill bad ideas. In one concept test, the idea of a peanut butter pudding was presented to mothers, who roundly rejected the thought. It was visualized as a product that would be sticky, gooey, and icky. Although actual taste tests of the developed product showed that children and their mothers found it delicious and smooth, the company—probably quite rightly—decided not to proceed with the product, believing that it would never move from the grocery shelf.

But there is a risk in concept tests. A test may show that a product idea gets high ratings, but the developed product itself may fail. There is the example of dry cereals containing freeze-dried fruits. Concept tests showed this idea to be highly acceptable, and the cereals were developed and introduced. They did not last long. They turned out to be a novelty item, and in the cereal business that is exactly what is not needed. Repeat buying is required, and this never developed.

Moskowitz[6] uses cereal as an example to describe a concept for purposes of consumer concept testing. This particular cereal concept statement, he says, should include:

- Authority statement(s) (dietitian, doctor, scientific evidence, tests)

- Nature of flavor (great taste, sweet and crunchy, graham and bran; stone-ground bran for better taste and health; low salt; high fiber)

- Health, nutrition (doctors and dietitians recommend for better health; provides roughage needed for better health; as recommended by doctors)

One form of the concept test is entirely *verbal*. It is descriptive entirely through words. There is a statement about what the product is and does, perhaps listing its major characteristics. Another form is *visual*, with an illustration (drawing or photograph) presented along with the description. Or it may take the form of a draft advertisement, which combines the description and illustration, usually in the form of a print advertisement. A third form of the concept test uses a *mockup* of the product. This is something that passes for a prototype, but is really only a dummy product (not in usable form) to help get across the idea of the product.

Marder Concept Test

Eric Marder Associates (New York) offers a concept-testing service using a mail survey in which questionnaires are sent to potential users of a new product. An enclosed booklet covers many products other than the one being tested, in order to eliminate focus of attention on the particular item being tested. Each page shows a picture of a product, provides a brief description, and indicates the price. Consumers first describe their frequency of monthly use of the product within the past month. For each product the consumer is then asked whether the picture is interesting, whether the description impresses favorably, and whether the product is worth the price indicated.

These queries are simply "sensitizing" questions to acquaint the person with the concept (price, picture, and theme). The key question follows, with each person telling how likely he or she is to buy each item. Ten stickers—only ten—are provided with each booklet. The person has the choice of placing all ten against a single product, a single sticker against each, or any choice in between. The booklet is set up mechanically so that only one sticker can be applied at a time. The consumer who wants to bloc vote has to work at it.

One sample of respondents is mailed Booklet A, another Booklet B. The two booklets are identical except for a single page. The procedure means that the firm sponsoring the test can be sure that basic comparisons of results between A and B are similar, and that differences in response to the concept are true differences.

Many research firms offer less complex concept tests. Most are done through personal interviewing, though some can be done by telephone if the concepts are simple enough. In the typical concept test, the concept is stated and the person is asked about interest in purchase. Some of the services outlined as STMs in Chapter 13 offer concept testing as one possibility in their systems.

Adopter

But at least one concept-testing system, sometimes mistakenly identified as an STM service (it isn't, because it really does *only* concept testing), produces results said to be really predictive. The Adopter system (Data Development Corp.) is designed "to forecast sales for those innovative new products that are distinctive enough to change consumer behavior."[7] An extensive study showed significant differences in consumer reactions to innovative products and more ordinary new products:

- Novel new products are usually accepted by only a small segment of interested prospects (meaning that concept scores may be mediocre).

- With a novel product, early attitudes may not predict later consumer behavior; attitudes may change as the consumer gets more experience with the product. Consumers cannot really anticipate their own or family use. They cannot predict how often they will use the product, even after first trial. (So self-predictions may be incorrect when consumers have limited information.)

- Repeat usage may follow a variety of patterns different from the standard decay rate assumed for less innovative products.

- Usage of innovative new products often does not follow the pattern of one-for-one substitution in an existing product category. (Comparative and substitution questions may be less meaningful or even deceptive, and source of business will be difficult to calculate.)

What all this means, it is argued, is that a new product, innovative or not, must find a sufficiently large number of adopters (committed ongoing purchasers) who buy often enough to create a good volume.

The test method designed to be consistent with all of these points includes a concept/product test, followed by a series of at least six opportunities to repurchase.

The concept/product test is conducted with a multicity random group of potential consumers. The typical starting sample size (those exposed to the concept) is 600. Each consumer respondent is recruited and interviewed at home, then offered the product in a personal callback interview and for "real money." Further sales waves are made by telephone calls, and the product is dropped off at the homes of purchasers.

Sales to the consumer on several occasions over a time period provide an observation of how much the consumer really wants to buy.

During the first eight years (the service was first offered in 1981), the firm claims that this method identified the winner in every case.

In-House versus Outside Testing

Generally, unless the user firm does a tremendous number of concept tests, it seems wise to use a research firm rather than do these tests in-house. Almost all research firms handling concept testing over the years have been able to establish norms by product category. They can report, for instance, whether a particular concept for a shaving cream rated in the top 10 percent, lowest 10 percent, or somewhere in between.

The marketing director of Cadbury-Schweppes used an imaginative way to concept-test a new line of drink mixes.[8] Afraid that potential consumers might be unable to respond accurately to a totally new idea, she turned the basic problem statement around. Instead of trying to find out how people responded to the product idea, she decided to learn the conditions under which people would use the proposed product. This meant determining how people chose brands and used products, then segmenting the market (a topic to be discussed in Chapter 15). It was a letdown to learn that there was not a big enough chunk of the market to warrant proceeding further with the beverage idea. We believe, however, that the method is productive.

CONSUMER PRODUCT TESTING

Unlike the concept test, consumer product testing measures what people think of the new or existing product only after actual trial of the developed product.

The consumer product test is certainly a useful and desirable technique. But like the concept test, it does not always successfully predict winners or losers in the marketplace. A product coming up with high marks in a consumer product test is not invariably strong in the actual market.

The product may fail because of factors other than the product itself. A firm with a good product may fail to make a good dent competitively because it lacks the funds to fight the competition, or because a competitor has built up so strong a reputation over the years that no amount of spending on advertising and other forms of promotion could get a worthwhile chunk of the market. A poor or marginal product, as long as it has even a low level of acceptance, may make it in the marketplace through massive spending on promotional efforts. One major-selling beer brand, for example, consistently scores low in blind product tests (where people try samples lacking brand identification).

Consumer product tests use several distinctly different basic forms in the collection of data. For a food or beverage, the test may be as simple as a one-time taste test, perhaps conducted at a mall. For a laundry detergent, only a longer-term in-home test can obtain a sound answer, with a sufficiently long trial period to test repeat use. The product may be placed with people at a mall with a request that they try it at home over an extended time period and the callback questions being asked over the telephone. Sometimes mail panels are used. One method rarely used today because of its cost is in-home placement of products, with either in-home or telephone callbacks.

Before getting into these basic testing procedures, we want to talk about some of the variables in how the products are presented to the tester. One variation has to do with whether the products in the test is presented on a blind (no brand identification) basis or on a branded basis. Another is whether only a single product is presented to the tester for rating (the monadic test), or whether a pair of products is presented (paired comparison).

Blind versus Branded Testing

There is almost always a need for blind testing, where products are presented to the testers without brand identification. This determines how the product, and only the product, is perceived by the tester. It provides basic guidance, when questions about reactions to specific attributes are also asked, as to how the firm can improve its product to make it more acceptable.

However, the branded test also has an important role. The results of such a test provide information about how people react to the product and the brand image, combined in a single rating. Identified brands typically score higher than blind products, unless the brand is relatively unknown or has a poor image. The combination rating is important because it indicates the probable ratings in the marketplace.

Moskowitz[6], cites the case of a consumer product test of 13 coffees. The instant coffee participants (50 percent women, 50 percent men) spent a long seven hours in the testing procedure. In the morning the panelists rated each product on a blind basis in terms of appearance, tried as black coffee, and then after adding sweetener and/or whitener. Consumers in the test tried each of the products and replied to a questionnaire about their purchase intent. After lunch—we said it was a long session—the same people went through the same procedure except that this time they were told each brand name.

Exhibit 14.2 shows abstracted results for purchase intent between the blind and branded results. It shows significantly better results for well-established brands when their identity in the test is revealed. The brand image carries through. Little of this is news to the astute marketer or marketing researcher, who already understands the brand's advantages or problems in the brand name.

Exhibit 14.2   **CHANGE IN PURCHASE INTENT POINTS**
FOLLOWING BRAND IDENTIFICATION

Maxwell House	+22	Nescafe (r)	+4
Maxim	+17	High Point	+4
Taster's Choice (r)	+15	Yuban	+2
Folgers	+14	Kava	−2
Sanka (d)	+13	Nescafe (d)	−2
Taster's Choice (d)	+18	Sunrise	−3
Brim	+10		

d=decaffeinated, r=regular.

Monadic versus Paired Comparison Testing

As we have explained, monadic testing is the presentation of only one test product at a time, obtaining a rating on that product alone or perhaps against the regular brand. Paired comparison testing means the presentation of two products to be tried, one against the other, and comparative preferences typically asked for. In either case, the ratings are not only for overall liking or preference, but usually cover many attributes or qualities of the product(s) as well.

Precautions must be taken, especially in the case of the paired comparison test. Studies over the years have shown that, all else being equal, the product tried first has a preferred posistion, and may, just because of position, get too high a proportion of preferred ratings. The more similar the two products are, the more likely this is to happen. So each product being tested has to be given first position with half of the sample of respondents. It is necessary to have a label affixed to the product saying "Try me first" or "Try me second." These are rotated to achieve equal average position for each product.

In the blind test, some sort of unbranded identification must be provided for the tester to identify the product to which he or she is responding. While numbers or letters assigned to the product might appear to be the answer, some numbers and letters are more preferred than others, and this preference tends to influence answers to statements about the product. One solution is to tie product identification to which one was tried first, and ask questions paralleling this sort of structure:

Which one did you prefer: the first or the second?

But then it is necessary to know which one *was* the first, and which the second. A simple but clever method is to color code the "Try me first" and "Try me second" labels. Let us say that two forms of the product, which we will define simply as A and B, are being tested. Here is the way the color coding might work:

	Blue label	White label
Try me first	A	B
Try me second	B	A

Since any one participant will see only one color of label, if there is any minor color bias operating, it will operate equally on the rating of each of the two products.

Which test is better, monadic or paired comparisons? There is no simple answer. On the monadic side, this is, in a sense, the way the real world operates. Consumers rarely make side-by-side choices, though sometimes they do so in a buying situation, particularly with consumer durables. But over the years, studies have shown that the same monadic test may give sharply differing results, probably because those replying have no anchor point on which to base responses.

The paired comparison test provides sharper results, because two definite things are being compared. But under some circumstances, these results too are not always consistent. It is also difficult to use paired comparison results for prediction of what will happen in the marketplace.

The One-Time Sensory Test

This common form of product test is different enough to warrant discussion. It is typically a relatively simple test.

A *flavor test* to determine which of two flavors of a product is preferred may require only a central location test, as in a shopping mall. In a high-traffic location, people can easily be intercepted. The procedure starts with making sure they are qualified (such as being heavy users of the product category), then having them sample the product and getting their reactions. Either the monadic or paired comparison presentation of the product(s) can be applied.

A firm offering toiletries may use a *sniff* test, simply getting reactions to one or more fragrances. But a cosmetics firm will need to know not only the immediate reaction to a fragrance, but the reaction over the period of at least a single use. So it will have to follow a procedure where reactions to a perfume or cologne, for instance, are also measured at the end of the particular one-time testing period.

MindView (Inner Response Inc., Charlotte, N.C.) offers a unique approach to consumer product testing. The firm's technique, coupled with some of the usual pencil-and-paper forms, makes use of the measurement of the galvanic skin response, which is perspiration caused by an emotional body reaction at less-than-conscious level. The equipment used is described later in this chapter.

In sensory testing (flavors and fragrances), where MindView is applicable, John Shimell,[9] president of Inner Response, argues that the consumer starts with a mind-set of what, say, a chocolate chip cookie should taste like. "When [a person] bites into the cookie," he says, "if it satisfies that mind-set of an acceptable cookie, the brain tends to relax, and in a sense enjoys itself." And as that relaxation takes place, the electrical impulses decline rapidly and show in the measurement obtained. But if the taste sensation is different, unusual, or unsatisfactory, the brain needs more input. Signals increase and the response curve rises. This pattern is common with new flavors. The mind has to get used to the new flavor while it is in the process of deciding whether or not the flavor is acceptable.

The approach will ". . . heighten the ability of the researcher to discriminate between alternative formulas, where paper and pencil tests may not be sensitive enough." It may also begin to establish optimal response curves for the "ideal" flavor or fragrance sensation.

Shimell warns that Inner Response's work in sensory testing is still in the early stages.

DEVELOPING AND EVALUATING ADVERTISING AND PROMOTION

The development and evaluation of advertising and promotion, at least in the past, have been far from exact sciences. But before we get into this thorny issue, we had better mention right off that we are grouping advertising and promotion together.

The definition of advertising, over the years, generally has been accepted as an impersonal and clearly paid message, with a clearly identified sponsor, generally aimed at selling goods or services. Advertising typically uses television, radio, print, outdoor media, and direct advertising.

The trouble these days is that it is no longer easy to distinguish between advertising and promotion. Promotion is defined as chiefly the same sort of mass communication, but provided editorially, without any sponsorship. And, of course, there is no payment by the advertiser.

But we are oversimplifying the definition of promotion, for in the field of retail selling it includes in-store aspects such as special displays, perhaps including identifying banners, cents-off offers, special-label offers, and many other activities that are not the usual identified advertising. But even if we rule out these in-store promotions, it is becoming more difficult to distinguish between the two. There is the *Reader's Digest* piece in the same format as an article that turns out to be a long ad. There is the television or radio MC or personality who personally tells you about and recommends a buying source, usually providing an 800 number. Many television game shows name specific products and sources, almost as a matter of course during the show. There is the television sit-com or sportscaster that displays brand names in one form or another. Of course, this doesn't just happen.

We therefore combine advertising and promotion here and use the simplistic term *advertising*.

There are two basic tools by means of which marketing research is able to contribute to advertising effectiveness: (1) research to develop the basic advertising appeals and (2) research to measure the effectiveness of advertising.

DEVELOPING BASIC ADVERTISING APPEALS

Three different methods have been applied to the development of advertising appeals: psychological (or motivational), sociological (focus groups), and anthropological (observation). The latter two have also been discussed in Chapter 7.

Psychological (Motivational) Studies

Ernest Dichter, legendary motivational researcher, most often used psychological tools within the framework of individual interviews. Dichter was once asked by a manufacturer of ice cream to determine the meaning of the product to consumers. He started by examining ice cream ads. Most plugged the superior quality and flavor of the particular brand. Not too exciting.

Dichter then had interviewers talk with people in depth about what ice cream meant to them. Most, particularly those past adolescence, had strong emotional feelings about it. Said one woman: "You want to get your whole mouth into it."

Dichter concluded that ice cream often symbolizes "uninhibited overindulgence or voluptuousness, via the mouth." The particular ice cream maker was advised to show the ice cream in his ads in lavish portions overflowing the plate or cone, thus inviting the viewers to sink their mouths right into it.[10] It is only fair to comment that while the creative types in agencies usually welcomed Dichter's recommendations as great ideas, marketing researchers generally had the attitude that these ideas were based on Dichter's creative genius rather than on dependable research. We tend to share these views.

Sociological (Focus Group) Studies

Discussion of the *focus group* technique in Chapter 10 showed how group interaction may lead to ideas that a single person would be unlikely to generate.

The group interview may be a helpful approach. For example, a company that was a leading mass marketer of economy products took over a smaller firm that made prestige goods. A group discussion alerted the creative staff of the advertising agency that a prominent display of the prestige make in the new owner's advertising might be dangerous. They had been far more impressed with the prestige make than with the economy make.[11]

Through focus groups, a soup manufacturer learned that the serving of a clear soup is regarded as a real treat, while soups containing solids suggest a substitute product made with inferior-quality solids or leftovers.

Anthropological Studies

In anthropological studies, the basic technique is from cultural anthropology, which studies culture as a key to understanding human behavior and attitude.

Use of the anthropological research approach applied to the advertising creative function means close and thorough observation of a small number of people to understand how a product fits into the life of a consumer (or a consuming family) and what bonds a person to a particular brand. But this approach, a British import apparently being increasingly accepted by U.S. advertising agencies, has taken on less offensive descriptive terminology by being called varying names, such as "account planning," "strategic planning," or just "planning."[12] Paraphrasing M. T. Rainey, former head of planning at the New York advertising agency Chiat/Day/Mojo and now with the London office, this means common sense by someone who has a sharp eye for culture. The person making these cultural observations (usually a creative agency type) goes into the marketplace to get a handle on the way people live. The planner immerses himself or herself thoroughly in the role of the consumer.

Here is how it worked for Arrow Shirts, an account of the Chiat agency.[13] Arrow arrived at the agency saddled by a consumer image as a conservative white dress shirt, though the firm had been making sports shifts for ten years. Merry Cutler, agency director of account planning, reports that "... we ... talked to both men and women; the men who wear the shirts and the women who often buy the men's clothes and do their laundry." Armed with basic attitude concepts, the planner is able to provide interpretation for what is said; the group respondent doesn't always say what he means.

The problem, as Cutler saw it, was to get the creative team thinking like Arrow consumers, away from the 100 percent Brooks Brothers type of preppie shirt. Arrow planning is about regular guys and their less-expensive shirts. It's about men who wear uniforms all week and who, when they get home, want to kick off their shoes, loosen their shirts, and relax. But the basic Arrow image had to be there: its strength was the white dress shirt.

The resultant commercial was the acclaimed "Higher and Higher" commercial, where "a solemn chorus of men in white shirts is gradually transformed into a gospel celebration of colorful sportswear." The Arrow sportswear tagline, "We've loosened our collar," and its visual transition from white shirts to sports shirts also grew from the planning stages of the campaign.

The technique has even been applied to the mail carrier. Making the rounds with the carrier made it plain to the researchers that most of the public see their mail carriers as friends, and many even know their first names. Guess what? The Postal Service began to feature mail carriers prominently in its advertising, thus capitalizing on an image asset.

There are other examples of anthropological studies as well.[14] The method has been used as an in-depth tool to obtain better understanding of consumers. It may provide a method of getting past the level of responses to questions by observing what people do instead of merely listening to what they say. In no way, however, does it replace survey research, however good a supplement it may be.

MEASURING ADVERTISING EFFECTIVENESS

We are distinguishing here between measurement of the impact of advertising within the framework of all of the various marketing inputs (previously described in Chapter 13) and the use of tools designed primarily to *predict* the impact of advertising. The tools that we will be describing are almost all concerned with the content of the advertising and with the way in which the material is delivered.

The measurement of the effectiveness of advertising and promotion is one of the most difficult kinds of marketing research. The old saw attributed to merchant John Wanamaker is no longer entirely relevant: "I know half of my advertising is working. The problem is I don't know which half." Astute marketers these days can find out, in advance or afterwards, about the performance of their advertising.

The trouble is that advertising is not the only element in the marketing mix helping to account for product success or failure. To have any sort of defensible measure of advertising effectiveness, it is necessary for a firm to have an advertising philosophy encompassing the particular product or service. The basic issue: What is the advertising intended to do? If the ultimate aim is to sell a product or service, it may be argued that it must go through two steps.

First, it must provide information. Second, it must persuade. The various copy-testing research services are essentially built around these two premises. Therefore most of the leading services provide scores both on awareness and memory (information retention) and on persuasion. There are a handful that measure only awareness and memory. A third group of methods are aimed at providing guidance about how the particular advertisement might be modified to be more effective. The three groups of copy-testing services and methods that we will discuss, then, are:

- Awareness, memory, and persuasion

- Awareness and memory

- Guidance studies

Users tend to be loyal to a particular service because of its norms and their familiarity with the service. About the only time a change is made is when a user becomes unhappy with how "helpful" the service is. Almost all advertising agencies resist having their ads tested, although the larger advertising agencies have developed their own methods of testing.

METHODS MEASURING AWARENESS, MEMORY, AND PERSUASION

All of the major services are solely or mainly measuring television commercials, largely because it is so expensive to produce a commercial and then to air it. However, some of these services have adapted their services to print and other media advertising as well. Our attention, however, will be only peripherally on these other forms.

All services follow a superficially similar pattern in their procedural steps, as shown in Exhibit 14.3. But the details, often crucially important, of how they operate often differ markedly from one service to the other.

Exhibit 14.3   THE PATTERN OF AWARENESS, MEMORY AND PERSUASION COPY TESTS

> Recruiting and Screening
> Advertising Exposure
> Measurement of Persuasiveness
> Measurement of Recall

The most frequently used services and their sponsoring research firms are:

- Apex Recall Plus and Persuasion Plus (ASI Market Research Inc., New York)

- Mapes and Ross (Princeton, N.J.)

- ARS (Research Systems Corporation, Evansville, Ind.)

- The PreTesting Company (Englewood, N.J.)

- Advertising Control for Television (ACT) (McCollum/Spielman, Great Neck, N.Y.)

- The Buy Test (The Sherman Group, Glen Cove, N.Y.)

To make our review of these six services as succinct as reasonable, we start with Exhibit 14.4, which compares them in outline form. We first review their similarities based on this exhibit, then examine the unique features of each.

Apex

Apex, the combination of Recall Plus and Persuasion Plus,[15,16,17] recruits viewers to tune their television sets at a particular hour to a specified cable channel. Participants are told that the survey concerns people's television viewing habits.

In the Recall Plus procedure, there is no contact other than the exposure the first day. During the second day there is measurement of recall (along with re-exposure of the commercial and asking of diagnostic questions, if desired).

Exhibit 14.4 **MAJOR CHARACTERISTICS OF SIX AWARE-NESS, MEMORY, AND PERSUASION COPY-TESTING SERVICES**

	Apex	Mapes and Ross	ARS	Pretesting	ACT	Buy Test
Syndicated			X			
Customized	X	X		X	X	X
Market Locations						
Specified standard markets	X	X*	X	X*	X*	
Participant Sampling						
Recruiting medium:						
Central location intercepts				X		
By telephone	X	X			X	
By mail			X			
Character of sample:						
General cross section	X*	X*	X			
User-specified target market				X	X	
Sampling method:						
Quota				X		
Probability	X	X	X		X	
Sample size per test	400*	200	800–120	100*	400	
Location of Test Procedure						
Mall research suite				X		
Hotel ballroom, meeting room			X		X	
In-home	X	X				
Degree of Forced Exposure						
Complete (captive audience)			X	X	X	
Partial (by invitation to view)	X	X				X*
None (those naturally exposed on-air)						X
Questioning at Test Location						
Questioning before exposure		X	X	X	X	
Questioning after exposure	X			X		
Later Questioning	X	X	X*		X	X

*See text for explanation.

In the Persuasion Plus procedure, a separate but comparable sample of viewers watch the show and, immediately following, exposure questions are asked about viewing, rating of the program, and brand preferences and considerations.

Samples are cable television homes, typically in two geographically dispersed cities where an unused channel is available for the research firm. Typically, 200 homes are drawn randomly from computer-generated lists of all CATV homes on the system. Although female viewers are the usual respondents, specialized samples can be drawn according to client needs.

Repeat exposures can be built in. Either finished or rough commercials can be used.

The method presents test commercials in a natural setting: placed within a program and received on the television at home. But there is forced exposure through the request to view, and if rough commercials are used, these may draw unusual attention to the ads. Nevertheless, the method seems to meet all of the requirements laid down for a valid pretesting service.

Mapes and Ross

In the Mapes and Ross service,[18,19] the audience is recruited by telephone to view a regularly scheduled prime-time program, generally a movie on a UHF channel or independent channel into which the test commercial has been inserted. Typically, the sample size for one test is 200 female viewers, 150 male viewers, or 100 male viewers and 100 female viewers. Tests are typically conducted in three geographically dispersed standard markets. (Additional options include target samples, children or teenage samples, custom diagnostics, 40 custom markets, and other media: magazine, radio, newspaper.)

Brand preferences are measured during the recruiting call, but on an open-ended basis, without mention of any brand name.

The post-exposure interview is a day-after telephone call. The brand preference question is asked again, followed by queries to obtain proven recall.

The major measurement is brand preference shift (the percentage preferring the brand following exposure, minus the proportion who preferred it pre-exposure). Norms by product category are available.

The system works, according to a major study of validity conducted by Mapes and Ross.[20] A total of 142 commercial tests was the base, covering all commercials tested by the system (excluding big-ticket items) during the period of May through September 1979. A total of 2,241 respondents participated. The validation procedure was elegantly simple.

Two weeks after each test, telephone interviews were completed with each respondent. With no connection to the test, these people were asked about purchases of the product category and brand within the past two weeks. These could then be compared with their earlier responses to the same questions during the copy-testing procedure.

The results showed that:

- Increased levels of purchase follow changes in brand preference as measured by the pre–post copy test shifts. In a matched control sample where people were not exposed to the test commercial, there was a lower level of test-brand buying.

- While proven recallers showed somewhat higher test-brand buying levels than those not proving recall, the higher buying level was largely due to those in the proven recall group who changed their preference toward the test brand.

ARS

ARS is the successor to Schwerin Research, the venerable and respected copy-testing firm that developed the before-and-after brand preference method. In the original Schwerin method, all testing was done in theaters, with admission by ticket to those who came to see a presumed preview of a television show. Following the show, which included the test and other commercials, the brand preferences were asked for a second drawing (with, of course, no reference to the commercials). This was the start of the before-and-after brand preference measurement.

The testing procedure used by ARS is still pretty much like that, but with more sophistication built in. Invitations to attend a screening of a preview of a television show are mailed to men and women whose names have been chosen randomly from telephone directories in four metro areas (located in the Northeast, the Midwest, the South, and the West). Between 100 and 150 men and women are selected in each city, and of this number about half receive a follow-up telephone recall. Because it is a broad sample, more than a single test commercial can be used. Specific target samples are not recruited for standard tests. Studies are run almost daily throughout the year.

Sessions are held in hotel ballrooms or meeting rooms, with television monitors and VCR equipment in the middle of the room, facing out, and respondents in a circle surrounding these, facing in. A live MC presides. Before exposure of the film, participants are asked to choose a free quantity of the brand in each of several product categories should their ticket be selected in a later drawing. Following the pilot film, including the test commercial and other unrelated commercials, there is a second lottery.

Three days following the session, some 50 percent of the attendees are contacted by telephone to check their recall. The Related Recall

Score is the percentage claiming to have seen the commercial and able to give some proof through playback of details. The recall scores are used primarily as diagnostic, not evaluative, measures.

The big measurement is ARS Persuasion, the gain in lottery selection from before exposure of the test commercial to after the exposure.

The system seems to work. Exhibit 14.5 shows that sales/shares are indeed related to persuasion scores, from data collected over a 30-year period, covering 200 in-market validations.

Exhibit 14.5   SALES/SHARE RESULTS VERSUS PERSUASION SCORES

(Sales/Share Results from Split-Cable or Nielsen Scanner Data)[21]

Persuasion Score	Sales Effect
0–1.9	None
2.0–3.9	Measurable only with multiple exposures
4.0–6.9	Measurable, often temporary
7.0	Stronger, lasting for a longer time period

CATS

In CATS (Comprehensive Advertising Tracking System)[22]—(Research Systems Corporation in conjunction with Nielsen), persuasive rating points produced through ARS are combined with Nielsen data on audience size "to read actual advertising delivery both in traditional GRP and Share of Voice terms and in the more comprehensive terms of Persuasive Rating Points and Share of Persuasive Power."

Since persuasive ratings have been explained, we will concentrate on the Nielsen input, details of which will be given in Chapter 18.

Nielsen provides a measure of gross rating points (GRPs) for the specific ad through NSI quarter-hour ratings in 16 markets, and their Monitor Plus service verifies airing of these commercials. Then the Nielsen GRPs are combined with persuasive power in the following way:

Persuasive rating points (PRPs) = GRPs × ARS Persuasive Power in use in any given period

PRPs are said to assist ongoing evaluation and planning. An example: In evaluating a current campaign, the question is whether a new commercial should replace the present one.[23] The firm is running an ad that produced a +9.0 persuasion score when tested 11 months before. A new ad has tested at 7.3. Should the new ad replace the old one?

Calculations show that delivery of the old commercial is at the 3.2 level, and indeed it should be replaced. While this is a fictional case, it makes good sense.

The PreTesting Company

Though The Pretesting Company offers a service that covers testing of television, its approaches to print, radio, and outdoor advertising; while essentially parallel, are so intriguing that we will review one of them. But we will start with television.[24] Respondents are recruited by mall intercept from a selection of 17 shopping malls throughout the United States, and are typically target-market people chosen by specifications set by the advertiser or its agency.

The standard test sample size is 100. But if a client needs a larger sample to examine results within subgroups, such as males versus females or children versus adults, the sample size is increased.

Each person is individually processed in the suite of a research firm. The participant first rates the product attributes of the ideal product and actual brands (within the product category), including the test brand and its major competitors. The respondent then looks at the Sweepstakes Catalog, which includes a numerous list of product categories and brands within each. The person selects the two preferred brands within each category if he or she is the winner that week.

The person is seated before a color television set and given a remote-control unit, as in Exhibit 14.6, with controls for channels labeled NBC, CBS, and ABC. The person is told that the networks need public feedback about prime-time programming, and that if he or she doesn't enjoy the programming on one channel, it is possible to switch back and forth. Before the start of the screening, the participant is given a questionnaire to fill in during course of the scanning, with dummy questions such as which of the three channels he or she would be more likely to choose for home viewing and probable frequency of at-home viewing.

Each "network" has three inserts of four commercials. These are simultaneous, so that switching from one network to another at any commercial point simply provides a continuation of the same commercial. In the three bundles of commercials, the test commercial is presented twice.

Advertising exposure then follows.

In the post-testing stage, the identical questions of the pre-testing phase are repeated (brand recall and sweepstakes) to measure impact,

**Exhibit 14.6   PRETESTING COMPANY TELEVISION
SETTING FOR COPY TESTING**

Source: Photo courtesy of The PreTesting Co.

and, as diagnostic aids, there are also queries about what was liked and disliked about the advertising.

In the case of print, the reading behavior of the viewer of a portfolio of print pages—both editorial and advertising—is recorded through a "PeopleReader," shown in Exhibit 14.7. Appearances can be deceiving. This apparent traditional banker's lamp is no such thing. The People-Reader contains two cameras. One videotapes the particular page of the material at which the person is looking; the other focuses on the person's eyes, recording the center of attention. At the end of the test, the two sets of results are coordinated and combined.

ACT

ACT (Advertising Control for Television)[25] is the McCollum/Spielman service that measures awareness, communication of the message, and purchase motivation. It provides diagnostics showing the strengths and weaknesses of the proposed ad, with the goal of providing insights for future creative work on the ad.

These are central location tests in four regions of continental United States. Recruiting is by WATS line, generally with a total of 400 respon-

**Exhibit 14.7   PEOPLEREADER USED IN PRETESTING
COMPANY PRINT COPY TESTING**

Source: Photo courtesy of The PreTesting Co.

dents (within 20 miles of the particular central location) being recruited. The client specifies the type of participants desired, determined by the kind of audience at which the advertisement is targeted.

Those approached are told that the purpose is to get public reaction to some proposed television shows. (This not only facilitates recruitment of participants, but it also ensures that there will be no abnormal concentration on advertising aspects when they participate.)

In the test, four groups of some 25 persons each are seated around television monitors. An on-screen video host is used to provide a standard presentation for the entire test, eliminating the possibility that variation from one presentation to another might influence results.

Following a general orientation, there are questions about demographics and brand/product usage. A half-hour variety show (including a station-break clutter sequence of commercials including the test commercial) is shown. Then questions are asked about reactions to the show and unaided brand recall and copy recall.

The test commercials alone are then shown.

The test commercials are followed by specific questioning about a market basket choice (for frequently purchased, single-choice products such as hair-coloring products, toiletries, or food), or by use of a constant-sum question (for product fields with multiple brand usage by an individual, such as snacks) where the respondent allocates a given number of points to one or more brands. In either case, the pre–post brand choice difference is then taken as the measurement of persuasion or attitude shift. More complex measurements are used with other categories such as major appliances, automobiles, and airlines. McCollum/Spielman produces results both on ad performance, in terms of brand awareness, communication and persuasion (with norms available from some 2,300 tests over 20 years of testing), and on diagnostics to answer the client's specific interest areas.

McCollum/Spielman has a somewhat parallel service (ACM) for the measurement of magazine advertising.

The Buy Test

In The Buy Test,[26] the test commercial is aired in selected markets. Viewers of the show (and commercial) may be located, through telephone calls, either after the fact or by recruiting them in advance to view the show. Follow-up telephone interviews provide the measurements that are a part of The Buy Test.

The sample of people tested is generally the target market in terms of demographics and product use or purchase.

Recall covers unaided measurements of both product category and brand, followed by probes of the visual and copy elements of the ad. The Buy Test also measures intent to buy, improvement in attitude about the product, and intent to tell others about the product. All of this is put together to arrive at a cumulative score. To come up with a positive rating, a person must have recalled the advertising, shown involvement in it, and then given positive responses to the persuasion queries.

After mall passersby are qualified and recruited, they are taken into a room, usually in very small numbers, where they are exposed to the advertising. For a television commercial, it is on a CTR; for radio, it is a tape on a simulated radio set; for a print ad, it is a single ad or a portfolio.

In the customary Sherman testing procedure, those meeting target requirements are recruited, generally as they pass by in the mall, but if necessary by telephone. They are taken into the viewing room and shown the test ad or asked to listen to the test commercial.

The other concerns are the number of times the test advertisement is exposed and the advertising environment within which it is exposed. The test ad is shown twice within a competitive environment of other ads, and the participant is checked for recall of ads within the context. There are questions designed to determine the attention value of the test commercial within its testing environment.

The many significant variations in the nature of the presentation raise real questions about the comparability of results between media. This should be of concern to the user in terms of the norms that the firm has available.

An Evaluation Summary of These Methods

There are several crucial requirements that the procedures measuring awareness, memory, and persuasion should meet. Currently, none meets all of these, and it may be impossible for any one method ever to do so.

First, viewing should be in the home, on the participant's own television set. This is a normal condition. Viewing under any other condition is artificial.

Second, the person's exposure to the advertising being tested should be as normal as possible, in the sense of paralleling the situation in which he or she would generally be exposed to it. This totally excludes the outmoded method of showing ads and getting reactions, or showing "shuffle-cards" that ask the person to react favorably or unfavorably to each of a series of possible advertising themes. Both of these draw attention to the advertising itself and make the respondent a conscious judge. That is *not* the way advertising works. The person experiences it in an environment of program content and other ads, if on television, and in a mix of editorial content and other ads, if in print form. At the person's option, it is either examined and considered or not even noticed.

Third, the test should include exposure of the proposed advertisement more than once. Krugman[27] has argued with both logic and evidence that more than a single exposure to a new advertisement is required to sway a person's thinking about the product. So a copy-testing procedure that depends on a single exposure seems open to question. Nevertheless, there are many such services.

Finally needed is a really sound method of determining whether the results are significant in a practical sense: Do they tell the advertiser whether or not to go ahead and use the tested ad? This gets into the whole question of norms. Some copy-testing firms boast that they have banks of norms built up over years of testing. Such claims may be true but misleading. Over many years there may have been many new-product forms, many new claims, many varying techniques of presenting material. If, indeed, there are norms offered, they should most likely be recent ones, done on a moving average basis, perhaps, covering the past 18 months or so. Another possibility is to have a study design where there is a test group (which is exposed to the test ad) and a control group (which is *not* exposed to the ad) to see how their reactions compare.

We now summarize briefly our impressions of how well each of the reviewed services meet these four standards. We admit that this summary completely ignores such aspects as quality and the contributions of service representatives of the service. Despite these shortcomings, our summary is shown in Exhibit 14.8.

Exhibit 14.8   DEGREE TO WHICH EACH SERVICE* MEETS FOUR STANDARDS

	Apex	Mapes and Ross	ARS	Pretesting	ACT	Buy Test
Normalcy of Test Situation						
In-home	X	X		X		X
Out-of-home			X		X	
Degree of Normal Exposure						
Captive audience				X	X	X
Semicaptive audience	X	X	X			
Number of Advertising Exposures						
One	X	X	X	X		X
More than one					X	
Practicality						
Norms	X	X	X	X	X	X

*As provided in standard service.

METHODS MEASURING AWARENESS AND MEMORY

Day-after-Recall (DAR)

This post-test for television commercials is often used as a pre-test by running the test ad solely for the purpose of testing. Before we talk about the specific procedure, we must explain why it was ever developed at all as a sole measuring tool, without any attempt to build in a persuasion measure. It was simply that at the time the method was being developed, its major proponent, Procter & Gamble, argued that no copytesting method could measure persuasion. Lacking that, the rationale ran, let's have our advertising agencies and brand people define exactly what kind of message they are attempting to get across in the commercial. We can have them tell this in advance and then provide measurements of how well they did it. Thus the following procedure was established within this framework of thinking.

A test or actual commercial is aired. The following day, program viewers are reached by telephone. There is careful checking to make sure that the person really was tuned to the channel airing the commercial at the particular time.

Respondents are asked to name the brands in the commercials they can recall during the particular telecast time, what was said, what was shown, and what the main idea was. Exhibit A.1 (Appendix A at the back of this book) shows a typical questionnaire.

The DAR produces results showing the percentage of those in the commercial audience watching the show before and after the commercial who can remember something specific about the commercial. It measures principally memory and recall. Burke, developer and main supplier of the service, has norms by product category put together over the years.

Since our early years in advertising research, we have felt that this method was little less than saying that we cannot determine how effective advertising is, so let's just find out how well it gets across the message we want to push. We think that measurement methods over the years have shown we are right.

Print Recall

In Print Recall (Starch),[28] a post-test procedure, an individual who has seen the particular issue of a publication page-by-page is asked, for each ad:

Do you remember seeing or reading [this]?

Those claiming to have seen or read the ad are asked whether any part of the ad was seen (this is termed "noting"). Also measured are (1) whether the person saw or read the name of the product or service anywhere in the ad, and (2) readership of the headline, illustration, copy, or logo.

One hundred selected publications, including consumer, business, and trade magazines, as well as newspapers, are covered, with a sample of 150 readers of a particular publication. In addition to the scores for each ad, Print Recall provides two-year normative data for product categories by size and color, to provide a better basis for interpreting results obtained for a particular ad.

Ballot Research[29]

Another continuing readership service, this abridged form of the regular Starch (Mamaroneck, N.Y.) service covers readership of advertising and editorial content of small, controlled (free, sent to a select mailing list), or widely dispersed publications, where personal interviewing would be too expensive. The contacts are made through a mail survey sent to 200 potential respondents, with the expectation of about 150 responses.

"Ballots" (stickers) are affixed to 60 preselected items (editorial content and advertising) in an issue. This marked issue is sent some two weeks after the subscriber has received his standard issue.

We have strong doubts about this method. There is simply far too much "volunteerism," or self-selection. It lacks any semblance of good sampling.

METHODS AIMED PRIMARILY AT GUIDANCE

There are several kinds of tests where the aim is primarily guidance in developing or polishing the advertisement rather than straight evaluation. These include mainly qualitative measurements, but they also cover one procedure that produces quantitative results as a basis for guidance.

Instead of producing numbers that report how good the particular ad is, diagnostics-only shows its strong and weak points, and suggests ways in which the ad might be changed to overcome or reduce its weaknesses. Sometimes these diagnostic tools are studies in themselves; sometimes they are tools tacked on to the evaluative measurement methods.

We will talk about several kinds of these diagnostic studies: a quantitative measurement, a one-on-one personal interview method, group interviews generally, use of interactive devices, and psychogalvanic skin response.

A Quantitative Measurement

Video Storyboard Tests (New York City) offers a unique and long-standing method (with more than 5,000 tests) of providing recommendations working from rough television commercials (storyboards).[30,31] It provides both quantitative measurements, with norms, and qualitative diagnostics.

The research firm has facilities to produce video animatics (on video-cassettes) from storyboards with soundtrack.

People meeting the target requirements of the advertiser or its agency are intercepted at malls in cities of the sponsor's choice. Each qualified person is then interviewed on a one-on-one basis. The commercial is exposed on a television screen without any other material. The sample size per test is 100.

Following exposure, the respondent is asked questions that measure communications, relevance, and persuasion. Scores are also provided for product uniqueness, competitive strengths, and commercial likes and dislikes.

Quantitative results are provided, and these can be compared with norms for one of dozens of product categories.

The firm also has a procedure for measuring stopping power, communications, relevance, and persuasion for magazine ads in various early stages of development.[32] The rough ad may be a black and white line drawing, a color line drawing, a color tight comp, or a finished ad (black and white or finished color).

The test ad is inserted in a 20-page "magazine," a folder containing both editorial material and control ads. The magazine is tailored to be consistent with the development stage of the rough test ad.

Mall intercepts are used to recruit 100 qualified respondents. Each is then separately given the magazine to preview, following which each is asked about recall (unaided, aided, and related). The person is then asked to refocus on the ad and is probed about detailed reaction.

Again, many normative data are available as a basis for comparison against the test ad's quantitative results, and the diagnostic probe results are reported.

Headlines, body copy, and illustrations are analyzed.

A One-on-One Personal Interview Method

Reader Impression Studies (Starch: Mamaroneck N.Y.)[33] is a method that provides a means of diagnostics testing for print advertisements. The method provides a qualitative measure of whether the particular ad is conveying its intended message.

The respondent reads as much of the ad as he or she wishes during a personal interview. Exhibit 14.9 shows the standard impression questions and the following probe questions.

Exhibit 14.9   QUESTIONS ASKED IN STARCH READER—IMPRESSION STUDIES

1. When you first looked at this advertisement, what was outstanding to you? Tell me more about it.
2. In your own words what did the advertisement tell you about the (product, service, or company)? Tell me more about it.
   What does that mean to YOU?
3. What did the picture(s) tell you? Tell me more about it.
   What does that mean to YOU?
4. In your own words, what did the written material tell you? Tell me more about it.
   What does that mean to YOU?

The method is offered either as a pre-testing system, where those in the target audience group can be located and personally questioned, or as a post-testing system, conducted as a special appendage to the ongoing Starch readership studies.

Group Interviews Generally

Because there are few standardized formats for group interviews, it is difficult to say just how groups are used to produce diagnostics about proposed ads in any medium. Each group interview, as explained in Chapter 10, is a carefully crafted, highly dynamic procedure aimed at solving the particular problem. So we have to talk mainly about generalities.

Whether it is a proposed television, radio, or print ad, group reactions to virtually all aspects of the commercial are typically examined: the personality (if any), the way in which the material was presented, how convincing each element was, and so on. Product Acceptance & Research helped a client determine which anchorperson or combination of anchorpersons would be accepted by the viewing public.[34] Focus groups were presented with a variety of anchorperson combinations within a television news format. The focus groups indicated the decision to be made, and after the show was on the air for a few weeks, periodic telephone surveys measuring viewing levels determined that the decision had been correct.

Use of Interactive Devices

Four interactive devices are used in connection with group interviews. Since their similarities are greater than their differences, we group them together: PEAC, Quick-Tally, the Preference Analyzer, and the Interactive Group System. They have three common aspects: All have very similar interactive hardware and software, all work within the group interview system, and all follow very much the same sort of testing procedure.

In each case, all in the group are provided with a laptop keyboard through which they can respond on an ongoing basis about their reactions to the commercial or print ad. The kinds of push buttons and the kinds of reactions vary somewhat from one system to another, but mostly they are aimed at an overall reaction.

All of these interactive systems provide an instant averaging of responses, and they have a facility for displaying group averages superimposed on a rerun of the commercial. One advantage is that reactions are measured at time of exposure rather than depending on memory. Because use of these interactive systems eliminates problems of literacy, they can be used with children or with non-English-speaking people, all on a comparable basis.

The testing procedure is virtually identical. There are two steps:

1. Exposure of the test material during which participants use the keyboard to record their reactions.

2. A rerun of the test material with a moving-level graph superimposed, giving the moderator a chance to stop the rerun at high and low points and probe the group for reasons.

The PEAC System[35] is somewhat more standardized than the others, mainly because it is offered as a service. Testing is done in a theater-type setting. It provides a second-by-second measurement of response primarily to television and radio material, but it can also be used with print material.

Responses to open-ended questions approved in advance by the user company are also part of the procedure.

Although we have referred to this procedure as more standardized than others, we must qualify that by stating that the study is customized to meet the needs of the buyer. For instance, participants are recruited to match the firm's target market profile, and specific questions are tailored to client needs.

Results can be analyzed by such subgroups as age, socioeconomic level, and product usage.

PEAC has been used to check a British Chiclet commercial on *The Spitting Image,* featuring lifelike puppets and described as "truely outrageous." The satirical ad featured Reagan and Gorbachev. In Canada the ad was seen as very funny; in the United States the Reagan segment had far less appeal.

Quick Tally[36] is a system somewhat similar to PEAC, using electronic equipment as described in Chapter 7. It too uses a laptop computer with a 12-button, hand-held electronic unit. In the advertising test procedure offered by the sponsoring firm, participants react to three kinds of stimuli:

- Ongoing reaction to commercials (live movies, etc.) on a sliding scale basis

- Category questions

- Strength of reaction

As with PEAC, bar graph averages can be superimposed on reruns of the commercial, and the moderator can stop the action and ask questions at appropriate times. If there are client observers present, they can see results immediately by predetermined subgroups.

The system of 50 participant units is portable.

The Preference AnalyzerII[37] (Ortek Data Systems) is an intractive system similar to the two preceding systems. In this case, the hand-held unit contains, instead of buttons, a dial with a range of 0–100. Participants dial the level of their reactions as the commercial (or other stimulus) is shown, and these are recorded on a second-by-second basis. Demographics generally have been recorded before the beginning of the screenings.

Up to 512 participants can be handled in a single session. Instant graphs are available, along with breakouts of the results by subgroups.

The method offers no provision for questions for playbacks from participants on reasons-why.

The Interactive Group Research System (Market Opinion Research, Detroit)[38] recruits between 25 and 50 respondents to come to a central location. Participants rate a commercial continuously on a hand-held dial offering a scale of 0–100. The audience can also use the dial to reply to any specific questions.

The usual focus group discussion follows, conducted with a cross section or selected portion of participants.

Psychogalvanic Skin Response

Meet MindView Involvement Index (Inner Response Inc., Charlotte, N.C.). This intriguing diagnostic copy analysis measure utilizes the psychogalvanic skin response, but with a measuring method vastly updated from that of only a decade ago. The psychogalvanic reflex is an aspect of the lie detector test, in which the autonomic nervous system, acting at an unconscious level, produces perspiration when emotions are aroused.

The problem with the old instruments was that they measured only one (the phasic) aspect of response, and it could measure only the presence of emotion without being able to identify whether it was in a positive or a negative direction.

Inner Response has developed MindView,[9] a machine that overcomes this problem. MindView is a lunchbox-sized computer, capable of handling as many as 64 respondents simultaneously, gathering separate records for each. It also can aggregate records when preprogrammed to do so.

A sensor is placed on the upper palm of the person's nondominant hand (because that hand is generally less calloused and more sensitive). A slip-through Velcro strap is used to attach the sensor firmly but comfortably on the hand. The sensor contains various electronic chips to heighten the electrical signal coming from the sympathetic nervous system.

A very slight electrical charge is introduced through a second sensor. The rate at which it comes out is measured by the second sensor. Rarely, someone might feel a very slight warming sensation, nothing more. A photograph of a person going through the test procedure is shown in Exhibit 14.10.

Selection of respondents is similar to that of most surveys using a central location. The nature of the sample depends on the client's needs and the nature of the target audience.

Respondents are always told at the start what the test is about. People are then asked whether they are right- or left-handed, and the sensor is placed on the nondominant hand. Then a standard video of about 45 seconds is shown as a control (to ensure that the level of reaction is similar to that of other samples). The test commercial follows.

The commercial is then rerun, with a graph showing high and low points of response superimposed. The graph reflects both the person's

Exhibit 14.10   **A PERSON BEING TESTED WITH MINDVIEW**

Source: Photo courtesy of Inner Response.

predisposition towards the material (interest) and the effect of the stimulus itself (appeal). The moderator probes for explanations of the high and low points.

Inner Response *always* also uses pencil and paper methods of measuring response, and these are regarded as the primary measure. The machine reactions are viewed as a critical secondary and diagnostic tool.

The firm points out that while its system measures the duration, intensity, and directional change of emotional response, it does not in itself identify the nature of the response (for example, joy, sadness). Such descriptions are obtained through questioning after exposure.

The opening segment of a 30-second Campbell Soup commercial, for example, showed a young boy in a swimming pool. Measurements indicated this was weak. The strength of the commercial appeared in the second half, with the familiar refrain of "mmm-mmm, good." The spot was cut to 15 seconds, starting at the midpoint with the refrain and then the boy climbing out of the pool.

A NEW DEVICE FOR PROMOTIONAL PRE-TESTING

A very real practical problem in promotion testing has been the cost of and time required for producing variations in packaging, price, on-shelf displays, and shelf space and placement. A possible solution has been recently suggested.

Computerized variations of these elements can now be produced. One of the practical problems in much promotional pretesting has recently been reported.[39] The testing can be done within a simulated environment. However the "Hypermarket" has yet to be tested, and its sponsor has a far too limited view of its utility (focus groups), if it is indeed viable.

Hypermarket uses software to simulate magazines, grocery stores, car dealerships, fast-food, and other retail outlets on a video screen. Subjects use a computer to select the aisle where they want to shop (or a magazine page selected from a series of pages that flip as the reader moves a control ball).

PRODUCT DELIVERY

In this discussion, the term *product* should be construed to mean both *product* and *service*.

To understand the ways in which marketing research can be helpful in marking product delivery, it is necessary first to talk about symbolism and imagery. For that is what product delivery is all about: the building of an aura around a particular product.

Broadcaster Paul Harvey has commented that symbols speak louder than words. He is probably right. A symbol—something that stands for or represents another thing—helps create an image. Imagery is the way we perceive things, how we screen things to arrive at an interpretation of reality. For example, when you listen to a drama on radio—if you do that at all—you fill in the background. Your imagination fills in the scenario, enriching and coloring the action. You visualize the appearance of the characters in line with our own expectations. Not so with television, where it is all spelled out for you.

Or take the case of the male or female model. If too much is revealed, the model may lack much appeal. Often what is not shown but merely subtly hinted at is far more effective. If a subtle mystique is built up around a beautiful woman who never allowed her photos, behavior, or words to get out of hand—Princess Grace, for instance—it will be hard for anyone to dig up material that will change that image. It is too entrenched. The reverse is true for such femmes fatales as Mae West and Marilyn Monroe.

The firmly established brand image works in parallel fashion. If you perceive a brand as having poor quality, it is extremely difficult for the supplier of that brand to take any step that will change your evaluation.

This imagery or perception is very important in marketing. A 1989 study by Opinion Research Corp.[40] showed that 89 percent of a sample of 1,010 people said that the reputation of a firm often determines whether they purchase that firm's product. Further, 71 percent reported that the more they know about a firm, the more favorable they feel toward it.

In the case of marketing, the name of the product or service, the package, and the personalizing of product delivery all contribute to imagery. However, the impact of these elements, though strong, is most often subtle. This requires considerable understanding and skill about how to use research to develop and measure the impact of these three areas of product delivery. It is generally dangerous to ask people directly how they like a particular logo or brand name. Respondents are likely to give an acceptable social reply rather than one they feel, maybe even subsconsciously, down deep. It seems unlikely that Tussy (note how close that is to "hussy") would have won over Angel in a name test for a cosmetics line. Yet Tussy became a highly successful cosmetics line.

There are some exceptions. In the personalizing of product delivery, direct questions seem entirely reasonable. The consumer's service experiences and expectations are highly conscious matters, with little subtlety involved. But we will show how somewhat different kinds of research approach seem best suited to each of these three areas of product delivery.

NAMING THE PRODUCT

There are three stages in naming the product: defining the problem (the need), developing possible names, and testing those names.

Defining the Problem

Definition of the problem, as with all marketing research, is the key to good results. In the case of naming the product, this means that the purpose of the name must be stated in terms of the overall marketing goals, and its expected contribution in such terms as imagery or perception of the firm's own name or that of its product or service.

Developing Possible Names

Few firms talk about how they decide on a name. Some depend on their own internal decisions, while others go to an outside specialist firm.

We recall the case of a major automobile manufacturer, some years ago, that was trying to come up with a model name that would appeal to the Canadian market. In the in-house discussions, one suggestion was the name Beaumont. That died in a hurry when a French-Canadian member of the team pointed out that this could easily be construed to mean "heap, big pile."

Negative as the example may be, it demonstrates the basic method of developing possible names: It is brainstorming, either informal or formal, either internal or external (using an outside specialist firm).

Internal discussions are unlikely to be productive. Skilled as a firm may be in marketing generally, it typically does not have in hand either the skills of brainstorming or the criteria needed for a good name.

Testing the Names

Once potential names have been generated, an image or perception test may be the way to determine the winner. In one case, a Canadian distiller was considering four different brand names for a particular whiskey: Carrington, Alberta, Grey Cup, and Rocky Mount. Carrington is a prestigious British family name. Alberta is a stolid, generally prosperous, grain-growing Canadian province. Grey Cup is the championship of the Canadian Football League; the celebrations typically begin on the morning of the event, ending only in the early hours of the following morning, and are somewhat analogous, in the spirit of the affair, to Mardi Gras in New Orleans. Rocky Mount needs no explanation.

A small sample of whiskey drinkers was provided with four shot glasses of whiskey, all from the same bottle, though the testers did not know this. The four jiggers were stationed on a tray, each just in back of a gummed label containing one of the four names, so that all four names were represented. The men were asked to sip and compare the brands and to state which they preferred and why. The big winner was Carrington, which was perceived as smooth and expensive. Alberta was described as bland. Rocky Mount was seen as harsh and raw. Grey Cup was described as high in alcoholic content and for the working man.

Use of Outside Specialists

There are services that for a fee will generate possible names for a company, a product, or a service. These do not use typical marketing research as we have discussed it, but we mention them because they appear to be valuable services. They all use what might be termed "logic" or "rationality" as a method. Both of the specialist firms we discuss start with one or more interviews with their clients to define the problem.

Salinon's Namestorming[41] has had some success. "Sensible Chef" was generated as the name for a new line of frozen foods. "Visual Edge" became the name for a new computer board.

After a client discussion to define the problem, a brainstorming session is held among key Salinon staff. This is followed by computer programs to generate possible new names.

Salinon offers a disk program, Namer, for the firm that wants to follow its general procedure on the firm's own premises. The program can be loaded into a hard disk on a PC-compatible.

The program brainstorms with the user. It provides several optional means for selecting names. One is "the original name generator," which helps the user build names from individual letters. If the user were IBM, for instance, the program would come up with product or service names that formed three words using those letters, in accordance with the product concept.

The "connotation sythesizer" helps the user select types of connotations to be associated with the name. With "the adaptive learning method," the user tells the computer what type of name is desired. The "phrase maker" gives the user a chance to enter favorite words or phrases, and "dodging profanities" is self-descriptive.

Namelab[42,43] is basically similar to Namestorming. Following discussion with the client to define the problem, a ranked list of messages to be expressed in the name is produced.

In developing possible names, the first step is building a dictionary of verbal terms (from various languages that contribute to American English) and symbol fragments (visible and appropriate elements of existing names in the category). These terms are synthesized into a word-making pattern that expresses the product category and messages. These may be natural words (Apple, Blue Cross) or coined words (Citibank, Kleenex).

Each promising name candidate is sharpened to stress impact, aesthetics, memorability, uniqueness, vocabulary fit, internal or external reference, and shelf appeal. The process produces a ranked list.

The final step is a focus group discussion among the target market group. The group is exposed to the test sequence of names and competitive names. They respond to questions about how well each name describes the product and the ideas each suggests about the product.

SYMBOLIZING THE PRODUCT

The symbol associated with the product is also an important ingredient. The identical margarine tested in a simulated product test where one sample was packaged with a crown, and the other without a crown, gave huge preferences to the crown. The sample was seen as far tastier and richer.

And now Nipper, the RCA dog, is being reintroduced.[44] Nipper first listened to his master's voice on a Victrola in 1894. Of course, Nipper is being updated, and now—perhaps much to his surprise, and perhaps chagrin at this late age—has a 2-month-old male puppy who is to be the real star of the commercials.

Research had much to do with the reintroduction. Most consumers, even the younger ones, were familiar with Nipper. While Nipper meant good, reliable products, he also stood for a stodgy company. That's why son-of-Nipper was brought into the picture.

PACKAGING THE PRODUCT

Packaging, particularly for foods, nonprescription drugs, and small household items that are commonly sold in self-service stores, has three functions. One, through visibility and appeal, is to get attention on the shelf. A second is image-building. A third is the convenience of storage and use for the consumer.

Good packaging cannot guarantee product success; there are too many other factors contributing to success or failure. But it can aid the chances of success.

With most fast-moving consumer goods, package design is so important and so specialized that most larger companies go to a specialist such as an industrial or package designer for assistance. Of course, those designing the package must start with a good idea of the imagery desired, the importance of shelf visibility, and consumer requirements for storage and use. Some marketing research, therefore, should have preceded this step of design.

Packaging Development

Focus groups can be used in the early stages of package development, for instance, much the same as in consumer product research. Drawings or mock-ups of various packages can be shown, and the interaction provided by group interviews will almost surely bring out some important points, many not previously considered by the firm.

Package Testing

The PreTesting Company, whose services in copy testing were described earlier in this chapter,[24] also offers package-testing services.

The testing place is a research facility in a shopping center. Consumers representing the target market are recruited through mall intercept interviews. In the research facility, an optional first step is to give each person six ads (one about the test product that includes an illustration of the package), followed by questioning about the message communication of each. This step is used only when introduction of the new product or line extension is to be accompanied with strong advertising support.

Persons are individually seated in front of a $5\frac{1}{2}$-foot rear projection screen and told that they will be shopping photographically within a supermarket. There are three product categories, and for each one the respondent is to make a first, second, and third brand choice. The person can, with the special equipment, move photographically back and forth on any shelf and focus in on any product, spending as much or as little time as wished. All the while a computer is measuring which products are being approached, and the duration for each. This stage is termed *purchase intent.*

The respondent is then seated in front of a large screen and is told that each of four shelf slides (one for each product category) will be shown. Each shows packages in actual size and in a natural and competitive shopping setting. The person is asked to locate a particular brand as quickly as possible, and to touch the product with a special pointer as soon as identifying the product. (This removes the slide from view and records reaction time.) However, the sought-for brand may or may not be part of the display; the intent is to minimize quick but false spotting.

Then the participant is asked to identify the test package in terms of package design and copy. This "intrusiveness test" indicates whether a low level of close-up approach in the preceding stage was due to a lack of interest or a lack of visibility.

The person then rates attributes of the test product, four other specific brands, and the "ideal" product. Purchase intent and reason are also ranked.

The PreTesting Company method of package testing seems sound. Our only reservation is the question of how the user makes an overall judgment. At what levels of performance do results suggest a "go"?

An on-shelf test may also be applied to the testing of names, at least for small, packaged goods. A small quantity of the proposed package, enough to provide a small display, is used to stock a simulated shelf display that includes competitive-brand packages. There are many research firms that offer facilities for this sort of display and research.

The respondent, who generally has been given "seed money," is asked to do some shopping off the shelf. With a controlled design, the "pull" of a package with one name can be checked against that of another.

Moskowitz[6] has applied similar basic techniques in testing cereal packages. However, there was no product trial, but simply a statement of product expectations. This was far more a conscious-reaction measurement.

Adult participants first evaluated two different dry cereals on several attributes. This provided a base line. Later they evaluated six different cereal packages, first on a blind basis (without any indication of brand or manufacturer), then the same packages, with rotated order, on an identified basis (with manufacturer and brand name). Panelists scaled each of the two cereals (12 packages) on the same set of attributes.

Even in this more conscious perception testing, panelists distinctly differentiated among the packages. The greatest differences in attributes such as acceptance, nutrition, and the like were tied to the illustrations on the box.

PERSONALIZING PRODUCT DELIVERY

Customer satisfaction about service is increasingly important to all kinds of business. Since most manufacturers produce quality products—

with consumers well aware of this—customer service in the product delivery is demanded. With retailers, as self-service and automation have increased, service has declined. Have you tried to locate someone in a supermarket or department store to give you assistance?

The moment of truth may be customer reaction to service.

Measurement of reaction to service can usually be directly asked, because the impact is so solidly and directly on the consumer. Questioning can be direct, with no need for subtlety. Also, most measurements of the effectiveness of service (or customer satisfaction) are specialized—that is, by the type of marketing.

Several research firms specialize in measuring customer satisfaction with service for almost any type of firm. Before we discuss any of them, we will outline the common stages of this measurement: *problem statement, listing the possibilities,* and *testing.*

We emphasize once again the importance of stating the problem—in this case, the needs and goals of the program. The usual way of going at this is an internal study, working with management and employees to determine the needs, goals, and operating difficulties to be overcome.

As for listing the possibilities, exploratory research may be used to develop ideas and perceptions of problems and possible solutions.

For testing, a quantitative customer study is generally conducted.

Finally, we must mention *recommendations for action* and *follow-up programs,* if only because the marketing research firms in this field stress these so much.

We agree that research of any sort without action on recommendations is meaningless. We are mildly concerned about the tremendous emphasis on follow-up programs. While we realize that these studies are not the automatic self-perpetuating brand/product movement studies, or those continuing studies of television audiences, we wonder whether the overemphasis on continuing studies of customer satisfaction may not be generated more by the needs of the research firm than by those of the user firm. The user firm ought to *know* whether it needs these ongoing studies.

Specialist Research Firms

After Maritz[45] determines what the company is trying to do in delivering service, a small sample of customers is questioned.

Their input is used to design questionnaires for the measurement of satisfaction level. Each is custom-designed to meet the particular needs of the company as suggested by the preliminary input. This quantitative measure is usually conducted with both customers and frontline employees.

The job is not considered finished at this point. Programs are introduced to respond to customer satisfaction issues. The firm feels that follow-up studies are needed to keep the program on track.

Elrick & Lavidge[46] handles its studies in much the same manner. A preliminary internal study examines internal sales, servicing, and operational techniques to determine how, when, and by whom contact is made with customers. This is followed by qualitative in-depth and/or focus group interviews with employees to determine their understanding of performance standards, to define any obstacles employees feel hinder their performance standards, and to help the research firm develop the critical issues and attributes of the business.

There are qualitative interviews with customers. These may be either focus group sessions or in-depth questioning. This phase leads to the development of a questionnaire.

The customer study measures and tracks how well the firm is meeting or exceeding customer expectations and shows what areas need improvement.

Self-Conducted Customer Satisfaction Studies

Some firms conduct their own customer satisfaction surveys. Exhibit A.2 (in the appendix at the back of the book) shows a questionnaire used in a telephone survey by Mercedes-Benz to evaluate customer satisfaction. Owners of cars 1 to 2 years old were studied. The questionnaire covers identifying items about the dealer, car, and owner. There are queries about the purchasing situation, delivery, servicing and repairs, parts, and warranty. All in all, says Robert S. Baxter, manager of marketing research for Mercedes-Benz of North America, the results "are used as benchmark measures for individual dealer evaluations. . . . Dealerships selling 250–400 cars [are] compared with those of comparable retail unit volumes. Areas of strength and deficiency are pointed out and corrective measures . . . recommended."

General Motors has a continuing program paralleling this, conducted by Maritz (under GM direction) since the program began in 1979.[47] The questionnaire covers satisfaction with the services of the dealer who sold the vehicle, sales staff relations during and following purchase, vehicle condition at time of delivery, how well the dealer handled any warranty service, overall satisfaction with the dealer making the sale, and an open-ended query asking how the dealer could improve customer satisfaction.

Buyers of new GM vehicles are mailed the questionnaire six months following purchase. The mailing includes both the questionnaire and a personalized cover letter signed by the division's general manager and mailed from a post office near the home office of the division. Typically, a 50 percent to 55 percent response is obtained from the nearly 3 million mailouts made annually.

Applications of the results of these studies seem useful. Dealers and all levels of management in the company and its divisions are urged to think of customer satisfaction and survey results as a company priority. Dealers are encouraged to use the information provided from the surveys to use research to identify further the causes of dissatisfaction. Dealers wanting more in-depth information can start by going to the company for additional data and diagnostic information.

ENDNOTES

[1] Kevin O'Malley, vice president, marketing, Farberware. Interview.

[2] D. C. McGill. "Hunting for a Better Cut of Coffee." *New York Times,* May 27, 1989.

[3] *MA.RET: The True Single-Source of Consumer Information.* Columbus, Ohio: Impact Resources, undated; *Impact Resources.* Columbus, Ohio: Impact Resources, undated; *Caveat Emptor! Buyer Beware.* Columbus, Ohio: Impact Resources.

[4] Florence Fabricant. "How Dry They Are: New Wave in Beers? *New York Times,* Aug. 16, 1989.

[5] C. L. Alford and J. B. Mason. "Generating New Product Ideas." *Journal of Advertising Research* 15, no. 6 (1975): 27–32.

[6] H. R. Moskowitz. *New Directions for Product Testing and Sensory Analysis of Foods.* Westport, Conn.: Food & Nutrition Press, 1985, 171 ff.

[7] *Adopter.* New York: Data Development Corp., undated.

[8] Ann Keely. "Goals Segmentation: A Tool for Evaluating Pre-prototype New Product Concepts." *Marketing Research,* 17–21.

[9] J. E. Shimell, president, Inner Response. Letter, June 28, 1990.

[10] Vance Packard. *The Hidden Persuaders.* New York: Washington Square Press, 1980, 97.

[11] D. B. Lucas. "Advertising Research and Measurement." Chapter 6 in *Marketing Manager's Handbook.* Chicago: Dartnell, 1983, 6–7.

[12] Andrew Old. "Planned and Delivered." *Advertising Age,* Jan. 1, 1990, sect. 1, 8 ff.

[13] Terry Kattleman. "Planning in Action." *Advertising Age,* Jan. 1, 1990, sect. 1, 38.

[14] Kim Foltz. "New Species for Study: Consumers in Action." *New York Times,* Dec. 18, 1989.

[15]*Advertising and Entertainment Research.* New York: ASI Market Research, undated.

[16]*Recall Plus.* New York: ASI Market Research, undated.

[17]*Apex: Recall Plus, Persuasion Plus.* New York: ASI Market Research, undated.

[18]*Mapes and Ross, Inc.* Princeton, N.J.: Mapes and Ross, undated.

[19]*How Emotion Drives Persuasion in Television and Print Advertising.* Mapes and Ross Advertising Research Foundation presentation, Mar. 3, 1987.

[20]H. R. Ross, Jr. "Recall versus Persuasion: An Answer." *Journal of Advertising Research* 22, no.1 (1982): 13–16.

[21]"Validation and Advertising Elasticity." *Basic Research Notes,* Research Systems Corp., April 1990.

[22]Margaret Henderson Blair. *Getting Your Money's Worth: Measuring and Managing the Impact and Effectiveness of Your Advertising Campaign.* Cost-Effective Advertising Techniques Conference, Toronto, Nov. 3, 1989.

[23]K. E. Rosenberg. *Managing Advertising Quality Beyond Copy Testing.* Advertising Research Foundation: Conference on Copy Research in the Age of Technology, May 3, 1988.

[24]*A Comparison of PreTesting Company Methodologies as Compared to Other Research Services, Including a Brief Outline of Each Service.* Englewood, N.J.: The PreTesting Company, undated.

[25]*ACT Ad Vantage.* Great Neck, N.Y.: McCollum/Spielman, undated, 15 pp.

[26]*The Buy Test.* Glen Cove, N.Y.: The Sherman Group, undated.

[27]H. E. Krugman, "Why Three Exposures May Be Enough." *Journal of Advertising Research* 12 (1972): 11–14.

[28]*The Starch Readership Service.* Mamaroneck, N.Y.: Starch-INRA-Hooper, undated.

[29]*Ballot.* Mamaroneck, N.Y.: Starch INRA Hooper, 1979.

[30]*Test Rough Commercials.* New York: Video Storybook Tests, undated.

[31]*Video Storyboard Tests.* New York: Video Storybook Tests, undated.

[32]*Print Ad Test.* New York: Video Storybook Tests, undated.

[33]*Impression Study.* Mamaroneck, N.Y.: Starch INRA Hooper, undated.

[34]*Case History: News Anchors.* Evansville, Ind.: Product Acceptance & Research, undated.

[35]*The Testing Technology That Measures Up to Your Creative.* Chicago: Viewfacts, undated.

[36]*Quick Tally Systems.* New York: Quick Tally Systems, undated.

[37]*Preference Analyzer II.* Beaverton, Oreg.: Ortek, 1989.

[38]Leona Foster and Debra Vandenbussche. "Interactive Group Research System: What It Can Do for You." *Marketing News from Market Opinion Research,* Fall 1988.

[39]Jon Lafayette. "Interpublic Updates Focus Groups." *Advertising Age,* Apr. 16, 1990, 54.

[40]"Facts of Life Time." *Psychology Today,* September 1989.

[41]*Namestorming by Salinon.* Dallas: The Salinon Corp., undated.

[42]R. A. Mamis. "Name-calling." *Inc.,* July 1984.

[43]*Namelab.* San Francisco: Namelab, 1982.

[44]"RCA's TV Ads Reintroducing Famous Dog-and-Victrola Logo." *News-Journal* (Daytona Beach), Sept. 14, 1990, page 4C.

[45]*Customer Satisfaction Research Presentation Augmentation.* Fenton, Mo.: Maritz, undated.

[46]*The Difference Between Satisfied and Dissatisfied Customers is . . . .* Atlanta: Elrick & Lavidge, undated.

[47]"On the Right Track: CSI Program Helps GM Dealers Monitor Customer Satisfaction." *Quirk's Marketing Research Review,* Feb. 1991, 6–7 ff.

15

MARKET SEGMENTATION

What's in This Chapter

In this chapter we show how the grouping of customers for the purposes of marketing has progressed from the mere review of demographic statistics to the inclusion of psychographics. We examine the major syndicated services in the field of marketing research, and we examine some of the benefits—and the hazards—of a firm's doing its own marketing segmentation.

Henry Ford introduced mass production to the United States in 1908, when he first offered the Model T. Priced at $825, it was a real buy. Ford said that it could be had in any color at all, as long as it was black.

It was not long before General Motors, by offering more varieties (and colors), overtook Ford. Today the consumer has the choice not only of many colors and combinations, but of many options such as automatic drive; electronically controlled windows, door locks, rear-view mirrors, and seat posistions; radio (FM–AM or none); varying seat materials and colors, and so many others that we won't try to list them.

SEGMENTATION

The U.S. population is dividing into smaller, clustered groups, each with its own special interests, life-styles, and affinity for particular products and services.

Preference for various kinds of potato chips varies with region and by other demographics.[2] Jalapeno-flavored chips do well in Texas, Cajun dills in Louisiana. In Washington State, one brand successfully offers a smoked wood-chip variety. There are several local brands sold throughout the country that have chips with the potato skin left on.

There is no longer a mass market for soaps. Instead, there are bath soaps and toilet soaps, soaps for people with oily or dry skin. For what purpose do you want a toothpaste: to prevent cavities or to keep your teeth white? What about mouthwashes: one to give you a pleasant breath, to help prevent cavities, or to cut down on plaque?

In coffees, we are now offered powdered or regular; Brazilian or Colombian; and even gourmet coffees with touches of chocolate or other exotic flavors. Vacuum brick packs sell well in the South. Folgers has recently introduced Folgers Singles, a coffee bag similar to a tea bag.[3] The mass market has shattered into segments. Markets are now small bits and pieces. Quaker Oats began years ago as a single, long-cook variety of oatmeal. Later, it introduced an instant form. Today, it is possible to buy either of these in several different flavors and package types.

Sales Areas Marketing Inc. (SAMI), a leading marketing research firm now part of Arbitron, reports that the number of cereal brands with sales of at least $1 million annually rose from 84 in 1979 to 150 in 1989; the number of food store toothpaste brands in the $1 million category rose from 10 to 31 over the same period.

The division of the population into smaller, more clustered groups has led to the development of specific products and services wanted by each group. Yes, people *are* different. Some live in rural areas, perhaps on farms. Others live in small communities of perhaps under 2,000 population.

Why the rush to segmentation? One basic reason is declining population growth. Companies have been forced to seek sales increases by adding new lines or offering product variations within a line. They have to try to steal customers from other companies in what is now turning out to be a limited market.

The competition is not only with domestic firms. Overseas firms have improved their technology and now actively compete in many fields thought to have been safely American.

Another reason is that manufacturing has now become so computerized. It is no longer as expensive to change from one product run to another. Firms have learned to produce relatively inexpensively on a small-scale basis.

Really new products are rare. Mostly, they now consist of line extensions, with the company's hope that it can extend its total sales. So both the need and opportunity are there.

We are talking about the grouping of customers or potential customers toward whom a marketing program for a product or service can be directed. While we happen to use the term *market segmentation*, equivalent terms include *market definition, market description, market analysis*, or *clustering*. Whatever the term, it is simply a matter of grouping people with common characteristics that make sense as marketing targets. The target must be reachable through one or more promotion methods or media.

SOME APPLICATIONS AND EXAMPLES

Segmentation has many practical marketing applications, only a few of which we will discuss here.

One application is the selection of a possible new site for a firm or its extension. Closely related is the selection of new markets that match current customer profiles. Another is helping to determine product nature (particularly line extensions). Also, segmentation can aid advertising both in media selection (Chapter 18) and in the advertising message (Chapter 14).

THE BASIC FORMS OF SEGMENTATION

There are three segmentation bases: consumer data, business and industrial data, and geographics.

Most market segmentation concerns the consumer market rather than the business market, chiefly because the business firm is closer to its customers and knows a lot about them without making formal studies. And, of course, studies of the business market typically concern firms rather than people.

Consumer Segmentation

Consumer segmentation falls into two groups: syndicated and proprietary. The syndicated services are available from their primary sources, more often from secondary sources, incorporated with other data.

The information may be pure demographics, an implied mix of psychographics from demographics, or pure psychographics. But we had better start with some definitions.

Demographics are vital statistics: age, sex, marital status, ethnicity, family size and composition, nature of housing (including whether rented or owned), occupation, education, and other statistical characteristics covered by the census.

Psychographics are the psychological attributes that constitute a person's life-style. They refer to the way the person enjoys living. They have much to do with the person's self-image and how he or she wants to be perceived. They concern, for instance, whether one wants to drive a Toyota or an Oldsmobile 98. Some who can afford the latter don't care to display their worth. (Of course, some who cannot really afford the larger car still drive it.)

Pure psychographic studies are generally used only in proprietary services, for the sole use of the firm doing the study (almost always a marketing firm or an advertising agency). That's because any purely psychographic study has to be tailored for specific needs and uses.

The syndicated sources basically use demographic statistics, though embellishing them in psychographic terms.

Business Segmentation

Business segmentation is the description of areas or customers (as a group) in terms of various kinds of statistics, such as nature or size of the business (number of employees or dollar volume).

Geographics

Almost all syndicated segmentation sources provide descriptions by geographics, descriptions that are essential in marketing research.

CONSUMER SEGMENTATION

SYNDICATES SOURCES

Many syndicated sources provide the marketer with demographics about specific markets. Some provide print information only, some supply disks, and some provide electronic availability through databanks. Our major interest in this text concerns demographics available in one or more electronic forms.

There are the old standby print sources, such as the *Sales and Marketing Management Annual Survey of Buying Power* and the *Editor and Publisher Marketing Guide*, both described in Chapter 2. These sources, both providing consumer statistics by MSAs, generally have little flexibility for ongoing use by the sophisticated marketer or marketing researcher. If they are needed, they are likely to have been added to the company library.

The Lifestyle Market Analyst (Standard Rate & Data Service, Wilmette, Ill.) annually publishes its *Lifestyle Marketing Analyst*.[4] On a market-by-market basis, it profiles markets in three dimensions: demographics, life-styles, and consumer segments. All 212 ADIs (see Chapter 2, Exhibit 2.1, for definitions of geographic terms) as well as 110 of the largest counties within the top ten ADIs in the United States are profiled demographically in the market profile section. The life-style profiles section outlines the nature of numerous hobbies, interests, and activities for five major life-style groups. The consumer segment provides 42 market segments, and for each ranks the ADIs by the percentage of households belonging to the segment. This section can aid the marketer in identifying and locating the markets most likely to buy or use a particular product or service.

ClusterPlus (Donnelley) classifies all households into 47 different clusters. The emphasis is on demographics (age, ethnicity, income, mobility, education, occupation, nature of housing) rather than psychographics. Exhibit 15.1 shows a few of the categories. ClusterPlus provides the current year's estimates of various demographics, along with five-year projections. The marketer should consider markets not only as they presently exist, but also as they are likely to be in later years.

Exhibit 15.1   SOME OF THE CLUSTERPLUS CATEGORIES[5]

1—Highest socioeconomic status, highest income, prime real estate areas, highest educational level, professionally employed, low mobility, homeowners, children in private schools

5—high income, high home values, high education level, professionally employed, low mobility, homeowners, homes built in 1950s and 1960s

10—High education level, average income, professionally employed, younger, mobile, apartment dwellers, above-average rents

15—Older, very low mobility, fewer children, above-average income and education, white-collar workers, older housing, urban areas

20—Areas with high proportion of group-quarters population, college dormitories, homes for the aged, mental hospitals and prisons, other institutions

25—Younger, mobile, fewer children, below-average income, average education, apartment dwellers

30—Low income, lowest educational level, families with one worker, farms, rural areas

35—Older housing, low income, average education, younger, mobile, fewer children, apartment dwellers, small towns

40—Older, very low income, low educational level, one-person households, retirees, few children, older homes and apartments

47—Urban blacks, very low income, low educational level, very high unemployment, female householders with children, older housing

Exhibit 15.2   SELECTED CLUSTERS FROM PRIZM

"Shotguns and Pickles"
Many small, outlying townships and crossroad villages which provide the nation's breadbasket, and other rural areas. Large families, school-age kids, headed by blue-collar craftsmen, equipment operators, and transport workers with high school education.

"Urban Gold Coast"
New York's Sutton Place and portions of Park Avenue

"Bohemian Mix"
Examples: Greenwich Village, Berkeley, Calif.

America's Bohemia, a largely integrated, singles-dominated, high-rise hodgepodge of white collars, students, divorced persons, actors, writers, artists, aging hippies, and races. While it is only a $5 cab ride from Manhattan's "East Side" to "The Village," the shift in perspective and income is dramatic.

"Public Assistance"
Example: South Bronx.

"Emerging Minorities"
Examples: Bedford-Stuyvesant, Harlem.

"Pools and Patios"
Upscale areas in a greenbelt surrounding a major city. The children have mostly grown and departed, leaving aging couples in empty nests too costly for young homemakers. The "good life" is assured by good educations, high white-collar employment levels, and double incomes.

Donnelley's TargetScan, a computerized search for areas that match specific demographic profiles, is more sophisticated. It is most useful simply because it can tell a chain retailer, for example, where it might seriously think about opening new outlets.

PRIZM (Potential Rating Index by ZIP Markets), from Claritas, has come up with 40 different demographic/life-style clusters. Every neighborhood in the United States has been classified into one of these clusters.[6,7] Exhibit 15.2 shows the names and descriptions of a few clusters. These PRIZM classifications are available for every ZIP code in the United States, and more recently their PRIZM + 4 even extends this to the ZIP + 4 level.[8]

PRIZM goes further. It ties in some major behavioral aspects: consumer purchasing, magazine subscriptions, and credit card information. It integrates media audience data, to be described in Chapter 18, for television (Nielsen and Arbitron), radio (Birch and Scarborough), and print media (SMB), meaning that the PRIZM data defining a company's market can also be used to select media that best reach that particular market. PRIZM is thus a database.

Since it is a database, it is logical that Claritas offers, with many options, a desktop marketing system. Compass, as Claritas terms it, starts with the amount of geographic concentration of the PRIZM data required by the user, typically by block group, census tract, ZIP, state, ADI, and MSA.

All this gets fairly close to the concept of a marketing information system discussed in Chapter 3. The program makes it possible to include the company's own sales data (such as number of customers and purchase dollars) by SIC at tract or ZIP level.

Since PRIZM has so thoroughly permeated segmentation, we must take a look at how it arrives at its data. Harvard-educated Jonathan Robbin, developer of the system and founder of Claritas, was a computer programmer in the 1950s, the early computer years.[1] He realized that the magnetic tapes of the 1970 census held essential marketing data—mainly demographics—in terms of census tracts, and that these could readily (with the computer) be broken down by ZIP code. So the Claritas computers began cranking out data such as social rank, mobility, ethnicity, stage in the family life cycle, and housing style. Through factor analysis, 87 percent of neighborhood variation was accounted for. Then the computer was instructed to rate each ZIP code on each element to place it in one of 40 clusters. Forty was seen as the ideal compromise between manageability and discriminating power. So in 1974 Claritas first offered its 40 life-style segments, arranged in pecking order and by ZIP code.

Since that time many new elements have been put into the system. In 1978 PRIZM entered data such as new-car purchases (from Polk), buying and reading habits (from Simmons and MediaMark, discussed later in this chapter), and television viewing (from local diaries of Nielsen, to be described in Chapter 18).

For the older marketing researchers (and marketers too), who are used to precision statistics, this sort of projection may be hard to accept. It may be even more bothersome that there is simply no way, given the data going into the system and their projection, to come up with any estimate of the probabilities that they are right. However, the marketer is hopeful that will make marketing efforts work better.

There is evidence that it does. The National Symphony found that far more "Money & Brains" people (cosmopolitan singles and couples) than "Furs & Station Wagons" (affluent suburbans) attended concerts. When children enter the family picture, the parents lose their mobility. The National Symphony began to promote in neighborhoods of "Bohemian Mixers" (childless couples), and in some of the areas where they promoted subscription sales jumped 25 percent.[1]

Vision (National Decision Systems, Encinitas, Calif.) set up its catego-

Exhibit 15.3   EXAMPLES OF VISION CLUSTERS

Suburban Gentry (one segment of "Suburban Wealthy"):
These are America's wealthiest, best-educated groups. They are highest in managerial/professional occupations, and household incomes are 11 times the national average. They represent less than 1 percent of all U.S. households.

They are located in the nation's top metro areas, such as Newport Beach, Calif. Concentrations are also found in Connecticut and in various parts of California, Washington, D.C., Maryland, and Hawaii.

The Good Life:
Eight of 10 of this group are in white-collar careers, most often in managerial/professional or technical/service work. Almost a fourth have incomes of $50,000 or more, and 93 percent have homes valued at $150,000 or more.

They are located in areas such as San Clemente, Calif., in other parts of California, in Hawaii, Washington, D.C., Nevada, and Connecticut.

Metro Hispanic Mix;
There are mainly poor, low-income Hispanics (singles and young families). They chiefly live in rented aparatments and duplexes in urban areas such as downtown Chicago. Most are blue-collar workers. Half have graduated from high school.

They eat at McDonald's and family steak restaurants. Occasionally they treat themselves to a meal at midscale restaurants, such as Denny's or Coco's. They enjoy rock radio music and go to movies. They listen to Spanish radio stations, watch little TV, though they may watch the late news. They do not read daily newspapers.

On the financial side, they carry Visa and MasterCard average balances of around $1,800. They make little use of checking accounts and mutual funds.

Imported beer and domestic wine are their main drinks.

---

ries with an emphasis on buying patterns, media preferences, and financial services used. Every household in the United States is classified into one of its 50 unique segments, based on the firm's analysis. By ZIP code, and more recently by the small grouping of ZIP + 4 (groups of only 10 to 15 households), every neighborhood in the United States has been put into one of its clusters.[9] Exhibit 15.3 presents examples of the clusters.

Compared with the average, the Suburban Gentry segment is seven times more likely to have asset management accounts, seven times more likely to use a brokerage service, four times more likely to have a home-equity line of credit, three times more likely to own other real estate, eight times more likely to own a sailboat larger than 25 feet, five times more likely to take a foreign vacation and spend $8,000 or more and to prefer places such as France and the Holy Land, five times as likely to read *Gourmet* magazine, three times more likely to read *Business Week*, slightly above average in subscribing to a newspaper, six times more likely to subscribe to the *New York Times*, four times more likely to listen to classical music, half as likely to enjoy jazz, and twice as likely to participate in aerobics classes.

Households in The Good Life segment, compared to the average, are:

- Four times as likely to have a home-equity line of credit.
- Three times as likely to use a brokerage service.
- Three times as likely to have asset management accounts.
- Twice as likely to own other real estate.
- Twice as likely to play racquetball and tennis; less likely to bowl.
- Twice as likely to buy imported beer; three times as likely to buy domestic wine.
- Five times as likely to tune their radios to jazz, three times more likely to tune them to classical.
- Six times more likely to take a foreign vacation and spend $6,000 or more (preferring places such as Japan and Mexico).
- Eight times as likely to own a sailboat 25 feet or larger.
- Five times as likely to subscribe to the *Architectural Digest* and to *Gourmet* magazine.
- Slightly under average in subscribing to a daily newspaper.

National Decision Systems (newly using the name Equifax Marketing Decisions) gets these data through its parent firm, Equifax Inc., with its own database of financial background of many individuals, since the parent firm is one of the three largest supercredit investigation firms in the United States (but note that these data are used only for area summaries and are not disclosed by individual). This financial database can even report on monies in savings accounts. Note that information identifying individuals is not released to a database user. A mailing, for instance, is handled on a one-time basis by a third party. The firm also obtains and merges data both from government and from some of the country's leading marketing research firms to enhance these data. It can provide its data to the user in either print form or disk form. It also has mapping facilities, which will be discussed later in this chapter.

The company offers many facilitating advantages to the user with its own computer system. Its Infomark, promoted as "the ultimate marketing machine,"[10] comes fairly close to providing the marketing information system described in Chapter 3. It is a means of integrating information from many different research sources and database vendors. The user's own database material can be incorporated. And all of this is provided in terms of whatever geographic breakouts are required. The system combines the power of a mainframe with the convenience of a desktop PC.

National Demographics & Lifestyles offers profiles of selected areas in categories based on personal activities (community and civic; cultural and arts; money-making; foreign travel; fishing and hunting; sports and leisure—golf, bowling, running, jogging); television sports viewing; domestic—automotive work, Bible/devotional, reading, crafts, gardening, plants; hi-tech—cable television viewing, electronics, computers.

CACI[11] offers a combination of demographics and buying power for every county and ZIP code.[12] There are 44 consumer types in its analysis. An example: the "B-4s" are trendsetters, middle-aged, upper-middle suburban dwellers who mainly own single-family homes. They are frequent travelers, first to buy a new product, frequently buy new clothes and home entertainment products, more frequently buy imported cars, and are likely to have equity loans.

On a print basis, CACI annually publishes two different volumes: *The Sourcebook of Demographics for Every ZIP Code*, and *The Sourcebook of Demographics and Buying Power for Every County in the USA*.

It provides population, demographics (such as distribution of age, race, education, employment), housing (year-round versus seasonally occupied), and market potential indexes calculated from CACI's own Acorn Market Segmentation System combined with Mediamark's consumer survey data. It offers geographic breakouts ranging from ZIP codes to the entire nation. For the researcher or marketer with a desktop computer and access to a mainframe, the database is available on magnetic tape. The user can manipulate the data in any way desired and present it in a format meeting company needs.

THE BASIC STUDIES FOR SYNDICATED PSYCHOGRAPHIC CLASSIFICATIONS

Syndicated categorizing is based on annual studies done either by Simmons Market Research Bureau (of the MRB Group) or by Mediamark Research.

Annually Simmons, the older of the two services, conducts its Media & Markets study in the United States.[13] This is based on personal, in-home interviews with some 19,000 people age 18 years and older.

Census data are the starting point. After the sampling areas have been chosen, trained personnel visit each area and list all houses, lots, schools, and apartments on a map. The firm's sampling department disperses single blocks within the block group as interviewing areas. Five interviewing points within each block group are chosen, with no substitutions. Respondents within each household are predesignated by sex.

The chief purpose of the study is to measure media audiences; it also acquires data on product usage. It is conducted in three phases.

In *Phase 1*, a personal interview covers magazine and newspaper readership, and it obtains an inventory of family members and their demographics. A questionnaire about product usage is left with the participant.

The questionnaire is picked up in *Phase 2*. It includes product categories information about purchase, dollars spent, and brand or type of product. The person who does most of the household's grocery shopping is asked mainly about the purchase of groceries and household items, covering items, services, and ownership from automobiles to women's wear.

Methods of buying are also covered: mall shopping, by mail, telephone, catalogs, etc.

The respondent's personal activities and involvements are also checked: community activities, contributions, memberships (civic clubs, fraternal orders, religious groups), and even daily travel.

The respondent checks his or her personal traits and interests (from affectionate to trustworthy, from interested in theories to support of the United Nations). Magazine and newspaper readership are checked again, to get cumulative figures. There is also a minor sort of check on radio listening and television viewing.

In *Phase 3*, only those in broadcast audiences are questioned, and the queries are about media exposure. This phase is conducted simultaneously with the spring and fall sweeps of Nielsen and Arbitron (see Chapter 18).

Annually Mediamark Research (MRI) makes a consumer study of some 20,000 adults,[14] covered in two 5-month personal interview surveys of 10,000 each. Sampling is thorough and precise.

The personal interview includes information on demographics, product usage, and media exposure of all those in a household age 18 and over. In the face-to-face interview, demographics and questions about media exposure are explained; a booklet is left for later pickup. (The specific media exposure questions are provided in Chapter 18).

PROPRIETARY CONSUMER SEGMENTATION STUDIES

Not offered for general marketing use, proprietary studies concentrate on the specific needs and goals of the particular marketing firm or advertising agency. Few, therefore, have been publicized. Unless the study is likely to help get business from specific marketers, it remains within the vaults of the owner, to be used only for the firm's own consumer marketing.

The Senior-Citizen Market

A study of the senior-citizen market segmented primarily for housing developers[15] found six groups of older Americans with varying housing desires and abilities. These were defined in terms of psychological, demographic and health factors, and of how they want to live in retirement. The six groups are shown and described in Exhibit 15.4.

Exhibit 15.4   SIX SENIOR-CITIZEN GROUPS SEGMENTED BY HOUSING NEEDS AND INTERESTS

Explorers:

These people want to do things their way. They are self-reliant, with no thought that their kids have an obligation to help them. They tend to be introverted. In moderately good health, they are on the younger side and generally better educated.

They typically have sold their homes for cash. They are unlikely to be interested in having cultural and recreational services, convenience services (maid and laundry), and health-care services (home health care, physicians' offices, and hospital) in the retirement complex.

Adapters:

These people are extroverted and open to change. They are the "socialites" among their peers. Personal relationships and material possessions are important to them. They are highly educated.

They are high in self-indulgence, helath, and wealth. They don't feel that their kids have an obligation to them.

They may live with spouse and children and like where they live. But they have thought about moving, and think about moving to an apartment or condo. They consider moving to a better climate and new life-style. They want to reduce their daily chores.

They want social support in a retirement community. They arc interested in recreational amenities such as a pool, par-three golf courses, and classrooms nearby. They want retirement housing that provides lifetime agreements with unlimited care and refundable entrance fees.

Pragmatists:

These people are somewhat extroverted and feel (mildly) that kids have an obligation to assist their parents.

While they are generally healthier than the other groups, they are somewhat less educated and have less money.

They are conservative and conformist. Although family-centered, they usually live alone. They do not want to think about moving, though they might consider moving to a nursing home or an adult housing complex, or to get help for themselves.

They want social supports and to live with people of the same religion. For their senior housing they want security guards, central dining facilities, beauty parlors, travel services, post office, and on-site nursing home at the retirement complex.

Attainers:
These are the youngest, most autonomous, self-indulgent, healthy, and wealthy. They are high in education and open to change. They don't think kids have any obligation to help parents.

They are impulse-oriented and are capable of realizing their objectives.

They are interested in getting what they want.

They generally own their homes and live with a spouse. They may have kids living at home.

They do not want to move into a retirement community offering a service package.

They have considered moving to another state—to a smaller home, to get cash from their present homes, or to live in a better climate with a new life-style and fewer chores.

They want movie theaters, cultural events, parks, and colleges on-site or close by. They want recreational facilities, from tennis to golf. They also want more and larger bathrooms, patios, and private garden space, and a wide range of kitchen amenities. They want a housing arrangement that offers monthly fees, but are less interested in lifetime agreements with unlimited care and refundable entrance fees.

Martyrs:
These are people resistant to change. They also feel that children should help parents. They are not well-educated, have little money, and are not in the bst health.

They cannot easily express and implement their values. They tend to rationalize their helplessness through denial and introversion.

They often live with children or relatives. If they live alone, they find the place difficult to maintain and want to leave their community.

They would like to move to a larger home, close to shops. They would consider an adult community, with medical care, and they want a physician's office, physical-therapy facilities, pharmacy, and a religious facility on-site.

Preservers:
Almost all have serious health problems.

They resist change. What little money they have they are concerned with preserving. They look for help—either within their family or from professionals—to maintain their quality of life.

They are likely to rent an apartment or live in older-adult housing in a high-rise. They generally live alone or with children or relatives. If they consider older adult housing, they want security, central dining, maid, maintenance, and housekeeping services. They want other on-site services, such as a religious facility and medical service. They want bathrooms equipped with safety seats and hand rails, wheelchair access, smaller bedrooms, kitchenettes, and a total housing and health-care package.

The Women's Market

Another specific segmentation study suggests that advertisers trying to reach women in the 1990s should understand women in terms of their attitudes toward career, marriage, and family. Commissioned by *Self*, a magazine for women, the study[16] reported that women 18–40 can be

Exhibit 15.5   SEGMENTS OF THE WOMEN'S MARKET

Searchers:
Generally young and married, want both careers and children but aren't sure in which direction to begin.

Traditionalists:
Home- and family-oriented. Some work outside the home but retain their basic family focus.

Strivers:
Career or work-oriented.

Copers:
Self-sufficient or divorced who, though forced to work, enjoy it.

Undecideds:
Mainly single and younger career-oriented, looking to marry but not ready for children.

Dreamers:
Work because they have to but are usually trapped between traditionalist and feminist roles.

Day-to-dayers:
Generally younger who haven't decided on career or family plans.

---

grouped into seven major life-style groups, with age only sometimes a factor. These are shown in Exhibit 15.5.

The advertiser implication, according to Marianne Howatson, publisher of the sponsoring magazine, is deciding which group is the target and determining the needs of such women. Only then can advertising be prepared to reach the women's market.

Should the Marketing Firm Commission Its Own Segmentation Study?

This $64,000 question, perhaps multiplied by 10 or more to reach the inflationary marketing costs of the 1990s, is a worrisome one. Only major marketers can afford the risk of such an investment. We have heard only of those that work, one of which we now describe.

It is the success story of a major ad agency (DDB Needham Worldwide) solicitation of a big account (Southwestern Bell's Mobile Systems).[17] The account was cellular telephones. Southwestern Bell knew the basic demographics of its market in the Dallas-Ft. Worth area: men 25–54, earning over $35,000, doing much traveling and spending 1 to 7 hours weekly in their cars on business or commuting. So the agency turned to its Life Style Study to match behavior and values with the demographics.

The targeted individuals were yuppies: self-confident, ambitious, outgoing, and physically active. They valued their time, considered themselves trendsetters, and enjoyed influencing business associates and friends.

Since the agency wasn't enthusiastic about using the yuppie approach, it developed a humorous campaign portraying a variety of animals as cellular phone users under headline appeals suggested by Life Style.

The approach not only secured the account but it worked, though Southwestern Bell declined to provide sales figures.

If available external segmentation database services do not meet the needs of a particular marketer, a custom segmentation survey may be required. But this should be a last resort. These studies are difficult and often expensive.

In setting up a segmentation study, the marketer must start with a good idea of the base to be used for the segmentation. This may have been acquired from insight gained over years of experience with the product category and brand, but even this sort of insight should be checked out by considerable exploratory, qualitative research with users and considered together with the perceptions of nonusers.

Even after the base for segmentation appears research-sound, it has to meet criteria for being marketing-sound. Can a marketing program be based on a segment of the base? Can the segment be reached through existing media? Is there a big enough slice in any of the segments? Is there another brand already slicing its piece in that manner? If all signs still seem to indicate moving ahead with the study, there is still one last crucial marketing question: Is this the sort of segmentation that will stimulate marketing ideas?

The study must be a solid study meeting the highest standards. It is a crucial study for the company, since results likely will affect marketing of the product for years to come (and perhaps for a far shorter time if the study is wrong). It is no place to skimp. The study must meet all of the rigorous survey requirements outlined elsewhere in this book.

The firm should employ a research company with considerable experience in segmentation studies, regardless of its skills in other areas. You wouldn't choose an orthopedic surgeon, no matter how skilled, to open your skull for a brain operation.

BUSINESS AND ECONOMIC SEGMENTATION

SOME STANDARD SOURCES

Business segmentation has not been nearly so well-developed as consumer segmentation, probably because business marketing is far less sophisticated. It is usually relatively simple for a firm to pinpoint its business customers and potential customers and then to promote directly to them. But since the consumer market is only today beginning to be spelled out in terms of names as well as characteristics, the marketing process there is more complicated, with the seller likely to be several steps removed from the ultimate consumer and having to use advertising media and middlemen.

There are few standard sources for such business and economic segmentation information. Some report the general business environment and outlook for a particular community, and others give more detail about specific kinds of business.

Many reports about the general business environment are in print form only and not available for PC use. We spend little time on them.

On a simple basis, business customers may be segmented by SIC code or by classifications within the yellow pages. Standard print sources such as the *Sales Management Annual Survey of Buying Power* and the *Editor & Publisher Market Guide*, both described in Chapter 2, can be used for obtaining general economic data and business statistics about level areas. But this is a long and laborious job. It is much easier these days to go the computer way.

Metro Insights (from Data Resources) describes the current economic profile for various communities in terms of industrial mix, employment, major employers, and measures of recent economic growth. Each area's economic strengths and weaknesses are profiled. Two-year forecasts of employment, income, and labor force are provided. There is an overview, including transportation, energy costs, education and health facilities, local government, and (where appropriate) military bases.

The service also describes the demographics: The population in terms of age, race, sex, and households with children are defined, as are population density and growth, and migration.

Metro Insights is available in both print and disk forms.

National Decision Systems offers a service covering shopping centers, available in both print and disk form. From this source the marketer can get the name, location, and size of any or all shopping centers with 100,000 square feet or more. That minimal size is about equal to the total of 33 football fields. A fair-sized shopping center occupies such an area.

National Decision Systems provides an overview of the total business environment in these centers, or a look at specific businesses classified by SIC codes. (See Chapter 2 for definition and description.) The firm also provides total daytime employment with each area.

BusinessLine[5] (Donnelley) has detailed information on 7.6 million businesses nationally. The service provides business name, SIC code, sales volume, and number of employees. Donnelley's Market Potential reports current annual sales data and potential sales for 21 types of retail stores.

Another Donnelley service, Shopping Center Profile,[5] offers information about shopping centers. For over 28,000 shopping centers, the service provides data for the name of the center, its address, year of opening, gross leasable area, current construction status, type of center (open or closed), anchor store tenants, number of stores, last expansion date, last renovation date, number of parking spaces, and name, address, and telephone number of the owner of the center.

Donnelley's database Conquest includes all of these data, as well as its ClusterPlus service, described earlier in this chapter, in addition to other material.

For business databases, Compass[18] (Claritas) can provide business summary counts (by SIC categories, total establishments, number of employees, and total sales) at the ZIP or tract level.

Compass is a desktop operating system. Among other programs it includes (such as PRIZM), it provides business summary counts (by total establishments, SIC counts, number of employees, and total sales) at the ZIP or track level. To these can be added daytime population counts (total employment by job type, seven types of business, along with payroll and sales information, and not only extending to ZIP and tract levels, but also covering ADI, DMA, MSA, and state levels.[18]

Business-Facts disk (Equifax Marketing Decision Systems)[19] are custom-built to the specific needs of the user firm. The user specifies the nature of the particular target business on one or more of 22 aspects such as SIC, size (sales or number of employees), and location. A disk is then prepared and the user can use it on a PC to target prospect analysis and identification, direct marketing, and overall sales development.

MarketPlace: Business[20] was first offered in October 1990 by Lotus Development Corporation. It provides information about 7 million businesses of various sizes.

The other possibilities for business databases will be discussed in Chapter 17.

MORE ABOUT GEOGRAPHIC SEGMENTATION

Almost all standard services providing segmented groups offer these on a geographic basis. It would make little sense to do anything else, for if the marketer had segmentation data only nationally, it would be impossible to use these data to target the specific markets desired. The basic list with definitions of the possible geographic breakouts a given source may offer is found in Chapter 2 (Exhibit 2.1).

The size of the market, depending on the service, varies from the total country down to city blocks.

Some consumer information companies provide estimates of census data in the years between the decennial censuses, and the unwary user may assume that these are correct. This is not necessarily so, particularly for areas such as counties or smaller. In one case,[21] a firm was considering a major investment in a county in another state. The projected rate from one source was double that from the other source. When a third supplier was consulted, the estimate was five times that of the lowest. The lowest estimate was used, not because the buyer had any more faith in it than in the others, but because it was believed that the conservative figures would be safest for the firm.

Since most suppliers of these kinds of information do not volunteer how their estimates are determined, they have to be asked. The buyer should understand the assumptions on which the estimates are based and the database on which the projections have been made. If the supplier was in business before the 1990 census, the buyer should find out how accurate its 1990 estimates were against the census data for that year.

Here are some additional terms used in geographic descriptions. *Geodemographics* covers the description of demographics by geographic areas. Similarly, *geopsychographics* is a breakout of psychographics by geographic segments. We suggest a third term, *geobusiness*, to characterize geographic segmentation by business and economic situation of specific areas.

CARTOGRAPHY IN GEOGRAPHIC SEGMENTATION

It is a cliché, in this case likely true, that a picture is worth a thousand words. A picture may even be worth a lot more than that if we talk in terms of tables of numbers. Most of us have trouble arriving at conclusions from massive tables. It is far easier to look at a coded or colored map to get a fast and lasting impression of the differences and possibilities in and between areas.

In terms of tables showing data by area, clearly the answer is to use mapping. Computer technology has made this simple. Depending on the data source, the map(s) can be displayed in varying colors or shading patterns (with almost unlimited possibilities, according to category, such as proportion of potential or actual customers, per capita spending in a particular product or service group, or sales achievement versus potential). There is no need for marketing personnel or management to wade through all of the detailed statistics. They are all there for fast viewing and absorption.

Most mapping sources can produce maps on paper, transparency film, or slides. Color transparency overlays are almost always a possibility.

With the Bureau of the Census 1990 TIGER work, even more will be possible. As we have said, the bureau, for the first time ever, is producing national maps showing every street and lane in the country. With the use of these maps, marketing mapping will really be down to a science.

Now we want to detail some of the sources and facilities available for this mapping. Some are for demographics only and some only for psychographics. Their mapping facilities are limited by geography according to what they choose to offer. We cover only a few of these sources, to provide some general knowledge of the kinds of products and the types of facility available.

OTHER THAN ON-LINE SOURCES

The Rand McNally Zip Code and Market Planner[22] is a print source with acetate overlay for use and reuse in presentations. It can be marked and erased for further use. The print volume includes detailed maps of states, vicinities, and urban areas overlaid with acetates showing 5-digit ZIP code boundaries.

National Decision Systems (new name: Equifax) builds computer-generated color maps to order, combining its database material and overlaying it with desired relevant client material. It can produce these maps by standard geographical units, by the user's sales territories, or within a radius specified by the user for analysis of actual or potential site locations). As an alternative, the buyer can purchase disks with specified database information to use within its own computer system to merge in-house data and create maps from appropriate mapping software.

But most segmentation sources offer mapping facilities within their computerized systems. Some offer a system that the users can combine with their own internal databases. Some even offer their own software systems to make it easier for the user.

Atlas*Graphics[23] is for the user firm that needs a national application, such as an analysis of a large number of sites or locations. The user specifies locations and defines trading area. (Specifications may be street intersections with a radius around each, or standard geographic specs such as ZIP codes, cities, counties, metro areas, or ADIs. Even merely a map showing trading areas—of whatever size or shape— anywhere in the United States may be specified.) The selected location data are then provided on disk or magnetic tape.

One form of Donnelley's Demographics On-Call[5] is Byways, street- level files for mapping, for all DIME areas of MSAs. Donnelley also of- fers GraphicProfile, a graphic program for computers, which leads to a printout. The marketing firm can plot its own data along with demo- graphics supplied by Donnelley.

Intelligent Charting Inc.[24] (Mt. Olive, N.J.) prepares maps when the client provides the material. The firm has its own database of consumer demographics (census demographics, Donnelley's ClusterPlus) for 7.5 million businesses (sales, employment, type of business, etc.) and will combine these as the client wishes with the client's own data (sales, sales quotas, response to advertising, direct marketing, and the like). Or it can display the radius around any location. Client data on tape or disk, reports, or printouts can be accepted.

On a geographic basis, the firm can construct maps showing data from areas as small as carrier routes and ZIP codes up to census regions and the total country. Client sales territories can be used. Depending on the size of the area the map covers, the map can show rivers, highways, roads, streets, airports, and other locations. It uses the 1990 U.S. Census TIGER files.

Compass[18] (Claritas), with its desktop system, makes it possible for the user to produce a profile of customers (PRIZM and their life-style characteristics, what other products they buy or use), market potential evaluation and performance, market evaluation for a new product, and more. All this and other databases can be loaded into or accessed through Compass, even including the company's own sales data, such as customer counts and sales volume. All of these data can be summarized down to the ZIP code level or any other geographic area, such as sales areas of the firm, that the user may wish.

With the cartographics of the system, it is possible for the user firm, on its own PC, to construct maps of any geographic area in the country, showing any of the many aspects of consumer or business characteris- tics in their measurements.

Vision (Equifax), in its Infomark System,[10] also offers on-line map- ping. The user firm, on its own PC, can construct marketing maps of al- most limitless variety, depending on company needs.

ZIP/Atlas (Strategic Mapping Inc., San Jose, Calif.) is yet another mapping program[25] that, along with use of other programs of the company, can be used on a PC or even a Macintosh. The user can take data files showing ZIP codes, count the entries having the same ZIP code, aggregate simultaneously two data fields with the same ZIP, reclassify into other geographic units (MSA, ADI, DMA) and construct new data files for mapping. It can also produce maps centered around a specific location, for use in establishing maps to aid in deciding on alternative locations for a particular business.

Scan/US,[26] offered by Urban Decision Systems Inc., is another desktop geomarket analysis system. It is the first system to make use of Microsoft Windows 3.0 program and its ease and convenient flexibility.

It can incorporate a broad variety of databases, including that of the user. The material in the memory can be analyzed at any geographic level, from the national to microneighborhood. Like other similar programs, it generates reports, charts, graphs, databases, and maps.

But the greatest difference is the ease with which the program can be used. The computer operator uses a mouse to magnify on the screen the general area in which he or she wants to work. The Microsoft connection makes it possible to move right into Microsoft Excel, for instance (or any other Windows application), with its extensive spreadsheet, and graphic display capabilities. Or the operator may want to define the most effective target area, a procedure that calls for a slightly different but still simple-to-use approach.

R. L. Polk & Company, along with Geographic Data Technology (of which Polk owns close to half), offers a computer database built on TIGER (Topologically Integrated Geographic Encoding & Referencing Line Files).[27] The service provides a printout of such elements for census tracts and block numbers as median household income, median age, and other data.

SOME CONCERNS ABOUT SEGMENTATION

We have a few problems with segmentation.

ARE PSYCHOGRAPHICS REALLY THERE?

Some, maybe most, of the syndicated sources of consumer descriptions imply psychographics that are not really there. These sources are based mainly on behavior results, and that is the way we think it should be.

A recent article from *The Public Pulse* (Roper Organization, a leading marketing research firm) suggests that life-style distinctions are most evident with the well-to-do. These people seek social status and recognition, but they don't feel constrained by social custom or rigid standards. Even the less affluent feel this way. The implication is that psychographic studies should pay more attention to actual behavior than to presumed psychological characteristics.

SOME PROPRIETARY STUDIES CLAIM TO MEASURE PSYCHOGRAPHICS

Some of the proprietary studies do claim to measure significant attitudes and life-styles. But psychographic descriptions based on one study are almost sure to be entirely different from those based on another research program, depending on what the sponsors were looking for. This doesn't mean that one can prove anything desired through such studies, only that the marketer has to make a decision as to which psychographic categorization styles seem to best fit the needs for the firm's products or services.

SOME PROPRIETARY STUDIES ARE AGAINST THE PUBLIC INTEREST

Do you remember the recent flap over R. J. Reynolds Tobacco Co.'s announcement that it was going to test-market a cigarette named Dakota? It was to be aimed at 18- to 20-year-old white women with a high school education or less, working in a service or factory job at the entry level. Comments made by Maura T. Payne of the tobacco firm were fascinating. She commented that Reynolds frequently employs market researchers to devise, as she put it, "the weirdest, most off-the-wall stuff . . . and there may be a tiny germ of an idea in there that's useful." She went to say, "Ninety-nine percent of what we get we don't use or wouldn't want to use."[28]

SOME SEGMENTATION STUDIES ARE NOT ALL THAT USEFUL

Some practical marketers argue that segmentation studies going beyond straight demographics are more showy than useful—that they make a real splash in a presentation but at bottom they really are not useful in either marketing planning or strategy. One advertising agency executive commented that he had never seen a segmentation study of any practical use in building advertising, for instance.

ENDNOTES

[1]Michael J. Weiss. *The Clustering of America.* New York: Harper & Row, 1988.

[2]Dena Kleiman. "All Across the Country, Chips Worth Their Salt." *New York Times*, May 23, 1990, B1.

[3]Jennifer Lawrence. "Folgers Puts Coffee in the Bag." *Advertising Age*, Jan. 21, 1991, 3.

[4]*The Lifestyle Market Analyst.* Wilmette, Ill.: Standard Rate & Data Service, dated annually.

[5]*Demographics On-Call.* Stamford, Conn.: Donnelley Marketing Information Services, 1987.

[6]*PRIZM: The Standard in Geo-Demographic Targeting.* Alexandria, Va.: Claritas, 1985.

[7]*PRIZM: Thumbnail Descriptions for Twelve Social Groups & Forty Life-Style Clusters.* Alexandria, Va.: Claritas, undated.

[8]*Claritas: The Target Marketing Company.* Arlington, Va.: Claritas, various brochures, undated.

[9]*Micro-Vision-50.* Encilitas, Calif.: Equifax, 1990.

[10]*Infomark.* Encinitas, Calif.: National Decision Systems, undated.

[11]*Make the Best Decisions Possible with CACI.* Fairfax, Va.: CACI Market Analysis, undated.

[12]*The Best Just Got Better.* Fairfax,Va.: CACI Marketing Systems, 1990.

[13]*Studies of Media and Markets.* New York: Simmons Market Research Bureau, 1989.

[14]*Ready for the 90's.* New York: Mediamark Research, 1990.

[15]James Gollub and Harold Javitz. "Six Ways to Age." *American Demographics*, June 1989, 28–29.

[16]Scott Donaton. " 'Self' Sorts Women by Attitudes." *Advertising Age*, Oct. 16, 1989, 32.

[17]J. M. Winski. "Research + 'Creative Leap' = Award-Winning Ads." *Advertising Age*, Sept. 24, 1990, 24.

[18]*Now There's a Powerful New Desktop Marketing System.* Alexandria, Va.: Claritas, undated.

[19]*Business-Facts Diskettes.* Encilitas, Calif.: Equifax Marketing Decision Systems, undated.

[20]Alan Radding. "Lotus Stirs Research Marketplace." *Advertising Age*, Jan. 13, 1991, 21.

[21]Judith Waldrop. "How Good Are the Numbers You're Buying?" *American Demographics* 12, no. 7 (July 1990): 20–22.

[22]*Introducing . . . The First and Only Atlas That Maps the Way to 5-Digit ZIP Codes!* Skokie, Ill.: Rand McNally, 1988.

[23]P. H. Lewis. "When Maps Are Tied to Data Bases." *New York Times*, May 28, 1989, F10.

[24]*Geo-Visual Solutions for Today's Business*. Mt. Olive, N.J.: Intelligent Charting, 1990.

[25]"New Products." *The Number News*, June 1990, 8.

[26]*Explore Windows of Opportunity*. Los Angeles: Urban Decision Systems, 1990.

[27]Patricia Strand. "Count on Cartography." *Advertising Age*, Dec. 10, 1990, 46.

[28]Anthony Ramirez. "New Cigarette Raising Issue of Target Market." *New York Times*, Feb. 18, 1990, News Section, 14.

16

USING THE CUSTOMER/ PROSPECT DATABASE

What's in This Chapter

In this chapter we show how the customer/prospect database is being used by marketing firms to personalize marketing efforts through the targeting of individuals. We detail the kinds of information found in these databases and we show by many examples how specific kinds of information can be used in both consumer and business marketing. We explain how these databases are built up and how they are used to expand the marketing horizon.

DEFINITION

A customer/prospect database, in the sense used here, is an electronic (computerized) bank of information about individual customers or prospects of a firm, accumulated from either the firm's internal sources (such as orders and inquiries), external sources (purchase of lists), or a combination of the two.

But no straight definition is enough. The marketing purpose has to be included. And the marketing purpose of such a databank is to make it possible for the marketing firm to personalize its marketing efforts with its customers: virtually to place marketing on a one-to-one basis.

The first use of such databases was by business-to-business marketers. The first use by consumer marketers was for services, including fund raising and travel. Except for catalogs, use of this sort of database marketing is relatively recent for consumer product marketers. However, in terms of the overall emphasis of this book, we stress the use of the database in the marketing of consumer goods and services.

The Implication: One-on-One Marketing

Database marketing is a method of moving from mass marketing to mass targeting to individual targeting. The marketer communicates with customers as individuals, mainly, but not always, in the form of direct marketing.

Not Single-Source Research

The single-source database was described in Chapter 13. The customer/prospect database is not the same thing at all. The single-source database is strictly a marketing research tool enabling researchers and marketers to arrive at judgments and make decisions about overall marketing strategy and tactics. Customer/prospect databases are essentially a system of marketing depending heavily on information in the system itself.

There is one other crucial difference. Even though its data collection methods are by individuals, single-source research is used in the form of group summaries. The customer/prospect database differs significantly in that the whole way through, from data collection to marketing, it deals with individuals.

We have briefly mentioned the clubs in which participants get special advantages as a result of their membership and use of the product or service. The general term applied to this kind of program is *frequency marketing*. In frequency marketing, the firm concentrates on making its customers more loyal and on encouraging them to purchase or use the product or service more frequently than they otherwise would.

While frequency marketing is a form of consumer/prospect database marketing, it is only one form. The broad concept of consumer/prospect database marketing extends to development of new customers; it is not limited to working with present customers to stimulate more of their business.

WHY INCLUDE CUSTOMER/PROSPECT DATABASE MARKETING AS MARKETING RESEARCH?

There is a simple answer. Customer/prospect database marketing *is* marketing research, the whole way through the process. It is only by constant refining of the list and the information in the list of customers or prospects that database marketing can be successful. True, the individual running such a program has to know many other aspects of marketing, such as advertising and promotion. But the underlying key to the entire process is constant, unending marketing research.

THE GALLOPING GROWTH OF CUSTOMER/PROSPECT DATABANKS

The Facts

Facts? As marketing researchers, we must admit that we lack hard statistics. Yet there are many indirect indications that customer/prospect databanks are growing rapidly.

One indication is the increasing number of marketing firms using such programs, as seen by specific company mentions in the trade press. A second is the number of specialists in the field offering their services. There are some very good reasons for this growth, and we want to talk about them.

The Increasing Costs of Marketing

Because broadcast media have a limited capacity, the costs of television, for instance, have skyrocketed. Costs of personal selling, too, are rising constantly. While we cannot vouch for the figure and the year is not current, the cost of a personal sales call in 1986 was reported to be $260.[1]

Fragmentation of Markets

Chapter 15 showed how the mass market has taken a back seat to small, segmented markets, with the resulting process of segmentation. The broad, mass market is almost a matter of history. Too many reached by the mass media are not really prospects for a specific product or service. The mass medium, itself, is almost a relic of the past.

Database marketing concentrates on those who have shown interest in the organization's product(s) or services(s). It has been argued[1] that 20 percent of a product's customers account for 80 percent of its volume. We cannot verify the particular figures, but certainly the general point is correct.

The Multiple Applications

There are four broad areas of application of the consumer/prospect database:

1. Public relations or image building

2. Concentrating on current customers

3. Recruiting new customers

4. Diagnostic: Fine-tuning the use of the tool

A customer/prospect database is sometimes used for public relations or image building to stimulate a favorable feeling toward the firm or its products. Japan's Shiseido Club has 10 million members. They receive a general-interest women's magazine that displays Shiseido cosmetics and supports the firm's retail stores and allied dealers. The brand is the dominant cosmetic brand in the country.[2]

In concentrating on current customers, the basic idea is to deal with them for one of two specific aims: increasing their total dollars of spending, or, in a deteriorating industry, to slow or halt the firm's declining dollar sales.

When an increase in dollar spending is the aim, one form may be to persuade the firm's customers to buy more frequently. For example, coupons may be offered to those who purchase the item only occasionally. "We can identify specific households and specific products," says William J. Ahearn, of Citicorp POS Information Services, "and automatically give . . . savings on a list of items."[3]

Another method of increasing spending by current customers is through cross-selling, where current customers are persuaded to buy other products or services in the company line. For instance, a particular cruise line[4] had two ships in the Caribbean. One followed a rather traditional Caribbean itinerary, including one day in the British Virgin Islands (which research indicated was the favorite port of call on the cruise). The other was a smaller ship that worked the BVI alone. The traditional cruise bookings were strong, the BVI weak. Inquiries from print advertising did not stimulate the desired volume. The solution was eventually found. Past general Caribbean tourists were sorted out of the customer list, and the BVI tour was cross-sold to them. A special last-minute discount offer filled the tour.

Barlow comments[5] that unfortunately the domestic auto industry has a far different problem. It is losing market share to imports. The domestic manufacturers consider themselves lucky if they achieve a loyalty of 30 percent, which means they get only one of three repeat buyers! So it is not a question of gaining market share at all, but one of simply holding down the losses.

The solution being attempted by the auto industry is to determine major likes of loyal purchasers, profile their life-styles (as outlined in Chapter 15), and custom-tailor the marketing approach to the particular segments.

More aggressive marketers often use the database system to recruit new customers. Sheraton Hotels offers points to its club members for each name suggestion that leads to a new member. The George Dickel Tennessee Whiskey Water Conservation Society[6] is a highly imaginative new-customer recruiting method. The distillery has a club headquarters, situated on the grounds of its Tullahoma, Tenn., headquarters. On the occasion of its opening weekend, several hundred members appeared for the event, which included dining, dancing, and, of course, drinking.

In a single year, 4,000 members paid $4.95 to buy a George Dickel Duel Kit (two shot glasses, a blindfold, napkins, and a scorecard). Members challenge competitive whiskey drinkers to a taste test. The gimmick was sufficiently successful to cause the distillery to raise the club's budget by a third in the following year.

Sometimes an aggressive database marketer goes directly after customers of the competition to establish its own database built on these customers. That is what Seagram's did on behalf of its own Glenlivet Scotch.[7] To a total of 500,000 drinkers of Johnny Walker Red, J&B, Cutty Sark, and Dewar's, it offered a choice of free old-fashioned glasses, a calculator, or a rebate if they would try Glenlivet. The names of some 1,000 new customers are now in the Seagram 5 million database.

A year later, a second mailing was made—a cassette tape describing the tradition and pride of the brand.[8] The campaign sold some 24,000 bottles of Glenlivet. Seventy percent of coupon redeemers recommended a friend for the special offer. Awareness and brand-attribute recall rose 100 percent among redeemers.

Through close and thorough monitoring of database results, the astute marketing firm can fine-tune its marketing techniques. The user who delves into the database can discover, with a fair degree of precision, which customers respond to which promotions. Mike Cox, vice president of marketing and planning at Donnelley Marketing, comments that manufacturers will be able to use direct-mail advertising and promotion more efficiently by knowing who buys, the recency of purchase, the frequency, amount items, and other details.[9]

THE KINDS OF INFORMATION IN THE DATABASE

Now we start being rather specific about the kind of information concerning the individual (or business firm) that may be in the customer/prospect database. After a quick summary of the ID items, we look at internal data (which apply to both the consumer and the business databases), then separately we consider the external data for a consumer database and the external data for a business database.

ID ITEMS

These include both access information (name, title, address, telephone number, ID number, time zone) and source of the name.

INTERNAL DATA

Shepard[10] comments that performance data (information on sales and promotion) are the most important data that direct marketers (we would add other types of marketers using customer/prospect databanks as well) have about their customers. Indeed they are; this is the end result of the total effort, and lacking that, there can be no effective use of the databank. And as we have said, these data apply both to the consumer and to the business database.

In establishing its own proprietary database, the marketing firm is, as we show later in this chapter, restricted to information about its customers that is already in its possession (such as orders, deliveries, charge accounts, and the like) or that it goes out of its way to accumulate.

The brief list of possibilities shown in Exhibit 16.1 gives an idea of the kinds of information sometimes available internally. Almost all, logically enough, center on buying. There are not too many databases, however, that can have these extensive records. Such enterprises as catalog firms, direct mail order companies, some retail establishments, and business marketers typically will have such information in their proprietary lists. More often, the proprietary list will include only the information under Purchases and Returns.

Exhibit 16.1   POSSIBLE DATABASE INFORMATION FROM INTERNAL COMPANY RECORDS

Date of Transaction

Purchase Method (where applicable)
Telephone, mail, personal

Purchases and Returns: Nature
Types of product, service
Dollar volume of each

Payment Method
Cash, company credit account, charge card, check

As you look at this list, remember that it is merely a list of items to be kept in the log of the purchasing by the individual, and that it does not represent the material coming from the summary and analysis of such data. We will be discussing later in this chapter what kinds of analyses of these records are useful. Some have already been suggested.

With the business marketing firm, this list is only the starting point if the database is to be an effective marketing tool. The listing must include the name or names of the right person(s) within the firm: the person(s) responsible for making the purchasing decisions and those placing the orders.

Customer information is generally restricted to the selling firm and is not made available to any other marketer. (We will see that some of the grocery sales information is an exception.)

EXTERNAL DATA FOR A CONSUMER DATABASE

The list given in Exhibit 16.2 is not by any means complete, but it is broad enough to give an idea of the range of possibilities.

Addition of Other Information

We won't try to cover all of the possibilities in any detail at this point. We will say only that it is possible to add information about those in a consumer database both in terms of many of the aspects listed in Exhibit 16.2 and in terms of media exposure, buying of other products, and psychographics.

Segmentation Analysis

Segmentation analysis, as explained in Chapter 15, is the grouping of people into similar segments, perhaps demographically or psycho-

Exhibit 16.2   CONSUMER DATABASE INFORMATION FROM AN EXTERNAL SOURCE

About the Dwelling
Type of dwelling unit (single or multiple)
Rented/owned
Possession of telephone

About the Household
Number
Composition (sex, age)
Number of children
Number employed
Income
Length of residence
Auto ownership
Ethnicity
Seasonal residency

Household Head or Purchaser
Sex, age
Occupation
Marital status
Ethnicity
Religion
Possession of savings account

graphically. In the kind of database marketing of concern in this chapter, a marketing firm that could define segments of the market for its goods or services might be able to market more effectively by taking different marketing approaches according to the nature of each segment. The steps are: (1) determine that segments exist, (2) measure the characteristics and attitudes of each segment, and (3) determine a cost-effective way to place all people in the customer or prospect database.

Here, marketing researchers really must show their skills. Questionnaires must be developed that will obtain the required information from a sample of those on the list, and since mail is the typical medium used in handling lists, this calls for a mail survey (described in Chapter 7) using sound survey sampling methods in the choice of those to be questioned (see Chapter 8). Obtaining sufficient raw data from which to make the necessary analyses to develop segments may require hundreds of questions. As we warned in Chapter 15, this sort of research requires unusual specialization. It is generally wisest to go to a research firm that is a specialist in the field of segmentation studies.

A less expensive way of handling segmentation of the list is for the marketer to purchase what appears to be the most applicable standard groupings of segments. We mention only three here, and briefly at that:

ClusterPlus, PRIZM, and Vision. There are more thorough discussions of these, along with some additional ones, in the segmentation chapter, Chapter 15.

Donnelley's ClusterPlus provides segments based entirely on demographics. PRIZM, offered by Claritas, classifies by a combination of demographics and life-styles. Vision, by National Decision Systems, segments using a combination of demographics and psychographics (buying patterns, media preferences, and financial services used).

If one of these seems to offer groupings that appear to make sense for the marketer's particular use, it is possible to have the segment supplier overlay every name on the database list with the resultant classification.

EXTERNAL DATA FOR A BUSINESS DATABASE

Typically, the breadth of external information in the business or industry database is far more restricted than that for the consumer database. For the individual buying firm, it can include (for each listed firm) the industry type (SIC number), its dollars of sales, and the number of company employees.

EXAMPLES OF DATABASE USE WITH CONSUMERS

Now that we have set the stage for what database marketing is all about, we are ready to consider some examples showing its use in marketing to consumers, by various kinds of manufacturers and by some different types of retailers.

BY MANUFACTURERS

Packaged Foods

General Foods, producer of a broad range of packaged foods, mails a four-color magazine *What's Hot for Kids* three times annually to families in its database with children between 4 and 14.[11] The magazine includes stories, puzzles, and coupons. The coupons are tailored to the household, so that two or three children living in the same block may get different coupons. The nature of the coupons will shift as usage patterns change.

Two similar 1990 magazines were aimed at 18–25-year-olds moving to new homes and to people who had responded to recipe offers.[12] The names of recent movers are available from change-of-address forms sent to the U.S. Postal Service.

Kraft General Foods is reportedly testing a direct marketing program in which coupons sent to households include an ID for each household.[13] Its 1990 Super Choices program promotes the company's light, low-fat, sugar-free, cholesterol-free, and caffeine-free brands, ranging from light cheese to Sanka and suger-free Jell-O. Coupon redeemers are automatically entered in a sweepstakes contest.

Hormel[14,15] has established a Kid's Kitchen Club. When the youngster spots the Hormel on-pack membership form and mails it in, he or she is rewarded with a patch, a newsletter, and a "Kidalogue," a catalog of items available with proof of purchase of various Hormel items. The completed application form provides a general demographic profile, as well as hobbies and interests. The program offers many applications. Hormel can make follow-up mailings to kids. It can send coupons and offer premiums, and it is possible to follow through on a personal basis using WATS lines.

Beverages

Coors Brewing Co. launched its Club Coors program in March 1990.[16] Its chief purpose was to increase the brand's sales to the occasional Coors user. Research showed that Coors, Busch, and Budweiser are all in the same brand set; people who predominantly buy one of these brands are often occasional buyers of another brand. Don Marable comments: ". . . It should be easier to influence someone who is already familiar with our brand to buy more of ours and less of the competitor's than those who do not have original Coors in their brand set."

The brewer is getting a good handle on these buyers both demographically and psychographically through coupon returns.

Enrollment of club members started in earnest on Memorial Day 1990. With a well-orchestrated promotion to dealers to provide floor space for a motion display, inviting beer purchasers to participate—with no strings attached—in a sweepstakes offering three grand prizes of a $15,000 vacation at a spot of the winner's choosing, and 10,000 prizes of a Coors Travel Club membership entitling the holder to discounts on hotel and condo accommodations, cruises, resort packages, and the like. The entry blank provided space for entering the name and address and the brands of beer bought most often, frequently, and occasionally.

Club Coors members receive direct mail. Frequent newsletters (the first one in the fall of 1990) give members "inside" information about the company, as well as providing coupons, refund offers, and self-liquidators.

Contact Lenses[17]

Bausch & Lomb has applied database marketing to its targeting of contact lens users for its lens care products. Although there are 24 million contact lens wearers in the United States, this is still only 25 percent of all households. Thus there is an opportunity for database marketing.

The database profiles millions of users and identifies the types of lens care product used by each, allowing the right message to be targeted to the right person. Since the profile also distinguishes prospects from customers, the most appropriate offer can be included, such as a free sample or high-value coupon to secure trial among users of competitive products. The bottom-line results of each promotion are tracked so that the most successful promotions can be applied in subsequent marketing efforts.

BY SERVICE FIRMS

We describe several types of service firms here: financial institutions, a transportation company, a cruise line, and a fast-food chain.

Financial Institutions

A national financial service advertises in selected business publications;[17] the ads include a toll-free number to use to request a free information kit. The operator, in addition to obtaining the name and address, asks a few questions about such things as the types of investments the caller made recently and approximate income. This produces sales leads. When the sales representatives call, they know the person's interests, specific product potential, and sufficient financial background to start a relevant conversation. Results of the sales contact are then entered into the firm's database.

In 1988, Chase Manhattan Bank decided to pursue the affluent market.[18] It decided to use the database approach instead of making a shotgun effort.

The first problem was to identify which Chase customers were "affluent," and to define these people in terms of demographics, life-style, and current use of financial products. There was also a need to combine customer data for all eight of the various Chase upscale services (including such products as jumbo mortgages and luxury auto financing), which were marketed separately, so that a customer who used three separate services would not be listed more than once.

Demographic data (such as income and family composition) and ownership information (home and auto) were entered into the database.

This permitted segmentation of the affluent into minimarkets and promotion to each. For instance, luxury auto owners could be identified. Based on length of ownership, they can be targeted with an auto loan promotion.

Transportation Companies

The 4 million customers of Amtrak take over 21 million trips annually.[18] The reservation and inquiry systems were the starting point for the database. Addresses were located for the names and telephone numbers already in the system. After adding demographics, the database was segmented into groups such as senior citizens, students, businesspeople, and families.

Amtrak was thus able to focus on the specific needs and motivations of each group. In addition, Amtrak could measure the value of each customer and spot potential sources of incremental income.

Twenty-five percent of Amtrak customers provided 65 percent of its business.

Auto Train, a passenger service that also moves vehicles and that operates between Virginia (just outside Washington) and Florida, offered a major revenue opportunity because of its well-defined audience and the long-term value of its customers. A V.I.P. (Very Important Passenger) program was started. News of fares and schedules, travel information, discounts, and promotions were provided. Distinct groups of passengers—snowbirds, summer vacationers and off-peak travelers—were identified, and unique communications were sent to each group by time of year and travel direction.

Based on the success of the V.I.P. effort, the company is moving into many more database-marketing initiatives to maximize revenue, build customer loyalty, and manage demand for its services.

A Cruise Line[4]

P&O Cruises (out of London) was operating many of its cruises with too many empty cabins. Operating costs are about the same whether the ship is full or only half full. While a cruise line is ready to offer big discounts to fill the ship, a sharply discounted promotion at best can merely change a potential loss into a break-even situation. If the promotion fails, it may add to the loss. So the cruise line wanted to rent the vacant staterooms at full price and at minimal promotion cost.

The cruise line had a long list of people who had traveled with it in the preceding four years. Since those on the list were already receiving the cruise program for each new year, it would be too expensive to have additional mailings to the entire list.

There was no way of predicting how frequently people on the list would take cruises. The POSH Club was established so that the mailing list would be self-selective. This was a free-membership group that was provided exclusive privileges and benefits related to cruise travel: a welcoming bottle of champagne, with the captain's compliments, in the passenger's cabin, an invitation to a "members only" cocktail party, vouchers against the price of shore excursions, chances to purchase club ties and silk scarfs, an award to the most-traveled passenger on the particular cruise, and a quarterly newsletter providing details of forthcoming cruises. These special privileges came at very little cost to P&O.

Fifteen percent of the list joined the club during a test and rollout. After the rollout mailing, the cruise line invited 3,000 of the new club members to a shore party for a preview of the next cruise program. Eight hundred appeared for the affair, which included drinks, snacks, film, and a talk.

No further member solicitations were ever needed. Recruiting is done during a cruise, where there is a relaxed environment, easy and friendly contact between passengers and staff, and a "charming" POSH Club representative. Since that first effort, there have been 16 shore parties annually. Most important, the number of POSH Club cruises went up from two to six in just a few years.

A Pizza Take-Out/Delivery Store[19]

Most new Pizza Hut units have no seating and offer no secondary items such as salad or garlic bread. They provide pickup or delivery service, with identical prices. The 1,000-odd nationwide outlets in this category also have their own computer systems.

The database located in each outlet provides a personal contact with customers. Daytona Beach's Todd Skelton comments: "The person taking the order can call the customer by name, and can ask 'Would you like the same thing you ordered last time?' "

The system records each customer's name, address, and telephone number. It provides details of the purchaser's previous order: date, type of pizza, price, and (if delivered) how long it took to get there.

The system provides the means of spotting dropout customers. If customers haven't reordered within 30 days, they will be telephoned to find out why not and whether there is anything wrong. They may be offered a discount on the next purchase if it is made within a stated time period.

BY RETAILERS

Retailers also are using database marketing. In the field of low-price, fast-moving merchandise, marketers rightly see the greatest promise in the one-on-one marketing of the consumer database.

Our examples include supermarkets, a department store, book-stores, an office supply firm, a catalogue firm, and a diamond retailer. The last is in contradiction to what is said in the previous paragraph. This contradiction merely demonstrates that an astute marketer some-times can break the rule.

Supermarkets

Probably more supermarkets than any other forms of business are using customer databanks. Up to 2,000 stores throughout the United States already have electronic couponing and promotion programs, according to *Supermarket News*.[20] Here we give only a prototype example.

Shoppers at a particular supermarket are invited to receive an ID card similar to a credit card, indicating membership in the store's pur-chasers' club. Each time purchases are made, the ID card is scanned electronically at the checkout counter. Purchases also are scanned, and depending on the system, the purchaser may receive discounts on se-lected items or purchase points (a stated number of earned purchase points accumulated will earn prizes for the member). The purchase data and the ID of the cardholder are entered into the databank.

Each month, cardholders are given a list of some 100 branded prod-ucts that qualify for rebates. Monthly statements to the recipient show purchases and earned credit to date. At the end of perhaps three months, these shoppers may receive a voucher that can be redeemed on store pur-chases; no cash is offered.

While the basic aim of the program is to eliminate the costly use of coupons, it offers many other potential advantages to the retailer, par-ticularly the chain retailer—the most likely supermarket retailer to use the method. One is the aiming of promotions to the nature of the clien-tele of a particular store.

The retailer running a store in a Hispanic area on the South Side of Chicago must run different kinds of promotions from a store in one of the affluent north-suburban areas.[21]

For a household of husband, wife, and two teenage boys, a promotion aimed at them should be far different from one for a 70-year-old couple living in the inner city. The teenagers, for example, will be heavy milk consumers. The store also will be able to calculate the probable percent-age of household grocery money it is getting, and that particular family may be spending only $30 of its $125 each week.

The Dallas-based Tom Thumb grocery chain[22] introduced scanner cards in a frequent-shopper program. Customers were urged to join the Tom Thumb Promise Club. Those who enroll use the card at the check-out counter, and this automatically credits store discounts to members when applicable items are part of the purchase. (There are discounts monthly on 125 specific items.) The card can also be used for check cashing or as a cash card, where the amount of the purchase is electronically debited from the customer's bank balance.

Members get "promise points" with each shopping visit. A monthly mailing provides a statement showing the total accumulated points and a newsletter describing the new promotions and special sales.

In the first month of a 6-month test, 6,000 shoppers applied for the card.

A store or a chain can also use its database to attract nonusers of a particular department to that department. Super Valu Stores, Minneapolis, which has its own database, can now separate out those people who bought bread in their stores but not in their bakery and can aim special bakery promotions at them.[23]

A store, through special efforts, can pursue competitors' customers. One store in a chain in one of the top 20 markets in the Midwest[24] was facing stiff competition; the store owners demanded a sound base plan targeting customers of the competition.

Shopper Database Marketing started with its own database, information from the store (including check-cashing files), and a telephone survey.

Among 15,000 shoppers within a 3-mile radius, 40 percent used the store as their regular, primary grocery store. But over 80 percent of those regular customers were secondary shoppers at competitive markets. Most had two or more supermarket check-cashing cards.

While a large pool of shoppers was available to increase the store's volume, a high proportion of the store's regular customers were at risk. The situation offered some promising marketing opportunities.

One was the start of a shopper database to build on. This would make it possible to target promotions of particular category items to users of the category. Customers of the competition could be targeted. Electronic couponing could be offered.

Several specialist firms offer services for setting up such programs. These include Citicorp POS Information Services, Advanced Promotion Technologies (APT), Donnelley Marketing, CheckRobot, and CNP Financial Corp. In May 1990 Citicorp's Reward America was in some 200 stores with over a half-million members.[25] APT was scheduled to be in 50 supermarkets by the end of 1990.

A Department Store

A major department store (which prefers not to be identified) wanted to use mailings of catalogs to likely high-income prospects in four selected markets. It began with a primary list of credit card users spending over $1,000 annually in retail establishments. The list was "cleaned" by eliminating current store charge accounts and third-party accounts (business establishments, for example).

Then 12 further screens were applied (of course, this is merely additional information about the prospects, so it is prospect database marketing). To remain on the list, a person had to meet at least three of these standards:

- A subscriber to one or more of four fashion magazines

- Falling within one of five Vision codes

- A subscriber to a city magazine

- A household of $60,000 or more income (life-style)

- New movers owning a house worth over $160,000

Each selected name received six catalogs (the same ones in each market). Results are shown in Exhibit 16.3. The promotion was successful. Response to direct mail sent to a less-targeted list would have been far less successful.

Exhibit 16.3   PROMOTION EFFORT AND RESULTS IN FOUR MARKETS

	Catalogs Mailed	Shoppers		Purchases in Four Months	Average Sales
		No.	Percent		
Market A	30,820	3,131	10.2%	$899,055	$117
Market B	13,377	1,057	7.9	344,159	138
Market C	30,820	1,515	4.9	357,679	116
Market D	25,005	2,234	8.9	645,108	122
Total	100,000	7,937	7.9%	$2,245,951	$121

Bookstores

Two retail bookstore chains recently started customer club plans so similar that we will talk about only one: Waldenbooks.[26] The other, B. Dalton, is almost as large and as well-known. Both concentrate their locations in shopping centers. Waldenbooks has 1,300 stores and over $1 million annual sales. B. Dalton has 800 stores.

The membership fee to join Waldenbooks club is a one-time $10. For the member there is a quick acceptance of personal checks and 10 percent off of the store price for any purchase. There is a $5 coupon given for each $100 of purchases.

What the member doesn't know is that the bar code on the membership card provides not only the accumulated dollar purchases, but a key to the member's reading selections, to be used as a guide in selection of books to be carried in stock.

An Office Supply Firm

Thomas G. Stemberg set up Staples, a discount supermarket for small businesses that offers office supplies at low prices on a self-service, cash-and-carry basis. By 1989 he had a chain of 27 in the Northeast corridor (Boston to Washington).[27]

Staples soon offered free membership cards to be filled in as the customer passes through the checkout counter. Though not at first used as an inducement, special discounts are now offered to those with membership cards.

When customers shop with a card, their purchases are logged against their card numbers. The company can then determine frequency of shopping and dollar volume, and it can analyze these by ZIP code, industry, demographics, and company size.

Now Staples can make stock and price changes and can focus promotion efforts based on the purchasing behavior of customers who buy less or purchase less frequently, thereby raising total volume.

A Catalog Firm

Cabela's is a major outdoor-product mail-order firm in Sidney, Nebr., which sells through a catalog.[28] Distribution of the catalog is controlled through a database. It has to be, to control costs. Typically, the firm annually makes a minimum of 9 mailings of catalogs ranging from 30,000 to 3 million.

Those not responding to the catalogs are quickly purged from the list. Names of new prospects are obtained through mailing list companies, magazines, advertising (hunting and fishing magazines), exchange with similar catalog firms, and asking current catalog recipients to suggest names.

Mailings are segmented by purchasing patterns. There are ten categories, from bow-hunting equipment to gift buyers.

A Diamond Retailer

Helzberg Diamonds, based in Kansas City, Mo., uses its customer database for a continuing expansion of business.[29]

Helzberg is primarily a chain of mall stores focusing on diamonds, precious gemstones, and karat gold.

When John Goodman, a young journalism graduate, joined the firm in 1979, he set up and began to use a database. At the time there were between 20,000 and 30,000 names in the house hand-maintained files. After moving to computerization, the files were segmented by geodemographics, dollar volume of spending, frequency of purchase, and method of payment. Names of house charge card holders were classified as to whether they were currently active, formerly active, or never active.

Today, the files contain some 90,000 names. Data for all stores are maintained in a single database, and weekly each of the 75 Helzberg shops in 30 markets forward names and addresses of all purchasers along with the date and amount of purchase.

The program offers many advantages to the firm. Markets requiring more promotional dollars can be spotted. Markets that could support an additional store become evident. Specific mail promotions can be aimed at appropriate customers: big spenders or holiday purchasers, for example. By having customers of all stores in the single database, it is also possible to ensure that all consumers get direct mailings covering the location of "new" stores.

Direct mail and mass media (including television and print) are used for promotion. Direct mail is used for solicitation of credit cards, for traffic generation, and for customer contact—never for mail order. Since almost all mailings are made to targeted groups, a single mailing is rarely to the entire list.

Sometimes the credit card solicitation offers a chance to participate in a drawing, such as for a Hawaiian vacation. On this particular promotion, the application for the charge card would result in a $50 gift certificate good on any charge card purchase of $100 or more.

Some mailings are packed with confetti, which falls to the floor as a greeting-card style mailing is pulled from the envelope. The outside of the card stresses "CELEBRATE" in bold, black letters surrounded by printed confetti on a white background. There's more printed confetti inside, with copy. "Celebrate" mailings may be used for many different purposes: inviting prospects living within a given radius to the opening of a new store, or inviting selected customers to special events such as a "Mother's Day celebration." A "celebrate" card generally offers a special incentive, such as a discount or a free jewel. One such promotion, offering a free sapphire to prospects bringing along a completed charge account application, attracted an average of 5,000 applications per store.

Helzberg catalogs are its largest distribution. All recent buyers meeting certain purchase frequency and dollar levels are sent annual Christmas holiday catalogs. At other times of the year, catalogs are mailed to various market segments throughout all Herzberg market areas.

Typically, personalized "love letters" are sent to heavy purchasers in early October (just before the start of the holiday buying). These go out on Barnett C. Helzberg Jr.'s personal, watermarked stationary. Homey and down-to-earth, they thank customers for honoring the firm with their business and letting the firm be a part of their family. They include no coupon and do not solicit a purchase. Flattered customers write or telephone Helzberg to thank him. The letters seem to help cement the bond between purchasers of jewelry and place of purchase.

EXAMPLES OF DATABASE USE WITH BUSINESS

Almost all marketing to business makes use of a sales force, through direct selling.

PHARMACEUTICALS

Key Pharmaceuticals manufactures chiefly cardiovascular medications, and its customers are physicians who prescribe rather than buy the products. Since the detail man (the customer representative who calls on the physician) never walks away with the order, the company sought other methods of measuring sales performance. It appears that a database might be the answer.[18]

A database was set up profiling each of the 200,000 cardiologists and general practitioners in Key's market universe. Each profile provides the physician's specialization area and prescribing level.

A reporting system was established to track the call activities of Key's 350 detail men. The reps complete a "call document" for each physician in their territory. The three-part form reports the products discussed during the call and the types of sample left for trial. The doctor gets one copy, one copy goes back into the database, and the rep keeps the third.

The database also guides much of Key's promotional effort. Mailings can be customized by a physician's specialty. More frequent programs can be targeted to high-volume prescribers. Key's sales managers and analysts can work with the database through their PC using the Epsilon Insight product. This program helps them answer specific questions about the reach, frequency, and success of the company sales and marketing efforts.

PUBLISHING

The *Harvard Business Review* supports its operation from its subscription revenue, since it runs little advertising.[19] It is essential for the publication to have very effective circulation activities. Most publisher service bureaus just maintain names at the lowest cost. So in 1981 Ernest Frawley, publisher of the *Review*, decided that it was time to set up a database, working with Epsilon. Frawley had had considerable experience with computers and fully realized the potential that a database would offer.

The database is detailed and flexible, offering a comprehensive profile of the subscribers with demographics. It is segmented.

Little wonder that the database has provided a number of important contributions to the *Review*. Complex targeted promotions are tracked and analyzed. Through segmentation the periodical has been able to tailor mailings on books and reprints according to wants and needs (such as finance, marketing, and other related areas).

The system accommodates well to the handling of overseas mailings, where the edition may be in English or in one of eight other languages.

There is some evidence that newspapers are about to jump onto the database bandwagon in terms of supplying assistance to the marketer. The *Spokesman Review* and the *Spokane Chronicle*, both Cowles newspapers in Spokane, are building small databases of readers with interests such as hunting or computers. They are using contests, promotions, and surveys to get the information. In early 1990 the newspapers, along with Ringling Bros., Barnum & Bailey Circus sponsored a contest that produced the names of 1,000 families with school-age children. The two newspapers also offered two books available for purchase by mail. The lists will be made available to local bookstores not using the two media in exchange for a run-of-press ad commitment.[30]

PRELIMINARY STEPS FOR THE MARKETING FIRM IN SETTING UP A DATABASE

For a marketing firm to establish and successfully use a customer/prospect database, considerable effort and diligence are required. The potential has to be defined, for this is an expensive effort. If the payoff is not worthwhile, the program should be discontinued before it gets very far.

If the signs are "go" after this step, the concept needs considerable and skillful pre-selling internally. Only then can the definitive steps in developing the database be taken.

DETERMINING THE POTENTIAL

There are three steps in determining the potential of a customer/prospect database for a particular marketer: defining the particular marketing objectives, targeting the logical marketing groups, and honing the examination. (Much of this discussion was stimulated by Jack Wolf, M/A/R/C.)

Defining the Specific Marketing Objectives

What can a database marketing program do for the firm? The answers have to be fairly specific. The process is very much like the one discussed in Chapter 5, where we talked about the potential values of a specific research study, and explained that it is crucial to weigh potential benefits against costs. But the stakes are far higher here. Now we are considering not a single marketing study, but a long-range decision involving basic company policy, even organization, and on a long-range basis.

It becomes important to examine what information about the customer or prospect can be helpful in specific results of greater marketing efficiency.

One of many inputs here may be from focus group interviews (see Chapter 10). Conducted separately with heavy users, light users, and nonusers, these may help establish desirable customer information requirements.

Targeting of Logical Market Groups

The exploratory work may help to identify the opportunities or lack of them. By this point in the preliminary work, it should be possible to come up with some hypotheses: possible plans that show some reasonable potential of success.

When this point has been reached, it may be time to try out—on a small scale—several alternative approaches.

Honing the Examination

Now it is time to see whether one or more of the promising approaches can be further sharpened to help ensure its success. There may be several important refinements to be considered. What additional information about those in the database might help generate better results? At what price? Anything additional, whether generated internally or purchased from an outside source, is going to carry a cost. Thus incremental cost versus incremental return must be determined.

INTERNAL PRE-SELLING OF THE CONCEPT

Let us assume that all indications up to this point are positive: There is virtual certainty that the marketing firm can benefit from the proposed database program. That is not necessarily a sign that the company is about to adopt it, however.

Senior management has to be sold on the idea, which is really almost revolutionary to the typical marketing firm. It is a whole new way of doing business. It requires integrated company thinking on a brand new approach. If the system is to be successful, it has to transcend the traditional product-marketing approach. For now, product marketing has to play second fiddle to this new, overall marketing approach. Senior management will require a lot of convincing, and the almost-certain high cost of the new approach won't make it any easier.

The necessary secondary role of product management won't make the plan easy to sell to the product managers either. Not only does it clearly downgrade their role, but if they continue to be judged on the basis of short-term results, so common now, their personal future will be in jeopardy. The pre-selling is not easy. Management has to change its thinking from short-term goals to overall corporate marketing goals.

SETTING UP THE DATABASE

The basic list may be either from internal records and efforts or from purchase of an external list.

USE OF INTERNAL RECORDS AND EFFORTS

Examining Existing Company Records[28]

The *nature* of company records was discussed earlier in this chapter. What now must be considered is the *sources* of such records.

These sources include customer files, merchandise orders, merchandise returns, service reports, credit applications, and, depending on the nature of the firm, may also include product-purchase registrations. (These used to be required for warranty registrations.)

Company Efforts to Obtain More Database Information

Database information already in the company archives may not be enough. Depending on the nature of the firm, it may be necessary to instruct those receiving telephone orders to ask for specific information about the purchaser, or for the checkout person to request additional personal information when cashing a check.

Retail Consumer Technology (East Windsor, Conn.) has developed a simple method of getting such data for retailers.[31] It is a difficult and involved process on an in-store basis. So what the firm does is use the customer's telephone number as a basis for filing customer information.

Cleaning the User Company List

Cleaning, as the term is used here, means the minimizing of errors in the list: inconsistencies (such as abbreviations) and duplications of identical listings. The cleaning process for lists of consumers also should include duplications caused by given names versus initials and the names of abbreviations of street names (Avenue, Street, Drive, Place, and the like).

For lists of businesses, such cleaning is also required. The name of a telephone company may appear on the company list as ATT, AT&T, American Telephone & Telegraph, Bell, or to complicate things even further, one of the regional Baby Bells or one of the company's subsidiaries.

Cleaning is essential for all efficient contact activity (clean mailings, letters, telephone calls).

Many external specialist firms can either provide software for the user to handle or will handle it on assignment. Epsilon has scrubbing software, customized to need, which standardizes name and address information into fixed field format. This assures that names are in suitable shape for mailing.

An Example

Tourism Canada, a federal government agency, wanted to attract American tourists. It had been making mailings primarily to people who fished, hunted, or engaged in for other outdoor activities. But in the early 1980s, the agency began to wonder whether it was losing much of its potential market. Were there Americans who visited Canada for other reasons, such as its cities, history, and culture? Were trips planned by the people themselves or with the assistance of a travel agency?

The agency included a detailed reply coupon and questionnaire in its next mailing. Respondents were asked questions about age, occupation, travel frequency, and travel interests.

The information was incorporated into the database. The database is constantly updated, and Tourism Canada now channels mailings and advertisements to the market segments. Responses to each mailing and ad are entered into the database. The family that travels by car, makes its own plans, and wants to visit historic cities, for example, gets the appropriate mailings.

Tourism Canada devised an ingenious method of measuring actual visits to Canada by these prospects. Each package of materials sent to a prospect after request includes a prepaid business response card which qualifies the sender to a premium or prize. But the trick is that the card must be mailed in Canada. So when a return card is received, Tourism Canada has positive evidence not only of the visit to Canada, but of at least one point that was visited.[32]

RECRUITING A LIST

Recruiting *can* be simple, though it is not inexpensive. For example, Oscar Meyer offered a lunch-meat cents-off coupon in newspapers in which the consumer had to fill in name and address before redeeming it.

BUYING A LIST

There are several major external specialist firms that have database lists available.

Performance Data System (TRW Marketing Services)

This service offers files covering some 140 million people throughout the United States. These files[33] hold an amazing amount of information about individuals. In addition to the usual demographics (sex, age, income, even recent movers and those with Hispanic surnames), they have the overlays of PRIZM and Acorn demographics (as described in Chapter 15). But they also have financial information (possession of various types of credit cards, bank balance, available purchase power). While an individual marketing firm can purchase a basic demographic list according to its specifications, it cannot buy a list based on financial aspects, since TRW (getting this information through its parent supercredit agency) considers this to be a breach of privacy. However, such lists combined with other aspects of classification will be supplied to a third party (such as a fulfillment agency) without disclosure of the nature of the list. The response to such a promotion, of course, might help to establish or expand the marketing firm's own database.

National Demographics & Lifestyles (NDL)

NDL has a ready-made list of 20 million, named the Lifestyle Selector. Mail responses to a detailed product registration questionnaire provide a broad range of demographic and life-style data.[34] A sample of one of these is shown in Exhibit 16.4.

OASYS (Opportunity Analysis System) is the software system available to the user.[35] NDL extends its information base by having the user's customers tell it about themselves and their reasons for use of the particular product or service. Information is supplemented with data about the customer's media habits and product category benchmarks (from Mediamark Research, described in Chapter 15), business and economic data for major markets, and behavior and life-style information (from NDL's The Lifestyle Census, covering over 30 million households, in every U.S. market).

NDL claims that the system, aimed at sales and marketing decision makers, can profile the market to design effective promotions and advertising strategies, provide input for new-product development and positioning, analyze sales potential and effectiveness, and aid in the efficiency of many other aspects of the marketing mix.

Call Interactive is a relative newcomer to this group. Set up jointly by American Express and AT&T in 1989, it is a database with some unique features that give it far more than the usual database potentials, though for our purposes here we stress those.[36]

The database of 89,000 residential names and addresses is keyed to 10-digit telephone numbers. While this is not a selective base except for geography, the firm offers several features that may make its use very attractive. Perhaps its most innovative feature is a high-quality digitized sound program, which means that incoming calls (in the case of database marketing, these would be either orders or information requests) are almost immediately answered by a polite, human-sounding voice. Instructions are taken and followed, even to the extent of recording credit card purchase information and checking authorizations.

Call Interactive has complete mailout fulfillment capabilities.

While the marketing user is not permitted to purchase any of the list, the user firm can use returns to start to set up its own database.

Call Interactive is prepared to manage and maintain the user's own data, on the user's premises or its own. Thus there is a lot of flexibility.

Select & Save[37] and Select & Save Plus[38]

There are some highly specialized firms in the business of providing consumer database lists. Computerized Marketing Technologies is one of the most important of these.

It generates amazing numbers—about 6.5 million annually—for its database. The total database currently is some 30 million. The firm ob-

Exhibit 16.4   A PANASONIC VCR PURCHASE INFORMATION CARD

Seal card here.

Panasonic® VCR PURCHASE INFORMATION CARD
IMPORTANT!   IMPORTANT!
Please fill out and return within the next 10 days.

Thank you for purchasing this Panasonic product. In order to serve you better in the future, we would appreciate your answering the following questions. Your assistance is greatly appreciated.

1 1. ☐ Mr.   2. ☐ Mrs.   3. ☐ Ms.   4. ☐ Miss   90M

First Name   Initial   Last Name

Street   Apt. No.

City   State   Zip

2 Date of Purchase.
Month   Day   Year

3 What is your model number? PV —
(Located in Operating Instructions Manual and Rear Panel of Product)

4 Type of store where purchased:
1. ☐ Received as a Gift
2. ☐ Department Store
3. ☐ Appliance/Radio/TV
4. ☐ Discount Store/
   Mass Merchandise
5. ☐ Video Speciality
6. ☐ Hi-Fi Store
7. ☐ Supermarket
8. ☐ Catalog Showroom
9. ☐ Membership Warehouse
10. ☐ Camera Store
11. ☐ Computer Store
12. ☐ Catalog Mail Order
13. ☐ Other:

5 Who had the most influence in the decision to buy this product? (check one only)
1. ☐ Your decision only
2. ☐ Spouse
3. ☐ You and Your Spouse
4. ☐ Children
5. ☐ Other:

6 Check the two (2) most important factors influencing your selection of this product:
1. ☐ Trust in Panasonic
2. ☐ Price
3. ☐ Quality
4. ☐ VHS Format
5. ☐ Features
6. ☐ Style/Appearance
7. ☐ Ease of Operation
8. ☐ Design
9. ☐ Size
10. ☐ Durability
11. ☐ Portability
12. ☐ Other:

7 Is this VCR:
1. ☐ First VCR owned
2. ☐ Replacement for another VCR
3. ☐ Additional VCR (own one other VCR)
4. ☐ Additional VCR (own 2 or more other VCRs)

8 Which of the following brands did you seriously consider before selecting Panasonic? (check all that apply)
1. ☐ Considered no other brand
2. ☐ Magnavox
3. ☐ Fisher
4. ☐ Sony
5. ☐ Quasar
6. ☐ RCA
7. ☐ Hitachi
8. ☐ Sanyo
9. ☐ G.E.
10. ☐ JVC
11. ☐ Sharp
12. ☐ Zenith
13. ☐ Toshiba
14. ☐ Other:

9 Where is the product used and who is (are) the primary users? (check one from each column)
A. 1. ☐ Living Room
2. ☐ Family Room/Den
3. ☐ Bedroom
4. ☐ School
5. ☐ Office
6. ☐ Outdoors
7. ☐ Other
B. 1. ☐ Yourself
2. ☐ Spouse
3. ☐ You and Spouse
4. ☐ Children
5. ☐ Other

10 Date of birth of person whose name appears above:
1   9
Month   Year

11 Marital Status:
1. ☐ Married
2. ☐ Divorced/Separated
3. ☐ Widowed
4. ☐ Single/Never Married

12 Occupation:

	You	Your Spouse
Homemaker	1. ☐	1. ☐
Professional/Technical	2. ☐	2. ☐
Executive/Administrator	3. ☐	3. ☐
Middle Management	4. ☐	4. ☐
Sales/Marketing	5. ☐	5. ☐
Clerical or Service Worker	6. ☐	6. ☐
Tradesman/Machine Oper./ Laborer	7. ☐	7. ☐
Retired	8. ☐	8. ☐
Student	9. ☐	9. ☐
Self Employed/Business Owner	10. ☐	10. ☐

13 What are the ages of all children living at home?
☐ None   ☐ 4 yrs.   ☐ 9 yrs.   ☐ 14 yrs.   ☐ 19 +
☐ Under 1   ☐ 5 yrs.   ☐ 10 yrs.   ☐ 15 yrs.
☐ 1 yr.   ☐ 6 yrs.   ☐ 11 yrs.   ☐ 16 yrs.
☐ 2 yrs.   ☐ 7 yrs.   ☐ 12 yrs.   ☐ 17 yrs.
☐ 3 yrs.   ☐ 8 yrs.   ☐ 13 yrs.   ☐ 18 yrs.

14 Which group describes your annual family income:
1. ☐ Under $14,999
2. ☐ $15,000-$19,999
3. ☐ $20,000-$24,999
4. ☐ $25,000-$29,999
5. ☐ $30,000-$34,999
6. ☐ $35,000-$39,999
7. ☐ $40,000-$44,999
8. ☐ $45,000-$49,999
9. ☐ $50,000-$59,999
10. ☐ $60,000-$74,999
11. ☐ $75,000-$99,999
12. ☐ $100,000 & over

15 Which of the following do you use regularly?
1. ☐ American Express, Diners Club, Carte Blanche
2. ☐ Bank credit card (Master Card, Visa)
3. ☐ Gas, Dept. store, etc. credit card(s)
4. ☐ Airline club/frequent flyer program
5. ☐ None of the above

16 For your primary residence, do you:
1. ☐ Own a house?
2. ☐ Rent a house?
3. ☐ Rent an apartment?
4. ☐ Own a townhouse or condominium?

(PLEASE CONTINUE ON BACK!)
(OVER)

Printed in Japan
VQAS0169 ®

Source: Reproduced with kind permission of National Demographics & Lifestyles.

.... Please fold here. ....

☞ **17** To help us understand our customers' lifestyles, please indicate the interests and
(CONTINUE HERE) activities in which you or your spouse enjoy participating on a regular basis:

1. ☐ Bicycling Frequently	20. ☐ Automotive Work	39. ☐ Coin/Stamp Collecting
2. ☐ Golf	21. ☐ Electronics	40. ☐ Collectibles/Collections
3. ☐ Physical Fitness/Exercise	22. ☐ Home Workshop/Do it Yourself	41. ☐ Our Nation's Heritage
4. ☐ Running/Jogging	23. ☐ Motorcycles	42. ☐ Real Estate Investments
5. ☐ Snow Skiing Frequently	24. ☐ Recreational Vehicles	43. ☐ Stock/Bond Investments
6. ☐ Tennis Frequently	25. ☐ Stereo, Records/Tapes/Discs	44. ☐ Veterans Benefits
7. ☐ Bowling	26. ☐ Avid Book Reading	45. ☐ Entering Sweepstakes
8. ☐ Camping/Hiking	27. ☐ Bible/Devotional Reading	46. ☐ Home Video Games
9. ☐ Fishing Frequently	28. ☐ Current Affairs/Politics	47. ☐ Household Pets (dogs, cats, etc.)
10. ☐ Hunting/Shooting	29. ☐ Health Foods/Vitamins	48. ☐ Money Making Opportunities
11. ☐ Power Boating	30. ☐ House Plants	49. ☐ Science Fiction
12. ☐ Sailing	31. ☐ Photography	50. ☐ Wildlife/Environment Issues
13. ☐ Crafts	32. ☐ Attend Cultural/Arts Events	51. ☐ Career-Oriented Activities
14. ☐ Crossword Puzzles	33. ☐ Charities/Volunteer Activities	52. ☐ Personal/Home Computers
15. ☐ Grandchildren	34. ☐ Fashion Clothing	53. ☐ Science/New Technology
16. ☐ Needlework/Knitting	35. ☐ Fine Art/Antiques	54. ☐ Self Improvement
17. ☐ Outdoor Gardening	36. ☐ Foreign Travel	55. ☐ VCR Recording/Viewing
18. ☐ Sewing	37. ☐ Gourmet Cooking/Fine Foods	56. ☐ Watching Cable TV
19. ☐ Walking for Health	38. ☐ Wines	57. ☐ Watching Sports on TV
		58. ☐ NONE OF THE ABOVE

18 From the above list, please indicate
the numbers representing the 3
most important activities for: You ☐☐☐☐☐☐   Spouse ☐☐☐☐☐☐

Thanks for taking the time to fill out this questionnaire. Your answers will be used for market research studies and reports — and will help us better serve you in the future. They will also allow you to receive important mailings and special offers from a number of fine companies whose products and services relate directly to the specific interests, hobbies, and other information indicated above. Through this selective program, you will be able to obtain more information about activities in which you are involved and less about those in which you are not. Please check here, if for some reason, you would prefer **not** to participate in this opportunity. ☐

tains the list through a "Speak Out America" advertisement run three times annually in free-standing inserts (FSI) in Sunday newspaper supplements, such as *Parade*. These reach some 100 million homes.

Each insert is a "survey." Those who respond are offered a packet of coupons good for discounts and free goods. But to qualify for all of these goodies, the consumer must answer questions about such elements as nature of residence (type and rental/ownership), family composition, household composition, working women and their demographics, buying patterns, pet ownership and nature, and attitude (such as voting for the sexiest man in America or the network news most trusted, aimed at basic attitudes possibly related to the product—for instance, attitudes that can be tied to environment awareness and health consciousness).

Select & Save gets information about 50 million households through FSIs and targeted direct mail. Consumers are given cents-off coupons and samples for filling in a questionnaire covering elements such as category use, brand preference, amount of consumption, purchase frequency, number of users in the household, multiple-brand users and special information such as the size of the household pet.[32]

Donnelley has the name of Carol Wright working for the firm. The direct-mail co-op covers some 45 million households in 351 metro markets. It offers Share Force, a market-targeting service, in which questionnaires on category and brand usage are distributed twice annually. Households are offered a small box of samples and coupons. A response of about 14 percent provides information on 6 million households. So advertisers can give samples or coupons to self-identified nonusers of their products, and if an ID is required to redeem the coupon, it can be the start of the firm's own database.[32]

CSI Telemarketing offers telephone surveys in a defined area around a supermarket that wants to build its own database. Questions are asked about the drugstore and supermarket used and about brand usage. Coupons aimed at getting noncustomers to visit the store can be sent to them.[32]

Lifestyle Selector processes warranty cards for many major manufacturers. The database has been expanded by collecting information on more than 12 million warranty respondents. Through creating a database for the manufacturer, it has the right to make the data provided by the buyers available to other firms. To a golf resort, for example, it can provide the names and addresses of people who travel and who play golf.[32]

EFFECTIVE USE OF THE DATABASE

While database marketing offers many obvious advantages, its effectiveness does not just happen. It requires thoughtful selection of names to be used in a particular marketing effort, careful media selection, sometimes the use of cooperating sponsors, the use of specific strategies and tactics to stimulate response, and ongoing management reports for evaluation and strategy.

SELECTION OF NAMES TO BE USED

Unless the list in the database is relatively small, as when there is only a single product or service—and there are very few databases like this—considerable care must be used if a particular marketing effort is to be successful. The majority of customer/prospect databases are far too large to be used en masse. In addition, there are generally a large number of products or services, and the one or the combination used in a marketing effort will be used with only a selected portion of the database. Further, the particular nature of the marketing effort may be more effectively aimed at only part of the database, even when the products or services are identical.

There are three ways to select the names for the particular effort: use of individual criteria, predictive models, or segmentation models.

Individual Criteria

It is possible to select names for the marketing effort in rather simple terms, using even a single criterion.

In one case, a good company selling a broad variety of goods through supermarkets does much of its promotion through mailings to customers and prospects, offering inducements such as premiums, free merchandise, cents-off coupons, and the like, each redeemable at one of its stores. It knows which people in the database purchase and which do not purchase its brand of coffee. It is simple enough to pull out the names of those who use coffee but do not purchase its brand, and then make a mailing of a high-value coupon in an effort to get them to purchase.

For a promotion of some other sort, the computer may be instructed to pull out the names of all those who bought the product within the past six months and who are women between the ages of 20 and 29. But both of these examples are rather hit-or-miss methods. With far more information available about each name in the database, there are more sophisticated and efficient methods.

Predictive Models

Predictive models make it feasible to select names on the basis of how likely those people are to respond, based on a previous statistical analysis.

This sort of model is built by analysis of the characteristics of each name against the amount of purchase response that is shown. Let us say that the particular marketer is a catalog firm offering a variety of merchandise by mail. The firm issues a single catalog a year, published in September. It keeps records on dollar amounts of purchases annually by each customer. It also knows a great deal about the demographics of its customers. By multiple regression statistics—developed through correlation analysis—it is possible to develop a regression equation that provides, let us say, for a weighting for each of family income, age, and census region, which estimates fairly accurately what total purchases are likely to be from a particular individual.

Now, the reason this catalog firm wants this information is that it plans to publish an expensive four-color catalog featuring gifts for the Christmas holiday season. It doesn't want to waste catalog money and postage on those who are likely to be low dollar-volume buyers. The predictive model won't solve the problem entirely, but it will certainly be a big help.

Segmentation Models

As we have said, segmentation places people into one of several groups, each of which has common characteristics based on previous statistical aspects such as demographics, psychographics, or needs.

The segmentation model makes it possible to pull out names falling into one or more of these segments, for use in a particular marketing effort. Marketing programs can be built to meet the requirements, needs, or interests of the particular segment.

PROPER MEDIA USE

There are two directions of media in database marketing. Both are essential for the interaction between marketer and customer or prospect. One media use is outbound: getting the message from the company to the prospect or customer. The other is inbound: getting the message from the prospect or customer to the company. Sometimes the two are combined, as when the prospect/customer talks to the company by telephone.

Outbound Media Possibilities

There is a wide range of choices, but we mention only the highlights here.

In *television*, a campaign can provide an 800 telephone number for further information.

In *radio*, for example, Campbell Soup times soup commercials next to reports on skiing conditions. Taco Bell places appetite-whetting commercials so as to catch homeward-bound commuters.[32] Radio talk shows (where listeners call in to talk) offer experts in varying fields such as finance, real estate, health, psychology, gardening, travel, or sports. The advertiser can select the type of show likely to include its prospects. A commercial delivered by a host is likely to have tremendous acceptance.

In *newspapers*, for example, the TMC (total market coverage) and SMC (selective market coverage) make it possible to focus on prospects in major markets where sales are greatest. The SMC is a specific geographic grid, and many newspapers now offer ads by SMC. In a mixed ethnic market, SMCs are often used for targeting specific ethnic groups.

In *magazines*, most of the over 1,400 magazines are highly segmented. The mass publications, such as the *Saturday Evening Post* (though now medically oriented and no longer a mass medium) and *Collier's*, disappeared many years ago. The segmentation may be by specialization or geography (regional and city magazines).

Many publications offer regional or even metro editions. It is possible to run an ad in a metro edition of *TV Guide* at a moderate price. *Time, Newsweek, U.S. News & World Report* also offer regional or local advertising.

The customized magazine is a special case. In recent years, R. R. Donnelley has introduced selective binding, a method of producing copies of magazines personalized for the individual subscriber, whose name can be used to provide the copy designed just for him or her. A number of national magazines using Donnelley as their production facility have gone to this procedure: *Harper's Magazine, Farm Journal, Time, People, Sports Illustrated,* and *Money.*

L. L. Bean, the Maine sporting goods cataloger, used *Harper's* in this way by having the magazine send a bound-in direct-response card requesting a free catalog next to a full-page ad. A number to track the respondent was inserted on each card.

In January 1990, the Time publications began offering their Target-Select plan[39] for special-binding issues of *Time, People, Sports Illustrated*, and *Money.* The program makes it possible for the operator of a database to have similar special offerings to those in the database list.

There seems to be incredible potential here for the database user to use a medium not formerly available to reach the particular specific list.

In *direct marketing*, both direct mail and telemarketing (the euphemistic term used to describe the frequently detested telephone solicitation) are outbound media possibilities. Direct marketing of the mail variety is the medium most commonly used to complete the sale in database marketing, and its results are the major source of additional inputs into the database. However, telemarketing is definitely effective in both ways, depending on the nature of the market.

The *use of multiple media* is another possibility. As an example of sound use of several media (television, radio, business publications), MCI started in the long-distance telephone business in 1968, grossing $14 million.[40] Sixteen years later its sales were $6 billion.

The company began by using the one-on-one sales technique in selling its long-distance service to businesses. After television was tested in Denver as a means of selling long-distance to residential consumers, thirty-second commercials with a toll-free number worked so well that the company realized television could also be used to market the service to business. Geographic targeting could be aimed at the markets then served by MCI.

But other media are also used. Radio is used during driving hours to reach managers and executives, again with a toll-free number in the commercials. Coupons in print ads in business publications such as *Forbes* and *Business Week* generate still more leads.

Inbound Media Possibilities

The inbound media are used by the customer/prospect primarily for placing an order, though sometimes to obtain information. In either case, the marketing firm naturally identifies the person (perhaps through an account number or a name, and the appropriate information is entered into the computer file: the ID number or name and address, the date (and perhaps the hour), and the nature and dollar amount of the order, or the nature of the request.

The telephone is one possibility. Toll-free (800) numbers are often used by the database marketer to provide a no-charge telephone number for buyers to place an order. This makes it easy for the purchaser. It instantly converts any other medium into a direct-response medium.

Procter & Gamble has used this system to get names and addresses in a rollout of a new detergent. (Television viewers were given an 800 number to get a free sample.) Now 900 numbers are a relatively new AT&T service. The caller pays 50 cents per call and gets a recorded message.

Coupon and write-in offers are the other major category of inbound media.

The firm that is seriously into database marketing always wants to be able to identify the respondent. If there are coupons redeemable at the store, these must require name and address of the user. If the marketing firm has mailed a coupon to those already on its list, these can be keyed with the particular ID number assigned the household. If there is a free offer—this is generally sent in by mail—name and address are required on the response.

PROMOTIONS AND RELATED DEVICES TO INCREASE EFFECTIVENESS

Couponing, whether by direct mail or media-enclosed (generally a newspaper), can be an effective device. One study[32] reports that coupons produced a sales increase of 250 percent for a supermarket product.

Sampling may also be a potent sales promotion method. The sales impact of 10 products in a John Blair Marketing's sample pack among nonusers showed gains in market share of from 5 percent (a brand with over half the volume in the category) to a top gain of over 35 times the current share (a new product with a low base).[32] Couponing plus sampling increased sales some 300 percent.[32].

Sweepstakes are another consumer-accepted marketing tool. Almost everyone will take a no-cost chance of being enriched, either by money or prizes. However, putting on a successful sweepstakes is a professional job, and since this is a marketing research book rather than a marketing book, we make no effort to try to tell you just how it should be done. It is a high-cost promotion, and there is no way to test-market it. It isn't possible to test a $1 million sweepstakes in Toledo and kill it if it is unsuccessful, unless the sponsor is willing to spend $1 million on the test alone.

Generally, sweepstakes, because of their prize levels, are restricted to higher-priced merchandise and services, such as an automobile, a hotel room, a magazine subscription (with the promise of renewals).

In terms of data for the databank, an entry automatically provides name and address. The entry form may even require additional information about the household, which will contribute to the databank.

The unique Target Chek system, offered by Moore Response Marketing Services,[41] is aimed at retailers. It features inclusion of an actual bank check (with the retailer putting it through the bank system) rather than a coupon. When the consumers receive the mailing including the check directed to them as individuals, the argument—probably correct—is that this has far more psychological impact than mere receipt of a coupon. The check can also be used as a data-gathering instrument, including demographics. From the fast clearance of checks (as opposed to coupon-clearing houses), results can be rapidly measured, including known characteristics versus total mailout list, redemption by store nature, and accumulation of new data about the redeemers.

Moore provides a house file, use of the client file, or a combination of the two. It cleans the file. It performs all the functions of a full-service direct-mail firm—but it is real database marketing with a novel twist.

Offers Cannot Be Static

Things change: What may be an effective premium one year may be totally wrong the next. One of the most dramatic changes has been in the reward system for frequent users: airlines and hotels. Largely because these heavy users often lack time to make use of additional flights or visits, and because these may not be available at times desired, some firms are now offering merchandise rewards. Sheraton, Holiday Inn, and Marriott now put out merchandise catalogs for their frequent users.[42]

OTHER METHODS OF INCREASING EFFECTIVENESS

COOPERATING SPONSORS

As shown in some of the examples, some producers of consumer goods seek partnerships with other business firms in making their database marketing more effective.

One advantage is the use of cross-promotions: In dealing with the consumer, you scratch my back and I'll scratch yours.

Sheraton Club members can earn bonus points by test-driving a new BMW and by purchasing it within 30 days of the test drive.

A well-chosen sponsor offers prestige, at no cost and perhaps more income. In Sheraton's case, there was the advantage of the prestige association with BMW, but without cost to Sheraton. BMW pays Sheraton for increasing traffic at its showrooms by covering the cost of the extra points.

Sheraton also offers premiums of other firms to its customers. The Sheraton Club 1990 awards catalog offered some 313 awards (55 overseas hotels, 103 domestic, 9 Canadian, 146 items ranging from a two-seater glider plane, an automobile, home electronic items, furniture, cameras, sporting goods, toys, small appliances, as well as instructions on obtaining catalogs for ordering from four mail-order houses).

The advantage to Sheraton: saving time in the search for the right merchandise. To the mail-order houses: increasing the size of their mailing lists.[6]

MANAGEMENT REPORTS FOR EVALUATION AND PLANNING

As with any ongoing system, the results of database marketing should be subject to a continuing evaluation. The nature of the continuing evaluation varies with the nature of the business. (Much of this discussion has been drawn from Geiger.[43]) A publisher has needs that are far different from the needs of a marketer of a low-price, fast-turnover item. However, there are some constants.

New customers should be examined in terms of numbers, geography, amount of spending, sales per customer by medium, and, depending on the firm's record-keeping, costs per customer and medium.

Existing customers merit equal review. Really basic is the loyalty rate—what sort of turnover there is. This should be reviewed by the length of time the customer has been on the list.

Both current and new customers should be profiled to spot heavy users who are the most loyal.

MAINTENANCE AND EXPANSION OF THE DATABASE

CONSTANT CLEANING

Things never remain the same. After only five years since you left college, your last job, or your last living quarters, when you go back, things are different—that world is not the same.

It is like that, too, in maintenance of a customer database. But things happen much faster than one might imagine.

A marketing consultant specializing in marketing planning reports that most business lists turn over by one-third annually.[44] But the figure varies wildly with the nature of the product or service. It is almost surely worse with consumer lists. We know that the proportion of those who move annually is high. What we don't know about the individuals in our database is how they are changing in their demographics and psychographics, unless we try to keep up with this through constant cleaning.

RECORDING RESPONSIVENESS

The database can be effective only if there is an ongoing monitoring of the responsiveness of its members. It is rather like being the manager, let's say, of a mutual fund. If you're a good one, you will know the continuing performance of each of your assets.

Managing the assets of the database membership is not all that different. The basic question is the degree to which each individual within the database is worth keeping there.

The choices, like those of a mutual fund, can be specifically spelled out, with specifics to be determined by the marketing firm. But we can mention what seems to be worth consideration.

The starting point is a record of the particular marketing effort: the total size and the nature of those approached, and the promotional effort (the kind of merchandise or service offered, its price, the advertising medium, and, if applicable, inducements to buy).

EXPANSION OF NUMBERS ON THE LIST

Once a marketing firm begins a database marketing program, simply because of the success of a one-on-one effort, it may want to expand its list. It may be possible to do this through its own internal efforts or through purchase of an outside list. We have already discussed the purchase of an outside list, so here we are concerned only with what the firm can do internally to expand the list.

There are two possibilities: ongoing internal procedures and response to special promotions.

Ongoing Internal Procedures

For a retailing firm, where buyers visit the premises, there are additional opportunities. Employees can be required, as an ongoing procedure, to get name and address for check cashing and completion of sales tickets. And, of course, names and addresses procured through credit cards should be a part of the procedure.

Response to Special Promotions

The marketing firm using a database for its marketing effort has a great way to expand its list. Every time it experiments with a new list, using whatever promotion effort, it can keep track of the names of those who respond. This is particularly useful for a firm using direct marketing as its basic method.

EXPANSION OF CASES AND INFORMATION IN THE DATABASE

Information about those in a database can be expanded in four ways, as described in Chapter 11. Three of these apply to the customer/prospect database: adding real cases, adding real information about existing cases, and adding implied information about existing cases.

Adding Real Cases and Information

The adding of real cases—names of people with similar characteristics to those already in the database— and unification of multiple sets of data on the same customer list (the use of separate but distinct information about those on the list) is the adding of hard data. Yes, there is often such information available. Sometimes it is in separate files within the firm's own records, which can occur when there are different brand groups or divisions within the firm. Less often it may be that an external source has specific information about some of those in the database of the marketing firm.

There is software available to handle the process. Duplicates of names appearing on more than one list can be purged. Data about the same customer in two or more lists can be consolidated.

There is little question about the strength of such additions. The publisher of *INC.!* Magazine showed ingenuity in use of the merge/purge technique in order to construct a list from which to build circulation rapidly when he first published the magazine. There was no prospect list of those he wanted to reach: small entrepreneurial firms unable to afford the team of various specialists used by larger companies.

So Bernard Goldhirsch developed a prime list with which to start his subscription drive. He merged a list of *The Wall Street Journal* subscribers with a list of companies whose volume could be identified. Non-business *Journal* subscribers and those connected with large firms were eliminated. The result was a list of executives of smaller firms who had demonstrated their responsiveness by subscribing to the *Journal*. The method worked. By using imaginative promotional techniques, *INC. !* was quickly able to develop a paid circulation of some 400,000, a large number for a business publication.[32]

Adding Implied Information

In the addition of implied information, an external source provides "data," if it can really be called that, about each person in the databank, all based on "averages." In this situation the source has determined averages for those living in the kind of neighborhood indicated by the address, and the marketing firm simply appends the presumed additional data to the person at the address. It may have to do with media habits, purchasing behavior, or life-styles. This is far from an exact process, impressive as it may appear. But we talk more about this in the last section of this chapter.

USING OUTSIDE SPECIALIST FIRMS

ADVANTAGES

Should the marketing firm use an outside specialist? (Much of this discussion is based upon Schwartz.) There may be one or more good reasons to do so. Start-up time will be much quicker. The outside specialist will have far less trial and error in the process.

The specialist is a source of advice, information, and systems. Going to an outside specialist means that the user firm can concentrate on what it does best: marketing. Maintaining and using a customer database system may be a tough job for a firm whose people are not skilled in the process, and it might even dilute the firm's overall marketing effectiveness.

THE ROLES OF AN OUTSIDE SPECIALIST

Some outside specialists actually can provide a ready-to-use system. Some will tailor a system to order. Some will undertake the expansion process. Some will perform the fulfillment process. A particular outside specialist firm may do one or more of these.

Providing a Ready-to-Use System

Citicorp POS Information Services Inc. had developed a virtually ready-to-use system for grocery retailers that came in several versions. The difference in the versions was the service to or the approach to customers; as far as the nature of the data produced is concerned, they were all parallel.[45] It was a system that rewarded customer loyalty in one form or another. It even included the installation of specialized computers, so it was a complete system. But there was one big difference between this and other systems for grocery retailers: Citicorp POS intended to build a massive database of purchase behavior related to 25–40 million households. All products—by brand, size, price, and frequency of purchase—were to be tied to a purchaser's address. That meant 30 billion transactions annually at the level of 25 million households. By the middle of 1990, there would be 1.5 million households whose purchase records were going into the databank. These would come through 500 stores of 19 chains. It was estimated that by the start of 1991 there would be a total of 1,400 stores from 25 chains.[46]

Citicorp would own the data. If the data could have been shown to be representative of supermarket purchasing throughout the country, the service would have had one tremendous advantage over the Nielsen ScanTrack service, which measures similar merchandise movement in supermarkets: It would have offered single-source data for every transaction.

The tests[47] got off to a thumping good start. Many retailers took on the program. But it was not to be. Like so many other massive database programs, it was simply too expensive a loss-producing center, so Citicorp, already having its own financial problems, dumped the program in late 1990.[48]

But the grandiose Citicorp system was not the only game in town. Vision[49] (Advanced Promotion Technologies, joint venture of P&G, Donnelley Marketing, Check-Robot, and Schlumberger) works with a conventional scanner-equipped checkout lane or with a new automated checkout machine. The shopper applying for a card fills out a profile questionnaire. The system uses a "smart card," the Vision Card, a plastic card with embedded microchip. This provides ID, tracks purchasing habits and keeps tabs of point status in frequent-shopper programs, can function as check approval or debit card, and may also serve as a conventional credit card (Visa).

An electronic cash register tape is displayed on a screen facing the shopper during the checkout process. It shows five items at a time (brand and price). Promotions are executed with instant rebates (manufacturer or retailer). Conventional pack cents-off are automatically shown on the tape, variable price pack offers are also feasible (based on product size or on a random basis). The system's printer can produce almost any type of coupon, activated by the UPCs. The system offers the flexibility of targeting almost any type of promotion to specific regions, chains, individual stores, or shoppers with specified buying habits.

Tailoring a System to the User's Needs[50]

M/A/R/C, one of the largest marketing research firms in the country, will develop a system to meet the buyer's needs. It begins with an assessment program and then will create and even manage the system.

There are some specialist firms with expertise in particular areas that will tailor a system to meet the needs of a user firm in that field. For example, Epsilon[17] offers special background and skills in database marketing for financial institutions and periodicals, and customizes systems to needs for firms in these marketing areas. SmartNames[51] customizes programs for insurance companies and banks, contractors, and publishers.

Across-the-Board Services

We have already mentioned that an outside specialist firm may offer either list expansion or fulfillment facilities. An example is SmartNames.

SmartNames can and will compile a database. It has its own Homes Database, a 28-million-name list, with 40 selections of optional data, including information about residence (owner/renter, dwelling type, age of home, market value, and number of bedrooms and baths), personal data (income, age, household size and composition, marital status, ethnic group, education, occupation, PRIZM, Vision coding, telephone number), and, of course, geography.

The firm can provide a list extension function, covering the gamut from addition of new names through enrichment by overlays. It can maintain a list, including the mundane but essential task of eliminating duplicates and updating addresses.

It will also run the system for the user firm. This includes production and mailout facilities, as well as response-tracking of individual members in the database.

SOME ISSUES AND LAST-MINUTE CHANGES

METHODS OF EXPANDING INFORMATION IN A COMPANY LIST

There are three methods of adding information about the names in a database list: questions asked of those listed, purchase of "hard" data about those on the list, and using cluster categories.

In the first case, the marketing firm, in sending material to its list, asks specific questions and generally offers some inducement for reply. Questions may be asked about use of other product categories or brands, product or other attitudes, or additional demographics or other characteristics. Such a procedure is sound. It is simply a specialized form of survey, a basic marketing research tool.

It is sometimes possible to locate an information source that will check a marketer's list against its own, and add additional information to any that match. This also appears to be a sound method, as long as the information of the supplier is dependable.

In using cluster categories, we are talking about categories for clusters (most often ZIP codes) to describe those living within certain areas. Several of these clusters were discussed earlier in this chapter, and we use one of these as an illustration here. (With some variations, the other clusters have been established in very much the same manner.)

Jonathan Robbin, under the aegis of his newly formed Claritas Corp., computer-analyzed each ZIP code into five groupings based on hundreds of characteristics: social rank, mobility, ethnicity, stage in family life cycle, and housing style. It was then possible to identify 34 factors accounting for 87 percent of the variation among ZIP code neighborhoods. Finally, Robbins had the computer rate each one simultaneously to place it into one of 40 clusters.[52] His system of PRIZM clustering was described in greater detail in Chapter 15.

Does the clustering method provide accurate descriptions? In terms of total individual clusters, the answer is yes. But not all individuals or households within the cluster follow the cluster pattern. You can check this out easily in terms of where you happen to live. You will almost surely find that most residents are reasonably homogeneous in terms of the five broad characteristics. But there is that family in the apartment next door, say, where both members clearly came from a lower class and are a lot younger (with children still in grade school). Or that family a few doors down the block who bought the smaller-than-average house in the area. The husband had to be told that you don't start your chain saw at 7 a.m. on a Saturday to start tree-trimming. They don't keep their grass well-mowed. The wife is one of the few women on the block who don't have weekly household help.

Yes, particular individuals or households can be misclassified. But in terms of the usefulness of the method in database marketing, we see no problem. The additional information is applied to the name on the marketer's list. Even with this additional information (which may be wrong), if the particular name does not prove productive, it can be dropped. And in most cases the additional information *is* likely to be correct.

INVASION OF PRIVACY

Computers provide the means for government and business to gather a great amount of information about an individual.[53] Telephone companies, with use of computers, provide a monthly bill showing the listing of all calls made. By use of a reverse directory (described in Chapter 8), it is a simple matter to get the names, occupations, and other pertinent information relating to the listed telephone numbers. Credit card firms keep similar records. So it is possible from computer records to know to what firms and individuals telephone calls are made and a great deal about a person's buying (what, when, and from whom). When you realize that to this can be added a person's credit records and Social Security records, there emerges an amazing inventory of a person's life: occupation, income, family, health, nationality, education, buying habits, and more.

Columnist James Kilpatrick[54] writes that it came out in a congressional subcommittee hearing that some 1,200 credit offices have files about 150 million Americans, and that computers can provide" . . . the most intimate details of our personal lives—where we shop, where we dine, what we buy, who [sic] we telephone."

There is serious concern about whether the consumer's privacy is being invaded. Does a credit-rating firm really have the right to make available to marketing firms information from the credit application and from bank reports about the individual (such as bank balance and repayment of loans).

A Harris poll reports that 79 percent of the public approve the idea of adding privacy to the fundamental rights of life, liberty, and the pursuit of happiness.[55] But that is only the starting point in an understanding of the feelings of the public. Fifty-four percent admit that they have bought something direct during the past year. But when it came to firms from whom they've ordered selling demographics about them, 69 percent said this is bad. Eighty-six percent are either concerned or very concerned.

However, when told that the seller's product was being aimed at the buyer's interests and budget, 67 percent found the practice acceptable. Seventy-five percent approved if personal and financial information is not passed on to other firms. A solid 88 percent voted acceptability when offered the option of excluding their names from the list.

There are pros and cons. On the privacy side, there is the issue of whether *anyone* has the right to turn over such personal information as finances to a business firm—especially when the information may be used, in a sense, against consumers—to expose them to unwanted telephone solicitations and junk mail, for instance. There is also the vague fear seldom expressed, that this might be a means of putting together dossiers on most of us, perhaps to be used by big government or some other ominous entity.

The issue is serious enough to be considered by Congress. In June 1990, a House subcommittee was considering revisions to the Fair Credit Reporting Act.[56] As of mid-1990, congressional action seemed a distinct possibility.

Two extremes of control were expressed by committee members. On the mild side, credit-reporting bureaus should be able to release records only if the consumer has a chance to bar such action. On the strong side, the records could be provided only for transactions initiated by consumers (use for direct-mail marketing and offering of pre-approved lines of credit would be prohibited). But no congressional action took place.

Some appealing arguments have been made by those favoring free exchange of such information. The exchange of financial information about consumers offers them some major advantages. One is (through the use of lists by marketing firms) learning about new products that they would otherwise never know about. Another is being offered inducements to purchase (coupons, for instance). And while not of major interest to our marketing students, perhaps, there may also be the consumer advantage of quick availability of credit.

Is there a good answer? We think so. But it is a program rather than an answer. The best approach may be to listen to Martin Abrams, director of consumer affairs and policy analysis, TRW Information Systems and Services.[57] Abrams suggests, first, that consumers should have the right to opt out of the program. When a person applies for credit (and we would add when a person fills in *any* sort of an order or request for information), he or she should be told of the clear right to specify that his or her name is not to be passed on to others for use in marketing goods and services.

Second, the firms with public databases (databases available for use by others, as opposed to databases built by firms for their own marketing use, such as Coors) should have their own rigorous principles. On-line services (names and addresses, with highly specific information about individuals or families) should be provided only for highly legitimate purposes, such as a granter of credit or an employer—something that can be specifically defined by law. Firms with public databases should make these available only in batch mode, so that the marketer gets only name and address and only for one-time use.

Abrams argues that if consumer privacy is protected, the database availability can only benefit consumers. It provides an opportunity to window-shop from the home, to visit the international shopping place without spending money for travel, to buy without stepping across the threshold. If an individual has a chronic illness, it may be a lot easier to buy pharmaceuticals less expensively by mail than to have them delivered by the local drugstore. But if the consumer's privacy is not protected, that same list may be sold to a life insurance company that may use the information to weed out those with specific ailments to solicit only the safer risks; in that case, the consumer's interests are damaged. That is unfair use of privileged information.

However, things are beginning to happen. Marketplace: Households, a database scheduled for release in March 1991, was withdrawn. This was a software program that would have provided data about 80 million Americans, including information about marital status, estimated income, and classifications such as "cautious young couples," "conservative seniors," and "accumulated wealth." The partners in the venture—Lotus Development Corp. and Equifax—could not face the concerns raised by consumers across the country, according to a company spokesman.[58] Marketplace: Business had also been withdrawn. This program, offered in October 1990, provided database material on 7 million businesses.[59]

Little wonder. Lotus had received 30,000 complaints within a short period. There was also a threat to boycott Lotus 1-2-3, the company's basic product.

New England Telephone & Telegraph Co. dropped plans to market a database of its 4.7 million customers, including names, addresses, and telephone numbers. A company spokesman explained that New York Telephone Co., a partner in the plan, had withdrawn, and that New England felt it was not feasible to go on alone. But there is some suspicion that it may have been the 400,000 who asked to be dropped from the database.

The matter of possible congressional action was again in the forefront in 1991, though both industry and congressional sources seem to agree that chances of any action during this year were infinitesimal.[60] No hearings were scheduled in early 1991 (though they are expected later) to consider a bill to create the Data Protection Board. The proposed board would be a watchdog lacking enforcement authority, so those firms in this form of database marketing are far less fearful than they were of the proposed 1990 bill.

There are pressures to have some sort of a bill. One of these is the increased expression of consumer concern, indicated by such events as the Lotus withdrawal.

Another pressure is the possibility of making it difficult for U.S. firms to transmit personal database material to the European Community. In 1992 the European Community becomes a virtual economic whole, and several of the member nations already have tough privacy laws. If a directive is issued by the European Community, it could hinder U.S. businesses in transferring personal data to and from Europe.

Although Congress did not act in 1991, it appears that some sort of privacy law is soon to be a reality in the United States.

INCREASE IN POSTAL RATES

In early 1991, significantly higher postal rates were introduced. Rates were increased 25 percent for promotional mailings, meaning that direct marketing began to be seriously reviewed by its users. At least two major results are predictable. First, the move from the old, blindly handled direct mail where straight mailing lists were used will increasingly shift to the kind of customer/prospect database marketing described in this chapter. Second, there will be increasing use of auxiliary media (such as television an cable) using toll-free telephone numbers to get names and addresses of prospective customers.[61]

ENDNOTES   [1]*1986 Annual Report, Epsilon.* Burlington, Mass.: Epsilon.

[2]*Frequency Marketing, Inc.* Milford, Ohio: Frequency Marketing, 1989.

[3]Leonard Sloane. "Electronic 'Coupons': Savings but No Scissors." *New York Times*, Apr. 21, 1990, 16.

[4]Catha Cowgill. "The Travel Market Wakes Up." *DM News*, May 15, 1989, 61.

[5]R. D. Barlow, president, Frequency Marketing. Interview.

[6]L. H. Towle. "What's New in Frequency Marketing." *New York Times*, Dec. 3, 1989.

[7]Joshua Levine. "Stealing the Right Shopper." *Forbes*, July 10, 1989, 104–105.

[8]Phyllis Feinberg. "The Seagram Database: Liquor Sells Quicker." *Database Marketing* 1, no. 1 (June 1990):15–17.

[9]Thomas Exter. "Advertising and Promotion: The One-Two Punch." *American Demographics*, March 1990, 18–21.

[10]Shepard (David) Associates. *The New Direct Marketing: How to Implement a Profit-Driven Database Marketing Strategy*. Homewood, Ill.: Dow Jones-Irwin, 1990.

[11]Julie Liesse and Ira Teinowitz. "Data Bases Uncover Brands' Biggest Fans." *Advertising Age*, Feb. 19, 1990, 3 f.

[12]Joe Schwartz. "Databases Deliver the Goods." *American Demographics*, September 1989, 23–24.

[13]Julie Liesse. "KGF Taps Data Base to Target Consumers." *Advertising Age*, Oct. 8, 1990, 3 f.

[14]Julie Liesse and Ira Teinowitz. "Data Bases Uncover Brands' Biggest Fans." *Advertising Age*, Feb. 19, 1990, 3 f.

[15]Bill Bernardo (Hormel). Letter, Mar. 9, 1990.

[16]Don Marable (Coors). Interview and correspondence.

[17]*Epsilon, The Database Marketing Company*. Burlington, Mass.: Epsilon, undated.

[18]*1985 Annual Report, Epsilon*. Burlington, Mass.: Epsilon.

[19]Renee McGaw. "Pizza Hut's Plan." *News-Journal*, Nov. 17, 1990, Section B, 5.

[20]"Electronic Marketing Set to Take Off in 1990s." *Supermarket News*, 1989, Oct. 9, 33.

[21]R. C. Blattberg. *Retailers and Scanning: What They Don't Know and What That Means for Marketing*. American Marketing Association, Sales Promotion Conference, June 7, 1989.

[22]Jan Larson. "Farewell to Coupons?" *American Demographics*, February 1990, 18.

[23]Thomas Exter. "Advertising and Promotion: The One-Two Punch." *American Demographics*, March 1990, 18–21.

[24]Gerald McMahon. "Grocers Need Shopper Data Base to Build Strong Relationships." *Marketing News*, Mar. 19, 1990, 26 f.

[25]Alison Fahey and Bradley Johnson. "Frequent Shopper Programs Ripen." *Advertising Age*, Aug. 6, 1990, 21.

[26]Edwin McDowell. "Waldenbooks to Begin Challenging Book Clubs." *New York Times*, Feb. 27, 1990, C17.

[27]"Perils of the Paper Clip Trade." *New York Times Magazine*, Part 2, June 11, 1989.

[28]Joe Schwartz. "Databases Deliver the Goods." *American Demographics*, 1989, September, 24.

[29]Gloria Savini. "24-Karat Database." *Direct Marketing*, March 1989, 36 f.

[30]Janet Meyers. "Papers Study Data-base Marketing." *Advertising Age*, Nov. 5, 1990, 60.

[31]Joseph Rydholm. "Trade Talk." *Quirk's Marketing Research Review*, October 1990, 36 f.

[32]Stan Rapp and T. L. Collins. *MaxiMarketing*. New York: McGraw-Hill, 1987, 49.

[33]*Source: TRW*. Orange, Calif.: TRW Target Marketing Services, 1990.

[34]*NDL Marketing Data Fits America Like a Glove*. Denver: National Demographics & Lifestyles, undated.

[35]*OASYS*. Denver: National Demographics & Lifestyles, 1988.

[36]*We Just Perfected the Most Phenomenal Interactive Communications System in the World*. Omaha: Call Interactive, 1989.

[37]*Select & Save—Mass Targeted Couponing*. New York: Computerized Marketing Technologies, undated.

[38]Roberta Reynes. "Data-Basics." *Promote*, Apr. 11, 1988, 14.

[39]*Breakthrough Technology for Magazine Advertising in the 1990s*. New York: Time Inc. Magazines, undated.

[40]"MCI: A Successful Break with Tradition." *Epsilon Marketing Letter* 2, no. 2 (1983): 6.

[41]*The Target Chek* (series of pamphlets). Libertyville, Ill.: Moore Response Marketing Services, undated.

[42]Betsy Wade. "Instead of Flights, Gifts or Money for Frequent Fliers." *New York Times*, Dec. 16, 1990, 3.

[43]Christopher Geiger. "Management Reports: Unlocking Your Database." *Epsilon Marketing Letter* 2, no. 2, 7–8.

[44]Grace Conlon. "Data-Driven Marketing." *Marketing Communications*, October 1987, 40.

[45]*Database Marketing Services*. Stamford: Citicorp POS Information Services, undated.

[46]Raymond Roel. "Citicorp Goes to the Supermarket." *Database Marketing* 2, no. 1 (June 1990): 11–14.

[47]Michael Freitag. "In This Computer Age, Who Needs Coupons?" *New York Times*, June 15, 1989, 1.

[48]Jack Honomichl. *Inside Research*. December 1990, 2.

[49]*VISION 1000—The Total Production Delivery Vehicle*. Deerfield Beach, Fla.: Advanced Promotion Technologies, undated.

[50]*Don't Think About Database Marketing Until You Can Test It*. Dallas: M/A/R/C, undated.

[51]*Direct Marketing's Greatest Hits*. Waltham, Mass.: SmartNames, undated.

[52]M. J. Weiss. *The Clustering of America*. New York: Harper & Row, 1988.

[53]P. H. Lewis. "Privacy: The Tip of the Iceberg." *New York Times*, Oct. 2, 1990, B7.

[54]James Kilpatrick. *A Conservative View*. July 20, 1990.

[55]"Consumer Privacy Concerns on the Rise." *Direct Marketing*, August 1998, 1 f.

[56]"Credit Privacy Law Too Lax, Legislators Say." *News-Journal* (Daytona Beach, Fla.), June 13, 1990, 3A.

[57]Martin Abrams, director of consumer affairs and policy analysis, TRW Information Systems and Services. Interview, May 20, 1990.

[58]"Software Firms Cancel Database after Privacy Invasion Complaints." *News-Journal*, Jan. 25, 1991, 12A.

[59]Alan Radding. "Consumer Worry Halts Data Bases." *Advertising Age*, Feb. 11, 1991, 28.

[60]S. W. Colford. "A Private Matter: Politicians Consider a Protection Board." *Advertising Age*, Feb. 11, 1991, 28.

[61]Kin Foltz. "Postal Rise May Cancel a Direct-Marketing Edge." *New York Times*, Feb. 19, 1991, C8.

REFERENCES

Rapp, Stan, and T. L. Collins. *MaxiMarketing*. New York: McGraw-Hill, 1987.

Shepard (David) Associates. *The New Direct Marketing*. Homewood, Ill.: Dow Jones-Irwin, 1990.

Stone, Robert. *Successful Direct Marketing Methods*. Lincolnwood, Ill.: NTC Business Books, 1989.

17

OTHER APPLICATIONS FOR MARKETING FIRMS

What's in This Chapter

In this chapter we look at how marketing research can be used by retailers and the service industry. We discuss some applications for specific product and service fields, such as automobiles, automotive-related products, computers, in-home foods, restaurant foods, health care, and health care services. Finally, in this chapter we start our discussion of media research, a topic that will be completed in Chapter 18.

Earlier chapters have reviewed many different kinds of research tools and approaches and have shown how each has been used in different applications. The same tools can be used in the various applications of research examined in this chapter. But most are useful only to the large firm that has the necessary funds to pay for them or that may get them from the home office.

Here are the major research tools we are talking about:

- Audits (some may be feasible for the small firm)

- Scanner results (even for the small firm if it has its own scanner installation)

- Use of invoices/shipments or electronic summaries of these

- Sales or shipments; the data from business firms rather than consumers: warehouses, pharmacies, physicians, hospitals

- Observation (shopper reports)

- Diary panels (recording of purchases, visits by salespeople, etc.)

- Focus groups

- Consumer surveys

- Personal-interview studies

- Self-administered pickup questionnaires

- Secondary research: use of available statistics, as in location and market potential studies

Many of the sophisticated tools reviewed in this chapter are syndicated or standard service offerings, meaning they are mostly for the manufacturer. But some are also offered to retailers and providers of services. A few are for chain stores and chain service firms; only a very few are for the smaller retailer or service firm wanting to do a straightforward, unsophisticated, but sound study.[1]

There are four main sections of this chapter. One discusses studies that are generally applicable to *any* retail or service business. The second considers studies applicable to retailers alone. The third reviews specialty areas of product and service research, and the final section examines media research.

STUDIES GENERALLY APPLICABLE TO ANY RETAIL OR SERVICE BUSINESS

Here we outline aspects of marketing research such as customer nature, market potential, location studies, and effectiveness of service delivery.

CUSTOMER NATURE

A study of the nature of customers is a statistical description of customers in terms of demographics, psychographics, or shopping habits.

The survey is the usual tool, although there is also the possibility of psychographic or other overlays on the data through the purchase of data-bank material from outside sources.

One such source is CCM,[2] Credit Cardholder Marketing information database. This is for the use of consumer-oriented marketing firms (retailers and service firms) having a sufficiently broad consumer base to warrant knowing a lot more about their actual and potential credit card customers. It is not for the small business.

With this database, the firm can combine bank and retail credit card information with consumer life-style characteristics (see Vision, described in Chapter 15) and a profitability index about credit cardholders. The financial data come from Equifax, the parent firm, one of the largest consumer credit firms in the United States. But these are not data on individuals; they are aggregates (call them averages, if you will) that maintain the privacy of individuals.

The information can be analyzed either by geographics or customer profiles. At the geographics level, breaks such as ZIP codes, county and larger groupings are possible. By customer profiles, it is possible to analyze market segments among new holders of credit accounts, those with high credit limits, those with high credit balances, or categories of the firm's own databases.

With Infomark,[3] the basic information system available from Equifax, it is possible to generate reports, graphs, bar charts, and maps for visual analysis.

MARKET POTENTIAL

There are several offerings of existing databanks—secondary data—that provide a measurement of market potential. On the consumer goods side is Compass Retail Sales Potential.[4] This database offers retail potential estimates of consumer spending by store type. The categories include apparel; footwear; major appliances; furniture; radio, television and musical instruments; jewelry and accessories; nonprescription drugs; personal care products; household textiles; housewares and small appliances; photographic equipment and supplies; stationery and greeting cards; books, magazines, and newspapers; prescription drugs; packaged alcoholic beverages; housekeeping supplies; tobacco products; toys; sporting equipment; hardware; paint and wallpaper; lumber and building materials; lawn and garden supplies; food in restaurants; flooring; groceries; and the auto aftermarket.

As with other Compass data, the estimates are available from the national level to the ZIP code level and are updated annually.

The information can be used for the development of sales and marketing areas, for site location, and for target marketing.

Donnelley offers a similar measurement in its Demographics On-Call[5], which provides the current year's potential sales volume for 21 types of retail store.

Donnelley also offers BusinessLINE, a detailed and summary count of business and commercial data by SIC codes. While this is mainly a resource for firms selling business goods and services, it also has implications for some sellers of consumer goods as well.

LOCATION STUDIES

These studies are usually done by or for large retail chains, but they are also done for many service firms and firms marketing to business. Generally, the major inputs are demographics (of the surrounding area or customers) and traffic patterns. We spend little time here on traffic patterns; the local government may be able to provide information in this area. If not, it is simple enough to set up a pattern of counting at key points and to record these counts by days and hours that the business plans to be open.

The data used to evaluate sites, in addition to traffic counts, are almost all secondary information in the form of databanks.

One such databank is the Compass Daytime Business Population,[6] which provides information about the number of employees (by type of work), businesses (and their nature), and payrolls. The data are available geographically from the national level to the ZIP code level. Some of the applications include site location (particularly for those retailers and service firms wishing to cater to the employee market, such as restaurants), business-to-business marketing, and demand estimates.

Another databank providing statistical data about businesses is one offered by National Decision Systems.[7] Its business facts base provides the number of business firms by types (SIC codes), total employment, and the ratio of employees to business. Also available are each firm's name, address, number of employees, and whether the address is a headquarters, a branch, or the single location. These data are available for any selected market area, such as a county, a radius around a site, or a ZIP code.

Dayton-Hudson, a diversified national retailer[8] manages chains of four different types: Dayton-Hudson fashion department stores, Target upscale discount fashion stores, Mervyn's family department stores, and Lechmere's, promotional hard lines. The parent firm makes preliminary store location decisions through use of desktop computers. It determines its own existing store traffic demographics annually. Then the demographics of possible new sites are compared with those for existing sites to get an idea of how well the new site will perform.

Mapping of Potential Sites

Mapping can make statistics easily understandable and contribute to the decision-making process. Plotting may be based on simple counts, on density by demographics, or on density by psychographics. Geographics may vary from census regions down to ZIP codes or the firm's own trading area. The 1990 census, through TIGER, will make the details of maps more accurate and more specific than ever before. Geographic mapping has been thoroughly discussed in Chapter 14.

With the assistance of Urban Decision Systems, we provide here a hypothetical example based on real locations and statistics.

A retail chain of products for home gourmet cooking is considering two different locations in the Washington, D.C., area. One is approximately at the intersection of Old Dominion Drive and Old Chain Bridge Road (McLean, Va.), the other at 21st and M Streets (Washington).

Management of the chain knows that proper location is probably the greatest factor in success or failure. The household units in the surrounding area must be of the right mix if there is to be a market. With its background in this kind of retailing, the firm has developed a weighting scheme for four population variables as follows:

Variable	Weighting Factor
Proportion of family incomes of $50,000 and more	2
Proportion of household sizes of 2 and more persons	1
Proportion of white families	1
Weekly per capita spending on food of $19 or more	1

This weighting results in a scale of market potential varying from 0 to 5 for any area.

Chain management knows that while its primary market area is within one-half mile of its store, it also needs backup support from less frequent buyers living within two miles.

Exhibits 17.1 and 17.2 are density maps for the two areas, showing the density of prospective customers in terms of the total weightings. The maps clearly show the superiority of the McLean location. It is definitely superior to the Washington location within the smaller radius. When the larger radius is added, the McLean location quality holds up, while the Washington location drops further.

Exhibit 17.1   MARKET VALUE OF McLEAN LOCATION

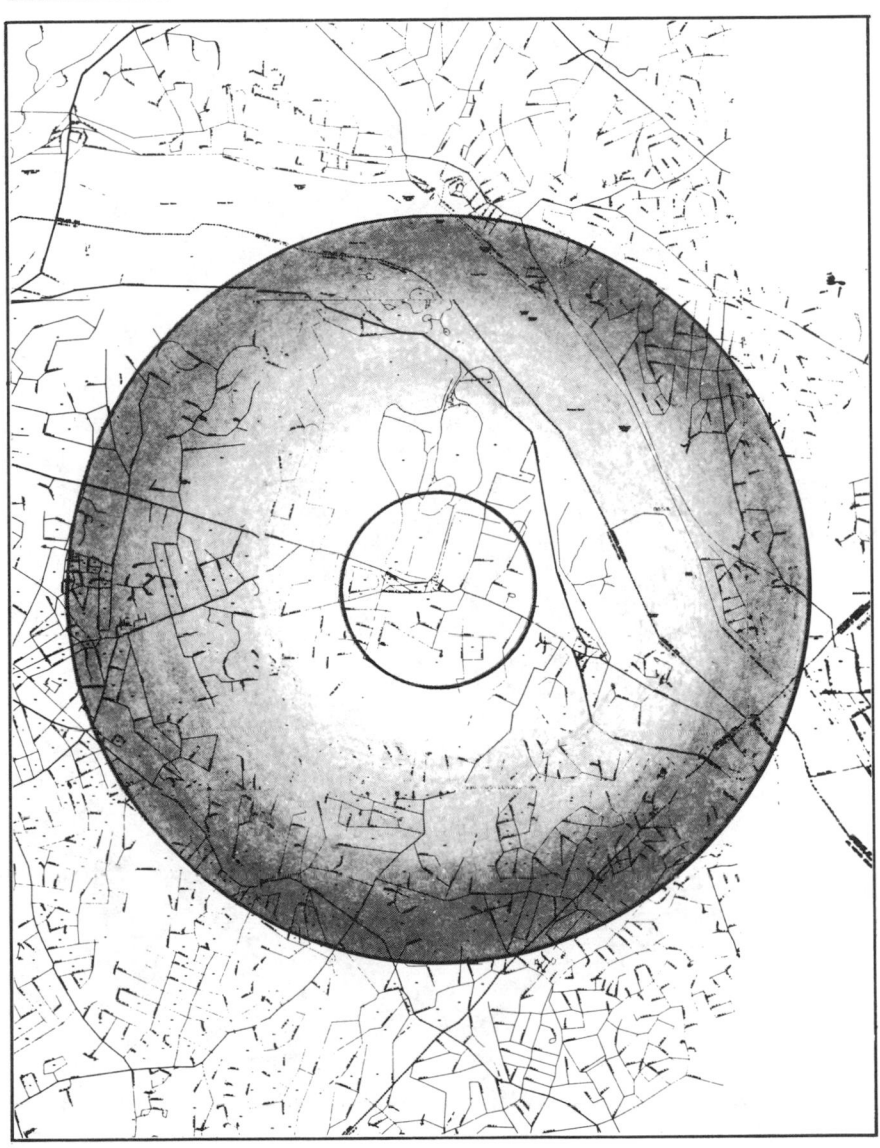

Source: Bureau of the Census.

- (4) Substantial density
- (3) Moderate density
- (2) Low density
- (0, 1) Little or no density

Exhibit 17.2   **MARKET VALUE OF 21ST & M STREETS LOCATION**

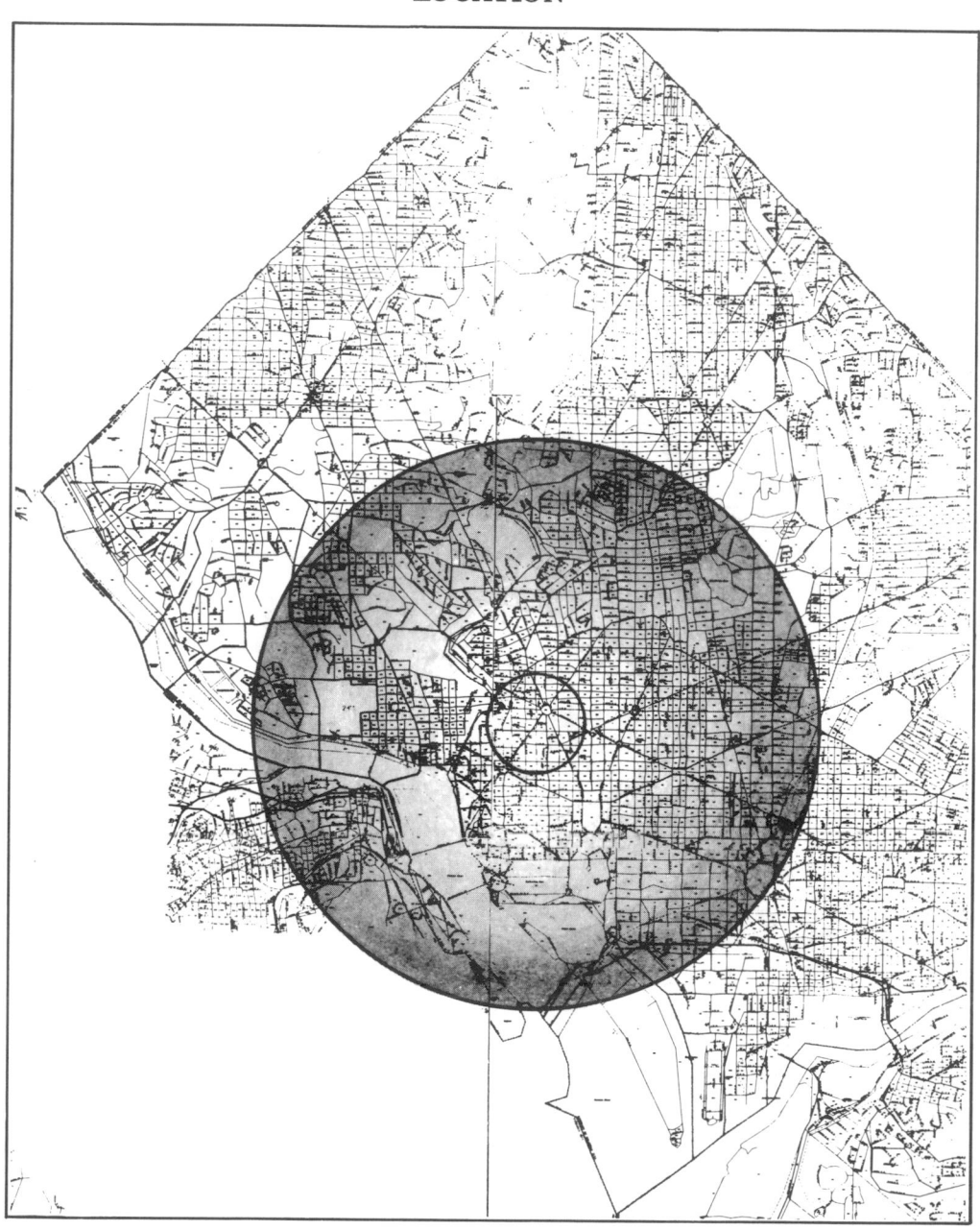

Source: Bureau of the Census.

EFFECTIVENESS OF SERVICE DELIVERY

This section considers shopping surveys; customized, full-scale studies of satisfaction with service delivery; and other studies of customer/client reaction.

Shopping Surveys

Shopping surveys are necessarily limited to retailing generally and to service marketing where there is a mingling of customers (hotels, motels, restaurants, and the like).

In the shopping survey, a fieldworker poses as a customer and, following a list of predefined steps, makes mental notes (later checking a list of specifics on a series of service or serviceperson's delivery of stated aspects). The shopper may simply note what aspects of delivery were or were not delivered, or he or she may note the quality or rating of delivery, adding explanatory notes.

This technique was first used over a half-century ago. In the middle 1930s, Elliott-Haynes, based in Montreal, then primarily in the credit-reporting business, was asked to do its first "service reporting," where an investigator posed as a customer and observed relationships with company employees in areas such as quality of service and personality.[9]

Major users of such surveys are retailers, such as tire dealers and service stations, fast-food outlets, hotels and motels. Here are some of the aspects typically covered (both for the firm and its major competition):

- Product or service quality
- Facility quality in various aspects
- Personnel courtesy
- Personnel efficiency
- Personnel service
- Personnel promotion of selected brands, items, features, benefits
- Items stocked, offered, on display
- Prices

Such studies are generally handled by an outside specialist firm. There are three reasons. First is impartiality: The outside firm has no ax to grind, one way or the other. Second is its skill. It can assist in constructing the points to be checked and determine how to check them.

Third, there is much less chance of the shopper's being detected by the employees, since it is most unlikely that any employee might know the individual. Of course, it is the user—the store or the service firm—that pays the charges for the outside firm.

One large marketing research firm, Elrick & Lavidge, specializes in shopping studies[10] in addition to its many other kinds of studies. The variety of projects on which they have shopped shows that the technique has many more applications than simply checking on service delivery. One project measured the degree to which employees were promoting features and benefits of telecommunications equipment. Another, conducted at tire dealerships, checked the extent to which employees were recommending specific brands of tires and accessories. In a third case, hamburgers were purchased in fast-food outlets to check employee performance and food quality.

The checks for one specialized shopper study, this one for hotels, included the following:

- At check-in, is the guest addressed by name? Is the term *sir* or *madame* used?

- Does the bellman place the luggage on a rack, making sure to hang up the flight bag? Does he offer information about the hotel and its services? Does he explain the amenities of the room?

- What is the bedroom condition at time of arrival? Is there dust on the window sills or television cabinet? How many hangers (wooden and padded) are there in the closet? Is there a Bible? Is there a functioning clock radio, television, blow-drier?

- Is the top sheet on the bed folded into a point to make it easy to turn down? A pencil mark is made on the sheets to check for changing.

- The bathroom is checked. Is there grime in the tub? Does the toilet tissue have a neat appearance? Are there adequate supplies of towels, washcloths, and toiletry items? The bathroom mirror is inconspicuously marked with soap, as the basis for a later check.

- The restaurant is visited for dinner. Is the table crumb-free? At dinner, does the waiter ask if something is wanted from the bar? The entrée is ordered first (to see whether the waiter will ask about appetizer and salad). Does the waiter inquire about wine?

- Honesty checks are made on bartenders and waiters, both of whom handle cash.

- How is message handling? Are messages delivered promptly and correctly?

- Room service is checked during the evening. Elapsed time from order to delivery is recorded. Correctness of delivered items is noted. Does the server use the guest's name? Is a chair moved to the table? After the server has left, a photo is taken of the tray as a check on presentation. Breakfast is ordered through room service, and again all of these same checks are made.

- A visit is made to the catering department (which basically serves business customers) to check on the ease and efficiency of discussing the booking of an anniversary party for 55 people. Services of the valet and use of the swimming pool and health club are also checked out.

To be effective, these checks should concentrate on what the *customer* thinks is important, and not *only* on what management thinks is important. There is evidence that management doesn't always know what the customer wants.[11] *The Wall Street Journal* conducted a survey among 403 adults in the United States who made 12 or more trips within previous 12 months. It learned that hotels should forget built-in bars and health clubs. Travelers are more interested in quiet rooms and daily newspaper delivery. Airlines should stress frequent-flier programs and provide more accurate information on delayed flights, better food, and wider seats, and they should forget on-flight telephones.

One of Marriott Corp.'s hotel chains is Courtyard by Marriott, segmented for travelers wanting moderately priced accommodations including high-quality rooms and such basic amenities as a restaurant, swimming pool, and exercise room.[12] During the development stage, before development of any architectural plans, thousands of business and vacation travelers were surveyed to determine their expectations and desires. One finding was that this market segment wanted a quiet residential environment where they could relax at the end of a busy business or travel day. Courtyard hotels are therefore limited in size (150 rooms) and are low-rise buildings somewhat similar in appearance to apartment complexes. There is a landscaped courtyard serving as the focal point for both the hotel and its rooms.

Room-design research showed that travelers wanted functionally designed rooms. So rooms were designed to have four functional areas—for working, relaxing, sleeping, and dressing. There is a large work desk, couch, coffee table, and king-sized bed. There is a dressing area outside the bathroom that includes a sink and full-length mirror.

Marriott conducts ongoing guest surveys, but since we have already talked about this kind of study, we will go on to another aspect of the Courtyard by Marriott research. Annual room decor is a continuing consideration. Furniture and decor styles constantly change. To keep current with what the market wants, Marriott fashions test rooms with varying decors and checks to determine which is most pleasing to its market.

Rental car firms should also forget in-transit phones. People are more interested in express check-in and clean cars and discounts than in computerized directions and accessories like power windows.

If needed, yet more proof is given by a survey of how frequent travelers rate hotel service, undertaken by Tim and Nina Zagat.[13] Over 4,000 frequent and professional travelers gave their opinions about some 850 business and vacation lodgings, including 17 chains in 38 cities. The major reasons for selecting a hotel were location, service, cleanliness, room quality, and price, in that order.

Location was the overwhelmingly important factor. But service, too, was important—ranging from "responsiveness at the front desk," to "getting my phone messages delivered on time." Room quality aspects that were of importance included size, location, view, furnishings, and charm.

Price, the fifth factor, was not that important. The accommodations were mainly paid for by companies, not individuals.

Two other items were in high demand: first-class restaurants and health clubs.

While *The Wall Street Journal* survey and the Zagat survey do not completely agree—they are samples of different kinds of people referring to different kinds of establishments—both suggest that service firms are not doing enough to find out what customers want. But there is a way to overcome this shortcoming: a customized, full-scale study of service satisfaction.

Customized, Full-Scale Studies of Service Satisfaction

Some marketing research firms are offering customized full-scale studies to provide measurement of customer reactions to the delivery of service. Since the general procedures, with two examples, have already been provided in Chapter 14, we will simply mention briefly one more service at this point: Service Satisfaction Measurement,[14] of Market Opinion Research, Detroit.

This continuing service is aimed at firms that have continuing and "formal" service satisfaction systems (where consumer reactions funnel in to a single central source, with records kept by name and telephone number). A day-after telephone interview with the customer measures reaction while the experience is still fresh in the customer's mind. Because of the day-after telephone feature, the service seems particularly applicable to utility, financial, and health care organizations.

Other Customer/Client Reaction Studies

Studies of customer/client reaction are often used by small-scale retailers or service firms as well as by the larger firms. They are typically do-it-yourself research projects. Done with care, they can be useful.

STUDIES APPLICABLE TO RETAILERS ALONE

We first discuss the several kinds of study applicable to almost any kind of retailer, then some specific services available to grocery retailers.

APPLICABLE TO ALMOST ANY RETAILER

Secondary Market Data

National Decisions Systems[15] offers comprehensive reports on the estimated dollars available for household spending for various products and services. The spending categories include:

- Restaurants (separate analyses for fast-food outlets, take-out chains, and independents, such as McDonald's, Taco Bell, and Wendy's; midscale (family-type) restaurants, such as Denny's and Ponderosa; and upscale, sit-down restaurants with full liquor service and typically higher-priced menu selections, such as Steak 'n Ale and Chart House)
- Financial services
- Apparel
- Footwear
- Department stores
- Auto aftermarket
- Jewelry
- Household furnishings
- Home improvement
- Sporting goods
- Toys
- Automotive services

Data are available for any size or shape market anywhere in the United States. Possible applications include strategic planning (national sales expansion strategy, quantification of high-potential marketing areas), merchandise planning (spotting of products and services with the greatest potential as a guide to choosing the best product mix), and site evaluation (quantifying the estimated demand at various proposed site levels as an aid in choosing a high-demand area, and analyzing the spending around existing sites to help identify those with the greatest growth opportunities).

Database Marketing

In Chapter 16 we discussed database marketing and how a firm goes about setting up its own database. While this applies mainly to large chain supermarkets, with a number of optional programs they can buy (see Chapter 16), such programs are limited neither to large retailers nor to grocery products.

You will remember the Stemberg example[16] in Chapter 16. Stemberg runs a discount "supermarket" chain for office supplies. Free customer memberships provide special discounts, and there are other benefits. For the chain, customer use of the membership card with purchases provides a means of checking individual buyer purchases in terms of dollar volume, frequency of buying, responsiveness to various sales promotion efforts (such as direct mail), and analysis of all this by demographics, type of business, company size, and ZIP code.

Such customer databases can be set up by any outlet having its own scanner system.

Combining Scanner Data at Store Level with Database Material

Market Metrics (Lancaster, Pa.) has a census-tract database encompassing some 500 different demographics for about 30,000 grocery stores across the country having $1 million or more all-commodity sales.[17] The firm also has descriptive information concerning each store's physical attributes.

The firm defines the trading area for each store through consideration of factors such as store size and reach, location of competitive stores, natural and man-made boundaries and barriers, and transportation routes.

The store scanner sales and promotion input and knowledge of the demographics (those related to store sales) of the trading area provide a way of measuring the effect of a demographic variable—perhaps house-hold income—on the velocity of sales of one or more brands within a par-ticular category. It also makes it possible for stores to analyze their mar-ket segments.

Wolfe[17] talks about the case of studying ready-to-eat cereals for a large West Coast retailer. One store type was found to have a predomi-nance of young families with a high proportion of children aged 6–17 years. Another type of store had a far greater concentration of older, empty-nest or retired households. The young-family stores showed high turnover of sweetened cereals, while the older-family stores had a pat-tern of high sales for brans and nutritional cereals.

APPLICABLE TO GROCERY RETAILERS

In Chapter 13 we described the national scanner services available for measurement of category and brand movement in supermarkets. How-ever, these were designed for and are sold primarily to manufacturers of food products and other products that move largely through supermar-kets. Only recently have the major suppliers of these services—Nielsen and Information Resources—turned their attention to tailoring their product to meet the needs of the larger chain supermarkets.

Tailoring National Scanner Data to Meet Chain Supermarket Needs

Pressures on the grocery chains are increasing. Profit margins are de-clining. Many new products are being introduced. Supplier promotions are at the same time more common and more complex. To keep up with what is happening, management needs more information to make in-formed judgments—information on both tactical and strategic aspects. Here are some of the specific topics that can be examined under each of the two aspects:

Tactical aspects
- Individual promotions
- Seasonal promotions
- The product mix
- New-product introductions
- Changes in price
- Market disruptions

Strategic aspects
- Stock management

- Shelf management
- Vendor performance
- Trends in categories, market share
- Pricing patterns
- Merchandising choices
- Advertising planning

Nielsen ScanTrack Reports for Retailers[18]

Nielsen offers hard-copy results from the major markets* in its national ScanTrack reports. The data, depending on needs of the users, can cover every item passed over the scanner at the checkout counter, with total item and category information available: DSD, drop shipments, transfers, and rack jobber placements. Data are available on a four-week basis updated weekly for tactical uses, or they are accumulated over longer time periods for use in strategic analysis and planning.

Electronic data access and/or tape delivery is offered optionally to give the users an opportunity to make their own analyses.

DataServer for Retailers

Operated at the retailer's office, this IRI program[19] is available to merchandising and marketing executives. It can use InfoScan data alone or combined with the user's own internal scanner, cost, warehouse, or DPP data. The program is accessed by a PC and can be utilized either through a mainframe on the user's premises to store the databank or on-line to IRI's own databank.

There are some built-in applications, but the user can also ask questions that will show, for instance, whether promotions are really paying off, how market share can be maintained, whether the right products are being stocked, or whether competition is ahead in introducing new items.

---

*The Eastern Region includes Albany, Baltimore, Boston, Hartford, New York City, Philadelphia, Syracuse, Washington; the Southeastern Region includes Atlanta, Birmingham, Charlotte, Dallas, Houston, Jacksonville, Miami, New Orleans, Orlando, Raleigh/Durham, Richmond, San Antonio, Tampa; the Midwestern Region includes Buffalo/Rochester, Cincinnati, Cleveland, Columbus, Detroit, Grand Rapids, Indianapolis, Louisville, Nashville, Pittsburgh; the West Central Region includes Chicago, Des Moines, Kansas City, Little Rock, Memphis, Milwaukee, Minneapolis, Oklahoma City, Omaha, St. Louis; and the Western Region includes Denver, Los Angeles, Phoenix, Portland, Sacramento, Salt Lake City, San Diego, San Francisco, Seattle.

FasTrac for Supermarket Buyers

Although designed primarily for the company *selling* a new product, FasTrac (Information Resources)[20] can also provide the supermarket buyer with the facts to make an intelligent business decision from the supermarket viewpoint, rather from the viewpoint of the brand. It provides information on what a new product will contribute to the bottom line and on how much the product adds to category sales, showing what happens in the buyer's own stores, not just in general.

InfoScan Supermarket Review

This retailer-aimed program from Information Resources[21] provides a summary of over 20,000 national and regional brands in almost 200 product categories of store-scanned sales. The quarterly reports (with an annual summary) cover total U.S. and major metro markets. Organized into eight store departments, the Review provides information on distribution, pricing, in-store merchandising, and volumetric data.

The retailing enterprise that participates in IRI's Retail Support program, described below, uses the Supermarket Review to track its performance and that of its vendors.

InfoScan Retail Support

Under this program,[21] IRI personnel work closely with representatives from retailers in all major U.S. markets. Merchandisers can use InfoScan data to tackle key business aspects such as promotion planning, category analysis, and maintenance of market share.

SPECIALTY AREAS OF PRODUCT AND SERVICE RESEARCH

There are several specialty areas that we consider: automobiles, automotive-related products, computers, in-home foods, restaurant foods, health care, and health care services.

AUTOMOBILES

In Chapter 13 we discussed the sales measurements available for automobiles. Because of the importance of this industry, there are also many types of specialized research available. They pretty much follow the patterns of research already established in this book.

Two major research firms specialize in the automotive field: R. L. Polk & Co. (Detroit) and J. D. Power and Associates (Agoura Hills, Calif.).

Akin to Test Marketing

No, there really is no test marketing, since one cannot test-market a car. But it *is* possible to measure *reactions of early buyers,* and that is just what the Power Early Buyer studies do.[22] They provide early feedback about new-model introductions and give manufacturer and dealer a chance to see promotional aspects that might be improved. These studies cover buyer loyalty, source of sales, price segmentation, demographic segmentation, and the shopping process.

Driver image is an important sales aspect, and the Power studies[23] show it. BMW is perceived as handled by a driver who is single, an up-and-coming executive, and aggressive. Jaguar drivers are seen as people who can afford to be self-indulgent, and BMW and Mercedes-Benz drivers are close behind. Oldsmobile and Alfa Romeo drivers lost many points in this area.

The Power Initial Quality Survey[24] is another measurement among early buyers. In one such study, made within the first 90 days of ownership, it was found that the upper-middle segment of cars was the most trouble-free, and within this segment the top five were Nissan Maxima, Toyota Cresida, Mazda 929, Chevrolet Celebrity, and Oldsmobile Ciera.

Reactions of *prospects of a particular class of car* make a competitive evaluation through the *product clinic,*[25] a test procedure used by all major U.S. automakers. As you will soon see, this is nothing more than a specialized form of the consumer product test (described in Chapter 14). Our example includes a product each from Chrysler, General Motors, Ford, and Honda.

Four maroon-colored new cars are scattered around a huge room in a hotel north of Manhattan. Represented are a Chrysler Acclaim, a Chevrolet Corsica, a Ford Tempo, and a Honda Accord, all of similar body design.

Participants in the product clinic are carefully screened by mail to ensure that they are prospects for the kind of car on which the study is made (in this case it was Chrysler's Acclaim, though the "guests" are not told this for fear it might prejudice their replies). A Chrysler clinic runs for up to 10 days to obtain between 100 and 150 participants.

The respondent is first asked to walk around the display space and reply to questions about such things as exterior and interior appearance, ease of entry, driving position, and comfort. This is followed by a driving test. While driving each of four similar cars, the guest is asked questions (by the accompanying guide) about acceleration, visibility, smoothness, and handling. The makes are rotated for equal average position in the testing, since "drivers tend to be tougher in evaluating the early cars and more generous as the day goes by."

There is a one-on-one personal and private interview with each respondent following the driving test. By the time this is finished, each person will have been asked some 1,000 questions.

Then comes a focus group interview, led by a skilled moderator. Probing questions about various characteristics of the test car stimulate group discussion. Members of the focus group mention lack of performance, amount of steering effort required, and road noise. These complaints pretty much mirror findings of the preceeding year. The lack of performance criticism really means that it requires too much pressure on the accelerator to get action, not that the car lacks quickness. The steering is modified to require a lighter touch. More insulation in the floor panels cut down on the noise.

Market Analysis

Polk provides data on the nature of *total* vehicles in operation (not just buyers of new cars). An annual report (as of July 1) shows the number of vehicles in operation by make and model year.[26] This is provided by county and by other breaks as required.

Auto dealers can gauge their mix of parts and volume of inventory. A sudden and dramatic sales drop pushes up inventory of cars and parts on hand.

From its Early Buyer studies,[22] Power provides demographics of buyers. Exhibit 17.3 shows, for example, the considerably higher economic and educational level of the Mercedes-Benz buyer versus the field, and indicates that the Mercedes purchaser is far more often male, married, and from a smaller household.

Exhibit 17.3   SELECTED DEMOGRAPHICS OF MERCEDES-BENZ BUYERS VS. INDUSTRY

	Mercedes-Benz	Industry
Median household income	$138,000	$43,120
Median age	49	43
Married	81%	65%
College graduate or more	63%	40%
Male	72%	58%
Median household size	2.00	2.87

Polk also offers a custom analysis by area, through its proprietary household AutoMIS,[27] which provides information such as:

- Vehicle description, automotive characteristics
- Demographics (sex and occupation of householder, age of oldest member of the household, estimated family income, number of persons in the household, number of adults in the household, presence of an adult female in the household, number of employed persons in the household, number of drivers in the household, length of residence)
- Life-styles (for subscribers to these services), geodemographic cluster coding such as PRIZM and Vision . . . housing (type of dwelling unit)
- Neighborhood data (median family income, median age, median school years completed by household head, percentage of professional/technical/managerial workers in the labor force, percentage of households with children, percentage of home ownership, percentage of single family dwelling units, median home value, percentage of auto ownership, percentage of move-ins within five years)

Since state privacy laws prohibit supplying names and addresses, the data are simply numerical summaries. Quarterly data are reported, and while the number in a quarterly summary will vary depending on sales, it typically runs about 1 million for cars and a half-million for trucks.

Because of these numbers, small areas can be examined with considerable confidence for making marketing decisions. The data, available through magnetic tape, can be used for such applications as product planning, marketing evaluation, advertising strategy, and marketing strategy.

Reactions to Automotive Advertising[28]

The single-make auto dealer is disappearing. The multiple-franchise dealer broadens the consumer choice and downplays dealer loyalty to the manufacturer. Women are major factors in car-purchasing choices. Imports are increasing. The appeal of utility vehicles (light trucks, compact pickups, jeeps, campers, and vans) has spiraled among the younger set, and the larger four-door, more luxurious cars have been in increasing demand with the aging of America.

So it is not surprising that life-style advertising—soft sell—does better than product advertising. Life-style advertising approaches the prospect with an appeal to personal style. Product advertising shows and talks performance. The life-style approach, McCollum/Spielman tells us, gets more attention. And it tends to be just as persuasive as the hard sell.

Dealer Attitude Survey

Undertaken by Power, the Dealer Attitude Survey[29] shows that dealers owning a particular franchise generally are more favorable to it than those not owning. Honda ends up with the top rating, with Yugo at the bottom. After a franchise appears successful to some 55 percent of its own dealers, dealers without the franchise usually start thinking of it as desirable.

Automobile Advertising Media

The Power Car and Truck Media Reports[30] are national surveys of drivers of new vehicles. There are separate studies each for cars and trucks; for simplicity, we consider only the automobile study.

This national mail study included 32,000 principal drivers of recently purchased new cars, covering eight car segments: basic small, lower middle, upper middle, sporty sedan, sports car, middle specialty, basic large, and luxury. The mailings covered 12 months of registrations (May 1988 through April 1989) and were sent to the field in two waves, each over a 3-month period. The response rate was 51 percent.

The questionnaire was extensive. It included:

Media exposure
- National magazines, newspapers (including supplements)
- TV viewing by day part (hours and minutes viewed yesterday)
- Cable network viewing (hours and minutes viewed yesterday)
- Radio listening by format

Marketing information
- Make/model
- Characteristics
- Delivery date
- Price
- Second-choice make
- Others seriously considered (up to three)
- Principal driver as decision-influencer
- Etc.

Life-style
- Twenty-eight categories of recreational activities attended, watched on TV, listened to on radio
- Participation in 34 categories of sports and other recreation activities
- VCR ownership and use

Demographics
- Eleven categories for principal driver
- Seven categories for households

The analyses are based on what *new car buyers* are doing mediawise and what they are like in life-style and demographics.

People with different tastes in cars have different tastes in media—scarcely a surprise. But the results make it possible to select media more effectively to reach the particular target audience.

Minority groups (blacks, Asians, Hispanics) tend to have less purchasing power, are younger, have larger families, and buy less-expensive cars. So it is scarcely surprising to find most of them buying basic small cars.

Among families with one or more members under the age of 18, the households are younger and less affluent. Where there is a child under 5, purchases are concentrated in the small, lower middle, and upper middle sizes. Where there are teenagers in the household (driving or pre-driving), the sportier cars, particularly the domestics, rise; these include the small sporty car, domestic sports car, and middle specialty car segments.

Single-person households go for small sporty imports, sports cars, and imports generally, while two-person households favor basic large and luxury cars, accounting for about half the sales in those two groups.

AUTOMOTIVE-RELATED PRODUCTS

American motorists spend more than $150 billion yearly to keep their cars and light trucks operating.[31] Repairs and service are done mainly at the dealership. Oil changes are chiefly bought at fast-service franchises. More than 80 percent of gasoline is purchaser-pumped. These and other automotive service purchases are measured by NPD Tracking Services.[32]

The larger auto companies conduct broad studies that indicate the ways in which particular dealerships are doing a good job or a poor one, and typically they tell the particular dealer. These studies are most often monthly consumer surveys, with monthly reporting.

The individual dealer can undertake his or her own survey on customer reaction to car servicing.[1] A suggested approach calls for telephone checks with customers within a couple of days following delivery of the serviced car to the customer, with perhaps a total of about 25 calls weekly, on a continuing basis.

Ratings can be obtained about the system of making appointments, promptness of attention to the appointment time, the courtesy and efficiency of the receiving person, the explanation of the repair procedure, accuracy of the repair cost estimate, delivery of the car on schedule, the reasonableness of the charges, quality of the service performed, interior cleanliness of the car on delivery, customer waiting facilities, courtesy and efficiency of the delivery person, the payment procedure, and the courtesy and efficiency of the cashier. For lower-than-average ratings, the customer is asked why the rating was so low. Following all these list-rating questions, a catch-all question is asked, such as "Do you have any (other) ideas on how we might improve our handling of service customers?"

Weekly, monthly, and annual summaries are made. The weekly and monthly figures are monitoring data to observe changes with time. The annual summary provides indications of improvement goals and shows where the dealer is doing well.

COMPUTERS

There are several methods of tracking retail trends for the computer market.

The National Computer Product Audit (Audits & Surveys) measures sales (in both units and dollars), inventories, brand and item shares, and distribution; it covers major chains and independents.[33] A parallel audit service, also described briefly above, is offered by NPD[32] and covers computer specialty stores. It offers retail audit data (manual and POS) of selected consumer electronic products sold through major department stores, discount houses, electronic mass merchandisers, and independent specialty retailers.

The IMS Sales & Inventory Report[34] reports monthly purchase and customer invoices and inventory records obtained from a panel of 400 chain and independent computer specialty stores (microcomputers, printers, software). The report provides tracking of a manufacturer's own sales and that of the competition. It is possible to identify customer buying patterns, retail sales units and dollars, brand shares, inventory levels, and the like.

A third service is the IMS Retail Distribution Report,[35] which monitors the initial stocking and repurchase of products, the percentage of dealers buying, and the average number bought. Possible applications include measurement of dealer penetration of client and competitive brands and speed of movement through the dealers' hands.

The IMS National Computer Retail Report,[36] samples over 500 retail stores, and its topics cover over 10,000 computer products. Data are collected monthly. Retail sales are measured through customer invoices. The service monitors product performance relative to competition, industry trends, brand shares, and brand/model sales in dollars and units.

IMSight is an on-line system providing access to the data in the three major IMS services: the National Computer Retail Report, NCR Regional Report, and Sales and Inventory Report. It makes it possible for marketing researchers or user firms with their own PCs to work from the database and make their own analyses and construct their own tables.

IN-HOME FOODS

Food at home has changed radically over the past two decades.[37] Working women—and now most households include a working woman—don't care to put a lot of time into food preparation. The Good Housekeeping Institute says that most women object to spending more than a half-hour preparing a meal. They are likely to buy foods requiring 20 minutes or less to prepare. Many do not want to use more than two pots for a meal, and they like microwave trays and boil-in bags. Pillsbury removed from a canned-corn label the instructions to put the contents into a pan and then heat it. The company received so many calls from consumers on how to proceed that the directions were replaced.

Most serious cooking occurs on weekends and special occasions. During the week, frozen dinners and take-out food, as well as restaurant eating, is more common. It is likely that each household member eats something different. The children may have canned spaghetti or hot dogs. Mom may have a salad and Dad a frozen dinner. NPD reports that pie, cake, and cookie baking has fallen dramatically. Only one-third of all chicken à-la-king served at home is made at home. It is the elderly who are the main at-home eaters.[38] They are the fastest-growing group using microwave ovens.

The NPD Group's National Eating Trends reports annually the foods and beverages prepared or consumed at home.[39] Measurements include end dishes (such as spaghetti) and ingredients (such as tomato paste). Over 4,000 different foods and beverages are reported from 2,000 households. Product categories include beverages/liquids, breakfast main items, lunch/dinner main items, side dishes, desserts/snacks, additive ingredients, and miscellaneous. The results are available in many formats, depending on the needs of the user.

The households are part of NPD's purchase panel, described in Chapter 7. The sample is drawn to match family census data in terms of income, household size, age of female head, female employment, and race; among nonfamilies there is a balance of income, age of eater, and sex. Diaries are used to keep track of the eating and are kept for two weeks. The sample is evenly distributed throughout the year so that an average two weeks of behavior is reported. Of course, the method necessarily means that seasonal and holiday patterns are obscured.

RESTAURANT FOODS

If people aren't eating as often in the home as they used to, where do they go to eat? On a market share basis, weekend night out with the kids is at hamburger fast-food restaurants (26 percent), followed by pizza (17 percent) and moderate upscale restaurants (10 percent).[40] These measurements are reported by CREST (Consumer Reports on Eating Share Trends), another NPD service,[41] also built on the diary panel of households reporting quarterly. Over 400,000 restaurant meal/snack purchases are recorded annually, and the major information recorded includes check size, reach, visit frequency, party size, deal usage, meal period, and product mix. Analyses can be provided by demographics and segments (such as life cycle, nutritional attitudes, nutritional behavior, and Vision clusters).

Audits & Surveys' National Restaurant Market Index[42] covers commercial restaurants open to the public. Annually, in May, enumerators visit some 6,000 restaurants (projectable to all commercial restaurants in the United States). Information is obtained from the chef, manager, or owner and by observation. Topics covered include usage of specific foods and supplies, brands of products in the kitchen (brands in use, including product types and package sizes), estimates of quantities of foods served or used, meals served (breakfast, lunch, dinner), and a specified list of equipment on hand.

Analysis of the data is by the nature of service offered (counter, table, drive-in), type of restaurant (hotel/motel, fast-food, counterservice, table-service), and geography (census regions, up to six-client sales regions).

On a more limited geographic basis, Restaurant Research Associates offers FlexiTrack, a restaurant research firm located in Tustin, Calif.[43,44] Usage and attitudes are tracked quarterly by telephone in 25 markets. Proprietary questions can be inserted to secure greater in-depth information. Neil Naroff, marketing vice president of Marie Callender's, a chain of coffee shops/family-style restaurants in the Western United States, comments that the service provides a good means of knowing what is going on before it becomes a serious issue.

To measure customer reaction, many restaurants place questionnaires on the guests' tables, hoping that they will take the few minutes required to respond to the questionnaires and leave them on the tables or drop them into a box on the way out.[45] But this simple technique may not work well. Too few may respond, and those who do are often overresponders, overwhelmingly either negative or positive. So here is how CheckPlease (a service offered by a division of Kapuler) works.[46] Over a one- or two-week period, as guests arrive, the host or hostess hands them a card (not a questionnaire) before they are seated, asking them whether they would like to take part in a survey. As an inducement, they are offered a discount or even a free meal on the next visit, a free beverage or course on the next visit, or even gourmet candies for agreeing to be questioned later.

A random sample of those who agree is interviewed very soon afterward by telephone. The questioning can be far more detailed than that table-top questionnaire. A plus to the restaurant is that the manager can follow up those who swear, for one reason or another, that they will never return. Exhibit 17.4 shows a sample questionnaire.

Exhibit 17.4   ABBREVIATED CONSUMER SATISFACTION SYSTEMS QUESTIONNAIRE

I'd like you to think back to your expectations when you visited _____ [restaurant] in _____ [location]—that is, what you expected the dining experience to be like.

I'll read you some features of the experience. For each, please tell me how satisfied you were that it met your expectations for this type of restaurant.

      [Features omitted for the protection of Kapuler and clients.]

How satisfied were you that the experience met your expectations for [each of the following]: extremely satisfied, very satisfied, somewhat satisfied, somewhat dissatisfied, or very dissatisfied.
- Greeting by host, hostess
- Promptness of seating
- Server friendliness
- Atmosphere
- General cleanliness
- Noise level
- Menu variety
- Value
- Portion size
- Food temperature
- Busing

Source: Reprinted with permission of Customer Satisfaction Systems.

The Red Lobster[47] restaurant chain is thoroughly committed to marketing research. It is the largest fast-food restaurant chain offering table service plus a full menu for both lunch and dinner. With its more than 400 outlets and with its over $1 billion sales, it tops its major competitors—Bennigans and Chi Chi's.

Red Lobster's major element of success may be its personal service. The waiter greets the customer with a smile, asking a friendly question or two, and spells out the day's specials. Serving personnel attend an intensive four-day training course before a restaurant opens, with monthly polishing classes. Important too are the decor, the menu, and the prices.

All of this did not just happen. Red Lobster runs a tight ship; its operation is based on continuing marketing research. There is a bimonthly survey that measures the quality of the dining experience. Exhibit 17.5 shows the questionnaire left at the table along with the check. A monthly mail survey gets consumer ratings of Red Lobster versus 15 competitors. Custom surveys help to evaluate new menu selections and other aspects of the operation.

Exhibit 17.5   RED LOBSTER CUSTOMER QUESTIONNAIRE

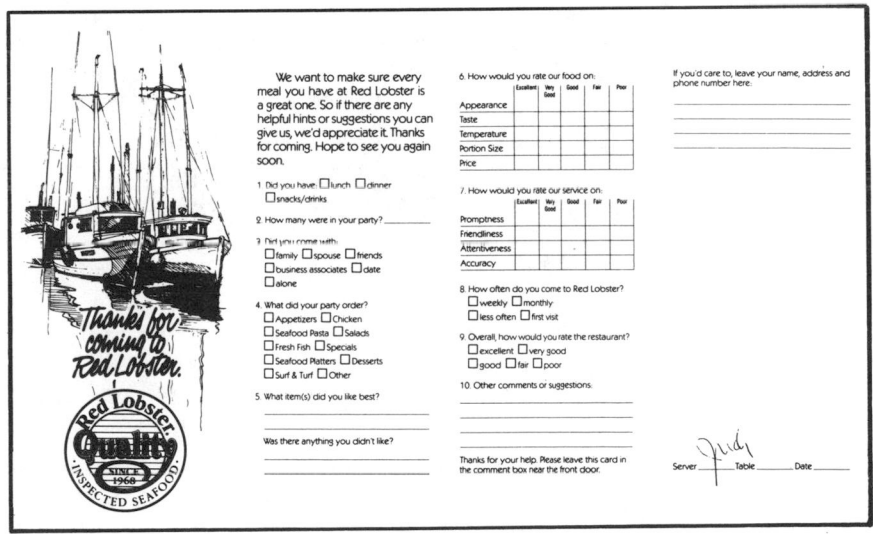

HEALTH CARE RESEARCH: FROM THE SUPPLIER'S VIEWPOINT

Marketing of health care can be divided into products and services that are wholesaled (provided by suppliers, mainly pharmaceutical manufacturers) and those that are retailed (hospitals, individual physicians, and other direct-selling medical services and suppliers). This first section of our discussion focuses on research directly pertinent to the supplier, and the second will explore research in health care services.

Health care measurements from the suppliers' viewpoint cover two main areas: market measurement and promotion.

Market Measurement

As with consumer goods, medical suppliers do not know how well they are doing by their own shipping records. Competitive measurements are needed for a real evaluation.

One measurement of the market is provided by services that check either the prescribing of various drugs or the movement of pharmaceuticals through hospitals.

One drug prescription measurement is the Scriptac database,[48] offered by the Dresden/Davis Organization, a Division of Pharmaceutical Data Services (PDS). Some 2,500 physicians report the frequency of writing prescriptions for various ethical drugs.

Audatrex,[49] an offering of IMS, provides monthly summaries of 1,000 physicians' prescriptions written (no patient names are used). Monthly reports are prepared. The major applications: measurement of new-product launches (the client's own or those of the competition) and indication of brand switching.

Monthly purchase of ethical and proprietary pharmaceuticals and diagnostics by hospitals is provided by the IMS syndication of U.S. Pharmaceutical Market Hospitals.[50] There are two sources of information. One is a panel of 350 representative hospitals with therapeutic beds listed in the American Hospital Association Directory or the Modern Hospital Directory. Federal hospitals are excluded. The other source is pharmaceutical wholesalers, which provide warehouse receipts for all relevant product categories.

IMS field personnel microfilm hospital purchase invoices, and the participating warehouses send monthly computerized information. Some of the data provided on a monthly basis are:

- New products
- Running 12-month dollar sales figures on products introduced within the past 12 months
- Total volume by manufacturer and class, including market share

Hospital pharmaceutical product movement by client diagnosis is provided by Hospital Data Services,[51] an offering of PDS. The sample is 80 hospitals (acute care, nonfederal government hospitals that are computerized), covering some 4 percent of all hospital discharges in the United States.

While the service is aimed mainly at pharmaceutical drug manufacturers, it may also be useful to hospitals. The measurements show product usage (including dosage distributions). In addition to their usefulness in general monitoring, results can be applied both to the observation of physician awareness and the monitoring of new-product launches.

The Beta Database,[52] a service of PDS, provides an ongoing analysis of prescriptions from patients who get their products through a third-party drug reimbursement plan. The data represent 2.2 million people in all 50 states. Data are reported by some 50,000 community pharmacies.

The analysis can be longitudinal, covering the same patient over a long period (as far back as 1982), regardless of the number of physicians treating that patient or the number of pharmacies the patient has dealt with.

Promotion

There are three types of physician promotion to which research has been applied: media advertising (more discreetly termed *journals* among the elite), direct mail, and detailing (sales calls on physicians).

The National Journal Audit[53] estimates monthly spending for ethical pharmaceutical advertising in health care publications. Some 350 medical journals and Standard Rate and Data Service figures are used to arrive at dollar figures. Competitive spending by product class and media class (in terms of therapeutic specialty) can be monitored. New-product introductions can be spotted and followed. The user has on-line access through Imspact.

The National Mail Audit[54] estimates the circulation and cost of ethical direct mail to practicing physicians and pharmacists. A sample of some 300 physicians and pharmacists forwards or reports all pharmaceutical mail received. Costs are estimated from factors such as printing, addressing and mailing, assembly and insertion, and postage. There is on-line access through Imspact. The major application is competitive analysis.

The National Detailing Audit[55] estimates the personal selling activity of pharmaceutical sales representatives directed to physicians in office-based practice. Dollar costs for these calls are estimated on the basis of annual expenses directly related to keeping a representative in the field.

Every month 2,800 office-based physicians report on personal visits by pharmaceutical company representatives. Reports show the number of calls, costs by product for each manufacturer, and similar information. The major applications are competitive analysis and better allocation of sales force effort. Data are accessible on-line through Imspact.

HEALTH CARE SERVICES: FROM THE RETAILER'S VIEWPOINT

Up to this point, our discussion of health care has focused on research to help the pharmaceutical manufacturer or supplier. Now we will examine the *provider* of health care services, mainly the hospital or other health care center.

This is such an important health area that the American Marketing Association has a divisional organization covering it, the Academy for Health Services Marketing, composed mainly of hospitals and similar service facilities, marketing professionals employed by such groups, and firms—mainly marketing research firms—that offer service to these entities.

A 1988 survey by the Academy for Health Services Marketing[56] provides a picture of the status of marketing research in such services, including chiefly hospitals, multihospital systems, and HMOs/PPOs, but also including many types of health service providers. Eighteen hundred questionnaires were mailed to those working in provider organizations. Since only 398 usable returns were received (22 percent), we can use the returns only as a guide to what is going on in the more sophisticated and more frequently using organizations, since these are the most likely to have responded. There were some pertinent findings.

Periodic, continuing surveys were reported by 90 percent, and one-shot studies by 94 percent. Exhibit 17.6 shows that telephone interviews and mail surveys were by far the most frequently used methods.

Exhibit 17.7 shows the proportion of respondents mentioning each of

Exhibit 17.6   RESEARCH METHODS USED BY HEALTH SERVICE PROVIDERS

Telephone interviews	82%
Mail questionnaires	82
Focus groups	64
Interviews at provider location	37
Premiums (gifts to respondents)	15
Mall interviews	8
Computerized interview stations	6
Interviews in respondents' homes	5
Other	8

Exhibit 17.7   TARGET UNIVERSES OF STUDIES WITHIN PAST YEAR

Patients	85%
General community	71
Physicians	71
Employees	44
Businesses	43
Women only	32
Seniors	31
Visitors	17
Volunteers	9
Donors	8
Men only	3
Other	14

a number of groups as their target universe of studies within the preceding year. Not surprisingly, patients (the market) topped the list, with the general community (potential market) close behind. Then physicians and employees (both internal staff) came into the picture, with various groups following thereafter. Eighty-four percent of these health service providers used external research firms, and among those using, the median number of research firms was two. Over half (52 percent) used PC software for the internal handling of survey results.

Exhibit 17.8 shows the nature of the problems for which research was used. The major kinds of problems were measuring image/awareness, potential for services, monitoring of key groups, measurement of consumer preferences, and support of strategic planning.

These kinds of health care facilities are increasingly taking a marketing viewpoint. There is more and more talk about marketing management, market share, and market research. Even the nonprofit institutions are taking a hard look at the bottom line and the important role played by marketing management and marketing research. There is

**Exhibit 17.8   KINDS OF PROBLEMS FOR WHICH
RESEARCH WAS USED**

Measure image/awareness	80%
Measure potential for services	76
Monitor key groups	76
Measure consumer preferences	68
Support strategic planning	59
Study advertising effectiveness	44
Measure use rates/market share	38
Determine media use habits	22
Support a merger/acquisition	9
Other	12

concern about sales quotas and product development. Rynne[57] comments that the health care firm has had to learn what competition is all about and that the key is market research.

NPD[32] through its Healthpoll, conducts continual telephone studies to measure consumer awareness toward hospitals and other health care organizations in selected communities where there is a demand for the service. This tracking study provides consumer reaction to the subscriber about that specific hospital and up to four competitors, including measurements such as awareness attitude ratings, choice for various specific health care needs, usage of various services and satisfaction—all with demographic breakouts. Piggyback questions for a single subscriber can be asked at the end of the questionnaire.[58]

Measurement of customer satisfaction is receiving increasing attention. While Sally K. Holmes,[59] director of market research, Harvard Community Health Plan, points out that this is relatively new in health care and has come a long way. But she also points out that many more specifics and fine-tuning are needed and that normative data are important.

Karowski and Pedroja[60] talk more definitively about patient satisfaction studies on which they worked together at University Hospital, Denver. The marketing emphasis is stressed. Karowski underlines the importance for a health facility to be getting from its patients recommendations to others (getting testimonials, as she puts it), and also mentions some specific marketing applications they got out of their work. These included positioning strategy (stressing in their promotion the quality of care and the state-of-the-art methods and facilities), use of the results in training new staff and employees before they were permitted to deal with customers, and in business development (obtaining managed-care contracts).

Pedroja developed the procedure. The data collection method was a mail questionnaire sent to each discharged patient within three weeks of discharge. It basically was a straightforward questionnaire. Following questions on overall satisfaction and whether the patient would recommend the facility to others, it measured the person's attitudes about each of the eight major areas where he or she would have had hospital contact: admitting, physicians, nursing care, housekeeping services, dietary services, guest relations, discharge, and billing. There was provision for open-ended comments. Demographics were built in.

A typical customer (patient) satisfaction questionnaire is shown in Exhibit 17.9.

At the same meeting of the Academy for Health Services Marketing, Hess and Hollinger[62] discussed how Viewtel can be used in the patient's hospital room to measure patient satisfaction. The series of questions is shown on the television in the patient's room, and the patient is provided with a hand-held unit similar to a remote television channel changer. Questions can be asked about the patient's reactions to the major aspects of the hospital stay.

One advantage of the system is its tendency to increase return rates. With the in-room procedure, response rates are bound to be close to 100 percent; with other methods (such as mail with follow-up mailing to non-respondents), they are not likely to go beyond 60 percent. People have found it enjoyable to work with the Viewtel unit. It is easy to use. If the patient is interrupted during the survey, nothing is lost; it can be returned to at a later time. The questions are asked while the person's attitudes and opinions are fresh and timely.

On the negative side, Hess and Hollinger mention that not every hospital room has television, that not all patients are in a position to handle a survey because of the nature of their illness, and that in some situations privacy of data entry may present problems.

Some in the field of health services marketing are concerned that these customer surveys may not always be accurate. Those done during or immediately after an illness may produce replies colored by stress and anxiety. If the study is done sometime following the visit, there may be memory loss. The person may be unable to describe specific reasons for level of satisfaction. There may be aspects unobservable to the untrained person.[63] At the Cleveland Clinic, therefore, three marketing researchers decided to use the technique of professional shopping common in retailing. Two shopping programs were developed, one using trained researchers, the other using telephone shopping. In a pilot program, nine shoppers (five with backgrounds as medical technologists) had their blood drawn for a variety of tests at an outpatient service of the clinic. The four professional shoppers also telephoned appointment secretaries of a particular medical department to determine the scheduling

Exhibit 17.9   PATIENT SATISFACTION QUESTIONNAIRE

PATIENT SATISFACTION SURVEY: INPATIENT SERVICES   *Survey Number* _____

DIRECTIONS: Please respond to each of the questions by circling the <u>one</u> number which best reflects
            your opinion relating to your most recent experience with _____ Hospital.

Who is completing this survey?

Patient	1
Other (Spouse/parent)	2

Please indicate your <u>overall</u> level of satisfaction with your hospital experience by circling the appropriate number on the scale to the right.

Extremely Satisfied								Extremely Dissatisfied
9	8	7	6	5	4	3	2	1

Were you admitted through the Emergency Department?

Yes	1
No	2

ADMISSION

	Yes, Definitely			Definitely Not	Does not apply
Was the admitting staff courteous?	5	4	3	2 1	9
Were you greeted with a smile?	5	4	3	2 1	9
Was the admitting process handled efficiently?	5	4	3	2 1	9
Was the amount of time between when you arrived at the hospital until you went to your room acceptable?	5	4	3	2 1	9
Approximately how long was it? *(Circle 999 for "Don't know")*	___ ___ ___ minutes				999
Were you informed of reasons for any delay in the admission process?	5	4	3	2 1	9

HOSPITAL SURROUNDINGS

	Yes, Definitely			Definitely Not	Does not apply
Did the hospital lobby and other public areas appear to be clean and neat?	5	4	3	2 1	9
Was your hospital room attractive?	5	4	3	2 1	9
Was your hospital room warm enough?	5	4	3	2 1	9
Were you given adequate instructions on operating the equipment in the room (i.e., bed, call button)?	5	4	3	2 1	9
Was the room kept clean by the housekeeping staff?	5	4	3	2 1	9
Was the housekeeping staff friendly and courteous?	5	4	3	2 1	9
Were telephone calls to the hospital answered with a greeting (i.e.,"Good Morning")?	5	4	3	2 1	9
Were directional signs in the hospital easy to follow?	5	4	3	2 1	9
Were noises disturbing to you during your hospital stay?	5	4	3	2 1	9

IF YES, what was the source of the noise(s)? (Circle all that apply)

Roommate	1	Talking/visiting by hospital staff	4	Other _____	7
Noise in the halls	2	Talking/visiting by other visitors	5	_____	8
Noise outside hospital	3	Crying children	6	_____	9

ITEM	Percent Always	Average Response	Always 1	2	Half the time 3	4	Never 5
MEALS							
Were you satisfied with the food in terms of:							
Choices available?	80.2%	1.7					
Temperature?	81.6	1.6					
Amount?	91.6	1.3					
Appearance?	87.0	1.5					
Taste?	74.5	1.9					
Did you receive the items you requested from your menu?	93.0	1.3					
If your meal was missed or held due to procedures you were receiving, were other arrangements made for your meal?	91.2	1.3					
Were you able to get snacks if you wanted them?	90.9	1.3					
Were your questions about the menu or diet answered to your satisfaction?	94.9	1.2					
PATIENT CARE							
I was given enough information about my medical condition by my doctor.	92.1	1.3					
I knew which doctor was "in charge" of my care.	93.7	1.2					
The doctors involved in my care treated me with dignity and respect.	95.8	1.1					
Special tests/procedures were explained to me by my doctor so that I understood the reasons for them.	95.3	1.2					
When appropriate, I was given choices/options for treatments.	91.5	1.3					
I was given enough privacy for examinations and special procedures (i.e. curtains were drawn)	97.9	1.1					
I knew which nurse was "in charge" of my care.	85.2	1.5					
The nurses informed me of my scheduled tests and procedures on a daily basis.	90.2	1.3					
The nurses involved in my care addressed me by the name I preferred.	97.6	1.1					
The nurse call button was answered promptly.	85.4	1.6					
The nurses involved in my care took the time to really *listen* to me and seemed to *understand* my fears and concerns.	91.8	1.3					
The nursing staff was sensitive to the needs of my family/visitors.	95.5	1.2					
I felt that there was a good reporting system between different shifts.	89.9	1.4					
Were concerns you expressed to your nurse about your care handled to your satisfaction?	94.0	1.2					

Source: Reproduced with permission of the American Marketing Association.

experience. We won't report on the actual results, but the procedures worked, and the program went into operation. It offers the potential advantage of shopping the competition.

Market segmentation has also been applied to actual and potential patients. The National Research Corp. (Lincoln, Nebr.) has segmented the market into 25 segments specifically for health care purposes.[64] Media can be used to reach those in the target market. It is even possible to set up specific target areas geographically, as with retailing.

Another study[65] suggests that the majority of health care consumers can be classified into four groups by the benefits they seek: quality, service, value, and economy. Yet another study[66] comes up with the value-conscious, the affluents, the old-fashioneds, and the professional want-it-alls.

We were highly impressed with the marketing research done in connection with the planning of the University of Michigan's complete replacement of its adult hospital and outpatient building.[67] The planning extended over a 5-year period, included some 33 separate studies, and covered over 3,200 patients and visitors (and 1,200 staff members). We report two of the kinds of study done, just to give an idea of the imaginative approaches that are possible.

Because the life of the patient may depend on the staff's ability to perform efficiently in emergency situations, full-scale mock-ups were perceived as the only way to get realistic reactions from the professional staff. Three different full-scale mock-ups were built: a private room and bath, a semiprivate room and bath, and an intensive-care room. Twenty-seven different situations were simulated (including aspects such as movement of the patient from the bed, use of sink, toilet, and shower, and emergency treatment). Results showed the proposed room sizes to be too small, and the room designs were accordingly modified.

Videotape simulation was used in designing a parking structure entrance. The basic question was where the entrance to a new visitor parking deck ought to be. One possibility was to have an entrance from the drop-off circle and another from the main road beside the parking deck. The other possibility was to have both deck entrances off the main road, away from the drop-off circle. Two simulations were used to take people through each of the proposed possibilities. Despite signs within the simulation directing people away from the drop-off circle and to the parking deck, results showed clearly that the visual cue lured drivers into the circle. Since this lure would draw visitors not needing to drop off anyone, it would have added to congestion in the circle. The two entrances to the parking deck were built on the street side.

While there isn't space to report everything that is happening in the way of marketing and marketing research with consumers in health care facilities, there is one more that is of high interest and significance. It is the story of the need for overnight research and the way this was solved at the Cleveland Clinic, as described by Janet R. Day, manager of market research at the Cleveland Clinic Foundation.[68]

Clinic management was shocked by a series of articles in the *Cleveland Plain Dealer* that reported first the fact that one of the senior physicians on the clinic's cardiovascular staff had been diagnosed as having AIDS, then that this was not immediately reported publicly, and lastly that he had died shortly afterwards, though he continued his patient work almost up to the end. The clinic was well-aware that poor handling of emergency situations such as this might affect its public image and its bottom line.

So the clinic undertook a series of studies, none of which, fortunately, showed any devastating results. An internal survey showed that there was little patient concern, and that there was no visible drop in admissions or increases in cancelations. One outside poll showed that there was awareness of the AIDS death but little belief that a patient could get AIDS through a health care contact. Another poll (one done on a continuing basis) showed very little drop in regarding the clinic as a high-quality center for cardiovascular care.

It turned out that the scare about image effects was much overrated. But because it took time—far too much time—to get these answers, the market research department decided it would gear up to handle measurements of such crises on an overnight basis.

Imagination and thought created a workable system. The market research department had worked successfully with three different research firms to set up its high-speed arrangements. The basic concept was to have prenegotiated contracts that would make it possible to move into a study rapidly without having to go through the usual long discussion process. Each of the firms is paid in advance to construct a telephone sample and put it on the shelf for use when needed. The questionnaire format is agreed in advance to be a closed-end series and to require no more than five to seven minutes of interview time. Because of speed requirements, there will be no callbacks. Clinic personnel will monitor a few of the early calls, and all calls will be made during evening hours. The usual sample size will be 300, and the samples will typically specify geographic (marketing) area with age and sex specifications.

The system has been tested, and it works. Results can be in hand within 48 hours. Admittedly, as Day says, there are prices to be paid for it. There is not as much questionnaire flexibility as one might like. There is lower precision because of lack of callbacks. And one cannot compare results with any earlier studies except those also using the overnight procedure.

These health care service firms have a major constituency that must be considered: physicians. Physicians are a crucial factor in the success of institutions, and most of these are well aware of it. Hospital and other institutions realize that there are high admitters and low admitters on their medical staffs, and that if too many are low admitters, the facility may be in financial trouble.

Health service firms do not overlook research about and from their medical staff. One such basic measurement is the physician profile, which is basically a description of physician activity, including admitting activity and outpatient referral activity.[69] The time period is 3–5 years. These data are recorded by age, specialty, and office location. They provide a means of spotting quickly those physicians whose production changes.

But the physician profile is just one of two major kinds of research about the medical staff. The other is measurement of staff values, staff attitudes, hospital needs, and staff loyalty. This may cover many specifics, such as the person's assessment of the hospital's reputation, facilities, and services provided to the physician. In the case of an unidentified 450-bed Midwestern hospital, it was decided that because of the highly competitive health-care environment, it was necessary to have a better understanding of the hospital's relationships with its medical staff.[70] The first phase of research was a series of focus groups conducted with key admitters, community medical leaders, and others whom it seemed politically wise to include. The groups were conducted in breakfast meetings. As compensation, participants were given a $50 dinner gift certificate to a local gourmet restaurant.

The focus groups gave some preliminary ideas of what the medical staff liked and disliked about the hospital, their day-to-day practice problems, and the hospital services they'd like to have. The results provided clues about the nature of information to be covered in the quantitative survey.

The quantitative survey provided medical reaction on topics such as evaluation of the hospital's various departments and nursing units, responsiveness to physician needs, ratings of the individual hospital in various respects compared with competitive hospitals, and what the physicians would like from the hospital to help enhance their professional practice.

MEDIA RESEARCH

Our discussion of media research is split between this chapter and Chapter 18. To make the topic more easily understandable, Chapter 18 will be restricted to "hard" media research—data used daily in buying and selling negotiations between the specific medium and its potential user. All other media research is covered here, including some kinds of study that are aimed at image-building rather than hard-sell material for potential advertisers.

USERS OF MEDIA RESEARCH

The individual medium pays the major share of costs of collecting data referring to the specific medium. Depending on the nature of the study, this is sometimes 100 percent. But there are many players in the business of selling or buying advertising space or time, and all of these benefit from media research. We first spell out the players in the game, then we take a look at how each player gains from continuing media research information, particularly from the hard forms of circulation data, monitoring, and audience data.

On the selling side, the major players include the individual medium and the medium's sales representative. On the buying side are the advertiser, the advertising agency, and the media-buying service. Exhibit 17.10 shows the applications by nature of the player.

Exhibit 17.10   **MARKETING APPLICATIONS OF MEDIA RESEARCH INFORMATION BY VARIOUS PLAYERS IN THE GAME**

The Advertising Medium
Sales planning and management
Pricing
Planning of editorial content
Promotion to increase subscribers or audience

The Medium's Sales Representative
Sales planning and management (for the medium)

The Advertiser
Media planning and buying
Planning competitive strategy

The Advertising Agency
Media planning (for the advertiser)

The Media Buying Service

Source: K. W. Endreson, "Everybody's Talking about Guest Relations but Nobody's Measuring It," *Marketing Is Everybody's Business,* Academy for Health Services Marketing, American Marketing Association, 1988, 148, 149. Reprinted by permission.

The Advertising Medium

The advertising medium, whether a large network television company (NBC, CBS, ABC) or a small local newspaper, uses data for sales planning and management. The basic tool is keeping track of how well the particular medium is doing against its competition (national, regional, or local) in terms of its share, a concept closely akin to the market share approach in measuring the relative success of a consumer item.

The small local radio station examines, by day and time period, the level of tuning and nature of listeners both for its own offerings and for those of the competition. It prepares a presentation aimed at particular prospects to show how a schedule including selective use of the station would offer greater marketing efficiency at lower cost.

Evaluation of "editorial" data is another important use of the hard data. (By editorial content, we mean the nonadvertising content: programming in the case of the electronic media, or news, fictional, or nonfictional material in the case of print media.) The television networks are constantly monitoring the audience size of their shows; a show that never earns a respectable rating or shows drastic drops or steady declines is likely to be axed. New shows that have passed screening tests are put to the final test by airing them. If the network thinks a particular show has a chance of being a real winner, it may be aired directly following a show with a high rating, to try to get a flow-over effect to give the new show a chance to build its own base of viewers.

Though a local television channel uses audience research in a generally similar way, the channel's options are greater, but limited. Network affiliates have limited local time to schedule; independents have their total time. But other than news and a bit of time filled by shows of local origin, much of the time of both affiliates and independents is filled with syndicated shows bought from producers or syndicators. Many of these are previously successful network shows. Past audience measurements provide the station with track records to help them make their selections.

A radio station faces somewhat different challenges in programming, since a greater proportion of its audience is exposed to the medium outside of the home—in automobile commuting and at work. Audience size measurements of the right type, therefore, often provide programming clues for the available time periods.

Some of these media measurements also provide guidance to the medium as to how to promote in order to increase audience or subscribers. The television networks regularly use promotion about new and existing shows, run during other time periods, to persuade potential viewers to watch. The placing of such promotions is guided by their knowledge of the demographics of the audience reached in various time periods. The newspaper circulation manager can spot the geographic portions of the coverage area where the circulation per household is low, but demographics come close to matching those of total circulation.

The Medium's Sales Representative

If the medium has a sales rep—most of the larger ones and some of the smaller ones do—the rep typically takes over the sales planning and management function already described as the first of the research uses by the medium.

The Advertiser

The advertiser's first use of media information is in media planning and buying. Media budgets are planned and appropriations made—except in the case of the very small advertiser, who is likely to base this on judgment calls—on the basis of media research data. It is simply a more efficient and effective way to handle the process.

The national advertiser, working closely with the advertising agency and its recommendations, makes the decision on the media budget and its allocation. The national advertiser is an active participant in major media purchases.

Astute local advertisers use media research data in much the same way. They typically include fast-food restaurants, department stores, supermarkets, banks, and auto and appliance dealers. Some of these, though locally franchised, are affiliated with a national or regional parent. Others are members of a chain organization. Thus many of these types of local advertisers receive continuing reports on specific local media and have the power to make media buying decisions based on these reports.

The advertiser is also aided in planning competitive strategy through the use of media research input. Some of these data provide competitive intelligence: what the competition is doing, by brand, in what media. This can be obtained in terms of dollars and time. Advertisers can even learn where they stand in terms of share of total dollar spending, and they can discover who the big spenders are and in what media they are to be found.

The Advertising Agency

The larger advertisers, as we have said, generally use advertising agencies. The agencies usually take on the role of recommending media plans, which, once approved, are then administered by them. Most larger ad agencies get their compensation from their clients by charging a commission on their media purchases. But in recent years things have changed somewhat. Some small breakaway agencies, emphasizing creative talents, have started to charge directly for these services and have assigned media buying to a separate service.

The Media-Buying Service

The media-buying shop specializes in buying spot television and radio advertising. Because it can buy on a large-scale basis, it is in a position to bargain harder and to charge its clients less than the advertising agency. While the ad agency must charge up to 15 percent commission on its media costs, the media-buying service may be able to charge less than 5 percent. Also, the media buyer is a tougher, more experienced buyer because of its volume of buying.

RESEARCH STUDIES FOR PRINT MEDIA

Print media sometimes undertake custom studies to help sell their space. But, as we have pointed out, the hard data on audience and print are really the basis for most buying of print media, and for these supplementary custom studies to have any acceptance at all, they must meet certain minimal quality standards. The trouble is that a list of such standards has been assembled only for audience studies, whether syndicated or proprietary,[71] and not for custom studies in general. So the buyer of print media looks a bit askance at any of these studies.

The Users

Custom studies of the sort reviewed here are aimed primarily at buyers: national (major advertisers, advertising agencies, and media-buying shops) or local (mainly retailers). This leads to several types of study:

1. Market definition
2. Audience reactions
   • Reactions to content
   • Purchasing behavior
   • Personality of the medium

We discuss these below, starting with network television and then going on to print media. Market definition is not included here, except in a general way; these audience numbers and nature will be discussed in Chapter 18.

NETWORK PROGRAM RESEARCH

The television networks try to develop their products (programs) systematically with the use of marketing research tools. They distribute programs, in the sense of buying most of these from production companies and selling them to affiliated stations and their small number of owned stations.[72] NBC, for example, goes through a thorough screening process.[73]

A typical fall season means that each of the three networks will need 20 to 30 new programs. The first step at NBC is a concept statement, an idea of what the program is going to be like. A concept test checks reactions of the potential audience at the idea stage, using telephone surveys and focus groups. If the idea passes this stage, the next step is a *pilot*. The pilot is the filming of a sample episode. Since pilots are expensive, running into the low millions, the decision to make a pilot is not an easy one. With some 40 pilots in the spring and up to another 20 during the year, each network is risking some quarter of a billion dollars on this phase of program development.

Only one of four pilots makes it to the airing stage. Of the pilots that do, two of three fail. This works out to about a 1 to 12 success ratio.

A likely pilot is tested in normal surroundings—the home—through arrangements that the network has with some 20 cable firms to show the test program on a spare channel. For each test of a pilot, some 500 adult respondents are recruited. Programs aimed at teenagers or children have samples supplemented with another 100.

Questions cover attitude toward the program and the key characters, the series premise, action, and humor. There are also several overall measures, including intention to view, and many competitive comparisons.

NBC has a single research firm handle all details relating to pilots, though it remains an NBC system. Audience Studies Inc. (ASI) prints the NBC-developed questionnaire, distributes it to the locations, ships the tapes to the cable system, recruits people (via telephone) to watch the show, conducts follow-up interviews and returns the completed questionnaires to NBC, which does its own analysis.

This is not a cut-and-dried predictive process. There is always the question of whether the pilot may be representative of the series to follow. Few programs test strong. Some programs that test weak end up in the schedule. There is another on-the-air testing problem. Since a network does not want to move a successful program out of the way for an untried product, new programs go against the strongest competition.

ABC went to a similar system of pilot testing about 1986. It uses Chilton Research to collect the data. CBS uses a theater technique. Thirty to forty people are invited into a conference room. A questionnaire is first administered, followed by the showing of the test show. The Stanton-Lazarsfeld Program Analyzer, a noncomputerized form of the current spate of button-pushing devices that require no central wiring, measures moment-to-moment reactions. Following this, three or four focus groups are conducted to get detailed reactions. In general, we feel the natural reaction within the home environment may offer more dependable results.

NBC also conducts concept tests for programming. A brief description of the program material following the pattern of *TV Guide* "Close-ups" is provided to potential viewers via telephone interviews. "The results are surprisingly useful for such a simple technique," reports Rubens.[73]

Scheduling research asks potential viewers whether they would watch a program if it were aired at the same time as several other specific shows. Promotion research utilizes surveys and focus groups to determine which aspects of a program, particularly about a made-for-TV movie, are appealing enough to use in print and on the air to build up viewing.

At NBC, product research about news is distinct from that about entertainment; so are the functions. News research evaluates competing programs. People are recruited to view various news programs.

PRINT MEDIA

The major research tools used by print media, other than the audience studies and promotion studies to be outlined in Chapter 18, are market definition, audience purchasing, subscriber motivation, product research, and image research.

Market Definition

Market definition is measurement of the actual or potential market, generally in numerical terms. Frequently, newspapers—especially those having no syndicated data to buy—conduct their own studies measuring the demographics and psychographics of their audience. This can help the advertiser in making comparative media selections. It can also be a highly useful internal tool.

The usual starting point is a demographic description of the circulation area in terms of common census-produced statistics.

An important part of market definition—for management guidance—is the spotting of areas in which circulation potential has not been realized. The research manager of one newspaper used census data to generate indexes of potential within census tracts, based on age, income, and education.[74] Tracts with high potential but low penetration were spotted, and the newspaper increased circulation by targeting its efforts in these tracts.

If a newspaper is not careful about building its circulation among the kinds of people to whom it caters, it may find itself in serious trouble. In the 1960s, Boston had three newspapers, each appealing to a different market segment:

- The *Herald* reached the upscale and well-educated.
- The *Globe* appealed to the middle-class.
- The *American* went to blue-collar workers and the lower class.

The merger of the *Herald* and the *American* created a dilemma. The new *Herald-American* gradually lost part of its top-level audience to the *Globe* and tried to compensate by appealing to the higher levels (blue-collar) of the *Globe.* Of course, it did not work.[75]

Sometimes the newspaper must undertake its own audience survey. Audience is different from circulation; circulation is a count of the number of copies actually distributed into homes or other places. Audience has to do with readership, and as Chapter 18 will show, typically includes measurements such as the number of readers and their frequency of reading. It also means a more definitive measurement of demographics and perhaps psychographics. Sometimes focus groups and surveys are integrated to help define the newspaper market. The *St. Paul Dispatch and Pioneer Press* used a combination of 10 focus groups and a survey of 1,600 to establish its market definition both to locate overlooked markets and for long-range planning.[75]

The Wall Street Journal has used research frequently to define its market. Median reader age is 49. Eighty-eight percent are are male; 81 percent are married. On the education side, 79 percent are college graduates, and 50 percent have done at least *some* graduate work. Financially, we know that the average household income of readers is $85,500, and that median net work is $448,700.

Occupationally, 79 percent are either CEOs or chief operating officers of their firms.[76] The *Journal* also reports that it reaches a higher percentage of professional women and young educated professionals than any other business publication.[77]

Audience Purchasing

Studies of audience purchasing may take one or more of three forms: total buying (nature and amount), principal local buying locations, and buying habits. These kinds of study are useful particularly for a local medium—one that covers a restricted market area. A survey of consumer buying habits may be a useful tool to help sell local retailers and consumer service firms on the idea of using the medium for advertising.

The concept is that a survey showing the shopping areas used for each of a selected number of products and services will help the medium sell retailers and consumer service firms in shopping centers where consumers do most of their shopping. Such a study can help the medium sell advertising to firms offering high-ticket goods by showing the high-ticket merchandise the audience is planning to purchase. As a side benefit, the study will also provide demographics of the medium's audience, enabling it to help its advertisers and potential advertisers properly slant their advertising toward the nature of the audience.

Exhibit A.3 (in the Appendix at the back of the book) shows a shopping-habits questionnaire provided by Suburban Newspapers of America, a national association of suburban newspapers, to its members for their use.

The introduction establishes that the respondent is the adult female head of the house, and Questions 1 and 2 are further qualifying questions to establish whether the sponsoring suburban newspaper is read by the respondent. Questions 3 and 4 measure generalized shopping habits, and Question 5 goes on to ask about where—in which of each of the three major shopping areas covered—the person visits or shops when buying each of eight different categories of items. Note that this list of items could be made far more specific, depending on the medium's needs. Question 6 inquires about the shopper's perceptions of five aspects of each of the three shopping centers. This list of aspects, too, could be expanded, if that were desirable. Question 7 asks about the number of stores typically visited when shopping for each of the same seven categories of items covered in Question 5. Question 8 covers the family's plans to purchase ten different major items, from luggage and outdoor furniture at the lower end of the scale to refrigerator or freezer and electronic home entertainment items (television and stereo) at the higher end. Again, it would be possible to add other items. From here on, the questionnaire covers psychographics (Questions 9, 10, 11) and demographics (Questions 12–17).

Subscriber Motivation

A unique problem for print media is why people subscribe or fail to renew. Unlike the electronic media, whose offerings are typically available without charge (except for cable television and specific channels that may levy additional charges when used), most print media have to extract subscription prices to survive.

The print medium, therefore, must know the needs of its actual and potential audience, and the degree to which the publication meets those needs. It often probes the degree to which its circulation-building methods reach prospects and meet those needs. Frequently, it undertakes studies to determine why people are *not* readers.

The Wall Street Journal has tackled motivation studies in two ways.[76] One is a study among subscribers who do not renew. The other is focus groups about why people decide to subscribe or buy, or why they do not. These have been conducted among would-be subscribers, new subscribers, and retail readers (newsstand purchasers). But no details of procedure or of results have been made public.

Product Research

One aspect of product research is the manner in which readers behave with the product—what parts of the publication are read? Such studies have been a publication tool at least since the 1940s. The person exposed to a particular issue is typically taken through the issue page by page and asked about readership of specific items (articles, features, ads), sections (news, comics, sports, classified), and pages. Questions may be asked about how well each of these is liked.

In the case of *The Wall Street Journal,* though we know that it has such studies made regularly, little about results or methods are publicized.[75] We do know that Starch has been used to measure reading habits and that customized questionnaires have been mailed to the circulation list.

We also know that average time spent on an issue is 48 minutes and that 25 percent regularly or often clip or save articles or features.

The *Journal* has measured reactions to its product largely through focus groups and later—after major changes in content and format—through a full-scale survey.

Twenty-four group interviews were conducted to get an idea of how readers felt. Both subscribers and newsstand buyers participated. During the process, various *Journal* editors had a chance to try out their ideas on participants.

A post-change study measured what readers thought of changes that had been made. Eighty-eight percent expressed strong to moderate approval of the new format and found the paper easier to read and understand. Few were strongly opposed to the new format.[76]

Image Research

The idea that an advertising medium has its own personality is not new; it may first have been applied to a study of MacLean's, a Canadian publication, some 30 years ago. More recently, the idea that brands have personalities has been promoted by a major advertising agency.[78] Since attribution of personality to an intangible is a perception, we will use the term *image*.

We are talking about how people *generalize* their feelings about a particular medium (assuming they have feelings about it), not their reactions to specific columnists, editorial policies, or program content. What is the total sum of the feelings and impressions that the public has about the particular medium?

If the medium were a person, how would it be described? What terms would be used—honest, thorough, inspirational, a leader, influential, or high-class? Or perhaps down-to-earth, middle-class, dependable? Or oversexed, overfrank, demeaning, sensational?

Image measurement is important to the medium in two ways. Both an image measurement and an image statement may help persuade the potential advertiser to spend marketing dollars in the medium. And if the image created with the target audience falls short of the market that the audience is looking for, the medium will lose audience.

The problem is that a person seldom states, or has even thought through, his or her total image of anything: a friend, a product, or a company. If you were asked to describe even your closest friend, except for those characteristics that are obvious to everybody (size, neatness, loudness and pitch of voice, color of eyes and skin, and the like), you'd have to take time to come up with all of the more important characteristics, close as you are to your friend.

The starting point of an image study is usually the *focus group interview,* described in Chapter 10. This provides an opportunity to learn the areas of imagery associated with the particular medium. Members and nonmembers of the medium's audience are assembled, depending on the needs of the study. The two groups should rarely be mixed, for their debates about the strengths and weaknesses of the medium may easily kill the breadth of discussion required to cover the range of image elements being explored.

In the focus group interview, the moderator may start with a question such as "What comes to mind when you hear the name of [*the medium*]?" The group participants can then go at it. The list of the major positive and negative elements associated with the medium will quickly become evident.

There are three important aspects of media image measurement: personality image, product image, and advertising image.

We all have distinct ideas about the personalities of our friends and associates. People see individual media as having some human personality aspects. A medium may be regarded as "warm" or "cold." One medium may be thought of as "dependable," another as "unreliable." Both people and media can be classed as "liberal" or "conservative."

When these personality questions are asked, often competitive media are included. Frequently, the image of the ideal medium is also covered to determine which aspects of the personality image are desirable. (In some media categories, the target audience group may be one that wants a "naughty" personality, for instance.) So these measures of competitive and ideal image are frequently included in gauging the product or personality image.

The product image concerns what people think of the product (the print medium). It has to do with such elements as general quality, completeness of coverage, quality of photography, quality of coverage, and personality, depending on what is relevant for the particular medium.

The advertising image measures the message people get from advertising appearing within the medium. For example, an unpublished Canadian study was conducted among readers of a news publication. Included for comparison was a lurid, sensational magazine. But even well-accepted products that were advertised there left a low-grade impression. "A really good product," said one respondent, "just would not advertise in a magazine of that nature." The comment by Marshall McLuhan many years ago that "the medium is the message" seems substantially correct.

Many descriptive terms might be used in asking about the nature of the advertising usually carried by the specific medium: prestigious, attractive, convincing, beautifully produced, believable, sold by well-known firms, and the like.

Starch offers an image measurement service for industrial publications. This takes the form of a competitive preference study and uses a mail survey to collect the data. It measures the comparative strengths and weaknesses of different publications covering the same market, concentrating on editorial service, graphic presentation, advertising content, and comprehensiveness.

ENDNOTES

[1] G. E. Breen and A. B. Blankenship. *Do-It-Yourself Marketing Research.* New York: McGraw-Hill, 1989.

[2] *Credit Cardholder Marketing Information.* Encinitas, Calif.: Equifax Marketing Decision Systems, 1990.

[3] *Infomark.* Encinitas, Calif.: National Decision Systems, undated.

[4] *Compass Retail Sales Potential.* Washington, D.C.: Claritas, 1989.

[5] *Demographics On-Call.* Stamford, Conn.: Donnelley Marketing Information Services, undated.

[6] *Compass Daytime Business Population.* Washington, D.C.: Claritas, 1989.

[7] *Your Single Source Guide for Demographic and Marketing Information.* Encinitas, Calif.: National Decision Systems, 1988.

[8] *Trends* 4, no.2 (1989):1.

[9] A. B. Blankenship. Chuck Chakrapani, and W. H. Poole. *A History of Marketing Research in Canada.* Toronto: Professional Marketing Research Society, 23.

[10] *Marketing Services.* Chicago: Elrick & Lavidge, 1988.

[11] Johnathan Dahl. "Giving People What They Don't Want." *The Wall Street Journal,* Nov. 30, 1989, B1 ff.

[12] W. H. Silverman. "The Role of Research in Developing and Maintaining Quality." *Profiling Tomorrow's Survivors,* Academy for Health Services Marketing, American Marketing Association, 1989, 10–12.

[13] W. L. Seldon, Jr. "Frequent Travelers Rate Hotel Service." *Marketing News,* 1989, July 31, 10.

[14] A. J. Morrison. "MOR's CATI-Based Service Satisfaction Measurement." *Marketing News from Market Opinion Research,* Fall 1988, 4.

[15] *Your Single Source Guide for Demographic and Marketing Information.* Encinitas, Calif.: National Decision Systems, undated.

[16] "Perils of the Paper Clip Trade." *New York Times Magazine,* Part II, June 11, 1989.

[17] M. J. Wolfe, "New Way to Use Scanner Data and Demographics Aids Local Marketers." *Marketing News,* Sept. 11, 1989, 1f.

[18] *Nielsen Scantrack Reports for Retailers.* Chicago: A. C. Nielsen Co., 1989.

[19] *DataServer for Retailers.* Waltham, Mass.: Information Resources Inc., undated.

[20] *This Week, He'll Kill 120 New Products.* Chicago: Information Resources Inc., undated.

[21] *Infoscan.* Chicago: Information Resources Inc., 1990.

[22] *Marketing Information for the Automotive Industry.* Detroit: Power, undated.

23"You Are What You Drive—or Does the Driver Make the Car?" *The Power Report* 14, no.3, (March 1990): 1 ff.

24"Upper Middle Segment Is the Most Problem-Free." *Power Report* no.3 (1990): 5 ff.

25Marshall Schuon. "Giving the Public What It Wants, Via Clinics." *New York Times,* May 26, 1989.

26*Standard Services.* Detroit: Polk Motor Statistical Division, 1988.

27*AutoMIS (Automotive Marketing Information System).* Detroit: Polk, 1990.

28"Spotlight on Automotive Advertising Audit." *McCollum/Spielman Topline,* no.30, undated.

29"Franchise Desirability Runs Either Hot or Cold." *Power Report* 14, no.3 (1990): 3.

30*1989 Power Car and Truck Media Reports.* Agoura Hills, Calif.: J. D. Power and Associates.

31"Self-Service Please . . . ." *NPD Insights,* January 1990.

32*Beyond Linear Solutions.* Port Washington, N.Y.: The NPD Group Inc.

33*The National Computer Product Audit.* New York: Audits & Surveys, undated.

34*Sales & Inventory Report.* New York: IMS, undated.

35*The National Computer Retail Distribution Report.* New York: IMS, undated.

36*National Computer Retail Report.* New York: IMS, undated.

37"Even Canned Corn Strains Abilities of Modern Cooks." *The Wall Street Journal,* July 25, 1985.

38"Dining in . . . ." *NPD Insights,* September 1989.

39*National Eating Trends: a Research Study on In-Home Food and Beverage Consumption.* Chicago: The NPD Group, undated.

40"Foodservice—Attracting Families with Children." *NPD Insights,* August 1990.

41*NPD CREST.* Park Ridge, Ill.: NPD CREST, undated.

42*National Restaurant Market Index.* New York: Audits & Surveys, undated.

43Stowe Shoemaker. Letter and materials. Jan. 9, 1991.

44"Marie Callender's, Food for Thought." *Quirk's Marketing Research Review,* August-September 1989, 14–15.

45"How to Survey Busy Retail Customers." *Customer Service Manager's Letter,* June 27, 1990.

46*CheckPlease.* Arlington Heights, Ill.: Customer Satisfaction Systems.

[47]D. C. McGill. "Why They Smile at Red Lobster." *New York Times,* Apr. 23, 1989, 1 ff.

[48]*Scriptac 1988 Desk Reference.* Philadelphia: Pharmaceutical Data Services, vol. 2.

[49]*Audatrex.* New York: IMS, undated.

[50]*The U.S. Pharmaceutical Market—Hospitals.* New York: IMS, undated.

[51]*Hospital Data Services, Inc., General Overview.* Philadelphia: Hospital Data Services, 1989.

[52]*Alpha Data Services.* Philadelphia: PDS, undated.

[53]*The National Journal Audit.* New York: IMS, undated.

[54]*The National Mail Audit.* New York: IMS, undated.

[55]*The National Detailing Audit.* New York: IMS, undated.

[56]David Marlowe (Ed.). *Building a Foundation for Effective Health Care Market Research.* Chicago: Academy for Health Services Marketing, 1990.

[57]Terry Rynne. *Emerging Trends in the 1990s: A Multi-Segment Perspective.* Conference, Academy for Health Services Marketing of the American Marketing Association, May 14, 1990.

[58]B. D. Gelb and K. M. Williamson. "Wringing Dollars Out of Data." *Profiling Tomorrow's Survivors,* Academy for Health Services Marketing, 1989, 72–75.

[59]S. K. Holmes, "*Emerging Trends in the 1990s: A Multi-Segment Perspective.*" Conference, Academy for Health Services Marketing of the American Marketing Association, May 14, 1990.

[60]Bettina Kurrowski and A. T. Pedroja. *Streamlining the Patient Satisfaction Survey While Improving Its Utility.* Conference, Academy for Health Services Marketing of the American Marketing Association, May 14, 1990.

[61]K. W. Endresen. "Everybody's Talking about Guest Relations but Nobody's Measuring It." *Marketing Is Everybody's Business.* Academy for Health Services Marketing, American Marketing Association, 1988, 147–150.

[62]Michael Hess, and W. A. Hollinger. *Measuring Hospital Patients' Satisfaction When and Where It Counts Most: In the Patient's Hospital Room.* Conference, Academy for Health Services Marketing of the American Marketing Association, May 15, 1990.

[63]W. R. Gombeski, Jr., C. E. Stone, and F. J. Weaver. "Improving Patient Services through a Professional Shopper Program." *Journal of Health Care Marketing* 6, no. 3 (1986).

[64]J. C. Jensen. "In Health Care Marketing, All Households Are Not Created Equal." *Profiling Tomorrow's Survivors.* Academy for Health Services Marketing, American Marketing Association, 1989, 17–22.

[65]Philip Kotler and R. N. Clarke. *Marketing for Health Care Organizations.* Englewood Cliffs, N.J.: Prentice-Hall, 1987.

[66]A. G. Woodside, R. L. Nielson, Fred Waters, and G. D. Muller. "Preference Segmentation of Health-Care Services: The Old-Fashioneds, Value Conscious, Affluents, and Professional Want-It-Alls." *Journal of Health Care Marketing,* June 1988, 14–24.

[67]J. R. Carpman and K. G. Trester. "Marketing Implications of Consumer-Responsive Health Facility Design." *Responding to the Challenge.* Academy for Health Services Marketing, American Marketing Association, 1986, 55–58.

[68]J. R. Day. *Fast Data—Stress Free (Establishing the Capacity to Do Overnight Research).* Conference, Academy for Health Services Marketing of the American Marketing Association, May 14, 1990.

[69] Rhoda Weiss. "Physician Strategies That Work." *Profiling Tomorrow's Survivors.* Academy for Health Services Marketing, American Marketing Association, 1989, 36–39.

[70]K. W. Endresen. "Medical Staff Research: State-of-the-Art Results." *Profiling Tomorrow's Survivors.* Academy for Health Services Marketing, American Marketing Association, 1989, 29–35.

[71]*ARF Guidelines for Newspaper Audience Studies.* New York: Advertising Research Foundation, 1990.

[72]Horst Stipp, and Nicholas Shiavone. "Research at a Commercial Television Network: NBC 1990." *Marketing Research,* Sept. 1990, 3–10.

[73]W. S. Rubens. "Program Research at NBC or Type I Error as a Way of Life." *Journal of Advertising Research,* March 1985, no.3, RC12–16.

[74]*Census ABC's: Applications in Business and Community.* Washington, D.C.: Bureau of the Census, 1989.

[75]W. J. Thorn and M. P. Pfeil. *Newspaper Circulation: Marketing the News.* New York: Longman, 1987.

[76]*The Wall Street Journal,* Centennial Edition, 1989.

[77]"Before You Deliver the Audience, You Have to Deliver the News." *Advertising Age,* Oct. 1, 1990, 6–7.

[78]J. T. Plummer. "How Personality Makes a Difference." *Journal of Advertising Research* 24, no. 6 (1986): 27–31.

18

APPLICATIONS FOR ADVERTISING MEDIA

What's in This Chapter

In this chapter we explore media research as a form of marketing research that emphasizes the custom analysis of data. We concentrate on the measurement of audiences in the major media: television, radio, magazines, and newspapers. We also look at print circulation as input into the buying of media. Finally, we consider the possibilities for media research in the future.

INTRODUCTION

DEFINITION OF MEDIA RESEARCH

Media research, as the term is used in this chapter, is survey or other information material used in the process of buying and selling media. Other forms of marketing research are also used by media, but these are primarily for use by their own managements and have been separately discussed in Chapter 17. The discussion in this chapter is strictly limited to the types of research that produce results that directly aid in the sale or purchase of advertising space or time. We are talking in this chapter only about the so-called "hard" data cited in negotiations for the sale or purchase of an individual advertising medium, such as ratings, audience size, or circulation. Other kinds of media measurement are used in attempting to build up a favorable attitude toward a medium to help support the sales effort. A study measuring reader image of a publication is an example. These "soft" data, sometimes called "qualitative" data (which they are not because they are often quantitative), were discussed in Chapter 17.

In an attempt to explain media research, Bill Rubens,[1] retired NBC vice president of research commented: "I see media research as just another form of marketing research. There's kind of a mystique sometimes associated with it because it has developed its own jargon, its own shorthand, and this is mainly because the various media research services have all developed their own terminology. But the essential differences between media and marketing research aren't really all that great. In media research you spend more time custom-analyzing the data, and in marketing research more time in custom-construction of the questionnaire."

But this doesn't mean you can forget the jargon in media research. You have to know it to follow the game, and so we present and define much of it.

Since advertising is the financial lifeblood of the typical medium, media research is extremely important to the medium. It has to produce consistent results to be acceptable to both buyer and seller. As we shall show, such lack of consistency has been the cause of considerable turmoil about network television audience measurements.

As background in understanding this numbers game, we will first take a look at the game itself (advertising dollars spent in the various media), the players in the game (the sellers and the buyers), and the medium of exchange in the game (the numbers used to sell and buy the media time and space and how these numbers are arrived at). The last of these, of course, constitutes media research.

THE MEDIA AND THEIR CHANGING IMPORTANCE

Media specialists will already know the meaning of most of the media. But because some are not so obvious, we provide a few of them here.

The television network is a parent company that provides programming to its stations, of which there are two types. Under federal law a network is permitted to own only a few local stations. Programs and ads are aired largely through affiliate stations, independently owned but associated with the network.

Cable television is the localized marketing, to subscribers, of a package of channels collected via satellite by the local distributor, or cable firm. In 1987 three-fourths of U.S. homes had cable television. Most cable systems offer some 36 channels versus the single channel offered by the television networks.

Syndication is the sale of the same program to many stations. The programs are typically reruns.

Exhibit 18.1 provides a look at how the various media currently stand in terms of advertising dollars, and the share of such dollar spending in each. Although the order of advertising expenditures for some of the media may be somewhat surprising to a few readers, we are more interested in the gains or losses in share from 1980 to 1989, shown in the last column.

Network television has been losing dominance for several reasons. One is the shift from mass markets to segmented markets, discussed in earlier chapters. Since using television for market segments is limited to such broad categories—and even then only in a general way—as sex, age, and income, advertising dollars are being shifted to media that offer greater possibilities in reaching various market segments.

The increasing role of the retailer is also changing the nature of media used. Through scanner use, as shown in Chapter 16, the retail operation now is learning more and more about its specific customers, even down to their names and addresses. So the retailer can use specifically keyed media, such as direct mail and even telephone.

There are new media, such as in-store advertising. Direct mail, through the customer/prospect databank, is almost a new medium, with new life. Direct mail can be directed to groups of people selected because they *are* either customers (for instance, of the retailer) or because they are of the right socioeconomic level, ethnic group, or other basis of segmentation.

With time, there will be more new media, such as interactive television, where the customer can respond to a commercial by using a device or a finger to order it via the television set. This is not a tool that can readily be used in network television with its tendency to reach mass markets.

This chapter concentrates on the measurement of audiences in the current major media. But if this chapter were being written four or five years from now, cable audience measurement would have to receive primary consideration rather than the casual attention we give it here.

**Exhibit 18.1   ESTIMATED ANNUAL U.S. ADVERTISING
MEDIA EXPENDITURES IN THREE
SELECTED YEARS[2,4]**
(in Millions of Dollars)

	1980		1985		1990		Gain/Loss in Share 1980/1990
Total	$53,550	100.0%	$94,750	100.0%	$128,640	100.0%	
Newspapers	14,794	27.6	25,170	26.7	32,281	25.1	−2.5
Direct mail	7,596	14.2	15,500	16.5	23,370	18.2	+4.0
Network television	5,130	9.6	8,060	8.6	9,383	7.3	−2.3
Magazines (including farm and business publications)	5,053	9.4	7,716	8.1	9,893	7.7	−1.7
National syndication and spot television	3,319	6.2	6,524	7.0	9,377	7.3	+1.1
Local television	2,967	5.5	5,714	6.0	7,856	6.1	+ .6
Yellow pages	2,900	5.4	5,800	6.2	8,962	6.9	+1.5
Local radio	2,740	5.1	4,790	5.1	6,609	5.1	=
Network and national spot radio	962	1.8	1,700	1.8	2,117	1.7	− .1
Outdoor	578	1.1	945	1.0	1,084	.8	− .3
Cable	53	a	724	a	1,789	1.4	+1.4
Miscellaneous	7,558	14.1	12,107	12.9	15,955	12.4	−1.7

[a]Less than .1 percent.

THE USERS OF MEDIA RESEARCH DATA

The individual medium pays the major share of the costs of collecting data referring to the specific medium. Depending on the nature of the study, this is sometimes 100 percent. (See Chapter 17.)

The advertising medium and the medium's sales representative use the hard data described in this chapter in their negotiations for the sale of advertising.

As explained in Chapter 17, the advertiser's first use of these hard data is in media planning and buying. Media budgets are planned and allocated—except in the case of the very small advertiser, who is likely to base this on judgment calls—on the basis of media research data. It is simply a more efficient and effective way to handle the process.

The national advertiser, working closely with the advertising agency and its recommendations, makes the decision on the media budget and its allocation. The national advertiser is an active participant in major media purchases.

Astute local advertisers use media research data in much the same way. They typically include fast-food restaurants, department stores, supermarkets, banks, and auto and appliance dealers. The latter two are by far the largest users of local television. Some, while locally franchised, are affiliated with a national or regional parent. Others are members of a chain organization. Many of these types of local advertisers receive continuing reports on specific local media and have the power to make media-buying decisions based on these.

The advertiser is also aided in the planning of competitive strategy through the use of media research input. Some of these data provide competitive intelligence: what the competition is doing, by brand and in what media. This information can be obtained in terms of dollars and time. Advertisers can learn where they stand in terms of share of total dollar spending, and who the big spenders are and in what media.

The larger advertisers generally use advertising agencies. Their agencies usually take on the role of recommending media plans, which, once approved, are then administered by them. Over the years advertising agencies got their compensation from their clients by charging a 15 percent commission on their media purchases. Few, however, now charge their clients that full 15 percent. Some agencies are on a prearranged-fee basis, covering a specified bundle of services. In recent years, things have changed in the sense that not all advertising agencies offer full services. Some small, breakaway agencies, often called "boutiques" and emphasizing creative talents, have started to charge directly for these services and have assigned media buying to a separate service.

The media-buying service specializes in buying spot television and radio advertising. It may be able to charge less than 5 percent and it is a tougher, more experienced buyer because of its volume buying.

But the media-buying service does most of its work for the larger advertisers. The major agency head of media is the major player in the game and decides which media buying can be done more efficiently (at lower cost) by the media-buying service.

AN INTRODUCTION TO MEDIA RESEARCH

THE GEOGRAPHY OF BUYING AND SELLING MEDIA

It may be surprising to learn that the type of numerical data used to buy or sell advertising space or time varies by whether the buying/selling is for national or local media. If the buyer advertises nationally or regionally, audience measurements are the usual kind of research data.

> *Audience* is defined as the number of people reached by a particular medium, whether television, radio, newspaper, or magazine.

If the advertising buyer is buying local media, as long as it is making comparisons between media, it likely depends on audience data, which provide intermedia data on essentially the same basis. But if the buyer is considering only newspapers, for instance, it may depend on circulation or on the rank of the newspaper in terms of advertising dollars.

> *Print media circulation* is the number of copies distributed by the particular periodical.
>
> For electronic media the term circulation is vague, almost meaningless. A liberal definition holds that it is the population in the geographic areas where the station signal can be received. A tighter definition states that it is the population in the geographic areas where there is a minimum, predetermined level of tuning to the station.
>
> Practically, circulation of electronic media is not used in media buying or selling, so we need not be further concerned with the term in connection with electronic media.

SYNDICATED VERSUS PROPRIETARY (CUSTOM) DATA

In almost all buying and selling of media, only results of syndicated data are used, for a simple reason: Both buyer and seller are using the same data; they know that the syndicated data are commonly accepted in the media marketplace.

This is not true with proprietary or custom data, which have typically been collected on behalf of the seller. The buyer does not know the quality of the data or whether there is some hidden bias favoring the medium. It is scarcely surprising that syndicated data constitute the general basis for pricing the time or space of the individual medium.

The Varieties of Media Research

As a result, media research takes many forms. There is monitoring, audience research (network and local television, national and local radio, magazines and newspapers), and circulation. All come in syndicated form.

There are other types of studies—almost all of a proprietary nature—for print media, and outdoor has some rather primitive research results. We now discuss each of these forms of media research.

MONITORING

DEFINITION

Monitoring tracks when and where electronic advertisements are run. It is not used with print media, since tear sheets (the particular advertisement on the page pulled from the publication) are sent to the buyer as proof of publication. As a side effect, monitoring provides detailed information about advertising content and spending, all by brands.

IMPORTANCE

Monitoring is of great importance to electronic media buyers: the advertiser, the advertising agency, and the media-buying service. It ensures that the buying firm gets what it pays for. But there is a big side benefit for the advertiser: It provides information on what the competition is doing.

The medium also benefits. On the internal side, it can use these data to help establish sales goals and budgets, and to measure its own market performance versus competitive media. It can spot accounts that it is missing and identify seasonal advertisers to approach.

On the external side, monitoring sharpens the sales tool in that the medium can show a potential advertiser what the competition is doing and where the potential buyer stands in advertising share. Further, the salesperson for the medium may be able to show the potential advertiser how to achieve a more efficient schedule by including the particular medium. And the medium can cater to present advertisers by showing their advertising shares and suggesting how to improve their schedules.

HOW IT STARTED

When radio came along in the 1920s, the advertiser and agency did not find it easy to verify that the advertising they had paid for had actually been broadcast. The Frank Seaman Advertising Agency (New York) asked an early marketing research firm, Crossley, to check to determine whether the commercial of its client Davis Baking Powder was really being broadcast by the stations being paid for it.[4] Crossley's local fieldworkers in various cities and towns across the country monitored stations over their sets. This was the first time that monitoring of an electronic medium occurred.

MONITORING OF TELEVISION AND RADIO SPOTS

General Technique

The monitoring of spots (commercials) in selected communities is accomplished either through the use of field representatives (who tune in and make notes or use electronic recording devices) or entirely by use of electronic recording devices.

We now outline three commercial monitoring services.

Broadcast Advertisers Reports

Broadcast Advertisers Reports (BAR, Arbitron), the granddaddy of television monitoring, started in 1953. Its original markets were New York, Philadelphia, and Baltimore. Originally, whole programs were sound-taped, with the commercial monitoring done later. As of 1989, BAR was monitoring in 75 markets, using tapes and covering spot television, network television and radio, cable television, and national barter syndication. For television, one random week of each four is monitored, with reports provided on incidence and "retail" dollars.[5]

BrandTraq is an Arbitron offering that tells an advertiser how its advertising schedule compares with its competition, and its network television audience delivery in the 17 largest ADIs. The system integrates BAR commercial scheduling data with Arbitron program ratings.[6]

Mediawatch

MediaWatch (Arbitron) is being rolled out in 75 markets. With this system, which uses a pattern-recognition technology, the entire commercial is "viewed" by computer. It is then matched to a library of known spots that is updated daily. Arbitron gets daily results by satellite. Media spending can be tracked by commercial execution and market, and the system can differentiate between television commercials and promotional spots.[7]

Monitor-Plus

This Nielsen service is offered in 23 markets covering half of U.S. households. Commercials are sampled by computer, with a matching of picture and sound patterns to a base of known spots that is updated daily. The monitoring covers 18 hours daily. Nielsen gets results electronically. Currently there are no expansion plans for this service.

AUDIENCE MEASUREMENT: INTRODUCTION

EFFECTS OF SPECIAL ASPECTS OF MEDIA

Nature of the Sales Effort

Today, almost all media except television prime time and some television specialty offerings are sold rather than bought. There just isn't enough prime time to meet the demand; also, some off-prime shows develop into hot numbers and many sports broadcasts fall into the same category. The networks are avid bidders for professional sports telecasts and for special events such as professional golf and tennis tournaments and the Olympics. But *most* television time slots—later and earlier than prime time—are sold. So is local television, and so are network and local radio. Print media, too, are sold, and this is especially true with magazines, where the recent proliferation has made more total magazine advertising space available than there is demand. Little wonder that so many magazines are having financial problems.

Pricing

In network television advertising—at least until the networks temporarily took steps to end the system—fractional changes in audience size meant millions of network advertising dollars. To a lesser degree, but still importantly, almost all media are priced according to their audience figures. Thus there is a tremendous demand for figures that don't jump around from one measurement period to another. Unfortunately, it appears that the demand for consistency is far greater than the demand for accuracy and precision.

Purpose of the Study

We make a distinction here between national and local measurements. Typically, a national study cannot and does not provide a sufficient sample size to permit local analyses, and that is why, for both television and radio, there are separate syndicated services for the two kinds of geographic bases.

Basic Methods of Audience Measurement

Our discussion is limited to measurement of audience size, though discussion later in the chapter shows that there are also measurements of audience characteristics.

The various syndicated media research services covering the electronic media use an assortment of measuring methods. Respondent recall (via telephone) is one method. Then there are paper diaries, left with the household, in which participants record their viewing or listening. There are also meters attached to the television set.

The two major syndicated print media studies conclude by asking almost identical questions in their personal-interview audience measurements for magazines, but they start out rather differently. One uses the "through the book" method, where the respondent is taken through a stripped-down version of the current publication with aided recognition questions as an early step. The other uses the "recent reading" technique in a face-to-face approach.

In measuring newspaper audiences, both major syndicated services use the "recent reading" approach.

Some Basic Audience Research Terms

Exhibit 18.2 lists the measurement terms commonly used in audience research, whether for television, radio, magazines, or newspapers. Since these terms are second nature to buyers and sellers of media, it is essential that the terminology be clearly understood before we proceed with our discussion.

Audience is the key term. If there could be only a single measurement in audience research, this would have to be it. The term *rating* is used with *audience*. *Duplication* means reaching the same household with a single medium more than once, and *frequency* is the numerical measure of how often the duplicating happens within a stated time period. *Reach* or *cume* refers to the number of different households reached by a medium.

All this is not so complicated as it may sound. Cumes for consecutive episodes of the same television program can be predicted when ratings are more or less steady, as with an established series or the news,[8,9] especially if the ratings are high. This simply means that there are fewer additional potential viewers to be added from one episode to the next.

<u>Exhibit 18.2</u>   **TERMS COMMONLY USED IN AUDIENCE**
RESEARCH
(Geographic terms are defined in Chapter 2.)

Audience
The total number of people exposed to a specific advertising medium program (electronic media) or issue of a print medium. Also see Rating.

Rating
The number of households or persons exposed to a specific program, network, station, or commercial. For television and radio, it covers only a 15-minute segment, not the entire program (although total program ratings are available on order). With all media using the term, it is projected audience size relative to the total population, stated as a percentage. A rating of 20 for a network show means that 20 percent of (television or radio) households were tuned to that show. Average audience for a print medium is the projected number of readers.

Duplication
Reaching the same household or person in one or more media exposures.

Frequency
The average number of times a household or person is reached by a program, station, or commercial, or by a print medium within a stated time period.

Reach, cume
The number of *different* households or persons exposed to a program, a specific publication, an advertisement, or a schedule (commercial or print ad) at least once during the measurement period. The net audience size over a time period after elimination of duplication.

AUDIENCE MEASUREMENTS OF TELEVISION

MORE TERMS

We have just considered a few terms commonly used in all quantitative media survey results. Now, in terms of television quantity data—most of these also apply to radio quantitative data—we have to add those listed and defined in Exhibit 18.3. Although we don't use these terms much in the following discussion, we list them because the media researcher and the media buyer, seller, or user must know them.

Two of the terms in Exhibit 18.3 require some elaboration. One is *day part*, used both in television audience reports and in discussion, referring to major segments of the day that affect audience nature, size, and rates. Day parts, for weekdays, are divided into several segments, shown in trade terms (to be literally correct, each category should end with the 59th minute of the time period) in Exhibit 18.4. Weekend definitions are a bit different. Saturday morning is considered childtime, and then there is weekend sports time. Also, on Sunday, prime time runs from 7 p.m. to 11 p.m.

**Exhibit 18.3   SOME ADDITIONAL TERMS USED IN
ELECTRONIC MEDIA RESEARCH
(Geographic terms are defined in Appendix B.)**

Day Part
Hour chunks of the day into which time analysis of audience reports are typically made.

Gross Rating Points (GRP)
The gross sum of all ratings for a schedule of spots or commercials (*not* programs), including duplications, reaching some persons or households more than once. Less frequently, it means the sum of all ratings for a particular time period. A television schedule producing 100 GRPs weekly does not reach 100 percent of the television households in that market during a week. GRPs are gross, not net. During a single week or other measurement period, some homes are reached only once, some twice, some more often.

GRPs are essentially reach times frequency. So it is important that the terms *reach* and *frequency* be understood.

Households Using Television (HUT)
The percentage of all households in the survey area having one or more sets in use during a particular time period. Size of total television audience at a given time.

Share of Audience
The audience viewing a particular show or program divided by HUT.

Exhibit 18.4   DEFINITIONS OF DAY PARTS

Early morning	6 a.m.– 9 a.m.
Daytime	9 a.m.– 4 p.m.
Fringe	4 p.m.– 7 p.m.
Access*	7 p.m.– 8 p.m.
Prime*	8 p.m.–11 p.m.
Late night	11 p.m.–on

---

*Access time is time when stations are given certain access to nonnetwork shows. Network shows are not permitted, with the exception of news shows, at the discretion of the individual station.

Share of audience literally means the proportion of all households using television (or radio) at a particular time that are tuned to a particular channel or program.

BASIC METHODS OF TELEVISION AUDIENCE MEASUREMENT

The basic measuring methods used are diaries, set meters, and people meters.

A media research *diary* is a form in which the participants keep records of their television viewing (or radio tuning) in a highly structured form. It typically is kept for a week and covers, by day of the week and time of day, station and program identification. Diaries are on a household basis, with a diary for each household set. Every person 12 years of age or over, or an adult surrogate, is asked to fill in the diary. Viewing of younger children (ages 2–5 and 6–11) is also recorded.

The *set meter* is an electronic device attached to the individual television set in the home. It automatically records the time, whether the set is on or off, and the channel to which it is tuned—all reported on a minute-by-minute basis.

The data are recorded in a home storage unit and are transferred to the research firm's central computer, generally between 2 a.m. and 6 a.m. the next day, through telephone lines. Since the participating home needs an expensive installation, this is operated with a relatively small panel of houses.

The *people meter* is a recently implemented special form of the set meter. In this case, each family member pushes buttons on a keypad to indicate viewing, and these data are automatically recorded simultaneously with set usage. Like the electronic meter, this too is conducted with a panel of participating families.

What Each Method Purports to Measure

Each of the three methods presumably measures total audience size. We use the words *purports* and *presumably* because, as you will shortly see, at least one of these methods—the people meter—is facing industry charges that it underestimates audience size. These audience figures are measured by station and programming for every day of the week and presumably for each hour of the day.

The straight set meter measures only whether the set is on or off. Total household demographics are known, to be sure. Figures showing total audience size and size by nature of household demographics are produced. Specific viewers and their demographics cannot be identified. These gross measurements are not specific enough to permit an advertiser to pinpoint its desired individual market.

Diaries and people meters provide demographic definitions for individual audiences: such aspects as sex, age, and certain other characteristics. Diaries obtain such data directly in connection with the diary procedure. In the people meter panels, such information is collected at the time of installation of the meter in the household unit.

People meters have added a method of measuring the demographics of of the audience to a particular show. The measurements of a show's demographics in syndicated services started about 25 years ago with the introduction of the diary technique as an addition to the straight set meter.

Here are some examples, as of early 1990. Children and teenagers were heavy in the audiences of "Mr. Belvedere," "Just the Ten of Us," and "The Hogan Family." The advertiser aiming for the 35–54 age group might do well to consider "L.A. Law," "Cheers," and "Murphy Brown." But if those targeted are in the 50+ age group, "Murder She Wrote," "Golden Girls," and "60 Minutes" come on strong. For an all-family orientation, "The Cosby Show" and "Roseanne" are good shows.

Audience Demographics, Overall Ratings, and Sweeps

While television time today is typically purchased on the age and sex composition of the audience rather than on the number of households watching a show,[10] the sweeps are highly competitive programming months aimed at getting the maximum ratings, since total ratings are still a factor in determining network prices. Sweeps months are February, May, August, and November.

The networks go all out in their programming for a sweeps month. These are not typical programs, and the networks and the industry generally are well aware of it. Though advertisers greet the sweeps ratings with some skepticism, the networks view them very seriously, for winning is important psychologically if for no other reason.

In the latest sweeps that we can report on here—February 1991— CBS topped NBC for the first time in three years.[11] But it won chiefly by getting big audiences for winners of the distant past: "The Ed Sullivan Show," "All in the Family," and "The Mary Tyler Moore Show." It seems curious that anyone except the networks would take such ratings seriously.

The Confusion

But there is confusion in the offering of these methods. After all these years of television, and of television research, one might think that a single kind of measurement approach had long since been proven superior, if only on a trial-and-error basis. Not so. The summary in Exhibit 18.5 shows that in current national measurements there is—at least as this book goes to press—only one basic national type of measurement (the people meter), but that local measurements currently don't use this measurement at all, but instead use the other two forms (diary and set meter).

Exhibit 18.5 **TELEVISION AUDIENCE MEASUREMENTS CURRENTLY OFFERED**

	National Measurement	Local Measurement
Diary		X
Set meters		X
People meters	X	

The Syndicated Television Audience Services

Nationally, the syndicated services include Nielsen and Arbitron's ScanAmerica. On a local basis, Nielsen and Arbitron are also in the picture, but each uses an almost completely different method of measurement.

NATIONAL MEASUREMENT: NIELSEN NATIONAL TELEVISION INDEX (NTI)[12]

The data collection method is the Nielsen people meter, pictured in Exhibit 18.6. The basic characteristics have already been described. The device is installed on all television sets in the panel households with each household member's sex, age, and other demographics programmed into the meter. Some total household demographics are also programmed in: education of the household head and household income.

A remote control keypad has a button for each household member, up to eight, to be activated when the person is viewing and when not. Guests can also be entered when present, with sex and age. There is a keyboard, placed on or near the set, that has a panel of lights to indicate the currently registered audience membership and to prompt (all lights flash, like a police car) for input when the set is turned on or the station changed.

Receiver tuning and audience measurement are recorded by half-minutes.

The NTI sample covers 4,000 households in all 50 states. It is a multistage, stratified-area, probability household sample, with blocks used as basis for a list starting with some 250,000 housing units. To avoid burnout, panel families are kept for no more than two years.

On-line facilities are available to download information onto client PCs.

Exhibit 18.6   THE NIELSEN PEOPLE METER

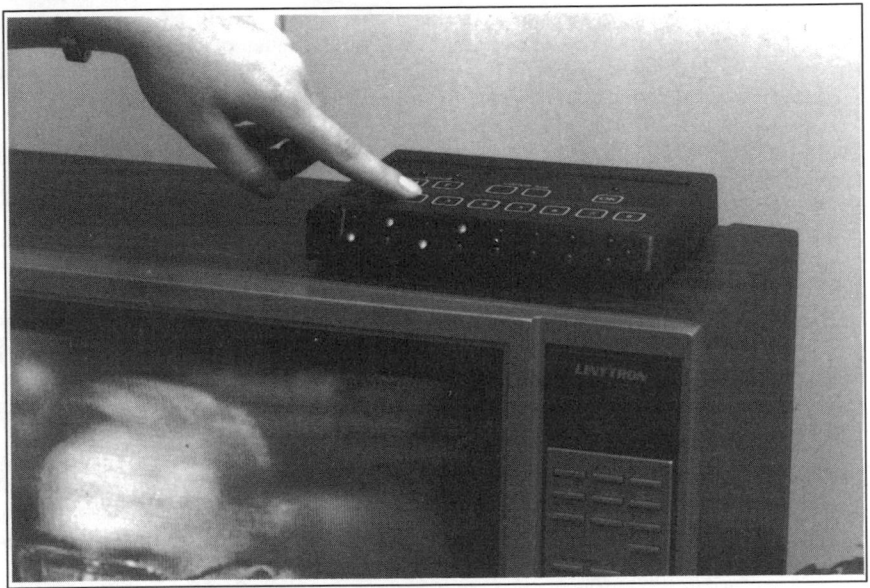

The Squabble

We report what the industry has to say about NTI in simulated newspaper column format, with appropriate dates starting in 1989.

August, 1989—A study by R. H. Bruskin & Associates[13] showed that two significant groups—college students and working women—were completely missed in the Nielsen in-home people meter measurement. Daily telephone calls were made with some 5,000 adult working women, and 2,200 personal interviews with students at 19 colleges across the country.[14]

January 1, 1990—The 1959 CONTAM study (commissioned by the Committee on Nationwide Television Measurement, including the three networks plus the National Association of Broadcasters) done by Statistical Research[15] led to four major recommendations about changes needed in the national Nielsen television meter procedures:

- Raise the acceptance level of panel invitation. Since the acceptance level is under 50 percent, this raises severe doubts about representativeness of the panel.

- Keep panel members for only one year. Currently, they are retained for two years, but button-pushing fatigue sets in before the end of that time, and ratings fall because some viewing is not reported.
- Simplify the use of meters to increase participation by children and visitors.
- Place more meters in panel homes, to cover all areas where there are sets (such as garages), including small-screen sets (screen size under 5 inches).

May 4—David L. Poltrack, CBS senior vice president of research, commented that since Nielsen had been unable to explain the serious ratings drop over the past three months, the network would seriously consider any better system.[16] Poltrack questioned how the Nielsen national service could show such large drops while the Nielsen local service in the 17 largest television markets—using different techniques—showed much smaller declines. Another unidentified senior network executive claimed that the unexpected decline indicated lack of controls to maintain integrity of the system.

May 10—Nielsen reported that an out-of-home television viewing study that it conducted among 4,000 viewers who kept diaries showed there was an average of between a 2 percent and 3 percent increase over the national Nielsen people meter ratings.[17] The study, logged over a four-week period, showed that this outside-the-home viewing was 35 percent at work, 21 percent in college dorms, 16 percent in hotel rooms, 9 percent at bars and restaurants, 4 percent in second homes, and 15 percent at other locations.

With the way that television network advertising is priced, according to Richard Montesano, vice president of marketing research at ABC, a 2.5 percent increase in audience is worth about $225 million. A Nielsen spokesman commented that the firm was "continuing to evaluate" whether to provide ongoing measurements of out-of-home viewing.

May 18—Alan Wurtzel, ABC's senior vice president of research, demanded two basic changes in the Nielsen measurement system.[18] One was a larger sample of people, the other a two-tiered basis of measurement.

On the first level of the proposed system would be measurement of the number of households viewing a program. On the second level would be a description of viewers as measured by people meters. The network argument is that since people quickly tire of the chore of people meter button pushing, this depresses the reported level of total household viewing.

Nielsen will examine possibilities, and if any appear worth pursuing, they will be explored, responded Nielsen executive vice president William G. Jacobi. The response was not greeted with enthusiasm by the networks, which may ask for a proposal on a new audience measurement system.

June 1—ABC announced that it will no longer base its network advertising rates on national Nielsen ratings produced by the people meter system.[19] ABC said that it had "serious questions" about the dependability of the ratings. Nielsen "stood by" its reports.

June 2—NBC and CBS joined ABC in rejecting current Nielsen ratings as the sole method for pricing from ratings. NBC expressed distrust of the Nielsen figures.[20] All three networks have moved to a system using an eight-year ratings regression for adjusting the current ratings.

July 19—Nielsen continues under fire from the networks.[21] Potential competition looms too. British Pergamon AGB PLC plans to re-enter the American market. (It withdrew several years ago following strong efforts beaten down by Nielsen.) Arbitron, Nielsen's competition in local television measurements, plans to go national with a new service in late 1991.

One aspect of the Nielsen figures that the networks do not understand at all is how in some cases households watching television held steady, yet fell sharply in some age groups. In March there was only a 2 percent drop in households watching all channels in prime time, but women ages 18–34 showed a drop of 8 percent. In April, late-night viewing slipped only 3 percent, but cascaded 13 percent among men under 35.

Advertising agency people are among the critics. Paul Isaacson, executive vice president of Young & Rubicam, suspects that the numbers are flawed.

Only a few over half of potential panel households agree to participate and only 47 percent continue. The low rate of participation, well below that accepted by the marketing research industry, may be a great distorting factor. Persi Diaconis, statistician at the University of Illinois, sees this as "an enormous potential source of bias." Nielsen Media Research executive vice president responds that a 47 percent cooperation rate is "an admirable achievement."

Analysis of Nielsen people meter data seems to support the case for error in the Nielsen data, and suggests some of the reasons. Considering just one group of users of the people meter—men aged 18–34—those watching for only 3 months report watching 17 percent more television than the total Nielsen sample, while those watching for one year are at about the overall level. This is pretty fair evidence that people *do* tire of pushing the people meter buttons.

Statistical Research recently did another study for the jointly sponsored Commission on National Television Audience Measurement (CONTAM).[22] This telephone survey of 26,000 homes showed that 26 percent more men aged 18–34 and 33 percent more children were watching television than was reported by Nielsen for the same period. Some panel members reported using the meters only when viewing; others reported using them any time they are in the room and television is on. William Rubens, retired NBC vice president for research, representing the networks with the research firm, says that there is no question that some portions of the Nielsen method are providing biased reports of public viewing.

The survey found 52 percent more visitors watching in other homes than Nielsen reported, and Nielsen understates other out-of-home viewing as well. Nielsen misses television viewing in bars, hotels, and other public places. Some 20 percent of the public vacations during any given week in the summer, and studies report that 80 percent watch television. These, too, are missed by the Nielsen method.

July 30—Without warning, the Nielsen figures for June rose, regaining most of the lost ground of the first quarter.[23] Only 1 percent fewer adults aged 18–49 viewed prime-time television than in June 1989. Adult daytime and late-night viewing also increased from the first quarter. The networks remained unhappy.

An ABC media executive commented that there had been no explanation of why the figures had gone down or why they then went back up, and that there was no way of predicting what might happen next.

August 6[24]—The time of decision is approaching. Nielsen network renewal contracts come up in September. What may happen is anyone's guess.

The networks are proposing a two-tiered measurement system. Tier One would be aimed at measuring household ratings, using people meters. The second tier, a quite separate panel, would measure demographic ratings through a combination of methods.

There is even a chance that the networks will consider possibilities other than the two-tier system or Nielsen. The Committee on Nationwide Television Measurement may come up with recommendations on a new system, and will welcome proposals from any research firms willing to meet such specs. AGB (Britain) has already met with the three big networks to decide whether there is enough interest for them to try once again in the United States.

September 10—A study sponsored by ABC showed that 77 percent of the 79 million Americans taking summer vacations away from home watch television an average of 3 hours daily. None of this viewing is measured by Nielsen.[25]

September 17—Willard Hadlock, executive vice president for media services at Leo Burnett, says that he knows that the networks are concerned that Nielsen is less reliable than it used to be. Nielsen, meanwhile, questions the coincidental method used in the CONTAM validation study.[26]

September 24—The three networks still have not renewed their Nielsen contracts, worth some $10 million. Relations with Nielsen continue, temporarily allowing the old contract to continue until the client cancels or renews.

But nothing has been resolved. Nielsen is expected to offer enhancements and experiments to improve the system.[27]

October 8—Acceptance of Nielsen ratings by the networks has been lost. But Nielsen points out that differences between the people meter findings and audiometer-diary findings in local markets are within sampling error range, so that these discrepancies should be discounted.[20]

October 15—To date in the young television year, the Nielsen data appear to be reasonably normal, according to the networks. So the NBC-designed method of establishing media rates using viewing data covering eight years has not been put into effect.[29]

October 22—The major television networks charge that a chief contributing factor to the fluctuating Nielsen ratings is a systematic sampling flaw, and that Nielsen should have foreseen it. The nature of the stated flaw will be revealed in two to four weeks, after the networks and Nielsen have had a chance to review the data on which the charge is based.[30]

November 19—Nearly 1.3 million men (18 and older) watch Monday night football, according to a November 1989 Nielsen study sponsored by ABC, NBC, ESPN, and Nielsen. Most of the viewing was done in the workplace, college dorms, hotels, and taverns. This is equivalent to a 1.5 rating.[31]

November—Nielsen announced "enhancement to national people meter service," to include "changes in field procedure, net methods to improve cooperation among sample homes, and streamlining the way household information is collected and processed."

But that wasn't enough for the networks. They asked interested research firms to submit ideas and methods for new ways to measure television viewing.[32]

November 26—Allen Banks, executive vice president–media director, Saatchi & Saatchi Advertising, questions whether there is anything wrong with the Nielsen television data. He questions whether the current network plan for adjusting current ratings based on eight years of rating information is defensible.[33] To improve network ratings, he suggests that they air better programs.

March 1, 1991—NBC drops adjustable program rating system. Spokesman said it drove too many advertisers to cable television and to the Fox network.[34]

March 4—CBS followed suit, with expectations that ABC would climb aboard.[36]

Sounds like the infighting is all over? We think not, believing that only the questionable methods of pricing are out. But there seem to be serious problems with the ratings measurements, and we doubt that these have gone away.

NATIONAL TELEVISION MEASUREMENTS: THE FUTURE

Nielsen Media Research

Nielsen Media Research is mulling a request from CONTAM to consider a system that would combine household tuning and people meters with other methods to determine whether such a system might produce better audience data.[20] Nielsen may have a new "passive" people meter on the way.[36] Reportedly, it is a miniaturized camera (no larger than a VCR) sitting on top of the television set that scans the room for familiar faces, and records, second by second, whether eyes are on the set. A minicomputer stores the facial image of each family member. The big advantage is that no viewer participation is required. But it will not measure visitor viewing. The device should be ready for testing about the middle of 1992.

There may, however, be a serious question as to whether potential participants will regard this camera as an intrusion on their privacy and refuse to participate in the system.

Arbitron's ScanAmerica

This is to be a national single-source measurement. Each member of a household logs in his or her television viewing (using a people meter), and records purchases of UPC items through use of an in-home data scan wand. Each person also provides additional information about buying by answering questionnaires. The intent is to be the only national television measurement service that can provide related information on buying, and therefore the only service that can make the purchase and evaluation of television far more realistically targeted than now.

We first describe the basic technique.[37] The household is the sampling unit.

Television viewing is recorded through the people meter shown in Exhibit 18.7. The meter is a sensing unit attached to the television set that measures whether the set is on or off and indicates the channel to which the set is tuned. It provides—as does the Nielsen people meter—a system for measuring viewing by individual household members. A unique feature is the on-screen prompt, a question mark at the top left corner of the television screen that prompts viewers to log in their viewing.

Purchases of UPC products are recorded in the home by use of a data scan wand, as shown in Exhibit 18.8. These purchases are recorded daily and are electronically collected via telephone lines in the middle of the night.

Exhibit 18.7   THE SCANAMERICA PEOPLE METER

Exhibit 18.8   THE SCANAMERICA IN-HOME DATAWAND

The purchase of items and services not covered by UPC codes are recorded in a daily diary and include large durable items such as cars and appliances, credit cards, banking, fast-food restaurants, and department stores.

The measurements include viewing by individuals (with results shown by the demographics of sex, age, and race/ethnicity), and by "buyergraphics": viewers defined by the products they buy.

So far there has been no strong outspoken industry reaction. This is probably because it is too early; There has been no experience with the service and how well it works. If it is to be acceptable, it will have to solve the problem of continuing consistency in audience level measurement. And it faces all the potential weaknesses of a panel that the Nielsen Television Index is currently charged with.

Another Arbitron Possibility

Arbitron has another iron in the fire: a passive people meter. In conjunction with Telemetric, a French company, Arbitron is developing a passive meter, which may be implemented into the ScanAmerica service as early as 1991. Here is the way it works in France: When the system is installed in a panel household, the representative of the research firm finds out which seats in each television reception area are generally used by which family member and the hours the particular family member is at home. If the programmed sensor detects a body in dad's favorite chair and he is typically home at that hour, he is counted as a viewer.

LOCAL MEASUREMENT: NIELSEN (NSI)[38,39,40,41]

The Nielsen service uses a combination of diary and meter methods. The particular method used depends on the area covered.

Technique for Diary Homes

The sample covers all 210 U.S. DMAs (Designated Marketing Areas), and includes 100,000 households (both listed and unlisted telephone numbers). In three of the "sweeps" months, the base is 100,000 households, but the July sweeps may be somewhat smaller. Other periods are measured on a more limited basis and are restricted to metered households.

All DMAs are covered in November, February, May, and July (the "sweeps" months), with limited studies in October, January, and March.

The procedure is as follows: A telephone call identifies the household, gets television set information, and obtains cooperation. About 55 percent of the predesignated sample is successfully recruited. Diaries are then mailed to the household. There is a one-week diary, as we have said, for each set in the household, to be used for any viewing of five minutes or more. As previously described, station or channel name or number and program name are recorded. The diary shows sex, age, and hours for each viewer. (The diary procedure is essentially parallel for all diary procedures—regardless of the research firm or whether a television or a radio audience is being measured.)

Technique for Metered Homes[42]

The meter, attached to the television set, electronically records and stores minute-by-minute tuning, with records transmitted daily to a central computer via telephone lines.

There were 23 DMA areas for metered homes as of May 1990, as shown in Exhibit 18.9. The number of homes in any one market ranges from the low 400s to the upper 500s. These are in addition to any diary households within each DMA.

Exhibit 18.9   **SAMPLE AREAS OF METERED HOMES (May 1990)**

Atlanta	Minneapolis
Boston	New York
Chicago	Philadelphia
Cincinnati	Phoenix
Dallas–Ft.Worth	Portland
Denver	Sacramento
Detroit	San Francisco–Oakland
Hartford	Seattle
Houston	St. Louis
Los Angeles	Tampa
Miami	Washington, D.C.
Milwaukee	

Since these metered homes are panel homes, in addition to standard audience measurements, audience flow can be provided, with lead-in and lead-out analysis.

Data tapes are available for those with PCs and mainframes. In addition, Nielsen Micro Services covers all Nielsen Media Research. It provides a software program for analysis of overnight metered area results. It can handle both Nielsen local ratings services. There are special programs to assist spot buying and evaluation of results and to compare the performance of a particular program with other user-chosen programs.

LOCAL MEASUREMENT: ARBITRON

Arbitron[43,44] uses three basic data collection methods in its measurement of local television audiences: diaries, meters, and people meters. Diaries alone are used in 200 markets (ADIs), a combination of meters and diaries in 17 markets, and people meters in one market.

Diary Homes

During the sweeps months, 100,000 households are sampled. Participants, over a one-week period, complete a standard diary to indicate when television and cable were on, who was viewing, and the channels or programs viewed.

Metered Households

The meter monitors whether the set is on or off and channel tuning. The equipment consists of two modular units: a television meter and a household collector. The meter provides the measurements, and the collector (a microcomputer) stores the meter input.

People Meter Households

At present, Denver is the only market with people meters, and the technique is the same as in ScanAmerica.

LOCAL MEASUREMENT: THE FUTURE

Arbitron had planned to convert its local measurements into single-source technology, as with the ScanAmerica plan. New York City was to have been retrofitted in 1991 and 6 new meter markets added. A target date of 1995 had been set for 20 local people meter markets.

That plan seems to have changed. Pittsburgh, St. Louis, and Phoenix may be so equipped this year.[45] This would bring Arbitron's total meter panel system to 17 markets. Strong objections of local television stations to the people meter concept seem to rule out inclusion of New York City.

If the people meter system isn't going in New York City, it seems unlikely to go anywhere else as a local television measurement method. No technology approaches the low cost of the diary system, making it doubtful that local television measurement will ever move completely to a people meter system.

AUDIENCE MEASUREMENTS OF RADIO

Telephone recall and diaries are the two methods used in making audience measurements of radio. There is a single national measurement service—Radio's All Dimension Audience Research (RADAR), and two services provide measurements of local radio audiences—Arbitron and Birch.

NATIONAL MEASUREMENT: RADAR (STATISTICAL RESEARCH INC.)

RADAR's method is telephone recall. A telephone call obtains recall for station listening covering the previous 24 hours, over a period of one week in the same households. A summer–fall study covers 24 weeks between May and October, and a winter-spring study covers 24 weeks between November and April.

First, a prelisting telephone call is made to a selected household in which all household members 12 and over are listed, a respondent is randomly selected, and cooperation is solicited. In the same call, the best time of day to reach respondents for later contacts is determined.

During the one-week survey period, a daily telephone call is made to obtain recall for station listening by 15-minute periods for the previous 24 hours of listening.

National random-digit dialing provides coverage of all telephones, listed and unlisted. There is a response rate of 65 percent. The actual and effective sample size is approximately 12,000 annually.

The usual audience estimates are provided. A follow-up report[46] gives complete tracking for a one-week schedule on a network. Data are provided in printed reports, but they are also available in electronic form, accessible through a PC.

LOCAL MEASUREMENT: ARBITRON

Arbitron's method is essentially a diary technique, run during sweeps periods, with a 7-day diary.

The sample is randomly selected by telephone (including unlisted numbers) for each of 260 local markets. The usual audience measurements are provided for each market.

ClusterPlus Lifestyle can be provided for the area but not for the audience. Product usage data can be provided from Simmons.

LOCAL MEASUREMENT: BIRCH[47]

Birch's method is similar to the RADAR technique, except that it is applied to local market measurement. The basic technique is daily telephone contacts over a 7-day period, covering recall of yesterday's listening activity between 5 a.m. and midnight. The measurements are conducted quarterly in continually surveyed markets: winter (December, January, February), spring (March, April, May), summer (June, July, August), fall (September, October, November); and in nonmonthly markets during the spring (December through May) and fall (June through November).

The initial telephone interview obtains cooperation and demographics (family size, income, occupation, and working women).

The questioning time for the 7-day period is 5 p.m. to 10 p.m. on weekdays, 10 a.m. to 10 p.m. on Sundays. Questioning covers yesterday's listening by day part and last night 7 p.m. to midnight. Start and stop times and location (home, car, or other out-of-home location) are asked for each listening period.

The sampling covers 250+ markets, 109 continuously and the remainder less frequently.

The quarterly report provides audience ratings by day part, hour by hour, by location (at-home, in-car, other away-from-home locations), by county, demographics, and ethnicity. It includes cume duplication tables and shows audience composition by media usage (weekday newspaper readership, television viewing) and product/service usage (airline travel, beer consumption, financial service usage, and the like).

For broadcasters, the BirchPlus Microcomputer Data Analysis System provides monthly and quarterly rating data on disk. Also available is respondent-by-respondent material, which permits special cross-tabulations.

For broadcast and agency subscribers, tapes are available that make it possible to develop materials such as quarterly summaries and monthly trends.

A SMALLER SQUABBLE

In addition to the squabble about how to measure television audiences, there is one about the methods of measuring radio audiences. But this one is a much smaller squabble. First, varying results of different techniques haven't hit radio that hard. Second, it seems to be—valid or not—chiefly a squabble instigated by Birch and aimed at the Arbitron diary method of measuring radio audiences.

Birch argues that Arbitron's diary technique may be outmoded for measuring radio audiences.[48] Here is their argument. It maintains that the diary method, after a test, was adopted in 1966 at a time when radio listening was relatively easy to measure. There was little competition on the AM band, and there was almost no FM. Now FM has exploded. Total stations have doubled, from 5,000 to 10,000. In the 1960s there were few working wives: The typical household was headed by a working male with the wife staying at home. Today communication has become oral rather than written. Our society has moved from writing to the telephone.

It is not surprising, argues Birch, that Arbitron shows the lowest completion rates of any of the three radio services, as shown in Exhibit 18.10. The discussion does not end there. One former user of Birch complained that after three years with the service, he went back to Arbitron because the Birch ratings fluctuated so much.[50]

A POSSIBLE DEVELOPMENT

As indicated, the chief complaints about current radio-tuning measurements are that diary measurements understate out-of-home tuning and

**Exhibit 18.10   AVERAGE RESPONSE RATES FOR THREE
RADIO AUDIENCE MEASUREMENT
RESEARCH SERVICES[49]**

	Method	Response Rate
Birch	Recall	61.8%
RADAR	Recall	60.0
Arbitron	Diary	43.3

that the electronic measurements miss them entirely. In late 1990, two members of Viewfacts obtained a patent for a device that seems to solve these problems.[51] It is a self-powered device that the person would carry and that would log tuning to stations wherever the person might be.

AUDIENCE MEASUREMENTS OF MAGAZINES

Simmons Market Research Bureau measures media audiences and other media aspects in its massive study[52] covering other topics as well, described in Chapter 15. Data are provided on 128 magazines.[53]

The sampling procedure, described in the earlier chapter, appears impeccable. But since we have not reviewed the way that the media data are collected, we do so now.

For measurement of the audience, the "through the book" method is used. The person is taken through the book, and aided recognition questions are asked.

Specifically, the interviewer carries a deck of cards, each containing the logo of one of the magazines being covered. The deck is handed to the respondent, who is asked to sort the cards into two piles, placing in one pile those he or she might have read or looked into in the past six months, and in the other pile those the person is sure that he or she has not read or looked into.

For each magazine that the respondent "might have read or looked into," a stripped issue (containing up to nine articles) is shown. The issue is sufficiently dated to permit time for the magazine to accumulate its total audience. The person is shown each of the articles and then asked whether the particular issue was seen. Following that, the number of days looked at is asked, and then follow other queries such as where the publication was seen and the overall rating.

Simmons generates reports showing, for each magazine, summaries of audience accumulation and reach, net unduplicated audiences for combinations of magazines, total and in-home audiences by demographics and psychographics, and qualitative measures of readership.

Database material about households and their members secured from a national study are used to describe the audiences of local television and radio stations. But the audience measurements are conducted by other research services independently of the national database study. There is no direct access to the replies of anyone to the Simmons Study of Media & Markets (SMM) databases. The responses of those measured by SMM are not melded into responses of those sampled in the audience study (conducted either by Arbitron or Nielsen).

To understand this projection system, one must begin with awareness of the starting database, SMM. This annual study is based on personal, in-home interviews with some 19,000 adults, more fully described in Chapter 15. Two of these annual studies are combined for use in the database. It is massive in the scope of its measurements about the household in total and its members, as the following abbreviated summary shows:

Product Usage and Purchase Behavior
Partial listing of products: toiletries (from deodorants to toothpaste), pharmaceuticals and drugs, women's cosmetics, beverages, tobacco products, camera and photography, stereos (including records and tapes), book clubs, games and toys, personal computers, banking and investments, insurance, home improvements and pet foods, take-out foods, florists, men's wear, women's wear, and telegrams and wires.
Partial listing of behavior: product usage and purchase behavior covering such elements as dollars spent, and brand or type of product, frequency of purchase or use, methods of buying, in-store, mail, telephone, catalogs, yellow pages.

Service Usage
Partial listing of services: hotels and motels, foreign travel, domestic travel, restaurants, sports events.

Newspaper Readership

Ownership
Partial listing: vehicles (automobiles, trucks, motorcycles), credit cards.

Personal Activities and Involvements
Partial listing: community activities (voting, getting in touch with a local communications medium, etc.), contributions, memberships (civic clubs, fraternal orders, religious groups, etc.), and even daily travel.

Personal Traits and Interests
(From affectionate to trustworthy, from interested in theories to support of the United Nations.)

Although the two methods of projection (one used by Arbitron, the other by Nielsen) vary in some of the details, each follows the same basic

Exhibit 18.11 **THREE STEPS IN PROJECTING DETAILED CHARACTERISTICS COLLECTED ON NATIONAL BASIS TO LOCAL AUDIENCE DATA**

Step 1.
Aggregating the SMM national data by small clusters within the four census regions.

Step 2.
Projecting these SMM data to larger areas (ADIs) used in reporting media audiences.

Step 3.
Profiling media audiences in terms of these SMM data.

steps shown in Exhibit 18.11. The projected SMM product/brand, demographic, and generic newspaper data are said to apply proportionately across the board to the local station audience.[54] Exhibit 18.12 shows a sample of a Simmons report of basic magazine audience data showing ratings, reach, and frequency expressed in thousands. But its reports go a lot further. It also produces tables showing duplication of each one of these 128 magazines versus each other one. Additionally, for each magazine, they show—separately for all adults, males, females, and female homemakers—median age, median individual employment income, and median household income.

The Simmons study also covers newspapers, television, radio, and other media. We will review their research in connection with newspapers, but not radio or television, since the continuing services previously reviewed for these media provide more timely information.

Mediamark, in connection with its twice-annual study described in Chapter 15, measures magazine audiences,[55] as well as radio, television, and some newspaper audiences (which we discuss later in this chapter), but since the television and radio audience measurements are far less used and less frequent than those previously discussed in this chapter, we do not examine these.

The sample for Mediamark was discussed in an earlier chapter, but the questioning procedure for the media measurements was not.

The "recent reading" technique is used in a face-to-face approach. The concept is that the number of people reading any issue of a magazine during its publication period equals the total number of people reading any issue over its total life. So people are asked whether they have read any issue during the past 30 days for a monthly, the past 7 days for a weekly, and so on. This is termed the *publication interval*, though it is not mentioned to the respondent.

People are first asked to sort a deck of magazine logo cards according to those they are sure they have read, those they are not sure they have read, and those they are sure they have not read within the past six months.

The person then sorts through the "sure they have read" pile to eliminate those magazines that have not been read during the most recent publication interval. Those who are certain they have read or looked into a specific magazine are considered part of that magazine's total audience. Audience members are then asked how frequently they read the magazine, and these replies are used to estimate cumulative audiences and turnover. Qualitative data such as place of reading (in-home, at work, on airplane), number of days the publication was read, amount of time spent reading it, actions taken as a result of reading it (cutting out or using cents-off coupons or recipes, sending for information about a product or for the product itself, or cutting out an ad or ads, or an article or articles), source of the issue, percentage of pages looked at, overall rating of the magazine, and the reader's interest in advertising in the magazine.

Since each wave of interviewing extends over five months, the data are simply totaled (with necessary weightings) and the totals used as representative of the total period.

The magazine results, covering some 166 publications, present basic information on cume audience, 4-issue reach and frequency. The qualitative data are available for each magazine. Demographics are also available for each.

Starch,[56] as mentioned in Chapter 14, also measures advertising readership in magazines. In a personal interview, respondents who have seen the particular issue of a publication are taken through the publication page by page and asked whether they remember seeing or reading each ad. Additional questions are asked about each ad seen or read, but these are not reviewed here because they are not part of the readership measurement.

The service covers 100 publications, including consumer, business, and trade magazines, and 150 readers of each publication are questioned.

Ballot Research[57] (Starch) is a mail survey version of the Starch service. This abridged form covers readership of advertising and editorial content of small, controlled (free, sent to a select mailing list), or widely dispersed publications, where personal interviewing would be too expensive. The contacts are made through a mail survey sent to 200 potential respondents, with the expectation of about 150 responses.

"Ballots" (stickers) are affixed to 60 preselected items (editorial content and advertising) in an issue. This marked issue is sent some two

Exhibit 18.12   **1989 SIMMONS BASIC AUDIENCE DATA FOR 128 MAGAZINES**

0001
M-3

0001
M-3

TOTAL ADULTS
REACH AND FREQUENCY

(IN THOUSANDS)

	U.S. TOTAL	AVERAGE AUDIENCE	RATING	TURNOVER RATE	REACH				FREQUENCY DISTRIBUTION			
					ONE	TWO	THREE	FOUR	1 OF 4	2 OF 4	3 OF 4	4 OF 4
AMERICAN BABY	178193	2277	1.3	.468	2277	3341	4035	4548	2053	1079	766	650
AMERICAN HEALTH	178193	2648	1.5	.496	2648	3963	4835	5487	2607	1323	888	669
ARCHITECTURAL DIGEST	178193	2143	1.2	.550	2143	3321	4133	4751	2472	1161	696	422
BABY TALK	178193	1726	1.0	.522	1726	2627	3235	3694	1836	897	572	390
BARRON'S	178193	1390	0.8	.466	1390	2039	2461	2774	1252	656	467	399
BETTER HOMES & GARDENS	178193	22609	12.7	.423	22609	32179	38107	42352	16977	10103	7836	7436
BON APPETIT	178193	3585	2.0	.424	3585	5106	6069	6771	2811	1558	1197	1205
BRIDE'S	178193	3174	1.8	.601	3174	5082	6442	7496	4218	1832	971	474
BUSINESS WEEK	178193	6568	3.7	.502	6568	9868	12057	13689	6528	3340	2216	1604
CAR AND DRIVER	178193	4817	2.7	.419	4817	6837	8109	9036	3707	2073	1608	1648
CHANGING TIMES	178193	2080	1.2	.546	2080	3214	3992	4584	2367	1119	678	419
COLONIAL HOMES	178193	1830	1.0	.476	1830	2701	3272	3696	1696	880	615	505
CONDE NAST LIMITED (NET)	178193	14196	8.0	.452	14196	20610	24693	27667	11897	6655	4882	4233
CONDE NAST LIMITED PLUS(NET)	178193	15831	8.9	.441	15831	22814	27223	30419	12784	7276	5448	4911
CONDE NAST PKG. WOMEN(NET)	178193	17114	9.6	.390	17114	23796	27881	30800	11676	6993	5728	6402
CONSUMERS DIGEST	178193	3268	1.8	.479	3268	4833	5858	6619	3045	1584	1101	889
COSMOPOLITAN	178193	11737	6.6	.420	11737	16669	19757	21992	8941	5114	3970	3968
COUNTRY LIVING	178193	6466	3.6	.461	6466	9449	11377	12795	5676	3049	2192	1878
CREATIVE IDEAS FOR LIVING	178193	2005	1.1	.570	2005	3147	3944	4556	2446	1114	638	358
CYCLE	178193	2118	1.2	.433	2118	3034	3618	4046	1711	935	708	692
CYCLE WORLD	178193	2034	1.1	.445	2034	2939	3520	3947	1710	921	682	634
DIAMANDIS MAG NETWORK(NET)	178193	13804	7.7	.350	13804	18633	21526	23579	8213	5033	4394	5939
DIAMANDIS MTRCYCL GRP(NET)	178193	3145	1.8	.379	3145	4336	5068	5597	2113	1225	1016	1242
DISCOVER	178193	3901	2.2	.437	3901	5607	6694	7491	3187	1744	1310	1250
EBONY	178193	8719	4.9	.328	8719	11581	13281	14487	4823	2967	2669	4029
ELLE	178193	2122	1.2	.514	2122	3213	3946	4497	2203	1090	706	497
ESQUIRE	178193	2528	1.4	.560	2528	3944	4925	5674	2998	1389	814	474
ESSENCE	178193	4012	2.3	.386	4012	5561	6517	7208	2763	1594	1307	1544
FAMILY CIRCLE	178193	18140	10.2	.442	18140	26164	31220	34877	14627	8395	6276	5578
THE FAMILY HANDYMAN	178193	3350	1.9	.460	3350	4889	5885	6620	2941	1565	1129	985
FIELD & STREAM	178193	10747	6.0	.400	10747	15045	17705	19622	7668	4457	3582	3916
FINANCIAL WORLD	178193	1350	0.8	.420	1350	1917	2275	2537	1047	579	448	463
FLOWER & GARDEN	178193	2519	1.4	.492	2519	3799	4579	5192	2450	1249	845	648
FOOD & WINE	178193	1793	1.0	.519	1793	2724	3351	3824	1891	928	595	410
FORBES	178193	3634	2.0	.475	3634	5362	6491	7329	3349	1752	1226	1002
FORTUNE	178193	4042	2.3	.526	4042	6167	7603	8685	4327	2123	1342	892
GQ/GENTLEMEN'S QUARTERLY	178193	4463	2.5	.561	4463	6967	8699	10019	5282	2467	1442	828
GLAMOUR	178193	7805	4.4	.475	7805	11513	13927	15710	7129	3789	2654	2137
GOLF	178193	2941	1.7	.379	2941	4056	4742	5238	1981	1147	951	1159
GOLF DIGEST	178193	3501	2.0	.358	3501	4754	5515	6061	2182	1291	1107	1480
GOLF DIGEST/TENNIS (NET)	178193	4773	2.7	.384	4773	6607	7738	8554	3263	1890	1555	1846
GOOD HOUSEKEEPING	178193	20947	11.8	.446	20947	30288	36167	40408	16965	9824	7302	6317
GOURMET	178193	2353	1.3	.442	2353	3393	4058	4547	1956	1059	789	743
HARPER'S BAZAAR	178193	2807	1.6	.587	2807	4455	5618	6515	3589	1595	876	455
HEALTH	178193	3095	1.7	.446	3095	4475	5361	6011	2604	1407	1040	961
HEARST GOLD BUY (NET)	178193	11688	6.6	.496	11688	17481	21286	24101	11261	5938	3994	2908
HEARST HOME BUY (NET)	178193	10790	6.1	.431	10790	15444	18381	20516	8539	4813	3662	3502
HEARST MAN POWER (NET)	178193	11002	6.2	.455	11002	16008	19213	21958	9379	5163	3761	3255
HEARST WOMAN POWER (NET)	178193	38291	21.5	.324	38291	50685	57800	62703	19612	13271	12271	17549
HOME	178193	2549	1.4	.524	2549	3885	4789	5470	2726	1332	844	568
HOME MECHANIX	178193	2955	1.7	.477	2955	4366	5290	5976	2744	1428	995	808
HOMEOWNER	178193	1984	1.1	.506	1984	2988	3659	4162	2013	1006	662	481
HG/HOUSE & GARDEN	178193	3030	1.7	.500	3030	4546	5553	6307	3014	1524	1016	753
HOUSE BEAUTIFUL	178193	3841	2.2	.549	3841	5948	7394	8493	4395	2085	1253	760
INC.	178193	1690	0.9	.442	1690	2437	2916	3268	1408	761	566	533
INSIDE SPORTS	178193	3722	2.1	.504	3722	5597	6846	7781	3739	1887	1248	908
JET	178193	7548	4.2	.326	7548	10007	11466	12502	4142	2546	2298	3517
LADIES' HOME JOURNAL	178193	14526	8.2	.406	14526	20430	24083	26711	10512	6152	4898	5149
LIFE	178193	12121	6.8	.547	12121	18746	23247	26630	13534	6701	4033	2362
LOS ANGELES TIMES MAGAZINE	178193	3564	2.0	.364	3564	4862	5653	6221	2273	1337	1136	1475
MADEMOISELLE	178193	4197	2.4	.540	4197	6463	8008	9178	4679	2252	1381	866
MCCALL'S	178193	15025	8.4	.455	15025	21856	26210	29381	12683	7098	5179	4420
MCCALL'S/WRK MOTHER (NET)	178193	16063	9.0	.451	16063	23307	27906	31249	13370	7543	5546	4790
MCCALL'S/WRK MOTH/HOM(NET)	178193	17440	9.8	.441	17440	25137	29988	33498	14042	8043	6023	5391
MCCALL'S/WRK WOMAN (NET)	178193	16584	9.3	.446	16584	23979	28658	32051	13573	7713	5725	5041
MONEY	178193	6015	3.4	.473	6015	8858	10709	12078	5474	2897	2038	1669
MOTHER EARTH NEWS	178193	1413	0.8	.476	1413	2036	2526	2853	1309	679	475	390
MS.	178193	1049	0.6	.529	1049	1605	1982	2267	1142	551	345	229
MUSCLE & FITNESS	178193	3535	2.0	.391	3535	4917	5772	6392	2477	1420	1155	1339
NATIONAL ENQUIRER	178193	20025	11.2	.399	20025	28013	32905	36397	13969	8396	6789	7243
NATIONAL GEOGRAPHIC	178193	23179	13.0	.382	23179	32042	37398	41194	15183	9357	7794	8859

Source: Reproduced with the permission of Simmons Market Research Bureau.

```
0002                                                                                                          0002
M-3                                                                                                           M-3
                                              TOTAL ADULTS
                                            REACH AND FREQUENCY
                                             (IN THOUSANDS)
                                                               REACH                    FREQUENCY DISTRIBUTION
                    U.S.    AVERAGE          TURNOVER  ───────────────────────────   ───────────────────────────
                    TOTAL   AUDIENCE  RATING   RATE    ONE    TWO    THREE   FOUR     1 OF 4  2 OF 4  3 OF 4  4 OF 4
```

	U.S. TOTAL	AVERAGE AUDIENCE	RATING	TURNOVER RATE	ONE	TWO	THREE	FOUR	1 OF 4	2 OF 4	3 OF 4	4 OF 4
NATURAL HISTORY	178193	1199	0.7	.493	1199	1791	2183	2476	1173	594	401	308
NEW WOMAN	178193	2855	1.6	.485	2855	4238	5149	5827	2711	1397	960	758
NEW YORK	178193	1496	0.8	.367	1496	2045	2381	2623	967	565	477	614
THE NEW YORKER	178193	2361	1.3	.529	2361	3611	4458	5099	2562	1242	780	515
NEWSWEEK	178193	19636	11.0	.434	19636	28158	33491	37333	15367	8945	6795	6225
THE N.Y. TIMES DAILY EDITION	178193	3303	1.9	.343	3303	4438	5121	5609	1952	1170	1026	1461
THE N.Y. TIMES MAGAZINE	178193	3640	2.0	.391	3640	5064	5947	6586	2554	1465	1190	1376
OMNI	178193	2780	1.6	.557	2780	4327	5396	6211	3261	1521	898	530
1,001 HOME IDEAS	178193	3524	2.0	.458	3524	5137	6179	6948	3076	1642	1188	1043
ORGANIC GARDENING	178193	2506	1.4	.443	2506	3615	4325	4847	2088	1130	841	788
OUTDOOR LIFE	178193	7782	4.4	.421	7782	11057	13116	14613	5987	3376	2613	2637
PARADE MAGAZINE	178193	66436	37.3	.244	66436	82662	91274	96955	22727	17582	18735	37912
PARENTS	178193	5595	3.1	.491	5595	8342	10152	11499	5385	2784	1890	1439
PEOPLE	178193	28678	16.1	.442	28678	41355	49230	54848	22471	13546	10174	8656
PERSONAL BEST MEDIA GRP(NET)	178193	6795	3.8	.477	6795	10033	12144	13705	6245	3301	2306	1854
PLAYBOY	178193	8829	5.0	.432	8829	12647	15063	16822	7039	3936	2986	2861
POPULAR MECHANICS	178193	5810	3.3	.461	5810	8487	10217	11491	5097	2733	1967	1693
POPULAR SCIENCE	178193	4421	2.5	.477	4421	6530	7908	8930	4088	2140	1493	1210
PREVENTION	178193	5727	3.2	.439	5727	8243	9846	11020	4695	2578	1931	1816
PSYCHOLOGY TODAY	178193	3254	1.8	.510	3254	4914	6023	6856	3330	1664	1087	774
READER'S DIGEST	178193	35737	20.1	.327	35737	47420	54161	58823	18646	12475	11453	16249
REDBOOK	178193	10378	5.8	.443	10378	14978	17904	20038	8537	4747	3534	3220
ROAD & TRACK	178193	3536	2.0	.434	3536	5070	6046	6761	2860	1568	1185	1148
ROLLING STONE	178193	5512	3.1	.465	5512	8078	9741	10969	4909	2616	1866	1578
SCIENTIFIC AMERICAN	178193	1949	1.1	.578	1949	3076	3867	4476	2436	1094	614	332
SELF	178193	3188	1.8	549	3188	4940	6144	7060	3663	1730	1038	629
SEVENTEEN	178193	3892	2.2	.469	3892	5716	6902	7779	3510	1853	1314	1103
SHAPE	178193	1929	1.1	.479	1929	2854	3461	3913	1806	934	648	524
SKI	178193	1333	0.7	.501	1333	2000	2445	2778	1332	669	445	331
SKIING	178193	1510	0.8	.429	1510	2158	2571	2872	1208	661	504	500
SMITHSONIAN	178193	6253	3.5	.408	6253	8806	10402	11559	4628	2630	2079	2222
SOAP OPERA DIGEST	178193	4850	2.7	.459	4850	7078	8518	9579	4245	2272	1639	1424
SOUTHERN LIVING	178193	7015	3.9	.467	7015	10291	12413	13977	6258	3347	2382	1990
THE SPORTING NEWS	178193	3673	2.1	.415	3673	5199	6158	6856	2794	1564	1221	1277
SPORTS AFIELD	178193	3597	2.0	.511	3597	5436	6667	7591	3695	1845	1202	849
SPORTS ILLUSTRATED	178193	20432	11.5	.381	20432	28224	32944	36298	13418	8193	6825	7862
STAR	178193	10958	6.1	.429	10958	15463	18627	20780	8612	4868	3717	3583
SUNDAY MAGAZINE NETWORK	178193	40439	22.7	.230	40439	50064	55358	58955	14400	10146	10574	23836
SUNSET	178193	3438	1.9	.309	3438	4499	5124	5548	1773	1095	1011	1689
TV GUIDE	178193	40204	22.6	.304	40204	52408	59327	64071	18977	13046	12446	19602
TENNIS	178193	1334	0.7	.513	1334	2018	2478	2823	1382	683	444	315
TIME	178193	24570	13.8	.438	24570	35334	42043	46851	19234	11403	8615	7599
TRAVEL & LEISURE	178193	2162	1.2	.576	2162	3407	4280	4951	2683	1211	684	373
TRUE STORY	178193	3712	2.1	.463	3712	5431	6545	7368	3292	1748	1252	1076
USA TODAY	178193	6326	3.5	.702	6326	10765	14163	16906	10971	3937	1537	462
USA WEEKEND	178193	29461	16.5	.283	29461	37799	42538	45813	13101	8779	8644	15388
U.S. NEWS & WORLD REPORT	178193	12099	6.8	.470	12099	17779	21444	24137	10762	5857	4151	3366
US	178193	4625	2.6	.580	4625	7309	9191	10636	5781	2620	1442	773
VANITY FAIR	178193	1487	0.8	.501	1487	2232	2729	3101	1489	747	497	368
VOGUE	178193	5441	3.1	.553	5441	8449	10516	12085	6279	2982	1775	1049
WALL STREET JOURNAL	178193	4768	2.7	.559	4768	7433	9274	10676	5609	2631	1544	892
WEIGHT WATCHERS	178193	2774	1.6	.435	2774	3980	4748	5311	2253	1331	929	898
WOMAN'S DAY	178193	15428	8.7	.409	15428	21732	25635	28441	11225	6578	5219	5419
WOMAN'S WORLD	178193	5155	2.9	.495	5155	7708	9396	10653	5030	2582	1738	1303
WORKBENCH	178193	1905	1.1	.361	1905	2594	3013	3315	1206	708	604	796
WORKING MOTHER	178193	1558	0.9	.579	1558	2461	3095	3584	1955	875	490	265
WORKING WOMAN	178193	2343	1.3	.494	2343	3500	4266	4838	2289	1164	786	599
WRK MOTHER/WRK WOMAN (NET)	178193	3567	2.0	.495	3567	5333	6801	7373	3488	1708	1199	906
DAILY NEWSPAPERS READ ANY	178193	113337	63.6	.201	113337	136156	146378	152290	23644	25869	33139	69637
WEEKEND/SUNDAY NEWSPAPERS READ ANY	178193	119349	67.0	.180	119349	140777	150133	155476	21370	24081	32236	77789

weeks after the subscriber has received the standard issue. We do not have too much confidence in a technique using a self-selected sample.

Gallup & Robinson (Princeton, N.J.) offers a similar approach to the basic Starch method of measuring readership of magazines. The personal interview begins by thorough questioning about specific magazines respondents report they have read. Copies of the advertisements are then shown, along with cards showing product brand names. Some of these are products and brand names not appearing in the particular issue, and these are used as a control to measure false recognition.

AUDIENCE MEASUREMENTS OF NEWSPAPERS

Simmons also covers newspapers in its audience measurements. The questioning technique used is somewhat different from that used for magazines. In newspaper measurements, the Simmons procedure calls for two interviews with each respondent—separated by a short time interval—using the "yesterday reading" method. The questioning covers both daily and Sunday newspapers (Sunday supplement results are accumulated by totaling results for all Sunday newspapers carrying the particular supplement).

For daily newspapers, respondents are first asked what newspapers they have read or looked into during the past six months. Then, excluding the day of the interview, they are asked when they last looked into an issue of the particular paper, and the amount read (but only the replies of those reading yesterday are counted). The same general procedure is followed for Sunday newspapers, with necessary changes.

Mediamark audience measurements also cover newspapers. The measurement technique basically parallels its magazine procedure. The interviewer has a list of daily and Sunday newspapers that circulate in the particular area. For the daily papers, respondents are asked which ones they have read or looked into in the past seven days; for Sunday papers the time period is four weeks. After the initial sorting out, respondents are asked about reading the daily newspapers yesterday, the Sunday papers within the past seven days. Qualitative questions about place of reading and how the paper was obtained are also asked of those who qualify as audience members.

Birch Scarborough conducts newspaper audience studies and currently serves 20 of the top 25 newspapers.[58] The measurement methods parallel those of Simmons and Mediamark except that there are no personal interviews. There are two telephone interviews asking about which of a list of daily newspapers the respondents have read or looked into in the past seven days. For the list of Sunday papers, the time period is four weeks. Respondents then are asked about reading the daily newspapers yesterday and the Sunday papers within the past seven days. Through a repeat interview, the technique also provides estimates of reach and frequency.

COMPUTERIZED INTERMEDIA PROJECTIONS: FUSION

"Fusion"[59] is the melding of data from two independent surveys to construct both additional cases and additional information about all the cases. The major application is media research. It has been used for some years in Europe (France and Germany) to combine print and television data, and more recently it has been applied in Canada.

Two Canadian surveys provide an example. One was an industry television survey measuring television viewing in the fall of one year. The other was a separate print media and product survey, measuring magazine reading, other media exposure, and product usage. Both surveys also measured demographics. Each was conducted in metropolitan Toronto. The base for the television survey was 2,283, and for the print study it was 925.

The print study was used as the recipient base on which to build the final melded product.

Respondents were matched from each of the two surveys on the basis of 87 variables common to each study. The linking variables were mainly demographics (sex, age, education, etc.), television usage (heaviness of usage, hours of viewing prime time, etc.), and other selected aspects (such as ownership of a cable converter and subscription to pay TV).

The fusion process was basically done within 18 control cells, though all 87 variables were used to get the best possible match. The cells involved combinations of sex, age, and education as typically used in defining target market groups such as males aged 25–34 with high school or higher education. Average issue data from the print study were adjusted to "true" television study audience data within each of 12 demographically defined adjustment cells.

Fusion provided additional demographics and psychographics, and additional material on buying behavior and intermedia relationships. Its basic goal was to offer media buyers the advantages of a single-source base, when there is no way that a single data collection method can obtain all of the desired information.[60]

Withers rationalizes that though the process may not carry the high standards of reproducing interrelationships that a true single-source study would, it might produce results on cumes that would be close enough to original results to be useful to media buyers. Results showed that this was not the general pattern.

We see no way to predict how accurately fusion produces total results. We know of no way to measure any error introduced by the process. We question a "study" in which accuracy cannot be estimated in advance.

COMPUTERIZED MEDIA PLANNING AND SCHEDULING

With the availability of a vast array of audience data about all major media, it is not surprising that computer specialists have come up with various programs for media planning and scheduling. The concept is simple: Enter all appropriate available audience data and with a statement of objectives the computer will churn out the data for decision making. Some of these programs cover only a single medium, such as television. Since the amount of detail we can cover in this book is limited, we will look at some of the multimedia programs.

These programs are designed variously for the advertiser, the advertising agency, or the advertising medium. The logic of the first two is clear, for these firms make and execute media plans. In the case of the advertising medium, the usefulness of these programs is in having a factually backed-up plan to sell to current or potential advertisers.

The MEMRI System (Microevaluation by Mediamark Research Inc.)[61] is designed chiefly for advertisers and their agencies. The program is aimed at producing optimal media schedules and providing reach and frequency. Basically, the schedules use efficient reach for a particular budget, although minimum and maximum insertions can be utilized in the program plan. Since the database can include category purchase data, such data can also be provided by category.

While reportedly user-friendly and available to users with a PC-compatible having a floppy drive and a hard disk, we see a major limitation. The user can use only Mediamark data, which provide only half-year audience measurements for television and radio, two important, constantly changing media. It is doubtful whether national measurements can be properly adjusted to produce dependable local data.

Mediamark is presently planning a multimedia reach and frequency model that will be able to use Nielsen or Arbitron data.[62]

The Harris Donovan program[63] provides reach and frequency data for several individual media to be included in a local media plan. It utilizes single medium data, avoiding production of numbers through random duplication. In random duplication, it is assumed that those hearing the radio campaign will be spread proportionately across those who did and did not see the newspaper campaign. The random duplication method can result in misleading results, such as a total reach figure that is too high. The Harris Donovan program does not take such a short cut—it uses *actual* duplication data.

The program is user-friendly. On a PC system the user enters the demographics of importance in the media plan, the proposed media and their schedules, and the program does the rest.

TAPSCAN (Birmingham)[64,65] offers a sophisticated media-scheduling program for use on a PC.

The *input* into the program includes television data from either Arbitron or Nielsen, at the user's choice. Radio data come from either Arbitron or Birch figures, and newspaper data from national Starch readership data. These data are loaded onto a standard computer disk.

Once targets have been set up, the local advertiser or agency can generate a plan or schedule that will produce the aims in terms of the specifics of audience, reach, frequency, and cost per thousand.

CAMEO (Management Science Associates, Pittsburgh) provides primarily television and frequency estimates for the media planner.[66] Depending on input about networks, programs and spots, it generates data about reach and frequency for network television (by day part), network cable, spot television (largely by day part), and other media.

CAMEO Express, by the same firm, uses only GRPs and demographics as inputs. Reach and frequency are reported for each plan and demographic, as required, for up to 100 plans and 12 inputs.

WISH (Management Science Associates, Pittsburgh) provides an allocation of the spot budget to try to weight each marketing area ideally into the requirements of the specific brand.[67,68]

PRINT CIRCULATION MEASUREMENT

THE CONCEPT

Circulation is a publisher's statement of the number and nature of circulated copies. It has a different meaning from audience. Audience concerns the total number of people reached; circulation has to do with number of copies only. In the case of most print media, a single copy is likely to reach more than just one person, so audience figures will be larger than circulation.

For publications offering advertising, circulation is usually verified by an independent audit of the publisher's records, necessary to provide assurance to advertisers that they are getting what they paid for.

This is parallel to the concept of a financial audit of records by a financial auditor. The Audit Bureau of Circulations (ABC) is a group financed by advertisers, advertising agencies, and publishers; it was organized over 75 years ago.

The Audit

There is an on-site inspection of the relevant publisher's records, conducted twice annually except for newspapers, where it is done once annually (by ABC, at least). In the audit, publisher claims for two previous statements are checked with distributors or subscribers as well. For example, publishers typically keep press run records by issue, as well as distribution and return records (including mail subscriptions). The nature of the records and the checks vary with type of publication.

ABC figures are net paid circulation determined on a daily basis and averaged over a five-day period.[69]

What the ABC Reports Show[70,71,72]

ABC reports cover two major aspects of circulation: (1) per-issue circulation, with breakouts by geography (nature of business, where applicable), and (2) circulation by nature of method (relevant methods for the specific publication such as subscription, single-copy sales, carrier, third-party or bulk sales where businesses make copies available to their patrons, such as hotels and airlines).

A typical one-page ABC report on *Southern Outdoors* is shown in Exhibit 18.13.

Formats of ABC Material

The Circulation Data Book is available in print format (either printouts or bound volumes) or in electronic format (disk, magnetic tape, or online).

THE USE OF CIRCULATION DATA IN THE SALE/PURCHASE OF NEWSPAPER SPACE

The sale and purchase of newspaper space is frequently made on the basis of circulation data. Usually, cost per thousand of circulation is the

Exhibit 18.13 AN AUDIT REPORT BY THE AUDIT BUREAU OF CIRCULATIONS

Audit Bureau of Circulations

PRINTED AND RELEASED
BY ABC APRIL, 1990

AUDIT REPORT: Magazine

SOUTHERN OUTDOORS
Montgomery, Alabama

CLASS, INDUSTRY OR FIELD SERVED: Hunting, fishing and outdoor enthusiasts.

1. AVERAGE PAID CIRCULATION FOR 12 MONTHS ENDED JUNE 30, 1989:

Subscriptions:	218,070
Single Copy Sales:	15,723
AVERAGE TOTAL PAID CIRCULATION	233,793
Advertising Rate Base/Circulation Guarantee	None Claimed
Average Total Non-Paid Distribution 17,714	

1a. AVERAGE PAID CIRCULATION of Regional, Metro and Demographic Editions:

None of record

2. PAID CIRCULATION BY ISSUES:

Issue 1988	Subscriptions	Single Copy Sales	Total Paid	Issue 1989	Subscriptions	Single Copy Sales	Total Paid
July/Aug.	226,223	14,277	240,500	Jan.	235,268	13,125	248,393
Sept.	211,134	13,892	225,026	Feb.	214,884	23,324	238,208
Oct.	211,781	13,391	225,172	Mar.	218,440	17,229	235,669
Nov./Dec.	208,823	24,298	233,121	Apr.	217,104	8,375	225,479
				May/June	218,972	13,598	232,570

AVERAGE PAID CIRCULATION BY QUARTERS for the previous three years and period covered by this report:

Calendar Quarter Ended	1985	1986	1987	1988	1989
March 31		245,868	240,245	236,150	240,757
June 30		225,468	237,601	223,204	229,025
September 30	236,444	222,981	225,635	232,763	
December 31	220,182	217,917	215,971	220,146	

AUDIT STATEMENT

The difference shown in average paid circulation in comparing this report with the Publisher's Statements for the period audited is 1,906 copies per issue deduction from paid circulation.

To Members of the Audit Bureau of Circulations:

We have examined the circulation records and other data presented by this publication for the period covered by this report. Our examinations were made in accordance with the Bureau's Bylaws and Rules, and included such tests and other audit procedures as we considered necessary under the circumstances.

In our opinion, the total average paid circulation for the period shown is fairly stated in this report, and the other data contained in this report are fairly stated in all respects material to average paid circulation.

March, 1990

Audit Bureau of Circulations

(04-1133-0 - #151489 - 387 - SER)

basis for choice. While this may provide a rough comparison of one news-paper to another, it is scarcely a useful measurement, popular as its sim-plicity makes it when only newspapers are being considered as media. It has the advantage of being hard fact, since the circulation figures are audited, but it does not take into account such aspects as the number of readers per copy and frequency of reading. Circulation data are a far cry from audience data.

The method provides no real comparison with the audience data common to so many of the other media. There are two reasons. One is that the measurement itself (circulation versus audience) is quite differ-ent. Second, the territorial boundaries used are different. Other media most often use the ADI; newspapers use the Newspaper Designated Market Area (NDMA), the commercial and residential zones nearest to the newspaper's central city.

Standard Rate & Data offers Circulation 91,[73] which provides an analysis of penetration for major newspapers (daily, weekly, and Sun-day), and 22 consumer magazines for all counties, metro areas and television-viewing areas (ADI, DMI), aimed at assisting the media plan-ner in selecting the right media for a particular campaign. Circulation and demographics are provided.

THE FUTURE OF MEDIA RESEARCH

THE CHANGING MEDIA

Fractionated Media

Parallel to the fractionation of markets, media are becoming increas-ingly segmented too, and they are likely to become even more so. Con-sider some examples.

We have had regional and segmented magazines for years, and they are on the increase. Even more startling is the personalized magazine described in Chapter 16, where an issue of a magazine may include ad-vertisements and editorial material aimed at the interests of the indi-vidual recipient.

In the field of electronic media there are low-power television sta-tions.[74] These are restricted to a few thousand watts (versus millions of watts for typical television stations), and they do not usually offer cover-age of even as much as 25 miles (up to 70 miles for typical television sta-tions). This is truly local television. It offers local retailers a chance to use a medium that had been too expensive for them and covered an audi-ence area much larger than they could use effectively.

The FCC decided to use low-power television to fill obvious gaps in television offerings, chiefly geographic and thematic gaps. In only three years, the number of such stations doubled to just over 800 (and located in every state except Rhode Island), and the FCC is predicting as many as 4,000 by the end of the 1990s.

The thematic gap does seem to be filling too. There is an "all rural" channel in Nebraska, and the Silent Network (Los Angeles) provides captioned shows for the deaf.

Low-power networks are appearing. Channel America owns 14 low-power stations and transmits to 42 affiliates. The low-power television station faces much the same kinds of programming choice that a larger station does. It may buy syndicated programming, air network programs, or produce its own shows. Most use a mix of these.

A Fifth Medium?[75]

On-line interactive information, says Cutler, will soon be adding a fifth medium to the four we know so well: television, radio, magazines, and newspapers. You will no longer have to walk into the store; the store will come to you. So will editorial material geared to your particular interests.

It may be termed an electronic newspaper or magazine, electronic publishing, on-line information, telecomputing, multimedia, or videotex. From a marketing viewpoint, this development will reduce mass marketing to an almost simple conversation between seller and buyer, virtually a one-on-one dialogue.

France, through its telephone lines, has the first electronic white and yellow pages and an around-the-clock electronic marketplace that offers over 12,000 consumer services. Available are tax advice and the latest on-line news. The lonely can tune into a channel to make contact with those of the other sex. Like-minded fishermen or marketing researchers can get in touch with one another. Other than time charges, the only costs are for merchandise ordered.

Although the United States currently has no medium of this sort, there are some beginnings, and when fiber optical lines (able to carry words, sounds, and pictures into the home on telephone lines) are in place, the new medium will be with us. This is likely to happen in the late 1990s.

IMPLICATIONS FOR MEDIA RESEARCH

Our crystal ball is rather murky. The specific implications of these changes for media research cannot be predicted with any certainty. The only thing that is completely certain is that present research methods are in no way ready to cope with these changes.

But let's speculate a bit. It seems reasonable to think that one tremendously large national sample of homes, including subsamples of almost every kind of household you can think of, may have to be the key. If it were huge enough and enough were known about all of its marketing characteristics, then perhaps subsamples could be used to handle the needs of specific marketing firms and specific marketing aspects. It would mean that, except on a localized basis, even the personal information (income, credit, and all other "private" data frequently used in database marketing, as described in Chapter 16) would have to be part of the file on the family.

The measurement process almost surely would have to be electronic to handle the masses of data systematically and with reasonable speed.

The setup and maintenance of this enormous sample would be so costly an operation that all the major research firms would have to underwrite it, as they gradually melded their present measurement systems into it. All would have input in deciding what kinds of information were to go into it and be available to come out of it. Data withdrawals by a particular research firm—or a marketing firm—would be charged on some sort of cost-related basis.

A dream? Very likely. But if something akin to this does not take place, media research will not keep up with all the emerging technological and social changes, and the controversy about media research can only increase.

ENDNOTES

[1] W. S. Rubens. *Interview*, Aug. 27, 1990.

[2] R. J. Coen. *Estimated Annual U.S. Advertising Expenditures 1980–1989*. Prepared for *Advertising Age*, undated.

[3] R. J. Coen. "Coen: Little Ad Growth." *Advertising Age*, May 6, 1991, 1, 16.

[4] A. M. Crossley. *The Public Wants* (unpublished manuscript). Princeton, undated.

[5] *BAR-Monitoring Methodology*. New York: Arbitron, February 1989.

[6] *BrandTraq*. New York: Arbitron Ratings, 1988.

[7] Ira Teinowitz. "Arbitron, Nielsen Set to Track TV Ads." *Advertising Age*, July 17, 1989, 13.

[8] Patrick Barwise and Andrew Ehrenberg. *Television and Its Audience*. Newberry Park, Calif.: Sage, 1988.

[9] G. J. Goodhardt, A. S. C. Ehrenberg, and M. A. Collins. *Television Audience*. Brookfield, Vt., 1987.

[10]Bill Carter. "For CBS, an Upset in the Ratings Race at a Critical Turn." *New York Times*, Feb. 5, 1991, B1.

[11]Bill Carter. "CBS Wins, NBC Loses in Reversals of Ratings." *New York Times*, Feb. 28, 1991, B1–2.

[12]*1989–90 NTI Reference Supplement*. Northbrook, Ill.: Nielsen Media Research, 1989.

[13]"Missing: Six Million Working Women and College Students." *Bruskin Report*, August 1989.

[14]Jeremy Gerard. "TV Networks Want Nielsen to Change Rating Methods." *New York Times*, Dec. 14, 1989.

[15]"Networks Urge Changes in People Meter System." *Marketing News*, Jan. 22, 1990, 6.

[16]Bill Carter. "As Viewers Seem to Vanish, CBS Seeks Rating Changes." *New York Times*, May 4, 1990, C1 ff.

[17]Bill Carter. "TV Viewing Cited Outside of Homes." *New York Times*, May 10, 1990, C15.

[18]Bill Carter. "Nielsen to Study Changes in Ratings." *New York Times*, May 18, 1990, C17.

[19]Bill Carter. "ABC Plans to Impose New Rating System." *New York Times*, June 1, 1990, 1 ff.

[20]Bill Carter. "NBC Weighs a Change on Viewer Count." *New York Times*, June 2, 1990, Y21, 23.

[21]Dennis Kneale. "Fuzzy Picture." *The Wall Street Journal*, July 19, 1990, A1, A4.

[22]"Are Audiences Down, or Are Measurement Systems Down on Them?" *The Numbers News*, July 1990, 7.

[23]Wayne Walley. "TV Usage Rebounds to 'Normal' Levels." *Advertising Age*, July 30, 1990, 3 ff.

[24]Wayne Walley and Scott Hue. "Nielsen under Siege." *Advertising Age*, Aug. 6, 1990, 1 ff.

[25]Wayne Walley. "Vacationers Turning to TV." *Advertising Age*, Sept. 10, 1990, 81.

[26]Howard Schlossberg. "Case of the Missing TV Viewers: Everyone Knows They're Gone, but No One Knows Why." *Marketing News*, Sept. 17, 1990, 1 ff.

[27]Wayne Walley. "Nets Force TV Showdown." *Advertising Age*, Sept. 24, 1990, 3.

[28]Randall Rothenberg. "Black Hole in Television." *New York Times*, Oct. 8, 1990, C14 ff.

[29]"Nets Don't Sweat Ratings Yet." *Advertising Age*, Oct. 15, 1990, 58.

[30]Wayne Walley. "Finding Nielsen Glitch." *Advertising Age*, Oct. 22, 1990, 1.

[31]Wayne Walley. "TV Ratings Windfall." *Advertising Age*, Nov. 19, 1990, 56.

[32]Jack Honomichi. "Dirty Linen." *Inside Research*, Jan. 1991, 4–5.

[33]Alicia Lasek. "Worry About Content, Not System, Nets Urged." *Advertising Age*, Nov. 26, 1990, S-2.

[34]Kim Foltz. "NBC to Drop System of Adjustable Ratings." *New York Times*, Mar. 1, 1991, C17.

[35]Eben Shapiro. "CBS Joins NBC in Dropping Audience-Gauging System." *New York Times*, Mar. 4, 1991, C9.

[36]Bill Carter. "TV Viewers Beware: Nielsen May Be Looking." *New York Times*, June 1, 1989, C1, C17.

[37]*ScanAmerica Information Packet.* New York: Arbitron, undated.

[38]*Nielsen Station Index Reference Supplement.* Northbrook, Ill.: Nielsen Media Research, 1989.

[39]*Nielsen Station Index: An Overview of the Local Market Television.* Northbrook, Ill.: Nielsen Media Research.

[40]*Audience Measurement Service.* Northbrook, Ill.: Nielsen Media Research, 1988.

[41]*Nielsen Station Index: Your Guide to Reports/Services.* Northbrook, Ill.: Nielsen Media Research, 1988.

[42]*Nielsen Station Index: Techniques and Data Interpretation.* Northbrook, Ill.: Nielsen Media Research, 1989.

[43]*Meter Service.* New York: Arbitron, 1987.

[44]*Description of Methodology.* New York: Arbitron, 1989.

[45]Jack Honomichl. "Street Talk." *Inside Research*, Dec. 1990, 6.

[46]*Network Radio Post Analysis.* Statistical Research Inc., undated.

[47]*How Birch Measures Radio: The Complete Birch Radio Sourcebook.* Birch/Scarborough Research Corp., 1989.

[48]*Radio Watchwords.* Radio Watch, 1989.

[49]Tom Birch. "Birch vs. Arbitron: Response Rate Key to Difference." *Ratings and Research*, Feb. 17, 1989.

[50]A. M. Arrate. "Ratings Slugfast Can't Product Winner." *Advertising Age*, Sept. 10, 1990, S-13 ff.

[51]E. L. Andrews. "New Device to Measure Audiences." *New York Times*, Sept. 29, 1990, Y18.

[52]*Studies of Media and Markets.* New York: Simmons Market Research Bureau, 1989.

[53]*Pioneering New Horizons Through Research*. New York: Simmons Market Research Bureau, undated.

[54]Marion Yuen, manager of technical services, Simmons Market Research Bureau. Letter, May 15, 1990.

[55]*Ready for the 90's*. New York: Mediamark, 1980.

[56]*The Starch Readership Service*. Mamaroneck, N.Y.: Starch INRI Hooper, undated.

[57]*Ballot*. Mamaroneck, N.Y.: Starch INRI Hooper, 1979.

[58]*Multi-Media Consumer Profile*. Coral Springs, Fla.: Birch Scarborough, undated.

[59]H. F. Dow. "Data Fusion: The Canadian Experiment," *Canadian Journal of Marketing Research* 8 (1989): 57–63.

[60]Hastings Withers. "Data Fusion—The Canadian Experiment. *Canadian Journal of Marketing Research* 9 (1990): 73–77.

[61]*MERI, Micro Evaluation by Mediamark Research Inc.* New York: Mediamark Research Inc., undated.

[62]Sylvia Cassel. Letter, July 25, 1990.

[63]*Computerized Intermedia Planning for Advertising Agencies*. Toronto: Harris Donovan Systems, 1989.

[64]*Multimedia Campaign Planner for Radio, Newspaper, and Television*. Birmingham: TAPSCAN, 1990.

[65]K. M. Foster (TAPSCAN). Letter, June 13, 1990.

[66]*CAMEO: Multimedia Reach & Frequency System*. Pittsburgh: Management Science Associates, undated.

[67]*WISH: National and Local Market Media Allocations*. Pittsburgh: Management Science Associates, undated.

[68]*Computerized Intermedia Planning for Advertising Agencies*. Toronto, October 1989.

[69]R. J. Thorn and M. P. Pfeil. *Newspaper Circulation: Marketing the News*.

[70]*How to Use ABC Information to Evaluate Business Publications*. Schaumberg, Ill.: Audit Bureau of Circulations, undated.

[71]*How to Use ABC Information to Evaluate Newspapers*. Schaumberg, Ill.: Audit Bureau of Circulations, undated.

[72]*How to Use ABC Information to Evaluate Magazines*. Schaumberg, Ill.: Audit Bureau of Circulations, undated.

[73]*Extra! Big News from SRDS*. Wilmette, Ill.: Standard Rate & Data Service, 1990.

[74]"Low Power TV Gains Strength." *New York Times*, May 14, 1990, C3.

[75]Blayne Cutler. "The Fifth Medium." *American Demographics*, June 1990, 25–29.

REFERENCES Beville, H. M., Jr. *Audience Ratings: Radio, Television, and Cable.* Hillsdale, N.J.: Lawrence Erlbaum, 1988.

Bogart, Leo. *Press and Public.* Hillsdale, N.J.: Lawrence Erlbaum, 1988.

Thorn, R. J., and M. P. Pfeil. *Newspaper Circulation: Marketing the News.* New York: Longman, 1987.

APPENDIX

SAMPLES OF QUESTIONNAIRES

Exhibit A.1   A DAY-AFTER-RECALL QUESTIONNAIRE

This is _____, from _____ Marketing Research. We are doing a study on television viewing.

1. Are you (May I speak to) the lady/man of the house?
   ( ) Yes
   [This may be a qualifying question on age or some other category, depending on target audience.]
   ( ) No
   May I speak to him (her)?
   [Continue after getting correct respondents.]

2. Yesterday _____ was shown on Channel _____ between _____ and _____ p.m. Did you, yourself, see any part of this show or not?
   ( ) Yes [If *yes,* go to Question 3.]
   ( ) No [Discontinue interview.]

3. While watching _____ yesterday, did you happen to see a commercial for [product category] or not?
   ( ) Yes [Go to Question 4.]
   ( ) No [Discontinue interview.]

4. What brand was it?
   _____

5. While watching the show yesterday, did you see a commercial for _____ _____ or not?
   ( ) Yes
   ( ) No

6. While watching the show yesterday, did you see a commercial for _____ _____ or not?
   ( ) Yes
   ( ) No

7. Now please tell me anything you remember about the _____ _____ commercial you remember you saw yesterday.
   [Probe] What else can you remember about the commercial?

8. What did the commercial look like? What did the commercial show?

9. What did the advertising say about _____?

10. What *ideas* were brought out in the commercial?
    What *other ideas* were brought out in the commercial?

(ASK ALL RESPONDENTS)
11. We are also interested in people's television-viewing habits. I'm going to tell you about some scenes and commercials from one part of the program. When I stop reading, would you tell me if you remember seeing *any part* of them?

Do you remember seeing any of the part near the beginning/middle/end of
_____ [before activity]?
Just after that, did you see any part of the _____
commercial when [during activity]?
Just after that, did you see any of the part when _____
_____ [after activity]?
[If two or more *no* answers, go to Question 12. Otherwise, go to Question 15.]

12. You mentioned you didn't see some/any of the parts I just read to you. During that time, were you out of the room at any time or not?
( ) Out, Don't know [Go to Question 15 if necessary.]
( ) Yes

13. While you were in the room, what were you doing during that time?

14. Did you change channels during that time or not?

15. These last questions are just to help us divide our interviews into groups. Yesterday did you, yourself, watch _____ on a color or black-and-white television set?

16. Are you, yourself, employed outside the home or not?
[If *yes*] Is that full-time or part-time?
[If *no*] Are you a student?

17. What is your age, please?

18. What is the last grade of school you, yourself, completed?
( ) Grade school (0–8)
( ) Some high school (9–11)
( ) High school graduate (12)
( ) Some college (13–15)
( ) College graduate (16+)
( ) Refused

Exhibit A.2   TELEPHONE QUESTIONNAIRE ABOUT AUTOMOBILE SERVICE

Hello, I am _____, representing
_____, a national marketing research company. We are conducting a survey on automotive service. Registration records show that someone in your household owns a 19____ Mercedes-Benz. Is that correct?

YES [ ]   No [ ] (TERMINATE)

May I speak to the person responsible for having maintenance and repair work done on the car? Are you he (she)?

YES [ ]   No [ ] (ASK TO SPEAK TO THAT PERSON. REPEAT INTRODUCTION IF NECESSARY.)

1. Is your Mercedes-Benz a gasoline or diesel-powered model?
    GASOLINE [   ] 7-1   DIESEL [   ] -2

2a. When it comes time to replace your Mercedes-Benz with another car, how
    likely will it be with another Mercedes-Benz product? Would you say:
    (READ CHOICES ALOUD AND CHECK ONE BOX.)
    DEFINITELY   [   ] 8-1
    VERY LIKELY   [   ] -2   (ASK QUESTION 2b, THEN SKIP TO
    SOMEWHAT LIKELY   [   ] -3   QUESTION 3a.)

    NOT VERY LIKELY   [   ] -4
    DEFINITELY NOT   [   ] -5   (SKIP TO QUESTION 2c.)

 b. Would you use the same dealer from whom you purchased your present
    car?
    YES [   ] 9-1   NO [   ] -2

 c. What are the most important reasons you are unlikely to purchase   10-
    another Mercedes-Benz? (PROBE FOR SPECIFIC REASONS.)

                                                                             11-

                                                                             12-

                                                                             13-

                                                                             14-

                                                                             15-

                                                                             16-

 d. What make and model series do you think you would most likely   17-
    buy?
                                                                             18-

    MAKE: _____   SERIES: _____   19-

                                                                             20-

                                                                             21-

3a. Considering all aspects of ownership of your Mercedes-Benz, how would
    you describe your overall satisfaction with the car? Would you say you
    were: (READ CHOICES AND CHECK ONE BOX.)

    COMPLETELY SATISFIED   [   ] -1   (SKIP TO QUESTION 4a.)
    VERY SATISFIED   [   ] -2
    FAIRLY WELL SATISFIED   [   ] -3
    SOMEWHAT DISSATISFIED   [   ] -4   (ASK QUESTION 3b.)
    VERY DISSATISFIED   [   ] -5

b. You indicate that you are less than completely satisfied with your   23-
   Mercedes-Benz. What do you feel should be necessary to have you
   completely or 100 percent satisfied with this car?   24-
   (PROBE: Anything else?)
                                                                         25-

                                                                         26-

                                                                         27-

                                                                         28-

                                                                         29-

                                                                         30-

4a. How would you rate the service department at the dealership where you
    bought your car? Would you rate it: (READ CHOICES AND CHECK ONE
    BOX.)

EXCEL-LENT [ ]	VERY GOOD [ ]	GOOD [ ]	FAIR [ ]	POOR [ ]
31-1	-2	-3	-4	-5

b. Why did you give the dealer's service department this rating?   31-
   (PROBE FOR SPECIFIC REASONS.)
                                                                    32-

                                                                    33-

                                                                    34-

                                                                    35-

                                                                    36-

5. Based on your experience, how would you rate the dealership which sold
   you your Mercedes-Benz on (ITEM CHECKED AT LEFT)? Would you say
   Excellent, Very Good, Good, Fair, or Poor? (REPEAT FOR REST OF
   ITEMS. CONTINUE TO BOTTOM, THEN RETURN TO TOP AND FIN-
   ISH. CHECK ONE BOX IN EACH ROW.)

   THEIR ABILITY TO GET WORK DONE ON TIME

Excellent	Very Good	Good	Fair	Poor
[ ] 37-1	[ ]-2	[ ]-3	[ ]-4	[ ]-5

   THEIR ABILITY TO MAKE IT AS CONVENIENT FOR CUSTOMER AS
   POSSIBLE IN GETTING NECESSARY REPAIRS

| [ ] 38-1 | [ ]-2 | [ ]-3 | [ ]-4 | [ ]-5 |

FAIRNESS OF PRICES FOR SERVICE
[ ] 39-1   [   ]-2   [   ]-3   [   ]-4   [   ]-5

OVERALL QUALITY OF REPAIR WORK
[ ] 40-1   [   ]-2   [   ]-3   [   ]-4   [   ]-5

THE WAY THEY TREAT THEIR CUSTOMERS
[ ] 41-1   [   ]-2   [   ]-3   [   ]-4   [   ]-5

THE JOB THEY ARE DOING TO IMPROVE THE QUALITY OF SER-
VICE AND REPAIR WORK WITHIN THE DEALERSHIP
[ ] 42-1   [   ]-2   [   ]-3   [   ]-4   [   ]-5

APPEARANCE OF SERVICE FACILITIES
[ ] 43-1   [   ]-2   [   ]-3   [   ]-4   [   ]-5
                                                                         44-

                                                                         45-

6. Thinking only about repairs you paid for yourself, not including routine
    maintenance such as oil changes and lubrication, how long has it been
    since you have had work done on this car? (CHECK ONE BOX.)
    UP TO 3 MONTHS AGO   [   ] 46-1
    3 BUT LESS THAN 6 MONTHS   [   ]   -2
    6 MONTHS BUT LESS THAN 1 YEAR   [   ]   -3
    1 YEAR BUT LESS THAN 2 YEARS   [   ]   -4
    NEVER   [   ]   -5   (SKIP TO QUESTION 10.)

7a. Think about the most recent time you had service or repair work done on
    this car that you paid for yourself. Not counting oil changes or lubrication,
    where did you go to obtain this service or repair work? (CHECK ONE
    BOX.)

    A MERCEDES-BENZ DEALER   [   ] 47-1 (ASK PART 7b.)
    GASOLINE STATION   [   ]   -2
    INDEPENDENT GARAGE   [   ]   -3
                                            (SKIP TO
    DEPARTMENT OR CHAIN   QUESTION 8.)
      STORE (SEARS, PENNEY'S,
      ETC.)   [   ]   -4
    SPECIALTY SHOP (MIDAS,
      AAMCO, ETC.)   [   ]   -5
    OTHER (PLEASE DESCRIBE): _____
    DID IT YOURSELF   [   ]   -6 (SKIP TO QUESTION 10a.)
                                                                     47-

  b. Was this work done at the same dealership where you bought the car?
     YES [   ] 48-1   NO [   ] -2

8. With regard to this most recent service visit, how satisfied were you with
    _____? Would you say completely satisfied, very satisfied, fairly
    well satisfied, somewhat dissatisfied, or very dissatisfied? (REPEAT FOR
    OTHER ITEMS. CHECK ONE BOX IN EACH ROW.)

	Com-pletely Satisfied	Very Satis-fied	Fairly Well Satis-fied	Some-what Dissat-isfied	Very Satis-fied
OVERALL QUALITY OF REPAIR WORK	[ ] 49-1	[ ] -2	[ ] -3	[ ] -4	[ ] -5
OVERALL CONVEN-IENCE FOR YOU IN OBTAINING THE SERVICE	[ ] 50-1	[ ] -2	[ ] -3	[ ] -4	[ ] -5
TREATMENT OF YOU AS A CUSTOMER	[ ] 51-1	[ ] -2	[ ] -3	[ ] -4	[ ] -5
FAIRNESS OF PRICES FOR SERVICE	[ ] 52-1	[ ] -2	[ ] -3	[ ] -4	[ ] -5
ALL THINGS CONSIDERED, YOUR OVERALL IMPRESSION	[ ] 53-1	[ ] -2	[ ] -3	[ ] -4	[ ] -5

54-

55-

9. For this most recent service work:

	Yes	No
a. Were all repairs performed that you requested?	[ ] 56-1	[ ] -2
b. Was the car ready when promised?	[ ] 57-1	[ ] -2
c. Did you receive an estimate of cost before work was begun?	[ ] 58-1	[ ] -2
d. Did you receive a follow-up contact by phone or in person inquiring about your satisfaction with the work?	[ ] 59-1	[ ] -2
e. Was there a guarantee on the service or repair work?	[ ] 60-1	[ ] -2

10a. Have you been contacted by your Mercedes-Benz dealership's service department within the past six months or so, by phone, mail, or in person, for purposes of service reminder or otherwise asking for your service business?

YES [ ] 61-1   NO [ ] -2

b. Is the dealer from whom you purchased your Mercedes-Benz *exclusively* a Mercedes-Benz dealer, or does he handle other makes of new cars through that same dealership?

EXCLUSIVE [ ] 62-1

HANDLES OTHER MAKES OF NEW CARS [ ] -2

11a. Think about the most recent time you had routine maintenance done on your Mercedes-Benz such as oil changes, lubrication, filter, and so forth. Where did you go to obtain this routine maintenance? (CHECK ONE BOX.)

A MERCEDES-BENZ DEALER [ ] 63-1 (ASK PART b.)
GASOLINE STATION [ ] -2 ⎤
INDEPENDENT GARAGE [ ] -3 ⎟
DEPARTMENT OR CHAIN
 STORE (SEARS, PENNEY'S,
 ETC.) [ ] -4 ⎬ (SKIP TO
                   QUESTION 12a.)
SPECIALTY SHOP (MIDAS,
 AAMCO, ETC.) [ ] -5 ⎟
OTHER (PLEASE DESCRIBE): _____
DID IT YOURSELF [ ] -6 ⎦

b. Was this work done at the same dealership where you bought this car?
YES [ ] 64-1   NO [ ] -2

12. In addition to your Mercedes-Benz, are there other cars in your immediate household?
YES [ ] 65-1 (ASK PART b.) NO [ ] -2 (SKIP TO QUESTION 13.)

b. Would you please tell me the make, series, and model year of each of these other cars? (ASK FOR EACH.) Was it bought new or used? (RECORD ANSWERS IN GRID.)

Make	Series	Model Year	Bought New	Used
_____	_____	_____	[ ]	[ ]
_____	_____	_____	[ ]	[ ]
_____	_____	_____	[ ]	[ ]

13. Finally, a few questions about you, to classify the sample. How old are you?

66-

_____
(Age in years)

67-

14. What was the last grade you attended in school?
NO SCHOOLING   [ ]68-1
SOME GRADE SCHOOL   [ ] -2
FINISHED GRADE SCHOOL   [ ] -3
SOME HIGH SCHOOL   [ ] -4
FINISHED HIGH SCHOOL   [ ] -5
SOME COLLEGE   [ ] -6
GRADUATED COLLEGE   [ ] -7
 OR MORE
POSTGRADUATE WORK   [ ] -8

15. And finally, is your total annual family income under $40,000 or is it $40,000 and over?

Under $40,000	[ ]	$40,000 and over	[ ]	
(ASK:)		(ASK:)		
Is that under $25,000	[ ]	Is that under $50,000	[ ]	
or		or		
$25,000 and over	[ ]	$50,000 and over	[ ]	69-

16.   May I have your name, please? (OBTAIN FULL NAME—PRINT.)

Mr./Mrs./Ms.   First Name   Last Name
House no. and street _____ 70-
City _____ State and zip code _____ 71-
Telephone number: _____   72-
                                              Time
Interviewer's name: _____ Date: _____ finished: _____
Validated by: _____ Date: _____

Source: Reproduced with permission of Mercedes-Benz of North America Inc.

Exhibit A.3   SHOPPING HABITS QUESTIONNAIRE BY SUBURBAN NEWSPAPERS OF AMERICA

INTRODUCTION. Hello, I am _____, representing the Suburban Newspapers Advertising Bureau. We are making a study of newspaper reading and shopping habits. In your household I am to talk to the adult female head of the family. (GET TO TALK TO DESIGNATED PERSON BEFORE PROCEEDING.)

1.   Which of these newspapers comes into your home regularly or is read regularly by someone when he or she is outside the house? (READ EACH NEWSPAPER NAME. RECORD RESPONSE BELOW.)

2.   Which of these newspapers do you, yourself, usually read? (READ EACH NEWSPAPER NAME. RECORD RESPONSE BELOW. TERMINATE INTERVIEW IF RESPONDENT DOES NOT READ YOUR LOCAL NEWSPAPER.)

	Question 1		Question 2	
	Regularly In-Home or Outside	Not Regularly In-Home or Outside	Read	Do Not Read
_____	[ ]	[ ]	[ ]	[ ]
_____	[ ]	[ ]	[ ]	[ ]
_____	[ ]	[ ]	[ ]	[ ]

3.   About how many times did you go shopping in the past seven days, not counting today?
0 [ ]   4 [ ]
1 [ ]   5 [ ]
2 [ ]   6 [ ]
3 [ ]   7 [ ]

4a.   Which of these shopping areas did you visit in those trips? [READ LIST AND CHECK WHICH ONE(S).]
Shopping Center A [ ]
Shopping Center B [ ]
Shopping Center C [ ]

4b.   Did you shop anywhere else? (WRITE IN.)

5. Which shopping areas do you visit when you go shopping or buying _____? (READ EACH ITEM SEPARATELY AND CHECK REPLY.)

	Shopping Center A	Shopping Center B	Shopping Center C
Groceries	[ ]	[ ]	[ ]
Furniture	[ ]	[ ]	[ ]
Small appliances (toaster, radio, etc.)	[ ]	[ ]	[ ]
Major appliances (TV, washing machine, etc.)	[ ]	[ ]	[ ]
Women's clothing	[ ]	[ ]	[ ]
Children's clothing	[ ]	[ ]	[ ]
Hardware	[ ]	[ ]	[ ]
Drugs and toiletries	[ ]	[ ]	[ ]

6. In general, which shopping area do you believe offers the following? (READ EACH ITEM AND RECORD REPLY TO EACH.)

	Shopping Center A	Shopping Center B	Shopping Center C
Best parking	[ ]	[ ]	[ ]
Greatest selection of merchandise	[ ]	[ ]	[ ]
Nearest location to you	[ ]	[ ]	[ ]
Best quality of stores	[ ]	[ ]	[ ]
Nicest atmosphere	[ ]	[ ]	[ ]

7. When you shop for _____ (READ EACH ITEM, ENTER REPLY), about how many stores do you visit?

Groceries	_____	Women's clothing	_____
Furniture	_____	Children's clothing	_____
Small appliances	_____	Hardware	_____
Major appliances	_____	Drugs and toiletries	_____

8. Which of these items is your family planning to buy during the next 12 months? (READ EACH ITEM AND CHECK RESPONSE.)

	Yes	No	Not Sure
Washing machine or dryer	[ ]	[ ]	[ ]
Dishwasher	[ ]	[ ]	[ ]
Refrigerator or freezer	[ ]	[ ]	[ ]
Range	[ ]	[ ]	[ ]
Power mower	[ ]	[ ]	[ ]
Television set	[ ]	[ ]	[ ]
Stereo equipment	[ ]	[ ]	[ ]
Luggage	[ ]	[ ]	[ ]
Outdoor furniture	[ ]	[ ]	[ ]
Home furniture	[ ]	[ ]	[ ]

9. Up to now, we've been talking about your shopping habits. Now I'd like to ask you some questions about some of your other attitudes and activities.

   Generally, do you consider yourself as someone who does one of the following? (READ BOTH CHOICES BEFORE ACCEPTING ANSWER.)
   Likes to try new products soon after they come on the market. [ ]

   Prefers to wait until the new products have proven themselves before trying. [ ]

10. During the past four weeks, about how many times, if any, have you entertained a group of four or more people in your home?
    Number of times _____

11. To which of these types of groups or clubs do you belong?

	Yes	No
School PTA	[ ]	[ ]
Local or political club or group	[ ]	[ ]
Volunteer fireman or policeman	[ ]	[ ]
Volunteer charitable or fund-raising group	[ ]	[ ]
Church group	[ ]	[ ]
Sports club	[ ]	[ ]

12. What age group should I put you in? (READ EACH GROUP UNTIL RESPONDENT REPLIES.)
    Under 30   [ ]   40–49   [ ]
    30–39   [ ]   50 or over   [ ]

13. What is the occupation of the head of the house? (READ EACH ONE)
    Managerial   [ ]   Unemployed   [ ]
    Blue-collar   [ ]   Wife   [ ]
    Student   [ ]   White-collar   [ ]
    Professional   [ ]   Retired   [ ]

14. What was the name of the last school attended by the head of the house? How far did he or she go? (CHECK ONLY TOP CATEGORY.)

	Some	Graduated
Elementary school (grades 1–8)	[ ]	[ ]
High school (grades 9–12, including technical or vocational school)	[ ]	[ ]
College (through bachelor's degree)	[ ]	[ ]
Postgraduate (toward master's, doctor's)	[ ]	[ ]

15. Please stop me when I read the group which includes your *family's total annual income*—including all family members and all sources of income. (READ LIST.)
    Under $20,000   [ ] $40,000 but under $50,000   [ ]
    $20,000 but under $30,000   [ ] $50,000 but under $60,000   [ ]
    $30,000 but under $40,000   [ ] $60,000 or more   [ ]

16. Do you *own* or *rent* your home?
    Own [ ]   Rent [ ]

17. Do you, yourself, have a car available to go shopping?
    Yes [   ]   No [   ]

18. Which of these types of credit card, if any, do you personally carry? (READ
    EACH ONE AND RECORD REPLY.)

	Carry	Do Not Carry
Bank card (Visa, etc.)	[ ]	[ ]
Gasoline	[ ]	[ ]
Department store (including mail order)	[ ]	[ ]
Hotel	[ ]	[ ]
Fee card (such as American Express, Diner's Club	[ ]	[ ]

19. Do you have a check-cashing card, such as the ones sometimes offered by
    grocery stores?
    Yes [   ]   No [   ]

20. (INTERVIEWER, PLEASE RECORD.)
    Sex of respondent: Male [   ]   Female [   ]
    Respondent name: _____
    Telephone number: _____
    Date of call: _____
    Interviewer signature: _____

_____

Source: Reproduced with permission of Suburban Newspapers of America.

INDEX